Every student succeeds.

- **New features and strategies designed to reach every student at every level**

COMMUNITY OF LEARNERS

• Students are able to move between levels, creating incentives for improvement while making sure every student is encouraged to achieve the lesson objectives.

Teachers reach every student with one lesson plan!

Beginning Kindergarten

The foundation of reading success is built in Kindergarten.

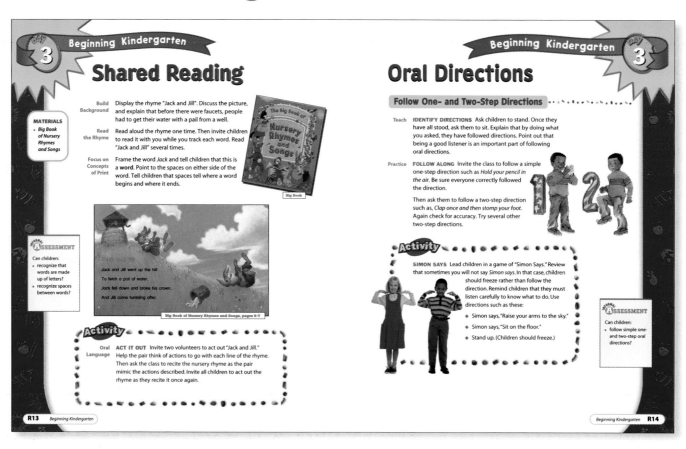

Shared Reading

MATERIALS
• Big Book of Nursery Rhymes and Songs

Build Background Display the rhyme "Jack and Jill". Discuss the picture, and explain that before there were faucets, people had to get their water with a pail from a well.

Read the Rhyme Read aloud the rhyme one time. Then invite children to read it with you while you track each word. Read "Jack and Jill" several times.

Focus on Concepts of Print Frame the word *Jack* and tell children that this is a **word**. Point to the spaces on either side of the word. Tell children that spaces tell where a word begins and where it ends.

ASSESSMENT
Can children:
• recognize that words are made up of letters?
• recognize spaces between words?

Big Book of Nursery Rhymes and Songs, pages 6-7

Activity
Oral Language **ACT IT OUT** Invite two volunteers to act out "Jack and Jill." Help the pair think of actions to go with each line of the rhyme. Then ask the class to recite the nursery rhyme as the pair mimic the actions described. Invite all children to act out the rhyme as they recite it once again.

R13 *Beginning Kindergarten*

Oral Directions

Follow One- and Two-Step Directions

Teach **IDENTIFY DIRECTIONS** Ask children to stand. Once they have all stood, ask them to sit. Explain that by doing what you asked, they have followed directions. Point out that being a good listener is an important part of following oral directions.

Practice **FOLLOW ALONG** Invite the class to follow a simple one-step direction such as *Hold your pencil in the air*. Be sure everyone correctly followed the direction.

Then ask them to follow a two-step direction such as, *Clap once and then stomp your foot*. Again check for accuracy. Try several other two-step directions.

Activity
SIMON SAYS Lead children in a game of "Simon Says." Review that sometimes you will not say *Simon says*. In that case, children should freeze rather than follow the direction. Remind children that they must listen carefully to know what to do. Use directions such as these:
♦ Simon says, "Raise your arms to the sky."
♦ Simon says, "Sit on the floor."
♦ Stand up. (Children should freeze.)

ASSESSMENT
Can children:
• follow simple one- and two-step oral directions?

Beginning Kindergarten R14

Beginning Kindergarten provides more readiness material to ensure that every child learns the basic skills needed to read.

Macmillan/McGraw-Hill Reading offers a wide array of Big Books for shared reading and skill development.

• ABC Big Books (6)
• Literature Big Books (12)
• Big Book of Nursery Rhymes and Songs
• Big Book of Phonics Rhymes and Poems
• Reading for Information Big Book
• Big Book of Decodable Stories

A strong, logically-sequenced phonics strand promotes phonemic awareness—an essential building block for the skill of reading.

Word building begins in Kindergarten.

Macmillan/McGraw-Hill Reading offers a wide array of manipulatives to support phonics instruction and word building.

- ABC Letter Cards
- Tactile ABC Cards
- Phonics Picture Cards/Posters
- Vocabulary Cards
- Story Pop-Out Cards
- Word Building Manipulative Cards

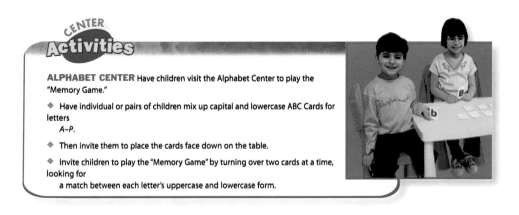

ALPHABET CENTER Have children visit the Alphabet Center to play the "Memory Game."

◆ Have individual or pairs of children mix up capital and lowercase ABC Cards for letters
   A–P.

◆ Then invite them to place the cards face down on the table.

◆ Invite children to play the "Memory Game" by turning over two cards at a time, looking for
   a match between each letter's uppercase and lowercase form.

Center Activities provide exciting, hands-on learning opportunities for every child. Children learn at their own level. Center set-up and management instructions are always provided.

Every student reads.
Every student succeeds.

Every student participates in the same whole-group activities at the beginning of each week.

Every student learns the SAME concept.

Every student learns the SAME skill.

Every student learns the SAME vocabulary.

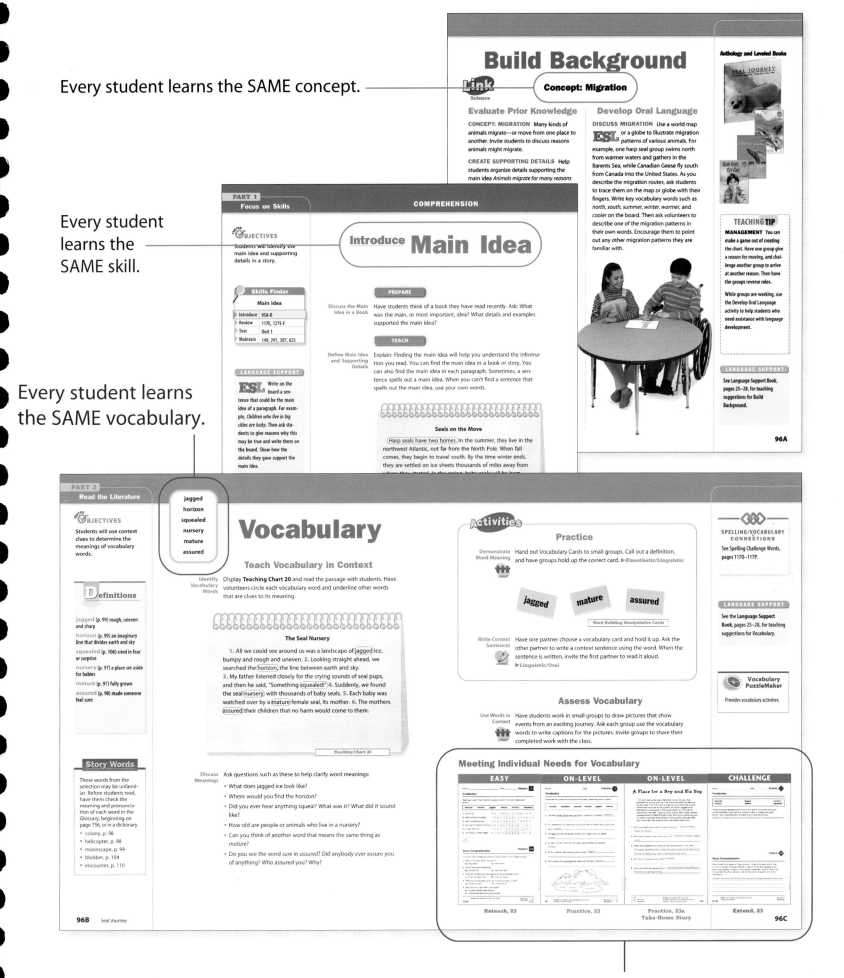

Leveled Books and Leveled Practice help every student succeed. Practice is available for every level.

Leveled Books and Leveled Practice help every student read and every student succeed.

After reading the weekly anthology selection, students move to the Leveled Books. Written for three distinct levels—Easy, Independent, and Challenge—each Leveled Book contains the **same concept, skills, and vocabulary** as the anthology selection. Lessons for every leveled book are included in the Teacher's Edition.

Anthology

Seal Journey

Selection Summary Students will read about a photographer and his son who go to Prince Edward Island to learn about the life cycle of harp seals.

Leveled Books

Easy

Independent

Challenge

Leveled Practice

EASY
Reteach

INDEPENDENT/ON-LEVEL
Practice

CHALLENGE
Extend

Shared learning experiences encourage every student to read and every student to succeed.

After reading, the small groups are brought back together for culminating whole-group activities. Since every student has been using the same concept, skill, and vocabulary, every student participates in the community of learners, regardless of level.

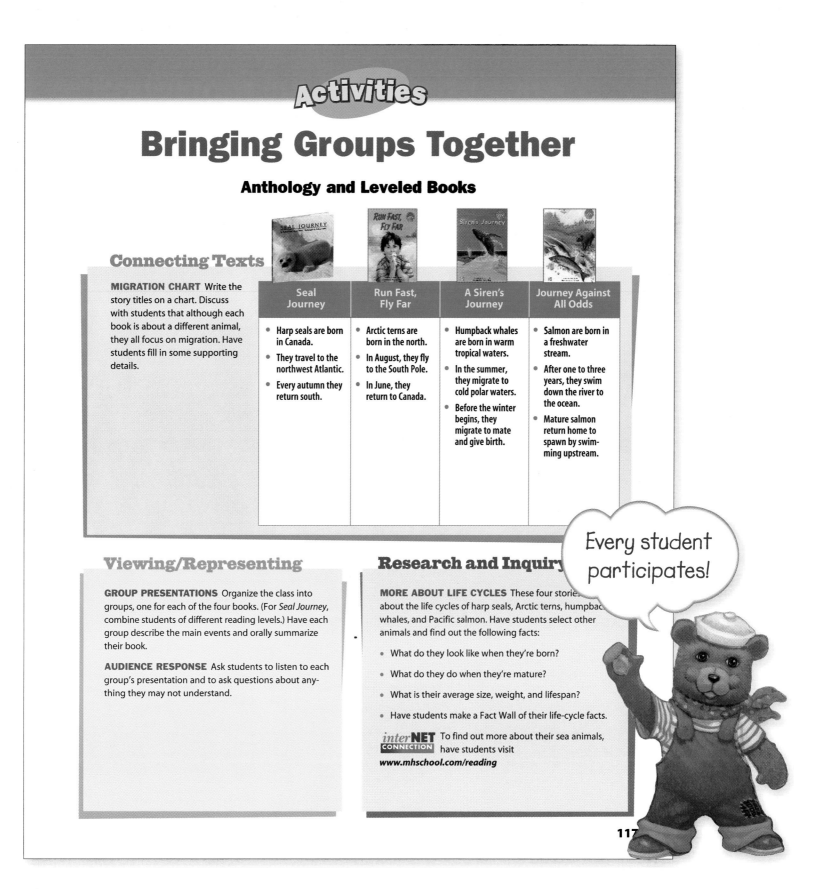

Activities

Bringing Groups Together

Anthology and Leveled Books

Connecting Texts

MIGRATION CHART Write the story titles on a chart. Discuss with students that although each book is about a different animal, they all focus on migration. Have students fill in some supporting details.

Seal Journey	Run Fast, Fly Far	A Siren's Journey	Journey Against All Odds
• Harp seals are born in Canada. • They travel to the northwest Atlantic. • Every autumn they return south.	• Arctic terns are born in the north. • In August, they fly to the South Pole. • In June, they return to Canada.	• Humpback whales are born in warm tropical waters. • In the summer, they migrate to cold polar waters. • Before the winter begins, they migrate to mate and give birth.	• Salmon are born in a freshwater stream. • After one to three years, they swim down the river to the ocean. • Mature salmon return home to spawn by swimming upstream.

Viewing/Representing

GROUP PRESENTATIONS Organize the class into groups, one for each of the four books. (For *Seal Journey*, combine students of different reading levels.) Have each group describe the main events and orally summarize their book.

AUDIENCE RESPONSE Ask students to listen to each group's presentation and to ask questions about anything they may not understand.

Research and Inquiry

MORE ABOUT LIFE CYCLES These four stories are about the life cycles of harp seals, Arctic terns, humpback whales, and Pacific salmon. Have students select other animals and find out the following facts:

• What do they look like when they're born?

• What do they do when they're mature?

• What is their average size, weight, and lifespan?

• Have students make a Fact Wall of their life-cycle facts.

interNET CONNECTION To find out more about their sea animals, have students visit **www.mhschool.com/reading**

> Every student participates!

The *Macmillan/McGraw-Hill Reading* lesson design ends each week by bringing groups together. The whole group is able to compare and contrast the four selections that have been read. Every student succeeds because every student has learned the same concept, skill, and vocabulary. Teachers succeed with one simple-to-use lesson design.

Macmillan/McGraw-Hill Reading's literature is sequenced for success.

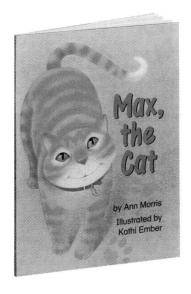

Decodable literature gives children the opportunity to apply phonics skills.

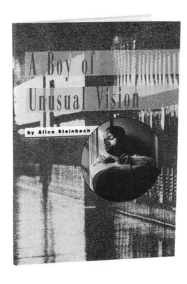

Nonfiction selections prepare students for the skills and strategies needed for outside reading.

Story selections reflect the **diversity of students** in the classroom.

Well-known authors, favorite characters, and award-winning literature are found in each grade.

Classics introduce students to some of the best literature of the past.

Macmillan/McGraw-Hill's unique partnership with *Time for Kids* ensures that every unit provides a range of nonfiction topics.

Reading is applied across the curriculum with expository text.

Macmillan/McGraw-Hill Reading provides a "Reading for Information Handbook" at the back of the Pupil Edition in Grades 1–6. The handbook allows students to apply the reading strategies that they've learned to real-life situations. The handbook prepares students for real-life reading and improves performance on standardized assessments.

This handbook provides reading experiences with expository text for:

• Reading Directions
• Reading Media
• Reading Online
• Reading Research
• Science
• Social Studies

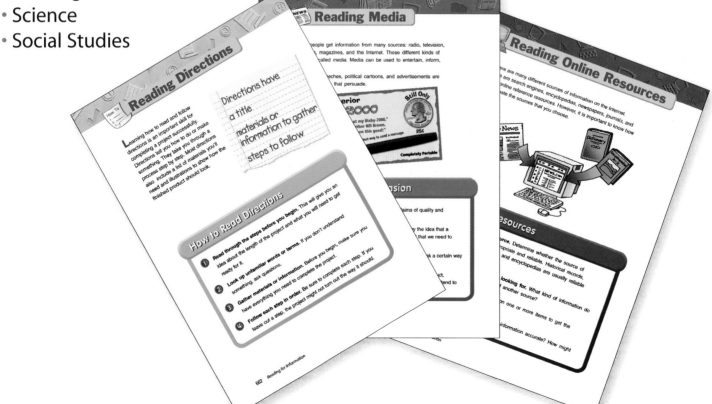

Assessment helps to ensure that students succeed in reading and on standardized tests.

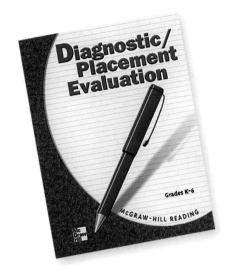

Diagnostic/Placement Evaluation includes individual inventories, running records, and placement tests.

Selection Assessment makes it easy to check skills, story vocabulary, and story comprehension on a weekly basis. **Comprehensive Assessment** provides unit, mid-year, and end-year tests for these important skills. **Reading Fluency Assessment** contains passages that assess student fluency.

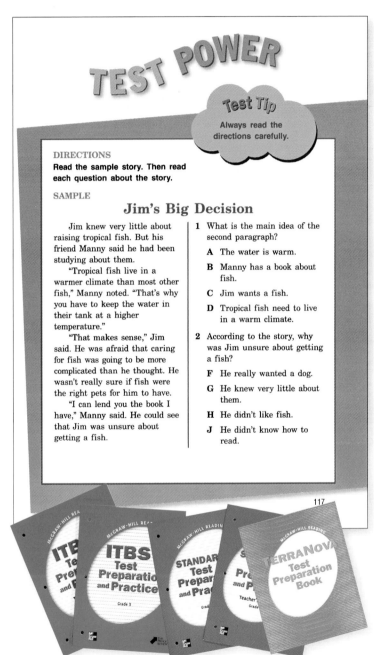

Test Power provides test preparation in the Pupil Edition. Weekly test-preparation practice for the skills and strategies of the nation's most recognized standardized tests are also available.

15

Technology extends the reading experience.

Accelerated Reader® Quizzes
Every Pupil Edition selection and every Leveled Book selection
for Grades 1–6 are correlated to an Accelerated Reader Quiz.

Vocabulary PuzzleMaker
Vocabulary PuzzleMaker can be used to create
customized crossword puzzles, word searches,
or word jumbles.

Adventures with Buggles Phonics CD-ROM

Exciting activities and colorful characters keep interest high as students use phonics in letter recognition, decoding, blending, and segmenting.

Handwriting CD-ROM

This easy-to-use handwriting component helps teachers customize worksheets and activities, including cross-curricular practice.

Grammar Tunes

Tunes complement every language and grammar skill found in each grade of *Macmillan/McGraw-Hill Reading*. Songs help students remember the discrete skills of language.

Test Generator

Featuring Test Check and Assessment and Reporting system, the Reading Test Generator can help with all your assessment needs.

MindJogger Videos

Quizzes review and reinforce unit content through an exciting game format.

Songs from A to Z

Compact discs and audiocassettes provide phonics songs that help children practice letter sounds.

Listening Library

Compact discs and audiocassettes contain readings of selected literature to enhance student understanding.

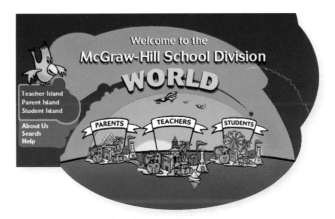

Internet Activities

The Macmillan/McGraw-Hill website has a full range of activities designed to support lessons from *Macmillan/McGraw-Hill Reading*.

Macmillan/McGraw-Hill Reading Authors

Dr. James Flood
Dr. Flood is Professor of Reading and Language Development at San Diego State University, and is involved with the study of teacher preparation and research in language arts and reading.

Dr. Diane Lapp
Dr. Lapp, the 1996 IRA Outstanding Teacher Educator of the Year, is Professor of Reading and Language Development in the College of Education at San Diego State University.

Dr. Jan Hasbrouck
Dr. Hasbrouck is Assistant Professor of Special Education and School Psychology at Texas A&M University, where she is also Director of the Collaborating Teachers Training program.

Donna Harrell Lubcker
Ms. Lubcker is Assistant Professor of Education at East Texas Baptist University, where she is responsible for Block III site-based classes. She supervises student teachers and Early Childhood classes.

Dr. James Hoffman
Dr. Hoffman is Professor of Language and Literacy Studies at the University of Texas at Austin, and serves on the board of the International Reading Association.

Angela Shelf Medearis
Angela Shelf Medearis is the author of more than 67 award-winning books for children, and has been translated into Spanish, French, Dutch, and Japanese.

Dr. Scott Paris
Dr. Paris is Professor of Psychology and Education at the University of Michigan.

Dr. Josefina Villamil Tinajero
Dr. Tinajero is a noted authority, researcher, and speaker in the field of elementary bilingual education.

Dr. Steven Stahl
Dr. Stahl is Professor of Reading Education at the University of Georgia, where he is also the director of the Reading Clinic.

Dr. Karen Wood
Dr. Wood is a Professor in the Department of Reading and Elementary Education at the University of North Carolina at Charlotte, where she has been a member of the faculty for over 15 years.

Macmillan/McGraw-Hill Reading Components

LITERATURE

	K	1	2	3	4	5	6
Pupil Editions	•	•	•	•	•	•	•
Readiness Pupil Edition		•					
Leveled Books: Easy	•	•	•	•	•	•	•
Leveled Books: Independent	•	•	•	•	•	•	•
Leveled Books: Challenge	•	•	•	•	•	•	•
ABC Big Books	•						
ABC Little Books	•						
Big Book of Phonics Rhymes	•						
Reading for Information Big Book	•						
Big Book of Nursery Rhymes	•						
Big Book of Decodable Stories	•						
Literature Big Books	•	•	•	•			
Take-Home Books and Daily Activities Blackline Masters	•	•	•	•	•	•	•

TEACHER'S MATERIALS

	K	1	2	3	4	5	6
Teacher's Editions	•	•	•	•	•	•	•
Readiness Teacher's Edition		•					
Daily Language Activities Transparencies		•	•	•	•	•	•
Daily Language Activities Blackline Masters		•	•	•	•	•	•
Writing Process Transparencies		•	•	•	•	•	•
Teaching Charts		•	•	•	•	•	•
Teaching Chart Transparencies		•	•	•	•	•	•
Graphic Organizer Transparencies		•	•	•	•	•	•
Skills Intervention Guide		•	•	•	•	•	•
Phonics Intervention Guide					•	•	•
Sentence Strips		•					
Handwriting Handbook	•	•	•	•			

SKILLS AND PRACTICE

	K	1	2	3	4	5	6
Practice Book Pupil Edition	•	•	•	•	•	•	•
Practice Book Teacher's Annotated Edition	•	•	•	•	•	•	•
Reteach Blackline Masters		•	•	•	•	•	•
Extend Blackline Masters		•	•	•	•	•	•
Phonics/Phonemic Awareness Practice Book Pupil Edition	•	•	•	•	•	•	•
Phonics/Phonemic Awareness Practice Book Teacher's Annotated Edition	•	•	•	•	•	•	•
Language Support: Lessons and Practice Blackline Masters	•	•	•	•	•	•	•
Grammar Practice Book Pupil Edition		•	•	•	•	•	•
Spelling Practice Book Pupil Edition		•	•	•	•	•	•
Word Building Manipulative Cards: Letters, Sounds, and Words	•	•	•				
Word Building Manipulative Cards: Words and Word Parts				•	•		•
Fluency Assessment		•	•	•	•	•	•

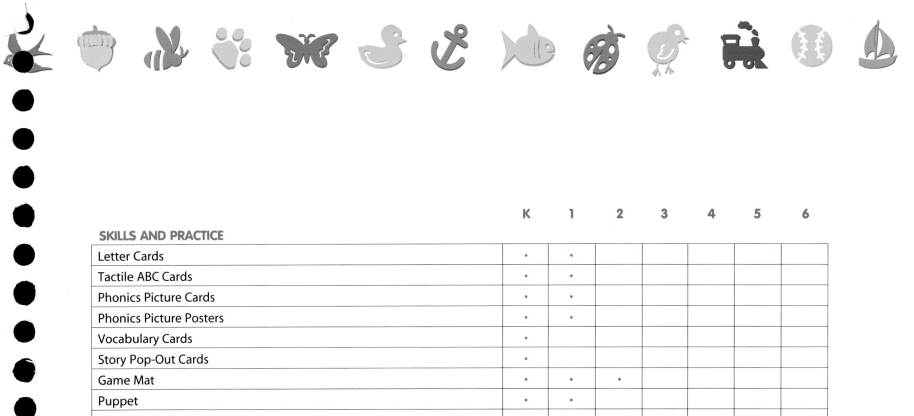

SKILLS AND PRACTICE	K	1	2	3	4	5	6
Letter Cards	•	•					
Tactile ABC Cards	•	•					
Phonics Picture Cards	•	•					
Phonics Picture Posters	•	•					
Vocabulary Cards	•						
Story Pop-Out Cards	•						
Game Mat	•	•	•				
Puppet	•	•					
Phonics Practice Readers		•					

ASSESSMENT	K	1	2	3	4	5	6
Diagnostic/Placement Evaluation Blackline Masters/Teacher's Edition	•	•	•	•	•	•	•
Unit Test Booklets Pupil Edition	•	•	•	•	•	•	•
Mid-Year Test Booklets Pupil Edition	•	•	•	•	•	•	•
End-Year Test Booklets Pupil Edition	•	•	•	•	•	•	•
Comprehensive Assessment Blackline Masters and Teacher's Manual (includes Unit, Mid- and End-Year)	•	•	•	•	•	•	•
Selection Assessments Pupil Edition		•	•	•	•	•	•
Selection Assessments Teacher's Annotated Edition		•	•	•	•	•	•
Standardized Test Preparation Practice Book	•						
Standardized Test Preparation Practice Book Teacher's Edition	•						
TerraNova Test Prep Pupil Edition		•	•	•	•	•	•
TerraNova Test Prep Teacher's Annotated Edition		•	•	•	•	•	•
SAT-9 Test Prep Pupil Edition		•	•	•	•	•	•
SAT-9 Test Prep Teacher's Annotated Edition		•	•	•	•	•	•
ITBS Test Prep Pupil Edition		•	•	•	•	•	•
ITBS Test Prep Teacher's Annotated Edition		•	•	•	•	•	•
Student Profile Booklet	•	•	•	•	•	•	•

TECHNOLOGY	K	1	2	3	4	5	6
Phonics: Adventures with Buggles CD-ROM	•	•	•	•			
Accelerated Reader® Quizzes		•	•	•	•	•	•
Internet Research and Inquiry Activities	•	•	•	•	•	•	•
Listening Library Audiocassettes and Compact Discs	•	•	•	•	•	•	•
Songs from A to Z Audiocassettes and Compact Discs	•	•					
Grammar Tunes Compact Discs	•	•	•	•	•	•	•
Test Generator	•	•	•	•	•	•	•
Handwriting CD-ROM	•	•	•	•	•	•	•
Vocabulary PuzzleMaker			•	•		•	
MindJogger Videos			•	•	•		

Notes

Notes

Every student reads.
Every student succeeds.

Macmillan McGraw-Hill

Macmillan/McGraw-Hill READING

Mc Graw Hill **Macmillan
McGraw-Hill**

New York   Farmington

Contributors

The Princeton Review, Time Magazine, Accelerated Reader

The Princeton Review is not
affiliated with Princeton
University or ETS.

Students with print disabilities may be eligible to obtain an accessible, audio version of the
pupil edition of this textbook. Please call Recording for the Blind & Dyslexic at 1-800-221-4792
for complete information.

Macmillan/McGraw-Hill

*A Division of The **McGraw·Hill** Companies*

Published by Macmillan/McGraw-Hill, a division of The McGraw-Hill Companies, Inc., Two Penn Plaza, NY, NY 10121

Printed in the United States of America

2 3 4 5 6 7 8 9 006/043 05 04 03 02

Macmillan/McGraw-Hill READING

Authors

James Flood

Jan E. Hasbrouck

James V. Hoffman

Diane Lapp

Donna Lubcker

Angela Shelf Medearis

Scott Paris

Steven Stahl

Josefina Villamil Tinajero

Karen D. Wood

Macmillan McGraw-Hill

New York   Farmington

Managing the

Computer Center

Working with Words Station

Writing Station

Reading and Listening Station

Word Box

Classroom

Social Studies Station

TEACHING TIP

MANAGEMENT

Provide children in each group with their own list of centers they will go to. Children can check off each center after finishing their work. Early finishers can read a book from the Reading Center.

Teacher Directed Small Group Instruction

Sample Management Plan

Group 1	Group 2	Group 3	Group 4
With Teacher	Reading or Writing Workstation	Working with Words Station	Cross-Curricular or Computer Station
Reading or Writing Workstation	**With Teacher**	Cross-Curricular or Computer Station	Working with Words Station
Working with Words Station	Cross-Curricular or Computer Station	**With Teacher**	Reading or Writing Workstation
Cross-Curricular or Computer Station	Working with Words Station	Reading or Writing Workstation	**With Teacher**

Creating WORKSTATIONS

Establishing independent workstations and other independent activities is the key to helping you manage the classroom as you meet with small groups.

Reading

Set up a classroom library for independent reading. Add Leveled Books as read during small-group instruction. Add other titles, also grouped by reading level. See the Theme Bibliography on pages T78–T79 for suggestions. Include titles based on discussions of students' fiction and nonfiction preferences.

- Self-Selected Reading
- Paired Reading
- Student Anthology selection from the Listening Library

Computer

Students can access the Internet to complete the Research and Inquiry activities suggested throughout the unit. Look for Internet connections in the following Research and Inquiry projects:

- Find Out More project at the end of each selection
- Cooperative Theme Project: Reflections of the Past
- Cross-Curricular Activities
- Bringing Groups Together project

Writing

Focus the unit's writing projects on Personal Narrative. Weekly writing assignments are found at the end of each selection. The unit writing process project, Writing Personal Narratives, can also be the focus of the Writing Station. Equip the Writing Station with the following materials:

- Samples of published personal narratives
- Personal Narrative writing samples, available in the **Teacher's Writing Resource Handbook**, pages 18–19

Working with Words

Selection Vocabulary
After reading each selection, ask students to create word cards and sort them using these categories:

- Sounds: beginning, middle, or end sounds, number of syllables
- Semantics: compounds, plural forms, parts of speech
- Student-determined categories

High-Frequency Words
Create cards for the words: a*sk, black, best, along, second,* and *anything.* Have students write the high-frequency words in sentences.

TEACHING TIP

MANAGEMENT
Incorporate workstation suggestions into a class assignment chart.

If classroom space is limited, shelve materials for each project and distribute them as you assign an activity.

Have students work in groups, pairs, or independently.

Cross-Curricular
STATIONS

Set up Cross-Curricular Stations to help extend selection concepts and ideas. Suggestions for Cross-Curricular activities can be found in the Teacher's Edition.

Science

- Mountain Animals, 24
- Grasslands, 54
- Test the Weather Report, 74
- Water Mammals, 102

Social Studies

- Map Skills, 28, 98
- California, 48
- Geographical Features, 72

Math
3 + 2

- Fractions, 34
- How Many Harvests?, 56
- Thunder and Lightning, 80
- Seal Math, 104

Art

- Special Places, 30
- Hidden Treasures, 58

...... Additional Independent Activities ......

The following independent activities are offered as a means to practice and reinforce concepts and skills taught in the unit.

PUPIL EDITION: READER RESPONSE

Story Questions to monitor the student's comprehension of the selection. The questions are leveled progressing from literal to critical thinking.

Story Activities related to each selection. Four activities are provided: one writing activity, two cross-curricular activities, and a research and inquiry activity in the Find Out More project. Students are encouraged to use the Internet for research.

LEVELED PRACTICE

Each week, Reteach, Practice, and Extend pages are offered to address the individual needs of students as they learn and review skills.

McGraw-Hill Reading

MULTI-AGE
Classroom

Using the same global themes at each grade level facilitates the use of materials in multi-age classrooms.

GRADE LEVEL	Experience Experiences can tell us about ourselves and our world.	Connections Making connections develops new understandings.
Kindergarten	**My World** We learn a lot from all the things we see and do at home and in school.	**All Kinds of Friends** When we work and play together, we learn more about ourselves.
Sub-theme 1	At Home	Working Together
Sub-theme 2	School Days	Playing Together
1	**Day by Day** Each day brings new experiences.	**Together Is Better** We like to share ideas and experiences with others.
2	**What's New?** With each day, we learn something new.	**Just Between Us** Family and friends help us see the world in new ways.
3	**Great Adventures** Life is made up of big and small experiences.	**Nature Links** Nature can give us new ideas.
4	**Reflections** Stories let us share the experiences of others.	**Something in Common** Sharing ideas can lead to meaningful cooperation.
5	**Time of My Life** We sometimes find memorable experiences in unexpected places.	**Building Bridges** Knowing what we have in common helps us appreciate our differences.
6	**Pathways** Reflecting on life's experiences can lead to new understandings.	**A Common Thread** A look beneath the surface may uncover hidden connections.

Themes: Kindergarten – Grade 6

Expression	Inquiry	Problem-Solving	Making Decisions
There are many styles and forms for expressing ourselves.	By exploring and asking questions, we make discoveries.	Analyzing information can help us solve problems.	Using what we know helps us evaluate situations.
Time to Shine We can use our ideas and our imagination to do many wonderful things.	**I Wonder** We can make discoveries about the wonders of nature in our own backyard.	**Let's Work It Out** Working as part of a team can help me find a way to solve problems.	**Choices** We can make many good choices and decisions every day.
Great Ideas	In My Backyard	Try and Try Again	Good Choices
Let's Pretend	Wonders of Nature	Teamwork	Let's Decide
Stories to Tell Each one of us has a different story to tell.	**Let's Find Out!** Looking for answers is an adventure.	**Think About It!** It takes time to solve problems.	**Many Paths** Each decision opens the door to a new path.
Express Yourself We share our ideas in many ways.	**Look Around** There are surprises all around us.	**Figure It Out** We can solve problems by working together.	**Starting Now** Unexpected events can lead to new decisions.
Be Creative! We can all express ourselves in creative, wonderful ways.	**Tell Me More** Looking and listening closely will help us find out the facts.	**Think It Through** Solutions come in many shapes and sizes.	**Turning Points** We make new judgments based on our experiences.
Our Voices We can each use our talents to communicate ideas.	**Just Curious** We can find answers in surprising places.	**Make a Plan** Often we have to think carefully about a problem in order to solve it.	**Sorting It Out** We make decisions that can lead to new ideas and discoveries.
Imagine That The way we express our thoughts and feelings can take different forms.	**Investigate!** We never know where the search for answers might lead us.	**Bright Ideas** Some problems require unusual approaches.	**Crossroads** Decisions cause changes that can enrich our lives.
With Flying Colors Creative people help us see the world from different perspectives.	**Seek and Discover** To make new discoveries, we must observe and explore.	**Brainstorms** We can meet any challenge with determination and ingenuity.	**All Things Considered** Encountering new places and people can help us make decisions.

UNIT
1

Contents

Reflections

Stories let us share the experiences of others.

written and illustrated by **Allen Say**

SKILLS			
Comprehension	**Vocabulary**	**Study Skill**	**Phonics**
• **Introduce** Story Elements	• **Introduce** Multiple-Meaning Words	• **Parts of a Book:** Use Parts of a Book	• **Review** Short Vowels
• **Review** Story Elements			
• **Introduce** Make Inferences			

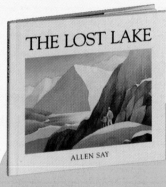

REALISTIC FICTION

written by **Linda Jacobs Altman**
illustrated by **Enrique O. Sanchez**

SKILLS			
Comprehension	**Vocabulary**	**Study Skill**	**Phonics**
• **Introduce** Problem and Solution	• **Introduce** Antonyms and Synonyms	• **Parts of a Book:** Use a Glossary	• **Review** Long *a* and Long *e*
• **Review** Problem and Solution			
• **Review** Make Inferences			

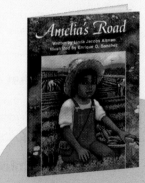

REALISTIC FICTION

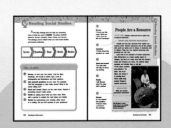

INFORMATIONAL TEXT

Unit Planner

	WEEK 1 The Lost Lake	**WEEK 2** Amelia's Road
Leveled Books	**Easy:** *The Stony Creek Bandit* **Independent:** *Martin's Journey* **Challenge:** *Lost and Found*	**Easy:** *Postcards from Mari Vic* **Independent:** *Home on the Range* **Challenge:** *The Story of Cesar Chavez*
✓ **Tested Skills**	☑ **Comprehension** Story Elements, 19A–19B, 41E–41F Make Inferences, 41G–41H ☑ **Vocabulary** Multiple-Meaning Words, 41I–41J ☑ **Study Skills** Parts of a Book, 40	☑ **Comprehension** Problem and Solution, 43A–43B, 65E–65F Make Inferences, 65G–65H ☑ **Vocabulary** Antonyms and Synonyms, 65I–65J ☑ **Study Skills** Parts of a Book, 64
Minilessons	**Phonics and Decoding:** Short Vowels, 35 **Genre:** Realistic Fiction, 21 **Context Clues,** 23 **Summarize,** 27 **Draw Conclusions,** 29	**Phonics and Decoding:** Long *a* and Long *e,* 55 **Genre:** Realistic Fiction, 45 **Summarize,** 47 **Character,** 53 **Context Clues,** 59
Language Arts	✎ **Writing:** Personal Narrative, 41K **Grammar:** Sentences, 41M–41N **Spelling:** Words with Short Vowels, 41O–41P	✎ **Writing:** Personal Narrative, 65K **Grammar:** Subjects and Predicates, 65M–65N **Spelling:** Words with Long *a* and Long *e,* 65O–65P

Activities

Curriculum Connections	Read Aloud: "The Paper Garden," 18E	Read Aloud: "Pack," 42E
	Stories in Art: *Gathering Watercress on the River Mole,* 18	Stories in Art: *Broadbottom, Near Glossop,* 42
	Science: Mountain Animals, 24	Social Studies: California, 48
	Social Studies: Map Skills, 28	Science: Grasslands, 54
	Art: Special Places, 30	Math: How Many Harvests?, 56
	Math: Fractions, 34	Art: Hidden Treasures, 58
	Science: Classifying Animals, 39	Social Studies: Climate and Crops, 63
🌿 **CULTURAL PERSPECTIVES**	Family Activities, 22	Cross-Cultural Communication, 52

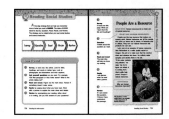

WEEK 3 Sarah, Plain and Tall	**WEEK 4** Seal Journey	**WEEK 5** Open Wide, Don't Bite!	**WEEK 6** Review, Writing, Reading Information, Assessment
Easy: *Sukey Johnson Builds a House* **Independent:** *Laura and the Great Quake* **Challenge:** *Trevor, Knight-In-Training*	**Easy:** *Run Fast, Fly Far* **Independent:** *A Siren's Journey* **Challenge:** *Journey Against All Odds*	*Self-Selected Reading of Leveled Books*	*Self-Selected Reading*

☑ **Comprehension** Story Elements 67A–67B, 93E–93F Problem and Solution, 93G–93H ☑ **Vocabulary** Antonyms and Synonyms, 93I–93J ☑ **Study Skills** Parts of a Book, 92	☑ **Comprehension** Main Idea, 95A–95B, 117E–117F Make Inferences, 117G–117H ☑ **Vocabulary** Multiple-Meaning Words, 117I–117J ☑ **Study Skills** Parts of a Book, 116	☑ **Comprehension** Problem and Solution, 119A–119B Main Idea, 127E–127F ☑ **Vocabulary** Multiple-Meaning Words, 127G–127H Antonyms and Synonyms, 127I–127J ☑ **Study Skills** Parts of a Book, 126	☑ **Assess Skills** Story Elements Make Inferences Problem and Solution Main Idea Multiple-Meaning Words Antonyms and Synonyms Parts of a Book ☑ **Assess Grammar and Spelling** Review Sentences, 129K Review Spelling Patterns, 129L ☑ **Unit Progress Assessment** ☑ **Standardized Test Preparation** 🌐 **Reading Social Studies** 129A
Phonics and Decoding: Long *i* and Long *o*, 83 **Genre: Historical Fiction,** 69 **Character,** 75 **Summarize,** 77 **Context Clues,** 81	**Phonics and Decoding:** /ū/ and /ü/, 101 **Genre: Narrative Nonfiction,** 97 **Suffixes,** 99 **Summarize,** 103 **Make Inferences,** 109	**Genre: Science Article,** 121	

✏️ **Writing:** Personal Narrative, 93K **Grammar:** Sentence Combining, 93M–93N **Spelling:** Words with Long *i* and Long *o*, 93O–93P	✏️ **Writing:** Personal Narrative, 117K **Grammar:** More Sentence Combining, 117M–117N **Spelling:** Words with /ū/ and /ü/, 117O–117P	✏️ **Writing:** Personal Narrative, 127K **Grammar:** Run-on Sentences, 127M–127N **Spelling:** Words from Health, 127O–127P	✏️ **Unit Writing Process:** Personal Narrative, 129E–129J

Read Aloud: "Dakota Dugout," 66E	Read Aloud: "Seal," 94E	Read Aloud: "The Dentist," 118E	👥 **GROUP** Cooperative Theme Project Research and Inquiry: Reflections of the Past, 129
Stories in Art: *Admiring the New House,* 66	Stories in Art: Burdick-Childs Family Quilt, 94	Stories in Art: *Tiger,* 118	
Social Studies: Geographical Features, 72	Social Studies: Map Skills, 98	Health/Science: Dental Hygiene, 120A	
Science Test the Weather Report, 74	Science: Water Mammals, 102	Science: Parts of a Tooth, 125	
Math: Thunder and Lightning, 80	Math: Seal Math, 104		
Social Studies: Maine, 91	Math: Estimating Distances, 115		
Farming, 82	The Inuit and Seals, 108		

UNIT 1

Unit Resources

LITERATURE

LEVELED BOOKS

📖 **Easy:**
- *The Stony Creek Bandit*
- *Postcards from Mari Vic*
- *Sukey Johnson Builds a House*
- *Run Fast, Fly Far*

📖 **Independent:**
- *Martin's Journey*
- *Home on the Range*
- *Laura and the Great Quake*
- *A Siren's Journey*

📖 **Challenge:**
- *Lost and Found*
- *The Story of Cesar Chavez*
- *Trevor, Knight-In-Training*
- *Journey Against All Odds*

LISTENING LIBRARY Recordings of the student book selections and poetry. Available on **audiocassette** and **compact disc**.

Macmillan/McGraw-Hill

ⓘ **Intervention** ▶
Easy Leveled Books
Skills Intervention Guide
Phonics Intervention Guide

SKILLS

LEVELED PRACTICE

Practice: Practice for comprehension, vocabulary, and study skills; plus practice for instructional vocabulary and story comprehension. Take-Home Story included for each lesson.

Reteach: Reteaching opportunities for students who need more help with assessed skills.

Extend: Extension activities for vocabulary, comprehension, story, and study skills.

TEACHING CHARTS Instructional charts for modeling vocabulary and tested skills. Also available as **transparencies**.

WORD BUILDING MANIPULATIVE CARDS Cards with words and structural elements for word building and practicing vocabulary.

LANGUAGE SUPPORT BOOK

ESL Parallel lessons and practice for students needing language support.

PHONICS/PHONEMIC AWARENESS PRACTICE BOOK Additional practice focusing on key phonetic elements.

FLUENCY ASSESSMENT Evaluation and practice for building reading fluency.

LANGUAGE ARTS

GRAMMAR PRACTICE BOOK Provides practice for grammar and mechanics lessons.

SPELLING PRACTICE BOOK Provides practice and home involvement activities.

DAILY LANGUAGE ACTIVITIES Reinforce grammar, mechanics, and usage skills. Available as **blackline masters** and **transparencies.**

WRITING PROCESS TRANSPARENCIES Model each stage of the writing process.

HANDWRITING HANDBOOKS Offer instruction and practice.

McGraw-Hill School
TECHNOLOGY

🔵 **VOCABULARY PUZZLEMAKER** Provides practice with instructional vocabulary.

🔵 **HANDWRITING CD-ROM** Offers instruction and practice.

🔵 **MINDJOGGER VIDEOS** Review grammar and writing skills.

interNET CONNECTION Extends lesson activities through Research and Inquiry Ideas.

Visit **www.mhschool.com/reading**

Resources for
Meeting Individual Needs

EASY	ON-LEVEL	CHALLENGE	LANGUAGE SUPPORT

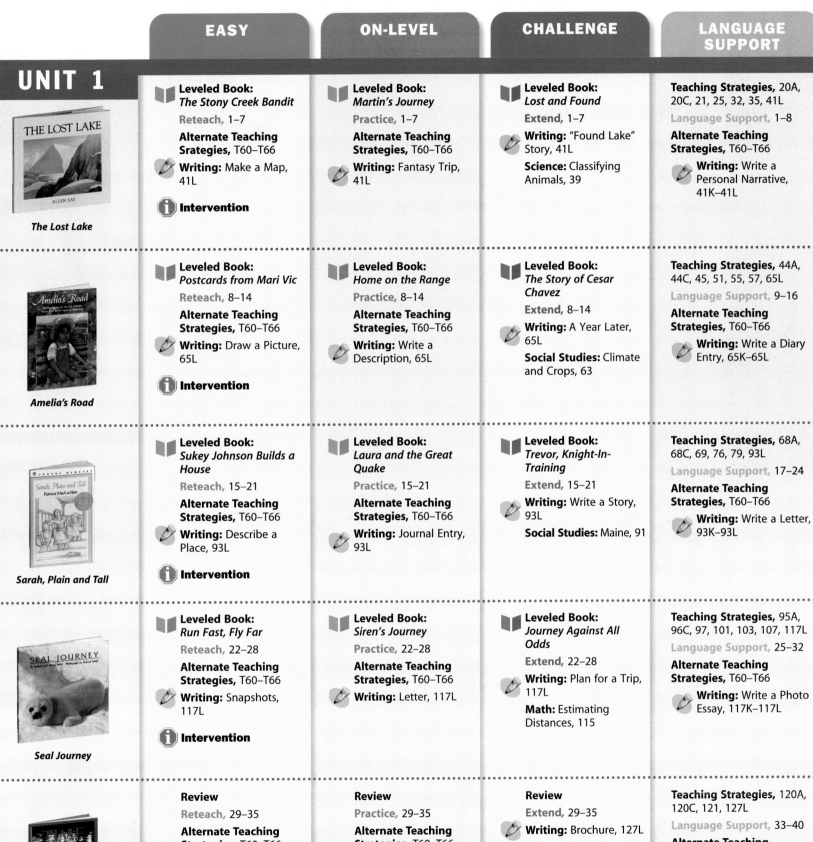

UNIT 1

The Lost Lake

Leveled Book: *The Stony Creek Bandit*

Reteach, 1–7

Alternate Teaching Strategies, T60–T66

Writing: Make a Map, 41L

ⓘ **Intervention**

Leveled Book: *Martin's Journey*

Practice, 1–7

Alternate Teaching Strategies, T60–T66

Writing: Fantasy Trip, 41L

Leveled Book: *Lost and Found*

Extend, 1–7

Writing: "Found Lake" Story, 41L

Science: Classifying Animals, 39

Teaching Strategies, 20A, 20C, 21, 25, 32, 35, 41L

Language Support, 1–8

Alternate Teaching Strategies, T60–T66

Writing: Write a Personal Narrative, 41K–41L

Amelia's Road

Leveled Book: *Postcards from Mari Vic*

Reteach, 8–14

Alternate Teaching Strategies, T60–T66

Writing: Draw a Picture, 65L

ⓘ **Intervention**

Leveled Book: *Home on the Range*

Practice, 8–14

Alternate Teaching Strategies, T60–T66

Writing: Write a Description, 65L

Leveled Book: *The Story of Cesar Chavez*

Extend, 8–14

Writing: A Year Later, 65L

Social Studies: Climate and Crops, 63

Teaching Strategies, 44A, 44C, 45, 51, 55, 57, 65L

Language Support, 9–16

Alternate Teaching Strategies, T60–T66

Writing: Write a Diary Entry, 65K–65L

Sarah, Plain and Tall

Leveled Book: *Sukey Johnson Builds a House*

Reteach, 15–21

Alternate Teaching Strategies, T60–T66

Writing: Describe a Place, 93L

ⓘ **Intervention**

Leveled Book: *Laura and the Great Quake*

Practice, 15–21

Alternate Teaching Strategies, T60–T66

Writing: Journal Entry, 93L

Leveled Book: *Trevor, Knight-In-Training*

Extend, 15–21

Writing: Write a Story, 93L

Social Studies: Maine, 91

Teaching Strategies, 68A, 68C, 69, 76, 79, 93L

Language Support, 17–24

Alternate Teaching Strategies, T60–T66

Writing: Write a Letter, 93K–93L

Seal Journey

Leveled Book: *Run Fast, Fly Far*

Reteach, 22–28

Alternate Teaching Strategies, T60–T66

Writing: Snapshots, 117L

ⓘ **Intervention**

Leveled Book: *Siren's Journey*

Practice, 22–28

Alternate Teaching Strategies, T60–T66

Writing: Letter, 117L

Leveled Book: *Journey Against All Odds*

Extend, 22–28

Writing: Plan for a Trip, 117L

Math: Estimating Distances, 115

Teaching Strategies, 95A, 96C, 97, 101, 103, 107, 117L

Language Support, 25–32

Alternate Teaching Strategies, T60–T66

Writing: Write a Photo Essay, 117K–117L

Open Wide, Don't Bite!

Review

Reteach, 29–35

Alternate Teaching Strategies, T60–T66

Writing: Comic Strip, 127L

ⓘ **Intervention**

Review

Practice, 29–35

Alternate Teaching Strategies, T60–T66

Writing: Dialogue, 127L

Review

Extend, 29–35

Writing: Brochure, 127L

Science: Parts of a Tooth, 125

Teaching Strategies, 120A, 120C, 121, 127L

Language Support, 33–40

Alternate Teaching Strategies, T60–T66

Writing: Write About an Experience, 127K–127L

INFORMAL

Informal Assessment

- Comprehension, 19B, 36, 37, 41F, 41H; 43B, 60, 61, 65F, 65H; 67B, 88, 89, 93F, 93H; 95B, 112, 113, 117F, 117H; 119B, 123, 127F
- Vocabulary, 41J, 65J, 93J, 117J, 127H, 127J

Performance Assessment

- Scoring Rubrics, 41L, 65L, 93L, 117L, 127L, 129J
- Research and Inquiry, 16J, 129
- Writing Process, 41K, 65K, 93K, 117K, 127K
- Listening, Speaking, Viewing Activities, 18E, 18, 20A, 20–39, 41D, 41L; 42E, 42, 44A, 44–63, 65D, 65L; 66E, 66, 68A, 68–91, 93D, 93L; 94E, 94, 96A, 96–115, 117D, 117L; 118E, 118, 120A, 120–125, 127D, 127L
- Portfolio, 41L, 65L, 93L, 117L, 127L
- Writing, 41K–41L, 65K–65L, 93K–93L, 117K–117L, 127K–127L, 129E–129J
- Cross Curricular Activities, 24, 28, 30, 34, 39, 48, 54, 56, 58, 63, 72, 74, 80, 91, 98, 102, 104, 115, 125
- Fluency, 36, 60, 88, 112, 122

Leveled Practice

Practice, Reteach, Extend

- **Comprehension**
  Story Elements, 1, 5, 15, 19
  Make Inferences, 6, 13, 27
  Problem and Solution, 8, 12, 20, 29
  Main Idea, 22, 26, 33
- **Vocabulary Strategies**
  Multiple-Meaning Words, 7, 28, 34
  Antonyms and Synonyms, 14, 21, 35
- **Study Skills**
  Parts of a Book: 4, 11, 18, 25, 32

FORMAL

Selection Assessments

- **Skills and Vocabulary Words**
  The Lost Lake, 1–2
  Amelia's Road, 3–4
  Sarah, Plain and Tall, 5–6
  Seal Journey, 7–8
  Open Wide, Don't Bite! 9–10

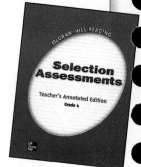

Unit 1 Test

- **Comprehension**
  Story Elements
  Make Inferences
  Problem and Solution
  Main Idea
- **Vocabulary Strategies**
  Multiple-Meaning Words
  Antonyms and Synonyms
- **Study Skills**
  Parts of a Book

Grammar and Spelling Assessment

- **Grammar**
  Sentences, 31–32
- **Spelling**
  Unit Assessment, 31–32

Fluency Assessment

- Fluency Passages, 6–9

Diagnostic/Placement Evaluation

- Informal Reading Inventory
- Running Record
- Placement Tests

Test Preparation

- Test Power, 41, 65, 93, 117, 127
- Additional standardized test preparation materials available

 Reading Test Generator

- Assessment Software

Assessment Checklist

Student .... **Grade** ....

Teacher ....

	The Lost Lake	Amelia's Road	Sarah, Plain and Tall	Seal Journey	Open Wide, Don't Bite!	Assessment Summary
LISTENING/SPEAKING						
Participates in oral language experiences.						
Listens and speaks to gain knowledge of culture.						
Speaks appropriately to audiences for different purposes.						
Communicates clearly.						
READING						
Uses a variety of word identification strategies, including						
• Multiple-Meaning Words						
• Synonyms and Antonyms						
Reads with fluency and understanding.						
Reads widely for different purposes in varied sources.						
Develops an extensive vocabulary.						
Uses a variety of strategies to comprehend selections						
• Make Inferences						
• Problem and Solution						
• Main Idea						
Responds to various texts.						
Analyzes the characteristics of various types of texts, including						
• Story Elements (Character, Setting, Plot)						
Conducts research using various sources, including					✓	
• Parts of a Book: Glossary, TOC and Headings, Index, Captions						
Reads to increase knowledge.						
WRITING						
Writes for a variety of audiences and purposes.						
Composes original texts using the conventions of written language such as capitalization and penmanship.						
Spells proficiently.						
Composes texts applying knowledge of grammar and usage.						
Uses writing processes.						
Evaluates own writing and writing of others.						

+ Observed   – Not Observed

Introduce the Theme

Reflections

Stories let us share the experiences of others.

DISCUSS THE THEME Write the theme statement on the board. Read it aloud with students. Explain that *reflections* has several meanings and that its meaning here is *thoughts and careful considerations.* Ask:

- What can stories tell us about other people's lives?

- What are some of your favorite stories? What makes them special to you?

- Do you prefer to read stories that are about real people and events or stories that are about imaginary people and events? Why do you feel that way?

- Some people share their stories through books. What are other ways people might share stories? (movies, letters, E-mail, pictures, newspaper articles, oral story-telling)

- Do you think it is possible to see yourself reflected in stories about other people? Give an example.

PREVIEW UNIT SELECTIONS Have students preview the unit by reading the table of contents and turning pages throughout the selections. Encourage students to read the selection titles and to notice the illustrations. Ask:

- How might these stories relate to the theme?

- What may be some similarities and differences among these stories?

- Are any of these selections about real people and real events? How can you tell?

As students read the literature and come to know the characters, settings, and events, have them consider the ways in which stories allow us to share the experiences of others. Discuss how reading may have helped students experience the cultures of distant lands. Have students describe memorable experiences they've read about that were previously unfamiliar. Finally, discuss any new activities students may have explored after reading about someone else's experiences.

THEME CONNECTIONS

Each of the five selections relates to the unit theme Reflections as well as to the global theme Experience. These thematic links will help students to make connections across texts.

The Lost Lake A father and son share a camping experience.

Amelia's Road The daughter of migrant workers reflects on a way to find a place that is all her own.

Sarah, Plain and Tall A mail-order bride starts a new life on the prairie and reflects on the life she left behind.

Seal Journey A father and son share the experience of photographing harp seals on Prince Edward Island.

Open Wide, Don't Bite! Readers learn what it's like to be an animal dentist.

Activity

Research *and* Inquiry

GROUP

Theme Project: Reflections of the Past

Have students work in teams to brainstorm ways in which older people can share their experiences and help others learn about the past. Have students choose a decade for a project that will include reflections on our past.

Make a Resource Chart Have students first list everything they know about the decade they chose. Then have them create a three-column chart like the one shown below. In the first column have them list **Questions** about the time period. In the second column have them list **Resources** that will help them answer the questions. When the research is finished, students can write **Answers** in the third column. Remind them to identify individuals and to cite sources properly.

Create a Presentation When their research is complete, ask students to choose a format or organizational structure for their presentations. For example, students could make a class newspaper, write a script for a video documentary, or create a multimedia presentation. Suggest that they use audio and visual aids in their presentations.

QUESTIONS	RESOURCES	ANSWERS
• What happened in my hometown or city during that decade?	• parents and neighbors, local historical society, newspapers, town Web site	
• What happened in the rest of the country? the world?	• newspapers, magazines, almanacs, Internet	
• What were relatives or other people I know doing at the time?	• relatives and friends, photo albums, school reports	

See **Wrap Up the Theme**, pages 128–129.

Research Strategies

Students may wish to interview relatives or other adults. Share these interview tips.

- Before the interview, prepare a list of questions.
- At the beginning of the interview, explain your purpose.
- During the interview, ask questions simply and directly. Make eye contact.

- Listen carefully to the answers. Ask follow-up questions if you want more information.
- Take notes. Don't forget to identify the person you interviewed, as well as any other sources.

*inter*NET **CONNECTION** Students can learn more about important events of the 20th century by visiting *www.mhschool.com/reading*

Poetry

Read the Poem

READ ALOUD Read "To" by Lee Bennett Hopkins aloud to students. Read the poem slowly, line by line. Afterward, ask:

- How does this poem relate to the unit theme Reflections?
- What everyday experiences does the narrator share?
- What do you notice about the opening and closing lines?

 LISTENING LIBRARY The poem is available on **audiocassette** and on **compact disc.**

CHORAL READING Assign small groups different portions of the poem to memorize and recite chorally. Have groups think about the **tempo**, the speed at which the poem moves, as they practice. After the readings, discuss whether the short lines create a faster or slower tempo or if the tempo doesn't change at all.

Learn About Poetry

STANZAS Explain:

- A **stanza** is a group of lines in a poem. A stanza forms one part of a poem or song.
- A line of space separates stanzas.
- Short poems may have only one stanza.

Have volunteers identify each stanza.

TEXT FEATURES Explain:

- Poets may set off a word, line, or stanza by using **capital letters**, **bold type** (darker type), or **italics** (slanted type). Italics, for example, may add emphasis or help lines stand out as a distinct section.
- **Indenting** is another way poets can emphasize or set off part of a poem.

Discuss why Hopkins may have italicized and indented the third stanza.

MEET THE POET

ABOUT LEE BENNETT HOPKINS Lee Bennett Hopkins has written and edited many poetry collections for children and young adults. His books include *Good Rhymes, Good Times!, Pass the Poetry, Please!,* and *Been to Yesterdays: Poems of a Life,* which won the Christopher Medal. He has also received numerous awards for his work as an educator and children's literacy advocate.

Reflections

To
make
this world
a whole lot
brighter

when
I
grow up
I'll
be
a writer.
I'll
write about
some things
I know—

*how to bunt
how to throw . . .
a Christmas wish
a butter dish . . .
a teddy bear
an empty chair . . .
the love I have inside
to
share . . .*

Yes.

To
make
this world
a whole lot
brighter,

when
I grow up
I'll
be
a
writer.

by Lee Bennett Hopkins

17

Poetry

LITERARY DEVICES: FIRST PERSON
Read the poem aloud emphasizing the words *I* and *I'll*. Explain that the words *I* and *I'll* indicate that the poem is written from a **first-person** point of view: The narrator, the person speaking in the poem, describes first-hand experiences using the pronoun *I*. Have students point out all the first-person clue words.

Then discuss the relationship between the poet and the narrator in this poem. Ask how old the narrator seems to be. Suggest that, in this poem, the author may be imagining the moment he first decided to be a writer.

Oral Response

SMALL-GROUP DISCUSSIONS Have students share personal responses to the poem and discuss these questions:

GROUP

- Why does the narrator want to be a writer?
- Why is it important for writers to write about things they know?
- What are some jobs that you are interested in doing when you grow up? How might each job help make the world a brighter place?
- The closing lines of the poem repeat the opening lines almost exactly. What is the effect of this repetition?
- What do you think of the poem's title?

WRITE A POEM

Rewrite the Poem Have students write their own version of this poem. Suggest that they copy the first stanza and last stanza and create a new middle. Have them begin by brainstorming ideas: What are some things they know well enough to write about someday? Which experiences could they write about to make this world brighter? Encourage students to share their reflections.

Make a Class Poetry Book Have students illustrate their poems and compile them in a class poetry book.

WRITING

17

Reaching All Learners

Concept
- Camping

Comprehension
- Story Elements

Vocabulary
- brand-new
- compass
- darted
- mug
- muttered
- talker

Anthology

The Lost Lake

Selection Summary Students will read about a father and son who set out to find a special place to camp and end up reflecting on the special relationship they have with each other.

Stories in Art focuses on the **comprehension** skill

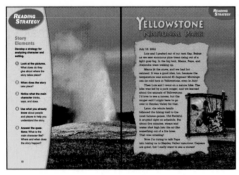

Reading Strategy applies the **comprehension** skill

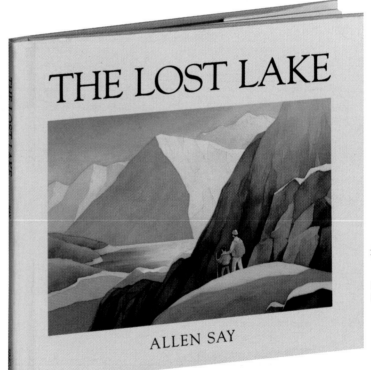

Listening Library

INSTRUCTIONAL pages 20–41

About the Author/Illustrator Born in Yokohama, Japan, Allen Say knew he wanted to be a cartoonist at the age of six. He describes as the happiest times of his life the four years as a young teen that he spent drawing and painting under his mentor, Noro Shinpei.

Say originally chose photography as his career and created illustrations only as a hobby. However, that changed when Say realized that working on books brought him the joy he knew as a boy in his mentor's studio.

Same Concept, Skills and Vocabulary!

Leveled Books

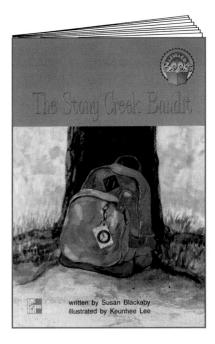

EASY
Lesson on pages 41A and 41D

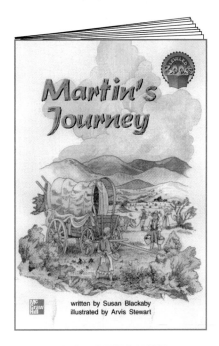

INDEPENDENT
Lesson on pages 41B and 41D

 Take-Home version available

CHALLENGE
Lesson on pages 41C and 41D

Leveled Practice

EASY
Reteach, 1–7 blackline masters with reteaching opportunities for each assessed skill

INDEPENDENT/ON-LEVEL
Practice, 1–7 workbook with Take-Home stories and practice opportunities for each assessed skill and story comprehension

CHALLENGE
Extend, 1–7 blackline masters that offer challenge activities for each assessed skill

Quizzes Prepared by Accelerated Reader®

WORKSTATION Activities

Social Studies . . .	Map Skills, *28*
Science	Mountain Animals, *24*
	Classifying Animals, *39*
Math	Fractions, *34*
Art	Special Places, *30*
Language Arts . .	Read Aloud, *18E*
Cultural Perspectives	Family Activities, *22*
Writing	A Personal Narrative, *38*
Research and Inquiry	Find Out More, *39*
🖥 **Internet Activities**	www.mhschool.com/reading

THE LOST LAKE

ALLEN SAY

Suggested Lesson Planner

Comprehension
Vocabulary
Phonics/Decoding
Study Skills
Listening, Speaking, Viewing, Representing

DAY 1

Read **Read Aloud Folktale,** 18E
"The Paper Garden"

Develop Visual Literacy, 18

☑ **Introduce Story Elements,** 19A–19B
Teaching Chart 1
Reteach, Practice, Extend, 1

Read **Reading Strategy: Story Elements,** 19
"Yellowstone National Park"

ℹ️ Intervention Program

DAY 2

Build Background, 20A
Develop Oral Language

Vocabulary, 20B–20C

brand-new	*darted*	*muttered*
compass	*mug*	*talker*

Teaching Chart 2
Word Building Manipulative Cards
Reteach, Practice, Extend, 2

Read **Read the Selection,** 20–37
☑ Story Elements

Genre: Realistic Fiction, 21

Cultural Perspectives, 22

ℹ️ Intervention Program

Curriculum Connections

Link Works of Art, 18

Link Science, 20A

Writing

✏️ **Writing Prompt:** Write a paragraph describing a quiet place you like to go to when you want to relax.

✏️ **Writing Prompt:** Imagine that you and your friend get lost while camping in the woods. Tell about the surprising and scary events that occur.

📓 **Journal Writing,** 37
Quick-Write

Grammar

Introduce the Concept: Sentences, 41M
Daily Language Activity
1. luke likes to hike L, .
2. did they bring enough food D, ?
3. luke's father carried the tent L, .

Grammar Practice Book, 1

Teach the Concept: Sentences, 41M
Daily Language Activity
1. will we eat fish for dinner W, ?
2. help me set up camp H, .
3. boy, am I tired B, !

Grammar Practice Book, 2

Spelling

Pretest: Words with Short Vowels, 41O
Spelling Practice Book, 1, 2

Explore the Pattern: Words with Short Vowels, 41O
Spelling Practice Book, 3

 Intervention Program Available

Meeting Individual Needs

 = Skill Assessed in Unit Test

 Intervention Program Available

DAY 3 — Read the Literature

Rereading for Fluency, 36

Story Questions and Activities, 38–39
Reteach, Practice, Extend, 3

Study Skill, 40
☑ **Parts of a Book**
Teaching Chart 3
Reteach, Practice, Extend, **4**

Test Power, 41

 Read the Leveled Books, 41A–41D
Guided Reading
Short Vowels
☑ **Story Elements**
☑ **Instructional Vocabulary**

 Intervention Program

DAY 4 — Build Skills

 Read the Leveled Books and Self-Selected Books

☑ **Review Story Elements,** 41E–41F
Teaching Chart 4
Reteach, Practice, Extend, 5
Language Support, 6

☑ **Introduce Make Inferences,** 41G–41H
Teaching Chart 5
Reteach, Practice, Extend, 6
Language Support, 7

Minilessons, 23, 27, 29, 35

Intervention Program

DAY 5 — Build Skills

Read Self-Selected Books

☑ **Introduce Multiple-Meaning Words,** 41I–41J
Teaching Chart 6
Reteach, Practice, Extend, 7
Language Support, 8

Listening, Speaking, Viewing, Representing, 41L

Minilessons, 23, 27, 29

Phonics Review,
Short Vowels, 35

Phonics/Phonemic Awareness Practice Book, 1–4

Intervention Program

Activity Science, 24; Social Studies, 28

Activity Art, 30

Activity Math, 34; Science, 39

Writing Prompt: Describe the perfect getaway for you and a parent or other relative. The destination can be real or fantasy.

Writing Process: Personal Narrative, 41K
Prewrite, Draft

Writing Prompt: Write a persuasive paragraph to convince a hesitant city dweller to "rough it" in the woods.

Writing Process: Personal Narrative, 41K
Revise

Meeting Individual Needs for Writing, 41L

Writing Prompt: At the beginning of the story, Dad isn't much of a talker and Luke is bored and lonely. Suppose that Luke writes to you for help. Write an advice column that includes Luke's letter and your advice.

Writing Process: Personal Narrative, 41K
Edit/Proofread, Publish

Review and Practice: Sentences, 41N
Daily Language Activity
1. put the sleeping bag in the tent P, .
2. our secret lake is awesome O, !
3. do you think it is going to rain D, ?

Grammar Practice Book, 3

Review and Practice: Sentences, 41N
Daily Language Activity
1. luke liked to watch his dad cook L, .
2. i think I hear a bear I, !
3. get some wood for the fire G, .

Grammar Practice Book, 4

Assess and Reteach: Sentences, 41N
Daily Language Activity
1. can we come back next year C, ?
2. we saw our lake below us W, .
3. watch out for falling rocks W, !

Grammar Practice Book, 5, 6

Practice and Extend: Words with Short Vowels, 41P
Spelling Practice Book, 4

Proofread and Write: Words with Short Vowels, 41P
Spelling Practice Book, 5

Assess and Reteach: Words with Short Vowels, 41P
Spelling Practice Book, 6

18D

Link
Language Arts

Read Aloud

The Paper Garden
a folktale by Tony Ramsay

A long time ago, on a beautiful island that lay on the sea like a new moon, there was an emperor. He lived in a palace which looked out onto the loveliest garden in the East. It was a garden full of peacocks and cherry trees. It had a lake as smooth as glass. And most precious of all, lining its twisting paths, were rows of golden kushiri flowers, so rare they grew nowhere else in the world.

One day as the Emperor was sitting in his garden a breeze blew in over the kushiri beds and made their leaves rustle like paper kites. The Emperor sniffed the air. Then, bending low, he looked carefully at the lake which lay in the middle of his garden. What he saw made his nose wrinkle in anger.

"The wind!" he cried. "The wind is ruffling my lake!"

And sure enough the lake had changed. A moment before it had looked like a silver mirror. Now it was like a rumpled blanket where someone had been sleeping.

Continued on pages T2–T4

Oral Comprehension

LISTENING AND SPEAKING Read the folktale aloud. Tell students to visualize the royal garden as you read. After reading, ask:

• What makes the royal garden a special place?

• Did you enjoy this folktale? What types of stories do you enjoy listening to most?

Explain that in a folktale the main character usually learns a lesson. Ask: What does the emperor learn?

GENRE STUDY: FOLKTALE Discuss literary devices used in "The Paper Garden."

• Comparisons, such as "a lake as smooth as glass," "like a rumpled blanket," "leaves rustle like paper kites," paint vivid pictures of the garden.

• Repetition provides rhythm. An angry emperor shouts, "Stop! … Stop, I command you!"

Activity Through movement, have students show the emotions of the people and the fragile state of the animals and plants in the garden.

▶ **Kinesthetic/Spatial**

Stories in Art

Like a story, a painting can show you time and place. It can also describe characters in a setting.

Look at this landscape painting. What can you tell about it? How does the artist create a quiet scene? How do the people feel in this setting? What makes you think so?

Close your eyes. What part of the painting do you remember? Why?

Gathering Watercress on the River Mole
by William F. Witherington
Owen Edgar Gallery, England

18

Analyze Character and Setting

VIEWING William F. Witherington uses color and perspective to create a peaceful outdoor scene in his painting. Ask students to tell how the artist makes the people seem a part of the country setting. Then have them tell what the colors of the painting reveal about the place.

Read the page with students, encouraging individual interpretations of the painting.

Ask students to analyze the characters and setting in the painting. For example:

- It is a quiet scene. All you would hear would be the people laughing and birds singing.

- The people are from an earlier time. Their clothes look different from mine.

REPRESENTING Have students role-play the scene in the picture. Encourage them to consider time, place, and weather.

Introduce Story Elements

OBJECTIVES

Students will make inferences about and analyze character and setting.

Skills Finder

Story Elements

Introduce	19A-B
Review	41E-F, 67A-B, 93E-F
Test	Unit 1
Maintain	163, 323, 527, 575

LANGUAGE SUPPORT

ESL Help students differentiate between character and setting by pointing to pictures of people and places. Ask students to respond with "character" or "setting" accordingly as you point. Invite a volunteer to take over your role as a pointer so you can observe students' understanding of this skill.

PREPARE

Discuss Familiar Characters and Settings
Have students pretend to be a favorite character from a book they have read. Ask: What do you look like? Where are you? How does this place make you feel?

TEACH

Define Character and Setting
Tell students: You can learn about the characters—the people or animals in a story—by noticing what they say, think, and do when they are alone or with other characters. Many times a character's actions are affected by the setting—where and when the story takes place.

Backyard Tent

Tracy was excited about sleeping in the tent that her dad had set up in the backyard. This would be her first time sleeping outside, and she was prepared for anything! She felt safe because inside the tent she had a flashlight, a book, blankets, a peanut butter sandwich, and a bottle of juice.

During the night, Tracy woke up to scratching noises. Her heart was beating fast, and she called out, "Who's there?"

Tracy laughed when the neighbor's dog came running into the tent and stole her sandwich. Tracy said, "I guess a backyard tent can also be a backyard restaurant!"

Teaching Chart 1

Read the Story and Model the Skill
Display **Teaching Chart 1.** Have students pay attention to clues about character and setting as the story is read.

MODEL I can tell by reading the title that the setting is in a backyard. The main character is Tracy, who is excited and a little nervous about sleeping outside in a tent.

Analyze Character and Setting
Have students underline clues that tell them what Tracy says, does, or feels and circle clues that describe the setting.

PRACTICE

Create a Setting and Character Chart
Using a Setting and Character chart, have students record the ways the setting affects what Tracy says and does. Help them begin filling in the chart and have volunteers complete it. ▶ **Linguistic/Logical**

SETTING	CHARACTER
backyard tent	Tracy is excited about sleeping in the tent.
outside	Tracy is prepared.
night	Tracy feels nervous.

ASSESS/CLOSE

Analyze Character and Setting
Ask students to compare themselves to Tracy. **How are they alike? How are they different?** (Sample answer: We both like adventure. I would be afraid to sleep outside by myself.) **What does Tracy do to make her setting more comfortable?** (She brings food and drink, something to read, a light, and blankets.) **What would you bring if you were sleeping in a backyard tent?** (Answers will vary.)

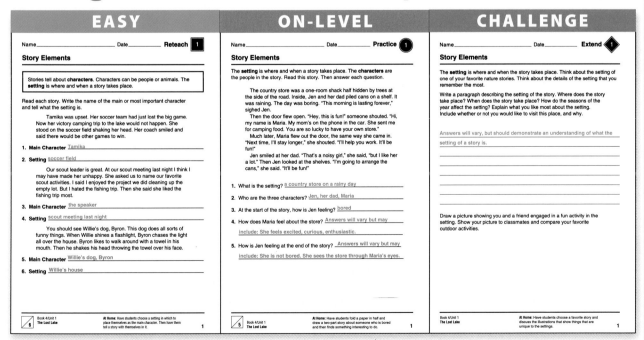

ALTERNATE TEACHING
STRATEGY
....

STORY ELEMENTS
For a different approach to teaching this skill, see page T60.

ℹ️ **Intervention** ▶ Skills
Intervention Guide, for direct instruction and extra practice in story elements

Meeting Individual Needs for Comprehension

EASY

Name_____ Date_____ **Reteach** 1

Story Elements

Stories tell about **characters**. Characters can be people or animals. The **setting** is where and when a story takes place.

Read each story. Write the name of the main or most important character and tell what the setting is.

Tamika was upset. Her soccer team had just lost the big game. Now her victory camping trip to the lake would not happen. She stood on the soccer field shaking her head. Her coach smiled and said there would be other games to win.

1. Main Character _Tamika_

2. Setting _soccer field_

Our scout leader is great. At our scout meeting last night I think I may have made her unhappy. She asked us to name our favorite scout activities. I said I enjoyed the project we did cleaning up the empty lot. But I hated the fishing trip. Then she said she liked the fishing trip most.

3. Main Character _the speaker_

4. Setting _scout meeting last night_

You should see Willie's dog, Byron. This dog does all sorts of funny things. When Willie shines a flashlight, Byron chases the light all over the house. Byron likes to walk around with a towel in his mouth. Then he shakes his head throwing the towel over his face.

5. Main Character _Willie's dog, Byron_

6. Setting _Willie's house_

Book 4/Unit 1
The Lost Lake 6

At Home: Have students choose a setting in which to place themselves as the main character. Then have them tell a story with themselves in it. 1

ON-LEVEL

Name_____ Date_____ **Practice** 1

Story Elements

The **setting** is where and when a story takes place. The **characters** are the people in the story. Read this story. Then answer each question.

The country store was a one-room shack half hidden by trees at the side of the road. Inside, Jen and her dad piled cans on a shelf. It was raining. The day was boring. "This morning is lasting forever," sighed Jen.

Then the door flew open. "Hey, this is fun!" someone shouted. "Hi, my name is Maria. My mom's on the phone in the car. She sent me for camping food. You are so lucky to have your own store."

Much later, Maria flew out the door, the same way she came in. "Next time, I'll stay longer," she shouted. "I'll help you work. It'll be fun!"

Jen smiled at her dad. "That's a noisy girl," she said, "but I like her a lot." Then Jen looked at the shelves. "I'm going to arrange the cans," she said. "It'll be fun!"

1. What is the setting? _a country store on a rainy day_

2. Who are the three characters? _Jen, her dad, Maria_

3. At the start of the story, how is Jen feeling? _bored_

4. How does Maria feel about the store? _Answers will vary but may include: She feels excited, curious, enthusiastic._

5. How is Jen feeling at the end of the story? _Answers will vary but may include: She is not bored. She sees the store through Maria's eyes._

Book 4/Unit 1
The Lost Lake 5

At Home: Have students fold a paper in half and draw a two-part story about someone who is bored and then finds something interesting to do. 1

CHALLENGE

Name_____ Date_____ **Extend** 1

Story Elements

The **setting** is where and when the story takes place. Think about the setting of one of your favorite nature stories. Think about the details of the setting that you remember the most.

Write a paragraph describing the setting of the story. Where does the story take place? When does the story take place? How do the seasons of the year affect the setting? Explain what you like most about the setting. Include whether or not you would like to visit this place, and why.

Answers will vary, but should demonstrate an understanding of what the setting of a story is.

_____

_____

_____

_____

_____

_____

Draw a picture showing you and a friend engaged in a fun activity in the setting. Show your picture to classmates and compare your favorite outdoor activities.

Book 4/Unit 1
The Lost Lake

At Home: Have students choose a favorite story and discuss the illustrations that show things that are unique to the settings. 1

Reteach, 1   Practice, 1   Extend, 1

OBJECTIVES

Students will make inferences about character and analyze setting.

Apply **Story Elements**

READING STRATEGY

Story Elements

Develop a strategy for analyzing character and setting.

1. **Look at the pictures.** What clues do they give about where the story takes place?

2. **When does the story take place?**

3. **Notice what the main character** thinks, says, and does.

4. **Use what you already know** about people and places to help you understand the story.

5. **Answer the questions:** What is the main character like? Where and when does the story happen?

19

READING STRATEGY

YELLOWSTONE NATIONAL PARK

July 18, 2002

Luis and I peeked out of our tent flap. Before us we saw enormous pine trees rising out of a light gray fog. In the big tent, Mama, Papa, and Alejandra were waking up.

Mama lit the stove, and we had hot oatmeal. It was a good idea, too, because the temperature was around 45 degrees! Mornings can be cold here in Yellowstone, even in July!

Then Luis and I went on a nature hike. The hike was led by a park ranger, and we learned about the animals of Yellowstone. I'd love to see a moose, but the ranger said I might have to go over to Hayden Valley for that.

Later, the whole family followed the hiking trail to the most famous geyser, Old Faithful. It erupted right on schedule. For about five minutes, steam and water shot high into the air like something out of a fire hose. That was amazing!

Now I'm trying to talk Papa into taking us to Hayden Valley tomorrow. Geysers are great, but I really want to see a moose!

PREVIEW Have students preview the journal entry. Explain that a journal entry is a personal narrative. It tells about a day in the life of the narrator. Ask:

• Who is writing? (a young boy; brother of Luis and Alejandra)

• Where does the story take place? (at Yellowstone National Park)

SET PURPOSES Tell students that they will apply what they have learned about the story elements character and setting as they read the journal entry.

APPLY THE STRATEGY Discuss this strategy for analyzing character and setting in a selection:

• Preview any illustrations to get an idea of the places involved.

• Look for words or phrases that tell you when the story takes place.

• Remember that an author may tell you about a character through that character's thoughts.

• Compare characters and settings to people and places you know in real life.

• Identify and describe the characters and setting.

Activity Have each student create a Setting and Character chart for the passage.

Build Background

Science

Concept: Camping

Anthology and Leveled Books

Evaluate Prior Knowledge

CONCEPT: CAMPING The characters in these stories have camping experiences. Have students share their own knowledge or experiences about camping.

COMPARE SETTINGS Have students list ways in which a camping setting is the same as or different from a home setting. Create a Venn diagram. ▶ **Logical/Visual**

CAMP		HOME
Different	**Alike**	**Different**
sleep outside or in a tent build a fire to cook use a flashlight to see	play games with family do chores	sleep indoors in a bed cook on a stove have electricity for lights

Graphic Organizer 14

PLAN A DAY Have students write a schedule of what they would do during a day of camping. For example, they may begin their day by washing in a stream at 7:00 in the morning and then eating breakfast cooked over a fire at 7:30 A.M.

Develop Oral Language

DISCUSS CAMPING If possible, bring in **ESL** camping supplies and have students identify and describe the function of each piece of equipment. Write the names of different camping equipment on cards. Students can choose a card, read the word, and then tell or act out how the equipment would be used on a camping trip. Then have students brainstorm a list of activities that could be a part of a camping trip in the woods. Write the list on the chalkboard, for example:

- hiking
- swimming
- canoeing
- fishing

Invite partners to pantomime one of the activities. Encourage the class to guess the activity and then use their five senses to describe what it would feel like to perform the activity outdoors.

LANGUAGE SUPPORT

See Language Support Book, pages 1–4, for teaching suggestions for Build Background.

BJECTIVES

Students will use context and structural clues to determine the meaning of vocabulary words.

compass
brand-new
muttered
darted
mug
talker

Vocabulary

Teach Vocabulary in Context

efinitions

compass (p. 31) an instrument for showing direction

brand-new (p. 22) never before used

muttered (p. 26) spoke in a low, unclear way

darted (p. 32) moved suddenly and quickly

mug (p. 22) a heavy drinking cup with a handle

talker (p. 21) a person who has much to say

Identify Vocabulary Words Display **Teaching Chart 2** and read the passage with students. Have volunteers circle each vocabulary word and underline other words that are clues to its meaning.

Walking in the Woods

1. Luke looked at the <u>needle</u> of his (compass) to see if he was <u>headed north.</u> **2.** His (brand-new) hiking boots hurt his feet because he had <u>never worn</u> them before. **3.** "Next time I will buy a larger pair of boots," Luke (muttered) qui-<u>etly</u> to himself. **4.** Luke and his dad took a break from hik- ing to watch as small birds (darted) through the trees, <u>mov-</u> <u>ing quickly</u> from branch to branch. **5.** Dad held his (mug) of <u>hot coffee</u> to warm his hands. **6.** "It's better to be a quiet <u>listener</u> than a (talker) when walking in the woods," Dad said. Luke smiled in agreement.

Teaching Chart 2

Story Words

These words from the selection may be unfamil- iar. Before students read, have them check the meaning and pronuncia- tion of each word in a dic- tionary or in the Glossary, beginning on page 756.

- canoeing, p. 21
- knapsack, p. 22
- poncho, p. 28
- glum, p. 31

Discuss Meanings Ask questions like these to help clarify word meanings:

- What is a compass used for?

- What word is the opposite of *brand-new?*

- If you muttered, did you use your hands or your mouth? How do you feel if you mutter about something?

- When the birds darted through the trees, were they moving fast or slow?

- What do you like to drink out of a mug?

- What is the base word of *talker?* Where would a talker be welcome? Not welcome?

Practice

Demonstrate Word Meaning

PARTNERS

Have partners take turns saying definitions, choosing the matching vocabulary cards, and using the words in sentences.

▶**Interpersonal/Linguistic**

compass   talker   darted

Word Building Manipulative Cards

Write Cartoon Captions

WRITING

Have partners draw cartoons about a camping adventure. Have them use vocabulary words to write captions for each frame. Invite pairs to share their finished work with the class.

▶ **Visual/Linguistic**

Assess Vocabulary

Use Words in Context

PARTNERS

Have students describe a real or imaginary place on a postcard, using as many vocabulary words as possible. Students should then exchange postcards with a partner and check for correct usage.

SPELLING/VOCABULARY CONNECTIONS

See Spelling Challenge Words, pages 41O–41P.

LANGUAGE SUPPORT

See the **Language Support Book**, pages 1–4, for teaching suggestions for Vocabulary.

Vocabulary PuzzleMaker

Provides vocabulary activities.

Meeting Individual Needs for Vocabulary

EASY	ON-LEVEL	ON-LEVEL	CHALLENGE

EASY

Name_____ Date_____ Reteach **2**

Vocabulary

Read each clue. Then find the vocabulary word in the row of letters and circle it.

brand-new	compass	darted	mug	muttered	talker

1. never used   d e (b r a n d n e w) t s z
2. use it to find direction   b e (c o m p a s s) r n y
3. moved fast   r e t (d a r t e d) n g l y
4. big cup with handle   c a l (m u g) r e j d m l
5. spoke unclearly   w e (m u t t e r e d) l a r g a
6. one who talks   m a c (t a l k e r) a y d

Story Comprehension   Reteach **3**

Write a ✔ next to every sentence that tells about "The Lost Lake."

✔ 1. Luke and Dad went on a camping trip.
___ 2. Dad often talked to Luke for hours at home.
___ 3. Dad liked to be with lots of other people at the lake.
✔ 4. Dad and Luke went looking for their own land.
✔ 5. Dad was like a mountain goat on the trail.
✔ 6. Dad and Luke had to look out for bears.
___ 7. Luke never tired while hiking in the woods.
✔ 8. Dad and Luke got to know each other better on their trip.

At Home: Have students retell the story of "The Lost Lake" in their own words.
2–3   Book 4/Unit 1 **The Lost Lake** **6**

Reteach, 2

ON-LEVEL

Name_____ Date_____ Practice **2**

Vocabulary

Answer each question, using the vocabulary word before each question in your response. Answers will vary.

1. **compass** Why might a hiker find a compass helpful? A compass helps a hiker locate directions.

2. **darted** Why might a squirrel have darted across your path? It might have darted because it was chased by a dog.

3. **muttered** Why might you have trouble understanding what a person said if he or she muttered? The muttered words would not be clear.

4. **mug** How is a mug different from a plate? A plate is flat and often holds food, a mug is a large cup that holds drinks.

5. **talker** What does it mean when we say that someone is a talker? We often mean that the person talks a lot without stopping.

6. **brand-new** How many times has something been worn when it is brand-new? When something is brand-new, it has never been worn.

At Home: Have students write sentences using each of the vocabulary words.
2   Book 4/Unit 1 **The Lost Lake** **6**

Practice, 2

ON-LEVEL

The Missing Compass

My name is Irina. This morning I got a compass for my birthday. It was just what I wanted. I went outside to try it out. I never knew before that the back door of our house faced north.

When Mom called me to come get a mug of lemonade, I left the compass in the grass. When I got back outside, it was gone. "Where is it?" I muttered. I began to get upset.

Then I saw the neighbor's dog, Chichi. He always wanted to play. I watched as he darted around the yard making playful growls. He was quite a talker. And there, dangling from his mouth was my brand-new compass.

The chase was on. I thought I'd never get the compass back, but Chichi saw my mug of lemonade on the steps. When he bent his head to drink it, I was able to grab the compass.

1. What gift did Irina get for her birthday? a compass
2. Where did she leave her brand-new gift? in the grass
3. How did Irina feel when she found her compass missing? She was getting upset.
4. How was Chichi moving? He darted quickly around the yard.
5. How did Irina's feelings change on her birthday? First, she was happy to receive a compass. She grew upset when she lost it, but was happy again after she found it.

At Home: Have students write how they feel when they lose something they like.
5 **The Lost Lake**   2a

Practice, 2a
Take-Home Story

CHALLENGE

Name_____ Date_____ Extend **2**

Vocabulary

brand-new	compass	darted	mug	muttered	talker

Suppose that you are on a hiking trip with a group of friends. You are keeping a journal about your trip. Write three journal entries using some of the words in the box. Use a separate piece of paper if you need more space.
Answers will vary but should include at least four vocabulary words used in the correct context and part of speech.

Extend **3**

Story Comprehension

Work with a partner. Choose one setting from "The Lost Lake." Write a short poem describing either Luke's or his father's feelings or reactions to the setting.
Answers will vary.

At Home: Read a poem about nature. Discuss how the poem reflects your feelings about nature.
2–3   Book 4/Unit 1 **The Lost Lake**

Extend, 2

20C

Comprehension

Prereading Strategies

PREVIEW AND PREDICT Have students read the title and preview the story, looking for pictures that give strong clues about the characters and the setting.

- What clues about the setting do the title and pictures give?
- Describe the characters by what you see in the pictures.
- What do you think this story will be about?
- How can you tell this story is realistic fiction, not fantasy? (The characters and the setting look real. The characters' actions seem real.) *Genre*

Have students record their predictions.

PREDICTIONS	WHAT HAPPENED
The main characters go camping.	
The story takes place near a lake.	

SET PURPOSES What do students want to find out by reading the story? For example:

- Where are the boy and the man going?
- What is important about the lost lake?

THE Lost Lake

by Allen Say

20

Meeting Individual Needs · Grouping Suggestions for Strategic Reading

EASY

Read Together Read the story with students. Have students use the Setting and Character chart to record important information. Comprehension and Intervention prompts offer additional help with decoding, vocabulary, and comprehension.

ON-LEVEL

Guided Instruction Choose from the Comprehension questions as you read the story with students. Have them use the Setting and Character chart during reading. You may wish to have students read the story first on their own.

CHALLENGE

Read Independently Before students read the story independently, remind them to think about the setting and how it affects what the characters say and do. Have students set up a Setting and Character chart as on page 21. After reading, students can use their charts to retell the story.

I went to live with Dad last summer.

Every day he worked in his room from morning to night, sometimes on weekends, too. Dad wasn't much of a talker, but when he was busy he didn't talk at all.

I didn't know anybody in the city, so I stayed home most of the time. It was too hot to play outside anyway. In one month I finished all the books I'd brought and grew tired of watching TV.

One morning I started cutting pictures out of old magazines, just to be doing something. They were pictures of mountains and rivers and lakes, and some showed people fishing and canoeing. Looking at them made me feel cool, so I pinned them up in my room.

Dad didn't notice them for two days. When he did, he looked at them one by one.

"Nice pictures," he said.

"Are you angry with me, Dad?" I asked, because he saved old magazines for his work.

"It's all right, Luke," he said. "I'm having this place painted soon anyway."

He thought I was talking about the marks I'd made on the wall.

21

Comprehension

☑ Apply Story Elements

STRATEGIC READING Before we begin reading, let's prepare Setting and Character charts. We can record story notes to help us better understand the story.

SETTING	CHARACTER

① **SETTING** What do we mean by the *setting* of a story? (the time and place of the story) **What do you notice about the two settings shown on pages 20 and 21?**

MODEL Those two settings look and feel very different. In the first picture, the characters are part of a grand outdoor scene. They look small, and no one else is around, yet they look like they are on an adventure. In the second picture, the characters somehow look lonely. Maybe that's because they are in separate rooms and facing opposite ways.

Genre

Realistic Fiction

Remind students that realistic fiction:

• features people, relationships, and problems very much like those in real life.

• is set in the present day.

• is set in places that could actually exist.

Activity After students read *The Lost Lake*, have them go over the text. Tell them to pick out details that make Dad and Luke seem like real people. They should go on to identify a problem confronting the two characters. Does this seem like a common problem faced by parents and children?

LANGUAGE SUPPORT

A blackline master of the Setting and Character chart is available in the **Language Support Book.**

Comprehension

2 **CHARACTER, SETTING** How do you think Luke is feeling at the beginning of the story? (bored and lonely) How is Dad feeling? (quiet and busy with work) Let's record their feelings and the setting on the Setting and Character chart.

SETTING	CHARACTER
home	Luke is bored and lonely. Dad is quiet and busy with work.

3 **CHARACTER** What has Dad done to make this Saturday morning different? (planned a camping trip) How does Luke feel when Dad tells him about the trip? How can you tell? (Luke seems excited. An exclamation point ends the first sentence. In the second, Luke implies the news woke him in a second.) How might Luke have awakened if Dad hadn't planned the trip? (Luke had been bored and lonely; he probably would have awakened unenthusiastically, thinking, "Just another day ahead.")

2 **3** That Saturday Dad woke me up early in the morning and told me we were going camping! I was wide awake in a second. He gave me a pair of brand-new hiking boots to try out. They were perfect.

In the hallway I saw a big backpack and a knapsack all packed and ready to go.

"What's in them, Dad?" I asked.

"Later," he said. "We have a long drive ahead of us."

In the car I didn't ask any more questions because Dad was so grumpy in the morning.

"Want a sip?" he said, handing me his mug. He'd never let me drink coffee before. It had lots of sugar in it.

22

CULTURAL PERSPECTIVES

FAMILY ACTIVITIES Explain that in many cultures a journey into the wilderness can be an important part of a young person's growing up.

RESEARCH AND INQUIRY Have students research the walkabout of Australia's Aborigines. Have them then write a paragraph that tells what they learned. ▶ **Interpersonal/Linguistic**

inter NET Students can find out **CONNECTION** more about the Aborigines of Australia by visiting **www.mhschool.com/reading**

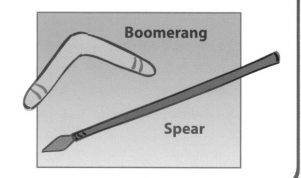

Boomerang

Spear

"Where are we going?" I finally asked.

"We're off to the Lost Lake, my lad."

"How can you lose a lake?"

"No one's found it, that's how." Dad was smiling! "Grandpa and I used to go there a long time ago. It was our special place, so don't tell any of your friends."

"I'll never tell," I promised. "How long are we going to stay there?"

"Five days, maybe a week."

"We're going to sleep outside for a whole week?"

"That's the idea."

"Oh, boy!"

23

Comprehension

④ SETTING Dad plans to take Luke to a special place, where his own father had taken him years ago. Try to imagine the setting in which you would find Lost Lake.

MODEL Luke's Dad says no one knows about the lake. In reading this statement, I begin to see a beautiful crystal-clear lake in a hard-to-find spot, maybe surrounded by tall trees and mountains. It's quiet and there is no sign of other people.

⑤ CHARACTER, SETTING Let's have a volunteer be Luke and another be Dad. Dad, how do you feel about getting away from work? Luke, how do you feel about going camping? *Role-Play*

Minilesson

REVIEW/MAINTAIN

Context Clues

Tell students that sometimes they need to reread a sentence or a paragraph to help them figure out an unfamiliar word. They are looking for context clues or information that will lead them to the meaning of the unfamiliar word.

• Have students find *knapsack* in the second paragraph on page 22.

• Then ask them to find context clues in the sentences around *knapsack* to help them identify its meaning. For example: "camping," "backpack," and "packed."

Activity Have students keep a list of unknown words as they read the story. Then have them record the clues that help them understand each word's meaning.

Comprehension

6 **CHARACTER, SETTING** How does the change of setting—from a city home to a mountain trail—affect Luke? (Luke is more active and talkative.) **How do you think Luke may be feeling now?** (excited and curious)

We got to the mountains in the afternoon.

"It's a bit of a hike to the lake, son," Dad said.

"I don't mind," I told him. "Are there any fish in the lake?"

"Hope so. We'll have to catch our dinner, you know."

"You didn't bring any food?"

6 "Of course not. We're going to live like true outdoorsmen."

"Oh . . ."

24

Activity

Cross Curricular: Science

MOUNTAIN ANIMALS Point out that animals that thrive in the mountains are sometimes different from those in cities, forests, and plains. Share the example of the mountain goat.

RESEARCH AND INQUIRY Have students research what kinds of animals live in mountain climates. Suggest they check science books, encyclopedias, or nature magazines. Then have students create a mural showing animals that live in hills and mountains.

▶ **Interpersonal/Spatial**

Mountain goat

Dad saw my face and started to laugh. He must have been joking. I didn't think we were going very far anyway, because Dad's pack was so heavy I couldn't even lift it.

Well, Dad was like a mountain goat. He went straight up the trail, whistling all the while. But I was gasping in no time. My knapsack got very heavy and I started to fall behind.

25

Comprehension

7 **CHARACTER, SETTING** Describe how Luke's dad is acting now. (He is making jokes and whistling.) Has Luke's dad changed, or is Luke seeing a side of his dad he's never seen before? (Possible answer: Luke's dad is more relaxed in this setting.) Act out, with gestures, the way Luke's dad is behaving. *Pantomime*

TEACHING **TIP**

CHARACTER, SETTING Organize the class into two groups. Have one group act like Luke's dad while he is still in the city. Have the other group show his actions on the mountain. Then ask the groups to switch roles. After the pantomime, have students brainstorm words that would describe Luke's dad in each setting.

LANGUAGE SUPPORT

ESL Check students' comprehension of vocabulary and idioms on these pages. Ask volunteers to explain in their own words the meaning of the phrases *a bit of a hike, catch our dinner, true outdoorsman, mountain goat,* and *in no time.*

If they have difficulty, guide students in looking for context clues to help them find the meanings of these phrases. Also encourage students to draw pictures or act out the phrases for further reinforcement.

Comprehension

8 **SETTING** As Luke and his dad continue hiking, the story's setting continues to change. Look at the picture on this page and compare it to the pictures on the pages we have already read. Describe how the setting has changed. (There are tall trees and many large rocks.)

8

Dad stopped for me often, but he wouldn't let me take off my pack. If I did I'd be too tired to go on, he said.

It was almost suppertime when we got to the lake.

The place reminded me of the park near Dad's apartment. He wasn't whistling or humming anymore.

"Welcome to the *Found* Lake," he muttered from the side of his mouth.

"What's wrong, Dad?"

"Do you want to camp with all these people around us?"

"I don't mind."

"Well, I do!"

"Are we going home?"

"Of course not!"

He didn't even take off his pack. He just turned and started to walk away.

26

Fluency

READ WITH EXPRESSION Lead students to understand that Dad and Luke have reached an emotional point in their journey and it is reflected in the dialogue on the page. Have partners take turns reading the dialogue on this page paying close attention to the punctuation marks. Ask them to consider how they would be feeling at this point if they were Luke. Remind students that reading with expression makes a story more interesting to the listener.

27

Comprehension

⑨ **CHARACTER, SETTING** Remember Dad told Luke that they were going to a place that no one else had found. Look at the picture on this page. What do you see? (There are many people camping at the lake.) How do you think Luke's dad feels? (unhappy) Why? (He wanted to go to a quiet place without other people.) Do you think Luke feels the same way? (No.) Why? (He is just happy to be away. He has never been here before, so he has nothing to compare it to.)

P/i **WORD STRUCTURE** Read the third paragraph on page 26. Find two words with the same ending. (whistling, humming) How were the base words changed when the endings were added? (dropped the final *e*; doubled the final consonant) *Graphophonic Cues*

Minilesson

REVIEW/MAINTAIN

Summarize

Tell students that it is a good idea to stop and summarize key points of the story as they read. This will be a review for them and will help them remember the story events.

• Ask students to think back and tell the main events of the story through page 27.

Activity Have students choose one of the following topics to summarize in one sentence:

• the characters' feelings as they started off on their trip.

• the situation at the Lost Lake.

P/i **PREVENTION/INTERVENTION**

WORD STRUCTURE Write *whistling* and *humming* on the chalkboard. Ask a volunteer to write under each word the corresponding base word. Lead students to see that the *e* was dropped in *whistle* and the last consonant was doubled in *hum* before *-ing* was added.

Ask students to brainstorm other words that follow these *-ing* rules, and list the words under the appropriate column on the chalkboard. Have students look for other *-ing* words on the pages they have already read in this story. (cutting, having, smiling, hiking) *Graphophonic Cues*

Comprehension

10 **CHARACTER** How has the setting changed Luke's and Dad's moods? Let's have two volunteers role-play Luke and Dad and tell how they feel about the Lost Lake. *Role-Play*

Let's record their feelings on our chart.

SETTING	CHARACTER
home	Luke is bored and lonely. Dad is quiet and busy with work.
Lost Lake	Luke is tired and confused. Dad is angry and disappointed.

Soon the lake was far out of sight.

Then it started to rain. Dad gave me a poncho and it kept me dry, but I wondered where we were going to sleep that night. I wondered what we were going to do for dinner. I wasn't sure about camping anymore.

10

28

Activity

Cross Curricular: Social Studies

MAP SKILLS Display a map of the Great Lakes. Tell students that these lakes are the largest group of freshwater lakes in the world. Have students

• locate and name the five Great Lakes.

• identify the two countries that border the Great Lakes.

• identify the lake that is entirely in the United States. ▶ **Logical/Spatial**

I was glad when Dad finally stopped and set up the tent. The rain and wind beat against it, but we were warm and cozy inside. And Dad had brought food. For dinner we had salami and dried apricots.

29

Comprehension

DECODING Find the word *sleep* on page 28 and *beat* on page 29. What sound do these two words have in common?

Graphophonic Cues

PREVENTION/INTERVENTION

DECODING Write *sleep* and *beat* on the chalkboard. Underline the phonograms *-eep* and *-eat* in the words as students pronounce them. Then circle the letters that stand for long *e* in each word.

• What other words end with *-eep* or *-eat*? (Sample answers: heat, meat, deep, peep) Do all of them have the /ē/ sound?

• Choose at least three of these words and use them in a single sentence. (Sample answer: In the heat of the day, the animals sleep without a peep.)

Graphophonic Cues

Minilesson

REVIEW/MAINTAIN

Draw Conclusions

Review that conclusions are decisions readers make based on information in the story and what they know from experience.

• Ask students to tell what conclusions they can draw about how Luke now feels about camping based on the information in the story so far.

Activity Ask students to write their conclusions about how other visitors feel about the Lost Lake. Have them share the reasons for their conclusions.

Comprehension

(11) **CHARACTER** Why do you think Luke says "I'm sorry about the lake, Dad"? (He knows how much his dad wanted the lake to be the way he remembered it.) **What does this tell you about Luke's character?** (He thinks about other people's feelings and not just his own.)

(11) "I'm sorry about the lake, Dad," I said.

He shook his head. "You know something, Luke? There aren't any secret places left in the world anymore."

"What if we go very far up in the mountains? Maybe we can find our own lake."

"There are lots of lakes up here, but that one was special."

"But we've got a whole week, Dad."

"Well, why not? Maybe we'll find a lake that's not on the map."

"Sure, we will!"

(30)

Activity

Cross Curricular: Art

SPECIAL PLACES Ask students to visualize a special place they might like to visit in the woods or mountains.

• Have them glue torn pieces (no cut pieces) of colored paper onto a full sheet of paper to make a picture of their secret spot. Ask students to visu-

alize a special place they might like to visit in the woods or mountains.

• Encourage students to experiment with different shapes and colors to create the different forms of nature in their picture. ▶ **Visual/Kinesthetic**

We started early in the morning. When the fog cleared we saw other hikers ahead of us. Sure enough, Dad became very glum.

"We're going cross-country, partner," he said.

"Won't we get lost?"

"A wise man never leaves home without his compass."

31

Comprehension

12 **CHARACTER, SETTING** What changes in the setting made Dad glum? (He saw several other hikers traveling in the same direction.) **Why do you think Luke is not surprised by his dad's reaction?** (He knows his dad wants to get away from crowds.)

SELF-MONITORING STRATEGY

REREAD Explain: Rereading a part of the story can help a reader to understand why the characters behave as they do. If students have trouble answering the questions above, have them reread page 26 to help them understand why Dad is glum when he sees other hikers on the trail.

Comprehension

13 **CHARACTER, SETTING** How do you think the setting makes Luke feel now? (lonely) What is it about the hills and mountains that makes him feel this way? (They are large and seem to go on forever.) Let's add this information to our chart.

SETTING	CHARACTER
Lost Lake	Luke is tired and confused. Dad is angry and disappointed.
mountains	Luke feels lonely.

So we went off the trail. The hills went on and on. The mountains went on and on. It was kind of lonesome. It seemed as if Dad and I were the only people left in the world. And then we hiked into a big forest.

At noontime we stopped by a creek and ate lunch and drank ice-cold water straight from the stream. I threw rocks in the water, and fish, like shadows, darted in the pools.

"Isn't this a good place to camp, Dad?"

"I thought we were looking for our lake."

"Yes, right..." I mumbled.

32

Visual Literacy

PERSPECTIVE

Discuss the illustration on page 32:

- What has the illustrator done to emphasize the large area where Luke and his dad are hiking? (The illustrator has drawn the characters small in comparison to the wilderness in which they are walking.)

- What impression does this leave on the reader? (Luke and his dad are struggling against the rugged wilderness to find their own secret place. It is not an easy task.)

- Find other pictures in this story where the illustrator has emphasized the setting over the characters.

LANGUAGE SUPPORT

ESL To help students better understand what is happening, talk about what it means "to go off the trail." Talk about why Luke's dad decided to go off the trail. Ask: What did Luke's dad have that would help prevent him and Luke from getting lost? Then invite students to talk about trails they have followed. (hiking trails, ski trails) Encourage them to explain why it is important to stay on a trail.

Comprehension

COMPOUND WORDS Look in the third paragraph on page 32 for a word without a hyphen that is made up of two smaller words. (noontime) What do you think this word means? *Semantic Cues*

33

COMPOUND WORDS Write the word *noontime* on the board. Invite a volunteer to draw a line between the two smaller words of the compound word and discuss their meanings. Then discuss what *noontime* means. (the time of day around noon) As a group, brainstorm other compound words that apply to camping. (campsite, campfire, backpack, moonlight)

Have volunteers write these words on the chalkboard and draw a line between the two words that make up each compound word. Discuss whether knowing the meaning of each part of a compound always gives you the exact meaning of the compound word.
Semantic Cues

Comprehension

(14) **CHARACTER, SETTING** What new fact about the setting does Luke learn from his dad? (They are traveling in bear country.) **How does this affect Luke's mood?** (He is afraid and begins to wish they had stayed at the Lost Lake.)

The forest went on and on.

"I don't mean to scare you, son," Dad said. "But we're in bear country. We don't want to surprise them, so we have to make a lot of noise. If they hear us, they'll just go away."

What a time to tell me! I started to shout as loudly as I could. Even Dad wouldn't be able to beat off bears. I thought about those people having fun back at the lake. I thought about the creek, too, with all those fish in it. That would have been a fine place to camp. The Lost Lake hadn't been so bad either.

(14)

It was dark when we got out of the forest. We built a fire and that made me feel better. Wild animals wouldn't come near a fire. Dad cooked beef stroganoff and it was delicious.

Later it was bedtime. The sleeping bag felt wonderful. Dad and I started to count the shooting stars, then I worried that maybe we weren't going to find our lake.

"What are you thinking about, Luke?" Dad asked.

"I didn't know you could cook like that," I said.

Dad laughed. "That was only freeze-dried stuff. When we get home, I'll cook you something really special."

"You know something, Dad? You seem like a different person up here."

"Better or worse?"

"A lot better."

"How so?"

"You talk more."

"I'll have to talk more often, then."

That made me smile. Then I slept.

34

Activity

Cross Curricular: Math

FRACTIONS Explain to students that campers need to eat a mixture of sweet and nutritional foods to give them energy for a hike.

- Write on the chalkboard the following ingredients and recipe for trail mix.

- Have students form hiking groups of four. Invite them to make enough trail mix for everyone in their group by doubling the recipe.

Trail Mix Recipe	
Raisins	+1/4 cup
Unsalted peanuts	+1/3 cup
Granola	+1/2 cup
Plain M&M's	+1/2 cup

(15)

35

Comprehension

(15) **CHARACTER, SETTING** What is happening in this picture? (Luke and his dad are talking to each other.) **Look at the picture on page 21. How is the picture on page 21 different from the one on this page?** (The settings are different. The characters on page 21 are not talking to each other.) **How has the setting affected the characters' actions?** (The outdoor setting has helped Luke and his dad learn new things about each other.)

Minilesson
REVIEW/MAINTAIN
Short Vowels

Have students say the sound of the short vowels *a, e, i, o,* and *u.* Then ask them to find examples of words with short vowel sounds on page 34.

- Ask students to name words with /e/ spelled *ea.* (bread, head, ready)
- Ask students to name words with /u/ spelled *ou.* (rough, tough)

Activity Organize the class into five groups, and assign a short vowel to each group. Have students brainstorm and list words that contain their vowel sound spelled different ways.

ⓘ **Phonics Intervention Guide**

LANGUAGE SUPPORT

ESL As students read page 34, help them understand that Luke doesn't feel very close to his father at this point. For example, when Dad says they have to make a lot of noise to scare the bears, Luke starts shouting and thinking about other safer places they could have gone because he doesn't trust his father to keep him safe. Later on Luke is worried that Dad won't be able to lead them to Lost Lake, but when Dad asks him what he's thinking he says, "I didn't know you could cook like that." And when his father says he'll start being more talkative, it makes Luke smile.

Comprehension

16 **CHARACTER, SETTING** How does the final setting affect the characters' feelings? (Luke and Dad are both happy.) Let's record this information on our chart.

SETTING	CHARACTER
home	Luke is bored and lonely. Dad is quiet and busy with work.
Lost Lake	Luke is tired and confused. Dad is angry and disappointed.
mountains	Luke feels lonely.
"their" lake	Luke and Dad are both happy.

RETELL THE STORY Ask volunteers to tell the major events of the story. Students may refer to their charts. Then have partners write one or two sentences that summarize the story. Have them focus on the different settings and how they affected the main characters. *Summarize*

STUDENT SELF-ASSESSMENT

- How did using the strategy of analyzing character and setting help me to understand the story?

- How did the Setting and Character chart help me?

TRANSFERRING THE STRATEGY

- When might I use these strategies again? In what other reading could a Setting and Character chart help me?

Dad shook me awake. The sun was just coming up, turning everything all gold and orange and yellow. And there was the lake, right in front of us.

For a long time we watched the light change on the water, getting brighter and brighter. Dad didn't say a word the whole time. But then, I didn't have anything to say either.

After breakfast we climbed a mountain and saw our lake below us. There wasn't a sign of people anywhere. It really seemed as if Dad and I were all alone in the world.

16 I liked it just fine.

36

REREADING FOR *Fluency*

PARTNERS Have partners reread aloud sections of the story where there is dialogue between Luke and Dad. Encourage students to express themselves as though they were having a conversation.

READING RATE When you evaluate rate, have the student read aloud from the story for one minute. Place a stick-on note after the last word read. Count words read. To evaluate students' performance, see the Running Record in the **Fluency Assessment** book.

i **Intervention** For leveled fluency lessons, passages, and norms charts, see **Skills Intervention Guide**, Part 4, Fluency.

MEET

ALLEN SAY

EL CHINO

ALLEN SAY

For Allen Say, who writes and illustrates many of his own stories, pictures always come first. When he makes up a story, he begins by drawing pictures without having words or even ideas to go with them. *The Lost Lake* grew out of pictures Say drew of a camping trip. He unexpectedly remembered hiking to a mountain lake many years before and finding the area completely ruined by litter.

Say has been an artist almost all of his life. He originally dreamed of being a cartoonist. At thirteen he already had a job drawing backgrounds for a famous cartoonist in Japan. Say eventually came to the United States. He never lost his interest in art and later began to write and illustrate stories.

Other books by this writer and illustrator that you might enjoy are *El Chino*, a book about Bill Wong, the first Chinese bullfighter, and *Tree of Cranes*, a book Say dedicated to the man he learned from and first worked for, the Japanese cartoonist Noro Shinpei.

(37)

LITERARY RESPONSE

QUICK-WRITE Invite students to record their thoughts about the story. These questions may help them get started:

JOURNAL

- How are you like Luke? How are you different?
- What do you think Luke and his dad learned about themselves while taking the camping trip?

ORAL RESPONSE Have students share their journal writings and discuss what part of the story they enjoyed most.

Comprehension

Return to Predictions and Purposes

Review with students their story predictions and reasons for reading the story. Were their predictions correct? Did they find out what they wanted to know?

PREDICTIONS	WHAT HAPPENED
The main characters go camping.	Luke and his dad go on a camping adventure to find a special place called the Lost Lake.
The story takes place near a lake.	The real Lost Lake is now a place crowded with people, so Luke and his dad hike until they find a lake they can call their own.

INFORMAL **ASSESSMENT**

STORY ELEMENTS

HOW TO ASSESS

- Have students draw conclusions about Luke from his words and actions.
- Ask how the story settings affect the relationship between Luke and Dad.

Students should recognize that Luke is easy-going and is willing to try new adventures with his dad. They should note that each new setting brought additional challenges that ended up strengthening the relationship between the two.

FOLLOW UP If students have trouble analyzing character, help them brainstorm words to describe Luke at the beginning and at the end of the story.

If students have trouble seeing the importance of setting, ask them why the Lost Lake will always be important to both Luke and Dad.

Story Questions

Have students discuss or write answers to the questions on page 38.

Answers:

1. in the apartment of Luke's father in the city and in the mountains *Literal/Setting*

2. city: Luke is bored, and his father works all the time; country: they hike, talk, and camp together *Inferential/Setting, Character*

3. He tries to take Luke to a special place. He pays attention to Luke and promises to talk more often. *Inferential/Character*

4. A boy and his father get to know each other better. *Critical/Summarize*

5. Sample answer: He might tell them that he and his father found a similar lake on their trip. *Critical/Reading Across Texts*

Write a Personal Narrative For a full writing process lesson see pages 41K–41L.

Story Questions & Activities

1. Where does the story take place?

2. How do the characters act in the two different settings?

3. How can you tell that Luke's father cares about him? Explain.

4. What is this story mostly about?

5. Imagine that Luke stepped into the painting on page 18. What do you think he would tell the people about his camping trip?

Write a Personal Narrative

Luke's camping story is drawn from his own experience. Write a personal narrative of your own about a time when you and your family took a trip somewhere. Where did you go? What did you do? Why is the trip still important to you? Use *I* when telling your story.

Meeting Individual Needs

EASY	ON-LEVEL	CHALLENGE

EASY

Name_____ Date_____ Reteach **2**

Vocabulary

Read each clue. Then find the vocabulary word in the row of letters and circle it.

brand-new	compass	darted	mug	muttered	talker

1. never used — d e (b r a n d n e w) t s z
2. use it to find direction — b e (c o m p a s s) r n y
3. moved fast — r e t (d a r t e d) n g l y
4. big cup with handle — c a l (m u g) r e j d m l
5. spoke unclearly — w e (m u t t e r e d) l a r g a
6. one who talks — m a c (t a l k e r) a y d

Story Comprehension Reteach **3**

Write a ✔ next to every sentence that tells about "The Lost Lake."

✔ 1. Luke and Dad went on a camping trip.
___ 2. Dad often talked to Luke for hours at home.
___ 3. Dad liked to be with lots of other people at the lake.
✔ 4. Dad and Luke went looking for their own lake.
✔ 5. Dad was like a mountain goat on the trail.
✔ 6. Dad and Luke had to look out for bears.
___ 7. Luke never tired while hiking in the woods.
✔ 8. Dad and Luke got to know each other better on their trip.

At Home: Have students retell the story of "The Lost Lake" in their own words.
Book 4/Unit 1 *The Lost Lake* 8
2–3

Reteach, 3

ON-LEVEL

Name_____ Date_____ Practice **3**

Story Comprehension

Read the statement below. Write **T** for true if the statement describes "The Lost Lake." Write **F** for false if the statement does not describe "The Lost Lake."

1. ___F___ Luke had lived with his Dad for many years.
2. ___T___ Luke had enjoyed cutting out pictures of mountains.
3. ___F___ Luke's Dad had never been camping before.
4. ___T___ Luke's Dad felt sad when they found Lost Lake.
5. ___F___ Luke's Dad didn't bring any food.
6. ___T___ Luke didn't know his dad could cook.

Write to tell why the following statements are not true. Answers may vary.

7. Luke was miserable sleeping in the tent. Luke felt cozy and warm as the rain and wind beat against the side of the tent.

8. Luke's dad still didn't talk much when they went back to the apartment in the city. Luke tells his Dad he seems different now. He talks more. Dad says he will talk more from now on.

At Home: Have students fold a paper in quarters and draw four important parts of the story using speech balloons. Then have students show and tell the story to a family member.
Book 4/Unit 1 *The Lost Lake* 8
3

Practice, 3

CHALLENGE

Name_____ Date_____ Extend **2**

Vocabulary

brand-new	compass	darted	mug	muttered	talker

Suppose that you are on a hiking trip with a group of friends. You are keeping a journal about your trip. Write three journal entries using some of the words in the box. Use a separate piece of paper if you need more space.

Answers will vary but should include at least four vocabulary words used in the correct context and part of speech.

_____

_____

_____

_____

Extend **3**

Story Comprehension

Work with a partner. Choose one setting from "The Lost Lake." Write a short poem describing either Luke's or his father's feelings or reactions to the setting.
Answers will vary.

_____

_____

_____

_____

At Home: Read a poem about nature. Discuss how the poem reflects your feelings about nature.
Book 4/Unit 1 *The Lost Lake*
2–3

Extend, 3

Use a Compass

Luke's father found his way in the mountains by using a compass. Try using a compass to find out in which direction from your home you would go to get to certain places in your community. Make a list of these places, such as your school, a park, or a friend's house. Then use a compass. Jot down the results.

Look at a Map

Where would you go to find a private place of your own? Look at a map to find a "lost lake." Use the map scale. Figure out how far you would have to travel to find a place where there are no roads or people. How would you get there?

2 mi.

0

2 km

0

Find Out More

In the story, Luke and his father hike through bear country. Use an encyclopedia or a library book to find out more about bears. For example, what kinds of bears live in your part of the country? What are their habits? What should you do if you come in contact with a bear while camping? Use what you learn to give a report to your class.

39

Story Activities

Use a Compass

Materials: compass, paper, pencil

PARTNERS Have pairs list their place ideas on a two-column chart that has the headings *Place* and *Direction*. When partners are using their compass, suggest that they take turns noting the direction and recording it on their chart.

Look at a Map

Materials: local maps that show urban and rural areas, index cards, paper, pencil

ONE Help students line up an index card with the map scale and mark the distances on the card. Students can then use this card to measure the distance to their own "lost lake." Have students take notes regarding the distance to their spot and how they would travel to get to it. Students can discuss their findings and offer travel ideas as a class.

Find Out More

RESEARCH AND INQUIRY Students may wish to research and report on other camping safety tips regarding food preparation, campfires, wildlife, and shelter.

*inter***NET CONNECTION** For more information on camping safety tips, students can visit ***www.mhschool.com/reading***

FORMAL ASSESSMENT

After page 39, see the Selection Assessment.

Activity

SCIENCE: CLASSIFYING ANIMALS Explain: Bears are **vertebrates** because they have a backbone. Animals without a backbone, such as jellyfish, are **invertebrates**. Have students make a two-column chart and label one column *vertebrate*, the other, *invertebrate*. Tell them to use the chart to classify these animals and others they choose.

spider *(invertebrate)* horse *(vertebrate)*
bird *(vertebrate)*   snake *(vertebrate)*

What to Look For Check responses to see that the student:

• creates a two-column chart and labels it correctly.

• classifies and lists animals in the correct columns.

CHALLENGE

Study Skills

PARTS OF A BOOK

⌖OBJECTIVES Students will:
- use a table of contents, glossary, and index to find information.

PREPARE Have students look at the front and back parts of books that contain a table of contents, a glossary, and an index. Display **Teaching Chart 3.**

TEACH Read the definitions for *table of contents, glossary* and *index*, while students refer to these sections of their books.

PRACTICE Have students answer questions 1–5. Review the answers with them. **1.** table of contents **2.** glossary **3.** page 78 **4.** to explain the important words used in the book **5.** Book parts help you to find the information you need.

ASSESS/CLOSE Have students use their textbook to find specific information such as the number of selections in a unit, a definition for a vocabulary word, and the page number of a topic you choose.

Study Skills

Use Parts of a Book

Where would you look in this book for the page on which "The Lost Lake" begins? The answer is the table of contents. Like many of your books, this book has different parts.

In the front of the book, you will find the table of contents. The **table of contents** lists the titles of the units or chapters and the selections. It also gives the page on which each of these begins. At the back of the book, the **glossary** gives the meaning of important words in the book. The **index** gives a list of topics and names.

TABLE OF CONTENTS
CHAPTER 1 3
CHAPTER 2 10
CHAPTER 3 20

GLOSSARY
backpack A bag for carrying things on the back.
back•pack (BAK´ pak) *noun, plural* backpacks.

INDEX
C
Compass, 78
Connecticut, 81–83

Use the sample parts of a book to answer these questions.

1 Where would you look to find out how many chapters a book has?

2 Where would you look to find the meaning of *backpack*?

3 Where would you look to find out how to use a compass?

4 Why do you think a book has a glossary?

5 How do book parts help you understand a book?

Meeting Individual Needs

EASY	ON-LEVEL	CHALLENGE
Name_____ Date_____ **Reteach 4**	Name_____ Date_____ **Practice 4**	Name_____ Date_____ **Extend 4**
Use Parts of a Book	**Use Parts of a Book**	**Use Parts of a Book**

EASY — Reteach, 4

Use Parts of a Book

Knowing the different **parts of a book** and how to use them can save time and provide important information.

On the lines below, write the letter that matches each book part with its description.

_c_ 1. Table of Contents a. defines important words in a book

_b_ 2. Index b. list of topics and important names in alphabetical order

_a_ 3. Glossary c. list of chapters, unit titles, or selections

Circle the letter of the correct response.

4. In what part of a book would you look to find a word's pronunciation?
   a. index
   (b.) glossary
   c. table of contents

5. To find on which page a chapter begins, you would look at the
   a. index
   b. glossary
   (c.) table of contents

6. To find the page on which a topic is discussed, you would look at the
   (a.) index
   b. title page
   c. table of contents

Book 4/Unit 1
The Lost Lake 6 At Home: Have students write a table of contents for a book they would like to read, or perhaps write. 4

ON-LEVEL — Practice, 4

Use Parts of a Book

Books can have many different **parts.** Write the name of a book part to answer each question.

Front of the book	Back of the book
title page	glossary
table of contents	index

1. The author's name is found on the same page as the book title.
   On which page in the book can you find these names? _on the title page_

2. Which book part is like a small dictionary? _glossary_

3. How can you find the first page number of a chapter? _Look in the table of contents._

4. Which part of a textbook gives a definition of a word? _glossary_

5. Which parts of a textbook are arranged in alphabetical order? _the glossary and the index_

6. Where would you look to find how many chapters a book has? _in the table of contents_

Book 4/Unit 1
The Lost Lake 6 At Home: Have students locate a book and discuss its parts with a family member. 4

CHALLENGE — Extend, 4

Use Parts of a Book

Suppose you wanted to write a book about favorite vacation spots in your state. There are several ways you could organize the information into chapters. One way would be to have a chapter for each region in the state. What are some other ways that the book could be organized?

Answers will vary. Some possibilities are by activity, by parks, by theme.

Use one of the methods of organization to make a sample table of contents. Include two or three subheadings in each chapter to identify places, such as specific state parks. Will your book contain a glossary and an index? If so, be sure to include them in your table of contents.

Vacation Fun in My State
Table of Contents

Answers will vary.

Now, on a separate piece of paper, design a title page for your book.

Book 4/Unit 1
The Lost Lake At Home: Read through the table of contents of a book. List other ways that the book could be organized. 4

Reteach, 4   Practice, 4   Extend, 4

Test Tip

Always answer all questions.

DIRECTIONS

Read the sample story. Then read each question about the story.

SAMPLE

Robert Plays Kickball

Robert wandered into the schoolyard where the other children were playing a fast-paced game of kickball. He had just moved to town and felt shy because he didn't know any of the children on the team.

A girl about his age walked up to him and said, "My name is Katie. I don't remember seeing you here before. Are you new here?"

Robert blushed. "Yes."

"Do you know how to play kickball?" The girl did not give him a chance to answer. "Because we play all the time. Would you like to be on my team?" Katie urged.

"That would be great," Robert responded happily.

1 What is the main idea of this passage?

(A) Robert makes friends with Katie.

B Robert just moved to town.

C Katie plays kickball.

D Robert felt shy.

2 At the beginning of the story, Robert was shy because—

F he didn't like school

G the new school was bigger

H he couldn't play kickball

(J) he didn't know anyone

Why are these answers correct? Explain.

41

Read the Page

Have students read the story, the questions, and the answer choices to themselves. Instruct students to choose the *best* answer choice and be prepared to discuss why it is the best choice.

Discuss the Questions

Question 1: This question asks students to find the main idea. Read each answer choice as a group and discuss why a choice might be incorrect *even though* it contains a fact that is stated in the passage. The main idea paraphrases the *whole* passage in a few words.

Question 2: This question requires students to understand why Robert is shy *at the beginning of the story*. Discuss what clues are given to determine why Robert felt shy. Answers: "He had just moved to town. . ." and ". . . he didn't know any of the children. . ."

Leveled Books

The Stony Creek Bandit

written by Susan Blackaby
illustrated by Keunhee Lee

EASY

The Stony Creek Bandit

Short Vowels

☑ Story Elements

☑ Instructional Vocabulary: *brand-new, compass, darted, mug, muttered, talker*

Answers to Story Questions

1. Any two of the following: mixed nuts, peanut butter, sardines, bread, chips, toothpaste.
2. Kiki probably felt embarrassed for blaming that girl. She might have learned that everyone is considered innocent until the truth comes out.
3. Yes, because their trap allowed them to catch the thieves in the act.
4. The story is mostly about catching a thief and solving a mystery.
5. Answers will vary but could include that he might have suggested using photography to catch the thief in the act.

The *Story Questions and Activity* below appear in the *Easy Book.*

Story Questions and Activity

1. Name two things that were missing from the campsite.
2. How do you think Kiki felt after the thief was found? What lesson might she have learned from this experience?
3. Do you think the scouts set a clever trap? Why or why not?
4. What is the story mostly about?
5. What idea might Luke from *The Lost Lake* have come up with to help the girls set a trap for the thief?

Design an Alert System

In the story, Judy, Kiki, and Lee set a trap to catch the thief. Design an alert system that will let you know when someone has been in your room. Draw a picture of your system and explain how it works.

from *The Stony Creek Bandit*

Guided Reading

PREVIEW AND PREDICT Discuss the illustrations up to page 11. Have students predict what the story is about. Chart their ideas.

SET PURPOSES Have students write why they want to read *The Stony Creek Bandit.* For example: *I want to learn what the girls do while camping.*

READ THE BOOK Use the following questions to guide students as they read or to check their understanding after they read the story independently.

Page 2: What story clue tells you that Skip is upset? (Skip looked worried.) *Character*

Page 6: Find the word *muttered* in the second paragraph. What does this word tell you about Kiki's mood? (It shows she's being negative.) *Vocabulary*

Page 12: How is the campsite described? (It was dark and still.) What were the only sounds to be heard? (the croaking of frogs and the chirping of crickets) *Setting*

Page 15: Find the words *mask, up,* and *box.* Say each word aloud. What vowel sound do you hear in each word? (short vowels /a/, /u/, /o/) *Phonics*

RETURN TO PREDICTIONS AND PURPOSES Review students' predictions and reasons for reading. Which of their predictions were accurate? Which questions were not answered?

LITERARY RESPONSE Discuss these questions with students:

- What will the girls do now that they know who the thief is?
- What will the girls remember to do with their camping supplies from now on?
- What is something unusual that has happened to you on a trip?

Also see the story questions and activity in *The Stony Creek Bandit.*

Leveled Books

Martin's Journey

written by Susan Blackaby
illustrated by Arvis Stewart

INDEPENDENT

Martin's Journey

☑ **Story Elements**

☑ **Instructional Vocabulary:**
brand-new, compass, darted, mug, muttered, talker

Guided Reading

PREVIEW AND PREDICT Have students read the title and look at the illustrations up to page 13. Have students discuss the illustrations and record their story predictions in a journal.

SET PURPOSES Students should decide what they would like to learn from the story before they read. Have them record a few questions they would like to have answered.

READ THE BOOK Have students read the story independently. When they finish, ask the following questions to emphasize reading strategies.

Pages 2–3: Where did the Ryde family's journey begin, and where will it end? (Missouri and Oregon) *Setting*

Page 4: In the context of the sentence what do you think *talker* means? (Someone who has a lot to say.) *Vocabulary*

Page 5: Reread the last paragraph. How would you describe Carrie's mood, based on what she says? (She is angry and feeling sorry for herself.) *Make Inferences*

Page 9: Why does the journey seem like an eternity? (It is raining, everything is wet, Carrie is sick, and Martin is restless.) *Setting*

Pages 13–16: How does Carrie's attitude change? Why? (At first she is unhappy with her new surroundings, but then she realizes there is much to be thankful for.) *Character*

RETURN TO PREDICTIONS AND PURPOSES Review students' predictions and reasons for reading the story. Which predictions were accurate?

LITERARY RESPONSE Discuss these questions:

• How might you feel if you had to move to a new home?

• Would you feel more like Martin or Carrie during the move? Why?

Also see the story questions and activity in *Martin's Journey*.

Answers to Story Questions

1. Martin and Carrie are a brother and sister in a pioneer family.
2. Martin and Carrie are traveling with their wagon train along the Oregon Trail.
3. Martin's parents laughed because they were relieved. They would now have help building their cabin.
4. Being with your family is the most important part of creating a home.
5. Answers will vary.

The *Story Questions and Activity* below appear in the *Independent Book*.

Story Questions and Activity

1. Who are Martin and Carrie?
2. Where are Martin and Carrie?
3. Why did Martin's parents laugh when the people came?
4. What is the main idea of the story?
5. If Carrie could speak with Luke and his father from *The Lost Lake*, what do you think they would talk about?

Design a Patch

Look at the pictures in this book. Then design a patch for a quilt that a pioneer might have. You might create a design or show something that reminds you of pioneer life—a wagon, a calico dress, a horse, or a bonnet or hat a pioneer might have had.

from *Martin's Journey*

Leveled Books

CHALLENGE

Lost and Found

☑ **Story Elements**

☑ **Instructional Vocabulary:** *brand-new, compass, darted, mug, muttered, talker*

written by Susan Blackaby
illustrated by Marianne M. Sachs-Iacob

Answers to Story Questions

1. Betsy and Greg were park rangers, They cleared and repaired trails and helped campers or hikers in trouble.

2. In the beginning of the story, Betsy thought Greg was a bit disorganized and "not together," but by the end she respected him for training his dog to be a Rescue Dog and knowing what to do to find Mark.

3. Answers will vary but should include wooded mountains, hiking trails, and the creek.

4. It was a story about finding a lost scout, a missing compass, and unexpected strengths in people.

5. Both were exploring unfamiliar territory, but the father in *The Lost Lake* was a more experienced hiker and did not venture out alone.

The *Story Questions and Activity* below appear in the *Challenge Book*.

Story Questions and Activity

1. What did Betsy and Greg do for a living? What did their job include?

2. Explain how Betsy felt about Greg at the beginning of the story and how her feelings had changed by the end.

3. Describe the setting of the story and how it contributed to Mark's getting lost.

4. What was the story mainly about?

5. How were the father from *The Lost Lake* and Mark the same? How were they different? Explain your answer.

Play a Part

Pretend you and your classmates are going to put on a play based on this story but from the scout troop's point of view. What might Carl and Mark's fellow scouts and the scout leaders be thinking, feeling, and saying when they realize the two boys have disappeared? Provide the dialogue for a short scene.

from Lost and Found

Guided Reading

PREVIEW AND PREDICT Have volunteers read the chapter titles and look at the illustrations up to page 14. Ask them to predict what the story will be about and record their predictions in their journals.

SET PURPOSES Have students write down what they want to learn from the story. Have them think of a few questions that they would like to have answered.

READ THE BOOK After students have read the story independently, return to the text to discuss the following questions.

Page 2: Find the word *muttered*. What does it mean? (to speak without clear pronunciation.) *Vocabulary*

Pages 4–5: What are some of the jobs Greg and Betsy complete on the trail? (They look for danger spots, make repairs, clear and mark trails, watch for wildlife, take soil and water samples, and add landmarks to the trail.) *Summarize*

Page 6–8: What do we learn about Carl and Mark based on their comments and behavior? (Mark likes adventure. Carl is more cautious.) *Character*

Page 12: Reread the third paragraph. What emotions does Betsy experience at one time and why? (embarrassment—it never occurred to her to use the dog; shock—she thought Greg was goofing off instead of helping; pride—because she is teaching Greg, she is proud of his idea) *Character*

RETURN TO PREDICTIONS AND PURPOSES Review students' predictions and reasons for reading. Which predictions were accurate? Which were not? Were all of their questions answered?

LITERARY RESPONSE Discuss these questions:

• What lesson do you think Mark has learned from his experience?

• In what ways does Greg show he will be a good forest ranger?

• What can you do to avoid becoming lost in a wilderness area?

Also see the story questions and activity in *Lost and Found*.

Bringing Groups Together

Anthology and Leveled Books

Connecting Texts

CHARACTER CHARTS Write the story titles on a chart. Discuss with students the main characters of each story, what problem they faced, and how it was resolved. Ask volunteers from each reading level to share their ideas, and write their suggestions on the chart. Compare the different ways the characters resolved their problems.

The Lost Lake	The Stony Creek Bandit	Martin's Journey	Lost and Found
• Dad and Luke don't talk much. • Dad and Luke go away together and learn to enjoy one another's company.	• Items that belong to the scout troop keep disappearing. • The girls set up a trap to catch the culprit.	• Carrie is unhappy about moving. • Carrie realizes that home is not a particular place, but wherever your family is.	• Mark and Carl leave their scout troop and then each other in the wilderness. • Greg proves himself to Betsy in an emergency. Mark is rescued after Carl asks for the rangers' help.

Viewing/Representing

GROUP PRESENTATIONS Divide the class into small groups, one for each of the four books read in the lesson. (For *The Lost Lake*, combine students of different reading levels.) Ask each group to choose an event from the book and pantomime it for the class. The audience must guess what event the group is portraying.

AUDIENCE RESPONSE Ask students to pay close attention to each group's pantomime. Have the audience tell what movements best portrayed the event. Allow time for questions after each presentation.

Research and Inquiry

MORE ABOUT HIKING AND CAMPING Have students research national parks in their area. Invite them to find out about:

• trails available in the park for hiking

• campground facilities

• points of interest

Have students display their findings on a bulletin board for others to read.

interNET CONNECTION To find out more about hiking and camping, have students visit
www.mhschool.com/reading

Review Story Elements

OBJECTIVES
Students will analyze character and setting.

Skills Finder

Story Elements

Introduce	19A-B
Review	41E-F, 67A-B, 93E-F
Test	Unit 1
Maintain	163, 323, 527, 575

TEACHING TIP

SETTING Ask a volunteer to read "The Special Place" aloud while the rest of the class keeps their eyes closed and visualizes what Luke sees and hears. Then ask them to use all of their senses to describe the setting they pictured in their mind. List their ideas on the chalkboard and ask them to tell how this place would make them feel.

SELF-SELECTED Reading

Students may choose from the following titles.

• The Lost Lake

LEVELED BOOKS

• The Stony Creek Bandit
• Martin's Journey
• Lost and Found

Bibliography, pages T78–T79

41E   *The Lost Lake*

PREPARE

Discuss Character and Setting

Review: To better understand the characters in a story, pay attention to their actions, thoughts, and words. A story's setting (when and where the story takes place) can affect how a character acts and feels. Ask students to name ways that the different settings affected the characters in the selection they just read.

TEACH

Read "The Special Place" and Model the Skill

Ask students to listen for clues about the character and the setting as you read the **Teaching Chart 4** passage with them.

The Special Place

Luke walked quietly up to the edge of the lake. Never in his life had he seen such a beautiful place. He noticed that the only sounds he could hear were woodpeckers drilling on nearby trees and a fish jumping up out of the water every once in a while.

He felt safe and peaceful in this special place that he shared with his dad. The sun seemed to bounce off the blue water and surround Luke with warmth. The mountains stood like tall soldiers protecting the lake. He sat on the beach knowing that he would remember this time and place forever.

Teaching Chart 4

Discuss clues in the passage that give readers information about the character and the setting.

MODEL I can tell that the special place is a beautiful outdoor setting. Luke is very relaxed here because the peacefulness of the lake makes him feel safe. He takes time to listen and observe the nature around him.

PRACTICE

Analyze Character and Setting Have students underline clue words in "The Special Place" that help them better understand Luke's character and circle clue words about the setting.

GROUP Then ask students how the setting affected the character's actions. (The peaceful setting prompted Luke to walk quietly and listen and observe. It made him feel relaxed as he sat on the beach.) ▶ **Logical**

ASSESS/CLOSE

Change the Setting Have students think of a different adventure for Luke and his dad in a new setting like a big city or an amusement park. Ask them to plan how the new setting will affect the characters. Then have partners write their version of the new adventure and share it with the class.

PARTNERS

ALTERNATE TEACHING STRATEGY

STORY ELEMENTS
For a different approach to teaching this skill, see page T60.

Intervention ➤ **Skills Intervention Guide,** for direct instruction and extra practice in story elements

Meeting Individual Needs for Comprehension

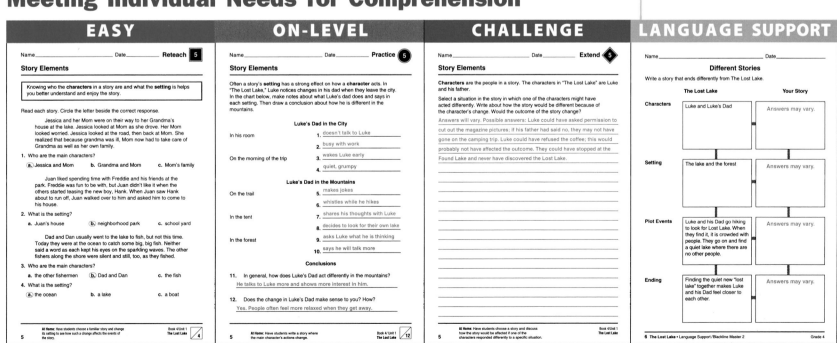

EASY — Reteach, 5

ON-LEVEL — Practice, 5

CHALLENGE — Extend, 5

LANGUAGE SUPPORT — Language Support, 6

OBJECTIVES

Students will make inferences about story characters.

Skills Finder

Make Inferences

Introduce	41G-H
Review	65G-H, 117G-H, 515G-H, 535G-H, 567G-H
Test	Unit 1, Unit 5
Maintain	147, 197, 225, 495

LANGUAGE SUPPORT

ESL Give students examples of clues that the author gives and help them make inferences from these clues. For example, on page 26: Dad stopped for me often, but he wouldn't let me take off my pack. Dad says, "Welcome to *Found* Lake."

Introduce Make Inferences

PREPARE

Discuss How to Make Inferences

Explain: Often an author does not specifically tell you something about a story character. While reading, you must look for clues in the story as well as think about your own experiences to learn more about a character's feelings. When you do this you are making inferences about a character.

TEACH

Read "One More Hill" and Model the Skill

Display and read aloud **Teaching Chart 5.** Ask students to look for clues in the text as well as to use their own experiences to determine how Luke feels about the hike.

One More Hill

Luke was thinking about what food or equipment he could spare to lighten his knapsack. His legs hurt as he and his dad climbed up yet another hill to find a special place to camp.

They stopped under a large shady tree near the top of the hill for lunch. While Dad cleaned up, Luke decided to climb the tree. His heart started racing when he saw the view.

"Ready to go, Luke?" asked Dad.

"Absolutely!" Luke cried as he climbed down. "Just one more hill!"

Teaching Chart 5

Ask volunteers to underline words and phrases in the passage that give clues about how Luke feels. Then ask students to think about how they might feel if they were Luke.

MODEL I know I would be tired if I were carrying a heavy knapsack and didn't know where I was going. I also know that I would get very excited if I learned that my special place was just over one more hill!

PRACTICE

Create an Inference Chart

GROUP

Have students work in groups to create an inference chart.

▶ Logical/Visual

STORY INFORMATION	MY EXPERIENCE	INFERENCES
heavy knapsack, legs hurt, climbing up a hill	I get tired when I walk a lot, especially if I am carrying something heavy.	Luke is tired and frustrated.
heart is racing	When I'm excited, my heart beats fast.	Luke is excited.

ASSESS/CLOSE

Make Inferences About a Character from a Familiar Story

Have students make inferences about a character from a familiar story. Students can write a paragraph about the character, citing clues from the text as well as their own experiences to back up their inferences.

ALTERNATE TEACHING STRATEGY

MAKE INFERENCES

For a different approach to teaching this skill, see page T62.

Intervention Skills **Intervention Guide,** for direct instruction and extra practice in inferences

Meeting Individual Needs for Comprehension

EASY

Name_____ Date_____ **Reteach** 6

Make Inferences

Authors do not always directly state what is happening or how characters are feeling in a story. Sometimes you have to use clues in the story and what you know from your own experiences to help you **make inferences.**

Read the story. Then write complete sentences to answer the questions.

Lucas sat perfectly still as Ms. Sanchez returned the tests. Lucas had studied very hard. He had even missed a camping trip to spend more time studying. When Ms. Sanchez gave Alex his test, he looked at it, then crumpled it up. Jean took hers and kissed the paper. Lucas reached out and took his test from Ms. Sanchez. He took one quick look. Lucas just sat and grinned.

1. How did Alex do on the test? How do you know?
   He probably did poorly because he crumpled up this test.

2. How did Jean do? How do you know?
   Jean probably did very well. She kissed the paper.

3. Was Lucas happy with his test results? How do you know?
   Yes. Lucas grinned.

4. Why do you think the room was so quiet?
   All the students probably were nervous about their grades.

Book 4/Unit 1
The Lost Lake   **At Home:** Have students explain how their own experiences in taking tests and finding out their grades helped them make inferences about the story.   6

Reteach, 6

ON-LEVEL

Name_____ Date_____ **Practice** 6

Make Inferences

In "The Lost Lake," the author does not always explain what the characters are feeling or why they act as they do. Therefore, you must **make inferences** about their feelings and actions by "reading between the lines." To make an inference, you can use clues provided by the author and similar experiences that you have had or heard about.

Answer each question by making an inference. Use story clues or personal experience to make each inference. Answers will vary.

1. Why do you think Dad decided to take Luke camping? He noticed nature pictures Luke had put up and figured Luke might enjoy camping.

2. How do you think Dad felt when he and Luke arrived at the Lost Lake? How can you tell? He felt disappointed. He didn't want to camp there with all the people around.

3. Why do you think Luke suggested to Dad that they find their own lake? He wanted to make his Dad feel better. He liked the idea of finding a secret place as his father and grandfather had.

4. When Luke noted that Dad talked more in the mountains, why did Dad say, "I'll have to talk more often, then?" Why did Luke smile when his Dad said this? He knew Luke liked it when he talked to him and wanted Luke to feel happy. Luke smiled because he thought their life would be better in the future.

5. Why did Dad and Luke just gaze at "their" lake and not say anything? They felt content. They were happy to be alone together.

Book 4/Unit 1
The Lost Lake   **At Home:** Write about why Luke's Dad became glum when he saw other hikers ahead of him.   6

Practice, 6

CHALLENGE

Name_____ Date_____ **Extend** 6

Make Inferences

An **inference** is a conclusion that you are able to draw after considering the facts in a story and relating them to your personal experience.

Make inferences to answer the following questions.
Answers will vary. Possible answers are given.

1. In "The Lost Lake," Luke's father was not angry with him for cutting out the magazine pictures. Why do you think that Luke's father wasn't angry? His father liked the pictures. They made him think of when he used to camp or hike. He may have realized that Luke was bored.

2. Why do you think that Luke and his father did not talk much in the city? Luke did not want to bother his father. His father was used to living alone.

3. Why is it important that Luke's father had a compass when they went off the trail? so they would not get lost

4. Do you think that Luke's father was happy at the end of the story? Explain. Yes, they found a lake and they were alone. His father became more talkative.

5. Do you think that the camping trip brought Luke and his father closer together? Explain. Yes, they communicated more. Luke learned new things about his father.

6. Do you think that the camping trip was important to Luke? Why do you think so? Yes, he wrote the story to tell about it.

Book 4/Unit 1
The Lost Lake   **At Home:** Have students make and exchange a list of clues. Discuss what they are able to infer from the clues.   6

Extend, 6

LANGUAGE SUPPORT

Name_____ Date_____

Alone and Together

1. Cut out the sentences below. 2. Paste the sentences that express what the people in the pictures are saying to each other, below each picture. 3. What do the words the characters say tell you about how they are feeling?

"I am bored."	"I cannot talk now, Son. I have to work."
"I am having fun with you, Dad!"	"I am having fun, too, Son."

Grade 4   Language Support/Blackline Master 3 • **The Lost Lake** 7

Language Support, 7

41H

OBJECTIVES

Students will identify the multiple-meaning words and determine their meanings.

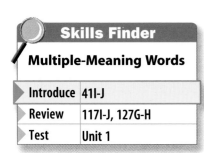

Skills Finder

Multiple-Meaning Words

Introduce	411-J
Review	117I-J, 127G-H
Test	Unit 1

TEACHING TIP

MULTIPLE-MEANING WORDS Students stumped by a multiple-meaning word can try thinking about the various meanings first. Then they can decide which meaning makes the most sense in the passage. Point out that noticing how a word is used in a sentence—for example, as an action word (verb), naming word (noun), or describing word (adjective)—can clarify which meaning the writer intended.

Introduce Multiple-Meaning Words

PREPARE

Discuss Multiple-Meaning Words

Explain: A word can have more than one meaning. For example, a *bank* can be a place where you keep your money or it can be land along a river. The way the word is used in the sentence tells the reader which meaning is being referred to. Sometimes the two meanings have different pronunciations, such as the verb *lead* and substance *lead*.

TEACH

Read "Danger Lake" and Model the Skill

Have students read the passage on **Teaching Chart 6.** Have them look for sentence clues to identify the meanings of *wind* and *bark*.

Danger Lake

Dad handed Luke a ⟨rope⟩ and told him to <u>wind</u> it ⟨around a tree.⟩ Just then a gust of <u>wind</u> ⟨off of Lost Lake lifted the tent⟩ from their hands.

Luke immediately set out after it. But as he ran, a ⟨dog's⟩ <u>bark</u> attracted his attention, and he didn't notice the tree branch in his path. Luke crashed into the branch, and the blow sent him sprawling.

"Are you all right?" Dad asked. Luke brushed himself off. The rough <u>bark</u> ⟨of the branch⟩ had left a scratch on his shoulder, but Luke said, "I'm OK, but from now on I think I will call this Danger Lake!"

Teaching Chart 6

Model using context clues for a multiple-meaning word.

MODEL The word *bark* in the second sentence of the second paragraph has more than one meaning. I will look for clues to help me determine the meaning. When the word *bark* is used with the word *dog's,* I know that it means the sound a dog makes.

Have students find clues and determine the meaning of the word *bark* in the third sentence of the third paragraph.

PRACTICE

Identify Multiple-Meaning Words

ONE

Have volunteers underline *bark* and *wind* each time the words appear in "Danger Lake." Then ask them to circle the words that provide clues to each word's meaning. Have students discuss the meanings. ▶ **Linguistic**

ASSESS/CLOSE

Write Sentences Using Multiple-Meaning Words

PARTNERS

On the chalkboard, write the multiple-meaning words shown below. Have partners choose a word and identify two different meanings. Then have each pair fold a sheet of paper into two sections. Using a different section for each meaning, have partners write a sentence and draw an illustration.

fly   light   pen   bat   palm   row

ALTERNATE TEACHING STRATEGY

MULTIPLE-MEANING WORDS

For a different approach to teaching this skill, see page T63.

 **Intervention** ▶ **Skills**

Intervention Guide, for direct instruction and extra practice in multiple-meaning words

Meeting Individual Needs for Vocabulary

EASY	ON-LEVEL	CHALLENGE	LANGUAGE SUPPORT

EASY — Reteach, 7

Name_____ Date_____ **Reteach** 7

Multiple-Meaning Words

Some words have **multiple meanings**, or more than one meaning. Use the other words in the sentences below as clues to help you decide which meaning is correct.

Circle the letter beside the correct meaning for the underlined word.

1. The camper used a <u>saw</u> to cut the log.
   (a.) a tool used to cut wood
   b. past tense of *see*
2. They got to the <u>park</u> early.
   (a.) a recreation area
   b. to leave a car in a place for a time
3. He wondered if he had the <u>right</u> directions.
   (a.) correct
   b. the opposite of left
4. His knapsack was <u>light</u>.
   (a.) not heavy
   b. cause to catch fire
5. We could not <u>bear</u> the crowds at the lake.
   a. a large animal
   (b.) put up with
6. It took just a <u>second</u> to the find the map.
   (a.) a very short amount of time
   b. next after the first

At Home: Have students choose three of the underlined words to use in sentences that show their other meanings.

7   Book 4/Unit 1 **The Lost Lake** /6

ON-LEVEL — Practice, 7

Name_____ Date_____ **Practice** 7

Multiple-Meaning Words

Many words are **multiple-meaning words**, or have more than one meaning. The context of the sentence will help you tell which meaning of the word is being used. Read each sentence below. Then circle the meaning of each underlined word.

1. Luke's Dad gave him a taste of the <u>sweet</u> coffee.
   a. good-tempered   (b. sugary tasting)
2. I could see the mountain path <u>snake</u> through the trees.
   a. long, thin animals   (b. wind around)
3. After he took out the camping stove, the knapsack was <u>light</u>.
   (a. not heavy)   b. traffic signal
4. The boy crashed into a low-hanging <u>branch</u>.
   (a. limb of a tree)   b. division of a library
5. It is important to <u>train</u> dogs not to chase animals in the woods.
   (a. teach)   b. railroad cars
6. The man was <u>patient</u> as he waited for his son.
   (a. calm, not complaining) b. getting medical advice
7. A <u>bat</u> flew in the trees under the night sky.
   a. stick used in baseball (b. a flying animal)
8. They <u>left</u> the path and struck out for the wilderness.
   a. opposite of right   (b. went away from)
9. In a <u>second</u>, the deer darted out of sight.
   a. after the first   (b. one-sixtieth of a minute)
10. They would <u>tire</u> too quickly if their packs were too heavy.
    (a. need rest)   b. part of a car wheel

7   At Home: Have students write sentences using words with different meanings.   Book 4/Unit 1 **The Lost Lake** /10

CHALLENGE — Extend, 7

Name_____ Date_____ **Extend** 7

Multiple-Meaning Words

Multiple-meaning words are words that have more than one meaning even though they are spelled the same way. For example, consider the word *bear*. It can mean a large wild animal: The bear was eating berries in the woods. It can also mean that you cannot put up with something: He could not bear to hear the loud sirens.

Each of the words below are multiple-meaning words. Write two sentences for each word to show different meanings for the word.

1. bottle	3. glasses	5. lie	7. dip
2. cooler	4. tire	6. trail	8. stick

Answers will vary. Possible sentences are given. 1. She was tempted to bottle up her feelings to hide her disappointment. They took a water bottle on their hike. 2. The cooler is filled with soft drinks. It is cooler today than yesterday. 3. He put his glasses on to read. They took plastic glasses on the picnic. 4. Their car had a flat tire. The hike did not tire them out. 5. It's not good to tell a lie. The dog went to lie down in the shade. 6. The trail went along the lake shore. The leader told the others not to trail behind. 7. They took a dip in the pool. There was a dip in the road. 8. He like the unusual shape of the stick of wood. The stamp did not stick to the envelope.

_____

_____

_____

_____

7   At Home: Ask the student to think of other multiple-meaning words. Discuss whether the use of the word as a noun or as a verb changes the meaning of the word.   Book 4/Unit 1 **The Lost Lake**

LANGUAGE SUPPORT

Name_____ Date_____

What Do They Mean?

1. Cut out the words below. 2. Look at the pictures and read the sentences under them. 3. Paste the correct word to fill in each blank.

bit	right	beat	left
bit	right	beat	left

You ___left___ your pack behind!

No I did not, it is ___right___ here!

To go up the mountain, follow the trail on your ___left___.

To go down the mountain, follow the trail on your ___right___.

Hey! That bug just ___bit___ me.

We should race! I bet I can ___beat___ you to that stream.

We should rest in the shade for a ___bit___.

My heart sure does ___beat___ hard when I run!

8 The Lost Lake • Language Support /Blackline Master 4   Grade 4

Personal Narrative

GRAMMAR/SPELLING CONNECTIONS

See the 5-Day Grammar and Usage Plan on sentences, pages 41M–41N.

See the 5-Day Spelling Plan on words with short vowels, pages 41O–41P.

Prewrite

WRITE A PERSONAL NARRATIVE Present this writing assignment: Luke's camping story is drawn from his own experience. Write a personal narrative of your own about a time when you and your family took a trip somewhere. Where did you go? What did you do? Why is the trip still important to you? Use *I* when telling your story.

VISUALIZE IDEAS Have partners take turns visualizing their family trips and describing the events and places to each other. Encourage them to use descriptive words to "paint a picture" of the trip for their partners to imagine.

Strategy: Focusing Questions Have students write answers to questions that ask *who, what, when, where,* and *why* about the family trip. Suggest:

- Who went on the trip?
- Whom did you meet on your trip?
- What season was it?
- Why did you choose this location?
- What did you take with you?

Draft

USE THE QUESTIONS Have students organize the answers to their questions in the order that the events happened on their trip. Stories should include details about the people and places students encountered on their trip.

Revise

SELF-QUESTIONING Ask students to assess their drafts.

- Have I answered the questions *who, what, when, where,* and *why?*
- Did I include descriptive details?
- Did I use the word *I* to tell my story?

 PARTNERS Have partners read parts of their stories to each other and comment on whether enough descriptive details are included.

Edit/Proofread

CHECK FOR ERRORS Students should reread their stories for spelling, grammar, punctuation, and proper word usage.

Publish

EXCHANGE STORIES Have students prepare final copies of their stories. Students can then exchange stories with partners and discuss what they liked best about each story.

TEACHING TIP

Technology Students can preview their story before printing by clicking on *File* and *Print Preview.* This allows them to see how their stories look on the page. They can then tinker with margins as necessary.

Supporting Details Have students review their drafts to make sure the descriptive details support the narrative.

 Handwriting CD-ROM

My Family Trip

Last summer my family and I visited an amusement park in Illinois. We looked at many travel brochures to decide where we wanted to go. Our neighbors had been to this park and told us all about it. We were glad we chose this spot!

We rode every ride and went to every show. My favorite ride was the Whirling Birdie. You stand in a room shaped like a circle. Your back is against the wall. Suddenly the room starts spinning and the floor drops down. I laughed so hard during this ride that I started crying!

I will never forget this trip because it meant a lot to me to share the rides, food, and shows with my family.

Presentation Ideas

MAKE POSTCARDS Have students create postcards that show pictures of the places their families visited. Create a display of the stories and postcards.

▶ **Viewing/Representing**

SHARE VACATIONS Designate a "Vacation Day." Have students wear things that remind them of their trips and then read their stories aloud to the class.

▶ **Speaking/Listening**

Listening and Speaking

LISTENING STRATEGIES
Have students:

- try to picture what the speaker is describing.
- ask questions about *who, what, when, where,* or *why.*

SPEAKING STRATEGIES
Encourage students to:

- tell what they like about each other's stories.
- suggest descriptive details to add to each other's stories.

Consider students' creative efforts, possibly adding a plus (+) for originality, wit, and imagination.

Scoring Rubric

Excellent	Good	Fair	Unsatisfactory
4: The writer • clearly answers the questions *who, what, when, where,* and *why.* • provides many descriptive details about the people and the setting. • uses the first-person point of view.	**3:** The writer • answers most of the questions *who, what, when, where,* and *why.* • provides a few descriptive details about the people and the setting. • uses the first-person point of view.	**2:** The writer • answers only a few of the questions *who, what, when, where,* and *why.* • provides descriptive details about either the people or the setting. • uses third-person point of view.	**1:** The writer • does not answer any of the questions *who, what, when, where,* and *why.* • provides little or no descriptive details about the people or the setting. • mixes points of view.

Incomplete 0: The writer leaves the page blank or fails to respond to the writing task. The student does not address the topic or simply paraphrases the prompt. The response is illegible or incoherent.

For a 6-point or an 8-point scale, see pages T107–T108.

LANGUAGE SUPPORT

ESL Ask students acquiring English to share their Focusing Questions with English-fluent partners. Suggest that they both make notes about descriptive words they might use to describe the people and setting.

PORTFOLIO Invite students to include their stories or another writing project in their portfolios.

Meeting Individual Needs for Writing

EASY	ON-LEVEL	CHALLENGE
Make a Map Have students draw a map of a campsite where they would like to stay. Have them label features such as roads, streams, or tent sites.	**Fantasy Trip** If students could take their families anywhere in the world, where would they go? Have them draw a picture of the place and write a paragraph explaining their reasons for choosing it.	**"Found Lake" Story** Ask students to suppose that Luke and his father stayed overnight at the original crowded Lost Lake on their way back to their car. Have them write a humorous story about what might have happened to the characters. How was the experience different from the one at their own "Lost Lake"?

41L

5 Day Grammar and Usage Plan

Ask students to use their fingers to draw a period or a question mark in the air after you read each of these sentences: *Where did they go(?) They went camping(.) Did it rain(?) The lake was crowded(.)*

DAILY LANGUAGE ACTIVITIES

Write the Daily Language Activities on the chalkboard each day or use **Transparency 1.** Have students correct the sentences orally. For answers, see the transparency.

Day 1
1. luke likes to hike
2. did they bring enough food
3. luke's father carried the tent

Day 2
1. will we eat fish for dinner
2. help me set up camp
3. boy, am I tired

Day 3
1. put the sleeping bag in the tent
2. our secret lake is awesome
3. do you think it is going to rain

Day 4
1. luke liked to watch his dad cook
2. i think I hear a bear
3. get some wood for the fire

Day 5
1. can we come back next year
2. we saw our lake below us
3. watch out for falling rocks

Daily Language Transparency 1

 DAY 1 Introduce the Concept

Oral Warm-Up Ask each student to finish this sentence: *I like to _____.*

Introduce Sentences The stories we read are made up of sentences.

Sentences
- A **sentence** is a group of words that expresses a complete thought.
- A **sentence fragment** is a group of words that does not express a complete thought.
- Every sentence begins with a capital letter.
- A **statement** is a sentence that tells something. It ends with a period.
- A **question** is a sentence that asks something. It ends with a question mark.

Present the Daily Language Activity. Have students write five statements and questions.

 WRITING Assign the daily Writing Prompt on page 18C.

Name_____ Date_____ **Grammar ❶**
Sentences

- A **sentence** is a group of words that expresses a complete thought.
- A **sentence fragment** is a group of words that does not express a complete thought.
- Every sentence begins with a capital letter.
- A **statement** is a sentence that tells something. It ends with a period.
- A **question** is a sentence that asks something. It ends with a question mark.

Decide if each group of words makes a sentence. If it does, rewrite the sentence adding a capital letter and a period or a question mark.
1. it was too hot outside
   It was too hot outside.
2. dad and Luke left in the morning
   Dad and Luke left in the morning.
3. when they hiked to Lost Lake
4. dad went up the trail   Dad went up the trail.
5. a mountain that no one else knew about
6. did they find a new "lost lake"
   Did they find a new "lost lake"?

Book 4 / Unit 1   Extension: Have students write two statements and
The Lost Lake   two questions about an outdoor adventure.   1

GRAMMAR PRACTICE BOOK, PAGE 1

 DAY 2 Teach the Concept

Review Sentences Ask students to tell the difference between a sentence and a sentence fragment.

Introduce Commands and Exclamations Explain that there are other kinds of sentences besides statements and questions.

Sentences
- A **command** tells or asks someone to do something. It ends with a period.
- An **exclamation** shows strong feeling. It ends with an exclamation mark.

Present the Daily Language Activity. Then have students give examples of commands and exclamations. Ask them to tell what punctuation belongs at the end of each of their sentences.

WRITING Assign the daily Writing Prompt on page 18C.

Name_____ Date_____ **Grammar ❷**
Types of Sentences

- A **statement** is a sentence that tells something. It ends with a period.
- A **question** is a sentence that asks something. It ends with a question mark.
- A **command** tells or asks someone to do something. It ends with a period.
- An **exclamation** shows strong feeling. It ends with an exclamation mark.

Write **statement** if the sentence tells something. Write **question** if the sentence asks something. Write **command** if the sentence tells or asks someone to do something. Write **exclamation** if the sentence shows strong feeling. Then put the correct end mark at the end of each sentence.

1. Dad and Luke hiked to Lost Lake
   statement .
2. What did they find when they got there
   question ?
3. Put your pack on and let's go
   command .
4. Luke wanted to camp by the creek
   statement .
5. Look out for bears
   exclamation !
6. How did they find their special lake
   question ?

2   Extension: Have students think of a special place. Then have
them write a statement, a question, a command, and an
exclamation about it.   Book 4 / Unit 1
The Lost Lake

GRAMMAR PRACTICE BOOK, PAGE 2

Sentences

DAY 3 — Review and Practice

Learn from the Literature Review sentences. Ask students to read the last sentence on page 31 of *The Lost Lake:*

> **A wise man never leaves home without his compass.**

Ask students to identify what kind of sentence this is. (statement) Then have them change the sentence into a question, a command, and an exclamation.

Identify Sentences Present the Daily Language Activity. Then have students find and copy examples of statements, questions, and exclamations from *The Lost Lake.* Ask them to make up commands that Luke and his father might say to each other.

 Assign the daily Writing Prompt on page 18D.

DAY 4 — Review and Practice

Review Sentences Hold up a card that shows a period, a question mark, or an exclamation mark. Ask students to make up a sentence that would have that end punctuation and then identify what kind of sentence it is. Then present the Daily Language Activity.

Mechanics and Usage Display and discuss:

Sentence Punctuation

- Every sentence begins with a capital letter.
- A statement ends with a period.
- A question ends with a question mark.
- A command ends with a period.
- An exclamation ends with an exclamation point.

 Assign the daily Writing Prompt on page 18D.

DAY 5 — Assess and Reteach

Assess Use the Daily Language Activity and page 5 of the **Grammar Practice Book** for assessment.

Reteach First ask students to write a period, a question mark, and an exclamation point on separate sheets of paper. Then say different types of sentences and have students hold up the appropriate ending punctuation.

Have students add the names of the different kinds of sentences and their ending punctuation to the classroom display wall.

Use page 6 of the **Grammar Practice Book** for additional reteaching.

 Assign the daily Writing Prompt on page 18D.

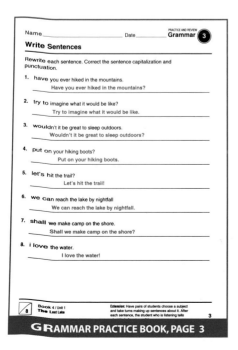

GRAMMAR PRACTICE BOOK, PAGE 3

GRAMMAR PRACTICE BOOK, PAGE 4

GRAMMAR PRACTICE BOOK, PAGE 5

5 Day Spelling Plan

DICTATION SENTENCES

Spelling Words

1. The baby drank from a bottle.
2. Take a rest after work.
3. Run ahead of me.
4. We will drink water.
5. A boat is at the dock.
6. A swing hung from the tree.
7. An old car can cause trouble.
8. I like to read magazines.
9. She is her happy self once more.
10. The deaf woman talks with her hands.
11. This bag is too large to lift.
12. A flock of sheep ate grass.
13. Friends can trust each other.
14. My aunt and cousin came by.
15. A loud noise came from the cannon.
16. He swept with a broom.
17. It is so pleasant in the sun.
18. She made a fist with her hand.
19. It rained for a couple of days.
20. Money is just one kind of wealth.

Challenge Words

21. Clean boots can look brand-new.
22. A compass points you in the right direction.
23. A fish darted in the water.
24. He walked off and muttered words.
25. He is not much of a talker.

DAY 1 — Pretest

Assess Prior Knowledge Use the Dictation Sentences at the left and **Spelling Practice Book** page 1 for the pretest. Allow students to correct their own papers. Students who require a modified list may be tested on the first ten words.

Spelling Words		Challenge Words
1. **drank**	11. lift	21. **brand-new**
2. rest	12. flock	
3. **ahead**	13. trust	22. **compass**
4. **drink**	14. cousin	23. **darted**
5. dock	15. cannon	24. **muttered**
6. hung	16. swept	25. **talker**
7. trouble	17. pleasant	
8. **maga-zines**	18. fist	
	19. couple	
9. self	20. wealth	
10. deaf		

*Note: Words in **dark type** are from the story.*

Word Study On page 2 of the **Spelling Practice Book** are word study steps and an at-home activity.

DAY 2 — Explore the Pattern

Sort and Spell Words Say the following words: *magazine, wealth, lift, flock, trouble.* Ask students what short vowel sound they hear in each word. (/a/, /e/, /i/, /o/, /u/) Have students read the Spelling Words aloud and sort them as below.

Words with

/a/ spelled *a*	/i/ spelled *i*
drank	drink
magazines	lift
cannon	fist

/e/ spelled *e*	/o/ spelled *o*
rest	dock
self	flock
swept	

/e/ spelled *ea*	/u/ spelled *u*
ahead	hung
deaf	trust
pleasant	
wealth	/u/ spelled *ou*
	trouble
	cousin
	couple

Word Wall Have students create a word wall based on the word sort and add more words from their reading.

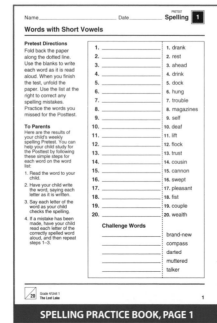

SPELLING PRACTICE BOOK, PAGE 1

WORD STUDY STEPS AND ACTIVITY, PAGE 2

SPELLING PRACTICE BOOK, PAGE 3

Words with Short Vowels

DAY 3 — Practice and Extend

Word Meaning: Endings Present the word *magazines*. Explain: adding -*s* to the end of some words can make them plural. Have students identify the Spelling Words that can be made plural by adding -*s*. Then have them write sentences using the plural form. Point out that -*s* is also added to some verbs for subject-verb agreement.

If students need extra practice, have partners give each other a midweek test.

Glossary Point out that a Glossary entry is usually listed as a base word without endings; other forms are shown at the end of the entry. Have partners:

• write each Challenge Word.

• underline base words of words with endings. (darted, muttered, talker)

• find the entry word in the Glossary.

• write forms of the words that are shown at the end of the Glossary entry.

DAY 4 — Proofread and Write

Proofread Sentences Write these sentences on the chalkboard, including the misspelled words. Ask students to proofread, circling incorrect spellings and writing the correct spellings. There are two spelling errors in each sentence.

> My cusin is one grade ahed of me in school. **(cousin, ahead)**
>
> We took a pleseant trip for a cuple of days. **(pleasant, couple)**

Have students create additional sentences with errors for partners to correct.

WRITING Have students use as many Spelling Words as possible in the daily Writing Prompt on page 18D. Remind students to proofread their writing for errors in spelling, grammar, and punctuation.

DAY 5 — Assess and Reteach

Assess Students' Knowledge Use page 6 of the **Spelling Practice Book** or the Dictation Sentences on page 41O for the posttest.

JOURNAL Personal Word List Have students add troublesome Spelling Words to their personal word list in their journals. Have students highlight the part of each word that they usually misspell.

Students should refer to their word lists during later writing activities.

SPELLING PRACTICE BOOK, PAGE 4

Name _____ Date _____ **Spelling** 4
Words with Short Vowels

drank	dock	self	trust	pleasant
rest	hung	deaf	cousin	fist
ahead	trouble	lift	cannon	couple
drink	magazines	flock	swept	wealth

Complete each sentence with a spelling word.

1. These _magazines_ always have funny stories I like to read.
2. Every morning, a large _flock_ of birds visits my bird feeder.
3. I _drank_ two glasses of milk this morning at breakfast.
4. A person's _self_ is who they are and how they are special.
5. Last week, the students _hung_ pictures on the classroom walls.
6. If you are in a hurry, you can go _ahead_ of me in line.
7. I like to _drink_ a glass of juice after school.
8. My _cousin_ Bob is my Aunt Tilly's son.
9. The clown at the circus was shot from a _cannon_.
10. He found the broom and _swept_ the floor.

Define It!
Write the spelling words that have the same meanings as the words or phrases below.
11. take it easy or sleep _rest_ 14. a place to tie a boat _dock_
12. two of something _couple_ 15. to raise up _lift_
13. not able to hear _deaf_ 16. a tightly closed hand _fist_

Challenge Extension: Ask students to write a "fill in the blank" sentence for each Challenge Word and then exchange papers with a partner to complete the sentences.
4 Grade 4/Unit 1 The Lost Lake 16

SPELLING PRACTICE BOOK, PAGE 5

Name _____ Date _____ **Spelling** 5
Words with Short Vowels

Proofreading Activity
There are six spelling mistakes in the letter below. Circle the misspelled words. Write the words correctly on the lines below.

Dear Cusin Bob,
I had a wonderful time with my dad this summer. We hiked into the mountains. Dad hiked ahed of me because I had truble climbing. I had to stop and reast a lot. But soon we found a lake. We drank water right from the lake! Once I thought we were lost. Dad said we could troust his compass to help us find our way. And he was right. It was the best vacation I ever had.
See you soon,
Luke

1. _cousin_ 3. _trouble_ 5. _drank_
2. _ahead_ 4. _rest_ 6. _trust_

Writing Activity
Write a letter to a friend about a holiday or vacation you once had. Use four spelling words in your writing.

_____
_____
_____
_____

18 Grade 4/Unit 1 The Lost Lake 5

SPELLING PRACTICE BOOK, PAGE 6

Name _____ Date _____ **Spelling** 6
Words with Short Vowels

Look at the words in each set below. One word in each set is spelled correctly. Use a pencil to fill in the circle next to the correct word. Before you begin, look at the sample sets of words. Sample A has been done for you. Do Sample B by yourself. When you are sure you know what to do, you may go on with the rest of the page.

Sample A (A) beest (B) best (C) beste (D) biest

Sample B (E) ring (F) ringe (G) raing (H) reing

1. (A) docke (B) dock (C) doick (D) dok
6. (E) lifft (F) lift (G) lifte (H) liaft
11. (A) megizines (B) magazines (C) magazanes (D) magizins
16. (E) sweept (F) swept (G) swiept (H) sweeped

2. (E) cannin (F) kannon (G) cannon (H) canin
7. (A) silf (B) sealf (C) selfe (D) self
12. (E) deaf (F) deef (G) def (H) daef
17. (A) welth (B) weelth (C) walth (D) wealth

3. (A) drinke (B) drienk (C) drink (D) drenk
8. (E) huhng (F) hung (G) hunge (H) hungh
13. (A) truste (B) troust (C) trost (D) trust
18. (E) pleasant (F) plesant (G) pleasint (H) plezant

4. (E) trubble (F) trouble (G) troubel (H) truble
9. (A) riste (B) rest (C) reist (D) reste
14. (E) flouck (F) flock (G) flok (H) flocke
19. (A) feste (B) fis (C) fist (D) fiste

5. (A) ahead (B) ahed (C) ahaed (D) ahede
10. (E) drenk (F) drienk (G) draenk (H) drank
15. (A) cousin (B) cusin (C) cousen (D) cuzin
20. (E) cuple (F) copple (G) cuppel (H) couple

6 Grade 4/Unit 1 The Lost Lake 20

41P

Concept
- **Migrant Workers**

Comprehension
- **Problem and Solution**

Vocabulary
- **accidental**
- **labored**
- **occasions**
- **rhythms**
- **shortcut**
- **shutters**

Reaching All Learners

Anthology

Amelia's Road

Selection Summary Students will read about a little girl who moves from place to place with her migrant family. Though she longs for a real home, Amelia manages to find a place for herself.

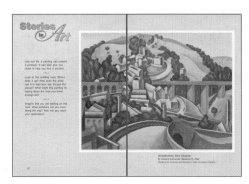

Stories in Art focuses on the **comprehension** skill

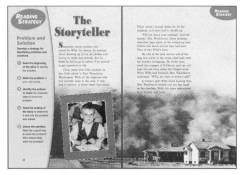

Reading Strategy applies the **comprehension** skill

Listening Library

INSTRUCTIONAL pages 44–65

About the Author *Amelia's Road* is one of many stories Linda Jacobs Altman has told about migrant workers. Altman also enjoys writing biographies of notable adults for young readers. Other books by Altman that students may enjoy are *Nobody Wants Annie, Cesar Chavez,* and *Women Inventors.*

About the Illustrator Born in the Dominican Republic, and currently living in Maine, Enrique O. Sanchez designed sets for *Sesame Street* before illustrating children's books. A 1993 Parents' Choice Award Honoree, his books include *Abuela's Weave* and *Saturday Market.*

Same Concept, Skills and Vocabulary!

Leveled Books

EASY
Lesson on pages 65A and 65D

INDEPENDENT
Lesson on pages 65B and 65D

CHALLENGE
Lesson on pages 65C and 65D

Leveled Practice

EASY

Reteach, 8–14 blackline masters with reteaching opportunities for each assessed skill

INDEPENDENT/ON-LEVEL

Practice, 8–14 workbook with Take-Home stories and practice opportunities for each assessed skill and story comprehension

CHALLENGE

Extend, 8–14 blackline masters that offer challenge activities for each assessed skill

Quizzes Prepared by Accelerated Reader®

WORKSTATION Activities

42B

Suggested Lesson Planner

READING AND LANGUAGE ARTS	DAY 1 — Focus on Reading and Skills	DAY 2 — Read the Literature

READING AND LANGUAGE ARTS	**DAY 1** *Focus on Reading and Skills*	**DAY 2** *Read the Literature*

• **Comprehension**
• **Vocabulary**
• **Phonics/Decoding**
• **Study Skills**
• **Listening, Speaking, Viewing, Representing**
	Read Aloud: Poetry, 42E
	"Pack"
	
	Develop Visual Literacy, 42
	
	☑ **Introduce Problem and Solution,** 43A–43B
	  Teaching Chart 7
	  Reteach, Practice, Extend, 8
	
	 Reading Strategy: Problem and Solution, 43
	"The Storyteller"
	
	ⓘ Intervention Program
		Build Background, 44A
		Develop Oral Language
		
		Vocabulary, 44B–44C
		
		| *accidental*
			occasions	*shortcut*

labored	*rhythms*	*shutters* | **Teaching Chart 8** Word Building Manipulative Cards Reteach, Practice, Extend, 9 **Read the Selection,** 44–61 ☑ Problem and Solution ☑ Make Inferences **Genre: Realistic Fiction,** 45 **Cultural Perspectives,** 52 ⓘ Intervention Program
• **Curriculum Connections**	**Link** Works of Art, 42	**Link** Social Studies, 44A
• **Writing**	**Writing Prompt:** Write three things that you would like others to know about the town where you live.	**Writing Prompt:** Imagine that you were just told that you and your family have to move to a new home. Describe how you feel about the news and why. **Journal Writing,** 61 Quick-Write
• **Grammar**	**Introduce the Concept: Subjects and Predicates,** 65M Daily Language Activity 1. Migrant farmers harvest the crops. 2. Amelia's parents work very hard. 3. Red delicious apples grow on trees. **Grammar Practice Book,** 7	**Teach the Concept: Subjects and Predicates,** 65M Daily Language Activity 1. Work hard in the hot fields The farmers work,. 2. Grow in a field The crops grow,. 3. Learned her name The teacher learned,. **Grammar Practice Book,** 8
• **Spelling**	**Pretest: Words with Long *a* and Long *e*,** 65O **Spelling Practice Book,** 7, 8	**Explore the Pattern: Words with Long *a* and Long *e*,** 65O **Spelling Practice Book,** 9

42C *Amelia's Road*   **Intervention Program Available**

Meeting Individual Needs

 = Skill Assessed in Unit Test

 Intervention Program Available

 Read EVERY DAY

DAY 3 — Read the Literature

 Read

Rereading for Fluency, 60

Story Questions and Activities, 62–63
Reteach, Practice, Extend, 10

Study Skill, 64
☑ Parts of a Book
Teaching Chart 9
Reteach, Practice, Extend, 11

Test Power, 65

Read the Leveled Books, 65A–65D
Guided Reading
Long *a* and *e*
☑ Problem and Solution
☑ Instructional Vocabulary

  ⓘ Intervention Program

Activity Social Studies, 48, Science, 54

Writing Prompt: Imagine that Amelia is a new student in your class. Write a paragraph that describes your class and school. What questions would you ask her? Make a short list.

Writing Process: Diary Entry, 65K
Prewrite, Draft

Review and Practice: Subjects and Predicates, 65N
Daily Language Activity
1. On hot summer days, people go swimming.
2. Can be found in grocery stores Apples can be,.
3. Move from place to place Migrant farmers move,.

Grammar Practice Book, 9

Practice and Extend: Words with Long *a* and Long *e*, 65P
Spelling Practice Book, 10

DAY 4 — Build Skills

 Read

Read the Leveled Books and Self-Selected Books

☑ **Review Problem and Solution,** 65E–65F
Teaching Chart 10
Reteach, Practice, Extend, 12
Language Support, 14

☑ **Review Make Inferences,** 65G–65H
Teaching Chart 11
Reteach, Practice, Extend, 13
Language Support, 15

Minilessons, 47, 53, 55, 59

 ⓘ Intervention Program

Activity Math, 56

Writing Prompt: Write Amelia a letter, and tell her about a special outdoor place you like to visit.

Writing Process: Diary Entry, 65K
Revise

Meeting Individual Needs for Writing, 65L

Review and Practice: Subjects and Predicates, 65N
Daily Language Activity
1. Live in shanties The workers live,.
2. Amelia and her family travel by car.
3. Packs up the car and goes away The family packs,.

Grammar Practice Book, 10

Proofread and Write: Words with Long *a* and Long *e*, 65P
Spelling Practice Book, 11

DAY 5 — Build Skills

 Read

Read Self-Selected Books

☑ **Introduce Antonyms and Synonyms,** 65I–65J
Teaching Chart 12
Reteach, Practice, Extend, 14
Language Support, 16

Listening, Speaking, Viewing, Representing, 65L

Minilessons, 47, 53, 59

Phonics Review, Long *a* and Long *e*, 55

Phonics/Phonemic Awareness Practice Book, 5–6

ⓘ Intervention Program

Activity Art, 58

Writing Prompt: Write a paragraph about the day Amelia left the accidental road. Describe how she felt and what she'll remember about her special place.

Writing Process: Diary Entry, 65K
Edit/Proofread, Publish

Assess and Reteach: Subjects and Predicates, 65N
Daily Language Activity
1. Amelia's kind teacher helps her.
2. Goes into the car The baby goes,.
3. Blankets, pots, and furniture fill the trunk.

Grammar Practice Book, 11, 12

Assess and Reteach: Words with Long *a* and Long *e*, 65P
Spelling Practice Book, 12

Read Aloud

Pack
a poem by Lee Bennett Hopkins

Pack
the boxes
into the car,
pile the dishes,
load in the clothes,
squeeze in the
pots and pans,
our two radios—
can't waste a
space—
everything goes.

Crowd in the Mama,
the Daddy,

the sister,
jam in the brother,
make room for my toes—
can't waste a space—
everything goes.

Bundle the memories
we're moving today
from
Scranton, PA,
to
Newark, NJ.

Oral Comprehension

LISTENING AND SPEAKING Read the poem aloud. Tell students to visualize the process of packing as they listen. Afterward, ask: Which words helped you imagine what it's like to pack a car on moving day? Then reread the poem. Discuss the different meanings of such "packing words" as *pile, load, squeeze, crowd,* and *jam.*

GENRE STUDY: POETRY Discuss the poet's use of rhythm, vivid words, and metaphor.

• What kind of pace, or rhythm, do the short words and phrases create? How does the fast pace affect the tone?

• In what way is the packing word *bundle* different from those such as *jam, squeeze,* and *crowd*?

• A metaphor is a type of comparison. What metaphor does the poet use in the last stanza? What two very different kinds of things are being compared?

Activity Read the poem aloud as four volunteers role-play the mother, father, sister, and brother. Encourage students to use props to act out the packing words. ▶ **Spatial/Kinesthetic**

Develop Visual Literacy

Link

Works of Art

Stories in Art

Like real life, a painting can present a problem. It can also give you clues to help you find a solution.

Look at this twisting road. Where does it go? How does the artist use it to lead your eye through the picture? What might this painting be saying about the road you travel through life?

Imagine that you are walking on this road. What problems will you meet along the way? How will you reach your destination?

Broadbottom, Near Glossop
by Edward Alexander Wadsworth, 1922
Bradford Art Galleries and Museums, West Yorkshire, England

42

Objective: Identify Problem and Solution

VIEWING Have students imagine that they are standing in front of this expressive painting by Edward Alexander Wadsworth. Discuss why a viewer is first drawn to the part of the road at the bottom of the painting. Invite them to share their feelings as their eyes travel down the road and through the town.

Read the page with students, encouraging individual interpretations of the painting. Ask students to identify possible problems and a solution that the painting evokes. Discuss how aspects of the painting symbolize

ways we encounter problems in real life. For example:

- The absence of people in the painting can mean that many problems must be faced alone.
- You can take different roads to solve problems.

REPRESENTING Have students work in small groups to create a mural of a road that traverses many problems. Then have them draw a solution, a "happier place" as the destination.

TESTED OBJECTIVES

Students will identify a problem and a solution in a reading passage.

Skills Finder

Problem and Solution

Introduce	43A-B
Review	65E-F, 93G-H, 119A-B, 633A-B, 663E-F, 691G-H
Test	Unit 1, Unit 6
Maintain	411, 545

LANGUAGE SUPPORT

ESL Read the passage aloud, pointing out key words and phrases that students may not understand, such as *caption* and *sparkle in her eyes*. Discuss their meanings and how each relates to a problem and solution in the passage.

Introduce Problem and Solution

PREPARE

Personalize Prompt students to think about times when they faced problems and tried to solve them. Ask: How did you feel as you were trying to solve the problem? How did you feel after the problem was solved?

TEACH

Define Problem and Solution Explain that a main character's actions often center on a problem. By thinking about how the character will solve it, you can gain a better understanding of the story.

Where Home Is

Paul was worried about his mother. She seemed so tired and the sparkle in her eyes was missing. As migrant farm workers, Paul's family traveled to find work harvesting crops. They had no one place to call home.

One evening before bedtime, Paul had an idea. The next day, he would draw a picture of his family. For a caption, he would write: HOME IS WHERE THE HEART IS. Paul borrowed pens and paper from his friend Anna. When he gave his drawing to his mother, her whole face lit up. His idea had worked!

Teaching Chart 7

Read the Story and Model the Skill Display **Teaching Chart 7.** As the passage is read aloud, direct students toward clues that identify the problem and solution.

MODEL The first sentence tells me that Paul is worried because his mother seems tired. The problem is that Paul doesn't know how to cheer up his mother and put the sparkle back in her eyes.

Identify Problem and Solution Have students circle the words that indicate the problem and underline the words that describe the solution.

ALTERNATE TEACHING STRATEGY
....
PROBLEM AND SOLUTION
For a different approach to teaching this skill, see page T64.

PRACTICE

Create a Problem and Solution Chart

Display a Problem and Solution chart. Have volunteers identify in their own words the problem faced by the character in the passage and the solution the character finds. Record their responses on the chart.

▶ **Linguistic/Logical**

GROUP

PROBLEM

Paul was worried about his mother.

STEPS TO SOLUTION

Paul imagined a gift for his mother.

Paul borrowed pens and paper.

SOLUTION

Paul's gift made his mother happy.

 **Skills Intervention Guide**, for direct instruction and extra practice in problem and solution

ASSESS/CLOSE

How Problem and Solution Create Plot

Ask students to explain whether or not they think Paul came up with a good solution to the problem. Then invite volunteers to suggest other actions Paul might have taken to cheer up his mother. Discuss with students how a story's problem and the actions the characters take to solve it create the story's plot.

Meeting Individual Needs for Comprehension

EASY

Name_____ Date_____ **Reteach** 8

Problem and Solution

> Like someone in real life, a character in a story may have a **problem**. What the character does to find a **solution** to the problem makes up the **plot**, or main events, of the story.

Read the story. Then answer each question.

> Sam felt left out. Willa and Lee were staying after school to build a rocket. Sam wanted to work on the rocket too.
> Sam decided to ask Willa and Lee if he could help. They said sure, but that he would have to ask Mr. Ward, the science teacher. Mr. Ward said Sam could help if it was okay with his Mom that he stay after school. Sam called his Mom and she told Mr. Ward it was fine for Sam to stay.
> Sam was a big help to Willa and Lee. He figured out how to get the rocket to blast-off. They launched the rocket the next day for the science class. All the kids cheered, and Sam was proud.

1. What was Sam's problem? Sam wanted to work on the rocket, but no one had asked him.

2. What did Sam do first to try to solve the problem? He talked to Willa and Lee to find out if he could help with the work.

3. What did Sam do next to help solve his problem? He went to get Mr. Ward's permission to help with the rocket.

4. What was the last thing Sam did to find a solution? Sam asked his mother for permission to stay after school and she gave it.

Book 4/Unit 1
Amelia's Road
4
At Home: Have students think of other ways Sam might have solved his problem.
8

ON-LEVEL

Name_____ Date_____ **Practice** 8

Problem and Solution

> The **plot** is the events of a story. It often has a **problem** and a **solution**. The problem is the main idea of a story. A character must find a solution, or answer, to the problem. Read the story and answer the questions.

> One by one, the kids in Ichiro's class stood up and told about a special talent. Everyone would take part. Soon it was Ichiro's turn. He gulped and then told his class that he was a good juggler and could juggle three balls at a time. Then the class asked Ichiro to juggle. "No problem," said Ichiro.
> But there was a problem. Ichiro couldn't juggle. Last year, his big brother Yoshi tried to teach Ichiro to juggle, but Ichiro found it too hard to do.
> Ichiro worried before remembering that he was a year older now. "Maybe I can do better," he thought. " I'll get Yoshi to help me try again." Sure enough, it worked. Juggling was easier now.
> Three weeks later, Ichiro and Yoshi put on a show for the class. Yoshi did all the tricky stuff. No one noticed that Ichiro did only the simple tricks. The class thought Ichiro was great!

1. Who is the main character? Ichiro

2. What is the problem? Ichiro said he could juggle, but he can't.

3. What idea helped with the solution? Ichiro realized he's a year older. Maybe he would find juggling easier now

4. What was the solution? Ichiro got his brother to help him.

5. How did Ichiro's solution benefit the class? Answers will vary but should include giving a demonstration that the class enjoyed.

Book 4/Unit 1
Amelia's Road
5
At Home: Have students work with someone at home to solve a problem.
8

CHALLENGE

Name_____ Date_____ **Extend** 8

Problem and Solution

> The main idea, or plan, of a story is called the plot. The plot may involve a **problem and solution**. Solutions to the problem can be simple and predictable or they can be more complicated and different from what you might expect.

Write a story about a problem that you were faced with and what the solution was.

Answers will vary but should include a problem and solution.

_____
_____
_____
_____
_____
_____
_____
_____
_____
_____
_____
_____
_____
_____
_____

Book 4/Unit 1
Amelia's Road
At Home: Have students retell the story they wrote with two different solutions to the problem.
8

Reteach, 8   Practice, 8   Extend, 8

OBJECTIVES

Students will identify a problem and a solution in a reading passage.

Apply Problem and Solution

READING STRATEGY

Problem and Solution

Develop a strategy for identifying problems and solutions.

1. **Read the beginning of the story** to identify the problem.

2. **State the problem** in your own words.

3. **Identify the actions or steps** the character takes to solve the problem.

4. **Read the ending of the story** to determine if and how the problem was solved.

5. **Check the solution.** Was this a good way to solve the problem? Who helped Willy solve his problem?

43

The Storyteller

September meant another new school for Willy. As always, he worried about showing up in his old clothes and having to make new friends. But he knew he had to go to school if he wanted to get anywhere in life.

Once, there were fifty students in this little school in East Wenatchee, Washington. With all the migrants who had recently come to the area, it now had to squeeze in three times that many.

READING STRATEGY

There weren't enough desks for all the students, and some had to double up.

"Tell me about your summer," said the teacher, Mrs. Washburne. Some students described days spent at the swimming hole. Others told about movies they had seen. Then it was Willy's turn.

He told of the dust storms and of the long trip north in the truck piled high with his family's belongings. He made them smell the oranges of California and see and hear the sea lions along the Oregon coast. When Willy had finished, Mrs. Washburne exclaimed, "Willy, you have a writer's gift!"

A writer's gift! Willy loved hearing that. Mrs. Washburne smiled and put her hand on his shoulder. Willy felt more appreciated than he had ever been.

PREVIEW Have students preview "The Storyteller." Remind them that fiction often tells about a character who faces and overcomes a problem. Have them skim the first paragraph to identify the main character of the story. (Willy)

SET PURPOSES Tell students that they will apply what they have learned about identifying problem and solution as they read "The Storyteller."

APPLY THE STRATEGY Discuss this strategy for identifying problem and solution in a selection.

• Locate the main character and his or her problem. These are usually introduced at the beginning of the story.

• Explain the problem to yourself.

• Step-by-step, discover how the problem was solved.

• Some problems are never solved. At the end of this story, was the problem solved? Were all the loose ends tied up?

• Decide whether you think the solution was good.

Activity Have each student create a Problem and Solution chart for the passage.

Build Background

Link
Social Studies

Concept: Migrant Workers

Anthology and Leveled Books

Evaluate Prior Knowledge

CONCEPT: MIGRANT WORKERS Ask students to share what they know about migrant farm workers. Also encourage them to share any experience or knowledge they may have of harvesting crops.

COMPARE LIVES Provide students with a general description of what life is like for migrant farm worker families. Then have students list ways the lives of children of migrant farm workers and non-migrant workers might be alike and different. Record their responses in a Venn diagram.

▶ Logical/Visual

CHILDREN OF NON-MIGRANT WORKERS		CHILDREN OF MIGRANT WORKERS
Different	Alike	Different

go to same school all year, have the same school friends all year, have a place to call home

go to school, do homework, help family with chores

go to different schools during the year, live in cabins in work camps

Graphic Organizer 14

PLAN A DAY Have partners write a schedule of what they think might be a typical day in the life of a family of migrant workers.

PARTNERS WRITING

Develop Oral Language

DISCUSS MIGRANT WORKERS Refer

ESL to an encyclopedia and, if possible, bring in magazine photos that show the work and living conditions of migrant farm workers. Ask students to generate a list of words associated with the life of a typical migrant farm worker family. Record the words on the chalkboard; for example:

- difficult
- harvest
- tiring
- strength
- unsettled
- diverse
- lonely
- crops
- moving
- picking

Ask students to take turns choosing a word from the list and using it in a sentence. Some students acquiring English may wish to work with an English-fluent partner for this activity.

TEACHING TIP

MANAGEMENT Have partners work on the Venn diagram and the Plan a Day activity. If any of your students come from migrant families, invite them to share their experiences.

As partners work independently, present the Develop Oral Language activity to students who require help. You may wish to write the words from the oral language activity on index cards to help students build their vocabulary.

LANGUAGE SUPPORT

See Language Support Book, pages 9–12, for teaching suggestions for Build Background.

TESTED OBJECTIVES

Students will use context clues to determine the meaning of vocabulary words.

labored

shortcut

occasions

rhythms

accidental

shutters

Definitions

labored (p. 46) worked

shortcut (p. 54) a quicker way of reaching a place

occasions (p. 48) important or special events

rhythms (p. 48) regular or orderly repeating of sounds or movements

accidental (p. 54) happening by chance

shutters (p. 47) movable covers for windows, usually attached to the frames by hinges

Story Words

These words from the selection may be unfamiliar. Before students read, have them check the meaning and pronunciation of each word in a dictionary or in the Glossary, beginning on page 756.

- shanties, p. 46
- cabin, p. 48
- footpath, p. 54

Vocabulary

Teach Vocabulary in Context

Identify Vocabulary Words   Display **Teaching Chart 8** and read it with students. Invite volunteers to circle each vocabulary word and underline other words that are clues to its meaning.

Amelia's Dream House

1. Amelia's parents were migrant workers who (labored) from sunrise until sunset picking crops. **2.** One afternoon, on her way home from school, Amelia took a (shortcut) through the fields rather than the road, which took longer. **3.** She was in a hurry to get back to the camp because it was her mother's birthday, one of the (occasions) everyone in the family liked to celebrate. **4.** Amelia was humming a new song, and she matched her steps to the song's changing (rhythms) and beat. **5.** It was (accidental) that she tripped on a rock. **6.** Then she looked across the field and saw her dream house with blue (shutters) around the windows.

Teaching Chart 8

Discuss Meanings   Ask questions to help clarify word meanings:

- If you spent the day relaxing, have you labored?
- How can a shortcut help you get somewhere quicker?
- List some events that were happy occasions.
- Do you prefer fast or slow rhythms?
- Can something accidental happen on purpose?
- Do shutters belong on windows or ceilings?

Practice

Demonstrate Word Meaning

PARTNERS

Have partners take turns choosing vocabulary cards from a pile and demonstrating the meaning of each word through pantomime, drawings, or verbal clues. ▶**Kinesthetic/Visual/Linguistic**

labored

shortcut

rhythms

Word Building Manipulative Cards

Write a Paragraph

WRITING

Have students write a short paragraph about something that happened to them by accident. Encourage them to use as many of the vocabulary words as they can.

Assess Vocabulary

Use Words in Context

PARTNERS

Have students write a diary entry about an event that happened during an imaginary trip, using as many vocabulary words as possible. Students can exchange completed entries with a partner and check for correct usage.

SPELLING/VOCABULARY CONNECTIONS

See Spelling Challenge Words, pages 65O–65P.

LANGUAGE SUPPORT

See the Language Support Book, pages 9–12, for teaching suggestions for Vocabulary.

Vocabulary PuzzleMaker

Provides vocabulary activities.

Meeting Individual Needs for Vocabulary

EASY

Name_____ Date_____ Reteach 9

Vocabulary

Use the words from the list to complete the sentence.

| accidental | labored | occasions | rhythms | shortcut | shutters |

1. She just happened to find the secret door; it was an ___accidental___ discovery.
2. The boys took a ___shortcut___ across the yard to catch the dog.
3. Birthdays are ___occasions___ I like to celebrate.
4. The farmers ___labored___ in the fields all day.
5. Our house has yellow ___shutters___ on all the windows.
6. We sat on shore and watched the ___rhythms___ of the waves.

Story Comprehension Reteach 10

Write the answers to these questions about "Amelia's Road."

1. Why did Amelia cry whenever her father took out the map? She didn't want to move so much. She longed to be settled in a home.
2. What work did Amelia do each morning before school? She worked with her family to pick apples.
3. How did Mrs. Ramos help Amelia at school? She learned her name and asked her to share what was special to her.
4. What happened by accident in the story? Amelia found a footpath to a tree and an old metal box to put her treasures in.

At Home: Have students write a paragraph about a place that is special to them.
9–10   Book 4/Unit 1 Amelia's Road 4

ON-LEVEL

Name_____ Date_____ Practice 9

Vocabulary

Fill in each blank with the correct vocabulary word from the list at the top of the page.

| accidental | labored | occasions | rhythm | shutters | shortcut |

1. The little doors on the outside of windows are called ___shutters___.
2. On some ___occasions___ the doors are blown closed by the wind.
3. Doors are not supposed to close by themselves, so when they do, it is ___accidental___.
4. The wind has a musical ___rhythm___ when it blows things around outside.
5. We have all ___labored___ to clean up after a windy day.
6. Cleaning up is hard work, and there is no ___shortcut___.

At Home: Have students play "I'm thinking of a word that means" with a family member using this vocabulary.
9   Book 4/Unit 1 Amelia's Road 6

ON-LEVEL

The Storm

The thunder made a loud crashing noise. Meg jumped and knocked over a plant. It was *accidental*, but as Meg *labored* to clean up the mess, she wished she didn't scare so easily.

Suddenly the rain began to come down heavily. Meg remembered that her window was open and raced to her room. She used her *shortcut*, the back stairs. Meg quickly closed her *shutters* and window. Then she listened to the *rhythms* of the heavy rain. On *occasions* like this, Meg found comfort curling up on her bed with a favorite book—safe and dry.

1. What was *accidental*? Meg knocking over the plant.
2. What did Meg wish as she *labored* to clean up the mess? that she didn't scare so easily
3. Why did Meg take a *shortcut*? Meg wanted to close the window before the rain got in her room.
4. What did Meg do to comfort herself on stormy *occasions*? She curled up on her bed and read a book.
5. What did Meg not like about the storm? Possible answers include: she does not like the loud noise made by the thunder; she does not like the rain coming in the windows.

At Home: Have students write and draw a cozy rain storm story.
5   Book 4/Unit 1 Amelia's Road   9a

CHALLENGE

Name_____ Date_____ Extend 9

Vocabulary

| accidental | occasions | shortcut | labored | rhythms | shutters |

Write three sentences using two of the vocabulary words in each sentence.

Answers will vary. Possible sentences are given. 1. The rhythms of the music made the time he labored in the fields go by quickly. 2. An accidental turn at the fork in the road led to a shortcut. 3. It was one of the many occasions that she walked by the house with the shutters.

Extend 10

Story Comprehension

Amelia found a special place beneath the tree at the end of the accidental road. She knew she would have to leave it soon. How did Amelia make herself feel better about having to leave?

Answers will vary. Possible answer: At her special place, Amelia buried a box filled with personal things. She told herself that she would be back.

Describe a place that is special to you.
Answers will vary.

At Home: Look at a map of your state. Select several destinations and determine how long it would take to drive to each place.
9–10   Book 4/Unit 1 Amelia's Road

Reteach, 9

Practice, 9

Practice, 9a
Take-Home Story

Extend, 9

Comprehension

Prereading Strategies

PREVIEW AND PREDICT Have students preview the story by reading the title and looking at the illustrations.

- Who do you think the story is about?
- Where do you think this story takes place?
- What do the girl's facial expressions tell you about how she feels?
- Do you think this story will be realistic or fantasy? How can you tell? (Realistic. The characters and setting seem real.) *Genre*

Have students create a Predictions chart and record what they expect to learn.

PREDICTIONS	WHAT HAPPENED
The girl is unhappy at the beginning of the story but happy at the end.	
The story has something to do with farming and a road.	

SET PURPOSES Encourage students to ask questions about the story. For example:

- Why is Amelia unhappy?
- Which road is Amelia's?

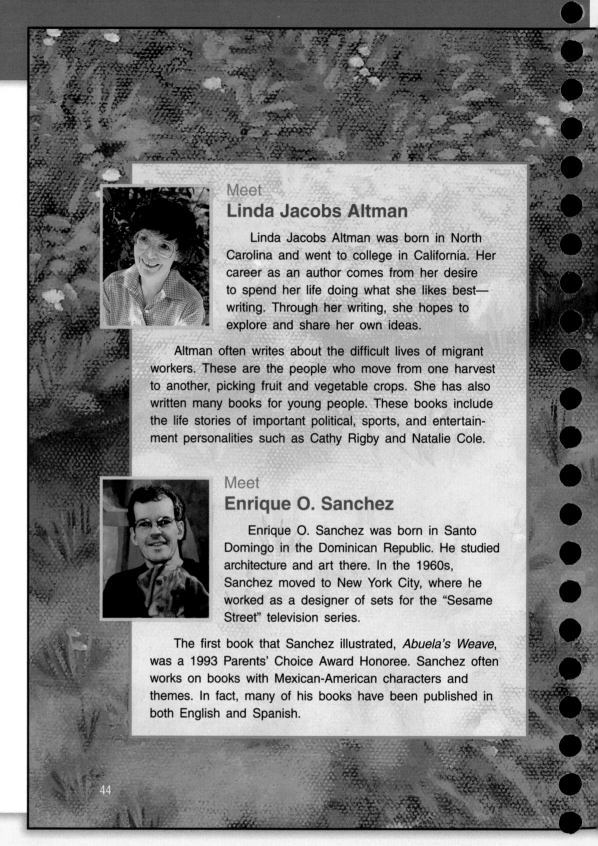

Meet
Linda Jacobs Altman

Linda Jacobs Altman was born in North Carolina and went to college in California. Her career as an author comes from her desire to spend her life doing what she likes best— writing. Through her writing, she hopes to explore and share her own ideas.

Altman often writes about the difficult lives of migrant workers. These are the people who move from one harvest to another, picking fruit and vegetable crops. She has also written many books for young people. These books include the life stories of important political, sports, and entertainment personalities such as Cathy Rigby and Natalie Cole.

Meet
Enrique O. Sanchez

Enrique O. Sanchez was born in Santo Domingo in the Dominican Republic. He studied architecture and art there. In the 1960s, Sanchez moved to New York City, where he worked as a designer of sets for the "Sesame Street" television series.

The first book that Sanchez illustrated, *Abuela's Weave*, was a 1993 Parents' Choice Award Honoree. Sanchez often works on books with Mexican-American characters and themes. In fact, many of his books have been published in both English and Spanish.

44

Meeting Individual Needs · Grouping Suggestions for Strategic Reading

EASY	ON-LEVEL	CHALLENGE
Read Together Read the story with students, or have them use the **Listening Library.** Have students use the Problem and Solution chart to record information about the main problem in the story. Comprehension and Intervention prompts provide additional help with vocabulary and comprehension.	**Guided Instruction** Use the Comprehension questions to check for understanding as students read the story or after they have played the **Listening Library.** Have students use the Problem and Solution chart to record information about the story as they read.	**Read Independently** Ask students to read the story independently. Remind them that recognizing the main problem and how it is solved will help them understand and appreciate the story. Have students set up a Problem and Solution chart like the one on page 45. After reading, they can use their charts to summarize the story.

Amelia's Road

Written by Linda Jacobs Altman
Illustrated by Enrique O. Sanchez

①

Comprehension

☑ **Apply Problem and Solution**

☑ **Apply Make Inferences**

STRATEGIC READING Let's make a Problem and Solution chart before we begin reading so we can record story notes.

PROBLEM

↓

STEPS TO SOLUTION

↓

SOLUTION

① **MAKE INFERENCES** Look at the picture on this page. What is the girl doing? How do you think she feels?

MODEL I see a girl working with other laborers in a field. I know that is hard work. She might feel hot and tired.

Genre

Realistic Fiction

Explain that realistic fiction:

• features characters and events in keeping with the real world.

• develops characters by showing how they act in different settings.

• may express a character's view of the world—for example, humorous, ironic, or tragic—through its tone.

Activity Have students look for details, in the text and illustrations, that tell how Amelia acts in different settings.

LANGUAGE SUPPORT

A blackline master of the Problem and Solution chart is available in the **Language Support Book.**

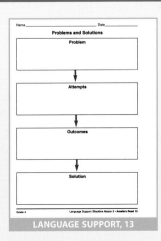

Name_____ Date_____
Problems and Solutions
Problem

↓

Attempts

↓

Outcomes

↓

Solution

Grade 4   Language Support (Blackline Master 3 • Amelia's Road 13

LANGUAGE SUPPORT, 13

45

Comprehension

② MAKE INFERENCES Where in the story do we learn how Amelia feels about roads? (the first line) Why do you think the writer opened the story this way? (The first sentence grabs the reader. It gets you wondering why Amelia hates roads so much so you read on.)

 **COMPOUND WORDS** Look at the word *sunstruck* in the second paragraph. What kind of word is it? (compound) Can you name the smaller words within this word that can help you figure out its meaning? (sun, struck) *Semantic/Syntactic Cues*

Amelia Luisa Martinez hated roads. Straight roads. Curved roads. Dirt roads. Paved roads. Roads leading to all manner of strange places, and roads leading to nowhere at all. Amelia hated roads so much that she cried every time her father took out the map.

② The roads Amelia knew went to farms where workers labored in sunstruck fields and lived in grim, gray shanties. *Los caminos*, the roads, were long and cheerless.

46

Fluency

READ WITH FLUENCY Have partners practice reading pages 46–47 aloud using an appropriate narrator's tone. Then invite pairs to take turns reading the pages to you. Evaluate each pair's reading rate and expression. If you wish, you can tape record each reading and play it back as you offer students pointers on the technique of reading aloud. Pronounce Spanish words for students before they begin reading. (lōs kä mē´ nōs)

PREVENTION/INTERVENTION

COMPOUND WORDS Write *sunstruck* on the chalkboard. Draw a vertical line between *sun* and *struck*. Tell students that the word is a compound made up of two words. Point out that they can use the smaller words that make up the compound to figure out its meaning.

Help students see that *struck* is the past tense of *strike* and that when this word combines with *sun* it forms a compound word that means "hit (or baked) by the sun."

Ask students to suggest other compound words formed with the word *sun.* (Sample answers: sunburn, sunglasses, sunlight, sunrise) *Semantic/Syntactic Cues*

They never went where you wanted them to go.

Amelia wanted to go someplace where people didn't have to work so hard, or move around so much, or live in labor camps.

Her house would be white and tidy, with blue shutters at the windows and a fine old shade tree growing in the yard. She would live there forever and never worry about *los caminos* again.

(3)

47

Comprehension

(3) **PROBLEM AND SOLUTION** What is Amelia's problem? How does she imagine solving it?

MODEL It is clear Amelia is tired of moving and wants to stay in one place where she doesn't have to work so hard. Her problem is that she wants a home. She believes that the solution to her problem is a white, blue-shuttered house where she can live forever.

Let's write Amelia's problem on our charts.

PROBLEM
Amelia longs for a home.

↓

STEPS TO SOLUTION

 DECODING/PHONICS Look at the words *windows* and *growing* on page 47. What sound do the letters *ow* represent in these words? (/ō/) *Graphophonic Cues*

PREVENTION/INTERVENTION

DECODING/PHONICS Point out that the letters *ow* can stand for the vowel sound heard in *mow* or the vowel sound heard in *cow*. Tell students that when they encounter an unfamiliar word that contains the letters *ow* they should try both sounds. Write the words *now* and *borrow* on the board. Ask a volunteer to circle the letters that represent the long *o* sound. *Graphophonic Cues*

Minilesson
REVIEW/MAINTAIN
Summarize

Remind students that a summary is a short statement that explains the main ideas of a passage or story. It should include only the most important ideas of the selection.

• Have students summarize in one or two sentences Amelia's feelings about roads.

Activity Ask partners to decide which sentences on pages 46 and 47 can be omitted without affecting the reader's ability to figure out and summarize the main idea. As a class, discuss and compare partners' suggestions.

Comprehension

 MAKE INFERENCES What kinds of experiences does Amelia miss because her family travels around so much? (having a best friend, going to birthday parties, having her own bed to sleep in)

 It was almost dark when their rusty old car pulled to a stop in front of cabin number twelve at the labor camp.

"Is this the same cabin we had last year?" Amelia asked, but nobody remembered. It didn't seem to matter to the rest of the family.

It mattered a lot to Amelia. From one year to the next, there was nothing to show Amelia had lived here, gone to school in this town, and worked in these fields. Amelia wanted to settle down, to belong.

"Maybe someday," said her mother, but that wonderful someday never seemed to come.

"Mama," Amelia asked, "where was I born?"

Mrs. Martinez paused for a moment and smiled. "Where? Let me see. Must have been in Yuba City. Because I remember we were picking peaches at the time."

"That's right. Peaches," said Mr. Martinez, "which means you were born in June."

Amelia sighed. Other fathers remembered days and dates. Hers remembered crops. Mr. Martinez marked all the important occasions of life by the never-ending rhythms of harvest.

48

Activity

Cross Curricular: Social Studies

CALIFORNIA Remind students that Amelia was born in Yuba City because the family was picking peaches then. Have a volunteer locate Yuba City on a map of California.

RESEARCH AND INQUIRY Have students find out where different crops are grown in California. Ask them to create a bulletin board display with pictures, captions, and labels.

▶ **Interpersonal/Spatial**

inter NET CONNECTION Students can learn more about California farms by visiting *www.mhschool.com/reading*

CALIFORNIA CROPS

Comprehension

(5) Look at the illustration on this page. What are Amelia and her family doing? How do you know? (They are carrying their belongings into cabin twelve at the labor camp. The first paragraph on the previous page mentions cabin number twelve and their car, which are both shown in the illustration.) *Use Graphic Features*

SELF-MONITORING STRATEGY

SEARCH FOR CLUES Searching for clues to meaning in the text and in illustrations confirms and enhances understanding and builds confidence. Encourage students to use this strategy whenever they need to make sense of what they are reading.

MODEL The last sentence on page 48 is a little difficult for me. I want to know more about how the author is using the word *occasions*. As I look back over the page, I see that Amelia is asking about when she was born. *Occasions* must mean important events.

49

Comprehension

6 Why do you think the author describes how hard Amelia and her family work? (Sample answer: to emphasize how difficult life is for migrant farm workers) *Evaluate Author's Purpose and Point of View*

Visual Literacy

VIEWING AND REPRESENTING

Have students spend a few moments studying the illustration on pages 50–51. Then discuss the details and the perspective of the picture. How do you know from looking at the illustration that Amelia is the main character? (She is toward the front of the picture and is the largest, most clearly drawn person in the illustration.)

Compare the illustration on pages 54–55. Why does the illustration show Amelia toward the back of the picture instead of toward the front? (This point of view emphasizes the road and the surroundings.)

6 The next day, everybody got up at dawn. From five to almost eight in the morning, Amelia and her family picked apples. Even though she still felt sleepy, Amelia had to be extra careful so she wouldn't bruise the fruit.

50

⑦

By the time she had finished her morning's work, Amelia's hands stung and her shoulders ached. She grabbed an apple and hurried off to school.

51

Comprehension

⑦ **MAKE INFERENCES** How did Amelia feel after picking apples for three hours? Can you show us how Amelia might have looked and acted as she hurried off to school? *Pantomime*

LANGUAGE SUPPORT

ESL Ask students to read aloud the sentences that describe how Amelia felt. Then have them pantomime the meaning of the words that describe specific feelings. For example, students might stretch and yawn to describe *sleepy*. They could rub their hands tenderly to show that they *stung*, and they might shrug their shoulders gently while frowning to show that their shoulders *ached*. You may also wish to have students describe each feeling in their own words and tell about a time when they experienced it.

Comprehension

8 Look at this illustration. Now pretend you're Amelia. Describe what you are doing and how you are feeling. (Amelia is showing other students a drawing of her dream house. She is probably happy and excited to be describing the house that means so much to her.)
Use Illustrations/Role-Play

CULTURAL PERSPECTIVES

CROSS-CULTURAL COMMUNICATION
Discuss Amelia's picture with the class. Point out that artwork is one way people communicate across cultures. Have a volunteer "interpret" Amelia's drawing for the class.

Activity Have students draw signs and symbols that communicate messages without words. Invite volunteers to draw examples on the chalkboard for the rest of the class to interpret.

▶ **Visual/Logical**

Last year, Amelia spent six weeks at Fillmore Elementary School, and not even the teacher had bothered to learn her name.

This year, the teacher bothered. She welcomed all the new children to her classroom and gave them name tags to wear. She wore a name tag herself. It said MRS. RAMOS.

Later, Mrs. Ramos asked the class to draw their dearest wishes. "Share with us something that's really special to you."

Amelia knew exactly what that would be. She drew a pretty white house with a great big tree in the front yard. When Amelia finished, Mrs. Ramos showed her picture to the whole class. Then she pasted a bright red star on the top.

By the end of the day, everybody in class had learned Amelia's name. Finally, here was a place where she wanted to stay.

53

Comprehension

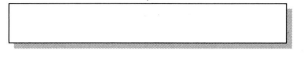

9 **PROBLEM AND SOLUTION** Amelia seems to be feeling better. What step toward solving her problem happened at school? Let's put the answer in our charts.

> **PROBLEM**
> Amelia longs for a home.

⬇

> **STEPS TO SOLUTION**
> Mrs. Ramos helps Amelia feel at home in the classroom.

⬇

>

p/i **MULTIPLE-MEANING WORDS** Read the first paragraph. What is one meaning of the word *bothered?* What do you think the word means in this sentence? *Semantic Cues*

Minilesson

REVIEW/MAINTAIN

Character

Remind students that good readers can figure out what a character is like by noting what the character says and does in the story. Character traits can be determined by spoken words, actions, and interactions with others.

- Have students reread page 53 and note what Mrs. Ramos says and does to make Amelia feel welcome. Ask them to describe Mrs. Ramos's character based on these story clues.

Activity Write a list of character traits on the board, such as *shy, friendly, mean, generous,* and *kind.* Have students brainstorm words and actions that a person with these traits might express.

p/i **PREVENTION/INTERVENTION**

MULTIPLE-MEANING WORDS
Have students reread the first sentence on page 53. Explain that the word *bother* has different meanings. One meaning is "to annoy"; the other is "to take the time or trouble." Guide students in discovering clues to help them decide which meaning makes the most sense in this context. (the second one)

Ask students to write two sentences using each meaning of the word *bother.* Have partners exchange sentences and identify the meaning used in each sentence. *Semantic Cues*

Comprehension

(10) **MAKE INFERENCES** We need two volunteers—one to role-play Amelia telling her mother about her wonderful day and another to play her mother responding.
Role-Play

Amelia couldn't wait to tell her mother about this wonderful day. Feeling as bright as the sky, she decided to look for a shortcut back to camp. That's when she found it.

The accidental road.

(10) Amelia called it the accidental road because it was narrow and rocky, more like a footpath that happened by accident than a road somebody built on purpose.

She followed it over a grassy meadow, through a clump of bushes, and down a gentle hill. There, where the accidental road ended, stood a most wondrous tree. It was old beyond knowing, and quite the sturdiest, most permanent thing Amelia had ever seen. When she closed her eyes, she could even picture it in front of her tidy white house.

Amelia danced for joy, her black hair flying as she twirled around and around the silent meadow.

54

Cross Curricular: Science

GRASSLANDS Tell students that the grasslands shown in the illustration might be used as pasture or for growing hay.

RESEARCH AND INQUIRY Have students find answers to these questions:

- What conditions are needed for grass to grow in abundance?

- What wildlife makes its home in meadows or grasslands? ▶ **Linguistic**

PRAIRIE ANIMALS

55

Comprehension

11 Look at the illustration. How does it add to the information given in the text? (It shows a footpath through a meadow.) *Use Graphic Features*

LANGUAGE SUPPORT

ESL Call students' attention to the expression "old beyond knowing" on page 54. Help them understand that this expression means that probably no one can remember when the tree wasn't there.

Invite students to talk about other things that are "old beyond knowing." Record their responses on the chalkboard. Then have each student choose one response and write a sentence about it.

Comprehension

12 **PROBLEM AND SOLUTION** If Amelia was happy when she met Mrs. Ramos, she was dancing for joy when she found the old tree. How did the tree take Amelia another step toward a solution to her problem? Let's put the answer in our charts.

PROBLEM
Amelia longs for a home.

STEPS TO SOLUTION
Mrs. Ramos helps Amelia feel at home in the classroom.

The old tree gives Amelia a place to come to every day and pretend to be home.

12 Almost every day, when work and school were over, Amelia would sit beneath the tree and pretend she had come home.

More than anywhere in the world, she wanted to belong to this place and know that it belonged to her.

But the harvest was almost over, and Amelia didn't know what she'd do when the time came for leaving.

56

Activity

Cross Curricular: Math

HOW MANY HARVESTS? Ask students to solve this problem: If Amelia is nine years old, and her family works at 6 labor camps a year, how many camps has Amelia lived in? (54)

RESEARCH AND INQUIRY Have small groups research the kinds of crops grown in different parts of the United States.

Students can write and exchange word problems based on their research. For example, they can calculate the total number of crops harvested in one season or determine the number of miles from one labor camp to the next.
▶ **Mathematical/Logical**

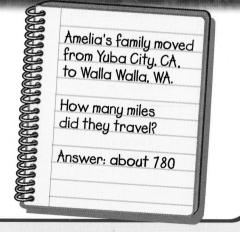

Amelia's family moved from Yuba City, CA, to Walla Walla, WA.

How many miles did they travel?

Answer: about 780

Comprehension

13 The last sentence of this page says that Amelia has come to, or thought of, a solution. Can anyone make a prediction about what the solution will be? (Sample answer: Amelia will draw a picture of the tree so that she can keep it with her wherever she goes.) *Make Predictions*

She asked everyone for advice—her sister Rosa, her parents, her brother Hector, her neighbors at camp, and Mrs. Ramos at school, but nobody could tell her what to do.

The answer, when it came, was nearly as accidental as the road.

57

LANGUAGE SUPPORT

ESL Help students understand the meaning of the word *advice* on page 57. List other words with similar meanings, such as *suggestions, helpful words,* and *opinions.* Invite students to tell what advice they would give Amelia. Write a brief summary of each suggestion on the board. At the end, ask the students to vote for the piece of advice they like best.

Comprehension

14 Look at the illustration of Amelia on page 58. In what ways does this illustration differ from pictures of her early in the story? From your reading of the story so far, how do you think Amelia has changed? (She doesn't seem unhappy now that she has found a place where she belongs.) *Compare and Contrast*

58

Activity

Cross Curricular: Art

HIDDEN TREASURES Have students make their own treasure boxes filled with personal items brought from home that stand for who they are. Then have students draw self-portraits, make maps of their neighborhoods, and write wish lists. Invite volunteers to share their boxes. Then have students seal them up. Invite them to hide their treasures in a special location in or around their homes, where they can retrieve the boxes at a later date.

▶ **Intrapersonal/Spatial**

Amelia found an old metal box that somebody had tossed into the trash. It was dented and rusty, but Amelia didn't care. That box was the answer to her problem.

She set to work at once, filling it with "Amelia-things." First she put in the hair ribbon her mother had made for her one Christmas; next came the name tag Mrs. Ramos had given her; then a photograph of her whole family taken at her last birthday; and after that the picture she'd drawn in class with the bright red star on it.

15

Finally, she took out a sheet of paper and drew a map of the accidental road, from the highway to the very old tree. In her best lettering, she wrote *Amelia Road* on the path. Then she folded the map and put it into her box.

When all the apples were finally picked, Amelia's family and the other workers had to get ready to move again. Amelia made one more trip down the accidental road, this time with her treasure box.

She dug a hole near the old tree, and gently placed the box inside and covered it over with dirt. Then she set a rock on top, so nobody would notice the freshly turned ground.

When Amelia finished, she took a step back and looked at the tree. Finally, here was a place where she belonged, a place where she could come back to.

16

"I'll be back," she whispered, and then she turned away.

59

Comprehension

15 What clue words can you find on this page that tell you to look for *steps in a process*? (first, next, then, after that, finally)

16 Do you remember your prediction about what solution Amelia would find for her problem? Compare your prediction to what happened on this page. *Confirm or Revise Predictions*

59

Comprehension

17 Amelia is moving again, but for the first time she isn't going to cry. It sounds like she found a solution to her problem. Let's write the solution in our charts.

> **PROBLEM**
> Amelia longs for a home.

> **STEPS TO SOLUTION**
> Mrs. Ramos helps Amelia feel at home in the classroom.

> The old tree gives Amelia a place to come to every day and pretend to be home.

> **SOLUTION**
> Amelia left some of her favorite things in a special place that she could return to.

RETELL THE STORY Invite volunteers to summarize what happens in the story. Students may refer to their charts. Then have partners write sentences summarizing the story. Remind them to focus on the main character's problem and how she solves it. *Summarize*

SELF-ASSESSMENT

- How did using the strategy of analyzing problem and solution help me to understand the story?

- How did the Problem and Solution chart help me to understand why the main character acted as she did?

TRANSFERRING THE STRATEGY

- When might I try using this strategy again? In what other kinds of reading?

Amelia skipped through the meadow, laughed at the sky, even turned cartwheels right in the middle of the accidental road.

When she got back to the camp, the rest of the family had already started packing the car. Amelia watched them for a moment, then took a deep breath and joined in to help.

17 For the first time in her life, she didn't cry when her father took out the road map.

60

REREADING FOR *Fluency*

PARTNERS Have students read a favorite section of the story to their partners. Remind them to read with feeling and expression.

READING RATE When you evaluate reading rate, have the student read aloud from the story for one minute. Place a stick-on note after the last word read. Count the words read. To evaluate students' performance, see the Running Record in the **Fluency Assessment** book.

> **i Intervention** For leveled fluency lessons, passages, and norms charts, see **Skills Intervention Guide**, Part 4, Fluency.

Author's Note

Amelia Luisa Martinez and her family, and thousands like them, are often referred to as migrant farm workers. This is because they usually have to move from one harvest to another, and they do not have stable homes. Many of the migrant workers come from different parts of the world, such as Mexico, South America, or the Caribbean. But many of them are American citizens, born in the United States.

Some of the male workers travel by themselves and return to their families after the harvest. Others travel with their families. Out of necessity, even their children work in the fields.

The constant work and moving about make it very difficult for the children to get to know a place or to make friends. In this story about Amelia, my hope is to show how one girl finds a favorite place.

61

Comprehension

Return to Predictions and Purposes

Review with students their predictions and reasons for reading the story. Were their predictions correct? Did they learn what they wanted to know?

PREDICTIONS	WHAT HAPPENED
The girl is unhappy at the beginning of the story but happy at the end.	Amelia was unhappy about living as a migrant farm worker and not having a permanent place to call home.
The story has something to do with farming and a road.	She resolved her problem by burying personal treasures at the end of an "accidental road," near her favorite tree—a place she could always come back to.

INFORMAL ASSESSMENT

PROBLEM AND SOLUTION

HOW TO ASSESS

- Have students identify the main problem and solution in the story.
- Have students explain how organizing a story along the lines of problem and solution advances the plot.

Students should be able to tell why Amelia was unhappy at the beginning of the story and explain why belonging somewhere was so important to her.

FOLLOW UP Complete a simple story map with students who are having difficulty connecting problem and solution with the development of the plot.

LITERARY RESPONSE

QUICK-WRITE Invite students to record their thoughts about the story. The following questions may help them get started.

JOURNAL

- How are you and Amelia alike? Different?
- How would you solve Amelia's problem?
- What do you think of Amelia's solution to her problem?

- What are some interesting things you learned about migrant workers?

ORAL RESPONSE Encourage students to share their journal writings and discuss why they think a sense of belonging is important. Which illustrations did they find most interesting? Why?

61

Story Questions

Have students discuss or write answers to the questions on page 62.

Answers:

1. They pick crops; they are migrant farm workers. *Literal/Setting*

2. She wants a permanent home of her own. *Draw Conclusions/Character*

3. No one else knows about it; she can pretend it is home. *Inferential/Character*

4. Amelia doesn't have a sense of belonging, since her family moves constantly. Amelia buries some treasures near a favorite tree. Now she has a place she can call her own. *Critical/ Summarize*

5. Both Amelia and Luke discover a place to call their own. *Critical/ Reading Across Texts*

WRITE A DIARY ENTRY For a full writing process lesson related to this suggestion, see pages 65K–65L.

Story Questions & Activities

1. What kind of work does Amelia's family do?

2. Why is Amelia unhappy about moving?

3. What makes the "accidental road" Amelia's special place? Explain.

4. In your own words, describe Amelia's problem in the story. Explain how she solves it.

5. How are Amelia and Luke in "The Lost Lake" like each other?

Write a Diary Entry

Think about a place that is special to you. Write a diary entry about the first time you went to that place. Be sure to explain how you felt while you were there.

Meeting Individual Needs

EASY	ON-LEVEL	CHALLENGE

EASY

Name_____ Date_____ **Reteach** 9

Vocabulary

Use the words from the list to complete the sentence.

accidental	labored	occasions	rhythms	shortcut	shutters

1. She just happened to find the secret door; it was an ___accidental___ discovery.

2. The boys took a ___shortcut___ across the yard to catch the dog.

3. Birthdays are ___occasions___ I like to celebrate.

4. The farmers ___labored___ in the fields all day.

5. Our house has yellow ___shutters___ on all the windows.

6. We sat on shore and watched the ___rhythms___ of the waves.

Story Comprehension **Reteach** 10

Write the answers to these questions about "Amelia's Road."

1. Why did Amelia cry whenever her father took out the map? ___She didn't want to move so much. She longed to be settled in a home.___

2. What work did Amelia do each morning before school? ___She worked with her family to pick apples.___

3. How did Mrs. Ramos help Amelia at school? ___She learned her name and asked her to share what was special to her.___

4. What happened by accident in the story? ___Amelia found a footpath to a tree and an old metal box to put her treasures in.___

9–10 | **At Home:** Have students write a paragraph about a place that is special to them. | Book 4/Unit 1 **Amelia's Road** 4

ON-LEVEL

Name_____ Date_____ **Practice** 10

Story Comprehension

Answer the questions about "Amelia's Road."

1. What are los caminos? ___the roads___

2. Why does Amelia hate los caminos? ___She hates the roads because she and her family are always on roads moving to a new place.___

3. What does Amelia have to do before she goes to school? ___She has to pick apples from dawn to eight o'clock in the morning.___

4. Why does Amelia like Mrs. Ramos more than the teacher at her last school? ___Mrs. Ramos remembered her name and gave her a red star. The other teacher never learned Amelia's name.___

5. What did Amelia know she could always go back to? ___She could always return to the old tree near the accidental road.___

6. For the first time, Amelia didn't cry when her family moved again. Why not? ___She had her special place that was permanent, the tree and the accidental road, which she knew would always be there.___

10 | **At Home:** Have students write a plan for making a new student feel at home. | Book 4/Unit 1 **Amelia's Road** 6

CHALLENGE

Name_____ Date_____ **Extend** 9

Vocabulary

accidental	occasions	shortcut	labored	rhythms	shutters

Write three sentences using two of the vocabulary words in each sentence.

___Answers will vary. Possible sentences are given. 1. The rhythms of the music made the time he labored in the fields go by quickly. 2. An accidental turn at the fork in the road led to a shortcut. 3. It was one of the many occasions that she walked by the house with the shutters.___

Extend 10

Story Comprehension

Amelia found a special place beneath the tree at the end of the accidental road. She knew she would have to leave it soon. How did Amelia make herself feel better about having to leave?
___Answers will vary. Possible answer: At her special place, Amelia buried a box filled with personal things. She told herself that she would be back.___

Describe a place that is special to you.
___Answers will vary.___

9–10 | **At Home:** Look at a map of your state. Select several destinations and determine how long it would take to drive to each place. | Book 4/Unit 1 **Amelia's Road**

Reteach, 10   Practice, 10   Extend, 10

Use a Product Map

Mrs. Martinez knows that Amelia was born in Yuba City, California. It must have been there because she remembers that her family was picking peaches. Where do crops grow in your state? Look at a product map. Make a list of the crops and the places where they grow.

Draw Your Dream House

Amelia drew the house that she would like to live in. Now it's your turn. Draw your own dream house and yard. Include all the features you would like your special house to have.

Find Out More

Amelia and her family were migrant farm workers. They picked different crops and moved from one harvest to another. What do you think life is like for Amelia's family? Start by looking up "migrant labor" in an encyclopedia. Use what you learn to list some problems that migrant farm workers and their families have.

63

Story Activities

Use a Product Map

Materials: reference books, the Internet, phone directory, butcher paper, crayons or markers

PARTNERS Have students look in various reference books or go online to find product maps of their state. They may also get information by contacting government agencies, such as the state Food and Agriculture Department. Have students pool their information to make a class product map of crops grown in their state.

Draw Your Dream House

Materials: drawing paper, colored pencils or crayons

ONE Have students imagine how their dream house would look. Ask them to sketch it first, then draw a final picture. You may wish to have students write descriptive paragraphs to go along with their pictures. Invite volunteers to present their dream homes to the class.

Find Out More

Materials: the Internet, encyclopedia

ONE Discuss some of the problems migrant workers face, and have the class brainstorm possible solutions. Ask students to prepare brief reports about the topic, and bind them in a class booklet.

*inter*NET To learn more about migrant
CONNECTION workers, have students visit
www.mhschool.com/reading

ᴼᴿᴹᴬᴸ ASSESSMENT

After page 63, see the Selection Assessment.

Activity

SOCIAL STUDIES: CLIMATE AND CROPS Direct students to research the climate of the southeast region of the United States. Then have them describe the climate and identify five crops found there. Have students repeat this process for other regions.

WHAT TO LOOK FOR Check responses. Did the student

- describe the climate accurately?
- name five crops grown in the region?

CHALLENGE

Study Skills

PARTS OF A BOOK

OBJECTIVES Students will:

- understand how to read a glossary entry.
- use a glossary to answer questions.

PREPARE Read the passage with students. Have students glance at the glossary in the back of their reading books. Display **Teaching Chart 9.**

TEACH Read aloud and discuss the entry in the sample glossary. Point out the different pieces of information. Tell students that the meaning given reflects how the word is used in *Amelia's Road*.

PRACTICE Have students answer questions 1–5. Review the answers with them.
1. a trail or path for walking; **2.** noun;
3. plural; **4.** two; **5.** to find the meaning of a word as it is used in a story.

ASSESS/CLOSE Have volunteers look up other words from the story and read the entries aloud to the class.

Study Skills

Use a Glossary

Do you know what a *footpath* is? What are *shanties*? The writer of this story uses some words you may not know. For help, you can look up these words in the glossary.

The **glossary** is in the back of the book. It is like a small dictionary, but it contains only words from the stories. A glossary tells you how to pronounce a word. It also gives you the word's meaning as it is used in the story. Glossary words are listed in alphabetical order.

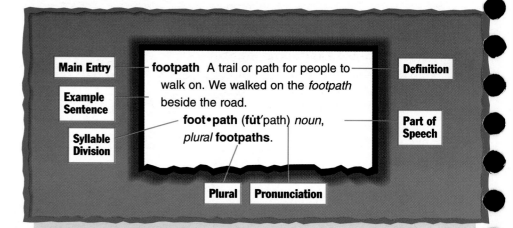

Main Entry — **footpath** A trail or path for people to walk on. We walked on the *footpath* beside the road. — **Definition**

Example Sentence

foot•path (fút′path) *noun*, *plural* **footpaths**. — **Part of Speech**

Syllable Division

Plural **Pronunciation**

Use the sample glossary entry to answer these questions.

1 What is the meaning of *footpath*?

2 What part of speech is the word *footpath*?

3 Is the word *footpaths* singular or plural?

4 How many syllables does the word *footpath* have?

5 When would you use a glossary instead of a dictionary?

Meeting Individual Needs

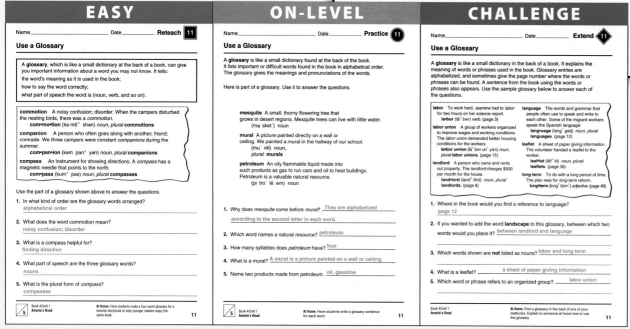

EASY

Name_____ Date_____ **Reteach** 11

Use a Glossary

A **glossary**, which is like a small dictionary at the back of a book, can give you important information about a word you may not know. It tells:
the word's meaning as it is used in the book;
how to say the word correctly;
what part of speech the word is (noun, verb, and so on).

commotion A noisy confusion; disorder. When the campers disturbed the nesting birds, there was a *commotion*.
com•mo•tion (ke mō′ shen) *noun, plural* **commotions**

companion A person who often goes along with another; friend; comrade. We three campers were constant *companions* during the summer.
com•pan•ion (kem pan′ yen) *noun, plural* **companions**

compass An instrument for showing directions. A *compass* has a magnetic needle that points to the north.
com•pass (kum′ pes) *noun, plural* **compasses**

Use the part of a glossary shown above to answer the questions.

1. In what kind of order are the glossary words arranged?
   alphabetical order

2. What does the word commotion mean?
   noisy confusion; disorder

3. What is a compass helpful for?
   finding direction

4. What part of speech are the three glossary words?
   nouns

5. What is the plural form of *compass*?
   compasses

Book 4/Unit 1
Amelia's Road   **At Home:** Have students make a four-word glossary for a favorite storybook to help younger readers enjoy the same book.   11

ON-LEVEL

Name_____ Date_____ **Practice** 11

Use a Glossary

A **glossary** is like a small dictionary found at the back of the book. It lists important or difficult words found in the book in alphabetical order. The glossary gives the meanings and pronunciations of the words.

Here is part of a glossary. Use it to answer the questions.

mesquite A small, thorny flowering tree that grows in desert regions. Mesquite trees can live with little water.
(me sket′) noun

mural A picture painted directly on a wall or ceiling. We painted a mural in the hallway of our school.
(mu′ rel) noun, plural **murals**

petroleum An oily flammable liquid made into such products as gas to run cars and oil to heat buildings. Petroleum is a valuable natural resource.
(pi tro′ lē em) noun

1. Why does mesquite come before mural? They are alphabetized
   according to the second letter in each word.

2. Which word names a natural resource? petroleum

3. How many syllables does petroleum have? four

4. What is a mural? A mural is a picture painted on a wall or ceiling.

5. Name two products made from petroleum. oil, gasoline

Book 4/Unit 1
Amelia's Road   **At Home:** Have students write a glossary sentence for each word.   11

CHALLENGE

Name_____ Date_____ **Extend** 11

Use a Glossary

A **glossary** is like a small dictionary in the back of a book. It explains the meaning of words or phrases used in the book. Glossary entries are alphabetized, and sometimes give the page number where the words or phrases can be found. A sentence from the book using the words or phrases also appears. Use the sample glossary below to answer each of the questions.

labor To work hard. Jasmine had to *labor* for two hours on her science report.
la•bor (lā′ ber) verb. (page 3)

labor union A group of workers organized to improve wages and working conditions. The *labor union* demanded better housing conditions for the workers.
la•bor un•ion (lā′ ber un′ yen) noun, plural labor unions. (page 15)

landlord A person who owns and rents out property. The landlord charges $500 per month for the house.
land•lord (land′ lôrd) noun, plural landlords. (page 8)

language The words and grammar that people often use to speak and write to each other. Some of the migrant workers speak the Spanish language.
lan•guage (lang′ gwij) noun, plural languages. (page 12)

leaflet A sheet of paper giving information. The volunteer handed a leaflet to the worker.
leaf•let (lēf′ lit) noun, plural leaflets. (page 36)

long-term To do with a long period of time. The plan was for long-term reform.
long•term (long′ tûrm′) adjective. (page 48)

1. Where in the book would you find a reference to language? page 12

2. If you wanted to add the word **landscape** to this glossary, between which two words would you place it? between landlord and language

3. Which words shown are **not** listed as nouns? labor and long-term

4. What is a leaflet? a sheet of paper giving information

5. Which word or phrase refers to an organized group? labor union

Book 4/Unit 1
Amelia's Road   **At Home:** Find a glossary in the back of one of your textbooks. Explain to someone at home how to use the glossary.   11

Reteach, 11   **Practice, 11**   **Extend, 11**

TEST POWER

DIRECTIONS

Read the sample story. Then read each question about the story.

SAMPLE

A Day at the Fairgrounds

Kee and Lin jumped out of the car and ran across the parking lot. Each wanted to be first inside the fairgrounds, but first they stopped in front of the fairground poster to see what they wanted to do first.

Green County FAIR

Blue Rides: Cost $2
Roller Coaster
Giant Steps

Green Rides: Cost $1
Ferris Wheel
Fun House
Bumper Cars

You must be over three feet tall to go on the rides.

The last ride is at 5:30 P.M.

1 How tall must you be to go on the rides?

Ⓐ Over 3 feet

B Over 2 feet

C Over 1 foot

D Over 4 feet

2 Which of these is NOT offered at the fairgrounds?

F Roller Coaster

G Giant Steps

H Fun House

Ⓙ Horseback Riding

65

Test Power

THE PRINCETON REVIEW

Read the Page

Have students read all of the information on the poster, the questions, and the answer choices. Tell students to select the best answer choice for each question.

Discuss the Questions

Question 1: This question requires students to locate information on the poster. It says "You must be over three feet tall to go on the rides." Have students eliminate answers that don't make sense.

Question 2: This question also requires students to locate information on the poster. This question is impossible to answer without first looking at the answer choices. Teach students to work through each answer choice and to eliminate answers they know are wrong. Remind students to pay attention to the fact that the question asks which ride is *not* offered.

Leveled Books

EASY

Postcards from Mari Vic

Long *a* and Long *e*
☑ **Problem and Solution**
☑ **Instructional Vocabulary:** *accidental, labored, occasions, rhythms, shortcut, shutters*

Postcards from Mari Vic

written by Janet Cassidy
illustrated by Diane Paterson

Answers to Story Questions

1. Barbara had just moved there. She hadn't met any kids her age yet.
2. Sometimes things happen that you never expect.
3. Mari Vic was leaving. She didn't know where her family would be staying or for how long they would stay at each location. Also, Mari Vic probably wouldn't have easy access to a telephone. The solution to their problem was that Barbara and Mari Vic would correspond with each other through postcards and letters until Mari Vic returned the following year.
4. It is about two girls who become friends and find a way to stay friends when one of them moves away.
5. Answers will vary but might include Amelia's buried box.

The *Story Questions and Activity* below appear in the *Easy Book*.

Story Questions and Activity

1. At the start of the story, why didn't Barbara have any friends?
2. What did Barbara's grandmother mean by "You never know"?
3. What problems did Barbara and Mari Vic have to face in order to stay in touch? What solution did they find?
4. What is this story mostly about?
5. If Amelia from *Amelia's Road* met Mari Vic at the next orchard, what do you think she might tell her about?

Design a Postcard

Pretend you are Mari Vic. First, design a postcard. Draw a picture on one side. On the other side, write a note to Barbara telling her about the new place where your family is staying.

from Postcards from Mari Vic

Guided Reading

PREVIEW AND PREDICT Display the front cover, read the title, and ask students to identify the main characters of the story. Have students describe what they see happening in the illustrations throughout the book.

SET PURPOSES Have students set a purpose for reading the story, such as discovering why the girl in the car is leaving.

READ THE BOOK Use the following questions to guide students as they read the story independently or to check their understanding after they read.

Page 5: What words on this page have the long *a* and long *e* sounds? What letters make these long vowel sounds? (away, always—*ay*; case—*a*; me, she—*e*; cream—*ea*; sneezed—*ee*) ***Phonics and Decoding***

Page 7: What words in the last paragraph help explain the meaning of *shutters*? (windows, closed, open) ***Vocabulary***

Pages 12–13: What is the problem in this story? (Mari Vic has to move, and the girls want to stay friends.) ***Problem and Solution***

Pages 14–15: What does Barbara do to solve the problem? (She addresses postcards and gives them to Mari Vic so they can write to each other and keep in touch.) ***Problem and Solution***

Page 16: Why do you think Barbara names the kitten Amigo? (because *amigo* means "friend" in Spanish and Mari Vic is Barbara's friend) ***Make Inferences***

RETURN TO PREDICTIONS AND PURPOSES Have students review their predictions and purposes for reading. Were their predictions accurate? Did they learn what they expected from the story?

LITERARY RESPONSE Discuss these questions:

- What do you think Barbara writes in her first letter to Mari Vic?
- What did Barbara teach Mari Vic about being a good friend?

Also see the story questions and activity in *Postcards from Mari Vic*.

Leveled Books

INDEPENDENT

Home on the Range

☑ **Problem and Solution**

☑ **Instructional Vocabulary:** *accidental, labored, occasions, rhythms, shortcuts, shutters*

Guided Reading

PREVIEW AND PREDICT Have students skim the Table of Contents and preview the illustrations through page 8. Have students describe the pictures they see. Ask them to predict who the story is about and who is at home on the range. Record their predictions on chart paper.

SET PURPOSES Have students set a purpose for reading the book, such as discovering what a cowboy does every day. Ask them to write in their journals questions they have about the story.

READ THE BOOK Have students read independently. Use the questions below to check their use of reading strategies.

Page 3: Who were the *vaqueros*? (They were enslaved people from Mexico trained to ride horses and handle cattle. They were the first real cowboys.) *Main Idea*

Page 8: How would you describe the typical cowboy? (His average age was 24, he was single, he was thin and wiry, and he was usually a Texan or a Southerner.) *Summarize*

Page 14: What do you think the *rhythms* of a horse's pace might sound like? (Sample answer: a steady beat of tapping hooves) *Vocabulary*

Page 15: How did the cowboys prevent cattle from starving in blizzards? (They kept the cattle in fenced pastures where they could be fed during the winter.) *Problem and Solution*

RETURN TO PREDICTIONS AND PURPOSES Ask students to compare their predictions to what actually happened in the story. Were their predictions accurate? Did they learn what they expected from the story?

LITERARY RESPONSE Discuss these questions:

- Would you like to be a cowboy? Why or why not?

- What would you like the most about being a cowboy? What would you like the least?

Also see the story questions and activity in *Home on the Range*.

Answers to Story Questions

1. Cowboys had to get the cattle to the nearest railroad, which was in Kansas.
2. The longhorns were not easy to manage. The herd might stampede, or cowboys could have other accidents. Cowboys tried to solve this problem by using special horses and by singing to the cattle to calm them.
3. Cowboys appealed to people's ideals. Most people thought the life of a cowboy was full of adventure and that cowboys were brave and daring.
4. The book tells about the life and work of cowboys of the Old West.
5. Sample answer: Cowboys moved from place to place in their jobs. They usually didn't settle down until they left the cattle business or started their own ranches.

The *Story Questions and Activity* below appear in the *Independent Book*.

Story Questions and Activity

1. Why did cowboys in the old days have to drive the cows from Texas to Kansas?
2. Why was being a cowboy a dangerous job? What were some of the ways he solved this problem?
3. Why do you think there were so many movies and television shows about cowboys?
4. What is the main idea of the book?
5. How were the cowboys of old like Amelia from *Amelia's Road*?

Cowboy Clothing

Do some further research to find out about the clothing cowboys wore and the gear they used. Make a drawing of a cowboy and label his clothing. Then pick one item of clothing, such as the cowboy's hat, and write a paragraph telling why it was important to the cowboy.

from Home on the Range

Leveled Books

The Story of Cesar Chavez

written by Janet Cassidy
illustrated by Ron Himler

CHALLENGE

The Story of Cesar Chavez

☑ **Problem and Solution**

☑ **Instructional Vocabulary:** *accidental, labored, occasions, rhythms, shortcuts, shutters*

Guided Reading

PREVIEW AND PREDICT Invite students to read the Table of Contents and preview the illustrations through page 15. Ask them to predict what the story is about.

SET PURPOSES Have students set a purpose for reading the story, such as learning why Chavez is shown leading marches. Have them think of a few questions they would like to have answered and record them in their journal.

READ THE BOOK Use questions such as the following to guide students as they read, or check comprehension after they read independently.

Page 4: Why did Cesar's family leave their farm? (They owed $4,000 in taxes and had to sell the farm.) *Cause and Effect*

Page 10: What does the phrase "nothing *accidental*" mean in the first paragraph? (It means that the action was done on purpose—it was no accident.) *Vocabulary*

Page 13: How did Chavez and his union get the growers to treat the workers fairly? (They picketed, marched, and boycotted the growers.) *Problem and Solution*

Page 14: How did Chavez feel about using violence to solve problems? (He strongly opposed the use of violence.) *Character*

Page 16: Why was Cesar Chavez a great man? (He devoted his life to helping migrant workers get the wages, working conditions, and respect that they deserved.) *Summarize*

RETURN TO PREDICTIONS AND PURPOSES Review students' predictions and reasons for reading. Which predictions were accurate? Did they find out what they wanted to know about Cesar Chavez?

LITERARY RESPONSE Discuss these questions:

* If you could interview Cesar Chavez, what three questions would you ask him?

* What has this story taught you about solving problems?

Also see the story questions and activity in *The Story of Cesar Chavez.*

Answers to Story Questions

1. Cesar Chavez formed the United Farm Workers union, which fought for better working conditions for migrant farm workers.
2. Chavez himself had experienced prejudice and didn't want there to be any within his union.
3. Chavez used peaceful marches, strikes, picketing, and sit-ins. He also fasted to call attention to the struggle.
4. Cesar Chavez worked hard to form a union and to help migrant farm workers get better working conditions.
5. Answers will vary.

The *Story Questions and Activity* below appear in the *Challenge Book.*

Story Questions and Activity

1. What is Cesar Chavez famous for?
2. Why do you think it was especially important to Chavez that the union be open to all workers, no matter what country they came from?
3. Some of the workers wanted to use violence to win the union's goals. What were some of the nonviolent solutions Chavez used to solve their problems?
4. What is the main idea of the book?
5. If Amelia from *Amelia's Road* could have spoken with Cesar Chavez, what do you think she might have told him?

Be an Activist

Read about the lives of Martin Luther King, Jr. and Mahatma Gandhi and jot down some notes about the ways they found to help people. Then think of a cause in your own neighborhood or state you might like to support. Make a list of three steps you could take to call attention to the problem and make your nonviolent protest for change.

from The Story of Cesar Chavez

Bringing Groups Together

Anthology and Leveled Books

Connecting Texts

PROBLEM AND SOLUTION CHART Write the story titles on a chart. Discuss the problems that the characters in each story faced. Have students recall how the characters solved their problems. List students' ideas on the chart.

Amelia's Road	Postcards from Mari Vic	Home on the Range	The Story of Cesar Chavez
• Amelia wants a place to call home. • Amelia buries her personal treasures by her favorite tree so that she always has a place to come home to.	• Mari Vic and Barbara are friends, but Mari Vic's family are migrant workers and they must move to a new town. • Mari Vic will send Barbara postcards to let her know where she is from time to time.	• Cattle roam freely all over the range. • Cowboys have roundups to gather the cattle together.	• Migrant workers earn low wages and live in poor conditions. • Cesar Chavez organizes the migrant workers and they have strikes to improve working conditions.

Viewing/Representing

GROUP PRESENTATIONS Organize the class into groups, one for each of the four books read in the lesson. (For *Amelia's Road*, combine students of different reading levels.) Have each group choose a character from the story and brainstorm what they learned about that character's life. Then have them dramatize an important event from the story involving their character, including thoughts the characters might have regarding the event.

AUDIENCE RESPONSE Have students observe the dramatizations and note how the main characters of the stories are similar and different. Allow time for each group to answer questions from the audience.

Research and Inquiry

MORE ABOUT COWBOYS AND MIGRANT WORKERS Have students list what they would like to know about migrant workers and cowboys. Then invite them to do the following:

• Research information on present-day cowboys.

• Interview a union representative to find out more about workers and their rights.

• Make a list of all the things they eat that are touched, gathered, or raised by migrant workers.

• Have students write and present reports about what they learn.

interNET
CONNECTION To find out more about cowboys, have students visit **www.mhschool.com/reading**

65D

OBJECTIVES

Students will identify problem and solution.

Skills Finder	
Problem and Solution	
Introduce	43A-B
Review	65E-F, 93G-H, 119A-B, 633A-B, 663E-F, 691G-H
Test	Unit 1, Unit 6
Maintain	411, 545

LANGUAGE SUPPORT

ESL Have students reread the last sentence of "Back at School." Help them understand that *beamed with pride* is an expression that describes how a person looks when he or she has done something of which to be proud. Ask a volunteer to pantomime someone who is beaming with pride. Point out how the student's face seems to light up or glow with pride.

SELF-SELECTED Reading

Students may choose from the following titles:

ANTHOLOGY
• Amelia's Road

LEVELED BOOKS
• Postcards from Mari Vic
• Home on the Range
• The Story of Cesar Chavez

Bibliography, pages T78–T79

Review Problem and Solution

PREPARE

Discuss Problem and Solution

Review: In many stories the actions of the main character are due to a problem the character faces. Point out that students can understand a story better when they identify the problem and think about its solution as they read.

TEACH

Read "Back at School" and Model the Skill

Ask students to listen for clues about the problem and its solution as you read **Teaching Chart 10** with them.

> **Back at School**
>
> It was Amelia's first day back at Fillmore Elementary. She hoped Mrs. Ramos would be her teacher again.
>
> Amelia entered her classroom, but she did not recognize anyone. The teacher's name was Ms. Carlson, and she barely looked up as Amelia sat down. "Oh, no," Amelia thought.
>
> Ms. Carlson asked if anyone had any questions. Timidly, Amelia raised her hand, and explained that she didn't know anyone. She asked if she could introduce herself. Ms. Carlson said that she thought that was a wonderful idea. Amelia beamed with pride.
>
> Teaching Chart 10

Ask a volunteer to circle the parts of the story that tell what Amelia's problem is. Then prompt students to think about how Amelia solved the problem and underline her solution.

MODEL Amelia was disappointed when she realized she knew no one in her class. She understood it was up to her to take the first step in getting to know the other students.

PRACTICE

Create a Problem and Solution Chart Have students create and complete a Problem and Solution chart for "Back at School."

ONE

PROBLEM
Amelia is disappointed and lonely in her new class.

STEP TO SOLUTION
Amelia raises her hand and asks to introduce herself.

SOLUTION
Amelia is proud of her wonderful idea.

ASSESS/CLOSE

Summarize Have students create a Problem and Solution chart from their every-day lives. Direct them to use their charts to summarize the story behind the problem.

ONE

ALTERNATE TEACHING STRATEGY
....

PROBLEM AND SOLUTION

For a different approach to teaching this skill, see page T64.

Intervention ▶ **Skills Intervention Guide**, for direct instruction and extra practice in problem and solution

Meeting Individual Needs for Comprehension

EASY	ON-LEVEL	CHALLENGE	LANGUAGE SUPPORT
Name_____ Date_____ Reteach **12**	Name_____ Date_____ Practice **12**	Name_____ Date_____ Extend **12**	Name_____ Date_____
Problem and Solution	**Problem and Solution**	**Problem and Solution**	**Road to a Solution**

EASY — Reteach 12

Problem and Solution

Knowing how to identify the **problem** a story character has and paying attention to how he or she goes about finding a **solution** will help you better understand the whole story.

Read the stories. Then write what the problems and the solutions are.

Sven is upset about his homework. He is trying to do a math problem but can't figure it out. He reads the directions over and over, but they don't make sense to him. Finally he gives up and goes to bed.
The next morning, Sven goes to school early so he can talk to his teacher. Mrs. Perry understands why Sven is confused and promises to teach the whole class how to solve the problem.

1. **Problem:** Sven can't figure out how to do his math homework.

2. **Solution:** Sven asks his teacher for help, and she shows him and the class what to do.

Tessa wants to add some new things to her special treasure box. She looks all over the house and can't find it in any of the usual places she keeps it.
Tessa sits down to think about where her box could be and remembers the last time she looked in it. She was at Lucia's house. She calls Lucia. The box is there!

3. **Problem:** Tessa can't find her special treasure box.

4. **Solution:** Tessa thinks calmly about when she last had the box and calls Lucia who has the box.

At Home: Have students make up a problem for a character. Then suggest they work with a friend to find some solutions.
12   Book 4/Unit 1 Amelia's Road 4

ON-LEVEL — Practice 12

Problem and Solution

In most stories, the main character faces some kind of **problem** and must find a **solution**, or a way to solve it. In "Amelia's Road," Amelia faces a big problem and smaller ones. Answer each question about the story. Answers may vary.

Problems

1. What was the problem with cabin number 12? It looked like every other cabin.

2. What was the problem with Amelia going to so many different schools? Amelia was in each school for such a short time that the teacher didn't know her name and she didn't make friends.

3. What is the problem with Amelia's parents not knowing her birthday? She feels lonely and different from the other children.

4. The big problem is how Amelia feels because her family moves so often. How does she feel and why is it a problem? She feels sad and that she never belongs. She wants something that is permanent and something to call her own.

Solutions

5. What did Amelia find that she could call her own? A permanent tree by the side of the accidental road.

6. What did Amelia do to make the road and tree her own home place? She filled a box with "Amelia-things" and buried it under the tree.

At Home: Have students write to describe a problem and a solution.
12   Book 4/Unit 1 Amelia's Road 6

CHALLENGE — Extend 12

Problem and Solution

Most stories you read include a **problem and solution**. Some solutions present themselves through a sequence of events. Sometimes the main character solves the problem. Other times someone else solves the problem. Think about the sequence of events that led to the solution of Amelia's problem in "Amelia's Road."

1. Describe the sequence of events that led Amelia to discover her road. Amelia went to school where her teacher gave everyone name tags. She drew a picture of her special house and got a star. She was so excited that she took a shortcut home and then found her road.

2. Amelia felt that she had found a home beneath the old tree. Was this a good solution to her problem? Explain. Answers will vary. Possible answer: It was a temporary solution good for her at the time.

3. How did Amelia decide to make the place around the old tree her home? She buried a treasure box near it and promised to come back.

4. Who solved Amelia's problem in the story? Amelia

5. Do you think the solution to Amelia's problem was a long-term solution for her? Explain. Answers will vary. Possible answer: Yes, Amelia felt she had a special place now.

At Home: Discuss problems faced by real people and by fictional characters. Compare how different people or characters solve similar problems.
12   Book 4/Unit 1 Amelia's Road

LANGUAGE SUPPORT

Road to a Solution

1. Help Amelia find the solution to her problem. 2. Cut out the icons she uses as part of her solution. 3. Paste the art in the correct places along Amelia's road.

14   Amelia's Road • Language Support/Blackline Master 6   Grade 4

Reteach, 12	Practice, 12	Extend, 12	Language Support, 14

65F

OBJECTIVES

Students will make inferences about a character's feelings.

Skills Finder

Make Inferences

Introduce	41G-H
Review	65G-H, 117G-H, 515G-H, 535G-H, 567G-H
Test	Unit 1, Unit 5
Maintain	147, 197, 225, 495

TEACHING TIP

MAKE INFERENCES

Remind students to think about what they've learned and what they already know when making inferences. Point out that applying prior experiences and knowledge allows them to understand the ideas they read and reach logical conclusions.

Review Make Inferences

PREPARE

Discuss Making Inferences

Review: Sometimes an author does not provide specific information, but instead provides clues about characters and why they do things. When you make inferences, you think about story clues and use common sense, logic, and what you already know to help you understand the characters and events in the story.

TEACH

Read "The Return" and Model the Skill

Read "The Return" with students. Encourage them to make inferences about Amelia's feelings and actions.

The Return

Her first school day was over, and Amelia was eager to go to her special place near the old tree. She walked in the direction of the meadow. At first, she couldn't find the footpath. Over the past year, the grass had grown high, almost hiding it.

As she neared the old tree, Amelia began to walk faster. When she reached the tree, she almost cried. The rock was still there! Amelia gave the old tree a hug.

Teaching Chart 11

Have students underline clues in the story that helped them make inferences about Amelia's feelings and actions.

MODEL Although the text doesn't say so, Amelia is nervous and worried about her special place. In the time she has been away it may have been disturbed in some way, which would mean that she would no longer have a place to call her own.

PRACTICE

Create an Inference Chart Have students create an inference chart about Amelia's feelings and actions. ▶ **Logical**

INFORMATION	INFERENCES
At first she couldn't find it.	Amelia was worried about not being able to find the accidental road.
She began to walk faster.	Amelia was worried that her secret place had been disturbed.
Amelia gave the old tree a hug.	Amelia is happy to find that her secret place is exactly as she left it.

ASSESS/CLOSE

Write a Different Ending for the Story

GROUP

Have groups of students discuss and then write different endings for "The Return." Ask groups to exchange their new versions and make new inferences based on clues in the revised text. Have students create a chart to record their inferences. ▶ **Interpersonal/Linguistic**

ALTERNATE TEACHING STRATEGY

MAKE INFERENCES

For a different approach to teaching this skill, see page T62.

Intervention ▶ **Skills**

Intervention Guide, for direct instruction and extra practice in making inferences

Meeting Individual Needs for Comprehension

EASY

Name_____ Date_____ Reteach **13**

Make Inferences

Sometimes you must read especially carefully to pick up clues about characters and events. When you use clues and what you know from your own life, you are **making inferences**.

The sunny room was filled with rows of plant experiments. There were books all along one wall. Margarita saw books about animals, the planets, electricity, and many other subjects. In the storage corner there were piles of safety goggles and plastic gloves. Margarita wasn't sure whether to go in or not. She just waited by the door.

The teacher waved for Margarita to come inside. He pointed to an empty seat and then introduced himself. Others in the room did the same. Before long, Margarita felt right at home.

Use clues in the story to answer the questions.

1. Where was Margarita? _at school_

2. What kind of room was she looking into? _science classroom_

3. How do you know what kind of room it was? _There were rows of plant experiments, books on science topics, safety goggles_

4. How do you think Margarita felt as she stood at the door? _She may have felt shy, or nervous about entering the room._

5. How do you know Margarita was probably a new student? _The teacher and other students introduced themselves._

Book 4/Unit 1
Amelia's Road
5

At Home: Have students make up an oral story, giving clues about the setting but not identifying it directly. Ask them to have someone infer the setting

13

Reteach, 13

ON-LEVEL

Name_____ Date_____ Practice **13**

Make Inferences

The author of a story doesn't always tell you what a character is feeling. Sometimes you have to **make inferences**, or figure it out, based on what the character says and does.

Answer each question. Tell what Amelia may be thinking. _Answers may vary._

1. Why does Amelia cry every time her father takes out the map? _She cries because she doesn't want to move to a new place again so soon._

2. What does Amelia think when she enters another grim, gray shanty at the labor camp? _She probably thinks about how ugly it is and that she wishes she could live in a pretty place._

3. How does Amelia feel when she says she want to settle down and her mother says, "Maybe someday." _Amelia may think that is too good to be true, and it will probably never happen._

4. How does Amelia feel when her parents can't remember when or where she was born? _She probably feels hurt and not very important._

5. Why is Amelia in such a good mood the day she finds the tree and the accidental road? _She had a good day at school._

6. How do you know Amelia can solve problems? _She figured out by herself how to feel better and how to make a place for herself._

Book 4/Unit 1
Amelia's Road
6

At Home: Have students create a small box of things that would make them feel special.

13

Practice, 13

CHALLENGE

Name_____ Date_____ Extend **13**

Make Inferences

An **inference** is a conclusion that you draw after considering all the facts and relating them to your own experiences. Inferences can be important in a story because they help you understand a character's feelings, motivation, and actions. Consider Amelia in "Amelia's Road." Then make inferences to answer these questions.

1. Why do you think Amelia wanted to hurry home on the day she met her teacher, Mrs. Ramos? _She wanted to tell her family about her wonderful day in school._

2. Do you think it bothered Amelia that her teacher did not bother to learn her name last year? Tell why. _Yes, because it made Amelia feel unimportant and temporary._

3. Why did the teacher this year give name tags? _She wanted everyone to get to know each other._

4. Why did Amelia save her name tag? _It helped Amelia feel like she belonged someplace._

5. Why did Amelia bury her treasure box near the old tree? _She felt like it was her home and her own special place._

6. Do you think that Amelia will return to her road? Explain. _Amelia will probably return since this is such a special place to her._

Book 4/Unit 1
Amelia's Road

At Home: Have students make inferences about what they will do at school the next day.

13

Extend, 13

LANGUAGE SUPPORT

Name_____ Date_____

Reading for Clues

1. What do these words and pictures tell us about Amelia and her family?
2. Match the numbers next to the sentences with the statements at the bottom of the page.
3. Some numbers may go with both statements.

1. Amelia's father drives a rusty old car.

2. The family gets up at dawn.

3. Amelia grabs an apple for her lunch.

4. The family moves into an old labor camp cabin.

5. Amelia picks fruit before school.

6. Amelia uses a box from the trash for her treasure box.

7. Amelia's family must keep moving from place to place.

Amelia's family does not have much money. _1,3,4,5,6_

Amelia's family works hard. _2,4,5,7_

Grade 4

Language Support/Blackline Master 7 • **Amelia's Road** 15

Language Support, 15

OBJECTIVES

Students will:

• identify antonyms and synonyms

• use antonyms and synonyms in a paragraph.

Skills Finder

Antonyms and Synonyms

Introduce	65I-J
Review	93I-J, 127I-J, 663I-J 691I-J, 723I-J
Test	Unit 1, Unit 6

TEACHING TIP

ANTONYMS AND SYNONYMS

• Some words have similar meanings and can be substituted for each other in a sentence. Many times, however, synonyms are not interchangeable.

• Words must be opposite or nearly opposite in meaning in order to be antonyms.

• To show contrasting ideas, writers often use antonyms.

Introduce Antonyms and Synonyms

PREPARE

Introduce Antonyms and Synonyms

Have students brainstorm a list of words that mean fast (quick, swift, speedy). Have them brainstorm a list of words that mean the opposite of fast (slow, gradual, unhurried).

TEACH

Define Antonyms and Synonyms

Explain: Synonyms are words with the same or similar meanings. They can replace each other in a sentence. Antonyms are words with opposite or nearly opposite meanings. They help writers to show contrasts.

The Old, Shady Tree

As she picked apples, Amelia daydreamed about her special place under the old tree. She pictured its many leafy branches, which gave shade from the noonday sunshine. These apple trees are young, but my tree is ancient, she thought. "If only I could be sitting under my tree right now, reading a book," she whispered to herself, "instead of standing here picking apples. It would be wonderful to feel a gentle breeze cooling my skin instead of this terrible, harsh sun."

Teaching Chart 12

Read the Passage and Model the Skill

Have students read **Teaching Chart 12** with you. Then model the skill for students.

MODEL The word old in the first sentence and ancient in the third sentence are synonyms; the word young is an antonym for old.

Ask a volunteer to identify the pair of words nearly opposite in meaning in the second sentence. Make sure students understand why shade and sunshine are antonyms.

PRACTICE

Identify Antonyms and Synonyms

Have students reread the passage and circle synonyms and underline antonyms. Then have the class brainstorm synonyms and antonyms for other words in the passage such as *special* (unique; common), *gentle* (delicate; rough), and *terrible* (awful; fine).

▶ **Linguistic/Logical**

ASSESS/CLOSE

Use Antonyms and Synonyms

List the following words in random order on the chalkboard: *straight; curved; narrow; wide; dirt; paved; grim; cheerful; unhappy; joyful; messy; tidy; permanent; temporary; difficult; easy.* Have students identify and record which words are synonyms and which ones are antonyms. Then have students use at least four of the pairs in an original paragraph about Amelia.

ALTERNATE TEACHING
STRATEGY

ANTONYMS AND SYNONYMS

For a different approach to teaching this skill, see page T65.

 **Intervention** **Skills**

Intervention Guide, for direct instruction and extra practice in antonyms and synonyms

Meeting Individual Needs for Vocabulary

EASY	ON-LEVEL	CHALLENGE	LANGUAGE SUPPORT

EASY

Name_____ Date_____ Reteach **14**

Synonyms and Antonyms

Synonyms are words that have almost the same meaning. Antonyms are words that have the opposite meaning.

Read each sentence. Write the word from the list that means almost the same as the underlined word.

| stay | happiness | completed | rushed |

1. She wants to remain in this town. ___stay___
2. I finished my drawing first. ___completed___
3. I hurried along the path to the lake. ___rushed___
4. The joy she showed made us smile. ___happiness___

Read each sentence. Write the word from the list that means the opposite of the underlined word.

| curved | silent | cried | always |

5. Follow the straight road north for two miles. ___curved___
6. The children were unusually noisy. ___silent___
7. She laughed just thinking of the movie. ___cried___
8. Marco is never late. ___always___

At Home: Have students list three pairs of synonyms and three pairs of antonyms.

14   Book 4/Unit 1 Amelia's Road 8

ON-LEVEL

Name_____ Date_____ Practice **14**

Synonyms and Antonyms

Synonyms are words that mean almost the same thing. Antonyms are words that have opposite meanings.

Write a synonym from the list to replace each underlined word.

| labored | smiled | strange | cried |

1. The baby sobbed when he was hungry. ___cried___
2. I have visited some weird places. ___strange___
3. The planters worked in the blazing sun. ___labored___
4. The friends grinned at each other when they won. ___smiled___

Write an antonym for the underlined word to complete each sentence.

| relax | curved | temporary | beautiful |

5. One road was straight, but the other was ___curved___.
6. The old cabin was grim, but the new house was ___beautiful___.
7. First Jeff would worry, and then he would ___relax___.
8. A rock is a permanent thing, but a flower is ___temporary___.

At Home: With a family member, have students list other synonyms and antonyms for the underlined words above.

14   Book 4/Unit 1 Amelia's Road 8

CHALLENGE

Name_____ Date_____ Extend **14**

Synonyms and Antonyms

Synonyms are words that have the same meaning. The words *rapid* and *quick* are synonyms. Antonyms are words that have opposite meanings. The words *weak* and *strong* are antonyms.

There are six pairs of synonyms in the box. Write the pairs of synonyms.

| shack | faithful | conquer | talk | make | chat |
| teach | shanty | create | instruct | win | loyal |

chat/talk; teach/instruct; conquer/win; shack/shanty; faithful/ loyal; create/make

Each word in the first box below has an antonym in the second box. Write each word and its antonym.

| deep | cautious | noisy | bright | gradual |
| quiet | quick | shallow | reckless | dull |

deep/shallow; cautious/reckless; noisy/quiet; bright/dull; gradual/quick

Write a short story using some of the pairs of synonyms and antonyms from your lists. Use a separate piece of paper to write your story.

At Home: Play a synonym/antonym game. Challenge each other to think up a synonym or an antonym for a given word.

14   Book 4/Unit 1 Amelia's Road

LANGUAGE SUPPORT

Name_____ Date_____

Picturing Antonyms

1. Choose the pair of antonyms below that goes with each sentence.
2. Write the words in the blanks. 3. Draw a picture in the box that tells about the sentence.

| bright/glum | trash/treasure |
| settle down/move around | straight/curved |

1. One of these roads is ___straight___.
   The other road is ___curved___.

2. He is feeling happy and ___bright___.
   She is feeling sad and ___glum___.

3. One person's ___trash___ is another person's ___treasure___.

4. The dog wants to ___settle___ ___down___.
   The cat wants to ___move___ ___around___.

16   Amelia's Road • Language Support/Blackline Master 8   Grade 4

Reteach, 14   **Practice, 14**   **Extend, 14**   **Language Support, 16**

65J

GRAMMAR/SPELLING CONNECTIONS

See the 5-Day Grammar and Usage Plan on subjects and predicates, pages 65M–65N.

See the 5-Day Spelling Plan on words with long *a* and long *e*, pages 65O–65P.

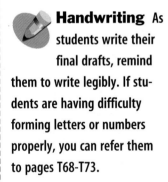

TEACHING TIP

Technology Show students how to capitalize, italicize, boldface, or underline to emphasize words that show strong feeling.

Handwriting As students write their final drafts, remind them to write legibly. If students are having difficulty forming letters or numbers properly, you can refer them to pages T68-T73.

Handwriting CD-ROM

Personal Narrative

Prewrite

WRITE A DIARY ENTRY Present this writing assignment: Think about a place that is special to you. Write a diary entry about the first time you went to that place. Be sure to explain how you felt while you were there.

BRAINSTORM IDEAS Help students brainstorm places that may be special to them, such as a garden, a tree house, a park, or a store. Have students choose their own special place.

Strategy: Make a Chart Ask students to recall their experiences with their place. When was the first time they went there? What happened? What made the place special? Have them fill in the chart.

Draft

USE THE CHART Students should tell the story of their special place in sequential order, as the events are listed on the chart. Remind them to use the word *I* and to include their feelings about their special place before, while, and after they discover it.

Revise

SELF-QUESTIONING Ask students to assess their drafts.

- Did I include my feelings and details about what happened?
- What would make my diary entry sound more realistic?
- Did I include the word *I* when telling about what happened that day?

PARTNERS Have students read their entries to a partner for feedback. Then have them add any details they think could improve the entry.

Edit/Proofread

CHECK FOR ERRORS Students should reread their entries for spelling, grammar, and sentence structure.

Publish

SHARE THE ENTRIES Students can take turns reading their entries aloud. Encourage listeners to tell writers if each entry sounds like a complete story.

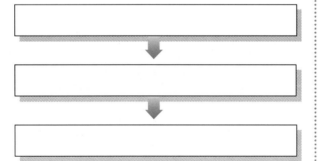

Dear Diary,

I thought today was going to be awful, but it was a great day! Mom and Dad said "Happy Birthday" to me this morning, but they didn't say anything about a party. I didn't see any gifts.

Dad told me to take out the trash. Some birthday! But when I got outside I looked up and saw a brand-new tree house in the branches of our oak tree. Wooden steps were nailed to the tree. I raced up the steps. Inside were all my friends, yelling "Surprise!"

The tree house has become our clubhouse. It's a great place to eat cookies, play games, talk, and make plans.

Presentation Ideas

ILLUSTRATE THE DIARY ENTRY Have students draw pictures of their special place to go with their diary entries.

▶ *Visual/Representing*

ACT IT OUT Have volunteers take turns pretending to be Amelia. Have them read their diary entries aloud to the class.

▶ *Speaking/Listening*

Consider students' creative efforts, possibly adding a plus (+) for originality, wit, and imagination.

Scoring Rubric

Excellent	Good	Fair	Unsatisfactory
4: The writer • retells events in a logical order. • relates feelings about the day and includes rich detail. • uses the word *I* in an authentic voice.	**3:** The writer • tells what happened that day in some detail. • adequately organizes material in a clear manner. • writes in first-person point of view and tells why the day is good.	**2:** The writer • explains his or her feelings but does not explain why he or she feels that way. • presents a few details about the day's events. • writes in first-person point of view, but not consistently.	**1:** The writer • does not express his or her feelings. • provides few or no details of the day. • has not written in first-person point of view.

Incomplete 0: The writer leaves the page blank or fails to respond to the writing task. The student does not address the topic or simply paraphrases the prompt. The response is illegible or incoherent.

For a 6-point or an 8-point scale, see pages T107–T108.

Meeting Individual Needs for Writing

EASY

Draw a Picture Have students draw pictures of the accidental road Amelia found. Then have them write captions for the pictures.

ON-LEVEL

Write a Description Students can write a description of the accidental road so Amelia can find it the next time she returns to the apple orchard. Have them draw pictures to go with the description.

CHALLENGE

A Year Later Students can write what happens a year later when Amelia's family returns to pick apples and she returns to the accidental road. They can draw a picture that includes a speech bubble of what Amelia is saying to the tree.

Listening and Speaking

LISTENING STRATEGIES
As diary entries are read aloud, have students:

• face the speaker and listen attentively.

• write down details they think could improve the entry.

SPEAKING STRATEGIES
Remind students to:

• vary volume and tone of voice in expressing personal feelings.

• use appropriate gestures when reading.

LANGUAGE SUPPORT

ESL English learners can work with a partner to dictate and write their diary entries.

PORTFOLIO Invite students to include their diary entries in their portfolios, or to add other examples of work they have written in first-person point of view.

5 Day Grammar and Usage Plan

Write complete sentences from *Amelia's Road* on sentence strips. Cut the strips to separate the subjects from the predicates. Display a strip and tell students it is a fragment. Then have students put the strips together to form complete sentences.

DAILY LANGUAGE ACTIVITIES

Write the Daily Language Activities on the chalkboard each day or use **Transparency 2.** Have students correct the sentence fragments orally, adding a subject or a predicate. For sample answers, see the transparency.

Day 1
1. Migrant farmers
2. Amelia's parents
3. Red delicious apples

Day 2
1. Work hard in the hot fields
2. Grow in a field
3. Learned her name

Day 3
1. On hot summer days, people
2. Can be found in grocery stores
3. Move from place to place

Day 4
1. Live in shanties
2. Amelia and her family
3. Packs up the car and goes away

Day 5
1. Amelia's kind teacher
2. Goes into the car
3. Blankets, pots, and furniture

Daily Language Transparency 2

65M   *Amelia's Road*

DAY 1 Introduce the Concept

Oral Warm-Up Say the following: *The dog. He sat down. Flew past.* Ask if each one is a sentence or a fragment.

Introduce Subjects Remind students that the subject tells who or what the sentence is about.

Subjects

- The **complete subject** includes all the words in the subject.
- The **simple subject** is the main word in the complete subject. It tells exactly whom or what the sentence is about.
- You can sometimes correct a sentence fragment by adding a subject.

Present the Daily Language Activity. Have students write sentences with two subjects but the same predicate.

 Assign the daily Writing Prompt on page 42C.

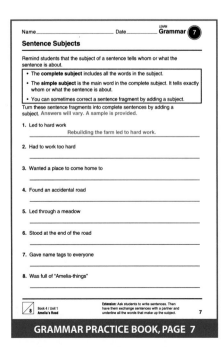

GRAMMAR PRACTICE BOOK, PAGE 7

DAY 2 Teach the Concept

Review Subjects Ask students to explain the difference between a complete and a simple subject.

Introduce Predicates The predicate tells what the subject does or is.

Predicates

- The **complete predicate** includes all the words in the predicate.
- The **simple predicate** is the main word in the complete predicate. It tells exactly what the subject does or is.
- You can sometimes correct a sentence fragment by adding a predicate.

Present the Daily Language Activity. Then have students write a subject on a strip of paper. Invite each student to select one and add a predicate.

 Assign the daily Writing Prompt on page 42C.

GRAMMAR PRACTICE BOOK, PAGE 8

Subjects and Predicates

Learn from the Literature Review subjects and predicates. Have students read the first two lines on page 46 of *Amelia's Road*:

> Amelia Luisa Martinez hated roads. Straight roads. Curved roads. Dirt roads. Paved roads.

Ask students which is a complete sentence and which are sentence fragments. Have them identify the complete subject and the complete predicate of the sentence. Then have them suggest ways to turn the fragments into sentences.

Write Subjects and Predicates
Present the Daily Language Activity. Have students form sentences using the sentence fragments from the Daily Language Activity for Days 1–3.

 Assign the daily Writing Prompt on page 42D.

Review Subjects and Predicates
Make a two-column chart with the heads *Subject* and *Predicate*. Invite students to fill in the chart with complete subjects and complete predicates from sentences in *Amelia's Road*. Then present the Daily Language Activity.

Mechanics and Usage Before students begin the daily Writing Prompt on page 42D, present the following:

Letter Punctuation

- Begin the greeting and closing in a letter with a capital letter.
- Use a comma after the greeting and the closing in a letter.
- Use a comma between the names of a city and a state.
- Use a comma between the day and year in a date.

 Assign the daily Writing Prompt on page 42D.

Assess Use the Daily Language Activity and page 11 of the **Grammar Practice Book** for assessment.

Reteach Give each student two large index cards. Ask students to draw and label a person, place, or thing on one card and write a complete predicate on the other. Collect the cards, placing the subjects and predicates in separate piles. Students can select a card from each pile, display the picture, and say a sentence that includes the chosen subject and predicate.

As students use interesting subjects and predicates in their sentences, have them add these words to the word wall.

Use page 12 of the **Grammar Practice Book** for additional reteaching.

 Assign the daily Writing Prompt on page 42D.

GRAMMAR PRACTICE BOOK, PAGE 9

Name_____ Date_____ PRACTICE AND REVIEW **Grammar** (9)

Write Complete Sentences

- The **subject** of a sentence tells whom or what the sentence is about.
- The **predicate** of a sentence tells what the subject does or is.

Complete each sentence fragment. Then tell if you added a subject or a predicate. Answers will vary.

1. Amelia and her family _____ predicate
2. Still felt sleepy _____ subject
3. Drew a picture of a pretty white house _____ subject
4. Everybody in the class _____ predicate
5. Danced for joy in the quiet meadow _____ subject
6. A narrow, rocky footpath _____ predicate

Book 4 / Unit 1 **Amelia's Road** — Extension: Have students write the subject of a sentence and have a partner add a predicate to complete the sentence. — 9

GRAMMAR PRACTICE BOOK, PAGE 10

Name_____ Date_____ MECHANICS **Grammar** (10)

Sentence Punctuation

- A sentence begins with a capital letter.
- Sentences that make statements end with periods.

Read each group of words. If the words are a complete sentence, write a capital letter at the beginning and put a period at the end.

1. roads that led to strange places
2. they pick peaches in June
   They pick peaches in June.
3. a neat white house with blue shutters
4. the family followed the harvest
   The family followed the harvest.
5. now they picked apples
   Now they picked apples.
6. her teacher never learned her name
   Her teacher never learned her name.
7. a rocky path through the meadow
8. the old metal box was dented
   The old metal box was dented.

10 — Extension: Have pairs of students take turns writing groups of words. The other partner must decide if the words are a sentence or a sentence fragment. If the words are a sentence fragment, the partner should... — Book 4 / Unit 1 **Amelia's Road** (8)

GRAMMAR PRACTICE BOOK, PAGE 11

Name_____ Date_____ TEST **Grammar** (11)

Complete the Sentences

Circle the letter of the words that make each fragment a complete sentence.

1. drew a picture of a white house
   a with blue shutters
   b Amelia
   c with a yard
   d in school

2. Mrs. Ramos
   a Amelia's teacher
   b her teacher last year
   c at school
   d welcomed the new children

3. got up at dawn
   a Amelia's whole family
   b picking apples
   c before school started
   d still sleepy

4. The accidental road
   a a sturdy, old tree
   b was rocky and narrow
   c through a meadow
   d a shortcut to camp

5. Amelia's dream house
   a had a tree in the yard
   b someplace neat and tidy
   c anywhere in the world
   d something special

6. could be easily bruised
   a had to be careful
   b The ripe fruit
   c grabbed an apple
   d was ready to be picked

7. led from the highway to the tree
   a was a shortcut
   b through the meadow
   c The narrow path
   d went down a gentle hill

8. The farm workers
   a the apple harvest
   b were ready to move on
   c one more trip
   d sun-drenched fields

Book 4 / Unit 1 **Amelia's Road** (8) — 11

GRAMMAR PRACTICE BOOK, PAGE 12

5 Day Spelling Plan

ESL Spanish speakers may associate the letter *e* with the long *a* sound in English. For example, the Spanish words *peso* (a unit of money) and *cena* (dinner) both have an *e* pronounced like long *a* in English. Point out that in English *e* may represent long *e* (*feed*) or short *e* (*fed*), but never long *a* (*fade*).

DICTATION SENTENCES

Spelling Words

1. The red cape is made of wool.
2. The sky is gray.
3. Meet us at the station.
4. We will travel by bus or by rail.
5. Trucks carry freight.
6. Friends do not always agree.
7. The teacher will check spelling.
8. Can you keep a secret?
9. Three children are in the family.
10. The woman walked with a cane.
11. Draw the sky with a blue crayon.
12. A cable is like a rope.
13. She will not fail the test.
14. They drank black tea.
15. Is a zebra black and white?
16. The metal desk is rusty.
17. Fruit is on the tray.
18. We ate raisin bread.
19. The bean plant was tall.
20. The house is clean and tidy.

Challenge Words

21. Seeing you at the park was accidental.
22. People labored hard in the fields.
23. Birthdays are happy occasions.
24. Dance to the rhythms of the music.
25. She wanted a white house with blue shutters.

DAY 1 — Pretest

Assess Prior Knowledge Use the Dictation Sentences at the left and **Spelling Practice Book** page 7 for the pretest. Allow students to correct their own papers. Students who require a modified list may be tested on the first ten words.

Spelling Words		Challenge Words
1. cape	11. crayon	21. **accidental**
2. **gray**	12. cable	22. **labored**
3. station	13. fail	23. **occasions**
4. rail	14. tea	24. **rhythms**
5. freight	15. zebra	25. **shutters**
6. agree	16. **rusty**	
7. **teacher**	17. tray	
8. secret	18. raisin	
9. **family**	19. bean	
10. cane	20. **tidy**	

*Note: Words in **dark type** are from the story.*

Word Study On page 8 of the **Spelling Practice Book** are word study steps and an at-home activity.

DAY 2 — Explore the Pattern

Sort and Spell Words Say *tray* and *tea*. Have students identify the vowel sound in each word. (/ā/ /ē/) Have students sort the Spelling Words as below.

Words with Long *a* Spelled

a-e	ay	ai	a
cape	gray	rail	station
cane	crayon	fail	cable
	tray	raisin	

eigh

freight

Words with Long *e* Spelled

ee	ea	e	y
agree	teacher	secret	family
	tea	zebra	rusty
	bean		tidy

Syllable Patterns List *raisin, station, cable, secret, zebra*. Have students divide them into syllables. Explain: When a syllable has a long vowel sound, it usually ends with a vowel (*rai-sin*). This is called an *open syllable*.

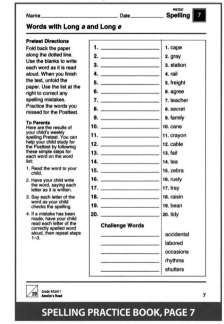

SPELLING PRACTICE BOOK, PAGE 7

WORD STUDY STEPS AND ACTIVITY, PAGE 8

SPELLING PRACTICE BOOK, PAGE 9

Words with Long *a* and Long *e*

Word Meaning: Synonyms Remind students that *synonyms* are words with similar meanings. Have partners think of synonyms for as many of the Spelling Words as they can. (Examples: station/depot, teacher/instructor, fail/lose, tidy/neat) Have students write a sentence for each Spelling Word and then rewrite to include the synonyms.

If students need extra practice, have partners give each other a midweek test.

Glossary Use the Glossary to review syllable division. Have partners

- look up each Challenge Word in the Glossary and find its syllable division.

- tap out the number of syllables as they say each word aloud.

- list the number of syllables in each Challenge Word. (accidental, 4; labored, 2; occasions, 3; rhythms, 2; shutters, 2)

Proofread Sentences Write these sentences on the chalkboard, including the misspelled words. Ask students to proofread, circling incorrect spellings and writing the correct spellings. There are two spelling errors in each sentence.

> The freight train arrived at the staytion.
> (freight, station)
>
> Do you agre not to tell a seacret?
> (agree, secret)

Have students create additional sentences with errors for partners to correct.

WRITING Have students use as many Spelling Words as possible in the daily Writing Prompt on page 42D. Remind students to proofread their writing for errors in spelling, grammar, and punctuation.

Assess Students' Knowledge Use page 12 of the **Spelling Practice Book** or the Dictation Sentences on page 65O for the posttest.

JOURNAL **Personal Word List** If students have trouble with any words in the lesson, have them add to their personal list of troublesome words in their journals. Have students underline the spelling patterns of long *a* and long *e*.

Students should refer to their word lists during later writing activities.

Name_____ Date_____ PRACTICE AND EXTEND **Spelling 10**
Words with Long *a* and Long *e*

cape	freight	family	fail	tray
gray	agree	cane	tea	raisin
station	teacher	crayon	zebra	bean
rail	secret	cable	rusty	tidy

Complete each sentence below with a spelling word.

1. The bus ___station___ is five miles from my house.
2. That ___freight___ train carries food to the city.
3. If I mix white and black together, I will have the color ___gray___
4. It is not a ___secret___ that she loves to dance.
5. Do you disagree, or ___agree___ with me?
6. The new ___teacher___ wrote her name on the chalkboard.
7. The dented metal looks red and ___rusty___
8. I will carry the cookies to the children on a ___tray___
9. Use a ___crayon___ to color in your coloring book.
10. The newest, fastest trains run on only one ___rail___

What Does it Mean?
Write the spelling word that has the same, or almost the same meaning.

11. flunk ___fail___   15. seed of a plant ___bean___
12. neat ___tidy___   16. a dried fruit ___raisin___
13. relatives ___family___ 17. hot drink ___tea___
14. striped animal ___zebra___ 18. walking stick ___cane___

Challenge Extension: Have students create Challenge Word scrambles. Then have students swap them with a partner and solve each other's word scramble.

10   Grade 4/Unit 1 Amelia's Road

SPELLING PRACTICE BOOK, PAGE 10

Name_____ Date_____ PROOFREAD AND WRITE **Spelling 11**
Words with Long *a* and Long *e*

Proofreading Activity
There are six spelling mistakes in the letter below. Circle the misspelled words. Write the words correctly on the lines below.

Dear Mrs. Ramos,
 Thank you for being so nice to me. I want to tell you a secret. Even though my family had to move to find work, I will come back to see you. I hope to build a small, tidy house near the big tree. I will live there forever with my pretty, grae cat, Kitty. When I move into my wonderful house, I will not fale to come and see you. You are the best teacher I ever had.

Your student,
Amelia

1. ___secret___   3. ___tidy___   5. ___fail___
2. ___family___   4. ___gray___   6. ___teacher___

Writing Activity
Where would you like to live? Write a letter telling a friend what your place will look like. Use four spelling words in your writing.

_____
_____
_____
_____

10 Grade 4/Unit 1 Amelia's Road   11

SPELLING PRACTICE BOOK, PAGE 11

Name_____ Date_____ POSTTEST **Spelling 12**
Words with Long *a* and Long *e*

Look at the words in each set below. One word in each set is spelled correctly. Use a pencil to fill in the circle next to the correct word. Before you begin, look at the sample sets of words. Sample A has been done for you. Do Sample B by yourself. When you are sure you know what to do, you may go on with the rest of the page.

Sample A
(A) ranne
(B) rane
● rain
(D) raine

Sample B
(E) nete
(F) neat
(G) neit
(H) neate

1. (A) teye (B) tea (C) tei (D) tae
2. ● cane (B) cain (C) caine (H) ceane
3. (A) ugree (B) agrey (C) aggre (D) agree
4. (A) rason (B) raisin (C) raesin (D) raysin
5. (A) tidee (B) tyde (C) tidi (D) tidy
6. (A) crayon (F) craiyon (G) crayen (H) craon
7. (A) zibra (B) zebra (G) zeebra (H) zeabra
8. ● capp (G) cape (G) caip (H) caipe
9. ● station (B) staytion (G) stashun (H) steation
10. (E) trai (F) traye (G) tray (H) trei
11. (A) famile (B) family (C) familee (D) famely
12. (E) rale (F) rael (G) raile (H) rail
13. (A) teecher (B) teachur (G) teacher (H) teacher
14. ● gray (F) grei (G) grai (H) graye
15. (A) frate (B) freight (C) freite (D) freaght
16. (E) cayble (F) caible (G) cable (H) cabl
17. ● bean (B) beene (G) beane (H) bene
18. (E) seecret (F) secrete (G) seicret (H) secret
19. (A) rousty (B) rusty (C) ruste (D) rustey
20. (E) fale (F) faile (G) fayle (H) fail

12 Grade 4/Unit 1 Amelia's Road

SPELLING PRACTICE BOOK, PAGE 12

65P

Concept
- **Coming to a New Home**

Comprehension
- **Story Elements**

Vocabulary
- **eerie**
- **huddled**
- **overalls**
- **pesky**
- **reins**
- **squall**

Reaching All Learners

Anthology

Sarah, Plain and Tall

Selection Summary Students will read about a mail-order bride who leaves Maine to start a new life as a wife and mother on the prairie. As the family adjusts to the changes and the new experiences, they have time to reflect on the things that are important to them.

Stories in Art focuses on the **comprehension** skill

Reading Strategy applies the **comprehension** skill

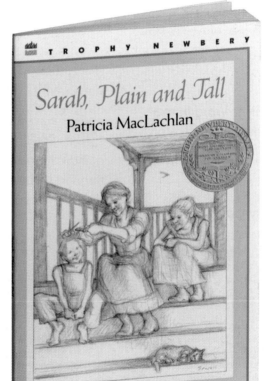

Listening Library

INSTRUCTIONAL pages 68–93

About the Author Patricia MacLachlan was born and raised in the West, moved to Connecticut to attend college, and now lives in Massachusetts. She believes children read "to find out who they are and where they fit into a complicated world." She writes, teaches children's literature, and plays cello.

About the Illustrator Burton Silverman is a well-regarded artist of realistic portraits and has received countless awards and honors. He paints using both oils and watercolors. His career spans five decades, and his works of art can be found in such major museums as the Philadelphia Museum of Art and the Brooklyn Museum.

Same Concept, Skills and Vocabulary!

Leveled Books

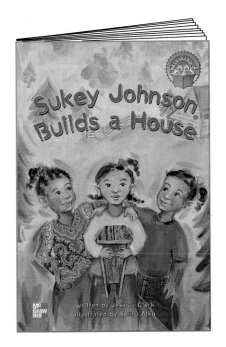

EASY
Lesson on pages 93A and 93D

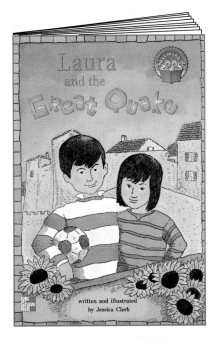

INDEPENDENT
Lesson on pages 93B and 93D

📖 *Take-Home version available*

CHALLENGE
Lesson on pages 93C and 93D

Leveled Practice

EASY
Reteach, **15–21** blackline masters with reteaching opportunities for each assessed skill

INDEPENDENT/ON-LEVEL
Practice, **15–21** workbook with Take-Home stories and practice opportunities for each assessed skill and story comprehension

CHALLENGE
Extend, **15–21** blackline masters that offer challenge activities for each assessed skill

Quizzes Prepared by **Accelerated Reader®**

WORKSTATION Activities

Social Studies . . .	**Geographical Features,** *72*
	Maine, *91*
Science	**Test the Weather Report,** *74*
Math	**Thunder and Lightning,** *80*
Language Arts . .	**Read Aloud,** *66E*
Cultural Perspectives	**Farming,** *82*
Writing	**A Letter,** *90*
Research and Inquiry	**Find Out More,** *91*
Internet Activities	**www.mhschool.com/reading**

Suggested Lesson Planner

READING AND LANGUAGE ARTS	DAY 1 — Focus on Reading and Skills	DAY 2 — Read the Literature

READING AND LANGUAGE ARTS

- Comprehension
- Vocabulary
- Phonics/Decoding
- Study Skills
- Listening, Speaking, Viewing, Representing

DAY 1 — Focus on Reading and Skills

 Read Aloud: Historical Fiction, 66E
"Dakota Dugout"

Develop Visual Literacy, 66

 Review Story Elements, 67A–67B
Teaching Chart 13
Reteach, Practice, Extend, 15

 Reading Strategy: Story Elements, 67
"The Arrival"

 Intervention Program

DAY 2 — Read the Literature

Build Background, 68A
Develop Oral Language

Vocabulary, 68B–68C

eerie	*overalls*	*reins*
huddled	*pesky*	*squall*

Teaching Chart 14
Word Building Manipulative Cards
Reteach, Practice, Extend, 16

 Read the Selection, 68–89
☑ Story Elements
☑ Make Inferences

Genre: Historical Fiction, 69

Cultural Perspectives, 82

Intervention Program

Curriculum Connections

Link Works of Art, 66

Link Social Studies, 68A

Writing

 Writing Prompt: Do you or your neighbor have a pet? Write a paragraph telling what you and the pet do together.

 Writing Prompt: Suppose you own a garden shop. Write a television advertisement telling the kinds of products you sell.

 Journal Writing, 89
Quick-Write

Grammar

Introduce the Concept: Sentence Combining, 93M
Daily Language Activity
1. Papa picked flowers. Sarah put them in her hair.
2. Old Bess was gentle. Jack was sly.
3. Rose laughed. Violet hooted.

Grammar Practice Book, 13

Teach the Concept: Sentence Combining, 93M
Daily Language Activity
1. Matthew plowed. Papa plowed.
2. Caleb can write with a pencil. Caleb can draw with a crayon.
3. Papa waited. Papa worried.

Grammar Practice Book, 14

Spelling

Pretest: Words with Long *i* and Long *o*, 93O
Spelling Practice Book, 13, 14

Explore the Pattern: Words with Long *i* and Long *o*, 93O
Spelling Practice Book, 15

 = **Skill Assessed in Unit Test**

 Intervention Program Available

Read EVERY DAY

DAY 3 — Read the Literature

Rereading for Fluency, 88

Story Questions and Activities, 90–91
Reteach, Practice, Extend, 17

Study Skill, 92
 Parts of a Book
Teaching Chart 15
Reteach, Practice, Extend, 18

Test Power, 93

 Read the Leveled Books, 93A–93D
Guided Reading
Long *i* and Long *o*
☑ **Story Elements**
☑ **Instructional Vocabulary**

 Intervention Program

 Activity Social Studies, 72, 91

✏ **Writing Prompt:** Tell about a time you learned how to do something new.

Writing Process: Letter, 93K
Prewrite, Draft

Review and Practice: Sentence Combining, 93N
Daily Language Activity
1. Sarah was plain. Sarah could cook.
2. Sarah planted. Papa plowed.
3. Sarah missed home. Maggie missed home.

Grammar Practice Book, 15

Practice and Extend: Words with Long *i* and Long *o*, 93P
Spelling Practice Book, 16

DAY 4 — Build Skills

 Read the Leveled Books and Self-Selected Books

☑ **Review Story Elements,** 93E–93F
Teaching Chart 16
Reteach, Practice, Extend, 19
Language Support, 22

☑ **Review Problem and Solution,** 93G–93H
Teaching Chart 17
Reteach, Practice, Extend, 20
Language Support, 23

Minilessons, 75, 77, 81, 83

Writer's Craft, 86

 Intervention Program

 Activity Science, 74

 Writing Prompt: Pretend you are Anna or Caleb. Write a letter to a friend telling him or her about the storm.

Writing Process: Letter, 93K
Revise

Meeting Individual Needs for Writing, 93L

Review and Practice: Sentence Combining, 93N
Daily Language Activity
1. Caleb fed the chickens. Anna fed the chickens.
2. Sarah walked slowly. Anna ran fast.
3. Sarah drank milk. Sarah ate bread.

Grammar Practice Book, 16

Proofread and Write: Words with Long *i* and Long *o*, 93P
Spelling Practice Book, 17

DAY 5 — Build Skills

 Read Self-Selected Books

☑ **Review Antonyms and Synonyms,** 93I–93J
Teaching Chart 18
Reteach, Practice, Extend, 21
Language Support, 24

Listening, Speaking, Viewing, Representing, 93L

Minilessons, 75, 77, 81

Phonics Review,
Long *i* and Long *o*, 83

Phonics/Phonetic Awareness Practice Book, 9–12

 Intervention Program

Activity Math, 80

✏ **Writing Prompt:** Suppose you are vacationing at the ocean. Write a letter to a friend describing the ocean and the beach.

Writing Process: Letter, 93K
Edit/Proofread, Publish

Assess and Reteach: Sentence Combining, 93N
Daily Language Activity
1. Sarah can ride Old Bess. Sarah can play with Seal.
2. Sarah nodded. Sarah turned away.
3. Papa likes the farm. Sarah likes the sea.

Grammar Practice Book, 17, 18

Assess and Reteach: Words with Long *i* and Long *o*, 93P
Spelling Practice Book, 18

Read Aloud

Dakota Dugout

historical fiction by Ann Turner

Tell you about the prairie years? I'll tell you, child, how it was.

When Matt wrote, "Come!" I packed up all I had, cups and pots and dresses and rope, even Grandma's silver boot hook, and rode the clickety train to a cave in the earth, Matt's cave. Built from sod, you know, with a special iron plow that sliced the long earth strips. Matt cut them into bricks, laid them up, dug into a hill that was our first home.

I cried when I saw it. No sky came into that room, only a paper window that made the sun look greasy. Dirt fell on our bed, snakes sometimes, too, and the buffalo hide door could not keep out the wind or the empty cries in the long grass.

The birds visited me, there was no one else, with Matt all day in the fields. A hawk came, snake in its claws, a heron flapped by with wings like sails, and a sparrow jabbered the day long on a gray fence

Continued on pages T4–T5

Oral Comprehension

LISTENING AND SPEAKING Read the selection aloud. Ask students to listen for clues that tell how people lived in this historical time. Discuss historical objects, such as boot hooks and paper windows. How did people use them? Now reread the selection and discuss other historical details students identify.

GENRE STUDY: HISTORICAL FICTION Discuss the characters and historical setting in "Dakota Dugout."

Explain that historical fiction:

• tells a story set in the past.

• shows characters that act and think like real people of the time.

• tells the story in time order.

Activity First point out sound words and phrases in the story, such as *flapped, jabbered, whish-hush, shoosh-hush,* and *ssst-ssst.* Those sound words helped create a vivid impression of life on the prairie. Now have students choose one description of the prairie and draw it. Ask students to write a caption for their drawing, using at least one sound word. ▶ **Intrapersonal/Spatial**

Develop Visual Literacy

Link

Works of Art

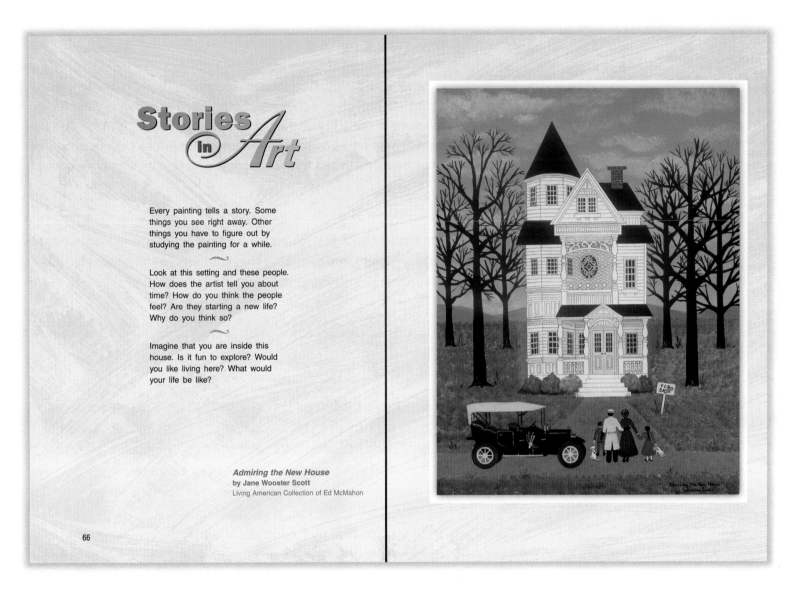

Stories in Art

Every painting tells a story. Some things you see right away. Other things you have to figure out by studying the painting for a while.

Look at this setting and these people. How does the artist tell you about time? How do you think the people feel? Are they starting a new life? Why do you think so?

Imagine that you are inside this house. Is it fun to explore? Would you like living here? What would your life be like?

Admiring the New House
by Jane Wooster Scott
Living American Collection of Ed McMahon

66

Objective: Analyze Character, Setting, and Plot

VIEWING In this American painting, Jane Wooster Scott uses size, perspective, balance, and color to give clues as to the feelings of the people in this picture. Have students look at the painting. Discuss how the size of the house compares to the size of the people. Then ask how size and color affect the mood of the piece.

Read the page with students, encouraging individual interpretations of the painting.

Ask students to support inferences they make about character, setting, and plot. For example:

- Since the artist paints the house so big, she must want to give the feeling that the event might seem over-powering to the people.

- The colors of the house and sky are bright and cheer-ful, welcoming the people inside.

REPRESENTING Have groups of students role-play the scene of the family as they stand before the house. Encourage them to talk about the feelings they have and the refurnishings and household chores that lie ahead.

66

Skills Finder

Story Elements

Introduce	19A-B
Review	41E-F, 67A-B, 93E-F
Test	Unit 1
Maintain	163, 323, 527, 575

Review Story Elements

^{TESTED} **OBJECTIVES**

Students will analyze character, setting, and plot.

LANGUAGE SUPPORT

ESL Ask a volunteer
to tell a simple
story about their day. Then, let
other students identify the
people, the place, and events of
the story. Repeat the activity.
Make the connections for
students between people and
characters, place and setting,
and what happens and plot.

PREPARE

Use a Familiar Story

Choose a story that students are familiar with, such as *Cinderella.*
Elicit the characters, setting and plot. Then ask: "What was the big
problem in the story and what finally happened?" (Cinderella's step-
mother was mean to her. She married the prince.) Often, plot—or
what happens in a story—involves a problem and its outcome.

TEACH

Read the Story and Model the Skill

Remind students that character, setting and plot are *story elements.*
Display **Teaching Chart 13.** Have students pay attention to clues
about character, setting, and plot as you read aloud.

Home Is with You

Pamela held her mother's hand as they walked into their
new apartment in New York City for the first time. The room
was dark and empty. None of the furniture from back home
in Virginia had arrived yet. Pamela looked around and burst
into tears. "I hate it," she sobbed. Mom held Pamela tight.
    After a minute, Pamela wiped her eyes and walked over
to the window. From outside, she thought she heard a
familiar sound. "Isn't that the ice-cream-truck song, just like
back home?" Mom nodded, then asked, "Want to get an
ice cream?" Pamela smiled at her mother. "Mom," she said,
"as long as I'm with you, I'll always feel at home."

Teaching Chart 13

MODEL This story seems to be about two people, Mom and Pamela.
They must be the main characters. Pamela is crying, so I think the
plot has to do with her feelings. If I keep reading, I will learn the
outcome, and find out how Pamela deals with her sadness.

Identify Setting and Plot

Ask students to underline words and phrases that tell something
about the plot and circle words that identify or describe the setting.

PRACTICE

Create a Story Elements Chart

GROUP

Using a Story Elements chart, have small groups organize the character, setting, and plot information from "Home Is with You."

> **Setting**
> A dark and empty apartment in New York City

> **What The Characters Want**
> Pamela wants her old home in Virginia. Mom wants Pamela to be happy in their new home.

> **Plot Problem**
> Pamela is homesick.

> **Outcome**
> Pamela finds something to like in her new home, and realizes family is an important part of home.

ASSESS/CLOSE

Use Story Elements

Have students imagine a new scene in Pamela and Mom's story. Ask them to write a list of characters, the new setting, and one line about the plot for the scene.

ALTERNATE TEACHING STRATEGY

STORY ELEMENTS
For a different approach to teaching this skill, see page T60.

Intervention ▶ **Skills Intervention Guide**, for direct instruction and extra practice in story elements

---

Meeting Individual Needs for Comprehension

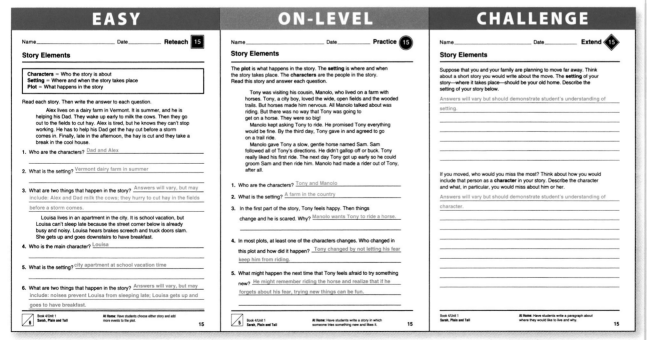

Reteach, 15   Practice, 15   Extend, 15

OBJECTIVES

Students will analyze character, setting, and plot.

Apply Story Elements

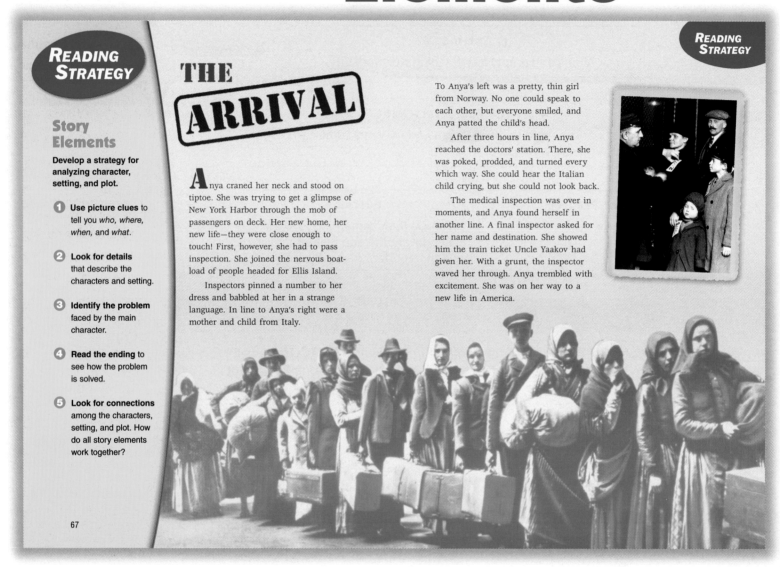

READING STRATEGY

READING STRATEGY

Story Elements

Develop a strategy for analyzing character, setting, and plot.

1. **Use picture clues** to tell you *who, where, when,* and *what.*

2. **Look for details** that describe the characters and setting.

3. **Identify the problem** faced by the main character.

4. **Read the ending** to see how the problem is solved.

5. **Look for connections** among the characters, setting, and plot. How do all story elements work together?

THE ARRIVAL

Anya craned her neck and stood on tiptoe. She was trying to get a glimpse of New York Harbor through the mob of passengers on deck. Her new home, her new life—they were close enough to touch! First, however, she had to pass inspection. She joined the nervous boat-load of people headed for Ellis Island.

Inspectors pinned a number to her dress and babbled at her in a strange language. In line to Anya's right were a mother and child from Italy.

To Anya's left was a pretty, thin girl from Norway. No one could speak to each other, but everyone smiled, and Anya patted the child's head.

After three hours in line, Anya reached the doctors' station. There, she was poked, prodded, and turned every which way. She could hear the Italian child crying, but she could not look back.

The medical inspection was over in moments, and Anya found herself in another line. A final inspector asked for her name and destination. She showed him the train ticket Uncle Yaakov had given her. With a grunt, the inspector waved her through. Anya trembled with excitement. She was on her way to a new life in America.

67

PREVIEW Have students preview "The Arrival." Explain that it is an example of historical fiction. Ask:

• When you know that a story is historical fiction, what do you know about the setting of the story? (It is probably set in the past.)

SET PURPOSES Tell students that they will apply what they have learned about analyzing character, setting, and plot as they read "The Arrival."

APPLY THE STRATEGY Discuss this strategy for analyzing character, setting, and plot in a selection.

• Preview any illustrations to get an idea of the people and places involved.

• Look for describing words or phrases that tell more about the characters and setting.

• At the beginning of the story, locate the main character and the problem he or she faces.

• At the end of the story, determine if and how the problem was solved.

• Think about how the plot and setting affect the characters and how the characters and setting affect the plot.

Activity Have each student create a Story Elements chart for the passage.

Build Background

Social Studies

Concept: Coming to a New Home

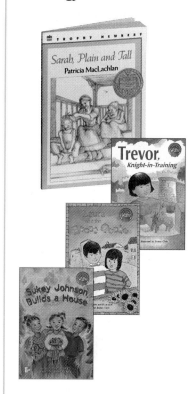

Evaluate Prior Knowledge

CONCEPT: COMING TO A NEW HOME
Tell students: by the time you are grown up you may have lived in several different homes. You might follow a job opportunity all the way across the country, or go to college in another state. All this moving around was not so common in the days when many Americans were farmers.

COMPARE HOMES Help students compare two places they have lived or their home to a friend's home. Create a chart to organize the information. ▶ **Logical/Visual**

OLD HOME	NEW HOME
Friends right in my building	A yard and a dog
The corner store	Going for walks on my own
My school	The county fair

PACKING UP Have students make a list or drawing of the most important things they would pack to take to a new home, for example, a favorite toy or photo.

WRITING   ONE

Develop Oral Language

DISCUSS COMING TO A NEW HOME

ESL Invite students to brainstorm a list of things that would be different if they moved to a new city. If possible, provide appropriate visual cues such as travel brochures, maps, and photographs from magazines. They may come up with a list something like this:

- my home
- my school
- where my parents work
- the weather

Ask students to form pairs and imagine that one partner lives in a new area and that he or she is talking to a friend from the old neighborhood. The person who has moved can tell the other person what is different about the new place. Invite students to use the items on the board to begin their descriptions.

TEACHING TIP

MANAGEMENT While advanced students are working independently on the Compare Homes and the Packing Up activities, you may wish to complete the Develop Oral Language activity with students who need extra help. Students who complete the Compare Homes and Packing Up activities early can act as tutors to students who may need to be guided through these more linguistically challenging activities.

LANGUAGE SUPPORT

See the **Language Support Book**, pages 17–20, for teaching suggestions for Build Background.

68A

OBJECTIVES

Students will use context and structural clues to determine the meanings of vocabulary words.

overalls

eerie

huddled

squall

reins

pesky

Vocabulary

efinitions

overalls (p. 75) loose-fitting trousers with a piece that covers the chest and attached suspenders

eerie (p. 80) strange in a scary way

huddled (p. 78) gathered close together in a bunch

squall (p. 78) a strong, gust of wind that arises very suddenly

reins (p. 83) narrow straps used to guide and control a horse

pesky (p. 85) troublesome or annoying

Teach Vocabulary in Context

Identify Vocabulary Words Display **Teaching Chart 14** and read the passage with students. Have volunteers circle each vocabulary word and underline other words that are clues to its meaning.

A Storm Is Coming

1. As Sarah slipped her legs into a pair of blue denim overalls, she looked out the window. **2.** The eerie color of the sky frightened her. **3.** It must have frightened the chickens, too, because they were all crowded together, huddled up close to the barn. **4.** A squall was on its way and could bring strong winds and heavy rain. **5.** Sarah watched her husband at the reins of the wagon, driving his horse toward the far fields. **6.** He was on his way to round up the pesky sheep that often annoyed him with their wandering.

Teaching Chart 14

Story Words

These words from the selection may be unfamiliar. Before students read, have them check the meaning and pronunciation of each word in the Glossary, beginning on page 756, or in a dictionary.

- advertisement, p. 69
- prairie, p. 69
- neighbors, p. 70
- whickering, p.70
- biscuit, p. 71

Discuss Meanings Ask questions like these to help clarify word meanings:

- How are overalls different from a dress?
- Describe how an eerie sky might look.
- Have you ever huddled near a campfire to keep warm? If so, what was that like?
- Why would a farmer worry about a squall more than a businessperson?
- How do reins help a driver control a horse?
- What is more pesky, a mosquito or a butterfly?

Practice

Demonstrating Word Meaning

PARTNERS

Have partners choose vocabulary cards from a pile. Each partner can pantomime a word while the other guesses its meaning.

▶**Kinesthetic/Linguistic**

reins   huddled   squall

Word Building Manipulative Cards

Write Context Sentences

WRITING

Have partners write context sentences, leaving a blank for each vocabulary word. Then, they can exchange papers to fill in the blanks or use vocabulary cards to show their answers. ▶ **Linguistic**

Assess Vocabulary

Use Words in Context

GROUP

Ask groups of six students to create a round-robin story using the vocabulary words. To begin, a student writes a sentence on a sheet of paper. The writer then passes the paper to the next student, who adds a new sentence using a different vocabulary word. The story is complete when all the words have been used. Have groups share their stories with the class.

SPELLING/VOCABULARY CONNECTIONS
See Spelling Challenge Words, pages 93O–93P.

LANGUAGE SUPPORT
See the **Language Support Book**, pages 17–20, for teaching suggestions for Vocabulary.

Vocabulary PuzzleMaker

Provides vocabulary activities.

Meeting Individual Needs for Vocabulary

EASY

Name_____ Date_____ Reteach **16**

Vocabulary

Read each clue. Then write the correct word from the list.

huddled	overalls	reins	squall	pesky	eerie

1. This word is an action word. ___huddled___
2. This word names a piece of clothing. ___overalls___
3. This word names a kind of storm. ___squall___
4. This word describes annoying behavior. ___pesky___
5. This word names something used with horses. ___reins___
6. This word describes something strange and scary. ___eerie___

6

Story Comprehension   Reteach **17**

Circle the letter beside the answer to each question about "Sarah, Plain and Tall."

1. Why did Sarah leave Maine and come to the prairie?
   a. to have a vacation   (b.) to answer Papa's ad
2. Who told Sarah there will always be things to miss?
   a. Papa   (b.) Maggie
3. How did Papa feel when Sarah helped with the roof?
   (a.) surprised   b. angry
4. What did Sarah want to learn to do?
   a. work in the field   (b.) drive a wagon

16–17   **At Home:** Have students write sentences using three of the vocabulary words.   Book 4/Unit 1 **Sarah, Plain and Tall** **4**

ON-LEVEL

Name_____ Date_____ Practice **16**

Vocabulary

Write a vocabulary word to replace each underlined word.

reins	eerie	squall	huddled	pesky	overalls

1. At the bottom of the tree, baby squirrels <u>gathered closely</u> together to keep warm. ___huddled___
2. Before the storm, a <u>strange, weird</u> stillness told us that the tornado was going to be even more frightening than we expected. ___eerie___
3. The new rider sat on the horse and gave the <u>straps</u> a little wiggle to get the animal to move. ___reins___
4. The <u>annoying</u> puppy kept whining for more food or a chance to go out and play. ___pesky___
5. When a sudden <u>gigantic wind</u> brings rain along with it, everyone runs for the shelter of their homes. ___squall___
6. The <u>pants with bib and straps</u> cover almost the whole body of the person wearing them. ___overalls___

16   **At Home:** Have students write an eerie story using as many vocabulary words as possible.   Book 4/Unit 1 **Sarah, Plain and Tall** **6**

ON-LEVEL

PRAIRIE SQUALL

Sally heard the wind whistle across the prairie as she put on her *overalls* and ran out to her horse in the barnyard. She was frightened as *eerie* clouds darkened the sky. A brief *squall* blew rain into her eyes. Sally's horse was frightened, too, and gave her a hard time. Sally grabbed the horse's *reins* and led the animal into the barn. There the chickens were *pesky* and running around. But the cows *huddled* together, waiting for the storm to end.

1. What kind of clothing is Sally wearing? ___overalls___
2. Define what the author means by "*eerie*". ___scary, frightening, dark___
3. What word describes the behavior of the chickens in the barn? ___pesky___
4. What did the other animals in the barn do during the storm? ___huddled___
5. Why did Sally run so quickly out to the barnyard? ___Answers will vary but should mention that she knew the animals would be frightened and she wanted to get them into the barn where they would be dry.___

5   Book 4/Unit 1 **Sarah, Plain and Tall**   **At Home:** Have students use the italicized words in new sentences.   16a

CHALLENGE

Name_____ Date_____ Extend **16**

Vocabulary

eerie	overalls	reins
huddled	pesky	squall

Suppose you were playing in a park far from your home when a storm comes. Think about how you might feel. Use some of the words above to write about what happened.

Answers will vary but should use vocabulary words correctly.

_____
_____
_____
_____

Extend **17**

Story Comprehension

Review "Sarah Plain and Tall." On the day Sarah drives to town, the other characters go about their usual daily activities. What do the other characters do while Sarah is gone?

Answers will vary. Possible answers: Jacob goes to work in the fields. Anna waters Sarah's plants and sweeps the porch. Caleb cleans the wood stove. Anna and Caleb take lunch to their father in the field. They feed the sheep. Anna sets the table. Jacob comes in from the field and lights the stove.

_____

16–17   **At Home:** Discuss how the daily activities of a character from "Sarah, Plain and Tall" may be similar to or different from your daily activities.   Book 4/Unit 1 **Sarah, Plain and Tall**

Reteach, 16   **Practice, 16**   **Practice, 16a**   **Extend, 16**
                                                   Take-Home Story

Comprehension

Prereading Strategies

PREVIEW AND PREDICT Have students read the title and preview the story, looking for pictures that give information about the characters, setting and plot.

- Where might this story take place?
- Does the story seem to be set in the past, the present, or the future?
- What clues about the characters are given by the title and the pictures?
- What do you think the story will be about?
- Will the story be realistic or a fantasy? Explain. (The characters and surroundings look realistic.) *Genre*

Have students record their predictions about the selection.

PREDICTIONS	WHAT HAPPENED
The characters live on a farm.	
Someone visits from the city.	

SET PURPOSES What do students want to find out by reading the story? For example:

- Who is Sarah, and why is she called *plain* and *tall?*
- Where and when does the story take place?

illustrated by Burton Silverman

68

Meeting Individual Needs • Grouping Suggestions for Strategic Reading

EASY

Read Together Read the story with students or have them use the **Listening Library.** Have students use the Story Elements chart to record information about the characters, setting, and plot. Comprehension and Intervention prompts offer additional help with decoding, vocabulary, and comprehension.

ON-LEVEL

Guided Instruction You may wish to have the students read independently first. Choose from the Comprehension questions as you read with students or after they have heard a **Listening Library** recording. Have them record information on their Story Elements charts.

CHALLENGE

Read Independently Have students read independently. Remind them that making inferences about the characters, setting, and plot will help them understand the story. Have students set up a Story Elements chart like the one on page 69. After reading, they can use their charts to summarize the story.

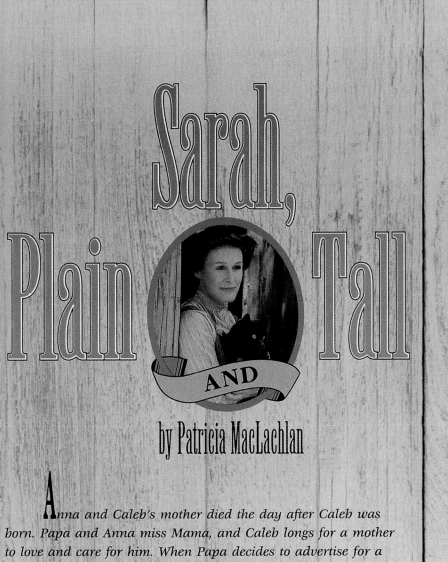

Sarah, Plain and Tall

AND

by Patricia MacLachlan

Anna and Caleb's mother died the day after Caleb was born. Papa and Anna miss Mama, and Caleb longs for a mother to love and care for him. When Papa decides to advertise for a wife, Sarah Elisabeth Wheaton answers the advertisement from Maine. After trading a few letters with Papa, Anna, and Caleb, Sarah decides to visit them in their prairie home for a month. She writes that they will recognize her at the train station because she is "plain and tall." Sarah brings Seal, her cat, and gifts from the ocean she loves so much. Papa, Caleb, and Anna wonder if Sarah will be content to stay and make her new home with them, so far from the sea. ①

69

LANGUAGE SUPPORT

A blackline master of the Story Elements chart is available in the **Language Support Book.**

LANGUAGE SUPPORT, 21

Comprehension

☑ **Apply Story Elements**
☑ **Apply Make Inferences**

STRATEGIC READING Before we begin reading, let's prepare Story Elements charts.

Setting

What the Characters Want

Plot Problem → **Outcome**

① **CHARACTER** On this page, we learn about the characters and what they want. Let's include this information on our charts.

What the Characters Want
Anna and Caleb want a mother. Papa wants a wife. Sarah wants to know if she would like to become part of a new family in a new place.

Genre

Historical Fiction

Explain that historical fiction:

• features events and settings typical of the period in which the story is set.
• develops characters by showing how they deal with real-life situations.
• may have one character tell the story from his or her point of view.

Activity After students have read *Sarah, Plain and Tall*, discuss this question: How might the story be different if told from the point of view of a character other than Anna?

69

Comprehension

(2) MAKE INFERENCES Who do you think is telling this story?

MODEL I notice that this story is being told by one of the characters. I wonder which character it is. Since this paragraph mentions all the main characters I read about in the introduction except for Anna, I think she must be the one telling the story.

(2) The dandelions in the fields had gone by, their heads soft as feathers. The summer roses were opening.

Our neighbors, Matthew and Maggie, came to help Papa plow up a new field for corn. Sarah stood with us on the porch, watching their wagon wind up the road, two horses pulling it and one tied in back. I remembered the last time we had stood here alone, Caleb and I, waiting for Sarah.

Sarah's hair was in thick braids that circled her head, wild daisies tucked here and there. Papa had picked them for her.

Old Bess and Jack ran along the inside of the fence, whickering at the new horses.

"Papa needs five horses for the big gang plow," Caleb told Sarah. "Prairie grass is hard."

Matthew and Maggie came with their two children and a sackful of chickens. Maggie emptied the sack into the yard and three red banty chickens clucked and scattered.

"They are for you," she told Sarah. "For eating."

Sarah loved the chickens. She clucked back to them and fed them grain. They followed her, shuffling and scratching primly in the dirt. I knew they would not be for eating.

The children were young and named Rose and Violet, after flowers. They hooted and laughed and chased the chickens, who flew up to the porch roof, then the dogs, who crept quietly under the porch. Seal had long ago fled to the barn to sleep in cool hay.

Sarah and Maggie helped hitch the horses to the plow, then they set up a big table in the shade of the barn, covering it with a quilt and a kettle of flowers in the middle. They sat on the porch while Caleb and

70

Matthew and Papa began their morning of plowing. ③
I mixed biscuit dough just inside the door, watching.
　"You are lonely, yes?" asked Maggie in her soft voice.
　Sarah's eyes filled with tears. Slowly I stirred the dough.
　Maggie reached over and took Sarah's hand.
　"I miss the hills of Tennessee sometimes," she said.
　Do not miss the hills, Maggie, I thought.
　"I miss the sea," said Sarah. ④
　Do not miss the hills. Do not miss the sea.
　I stirred and stirred the dough.
　"I miss my brother William," said Sarah.

71

Comprehension

③ After Sarah and Maggie finish setting the table, they sit down on the porch to visit. What do you think they will talk about? Why? (Sarah and Maggie may talk about their lives. Sarah has just arrived on the prairie. Maggie may want to help Sarah adjust to her new life. Maggie may want to know about Sarah's life in Maine.) *Make Predictions*

④ **MAKE INFERENCES** Why is Anna thinking, *"Do not miss the hills. Do not miss the sea"*? (She has a strong desire for Sarah to stay with them on the prairie. Anna is afraid she will lose Sarah if Sarah misses the sea too much.)

SYNONYMS Sometimes authors use synonyms to make their writing more interesting. Can you find a place where the author did that on this page? (mixed, stirred) *Semantic Cues*

PREVENTION/INTERVENTION

SYNONYMS Write the words *mixed* and *stirred* on the chalkboard. Ask volunteers to pantomime *mixing* and *stirring* dough. Explain that the reason for using two different words is to make the writing more interesting. Then, point out that the author uses the word *miss* several times in the passage. Tell students that a thesaurus is a book that lists synonyms. Help them find these synonyms for *miss* in a thesaurus: *crave, want, long for, desire, yearn for, need.* Ask students if they think using any of these words in place of *miss* would improve the writing. *Semantic Cues*

Comprehension

⑤ How does Sarah describe her aunts?
(She says they squawk like crows.)
Which word is a clue that the comparison
Sarah is making is a simile? (like) *Compare
and Contrast*

⑥ Maggie says she has something for
Sarah, then she gets a low wooden
box out of the wagon. Can you guess what
is in the box? *Make Predictions*

⑤ "But he is married. The house is hers now. Not mine any longer. There are three old aunts who all squawk together like crows at dawn. I miss them, too."

"There are always things to miss," said Maggie. "No matter where you are."

I looked out and saw Papa and Matthew and Caleb working. Rose and Violet ran in the fields. I felt something brush my legs and looked down at Nick, wagging his tail.

"I would miss you, Nick," I whispered. "I would." I knelt down and scratched his ears. "I miss Mama."

"I nearly forgot," said Maggie on the porch. "I have something more for you."

⑥ I carried the bowl outside and watched Maggie lift a low wooden box out of the wagon.

72

Cross Curricular: Social Studies

GEOGRAPHICAL FEATURES Display a landform map of the U.S. and point out the prairie lands of the West. Explain that when the settlers first came to the prairie, it looked like a sea of grass. Now, much of the prairie is covered by farms and towns.

RESEARCH AND INQUIRY Invite students to gather information about the Tallgrass Prairie National Preserve in Kansas. They can use what they learn to draw before and after prairie pictures.
▶ *Logical/Spatial*

"Plants," she said to Sarah. "For your garden."

"My garden?" Sarah bent down to touch the plants.

"Zinnias and marigolds and wild feverfew," said Maggie. "You must have a garden. Wherever you are."

Sarah smiled. "I had a garden in Maine with dahlias and columbine. And nasturtiums the color of the sun when it sets. I don't know if nasturtiums would grow here." **(7)**

"Try," said Maggie. "You must have a garden."

We planted the flowers by the porch, turning over the soil and patting it around them, and watering. Lottie and Nick came to sniff, and the chickens walked in the dirt, leaving prints. In the fields, the horses pulled the plow up and down under the hot summer sun.

Maggie wiped her face, leaving a streak of dirt.

"Soon you can drive your wagon over to my house **(8)** and I will give you more. I have tansy."

73

Comprehension

(7) SETTING This paragraph has a lovely description of the setting. Let's put this information in our charts. What else can you remember about the setting so far?

Setting
Summertime, a farm on the prairie with a house, a garden, animals and fields.

What the Characters Want
Anna and Caleb want a mother. Papa wants a wife. Sarah wants to know if she would like to become part of a new family in a new place.

Plot Problem	**Outcome**

(8) Let's put together some information from the text about Maggie and see if we can draw a conclusion about why she gives Sarah some plants to build a garden. First, she knows Sarah misses her home. Second, like Sarah, she also misses the home she left to move to the prairie. Third, she has even more plants for Sarah at her house. Think about all of those things, and then explain why Maggie gives Sarah plants to start a garden. (Maggie wants Sarah to feel at home. She hopes Sarah will stay and become her friend.) ***Draw Conclusions***

WORD STRUCTURE Look at the verbs *smiled, planted, walked, pulled, wiped*. What do all these verbs have in common? (They end in *-ed*.) ***Syntactic Cues***

Comprehension

9 MAKE INFERENCES What can you infer about Sarah from the fact that she follows the wagon for a long time? (She is sorry to see her neighbors leave.) What can you infer from the fact that Anna and Caleb run to bring her back? (They are nervous about her going away.)

10 What do you think is going to happen next? (bad weather) What clues tell you that? (strange clouds, still air) *Make Predictions*

Sarah frowned. "I have never driven a wagon."

"I can teach you," said Maggie. "And so can Anna and Caleb. And Jacob."

Sarah turned to me.

"Can you?" she asked. "Can you drive a wagon?"

I nodded.

"And Caleb?"

"Yes."

"In Maine," said Sarah, "I would walk to town."

"Here it is different," said Maggie. "Here you will drive."

Way off in the sky, clouds gathered. Matthew and Papa and Caleb came in from the fields, their work done. We all ate in the shade.

"We are glad you are here," said Matthew to Sarah. "A new friend. Maggie misses her friends sometimes."

Sarah nodded. "There is always something to miss, no matter where you are," she said, smiling at Maggie.

Rose and Violet fell asleep in the grass, their bellies full of meat and greens and biscuits. And when it was time to go, Papa and Matthew lifted them into the wagon to sleep on blankets.

9 Sarah walked slowly behind the wagon for a long time, waving, watching it disappear. Caleb and I ran to bring her back, the chickens running wildly behind us.

"What shall we name them?" asked Sarah, laughing as the chickens followed us into the house.

I smiled. I was right. The chickens would not be for eating.

And then Papa came, just before the rain, bringing Sarah the first roses of summer.

10 The rain came and passed, but strange clouds hung in the northwest, low and black and green. And the air grew still.

74

Activity

Cross Curricular: Science

TEST THE WEATHER REPORT The National Weather Service in Washington, D.C., provides weather reports for the entire country. They use satellites, maps, and computers to measure temperature and humidity every hour, and wind speed and direction every minute. But how accurate are they?

Have students copy a five-day weather forecast from a newscast or a newspaper, then create a chart to compare the forecast with actual conditions.

interNET CONNECTION To learn more about weather forecasting, have students visit **www.mhschool.com/reading**

San Antonio, TX

	Mon	Tues	Wed	Thu
Forecast	hi 86 lo 65	hi 90 lo 70	hi 90 lo 70	hi lo
Actual Weather	hi 92 lo 70	hi 90 lo 70	hi 95 lo 75	hi lo

In the morning, Sarah dressed in a pair of overalls ⑪ and went to the barn to have an argument with Papa. She took apples for Old Bess and Jack.

"Women don't wear overalls," said Caleb, running along behind her like one of Sarah's chickens.

"This woman does," said Sarah crisply.

Papa stood by the fence.

"I want to learn how to ride a horse," Sarah told him. "And then I want to learn how to drive the wagon. By myself."

Jack leaned over and nipped at Sarah's overalls. She fed him an apple. Caleb and I stood behind Sarah. ⑫

"I can ride a horse, I know," said Sarah. "I rode once when I was twelve. I will ride Jack." Jack was Sarah's favorite.

75

Comprehension

⑪ **CHARACTER** What do you learn about Sarah from her dress, her thoughts, and her actions?

MODEL Sarah dresses in overalls. That tells me she is practical and wants to work. When she argues with Papa, that shows me that she will stand up for her beliefs. When she takes apples to the horses, I realize she loves and cares for animals. All of those things tell me that Sarah is practical, strong, and caring.

⑫ How do you think Sarah speaks when she argues with Papa? How do you speak when something is important to you? We can continue reading this dialogue onto the next page with a volunteer reading for Papa. *Role-Play*

PHONICS/DECODING Listen to the following words from this page: *argument, behind, crisp, told*. Now listen again, but pay special attention to the ending blends. Can you spell the ending sounds? *Graphophonic Cues*

Minilesson

REVIEW/MAINTAIN

Character

Remind students that a person's character—his or her personality—can be revealed by what he or she says and does.

• Have students reread pages 74 and 75 to find clues about Sarah's personality. Discuss how Sarah's words and actions show that she is a strong-minded woman who is not afraid to try something new.

Activity Have students brainstorm character traits of people they admire and respect. Then have them use words, drawings, and pictures to create a class collage of character traits.

PREVENTION/INTERVENTION

PHONICS/DECODING Write these words on the chalkboard: *argument, behind, crisp, told*. Underline the consonant blends as students pronounce the words. (/-nt/, /-nd/, /-sp/, /-ld/) Challenge students to choose the ending blend that they have the most difficulty with, and list as many words as they can think of with that ending. (Possible answers: *sent, friend, clasp, bald*) Then, have students pronounce the words from their list. *Graphophonic Cues*

Comprehension

13 **PLOT** Sarah and Papa just worked out a problem. What did Sarah want? What did they agree on? (Sarah wanted to learn to ride a horse and she wanted it to be Jack. Then, she wanted to learn to drive a wagon. They agreed that Papa would teach her to drive a wagon and that she could drive to town by herself.)

Papa shook his head. "Not Jack," he said. "Jack is sly."

"I am sly, too," said Sarah stubbornly.

Papa smiled. "Ayuh," he said, nodding. "But not Jack."

"Yes, Jack!" Sarah's voice was very loud.

"I can teach you how to drive a wagon. I have already taught you how to plow."

"And then I can go to town. By myself."

"Say no, Papa," Caleb whispered beside me.

"That's a fair thing, Sarah," said Papa. "We'll practice."

A soft rumble of thunder sounded. Papa looked up at the clouds.

"Today? Can we begin today?" asked Sarah.

"Tomorrow is best," said Papa, looking worried. **13** "I have to fix the house roof. A portion of it is loose. And there's a storm coming."

76

Visual Literacy

VIEWING AND REPRESENTING

Encourage students to look at all the illustrations in the selection. Ask them:

- What kinds of illustrations do you see? (photographs and paintings)

- Who is in the photographs? (Actors who play the main characters: Sarah, Papa, Caleb, and Anna.)

- Do the characters look the same in the photographs and the paintings? (yes) Can you imagine a reason for that? (*Sarah, Plain and Tall,* was first a book, then a movie, and then a story excerpt for this book. The paintings were based on the actors who played the characters in the movie.)

LANGUAGE SUPPORT

ESL Write *sly* and *stubborn* on the board. Read aloud the sentence in which each word appears and ask students to guess the word's meaning. Guide them to understand that *sly* means "tricky" or "deceptive" and that when people or animals are *stubborn,* they are not easily influenced by what others want them to do.

Ask students to give examples of animals that possess each of these qualities. For example, some people may think that foxes and crows are sly, while donkeys and elephants are stubborn. Ask ESL students what animals represent these qualities in their native cultures.

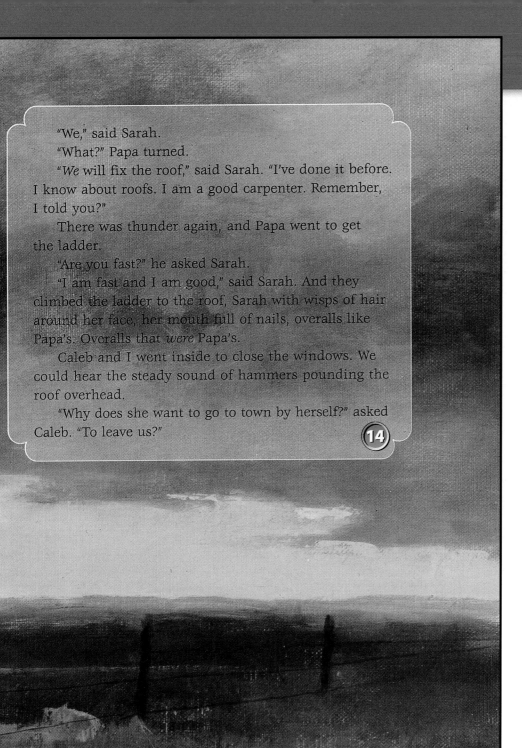

"We," said Sarah.

"What?" Papa turned.

"*We* will fix the roof," said Sarah. "I've done it before. I know about roofs. I am a good carpenter. Remember, I told you?"

There was thunder again, and Papa went to get the ladder.

"Are you fast?" he asked Sarah.

"I am fast and I am good," said Sarah. And they climbed the ladder to the roof, Sarah with wisps of hair around her face, her mouth full of nails, overalls like Papa's. Overalls that *were* Papa's.

Caleb and I went inside to close the windows. We could hear the steady sound of hammers pounding the roof overhead.

"Why does she want to go to town by herself?" asked Caleb. "To leave us?"

(14)

(77)

Comprehension

(14) **PLOT** Caleb finally says out loud what everyone has been worried about. **What is it?** (He thinks Sarah might want to leave them.) **Can you see how the plot is closely related to what the characters want? Let's record this information on our chart.**

Setting
Summertime, a farm on the prairie with a house, a garden, animals and fields.

What the Characters Want
Anna and Caleb want a mother. Papa wants a wife. Sarah wants to know if she would like to become part of a new family in a new place.

Plot Problem	**Outcome**
Papa, Anna, and Caleb hope that Sarah will stay with them, but Sarah is homesick for her home in Maine and for the sea.	

Minilesson

REVIEW/MAINTAIN
Summarize

Explain that summarizing a story's events can often help readers find meaning and order in what they have read.

- Have pairs of students brainstorm key events that have happened in the story so far. Ask them to discuss how following the events of the story up to this point will help them understand the plot as it develops.

Activity Have students write paragraphs describing what they do to prepare for school. Then ask them to read aloud their paragraphs to partners, and have partners summarize what they heard.

Comprehension

15 What problem do the characters face on this page? (the squall) What is part of the solution to the problem? (getting the animals to safety) What about the crops? Is there a solution for them? (no) *Problem and Solution*

I shook my head, weary with Caleb's questions. Tears gathered at the corners of my eyes. But there was no time to cry, for suddenly Papa called out.

"Caleb! Anna!"

We ran outside and saw a huge cloud, horribly black, moving toward us over the north fields. Papa slid down the roof, helping Sarah after him.

"A squall!" he yelled to us. He held up his arms and **15** Sarah jumped off the porch roof.

"Get the horses inside," he ordered Caleb. "Get the sheep, Anna. And the cows. The barn is safest."

The grasses flattened. There was a hiss of wind, a sudden pungent smell. Our faces looked yellow in the strange light. Caleb and I jumped over the fence and found the animals huddled by the barn. I counted the sheep to make sure they were all there, and herded them into a large stall. A few raindrops came, gentle at first, then stronger and louder, so that Caleb and I covered our ears and stared at each other without speaking. Caleb looked frightened and I tried to smile at him. Sarah

78

carried a sack into the barn, her hair wet and streaming down her neck. Papa came behind, Lottie and Nick with him, their ears flat against their heads.

"Wait!" cried Sarah. "My chickens!"

"No, Sarah!" Papa called after her. But Sarah had already run from the barn into a sheet of rain. My father followed her. The sheep nosed open their stall door and milled around the barn, bleating. Nick crept under my arm, and a lamb, Mattie with the black face, stood close to me, trembling. There was a soft paw on my lap, then a gray body. Seal. And then, as the thunder pounded and the wind rose and there was the terrible crackling of lightning close by, Sarah and Papa stood in the barn doorway, wet to the skin. Papa carried Sarah's chickens. Sarah came with an armful of summer roses.

79

Comprehension

 What do you learn about Sarah by the way she dashes out into the squall to save her chickens? (She loves and cares for animals.) This isn't the first time that the author has chosen to show Sarah caring for animals. She brought her cat with her for a month visit, she wouldn't eat the chickens, and she brought apples to the horses. What makes this part of Sarah's character so important to the author? (Answers will vary. It shows that she gets very attached. It might mean she would be a good mother.)
Author's Purpose, Point of View

Comprehension

17 How does Sarah say that Maine and the prairie are alike? (Both places have squalls.) *Compare and Contrast*

18 **MAKE INFERENCES** What does it mean when Caleb smiles and smiles until he can smile no more? (He is happy that Sarah and Papa are together.)

TEACHING TIP

CONTEXT CLUES To place Caleb's comment, "Look what is missing from your drawing!" in context, explain that, earlier in the novel, Sarah had drawn a picture of the prairie fields using only dark charcoal. Looking at her drawing, Sarah had remarked that something was missing. Caleb pointed out the colors of a prairie storm—blue, gray, and green, the same colors of the sea when it storms—are missing from the picture.

CALEB

Sarah's chickens were not afraid, and they settled like small red bundles in the hay. Papa closed the door at last, shutting out some of the sounds of the storm. The barn was eerie and half lighted, like dusk without a lantern. Papa spread blankets around our shoulders and Sarah unpacked a bag of cheese and bread and jam. At the very bottom of the bag were Sarah's shells.

Caleb got up and went over to the small barn window. "What color is the sea when it storms?" he asked Sarah.

"Blue," said Sarah, brushing her wet hair back with her fingers. "And gray and green."

Caleb nodded and smiled.

17 "Look," he said to her. "Look what is missing from your drawing."

Sarah went to stand between Caleb and Papa by the window. She looked a long time without speaking. Finally, she touched Papa's shoulder.

"We have squalls in Maine, too," she said. "Just like this. It will be all right, Jacob."

Papa said nothing. But he put his arm around her, and leaned over to rest his chin in her hair. I closed my eyes, suddenly remembering Mama and Papa standing that way, Mama smaller than Sarah, her hair fair against Papa's shoulder. When I opened my eyes again, it was Sarah standing there. Caleb looked at me and smiled and **18** smiled until he could smile no more.

We slept in the hay all night, waking when the wind was wild, sleeping again when it was quiet. And at dawn there was the sudden sound of hail, like stones tossed against the barn. We stared out the window, watching the ice marbles bounce on the ground.

80

Activity

Cross Curricular: Math

THUNDER AND LIGHTNING The sound of thunder is caused by a rapid expansion of air that instantly heats up when lightning strikes. Because light travels faster than sound, we see a lightning flash before we hear thunder.

RESEARCH AND INQUIRY Have students research thunderstorms, and find an equation for calculating the distance of lightning from an observer. Then, have them create a graph that demonstrates this equation for intervals of 10, 20, 30, 40, and 50 seconds.

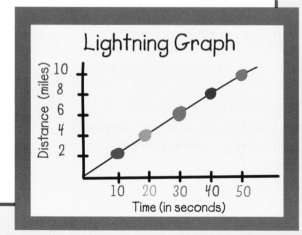

And when it was over we opened the barn door and walked out into the early-morning light. The hail crunched and melted beneath our feet. It was white and gleaming for as far as we looked, like sun on glass. Like the sea. **(19)**

It was very quiet. The dogs leaned down to eat the hailstones. Seal stepped around them and leaped up on the fence to groom herself. A tree had blown over near the cow pond. And the wild roses were scattered on the ground, as if a wedding had come and gone there. "I'm glad I saved an armful" was all that Sarah said.

81

Comprehension

(19) Here, the hail-covered prairie is compared to the sea. Why do you think the author has Anna make this comparison? (Answers will vary. The author wants to remind us of the main problem in the story: Anna, Caleb, and Papa want Sarah to live with them on the prairie, but Sarah is homesick for Maine and the sea.) *Author's Purpose*

Minilesson
REVIEW/MAINTAIN
Context Clues

Remind students that similes (comparisons that use the words *like* or *as*) and metaphors (comparisons that do not use those words) can help determine the meaning of an unfamiliar word.

• Have students read the last paragraph on page 80. Discuss how the author uses both a simile and a metaphor to describe hail.

Activity Invite students to choose another storm phenomenon, such as lightning, and have them write both a simile and a metaphor that might help someone understand the phenomenon.

Comprehension

(20) CHARACTER Sarah has helped with the roof, plowed and replanted the damaged field, and now Papa is keeping his promise to teach her to ride a horse. What does this tell you about Papa? (Papa is honest and reliable. He appreciates Sarah's hard work and understands why it's important to Sarah to be able to drive the wagon and go into town by herself.)

Only one field was badly damaged, and Sarah and Papa hitched up the horses and plowed and replanted during the next two days. The roof had held.

"I told you I know about roofs," Sarah told Papa, making him smile.

Papa kept his promise to Sarah. When the work was done, he took her out into the fields, Papa riding Jack who was sly, and Sarah riding Old Bess. Sarah was quick to learn.

(20) "Too quick," Caleb complained to me as we watched from the fence. He thought a moment. "Maybe she'll fall off and have to stay here. Why?" he asked, turning to me. "Why does she have to go away alone?"

82

CULTURAL PERSPECTIVES

FARMING Throughout the world farming is one of the most important occupations. Everyone needs food. Almost all the food you eat is raised on farms, and half the area of the United States is farmland.

RESEARCH AND INQUIRY Have students do research to learn about agriculture in another country, such as rice farming in India or banana crops in Ecuador. Then, have them present their findings in a paragraph with an illustration.

World Agriculture	
Country	Farmland
U.S.	50%
Thailand	34%
Spain	31%
Senegal	27%

"Hush up, Caleb," I said crossly. "Hush up."

"I could get sick and make her stay here," said Caleb.

"No."

"We could tie her up."

"No."

And Caleb began to cry, and I took him inside the barn where we could both cry.

Papa and Sarah came to hitch the horses to the **(21)** wagon, so Sarah could practice driving. Papa didn't see Caleb's tears, and he sent him with an ax to begin chopping up the tree by the pond for firewood. I stood and watched Sarah, the reins in her hands, Papa next to her in the wagon. I could see Caleb standing by the pond,

83

Comprehension

(21) **CHARACTER** Anna is cross with Caleb, but she, too, starts to cry when Sarah leaves. What does this tell about Anna? (That she is not as brave as she pretends to be, that she feels the same way Caleb does)

Minilesson

REVIEW/MAINTAIN

Long *i* and Long *o*

- Read page 83 aloud and have students raise their hands every time they hear you say a word with long *i*. List the words on the chalkboard. (*I, tie, cry, inside, driving, by, firewood*) Have students identify the three spellings for long *i*. (*i, ie,* and *y*)

- Repeat the process for long *o*, reading aloud page 82 and listing the words *only, told, know, old, go,* and *alone*. Add the word *loaded* to the list. Then have students identify the four spellings for long *o*. (*o, ow, o_e,* and *oa*)

Activity Have students make a class word wall of long *i* and long *o* words they discover in the story. Use different colored markers to highlight the different spelling patterns.

 Phonics Intervention Guide

Comprehension

22 Let's look closely at what is happening on this page. Sarah gets dressed and gathers apples and hay for the horses. Papa says to be home before dark, and Sarah tells the children to take care of Seal. Then, Sarah drives away. Where do you think she is going? What do you think will happen next? **Explain.** (Sample answer: Sarah is going to town. She will come back before dark, otherwise she would have said goodbye and taken Seal with her.) *Make Predictions*

one hand shading his eyes, watching, too. I went into the safe darkness of the barn then, Sarah's chickens scuttling along behind me.

"Why?" I asked out loud, echoing Caleb's question.

The chickens watched me, their eyes small and bright.

The next morning Sarah got up early and put on her blue dress. She took apples to the barn. She loaded a bundle of hay on the wagon for Old Bess and Jack. She put on her yellow bonnet.

"Remember Jack," said Papa. "A strong hand."

"Yes, Jacob."

"Best to be home before dark," said Papa. "Driving a wagon is hard if there's no full moon."

"Yes, Jacob."

Sarah kissed us all, even my father, who looked surprised.

22 "Take care of Seal," she said to Caleb and me. And with a whisper to Old Bess and a stern word to Jack, Sarah climbed up in the wagon and drove away.

84

"Very good," murmured Papa as he watched. And after a while he turned and went out into the fields.

Caleb and I watched Sarah from the porch. Caleb took my hand, and the dogs lay down beside us. It was sunny, and I remembered another time when a wagon had taken Mama away. It had been a day just like this day. And Mama had never come back.

Seal jumped up to the porch, her feet making a small thump. Caleb leaned down and picked her up and walked inside. I took the broom and slowly swept the porch. Then I watered Sarah's plants. Caleb cleaned out the wood stove and carried the ashes to the barn, spilling them so that I had to sweep the porch again.

"I *am* loud and pesky," Caleb cried suddenly. "You said so! And she has gone to buy a train ticket to go away!"

"No, Caleb. She would tell us."

"The house is too small," said Caleb. "That's what it is."

"The house is not too small," I said.

I looked at Sarah's drawing of the fields pinned up on the wall next to the window.

"What is missing?" I asked Caleb. "You said you knew what was missing."

"Colors," said Caleb wearily. "The colors of the sea."

Outside, clouds moved into the sky and went away again. We took lunch to Papa, cheese and bread and lemonade. Caleb nudged me.

"Ask him. Ask Papa."

"What has Sarah gone to do?" I asked.

"I don't know," said Papa. He squinted at me. Then he sighed and put one hand on Caleb's head, one on mine. "Sarah is Sarah. She does things her way, you know."

ANNA

85

Comprehension

23 Papa, Anna, and Caleb watch Sarah drive away. What do you think each might be thinking? Who would like to volunteer to play Papa, Anna, and Caleb and tell us how they feel? *Role-Play*

Fluency

READ DIALOGUE Have students find the question marks and exclamation marks in the dialogue on the second half of this page, beginning with line 16. Remind them that these punctuation marks tell them how to read dialogue aloud, with the question mark indicating a rising tone—and the exclamation indicating emphasis. Invite groups of three students to take the parts of Caleb, Anna, and Papa as they read the dialogue aloud.

Comprehension

24 **CHARACTER** Anna is confused about whether Sarah is coming back. What does she say, feel, and do that show her confusion? (She tells Caleb that Sarah will come back; she feels afraid to ask her father if that is true; she sets four plates on the table for dinner.)

"I know," said Caleb very softly.

Papa picked up his shovel and put on his hat.

"Ask if she's coming back," whispered Caleb.

"Of course she's coming back," I said. "Seal is here." But I would not ask the question. I was afraid to hear the answer.

We fed the sheep, and I set the table for dinner. Four plates. The sun dropped low over the west fields. Lottie and Nick stood at the door, wagging their tails, asking for supper. Papa came to light the stove. And then it was dusk. Soon it would be dark. Caleb sat on the porch steps, turning his moon snail shell over and over in his hand. Seal brushed back and forth against him.

Suddenly Lottie began to bark, and Nick jumped off the porch and ran down the road.

"Dust!" cried Caleb. He climbed the porch and stood on the roof. "Dust, and a yellow bonnet!"

86

Slowly the wagon came around the windmill and the barn and the windbreak and into the yard, the dogs jumping happily beside it.

"Hush, dogs," said Sarah. And Nick leaped up into the wagon to sit by Sarah.

Papa took the reins and Sarah climbed down from the wagon.

Caleb burst into tears.

"Seal was very worried!" he cried.

Sarah put her arms around him, and he wailed into her dress. "And the house is too small, we thought! And I am loud and pesky!"

Sarah looked at Papa and me over Caleb's head.

"We thought you might be thinking of leaving us," I told her. "Because you miss the sea."

Sarah smiled.

"No," she said. "I will always miss my old home, but the truth of it is I would miss you more."

Papa smiled at Sarah, then he bent quickly to un-hitch the horses from the wagon. He led them to the barn for water.

Sarah handed me a package.

"For Anna," she said. "And Caleb. For all of us."

The package was small, wrapped in brown paper with a rubber band around it. Very carefully I un-wrapped it, Caleb peering closely. Inside were three colored pencils.

"Blue," said Caleb slowly, "and gray. And green."

Sarah nodded.

Suddenly Caleb grinned.

"Papa," he called. "Papa, come quickly! Sarah has brought the sea!"

87

Comprehension

(25) MAKE INFERENCES When Sarah returns, Caleb says, "Seal was very worried!" What does Caleb really mean? (He himself was worried.)

(26) MAKE INFERENCES Has Sarah really "brought the sea," as Caleb says? What does he mean? (He means that Sarah has brought the colors of the sea and can now draw pictures of the setting she loves so much.)

WORD STRUCTURE/COMPOUND WORDS There are two compound words on this page. What are they? (wind-mill, windbreak) *Semantic Cues*

PREVENTION/INTERVENTION

WORD STRUCTURE/COMPOUND WORDS Write the words *windmill* and *windbreak* on the blackboard. Ask a volunteer to break the compound words into their parts. Talk about the meanings of these word parts. Then, have students suggest definitions for the compound words based on their word parts. Introduce students to these other compound words with *wind:* windbreaker, windshield, windsock, windbag, wind tunnel, windswept, whirlwind. *Semantic Cues*

Comprehension

(27) PLOT How did the story turn out? Let's fill in the outcome on our Story Elements charts.

Setting
Summertime, a farm on the prairie with a house, a garden, animals and fields.

What the Characters Want
Anna and Caleb want a mother. Papa wants a wife. Sarah wants to know if she would like to become part of a new family in a new place.

Plot Problem
Papa, Anna, and Caleb hope that Sarah will stay with them, but Sarah is homesick for her home in Maine and for the sea.

Outcome
Sarah will always miss the sea, but she would miss Anna, Caleb, and Papa more. She will marry Papa and be a mother to Anna and Caleb.

RETELL THE STORY Ask volunteers to tell the plot, the major events that happen in the story. Students may refer to their charts. Then have partners write one or two sentences that summarize the story. Have them focus on the problem of the story and how it is solved. *Summarize*

We eat our night meal by candlelight, the four of us. Sarah has brought candles from town. And nasturtium seeds for her garden, and a book of songs to teach us. It is late, and Caleb is nearly sleeping by his plate and Sarah is smiling at my father. Soon there will be a wedding. Papa says that when the preacher asks if he will have Sarah for his wife, he will answer, "Ayuh."

Autumn will come, then winter, cold with a wind that blows like the wind off the sea in Maine. There will be nests of curls to look for, and dried flowers all winter long. When there are storms, Papa will stretch a rope from the door to the barn so we will not be lost when we feed the sheep and the cows and Jack and Old Bess. And Sarah's chickens, if they aren't living in the house. There will be Sarah's sea, blue and gray and green, hanging on the wall. And songs, old ones and new. And Seal with yellow eyes. And there will **(27)** be Sarah, plain and tall.

88

REREADING FOR *Fluency*

PARTNERS Have students choose a favorite section of the story to read to a partner. Encourage students to read with feeling and expression.

READING RATE When you evaluate rate, have the student read aloud from the story for one minute. Place a stick-on note after the last word read. Count words read. To evaluate students' performance, see the

Running Record in the **Fluency Assessment** book.

(i) Intervention For leveled fluency lessons, passages, and norms charts, see **Skills Intervention Guide**, Part 4, Fluency.

Meet
PATRICIA MACLACHLAN

Although Patricia MacLachlan did not write as a child, she made up stories in her head. She imagined kings and queens, heroes and villains. When MacLachlan became an adult, kings and queens no longer captured her imagination. Instead, her children and the relatives she had known and heard about as a child became models for her characters.

MacLachlan becomes old friends with the people in her stories before she begins to write. "I ... have all sorts of conversations with myself and with characters I make up. . . . I talk with characters in the car, over a sink full of dishes, in the garden."

MacLachlan's story ideas may begin with people, but she also thinks a lot about the setting. Because she was born in Wyoming and raised in Minnesota, she says, "the western landscape has always been a powerful force in my life."

In the Newbery Award-winning story *Sarah, Plain and Tall*, character and place cannot be separated. Sarah, a mail-order bride—like one of MacLachlan's distant relatives—leaves her home on the eastern seacoast to begin a new life in the West. To the prairie she brings her love of Maine and her longing for the sea.

Other books by MacLachlan that you might enjoy are *The Facts and Fictions of Minna Pratt* and *Arthur, for the Very First Time.*

89

Comprehension

Return to Predictions and Purposes

Review with students their story predictions and reasons for reading the story. Were their predictions correct? Did they find out what they wanted to know?

PREDICTIONS	WHAT HAPPENED
The characters live on a farm.	The story takes place on a farm on a prairie far from the sea.
Someone visits from the city.	The visitor is Sarah from Maine, and she decides to stay.

INFORMAL
ASSESSMENT

ANALYZE CHARACTER AND SETTING

HOW TO ASSESS

• Can students draw conclusions about Sarah's character from her actions?

• Can students tell how the setting affects Sarah?

Students should recognize that Sarah usually does what she thinks is right, that she can be stubborn, and that she is loving toward all the other characters in the story.

FOLLOW UP If students have trouble analyzing character, help them brainstorm words to describe Sarah, and have students provide supporting details.

If students have trouble understanding the importance of setting, ask them how the prairie and the sea are alike and different.

LITERARY RESPONSE

QUICK-WRITE Invite students to record their thoughts about the story. These questions may help them get started:

• How would you describe the family before Sarah's arrival?

• What do you think of the way the family solves the problem of needing a wife and mother?

ORAL RESPONSE Have students share their journal writings and discuss the parts of the book they enjoyed the most.

COMPARE MEDIA If possible, show students a film version of *Sarah, Plain and Tall*. (See page T79.) Ask them to compare and contrast the film with the written story.

Story Questions

Have students discuss or write answers to the questions on page 90.

Answers:

1. Anna, Caleb, Papa, Sarah *Literal/Details*

2. Possible answer: Maine is Sarah's home. *Inferential/Problem and Solution*

3. Possible answer: Sarah leaves her home to travel to a place she has never seen. *Inferential/Draw Conclusions*

4. Possible answer: Sarah leaves Maine to live on the prairie. The children fear she will leave. Sarah stays because she would miss the family more than she misses the sea. *Critical/Summarize*

5. Both Amelia's father and Anna and Caleb's father work on farms. But Anna and Caleb's father owns his farm, whereas Amelia's father works for others. *Critical Reading/Across Texts*

WRITE A LETTER For a full writing process lesson see pages 93K–93L.

Story Questions & Activities

1. Who are the main characters in the story?

2. Why does Sarah miss Maine so much?

3. What makes you think that Sarah is adventurous? Explain.

4. How would you sum up the events in this story?

5. Compare the work done by Anna and Caleb's father with the work done by Amelia's father in "Amelia's Road." How is the work alike? What makes it different?

Write a Letter

Have you ever been caught in a storm? Write a letter to a friend about a time when the weather turned bad. Be sure to describe how you felt before, during, and after the storm. Use the correct form for writing a friendly letter.

Meeting Individual Needs

EASY

Name_____ Date_____ Reteach 16

Vocabulary

Read each clue. Then write the correct word from the list.

| huddled | overalls | reins | squall | pesky | eerie |

1. This word is an action word. _huddled_

2. This word names a piece of clothing. _overalls_

3. This word names a kind of storm. _squall_

4. This word describes annoying behavior. _pesky_

5. This word names something used with horses. _reins_

6. This word describes something strange and scary. _eerie_

Story Comprehension   Reteach 17

Circle the letter beside the answer to each question about "Sarah, Plain and Tall."

1. Why did Sarah leave Maine and come to the prairie?
   a. to have a vacation   (b.) to answer Papa's ad

2. Who told Sarah there will always be things to miss?
   a. Papa   (b.) Maggie

3. How did Papa feel when Sarah helped with the roof?
   (a.) surprised   b. angry

4. What did Sarah want to learn to do?
   a. work in the field   (b.) drive a wagon

At Home: Have students write sentences using three of the vocabulary words.
16–17   Book 4/Unit 1
                                               Sarah, Plain and Tall   4

ON-LEVEL

Name_____ Date_____ Practice 17

Story Comprehension

Write the names of the characters that fit each description.

1. All her life, she had lived near the sea. _Sarah_

2. They were neighbors who brought chickens. _Matthew and Maggie_

3. He doesn't remember his mother. _Caleb_

4. He brought roses for Sarah. _Papa_

5. She knew how to drive a wagon before Sarah did. _Anna_

6. They huddled in the barn during the squall. _Sarah and the family_

Answer each question.

7. Why is Caleb worried when Sarah drives away? _He thinks she may be going to town to buy a train ticket. Then she will go back to her home, and Caleb will never see her again._

8. Why do you think it was so important to Sarah that she learn to ride a horse and drive a wagon? _She would have more freedom to come and go and could go to town whenever she liked._

17   At Home: Have students write a new chapter in which   Book 4/Unit 1
     Anna or Caleb teaches Sarah a new task.   Sarah, Plain and Tall   5

CHALLENGE

Name_____ Date_____ Extend 16

Vocabulary

| eerie | overalls | reins |
| huddled | pesky | squall |

Suppose you were playing in a park far from your home when a storm comes. Think about how you might feel. Use some of the words above to write about what happened.

Answers will vary but should use vocabulary words correctly.

_____
_____
_____
_____
_____

Extend 17

Story Comprehension

Review "Sarah, Plain and Tall." On the day Sarah drives to town, the other characters go about their usual daily activities. What do the other characters do while Sarah is gone?

Answers will vary. Possible answers: Jacob goes to work in the fields.
Anna waters Sarah's plants and sweeps the porch. Caleb cleans the wood
stove. Anna and Caleb take lunch to their father in the field. They feed the
sheep. Anna sets the table. Jacob comes in from the field and lights the
stove.

At Home: Discuss how the daily activities of a character from "Sarah, Plain and Tall" may be similar to or different from your daily activities.
16–17   Book 4/Unit 1
                                               Sarah, Plain and Tall

Reteach, 17   Practice, 17   Extend, 17

90   *Sarah, Plain and Tall*

Make a Plan

Make a plan for Sarah's garden by listing the plants and seeds she will use. Decide on a plan for arranging the flowers or vegetables in the garden. You can put tall flowers in the back and shorter ones in the front. You can also arrange the flowers by color. An encyclopedia or a garden book can help you decide.

Paint a Picture

Many famous artists have painted the sea. Find a picture of the sea that you like. Then paint your own picture. Use watercolors to show the water. Give your painting a title, and sign it in one corner.

Find Out More

When a bad storm comes, the family members in the story have to stay in the barn until the storm passes. Use an encyclopedia or a science book to find out how a thunderstorm forms. Make a diagram of what you discover.

91

Story Activities

Make a Plan

GROUP Encourage groups of students to research different kinds of flowers and vegetables, paying attention to the dimensions and color of each plant at maturity. Then have groups plan and draw a garden. After drawing and labeling the garden, invite groups to share it, explaining their method for organization.

Paint a Picture

ONE Display pictures and paintings of the sea, and lead students in a discussion of the use of colors and brush strokes used to portray different moods of the sea. Provide painting materials. Have students paint a sea picture, write a title on it, and sign it. Display paintings on a bulletin board.

Find Out More

PARTNERS **RESEARCH AND INQUIRY** Have partners research thunderstorms in an encyclopedia, in a video, or on the Internet. Together, they should create a diagram that explains how a storm is formed.

*inter***NET** **CONNECTION** For more information about storm safety, students can visit **www.mhschool.com/reading**

Activity

SOCIAL STUDIES: MAINE Have students research the many species of shellfish inhabiting the waters along Maine's 5,500-mile coastline. Then have them choose one species and write a paragraph on how it develops its shell. Finally, have them draw a diagram of the shellfish.

What to Look For Check students' writing to make sure:
- they have organized their explanations step by step.
- they have explained a process clearly and concisely.

FORMAL ASSESSMENT

After page 91, see the Selection Assessment.

91

Study Skills

PARTS OF A BOOK

OBJECTIVES Students will:

• Identify parts of a Table of Contents.

PREPARE Preview the Table of Contents and point out its major parts. Point out that a chapter may be divided into sections, each of which may begin with a heading. Display **Teaching Chart 15**.

TEACH Review the Study Skills page. Invite volunteers to calculate the number of pages in each chapter.

PRACTICE Have students answer questions 1–5. Review the answers with them. **1.** Six **2.** Early History **3.** Page 30 **4.** The Maine Coast **5.** Possible answer: To learn the book's topics and where to find them.

ASSESS/CLOSE Have students look at the Table of Contents in a science or social studies book, then answer questions 1–4 based on this new Table of Contents.

Study Skills

Use a Table of Contents and Headings

"Sarah, Plain and Tall" is one selection in a much longer book. Longer books often have different parts. The **table of contents** is one of these parts. It lists the name of each unit, chapter, selection, and article. It also tells the page on which these begin. A chapter may be divided into sections. Each of these sections may begin with a heading. A **heading** is like a title. It tells what the section is about.

Page Number

TABLE OF CONTENTS
1. The State of Maine....5
2. Early History...........22
3. Recent History.........30
4. Recreation...............38
5. Tales and Stories.....45
6. Places to See...........54

Chapter Number **Chapter Title**

Chapter 4
RECREATION **Heading**
The Maine Coast
   Maine has many miles of coastline. It has both sandy and rocky beaches. The coast of Maine is beautiful. It attracts photographers, painters, and people who just want to see the scenery.
Winter Sports **Heading**
   Maine has nearly 60 ski areas. Each year, thousands of people travel from all over the country to take advantage of the beautiful slopes. Even when weather

Use the table of contents and chapter headings to answer these questions.

1 How many chapters are there in the book?

2 What is the title of Chapter 2?

3 On what page does Chapter 3 begin?

4 What is the first part of Chapter 4 about?

5 Why would you check the table of contents before reading a book?

Meeting Individual Needs

EASY	ON-LEVEL	CHALLENGE
Name_____ Date_____ Reteach 18	Name_____ Date_____ Practice 18	Name_____ Date_____ Extend 18
Use a Table of Contents and Headings	**Use a Table of Contents and Headings**	**Use a Table of Contents and Headings**

EASY — Reteach, 18

Use a Table of Contents and Headings

The **table of contents** gives you an idea of what the chapters in a book are about. It also gives page numbers. **Headings** in a section of text also give you an idea of what you will read about.

Table of Contents
Chapter 1. History of Horses 8
Chapter 2. Work Horses 20
Chapter 3. Race Horses 32
Chapter 4. Wild Horses 40
Chapter 5. Ponies 52

Chapter 2 Work Horses
On the Farm
   This breed of horses is the strongest and heaviest of all other horse breeds. Years ago these horses did the work that heavy farm machinery does today. They pulled wagons great distances and hauled plows through the fields.
Coach Horses
   Another type of work horse is called the Heavy Harness Horse, or the Coach Horse. These horses are good for light farm work, pleasure riding, or pulling coaches or buggies.

Use the samples to answer these questions.
1. What is the whole book about? Possible answer: Horses, their history, types of horses, and ponies.
2. What is the title of Chapter 4? Wild Horses
3. To learn about ponies, which chapter would you read? Chapter 5
4. What is the first heading in Chapter 2? On the Farm
5. What page would you check to read about race horses? page 32

Book 4/Unit 1
Sarah, Plain and Tall
At Home: Have students find the Table of Contents in a book and explain how it helps readers.   18

ON-LEVEL — Practice, 18

Use a Table of Contents and Headings

Answer the questions about the table of contents and the following section.

Table of Contents
UNIT 1 -   Covered Wagons Going West 12
Chapter 1 Planning the Route/Provisions.....................16
Chapter 2 Sleeping and Eating on the Trail.................36
UNIT 2 -   Prairie Hardship and Happiness 56
Chapter 3 Building and Hard Work...........................60
Chapter 4 The First Winter....................................82

Weather on the Trails
The weather made life on the trail hard. If it was too hot, the animals could get sick. If it rained too much, the rivers would flood. Winter months were dangerous because of snow storms. But on cool, summer nights, families would gather around the campfire to cook, share food, and sing songs.

1. How many chapters are there in this book? four
2. What are the two main parts of the book called? units
3. How is the first unit different from the second unit? The first unit is about the trail west and covered wagon life; the second unit is about building a home on the prairie.
4. In which chapter might the heading "Weather on the Trails" be found? 2
5. About how many pages are there in a chapter? 20 pages

Book 4/Unit 1
Sarah, Plain and Tall
At Home: Have students write unit and chapter heads for the topic of "Great Sports Stars."   18

CHALLENGE — Extend, 18

Use a Table of Contents and Headings

Here is the **table of contents** from a book that recounts the story of a family's move west and their adventures. The table of contents contains chapter numbers, page numbers, and **headings** for chapter titles and titles of sections within each chapter. Use the table of contents to answer the questions below.

Table of Contents
Chapter 1 Preparations
   The News 3
   Supplies 8
   Good-byes 15
Chapter 2 The Journey
   The Wagon Train 21
   Fording the River 36
   A Terrible Storm 42
   Crossing Mountains 50

1. What is the title of Chapter 2? What do you think the chapter is about? Tell why. The Journey. It probably tells about the family's journey west and some of the difficulties they encountered. Some of the headings are clues that there were difficulties.
2. On what page does Chapter 1 begin? How do you know? page 3; the first page number for the chapter is page 3.
3. How many section headings are there in Chapter 1? 3
4. Write sample table of content entries for chapter 3. Include in your entries the chapter title and 3 subheads with page numbers.

Book 4/Unit 1
Sarah, Plain and Tall
At Home: Look through several books at home. Discuss why some of the books have table of contents and some do not.   18

Reteach, 18   **Practice, 18**   **Extend, 18**

TEST POWER

THE PRINCETON REVIEW

Test Power

Test Tip
Check your understanding as you read the story.

DIRECTIONS

Read the sample story. Then read each question about the story.

SAMPLE

Whales

The largest creature on land or in the ocean is the blue whale. The blue whale can weigh up to 150 tons and can be 100 feet long. Although a newborn whale already weighs about 1.8 tons, it will double its weight within its first week.

Whales live in the ocean, but they are not fish. Like humans, whales are mammals. Whales breathe air through lungs, give birth to live young rather than lay eggs, and are warmblooded.

A whale breathes through its "blowhole," two nostrils at the top of its head. Some whales can stay underwater for two hours before they need more air.

1 How large can a blue whale become?

   A 1.8 tons

   B 100 tons

   Ⓒ 150 tons

   D 2 tons

2 Which is a **FACT** from the story?

   F Whales eat fish.

   Ⓖ A whale is not a fish.

   H A whale can weigh up to 550 tons.

   J Whales are the smallest creatures on Earth.

93

Read the Page
Have students read all of the information in the passage. Instruct students to pay attention to details.

Discuss the Questions

Question 1: This question requires students to recall a supporting fact. Remind students that they should *not* rely on their memories. They should always refer back to the passage. Instruct students to verify answers.

Question 2: This question requires students to determine which of the four choices is a FACT from the story. Read the answer choices as a group. Direct students back to the passage. Emphasize the importance of verifying the correct answer. Explain that all the incorrect answers will be close to the best answer, but a detail will make them false. Have students eliminate wrong answers.

Leveled Books

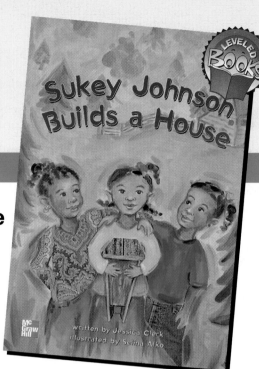

written by Jessica Clerk
illustrated by Selma Alko

---

i **Intervention** **Skills**
Intervention Guide, for direct instruction and extra practice in vocabulary and comprehension

---

Answers to Story Questions

1. Latesha had to give up her room to make room for Sukey.
2. Sukey is brave and honest. Her willingness to ask Latesha what is bothering her opened up the possibility of her sharing a room with Jas.
3. Sukey knew that the bat had a new home, just as she did.
4. It is a story about change and wanting to be accepted and loved. It is also about adapting to life in a new home.
5. Answers will vary.

The *Story Questions and Activity* below appear in the *Easy Book*.

Story Questions and Activity

1. What was the cause of Latesha's anger?
2. What kind of a person is Sukey? How does that further the story?
3. In what way did Sukey identify with the bat in the story?
4. What is the story mainly about?
5. If Sukey had to go to live on the prairie with Sarah Elisabeth Wheaton and her new family from *Sarah, Plain and Tall*, what do you think would happen? What would they talk about?

Bats and Bat Houses
Research bats and bat houses. Write a paragraph about them, explaining why building bat houses is helpful to the bats.

from Sukey Johnson Builds a House

EASY

Sukey Johnson Builds a House

Long *i* and Long *o*
☑ Story Elements
☑ Instructional Vocabulary: *eerie, huddled, overalls, pesky, reins, squall*

Guided Reading

PREVIEW AND PREDICT Have students look at the Table of Contents and discuss the illustrations up to page 5. Invite students to predict what the story will be about. List students' responses on a chart.

SET PURPOSES Encourage students to record in their journals reasons they would like to read *Sukey Johnson Builds a House*.

READ THE BOOK Have students read the story independently as you observe their reading behaviors. Use the following questions to guide students' reading.

Page 2: What do you know about Sukey Johnson by the end of page 2? (Her parents are not alive. She has lived in the city, but she is moving to the country to live with her cousins. She is sad, but she is trying to be brave.) *Character*

Pages 3–5: Why does Sukey think Latesha does not like her? (Latesha won't look Sukey in the eye when they meet, doesn't talk to her much, and stomps off when Sukey is given her room.)
Make Inferences

Page 7: Which words on page 7 have the long *i* sound spelled with just the letter *i*? (I, wild, I'm, find, outside) *Phonics*

Page 9: Reread the second sentence. What does *eerie* mean? (unfamiliar and frightening) *Vocabulary*

Page 16: How does Sukey's view of bats change? Why? (At first she thinks bats are creepy. But now she thinks they are graceful. She has learned about bats and living in the country.) *Cause and Effect*

RETURN TO PREDICTIONS AND PURPOSES Have students review their predictions listed on the chart. Ask which predictions were accurate and why. Encourage students to talk about whether their reasons for reading were fulfilled.

LITERARY RESPONSE Discuss these questions:

- How is this story an example of realistic fiction?
- What does the main character do that makes her seem real?

Also see the story questions and activity in *Sukey Johnson Builds a House*.

Leveled Books

INDEPENDENT

Laura and the Great Quake

- ☑ **Story Elements**
- ☑ **Instructional Vocabulary:** *eerie, huddled, overalls, pesky, reins, squall*

Guided Reading

PREVIEW AND PREDICT Preview the book to page 10. Discuss each picture, and invite students to write their story predictions in their journals.

SET PURPOSES Ask students to think about what they want to learn from the story. For example, they may want to know where the story takes place.

READ THE BOOK Have students read the story independently. Then ask the following questions to emphasize reading strategies.

Pages 4–5: When Laura looks at her surroundings in Assisi and listens to Nonna's stories, what does she think about? (people and events that were part of that setting, during the Middle Ages) *Setting*

Page 7: What can you conclude about Laura's character and Daniele's character, based on how they responded to the paintings? (Laura likes art and beautiful things; she wants to stay and look at everything. Daniele, being more interested in soccer, only thinks of the building in terms of his favorite sport.) *Character*

Page 9: Why does Laura think it's *eerie* that her brother might be human? (She's not used to seeing her brother perform acts of kindness.) *Vocabulary*

Pages 11–14: What does Daniele do that shows his care and concern for others? (He volunteers to get breakfast, cleans up, and thinks of an excuse that might encourage his grandmother to move.) *Character*

RETURN TO PREDICTIONS AND PURPOSES Have students review their predictions and purposes for reading. Were their predictions correct? Were their questions about the characters answered?

LITERARY RESPONSE Discuss these questions:

- Do you think Laura really disliked her brother as much as she said? Explain.

- What kind of problems do you think the family will face now that the grandmother has moved in? Do you think they will solve these problems? Explain.

Also see the story questions and activity in *Laura and the Great Quake.*

Answers to Story Questions

1. Daniele was never around when it was time to do his chores; Laura got stuck doing his chores as well as her own.
2. They must have been close because they e-mailed each other rather often.
3. The story takes place mostly in Assisi, a town in Italy. Assisi has a beautiful cathedral.
4. The story is about a girl's visit with her grandmother in Assisi, and the earthquake that forced the grandmother to move to Florence to live with the rest of the family.
5. Answers will vary.

The *Story Questions and Activity* below appear in the *Independent Book.*

Story Questions and Activity

1. What caused Laura's anger toward Daniele?
2. What kind of relationship did Laura and her cousin Celia have?
3. Describe the setting of this story.
4. What is the story mostly about?
5. If Sarah from *Sarah, Plain and Tall* could speak with Nonna and offer her some words of consolation, what do you think she would say?

Modern-Day Fresco

Laura and Daniele painted a "fresco" in their Nonna's room to cheer her up. If you could paint a fresco in your room, what would you want it to look like? Draw or paint a picture of your ideal fresco.

from Laura and the Great Quake

Leveled Books

CHALLENGE

Trevor, Knight-in-Training

☑ **Story Elements**

☑ **Instructional Vocabulary:**
eerie, huddled, overalls, pesky, reins, squall

Answers to Story Questions

1. Trevor was merely a shepherd boy from a small village.
2. Master Roger was a proud old man and would have refused assistance if the idea had not been proposed to him the way it was.
3. Master Roger recognized Trevor's hard work and began to appreciate him.
4. The story is about a boy's adjustment to living and working in a castle, far away from his village and his mother.
5. Answers will vary.

The Story Questions and Activity below appear in the Challenge Book.

Story Questions and Activity

1. Why was Trevor concerned that he wouldn't fit in at the castle?
2. What was the reason that Becca asked Master Roger to train Trevor?
3. How did Master Roger's attitude change toward Trevor and why?
4. What is this story mostly about?
5. Compare the change in setting for Trevor with the change in setting for Sarah from *Sarah, Plain and Tall.* Explain how each character was affected by the place to which he or she moved.

A Coat of Arms

You will need: scissors and crayons, paints, or markers

A knight wore a "coat-of-arms" on his shield so that he could be recognized in tournaments and in battle. Sometimes, the shield had symbols or animals that had special meaning for the knight. Cut out a shield shape from paper or cardboard and decorate it with your personal "coat-of-arms."

from Trevor, Knight-in-Training

Guided Reading

PREVIEW AND PREDICT Have students preview the illustrations up to page 12. Then have students write what they think will happen in the story in their journals.

SET PURPOSES Before students read the story, have them write several questions in their journals about what they would like to learn from the story.

READ THE BOOK To further develop the targeted reading strategies, ask the following questions after students read the story.

Page 3: Do you think Trevor has reason to worry about being accepted at the castle? How would you describe his personality? (Sample answer: No; he has already proven himself by tending to the sheep and by being concerned about his mother. So, he should be accepted at the castle.) *Character*

Page 9: Why do you think Trevor spends free time watching the squires and visiting the armorer's shop? (Sample answer: He has dreams of becoming a knight.) *Character*

Page 12: Based on story clues, what do you think *squall* means? Why would Wat be so concerned about getting the armor out of the *squall*? (A sudden, violent wind with rain; the rain would make the metal armor rust.) *Vocabulary*

Page 13: What do you think Trevor made? Why? (Answers will vary.) *Make Predictions*

RETURN TO PREDICTIONS AND PURPOSES Have students review their predictions and compare them with the story events. Were their predictions accurate? Did they learn new information that answered the questions in their journals?

LITERARY RESPONSE Discuss these questions:

• Do you think Trevor would make a good knight? What do you know about his character that will help you decide?

• Would you like to be a knight-in-training? Why or why not?

Also, see the story questions and activity in *Trevor, Knight-in-Training.*

Bringing Groups Together

Anthology and Leveled Books

Connecting Texts

RELOCATION CHARTS Write each selection title on a chart. Invite volunteers from each reading level to explain why the characters of each book move away from their home. Discuss the emotions each character expresses as a result of the move. Write students' responses on the chart.

Sarah, Plain and Tall	Sukey Johnson Builds a House	Laura and the Great Quake	Trevor, Knight-in-Training
• Sarah may move if she marries Papa. • She misses the people and the ocean.	• Sukey's dad dies, so Sukey moves in with her cousins. • She is afraid the cousins will not like her.	• Grandmother moves in with her family when her home is destroyed. • She does not want to leave her house and her friends.	• Trevor moves to a castle to work. • He is afraid he will not be accepted.

Viewing/Representing

INTERVIEWS Organize the class into four groups, according to the leveled book students read. (For *Sarah, Plain and Tall*, combine students of different reading levels.) Have group members work together to write an interview in which the main character answers questions relating to his or her feelings about moving to a new place. Invite groups to dramatize their interviews.

AUDIENCE RESPONSE Have students listen to each interview and ask questions at the end of the dramatization. Have presenters answer the questions while still in character.

Research and Inquiry

MORE ABOUT PEOPLE WHO RELOCATE These four fictional stories each involve a character who moves to a new place. Explain that real people also face adjustments when they move. Invite students to research techniques for making relocation easier. Have students find out:

• How to make a move: packing, hiring a van, calling utility companies, and so forth.

• How to learn the ropes in a new school and neighborhood.

• How to keep in touch with old friends and make new ones.

Have students create short how-to guides with pictures and lists. They can illustrate a cover and staple it to their book.

interNET CONNECTION To find out more about moving and adjusting to a new home, have students visit **www.mhschool.com/reading**

OBJECTIVES

Students will make inferences about and analyze character, setting, and plot.

Skills Finder

Story Elements

Introduce	19A-B
Review	41E-F, 67A-B, 93E-F
Test	Unit 1
Maintain	163,323,527,575

TEACHING TIP

SETTING Ask students to name the setting from their favorite movie or TV show. Encourage them to consider how a different setting could completely change a story.

SELF-SELECTED Reading

Students may choose from the following titles.

ANTHOLOGY

• Sarah, Plain and Tall

LEVELED BOOKS

• Sukey Johnson Builds a House
• Laura and the Great Quake
• Trevor, Knight-in-Training

Bibliography, pages T78–T79

Review Story Elements

PREPARE

Discuss Character, Setting, and Plot

Review: To make inferences about the characters in a story, students should pay attention to the actions, words, thoughts, and feelings. The setting can affect how the characters act, speak, think, and feel. The setting can also affect the plot, or what happens in a story. Ask students how the setting affects Sarah, a main character in the story they just read.

TEACH

Read the Passage and Model the Skill

Display **Teaching Chart 16.** Ask students to pay close attention to character and setting as you read the passage aloud.

Flowers for Sarah

Looking at the bright orange of the marigolds and sunny yellow of the zinnias made Sarah forget for a moment how much she missed the sea. "These will make a pretty garden," she thought. She dug into the damp soil to make a home for each plant. The sun was hot, and Sarah was glad she was wearing her broad-brimmed hat to shade her face. She took her water can and began to water a newly planted flower. A few drops spilled on her feet, and she laughed. Maggie, watching from the porch, smiled. "Maybe you'll put down roots in the soil, too," she said. "Maybe so," Sarah replied.

Teaching Chart 16

Discuss clues in the passage that help readers make inferences about the setting, character, and plot.

MODEL I can tell Sarah loves flowers because they make her forget about her home by the sea. I can tell she is beginning to like her new home because she is glad and is taking time to make it pretty.

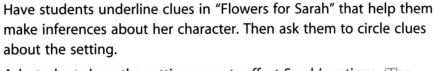

PRACTICE

Make Inferences About Character, Setting, and Plot

ONE

Have students underline clues in "Flowers for Sarah" that help them make inferences about her character. Then ask them to circle clues about the setting.

Ask students how the setting aspects affect Sarah's actions. (The flowers help Sarah forget her homesickness. The hot sun makes her appreciate the shade of her hat. The water in the watering can causes her to make a joke and feel playful.)

ASSESS/CLOSE

Write and Present an Old Tale

Have students create a new setting for a favorite tale or fable, such as "The Three Bears" or "The Ant and the Grasshopper." Ask them how the new setting will affect the characters. Have each group write its version of the story and share it with the class.

ALTERNATE TEACHING STRATEGY

STORY ELEMENTS

For a different approach to teaching this skill, see page T60.

i Intervention Skills Intervention Guide, for direct instruction and extra practice in story elements

Meeting Individual Needs for Comprehension

EASY	ON-LEVEL	CHALLENGE	LANGUAGE SUPPORT
Reteach, 19	Practice, 19	Extend, 19	Language Support, 22

EASY

Name_____ Date_____ Reteach **19**

Story Elements

As they read good readers keep track of the most important story elements: **characters**, **setting**, and the events that make up the **plot**.

Read the story. Then fill in the story map that follows.

Jackie spent most of the day at the department store. Her mom had suggested that she look for holiday gifts that didn't cost too much. Jackie wanted to find just the right gift for each of her three friends. And she did. She found a glass horse for Jennifer, a cloth purse for Ariel, and a book about lighthouses in Maine for René.

When Jackie returned home that evening, she and her mom went to work with lots of boxes and wrapping. They made each package as special as the gift inside. After dinner, Jackie was ready to deliver her gifts.

1. Characters	Jackie, mom
2. Setting # 1	department store during the day
3. Setting # 2	Jackie's home that evening
4. Event	Jackie goes to the department store.
5. Event	She finds three perfect gifts.
6. Event	She returns home.
7. Event	She wraps the gifts with her mother.
8. Ending	Jackie is ready to deliver the gifts.

At Home: Have students make a similar story map for a story they especially like.

19   Book 4/Unit 1 *Sarah, Plain and Tall* 8

ON-LEVEL

Name_____ Date_____ Practice **19**

Story Elements

Character and **setting** are closely linked to the **plot** of "Sarah, Plain and Tall." Sarah misses her home in Maine, but she also likes her new home on the prairie. Understanding what she likes about both places can help you understand Sarah's character.

In the chart below list what Sarah misses about her life in Maine and what she likes about her life on the prairie.

Misses About Maine	Likes About the Prairie
1. the sea	2. the family
3. her brother	4. neighbors
5. her aunts	6. chickens
7. her garden	8. Jack, the horse

9. Use the chart, the details from the selection, and your personal experience to describe the character of Sarah. caring; sensitive; determined; independent; shy; devoted; appreciates family, friends, and nature

10. Write a short description of the plot on the following lines. Answers will vary but should include: Anna and Caleb live on the prairie with their father. Sarah comes from her seaside home in Maine to visit and perhaps become their new mother. Everyone gets along well, but Sarah misses her home and the freedom she had there. Once she learns to ride a horse and drive a wagon, she feels free on the prairie, too. Everyone is happy because Sarah will stay with the family.

19   **At Home:** Have students draw the prairie or the sea.   Book 4/Unit 1 *Sarah, Plain and Tall* 10

CHALLENGE

Name_____ Date_____ Extend **19**

Story Elements

Think about Anna and Caleb in "Sarah, Plain and Tall." Both **characters** are afraid that Sarah is not going to come back when she goes to town alone. Why do you think they feel this way? How do Anna and Caleb feel about Sarah and why? Write a paragraph describing your thoughts. Include details to support your thoughts.

Answers will vary but should demonstrate student's understanding of character.

_____

Why do you think Sarah wanted to go to town alone? Did you think that she might not come back? Explain.

Answers will vary.

_____

On a piece of paper, illustrate a scene from "Sarah, Plain and Tall."

19   **At Home:** Have students look through a book with illustrations. Are the illustrations in color? Discuss how the illustrations enhance the story.   Book 4/Unit 1 *Sarah, Plain and Tall*

LANGUAGE SUPPORT

Name_____ Date_____

Past and Present, Near and Far

1. Think about the people, places and things that happened in the story, *Sarah, Plain and Tall.* 2. Write the words where they belong in the Venn Diagram.

the sea	Mama	a flower garden	Maggie and
the prairie	Sarah	horses	her children
the storm	chickens	Papa	the barn
	Seal the cat		Sarah's brothers

In the Past or Far Away
the sea
Mama
the storm
Sarah's brothers
Sarah

Past and Present
a flower garden
Sarah
Seal the cat
the storm

In the Story Now
the prairie
horses
Maggie and
her children
Sarah
chickens
Papa
the barn
Seal the cat

22 *Sarah, Plain and Tall* • Language Support / Blackline Master 10   Grade 4

Reteach, 19   **Practice, 19**   **Extend, 19**   Language Support, 22

93F

OBJECTIVES

Students will review problem and solution.

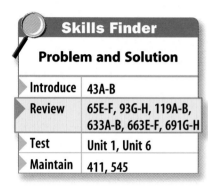

Skills Finder

Problem and Solution

Introduce	43A-B
Review	65E-F, 93G-H, 119A-B, 633A-B, 663E-F, 691G-H
Test	Unit 1, Unit 6
Maintain	411, 545

Review **Problem and Solution**

PREPARE

Discuss Meaning of Problem and Solution
Explain: In many stories, the characters' actions center on a problem. Thinking about the problem and how it is solved can make the characters and the story easier to understand.

TEACH

Read the Passage
Display and read **Teaching Chart 17.** Focus students' attention on the problem and how it is solved.

Painting the Sea

Sarah frowned. Her drawing of the sea just didn't look right in pencil and charcoal. What she <u>needed were paints and colors</u>. With those she could show the children the beautiful blues and greens of the sky and water back in Maine. Papa would see, too. Perhaps then <u>they would understand a little better what those things meant to her.</u>

Sarah put her drawing aside. She'd get the paints she needed somehow. Money wasn't the problem. She had that, but (the only store was miles away, which was too far to walk.) She quickly decided what she'd do. "I'll just have to learn to drive the wagon," she told herself. "Tomorrow I'll have my first lesson."

Teaching Chart 17

Model the Skill
Ask a volunteer to find and underline the words that tell what Sarah wants. Have another volunteer circle the words that tell why Sarah has a problem getting what she wants. Help students think about Sarah's problem and how she solves it.

MODEL Sarah wants green and blue paint, but it is too far to walk to town to buy some. She decides to solve the problem by learning to drive the wagon to town.

PRACTICE

Create a Problem and Solution Chart

ONE

Have students create a Problem and Solution chart. Help them get started. ▶ **Linguistic/Logical**

PROBLEM	SOLUTION
Sarah's sea painting doesn't look right.	She needs blue and green paint.
The paint store is far away.	Sarah decides to learn to drive the wagon.

ASSESS/CLOSE

Use a Chart to Summarize

Have students create a Problem and Solution chart for a familiar story. Have them use their charts to summarize the story.
▶ **Linguistic/Logical**

PROBLEM	SOLUTION
Cinderella needs a dress for the ball.	Her fairy godmother makes a dress for her.
The prince wants to find Cinderella.	He uses her lost shoe to figure out who she is.

ALTERNATE TEACHING STRATEGY
....

PROBLEM AND SOLUTION

For a different approach to teaching this skill, see page T64.

ⓘ Intervention ▶ **Skills Intervention Guide**, for direct instruction and extra practice in problem and solution

---

Meeting Individual Needs for Comprehension

EASY	ON-LEVEL	CHALLENGE	LANGUAGE SUPPORT
Problem and Solution	**Problem and Solution**	**Problem and Solution**	**Spin for Solutions**

EASY — Reteach 20

Name _____ Date _____ Reteach **20**

Problem and Solution

Sometimes one character's **problem** can affect other characters in the story. Often the other characters help find a **solution** to the problem.

Read the story. Then fill in the chart that follows.

Kelly wanted to get a pet. All her friends had pets.
Kelly had asked for a puppy for the past two birthdays, but she didn't get one. Her parents always seemed to avoid the issue. Kelly decided to explain to them how she felt.
Her mom and dad said there would be no one at home to walk the dog during the day. Dad asked, "What about a cat?"
But Kelly and her mom were worried that a cat would be too lonely by itself all day. "What about two kittens?" asked Dad. "They could keep each other company." Kelly liked the idea!

Kelly's Problem	Kelly's Solution
She wants a pet of her own.	1. She explains how she feels to her parents.
Mom and Dad's Problem	Dad's Solution
2. There would be no one to walk a dog.	3. Get a cat instead.
Mom and Kelly's Problem	Dad's Solution
4. The cat would be lonely.	5. Get two kittens.

Book 4/Unit 1
Sarah, Plain and Tall — 5

At Home: Have students extend the story, adding new problems caused by the kittens and some possible solutions. — 20

ON-LEVEL — Practice 20

Name _____ Date _____ Practice **20**

Problem and Solution

Read the story and answer each question. Answers may vary.

Molly found a ring on her way to play baseball. "What a pretty ring," thought Molly. "I should ask if anyone lost it." Then Molly heard the baseball coach call her name. She shoved the ring in her pocket and took off for baseball practice. Molly forgot all about the ring.
The next day, Molly heard Keisha say she'd lost her ring. Molly had left the ring at her house. She worried all that day because it was a day later and people might think she had wanted to keep the ring. Maybe she should just leave the ring at home and not mention it.
When Molly saw Keisha the next day, she knew she had to give the ring back. Keisha looked so sad. Molly knew it was better to give her the ring, no matter what the others thought.
"My ring!" shouted Keisha as Molly handed her the ring. She hugged Molly. No one asked when Molly had found it. Everyone was just happy Keisha had her ring back. So was Molly!

1. What was Molly's problem?
She found a ring and forgot to return it.

2. What solution did Molly think of at first?
She could just leave the ring at home and forget about it.

3. How did Molly learn that leaving the ring at home was the wrong solution?
Keisha looked so sad and really missed her ring.

4. What solution worked?
Molly gave Keisha her ring.

5. What would your solution have been?
Answers will vary but should mention returning the ring.

Book 4/Unit 1
Sarah, Plain and Tall — 5

At Home: Have students tell about a time they lost something that somebody needed and how that problem was solved. — 20

CHALLENGE — Extend 20

Name _____ Date _____ Extend ◆20

Problem and Solution

Most **problems** have **solutions**. Often a problem can be solved more easily by working with someone than by working alone. Write about a problem in "Sarah, Plain and Tall" where the characters worked together to solve it.

Answers will vary. Possible answer: The roof needed repair. Sarah and Jacob worked together to finish the work. The roof held through the squalls.

Suppose your school needs some new art or sports supplies. Think of ways to help your school. Would you try to solve the problem by yourself or together with other people? Explain your decision.

Answers will vary but should demonstrate an understanding of problem and solution.

Book 4/Unit 1
Sarah, Plain and Tall

At Home: Have students talk about daily problems students typically encounter. Discuss which problems are best solved alone and which problems are better solved with others. — 20

LANGUAGE SUPPORT

Name _____ Date _____

Spin for Solutions

1. Color the pieces that would help solve Anna and Caleb's problem *red*.
2. Color the pieces that would not help *blue*. 3. You and a partner take turns spinning the arrow six times each. 4. See who gets the most red pieces of the "pie" and solves the problem first.

Grade 4   Language Support/Blackline Master 11 • Sarah, Plain and Tall 23

Reteach, 20   Practice, 20   Extend, 20   Language Support, 23

93H

OBJECTIVES

Students will review synonyms and antonyms.

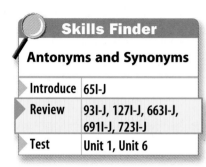

Skills Finder	
Antonyms and Synonyms	
Introduce	65I-J
Review	93I-J, 127I-J, 663I-J, 669I-J, 723I-J
Test	Unit 1, Unit 6

TEACHING TIP

SYNONYMS Encourage students to draw on personal experience as they work with synonyms. Make the listening activity less complicated by reading the passage twice. The first time students can listen for word pairs that are antonyms. During the second reading, they can listen for synonyms.

Review Antonyms and Synonyms

PREPARE

Discuss Meanings of Antonyms and Synonyms

Explain: Words that have opposite meanings, such as *huge* and *tiny*, are antonyms. Words that have the same or almost the same meaning, such as *small* and *little*, are synonyms.

TEACH

Read the Passage and Model the Skill

Have students listen for antonyms and synonyms as you read **Teaching Chart 18.**

Something for Sarah

They wanted to make something special for Sarah. So one day, while Sarah was at work in her garden, the two children took some paper and the pencils and ran out to the barn. Anna and Caleb couldn't wait to use the colored pencils. Anna drew a little blue pond with a big blue sky above it. Caleb drew a beautiful green tree surrounded by pretty green grass. The next time Sarah seemed sad about missing her old home, they would give her the pictures. They knew their pictures would make Sarah happy.

Teaching Chart 18

MODEL I think the sentence describing Anna's picture contains antonyms. It says one part of the picture, the sky, is very big. The other part, the pond, is little. *Big* and *little* have opposite meanings, so the two words are antonyms.

PRACTICE

Identify Synonyms and Antonyms

GROUP

Have volunteers circle antonym pairs and underline synonyms. Then have students discuss the meanings of each pair of words.

ASSESS/CLOSE

Use Antonyms and Synonyms in a Paragraph

Have students think of an antonym and a synonym for each word below. Then have them use each pair of words in a sentence. They may wish to draw pictures to accompany their sentences.

kind   start   wide

ALTERNATE TEACHING STRATEGY

ANTONYMS AND SYNONYMS

For a different approach to teaching synonyms and antonyms, see page T65.

 **Intervention** Skills

Intervention Guide, for direct instruction and extra practice in antonyms and synonyms

Meeting Individual Needs for Vocabulary

EASY	ON-LEVEL	CHALLENGE	LANGUAGE SUPPORT

EASY

Name_____ Date_____ Reteach 21

Synonyms and Antonyms

Synonyms are words that have almost the same meaning.
Antonyms are words that have the opposite meaning.

Read each sentence. Write the word from the list that means almost the same as the underlined word.

closed	glad	huge	smiled

1. After everyone was inside, we shut the door and ___closed___ the windows.
2. Large clouds covered the sky and ___huge___ drops of rain fell.
3. We were happy to be safe, and Papa was ___glad___, too.
4. I grinned and Papa ___smiled___ back.

Read each sentence. Write the word from the list that means the opposite of the underlined word.

softly	followed	dark	outside

5. The children talked loudly, but she spoke ___softly___.
6. The light faded and we were left in the ___dark___.
7. Inside it was calm, but ___outside___ it was stormy.
8. Papa led the way to the house, and we ___followed___.

At Home: Have students think of two pairs of synonyms and two pairs of antonyms to write in sentences.
21   Book 4/Unit 1 Sarah, Plain and Tall 8

ON-LEVEL

Name_____ Date_____ Practice 21

Synonyms and Antonyms

Synonyms are words that mean almost the same thing. Antonyms are words that have opposite meanings.

Write a synonym from the list to replace each underlined word.

noisy	tender	teach	squall	thin

1. Hannah wore a skinny ribbon in her hair. ___thin___
2. Tim's mom will show him how to do long division. ___teach___
3. David was very gentle with his baby brother. ___tender___
4. The loud music kept Jena from concentrating. ___noisy___
5. A wind blew up just as the game started. ___squall___

Write an antonym for the underlined word to complete each sentence.

cruel	silence	always	arrive	solution

6. First the room was filled with sound and then ___silence___.
7. One twin was kind and the other one was ___cruel___.
8. When Kevin has a problem, he finds a ___solution___.
9. As we leave the cafeteria, another class will ___arrive___.
10. I never eat peas, but I ___always___ eat carrots.

21 At Home: Have students write a synonym for every underlined word in the pairs of antonyms.
Book 4/Unit 1 Sarah, Plain and Tall 10

CHALLENGE

Name_____ Date_____ Extend 21

Synonyms and Antonyms

Write your own synonyms for the words below.

happen	party	confident	hard	pursue

Possible answers: happen/occur; party/celebration; confident/certain; pursue/chase; rigid/hard

Write your own antonyms for the words below.

hard	clean	happy	gather	success

hard/soft; clean/dirty; happy/sad; gather/scatter; success/failure

Begin a short story using at least three words from the first box of synonyms. Write three sentences. Then rewrite the sentences using the antonym of each word. How does your story change?

_____
_____
_____
_____
_____
_____

At Home: Make a list of common synonyms and antonyms.
21   Book 4/Unit 1 Sarah, Plain and Tall

LANGUAGE SUPPORT

Name_____ Date_____

Matching Game

1. Draw a solid line between synonyms (words that mean the same thing).
2. Draw a dotted line between antonyms (words that mean the opposite).

smile	cloudy
loud	squall
afraid	whisper
out loud	cry
storm	frightened
sunny	very softly
murmur	quiet

24 Sarah, Plain and Tall • Language Support/Blackline Master 12   Grade 4

Reteach, 21   Practice, 21   Extend, 21   Language Support, 24

93J

Personal Narrative

GRAMMAR/SPELLING
CONNECTIONS

See the 5-Day Grammar and Usage Plan on sentence combining, pages 93M–93N.

See the 5-Day Spelling Plan on words with long *i* and long *o*, pages 930–93P.

TEACHING TIP

Technology
Show students how to use the toolbar to set the tab spacing, thereby ensuring consistency of indentations.

Handwriting CD-ROM

Prewrite

WRITE A LETTER Present this writing assignment: Have you ever been caught in a storm? Write a letter to a friend about a time when the weather turned bad. Be sure to describe how you felt before, during, and after the storm. Use the correct form for writing a friendly letter.

FOCUSING CONTENT Lead students in a discussion about the purpose of the letter. Review the parts of a friendly letter. Remind students that they are to tell about their own experiences, so the letter should be written in first-person point of view.

Strategy: Complete a Chart Have students write these headings on a three-column chart: *Before the Storm, During the Storm, After the Storm.* Have students list what they saw, heard, and felt in each category.

BEFORE THE STORM	DURING THE STORM	AFTER THE STORM

Draft

REVIEW THE CHART Suggest that students review their charts and choose the information that clearly describes a time they were caught by bad weather. Remind them that a friendly letter should include a greeting and a closing signature.

Revise

SELF-QUESTIONING Ask students to assess their drafts.

• Did I use the correct letter format?

• Is this a letter I would write to a friend?

• Did I describe being caught in bad weather in a way that my friend could picture it in his or her mind?

PARTNERS

Have each student trade letters with a peer to get another point of view.

Edit/Proofread

CHECK FOR ERRORS Students should reread their letters for spelling, grammar, letter format, and punctuation.

Publish

SHARE THE LETTERS Have students "mail" their letters to classmates. Ask recipients to comment on the contents of the letters, noting which descriptions are clearest.

Dear Sammy,

It's been hot and dry here all summer. The water supply was so low that Mom and Dad weren't allowed to water the lawn. So when rain came, we were very happy.

But we didn't expect so much! We ran around shutting the windows. All night lightning flashed and thunder roared. Rain poured down. I could hear it pattering the roof and splashing through the rain gutters.

The next morning the rain stopped. But what a surprise we got when we went outside. We couldn't leave the porch because water covered the streets! Our electricity and plumbing weren't working. Rescue workers came by in boats and rowed us to a shelter. We had to stay there all that day and night until the water went down.

Your friend,
Sal

Presentation Ideas

ILLUSTRATE THE LETTER Have students draw pictures of themselves or their homes before, during, and after the storm.

▶ Viewing/Representing

MAKE A DOCUMENTARY Invite students to make a tape-recorded documentary about extreme weather. Volunteers can introduce the letters before individual students read them aloud.

▶ Speaking/Listening

Consider students' creative efforts, possibly adding a plus (+) for originality, wit, and imagination.

VIEWING STRATEGIES
Have students tell how specific details in one another's drawings show the differences before, during, and after the storm.

SPEAKING STRATEGIES
Remind students that, in reading their letters aloud, they should talk as though to a friend, vary tone and volume, and make eye contact with listeners.

LANGUAGE SUPPORT

ESL Ask students acquiring English to share their description and comparison charts with English-fluent partners. Invite the partners to check the words and phrases in the chart and offer corrections and additional suggestions, if they wish.

Invite students to include **PORTFOLIO** their letters or another writing project in their portfolios.

Scoring Rubric

Excellent	Good	Fair	Unsatisfactory
4: The writer	**3:** The writer	**2:** The writer	**1:** The writer
• uses many details to describe the events of the extreme weather in logical sequence.	• uses several details to describe the events of the extreme weather in logical sequence.	• uses just a few details to describe the events of the extreme weather.	• does not write about the events of the extreme weather.
• writes with a style that makes the letter seem real.	• consistently writes in first-person point of view almost all the time.	• does not show a clear sequence of events.	• includes no descriptive details.
• uses correct letter format.	• generally uses correct letter format.	• attempts to use letter format, but does not include all parts.	• does not use a letter format.

Incomplete 0: The writer leaves the page blank or fails to respond to the writing task. The student does not address the topic or simply paraphrases the prompt. The response is illegible or incoherent.

For a 6-point or an 8-point scale, see pages T107–T108.

Meeting Individual Needs for Writing

EASY

Describe a Place Have students think about a place they would miss if they were to move. Have them draw a picture of it and tell why the place is special.

ON-LEVEL

Journal Entry Have students write a journal entry about a day in the life of a person living on the prairie. What do they need to do to prepare food? What jobs must they do in the fields? Remind them to write from a first-person point of view.

CHALLENGE

Write a Story Have students write about the trip Sarah made to town by herself. What was Sarah doing in town? What did she see?

5 Day Grammar and Usage Plan

 ESL Write the words *and, but,* and *or* on the board and ask students to make up two-part sentences using these connectors. Give examples to get them started, if necessary.

DAILY LANGUAGE ACTIVITIES

Write each day's activity on the board or use **Transparency 3**. Have students join the sentences orally. For sample answers, see the transparency.

Day 1
1. Papa picked flowers. Sarah put them in her hair.
2. Old Bess was gentle. Jack was sly.
3. Rose laughed. Violet hooted.

Day 2
1. Matthew plowed. Papa plowed.
2. Caleb can write with a pencil. Caleb can draw with a crayon.
3. Papa waited. Papa worried.

Day 3
1. Sarah was plain. Sarah could cook.
2. Sarah planted. Papa plowed.
3. Sarah missed home. Maggie missed home.

Day 4
1. Caleb fed the chickens. Anna fed the chickens.
2. Sarah walked slowly. Anna ran fast.
3. Sarah drank milk. Sarah ate bread.

Day 5
1. Sarah can ride Old Bess. Sarah can play with Seal.
2. Sarah nodded. Sarah turned away.
3. Papa likes the farm. Sarah likes the sea.

Daily Language Transparency 3

93M   *Sarah, Plain and Tall*

DAY 1 Introduce the Concept

Oral Warm-Up   Read this aloud: *Sarah planted zinnias. Sarah planted marigolds.* Ask students to use one sentence to tell what Sarah planted.

Introduce Sentence Combining
Present and discuss the following:

Conjunctions

- A **conjunction** joins words or groups of words. *And, but,* and *or* are conjunctions.

- Two related sentences can be joined with a comma and *and, but,* or *or.*

- A sentence that contains two sentences joined by *and, but,* or *or* is called a **compound sentence.**

Present the Daily Language Activity and have students respond orally. Then ask them to write compound sentences using the conjunctions *and, but,* and *or.*

 Assign the daily Writing Prompt on page 66C.

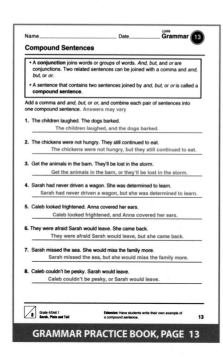

GRAMMAR PRACTICE BOOK, PAGE 13

DAY 2 Teach the Concept

Review Sentence Combining
Remind students that compound sentences make writing more interesting.

More About Sentence Combining
Subjects and predicates can be joined with *and* or *or* to form compound subjects and predicates.

Compound Sentences

- You can combine two sentences by joining two subjects or two predicates with *and* or *or.*

- A **compound subject** contains two or more simple subjects that have the same predicate.

- A **compound predicate** contains two or more simple predicates that have the same subject.

Present the Daily Language Activity. Have students write sentences with compound subjects and predicates.

Assign the daily Writing Prompt on page 66C.

GRAMMAR PRACTICE BOOK, PAGE 14

Sentence Combining

Learn from the Literature Review sentence combining. Read the first and last sentences in the next to last paragraph on page 75 of *Sarah, Plain and Tall*:

> **Jack leaned over and nipped at Sarah's overalls. Caleb and I stood behind Sarah.**

Have students identify which sentence includes a compound subject and which one includes a compound predicate.

Combine Sentences Present the Daily Language Activity, having students respond orally. Then have them look for compound sentences on page 72. Ask them to identify the sentences that include compound subjects or compound predicates.

 Assign the daily Writing Prompt on page 66D.

Review Sentence Combining Write on separate index cards simple sentences about the story characters. Distribute the cards to partners. Have students share aloud or in writing compound sentences that can be formed from the ones they receive. Present the Daily Language Activity.

Mechanics and Usage Display and discuss:

Sentence Punctuation

- Use a comma before *and, but,* or *or* when you join two sentences to form a compound sentence.

- Begin every sentence with a capital letter.

Point out that the second part of a compound sentence does not begin with a capital letter.

 Assign the daily Writing Prompt on page 66D.

Assess Use the Daily Language Activity and page 17 of the **Grammar Practice Book** for assessment.

Reteach Write the conjunctions and simple subjects and predicates from the sentences in the Daily Language Activities on large cards. Distribute one card to each student and have them hold them up. Ask them to arrange themselves so that they form a variety of compound sentences. You might make more than three conjunction cards.

Have students write their compound sentences on a class chart.

Use page 18 of the **Grammar Practice Book** for additional reteaching.

 Assign the daily Writing Prompt on page 66D.

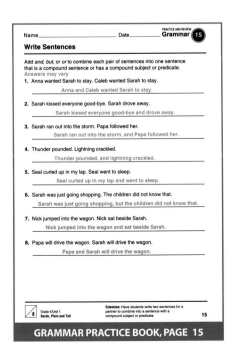

GRAMMAR PRACTICE BOOK, PAGE 15

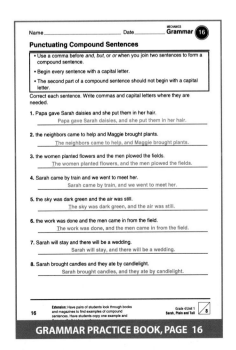

GRAMMAR PRACTICE BOOK, PAGE 16

GRAMMAR PRACTICE BOOK, PAGE 17

5 Day Spelling Plan

DICTATION SENTENCES

Spelling Words

1. The tiger walked on the ledge.
2. We will drive to the beach.
3. Did she reply to your letter?
4. The car started to roll down the hill.
5. Write a short note, please.
6. The crow has a big nest.
7. We planted an oak tree.
8. Iron the dress, please.
9. You and your brother look alike.
10. There is a large supply of water.
11. Slice one tomato.
12. Scrub the stove, please.
13. Put the pan below the sink.
14. He gave a groan when he saw his grade.
15. What is the title of the song?
16. The pine is a tall tree.
17. The sky overhead is cloudy.
18. We chose a black cat.
19. Is that egg hollow?
20. File out of the school.

Challenge Words

21. The flute made an eerie sound.
22. People huddled in the shed.
23. A pesky fly buzzed around.
24. Don't drop the reins!
25. I got wet in the squall.

DAY 1 — Pretest

Assess Prior Knowledge Use the Dictation Sentences at the left and **Spelling Practice Book** page 13 for the pretest. Allow students to correct their own papers. Students who require a modified list may be tested on the first ten words.

Spelling Words		Challenge Words
1. tiger	11. tomato	21. **eerie**
2. **drive**	12. **stove**	22. **huddled**
3. reply	13. below	23. **pesky**
4. roll	14. groan	24. **reins**
5. note	15. title	25. **squall**
6. **crow**	16. pine	
7. oak	17. **overhead**	
8. iron	18. chose	
9. alike	19. hollow	
10. supply	20. file	

*Note: Words in **dark type** are from the story.*

Word Study On page 14 of the **Spelling Practice Book** are word study steps and an at-home activity.

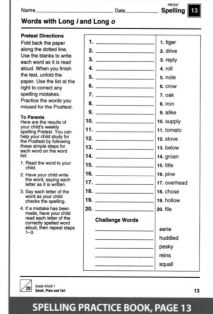

SPELLING PRACTICE BOOK, PAGE 13

WORD STUDY STEPS AND ACTIVITY, PAGE 14

DAY 2 — Explore the Pattern

Sort and Spell Words Say *drive* and *stove*. Ask students what vowel sound they hear in each word. (/ī/; /ō/) Have students sort the Spelling Words as below.

Words with Long *i* Spelled

i-e	*i*	*y*
drive	tiger	reply
alike	iron	supply
pine	title	
file		

Words with Long *o* Spelled

o	*o-e*	*ow*	*oa*
roll	note	crow	oak
tomato	stove	below	groan
overhead	chose	hollow	

Spelling Patterns In the spelling pattern CVCe (consonant-vowel-consonant-e), the silent *e* helps make the vowel sound long. Ask: What would happen if you forgot the silent *e* in *pine* or *note*? Have students write more words with the pattern CVCe.

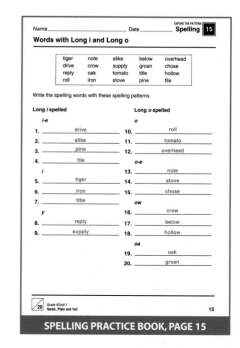

SPELLING PRACTICE BOOK, PAGE 15

Words with Long *i* and Long *o*

DAY 3 — Practice and Extend

Word Meaning: Analogies Remind students that an analogy is a comparison between two things that are alike in some way. Give this example: *tiger:animal::oak: tree.* A tiger is a kind of animal, and an oak is a kind of tree. Ask students to complete the following analogies using spelling words and then create their own: *bed:bedroom::_____:kitchen (stove); fly:plane::_____:car (drive); _____:bird::pine:tree (crow).*

If students need extra practice, have partners give each other a midweek test.

Glossary Use the Glossary to identify word histories. Have partners:

- look up *squall* in the Glossary.
- find the word history for *squall.*
- write the year *squall* first appeared in the English language. (1699)
- write the Swedish word on which *squall* is probably based, and its meaning. (*skval,* "rushing water")

Spelling 16 — PRACTICE AND EXTEND

Name_____ Date_____

Words with Long *i* and Long *o*

tiger	note	alike	below	overhead
drive	crow	supply	groan	chose
reply	oak	tomato	title	hollow
roll	iron	stove	pine	file

Complete each sentence below with a spelling word.

1. If your shirt gets wrinkled, you can use my ___iron___ .
2. When I grow up, my mom will teach me to ___drive___ a car.
3. A large black ___crow___ flew into the clouds.
4. The ___title___ of this story is Sarah, Plain and Tall.
5. The ___tiger___ took a nap in its cage at the zoo.
6. Mom used the top of our ___stove___ to fry onions.
7. Acorns are seeds from big ___oak___ trees.
8. At the office, all papers are kept in a ___file___ .
9. A ___pine___ tree has long, thin needles for leaves.
10. I keep a large ___supply___ of dog food in the house.

What Does it Mean?
Write the spelling word that has the same, or almost the same, meaning.

11. empty ___hollow___ 15. under ___below___
12. answer ___reply___ 16. above ___overhead___
13. picked out ___chose___ 17. moan ___groan___
14. the same or similar ___alike___ 18. letter ___note___

Challenge Extension: Have students write fill-in sentences for each Challenge Word. Have each student exchange sentences with a partner and fill each other's sentences.

16 Grade 4/Unit 1
Sarah, Plain and Tall 18

SPELLING PRACTICE BOOK, PAGE 16

DAY 4 — Proofread and Write

Proofread Sentences Write these sentences on the chalkboard, including the misspelled words. Ask students to proofread, circling incorrect spellings and writing the correct spellings. There are two spelling errors in each sentence.

> I ⟨choze⟩ a ⟨rol⟩ and cheese to eat. (chose, roll)
>
> A ⟨tigger⟩ rested ⟨beloe⟩ the tree. (tiger, below)

Have students create additional sentences with errors for partners to correct.

 Have students use as many **WRITING** Spelling Words as possible in the daily Writing Prompt on page 66D. Remind students to proofread their writing for errors in spelling, grammar, and punctuation.

Spelling 17 — PROOFREAD AND WRITE

Name_____ Date_____

Words with Long *i* and Long *o*

Proofreading Activity
There are six spelling mistakes in the paragraph below. Circle the misspelled words. Write the words correctly on the lines below.

Sarah just got back from town. She brought us a ⟨suply⟩ of food for dinner. She cooked rich, delicious ⟨tomado⟩ soup on the ⟨stoov.⟩ Then she made us warm, brown dinner ⟨rowls.⟩ We ate outside, in the shade of the huge, old ⟨oke⟩ tree. ⟨Overhed,⟩ the birds sang to each other in the branches. It was a wonderful day, and I was very happy.

1. ___supply___ 3. ___stove___ 5. ___oak___
2. ___tomato___ 4. ___rolls___ 6. ___overhead___

Writing Activity
Sarah liked to drive to town. Write a short story about a drive you would like to take. Use four spelling words in your writing.

_____
_____
_____
_____

18 Grade 4/Unit 1
Sarah, Plain and Tall 17

SPELLING PRACTICE BOOK, PAGE 17

DAY 5 — Assess and Reteach

Assess Students' Knowledge Use page 18 of the **Spelling Practice Book** or the Dictation Sentences on page 93O for the posttest.

Personal Word List If students **JOURNAL** have trouble with any words in this lesson, have them add to their personal lists in their journals. Suggest that students look up the definition of each troublesome word in the dictionary and then paraphrase the definition.

Students should refer to their word lists during later writing activities.

Spelling 18 — POSTTEST

Name_____ Date_____

Words with Long *i* and Long *o*

Look at the words in each set below. One word in each set is spelled correctly. Use a pencil to fill in the circle next to the correct word. Before you begin, look at the sample sets of words. Sample A has been done for you. Do Sample B by yourself. When you are sure you know what to do, you may go on with the rest of the page.

Sample A (A) groo ● grow (C) groe (D) groh
Sample B ● vote (F) vot (G) voat (H) voot

1. (A) driv ● drive (C) driev (D) dryve
2. ● crow (F) craw (G) croe (H) croo
3. (A) pyn (B) pihn (C) pien ● pine
4. (E) alick (F) aliek ● alike (H) alik
5. ● oke (F) oak (G) ok (H) oek
6. ● below (F) bilow (G) beloe (H) beloo
7. (A) fil ● file (C) fiel (D) fyel
8. (E) supplie (F) suply (G) suppley ● supply
9. (A) grone (B) groen ● groan (D) graon
10. (E) nowt (F) noot (G) noet ● note
11. (A) tornado ● tomato (C) toomatoe (D) tomatoe
12. (E) stoove (F) stov ● stove (H) stohve
13. ● overhead (B) ovuhead (C) overhed (D) overhad
14. (E) choos ● chose (G) chois (H) choss
15. (A) hollo (B) holluh (C) holloh ● hollow
16. ● tiger (F) tiegr (G) tyger (H) tigger
17. (A) iorn (B) ivern ● iron (D) iern
18. (E) rol ● roll (G) rool (H) rowl
19. (A) tiltell (B) titel (C) tietl ● title
20. (E) replyve ● reply (G) replie (H) repli

18 Grade 4/Unit 1
Sarah, Plain and Tall 20

SPELLING PRACTICE BOOK, PAGE 18

93P

Concept
- Migration

Comprehension
- Main Idea

Vocabulary
- assured
- horizon
- jagged
- mature
- nursery
- squealed

Reaching All Learners

Anthology

Seal Journey

Selection Summary Students will read about a photographer and his son who go to Prince Edward Island to learn about the life cycle of harp seals.

Stories in Art focuses on the **comprehension** skill

Reading Strategy applies the **comprehension** skill

Listening Library

INSTRUCTIONAL pages 96–117

About the Author/Photographer In 1981, Richard Sobol was commissioned by a French photo agency to take pictures of the harp seal hunt. His photographs showed the cruelty and inhumanity of the seal fur trade and helped bring attention to the need for laws to protect the seals. In 1990, he returned with his son Jonah to photograph the now protected seals. He turned his experiences into a book. Sobol's goal in writing nature books for children is both to inform and entertain young readers.

Same Concept, Skills and Vocabulary!

Leveled Books

EASY
Lesson on pages 117A and 117D

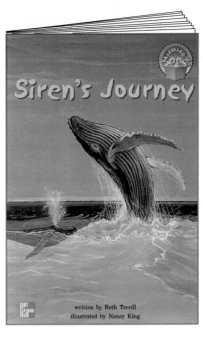

INDEPENDENT
Lesson on pages 117B and 117D

CHALLENGE
Lesson on pages 117C and 117D

Leveled Practice

EASY
Reteach, 22–28 blackline masters with reteaching opportunities for each assessed skill

INDEPENDENT/ON-LEVEL
Practice, 22–28 workbook with Take-Home stories and practice opportunities for each assessed skill and story comprehension

CHALLENGE
Extend, 22–28 blackline masters that offer challenge activities for each assessed skill

Quizzes Prepared by Accelerated Reader®

WORKSTATION Activities

Social Studies ... Map Skills, *98*

Science .... Water Mammals, *102*

Math .... Seal Math, *104*
Estimating Distances, *115*

Language Arts .. Read Aloud, *94E*

Cultural Perspectives...... The Inuit and Seals, *108*

Writing .... Photo Essay, *114*

Research and Inquiry ...... Find Out More, *115*

Internet Activities .... www.mhschool.com/reading

Suggested Lesson Planner

READING AND LANGUAGE ARTS

- ● Comprehension
- ● Vocabulary
- ● Phonics/Decoding
- ● Study Skills
- ● Listening, Speaking, Viewing, Representing

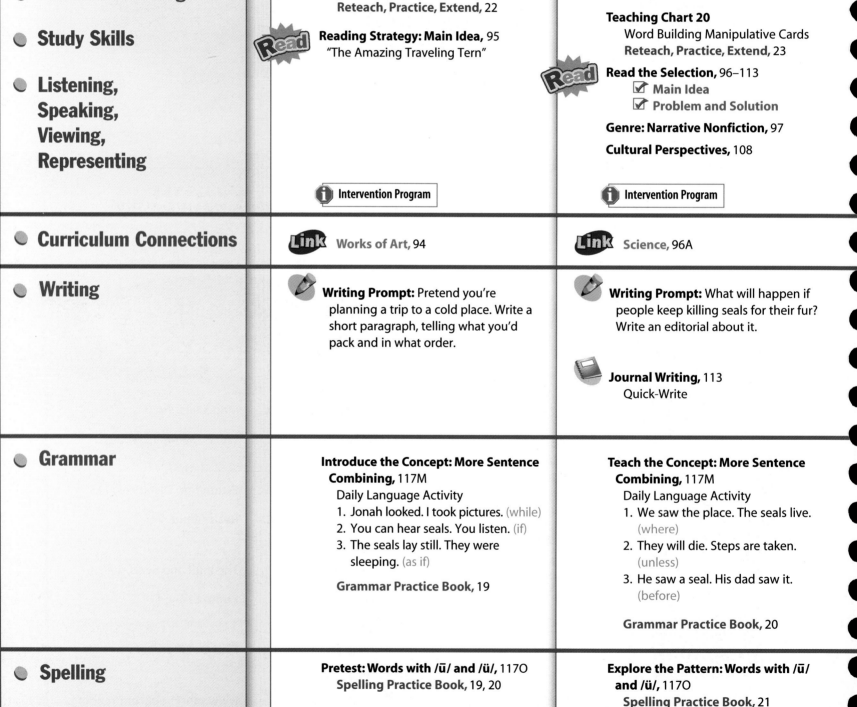

DAY 1 — *Focus on Reading and Skills*

Read **Read Aloud: Poetry,** 94E
"Seal"

Develop Visual Literacy, 94

☑ **Introduce Main Idea,** 95A–95B
   Teaching Chart 19
   Reteach, Practice, Extend, 22

Read **Reading Strategy: Main Idea,** 95
"The Amazing Traveling Tern"

ⓘ **Intervention Program**

DAY 2 — *Read the Literature*

Build Background, 96A
Develop Oral Language

Vocabulary, 96B–96C

assured	jagged	nursery
horizon	mature	squealed

Teaching Chart 20
Word Building Manipulative Cards
Reteach, Practice, Extend, 23

Read **Read the Selection,** 96–113
☑ Main Idea
☑ Problem and Solution

Genre: Narrative Nonfiction, 97

Cultural Perspectives, 108

ⓘ **Intervention Program**

● Curriculum Connections

Link Works of Art, 94

Link Science, 96A

● Writing

Writing Prompt: Pretend you're planning a trip to a cold place. Write a short paragraph, telling what you'd pack and in what order.

Writing Prompt: What will happen if people keep killing seals for their fur? Write an editorial about it.

Journal Writing, 113
Quick-Write

● Grammar

Introduce the Concept: More Sentence Combining, 117M
Daily Language Activity
1. Jonah looked. I took pictures. (while)
2. You can hear seals. You listen. (if)
3. The seals lay still. They were sleeping. (as if)

Grammar Practice Book, 19

Teach the Concept: More Sentence Combining, 117M
Daily Language Activity
1. We saw the place. The seals live. (where)
2. They will die. Steps are taken. (unless)
3. He saw a seal. His dad saw it. (before)

Grammar Practice Book, 20

● Spelling

Pretest: Words with /ū/ and /ü/, 117O
Spelling Practice Book, 19, 20

Explore the Pattern: Words with /ū/ and /ü/, 117O
Spelling Practice Book, 21

Meeting Individual Needs

 ✓ = Skill Assessed in Unit Test

ⓘ **Intervention Program Available**

 DAY 3 *Read the Literature*

Rereading for Fluency, 112

Story Questions and Activities, 114–115
  Reteach, Practice, Extend, 24

Study Skill, 116
  ✓ Parts of a Book
  Teaching Chart 21
  Reteach, Practice, Extend, 25

Test Power, 117

 Read the Leveled Books, 117A–117D
  Guided Reading
  /ū/ and /ü/
  ✓ Main Idea
  ✓ Instructional Vocabulary

ⓘ Intervention Program

DAY 4 *Build Skills*

 Read the Leveled Books and Self-Selected Books

✓ **Review Main Idea,** 117E–117F
  Teaching Chart 22
  Reteach, Practice, Extend, 26
  Language Support, 30

✓ **Review Make Inferences,** 117G–117H
  Teaching Chart 23
  Reteach, Practice, Extend, 27
  Language Support, 31

Minilessons, 99, 101, 103, 109

Writer's Craft, 110

ⓘ Intervention Program

DAY 5 *Build Skills*

 Read Self-Selected Books

✓ **Review Multiple-Meaning Words,** 117I–117J
  Teaching Chart 24
  Reteach, Practice, Extend, 28
  Language Support, 32

Listening, Speaking, Viewing, Representing, 117L

Minilessons, 99, 103, 109

Phonics Review,
  /ū/ and /ü/, 101

Phonics/Phonemic Awareness Practice Book, 13–16

ⓘ Intervention Program

 Activity Social Studies, 98

 Activity Science, 102

Activity Math, 104, 115

Writing Prompt: Imagine you're an adult harp seal. Write a paragraph about how you've changed since you were born.

Writing Process: Photo Essay, 117K
Prewrite, Draft

Writing Prompt: Ask Jonah what he did before and after he saw the seals. Write a paragraph about your conversation.

Writing Process: Photo Essay, 117K
Revise

Meeting Individual Needs for Writing, 117L

Writing Prompt: What did you know about seals before reading *Seal Journey*, and what do you know now? Tell the author in a letter.

Writing Process: Photo Essay, 117K
Edit/Proofread, Publish

Review and Practice: More Sentence Combining, 117N
Daily Language Activity
1. He looks out the window. We fly. (while)
2. We watched the seals. It got dark. (until)
3. Jonah put down the seal. It was time to go. (because)

Grammar Practice Book, 21

Review and Practice: More Sentence Combining, 117N
Daily Language Activity
1. I was happy. The seals were safe. (because)
2. I took pictures. I arrived. (when)
3. The pup swims. It learns how. (after)

Grammar Practice Book, 22

Assess and Reteach: More Sentence Combining, 117N
Daily Language Activity
1. The seals head north. The ice melts. (when)
2. Seals were hunted. People cared. (until)
3. We walked softly. We were nervous. (because)

Grammar Practice Book, 23, 24

Practice and Extend: Words with /ū/ and /ü/, 117P
Spelling Practice Book, 22

Proofread and Write: Words with /ū/ and /ü/, 117P
Spelling Practice Book, 23

Assess and Reteach: Words with /ū/ and /ü/, 117P
Spelling Practice Book, 24

Link Language Arts

Read Aloud

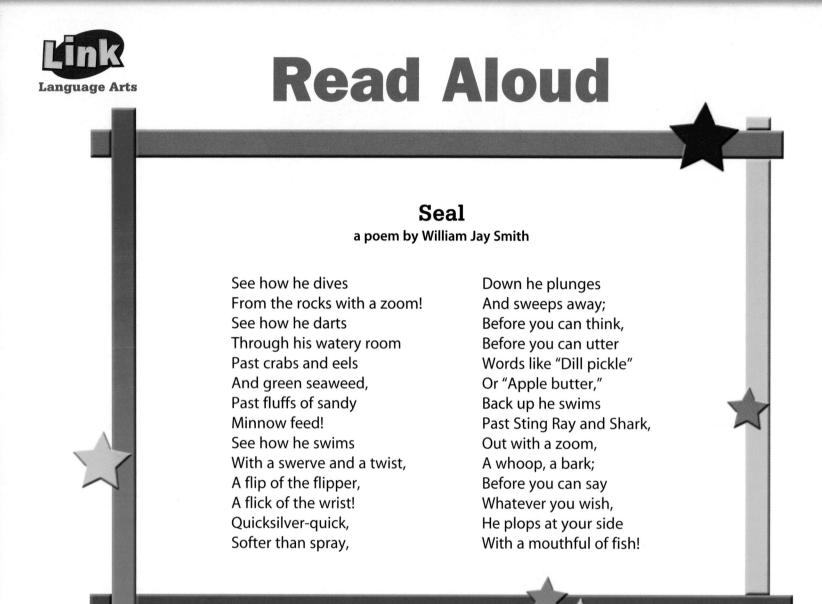

Seal
a poem by William Jay Smith

See how he dives
From the rocks with a zoom!
See how he darts
Through his watery room
Past crabs and eels
And green seaweed,
Past fluffs of sandy
Minnow feed!
See how he swims
With a swerve and a twist,
A flip of the flipper,
A flick of the wrist!
Quicksilver-quick,
Softer than spray,

Down he plunges
And sweeps away;
Before you can think,
Before you can utter
Words like "Dill pickle"
Or "Apple butter,"
Back up he swims
Past Sting Ray and Shark,
Out with a zoom,
A whoop, a bark;
Before you can say
Whatever you wish,
He plops at your side
With a mouthful of fish!

Oral Comprehension

LISTENING AND SPEAKING Read the poem aloud. Suggest students visualize, as you read, the pictures the poet paints with words. Afterward, ask:

• What is a "watery room"?

• In the poem, what is "softer than spray"? Why?

Then reread the poem. Explain that a poem's **tempo** is its speed or pace when read aloud. Discuss why a fast tempo is appropriate for this poem.

GENRE STUDY: POETRY Discuss some of the literary devices and techniques used in "Seal."

• Have students list the verbs in the poem and explain how these words help them picture the way the seal moves. Have students point out other vivid words in the poem, such as the nouns *fluffs*, *swerve*, and *mouthful*.

• Have students write down the last word of each line and then identify the poem's ABCB rhyme scheme.

• Discuss how the poet uses alliteration (the repetition of beginning sounds) and assonance (the repetition of vowel sounds) in lines such as, "A flip of the flipper/A flick of the wrist."

Activity Have volunteers act out the seal's movements as you read the poem aloud. Ask, "How did the colorful verbs influence your movements?"

▶ **Kinesthetic/Linguistic**

Develop Visual Literacy

Link

Works of Art

Stories in Art

Like stories or essays, a work of art can have a main idea and details that support it.

Look at this early American quilt. What do you see? What story might the quilt be telling? What does it say about a place and its people? What is the story's main idea?

Look at each of the squares in the quilt. How does each square add a detail to the story being told in the quilt? If you could step into one of the squares, which square would you choose? Why?

Burdick-Childs Family Quilt, 1876
The Shelburne Museum, Shelburne, VT

94

Objective: Identify Main Idea and Supporting Details

VIEWING Have students look closely at the clothing, architecture, and furniture shown in the quilt. Ask: "How do the styles help the viewer know that the quilt is old? What kinds of animals are depicted?" Have students discuss why those particular animals might have been chosen by the artist.

Read the page with students, encouraging individual interpretations of the quilt. Ask students to try to discover the main idea of the story being told in the quilt by looking at the details in the individual squares. For example:

- The people are engaged in a variety of activities.
- Some buildings seem to be in a city or downtown area. Others stand alone or seem to be set in the country.

REPRESENTING Have students pick one or two squares from the quilt and act out a little play, paying careful attention to the details shown.

94

OBJECTIVES

Students will identify the main idea and supporting details in a story.

Skills Finder	
Main Idea	
Introduce	95A-B
Review	117E, 127E-F
Test	Unit 1
Maintain	149, 291, 307, 623

LANGUAGE SUPPORT

ESL Write on the board a sentence that could be the main idea of a paragraph. For example, *Children who live in big cities are lucky*. Then ask students to give reasons why this may be true and write them on the board. Show how the details they gave support the main idea.

Introduce Main Idea

PREPARE

Discuss the Main Idea in a Book
Have students think of a book they have read recently. Ask: What was the main, or most important, idea? What details and examples supported the main idea?

TEACH

Define Main Idea and Supporting Details
Explain: Finding the main idea will help you understand the information you read. You can find the main idea in a book or story. You can also find the main idea in each paragraph. Sometimes, a sentence spells out a main idea. When you can't find a sentence that spells out the main idea, use your own words.

Seals on the Move

(Harp seals have two homes.) In the summer, they live in the northwest Atlantic, not far from the North Pole. When fall comes, they begin to travel south. By the time winter ends, they are settled on ice sheets thousands of miles away from where they started. In the spring, baby seals will be born here. When the ice melts in April, all the seals, including the new pups, swim back north to their summer home.

Teaching Chart 19

Read the Story and Model the Skill
Display **Teaching Chart 19.** Model identifying a main idea.

MODEL Sometimes, as in this paragraph, the first sentence tells the main idea. I can tell that *harp seals have two homes* is the main idea. The rest of the paragraph gives supporting details that tell where the homes are.

Find Main Idea and Details
Have students circle the sentence that shows the main idea of the paragraph. Ask them to underline details that support the main idea.

PRACTICE

Create a Main Idea and Supporting Details Chart

Using the Main Idea and Supporting Details chart, have students list the main idea and supporting details in the selection. Encourage students to paraphrase long details.

▶ **Linguistic/Spatial**

ONE

MAIN IDEA	SUPPORTING DETAILS
Harp seals have two homes.	In the summer, they live in the northwest Atlantic.
	When fall comes, they travel.
	In the winter and spring, they live on ice sheets thousands of miles south.
	In April, they head back north.

ASSESS/CLOSE

Identify Main Idea and Details

Ask students to identify the main idea in another story or article they have read. Have them name three supporting details, too, and explain how each helps to make the main idea clearer.

ALTERNATE TEACHING STRATEGY

MAIN IDEA
For a different approach to teaching this skill, see page T66.

Intervention ▶ **Skills**
Intervention Guide, for direct instruction and extra practice in main ideas

Meeting Individual Needs for Comprehension

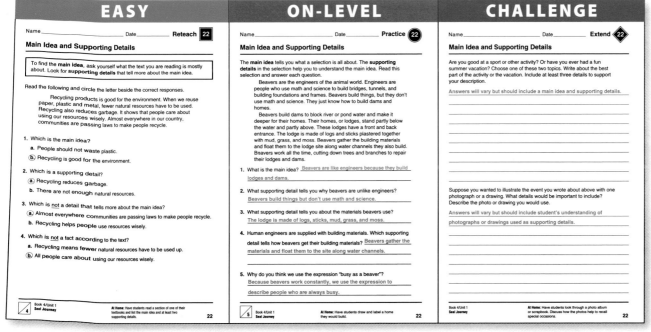

Reteach, 22   Practice, 22   Extend, 22

^{TESTED} **OBJECTIVES**

Students will identify the main idea and supporting details in a selection.

Apply Main Idea

READING STRATEGY

Main Idea

Develop a strategy for finding the main idea and supporting details.

1 **Read the title.** Does it give you any clues about the article?

2 **Identify who or what** the article is about.

3 **Look for facts and important details.** What do they tell about? Can you figure out the main idea from them?

4 **Are there charts or maps** with supporting details? Use them to guide your thinking.

5 **State the main idea** in your own words. Is there a similar sentence in the article?

95

The Amazing Traveling Tern

The Arctic tern is about the size of a small crow. It is one of the most amazing travelers of all the animals on Earth.

The Arctic tern makes its home in the Arctic regions near the North Pole. It nests along northern coasts from Canada to Norway to Siberia. It lives in colonies and lays one to three eggs at a time.

READING STRATEGY

Once the eggs hatch, the parents catch small fish to feed their young. Then, as winter approaches, the birds get ready to migrate.

And what a migration it is! In the next few months, the Arctic tern flies 10,000 miles, all the way to Antarctica. When winter ends, it returns to its breeding ground in the Arctic. Over a lifetime, an Arctic tern might fly the distance from the Earth to the moon—240,000 miles!

The Arctic tern rarely lands during its trip. It can hover over water and dive for fish. It can scoop insects out of the air as it flies. Unlike some other sea birds, terns spend most of their lives in the air.

Many animals migrate, but few travel halfway around the world each year. The Arctic tern is truly one of nature's amazing travelers.

Baffin Island
NORTH AMERICA
ATLANTIC OCEAN
PACIFIC OCEAN
SOUTH AMERICA

PREVIEW Have students preview "The Amazing Traveling Tern." Point out that it is a nonfiction article. Ask:

• What do the title and illustrations tell you about the topic of this article? (It is about a kind of bird that travels far.)

• If there were no title or illustrations, how could you find the topic? (Read the article.)

SET PURPOSES Tell students that they will apply what they have learned about identifying main idea and supporting details as they read "The Amazing Traveling Tern."

APPLY THE STRATEGY Discuss this strategy for identifying main idea and supporting details in a selection.

• Let the title of the article give you an idea about the topic of the selection.

• Look at the first paragraph or two to learn what the selection is about.

• Find important details and facts that will help you decide what the main idea is.

• Add details from charts and maps to your understanding of the main idea.

• Restate the main idea and look for a main idea statement or topic sentence in the passage itself.

Activity Have each student create a Main Idea and Supporting Details chart for the article.

Build Background

Link Science

Concept: Migration

Evaluate Prior Knowledge

CONCEPT: MIGRATION Many kinds of animals migrate—or move from one place to another. Invite students to discuss reasons animals might migrate.

CREATE SUPPORTING DETAILS Help students organize details supporting the main idea *Animals migrate for many reasons* by using the following graphic organizer to note main idea and supporting details.

> **DETAILS**
> to find more space
>
> to find more water
>
> to find food
>
> to go to warmer climate
>
> **MAIN IDEA**
> Animals migrate for many reasons.

Graphic Organizer 21

EXPLAIN MIGRATION Have partners   work together to write a paragraph explaining why animals migrate. Encourage them to refer to Graphic Organizer 21. Have them tell where the animal lives, why it wants to move, where it goes, and what it finds when it gets to its new home. Paragraphs may be based on fact or completely imaginary.

PARTNERS   WRITING

Develop Oral Language

DISCUSS MIGRATION Use a world map **ESL** or a globe to illustrate migration patterns of various animals. For example, one harp seal group swims north from warmer waters and gathers in the Barents Sea, while Canadian Geese fly south from Canada into the United States. As you describe the migration routes, ask students to trace them on the map or globe with their fingers. Write key vocabulary words such as *north, south, summer, winter, warmer,* and *cooler* on the board. Then ask volunteers to describe one of the migration patterns in their own words. Encourage them to point out any other migration patterns they are familiar with.

TEACHING TIP

MANAGEMENT You can make a game out of creating the chart. Have one group give a reason for moving, and challenge another group to arrive at another reason. Then have the groups reverse roles.

While groups are working, use the Develop Oral Language activity to help students who need assistance with language development.

LANGUAGE SUPPORT

See Language Support Book, pages 25–28, for teaching suggestions for Build Background.

OBJECTIVES

Students will use context clues to determine the meanings of vocabulary words.

jagged
horizon
squealed
nursery
mature
assured

Vocabulary

Teach Vocabulary in Context

Identify Vocabulary Words Display **Teaching Chart 20** and read the passage with students. Have volunteers circle each vocabulary word and underline other words that are clues to its meaning.

Definitions

jagged (p. 99) rough, uneven and sharp

horizon (p. 99) an imaginary line that divides earth and sky

squealed (p. 106) cried in fear or surprise

nursery (p. 97) a place set aside for babies

mature (p. 97) fully grown

assured (p. 98) made someone feel sure

The Seal Nursery

1. All we could see around us was a landscape of (jagged) ice, bumpy and rough and uneven. 2. Looking straight ahead, we searched the (horizon,) the line between earth and sky. 3. My father listened closely for the crying sounds of seal pups, and then he said, "Something (squealed!") 4. Suddenly, we found the seal (nursery) with thousands of baby seals. 5. Each baby was watched over by a (mature) female seal, its mother. 6. The mothers (assured) their children that no harm would come to them.

Teaching Chart 20

Story Words

These words from the selection may be unfamiliar. Before students read, have them check the meaning and pronunciation of each word in the Glossary, beginning on page 756, or in a dictionary.

- colony, p. 98
- helicopter, p. 98
- moonscape, p. 99
- blubber, p. 104
- encounter, p. 110

Discuss Meanings Ask questions such as these to help clarify word meanings:

- What does jagged ice look like?
- Where would you find the horizon?
- Did you ever hear anything squeal? What was it? What did it sound like?
- How old are people or animals who live in a nursery?
- Can you think of another word that means the same thing as *mature*?
- Do you see the word *sure* in *assured*? Did anybody ever assure you of anything? Who assured you? Why?

Practice

Demonstrate Word Meaning GROUP

Hand out Vocabulary Cards to small groups. Call out a definition, and have groups hold up the correct card. ▶**Kinesthetic/Linguistic**

 jagged   mature   assured

Word Building Manipulative Cards

Write Context Sentences WRITING

Have one partner choose a vocabulary card and hold it up. Ask the other partner to write a context sentence using the word. When the sentence is written, invite the first partner to read it aloud. ▶**Linguistic/Oral**

Assess Vocabulary

Use Words in Context GROUP

Have students work in small groups to draw pictures that show events from an exciting journey. Ask each group to use the vocabulary words to write captions for the pictures. Invite groups to share their completed work with the class.

See Spelling Challenge Words, pages 1170–117P.

SPELLING/VOCABULARY CONNECTIONS

LANGUAGE SUPPORT

See the **Language Support Book**, pages 25–28, for teaching suggestions for Vocabulary.

Vocabulary PuzzleMaker

Provides vocabulary activities.

Meeting Individual Needs for Vocabulary

EASY — Reteach 23

Vocabulary

Read each clue. Then find the vocabulary word in the row of letters and circle it.

assured	horizon	jagged	mature	nursery	squealed

1. grown up — b e t u (m a t u r e) p l s w
2. earth and sky boundary — l (h o r i z o n) j g f d a z c
3. told in a positive way — k a w j w (a s s u r e d) b c
4. an area for babies or young — h a y (n u r s e r y) l t e r
5. a high, shrill cry — r e w a r (s q u e a l e d) t
6. with sharp, uneven edges — m u w a (j a g g e d) l a c q

Story Comprehension — Reteach 24

Circle the letter beside the answer to each question about "Seal Journey."

1. What is the topic of this selection?
   (a.) harp seals   b. polar bears
2. Which describes the setting?
   (a.) cold and icy   b. warm and rainy
3. What do mothers and their pups do to recognize each other?
   a. They lick each other.   (b.) They rub noses.
4. What special thing did Jonah get to do before going home?
   (a.) He held a pup.   b. He fed a pup.
5. Why were the pups killed in the past?
   (a.) Hunters wanted their white fur.
   b. The animals were disturbing people.

At Home: Have students draw a picture of a seal pup.
23–24   Book 4/Unit 1 Seal Journey   5

ON-LEVEL — Practice 23

Vocabulary

Substitute the correct word from the list for each underlined word or words.

nursery	squealed	assured	horizon	jagged	mature

1. The baby made a loud, shrill sound as it looked for its mother. squealed
2. In a snowstorm, we sometimes cannot see the line where the sky and land meet. horizon
3. The adult animals are almost always much bigger than the babies. mature
4. At night, sounds come from the place where babies are cared for. nursery
5. Some icebergs have sharply pointed edges. jagged
6. Many people are convinced that seals are harmless. assured

At Home: Have students write a paragraph using as many vocabulary words as possible.
23   Book 4/Unit 1 Seal Journey   6

ON-LEVEL — Practice 23a

A Place for a Boy and His Dog

On warm spring evenings, Matt likes to sit on the dock that stretches out into the lake. He looks at the line where the lake and the sky meet. Then the bright, orange sun sinks below the horizon. Sometimes the sunset forms a pattern of brilliant, jagged colors. Matt listens to the sounds in the woods behind him. With all the baby birds in the trees, it sounds like a nursery. Matt's puppy always squealed when he heard the baby birds. Now he's a mature dog and is used to those baby birds. Sitting in this beautiful place year after year makes Matt feel assured that he will always like it here.

1. What does Matt look at when he sits on the dock? the sun sinking below the horizon
2. What kind of pattern does the sunset form? a pattern of brilliant, jagged colors
3. Matt's dog squealed as a puppy but has stopped doing it now. Why? The puppy squealed when it heard the noise made by the baby birds. Now he's a mature dog used to hearing the baby birds.
4. What do the baby birds sound like? a nursery
5. What does Matt feel assured about? that he will always like sitting on the dock on a spring evening

At Home: Have students write a story with illustrations using some of the vocabulary words to describe a special and beautiful place.
5   Book 4/Unit 1 Seal Journey   23a

CHALLENGE — Extend 23

Vocabulary

assured	jagged	nursery
horizon	mature	squealed

Draw pictures to illustrate each of the words above. More than one word can be illustrated in each picture. Include a label or caption with each picture. Use a separate piece of paper if you need more space.
Captions or labels should show an understanding of vocabulary definitions.

Story Comprehension — Extend 24

Write a brief book review of "Seal Journey." What is the story about? Did you like it enough to tell your friends to read it? In the first paragraph, tell what "Seal Journey" is about. In the second paragraph, explain whether or not you liked the story and why. Use another piece of paper if you need more space.
Answers will vary, but should show student's comprehension of the story.

At Home: Have students tell a story for each of their vocabulary illustrations.
23–24   Book 4/Unit 1 Seal Journey

Reteach, 23   Practice, 23   Practice, 23a Take-Home Story   Extend, 23

96C

Comprehension

Prereading Strategies

PREVIEW AND PREDICT Have students read the title and preview the story, looking mainly at the pictures.

- What does the title tell us about the selection?

- Describe the climate of the setting.

- Will the selection contain facts about seals? How can you tell? (yes; photographs come from real life.) *Genre*

- What might you learn about seals?

Have students record their predictions.

PREDICTIONS	WHAT HAPPENED
The story tells of a father and son visiting the home of seals.	
We will learn about mother seals and their babies.	

SET PURPOSES What do students want to find out by reading the story? For example:

- Where do seals live?

- What are baby seals like?

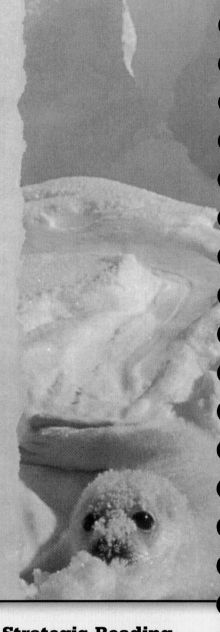

MEET
Richard and Jonah Sobol

Richard Sobol followed the battle to end the seal hunt for many years. On a trip to Canada, bad weather kept him from photographing the seals. He knew he would return.

On his next trip, Sobol took along his son Jonah. They spent a day on the ice with the seals. Jonah had many thoughts and questions. These ideas formed the heart of *Seal Journey*.

Sobol also created a book for children about the African elephant. He hopes his books will help children respect wildlife.

96

Meeting Individual Needs · Grouping Suggestions for Strategic Reading

EASY	ON-LEVEL	CHALLENGE
Read Together Read the story with students. Have students needing language support first use the **Listening Library.** Have students list Main Ideas and Supporting Details on their charts. Comprehension and Intervention prompts offer additional help with decoding, vocabulary, and comprehension.	**Guided Instruction** You may want to have the students read the story first. Then, choose from the Comprehension questions as you read the story with students. Have them list main ideas and supporting details on their charts as they read.	**Read Independently** Have students read the story on their own. Remind them that identifying the main idea and supporting details will help them understand the selection.

SEAL JOURNEY

by Richard and Jonah Sobol ▪ photographs by Richard Sobol

The life cycle of the harp seal is one of the great wonders of nature. Each autumn the seals begin a remarkable journey that carries them over three thousand miles. At a steady flow throughout the winter months, hundreds of thousands of mature harp seals swim through iceberg-filled waters from their summer homes in the northwest Atlantic, just below the North Pole, to the solid ice packs in the Gulf of St. Lawrence in eastern Canada. Once they reach the great sheets of winter ice, each female harp seal will claim her own space on which to give birth to a single pup. Thousands upon thousands of harp seal pups, more than anyone could ever count, are born and nurtured here each spring, transforming this frozen wilderness into a vast nursery.

 1

97

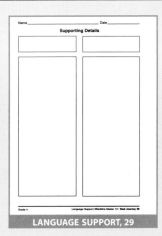

Comprehension

☑ **Apply Main Idea**

☑ **Apply Problem and Solution**

STRATEGIC READING Almost everything you read will have at least one main idea. Supporting details help to make the main idea clearer. Before we begin reading, let's prepare a Main Ideas and Supporting Details chart to help us keep track.

MAIN IDEAS	SUPPORTING DETAILS

1 In your own words describe the "remarkable journey" the harp seal makes. (Starting in autumn and continuing through the winter months, harp seals swim thousands of miles south to the winter ice sheets, where the baby harp seals are born.) *Summarize*

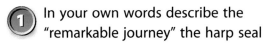

Narrative Nonfiction

Explain that narrative nonfiction:

- presents facts about a topic in the context of a real-life story.
- usually describes events in time-order.
- may include photographs, illustrations, and other graphic elements, such as charts.

Activity After students read *Seal Journey*, have them identify examples of photographs, illustrations, and other graphics used in the story. Discuss how these visuals help the reader understand the information presented.

Comprehension

2 **MAIN IDEA** Sometimes a main idea in a story is stated right up front. On page 97, the first sentence states one of the selection's main ideas. What are some details that support the main idea? Use your Main Ideas and Supporting Details chart.

MAIN IDEAS	SUPPORTING DETAILS
The life cycle of the harp seal is one of the great wonders of nature.	Each year seals make a journey of 3,000 miles.
	They swim through iceberg-filled waters.
	Thousands of pups are born in the spring.

3 **MAIN IDEA** Sometimes the main idea of a paragraph is not stated. Read the third paragraph on this page. What do you think is the main idea? Which details helped you decide what the main idea was?

MODEL I think the main idea of the paragraph is that Jonah is very excited to be visiting the seal nursery. He has dreamed about it. Now that his father has told him he is going to go, he cannot stop asking questions about it.

2 At the same time a second breeding population gathers on pack ice in the Barents Sea off the northern coast of Russia, while a third and smaller group comes together east of Greenland.

This year I had come to Charlottetown, Prince Edward Island, which is used as a base camp for scientists to observe the newborn harp seal pups. This was the third time that I had made this journey on assignment for a French photo agency. The first trip had been in 1981 when I set out to show the cruelty of the seal hunt that was then taking place. Now I was here to tell the story of the seals' survival and to photograph the beginnings of life out on the ice.

My eight-year-old son, Jonah, had been dreaming of seeing the seals, and I invited him to come along with me. "Can I really come with you?" he said in disbelief when I first asked. After that his **3** questions were endless. "Will I get to see newborn seals?" "How cold will it be?" "How will we get onto the ice?" I answered as many questions as I could until finally I assured him that the best answers would come from his own observations out on the ice.

The seal colony was located about a hundred miles north of Prince Edward Island and the only way to reach it was by helicopter. Jonah sat in the front next to the pilot. After we took off, the pilot held up his map, showing Jonah the spot where we would find the

98

Activity

Cross Curricular: Social Studies

MAP SKILLS Display a map of the North Pole and surrounding areas. Have students locate the North Pole, Greenland, the Barents Sea, Canada, Russia, and Alaska.

RESEARCH AND INQUIRY Have students consult an encyclopedia to learn about the exploration of the North Pole. Suggest they create a map showing the routes of famous polar explorers.
▶**Mathematical/Spatial**

*inter***NET** **CONNECTION** Students can learn more about the North Pole by visiting **www.mhschool.com/reading**

Comprehension

④ PROBLEM AND SOLUTION Jonah and his dad want to find the seals, but at first, they see none. How do they find the seals? (They search the horizon and listen to the pilot.)

TEACHING **TIP**

MAP SKILLS Remind students that a map is only a symbolic picture of what a place looks like. Show them a map of the United States. Ask, for example: Is Arizona really purple? If you go to Albany, New York, will you see a star painted on the street to show that it is the state capital?

---

seals. The map, though, showed an ocean of blue, not miles and miles of white jagged ice, looking like a moonscape, that we had been flying over all this March morning. The snow-covered farmlands of Prince Edward Island had quickly faded from view. We now flew over wide swatches of packed ice sandwiched between small strips of open water. Searching the horizon, we eagerly waited for our first glimpse of the seals. The pilot smiled as he pointed outside and said, "Look down now, there they are. The seals have returned once again." Below us tiny brown specks dotted

99

Minilesson
REVIEW/MAINTAIN
Suffixes

Remind students that suffixes are endings that change a word's meaning and part of speech.

- On page 99, have students find the words *quickly* and *eagerly*.
- Point out that the suffix *-ly* can mean "in a certain way or manner." Using this information, have students define *quickly* and *eagerly*.

Activity Have students create a list of words that end with the suffix *-ly*. Encourage them to underline the base word and circle the suffix in each word.

Comprehension

 **COMPOUND WORDS** Read the sentence on page 101 that contains the word *newborn*. What two words are combined to form the word *newborn*? What does the word *newborn* mean? *Semantic Cues*

100

Fluency

READ WITH EXPRESSION The paragraph on page 101 beginning, "As soon as we stepped . . ." describes a still landscape that is cold and uncomfortable for humans. Ask students how they might read this paragraph aloud to emphasize these points. One way might be to read quietly and slowly to show the stillness. Another way might be to emphasize words and phrases that show how uncomfortable humans are. Have students experiment with ways to read this paragraph aloud.

PREVENTION/INTERVENTION

COMPOUND WORDS Remind students that they can use words they know to help them read and understand other words.

- Write the word *newborn* on the chalkboard, using a different colored chalk for each of the smaller words within the compound word.

- Have students identify the two small words.

- Help students define the words *new* and *born*. (having existed only a short time; brought into life)

Have students explain the meaning of the word *newborn*, using the definitions of the two smaller words. (recently brought into life) *Semantic Cues*

the ice, first a few, then more and more, looking like chocolate sprinkles scattered on top of a huge bowl of vanilla ice cream.

⑤

As soon as we stepped out of the helicopter, we could hear the soft cries of hungry newborn pups. These were the only sounds that drifted through the stillness of this frozen landscape. It was springtime but the air was very cold—five degrees below zero. The wind bit into our skin. As we walked toward the seals, the snow swished and swirled under our clunky survival boots. We were careful to avoid the smooth round holes in the ice—bobbing holes— that the mother seals dive in and out of to return to the water to feed on small shrimp or fish, or just to swim.

101

Comprehension

⑤ **MAIN IDEA** The paragraph that begins with the words "As soon as we stepped out" has an important idea. But it is not stated. Read all the details in this paragraph. Then put the main idea in your own words. (This environment is comfortable for seals, but not for humans.)

Minilesson
REVIEW/MAINTAIN
/ū/ and /ü/

Say the words *cube* and *moon* emphasizing the vowel sounds /ū/ and /ü/ respectively.

• Write the words *cube* and *moon* on the board as column heads.

Activity Help students find words on page 101 that contain these vowel sounds. Ask them to say the words aloud and tell in which column they belong. (/ū/: huge; /ü/: soon, boots, smooth) Have them look for other words in the selection with these sounds and add them to the chart in the appropriate columns.

 Phonics Intervention Guide

LANGUAGE SUPPORT

ESL Ask: What do the authors mean when they say, "The wind bit into our skin"? (It felt like the wind was biting us.)

Explain that an author sometimes uses words that don't really mean exactly what they say. The wind didn't really take a bite out of the authors' skin. But it felt as though it did. An author chooses phrases such as these to make a point in a clearer, more interesting way.

Ask students if they can think of other ways the wind or the sun might feel. Then, write their sentences on the chalkboard, and have everyone read them.

101

Comprehension

⑥ **MAIN IDEA** What's the main idea of the first paragraph? (Seals are great swimmers, but require air.) **What are three facts that support the main idea?** (They can hold their breath for a long time; they can dive deep; every few minutes they pop up through holes in the ice to breathe.) Let's add this to our chart.

MAIN IDEAS	SUPPORTING DETAILS
The life cycle of the harp seal is one of the great wonders of nature.	Each year seals make a journey of 3,000 miles.
	They swim through iceberg-filled waters.
	Thousands of pups are born in the spring.
Seals are great swimmers, but need to breathe air.	They are mammals.
	They hold their breath for long periods.
	They pop up every few minutes to breathe.

Seals are great swimmers but, like other mammals, they require air to breathe. They are able to hold their breaths for long periods of time and dive deep into the water. Every few minutes they pop up through bobbing holes onto the ice to fill their lungs with air and to check on their pups.

As we walked closer to a small group of seals, we heard a sharp, deep cry, like a cat screeching in the night. We climbed along a large ridge of ice to get a better look. Up ahead, we spotted a female seal twisting one way,

102

Cross Curricular: Science

WATER MAMMALS Seals are not the only mammals that spend a great deal of time in the water. Others include: whales, dolphins, otters, hippopotami.

RESEARCH AND INQUIRY Have students create a chart with pictures of other mammals that spend much of their time in the water. Encourage volunteers to share what they have learned.
▶**Logical/Mathematical**

Comprehension

7 On page 103, we read that Jonah and his dad come face to face with a newborn seal pup and its mother. What do we learn about the first few days of a harp seal's life? (Pups are yellow and wet at birth. They nestle close to their mothers for warmth and comfort. After two days, the sun changes the pup's coat from yellow to lush white.) *Sequence of Events*

then another, again and again. There was a sense of great excitement in her movements and cries. Jonah tugged at my sleeve and pointed to a newborn pup, only minutes old, that was lying beside the mother seal. It was still wet and yellow from its birth.

He did not look at all like the cuddly white ball of fur that we were expecting. It will take a day or two in the sun for this birth-stained scraggle to be transformed into a lush baby known as a "whitecoat." Jonah said he felt sorry for the tiny pup, outside on frozen ice, having just left the warmth of his mother's womb. Now, as the steam rose up from his scruffy, gooey coat the mother moved closer to him, to reassure him and share her warmth. As they nestled together in the warm glow of the sunlight, it was easy to see the dark markings on the mother seal's back. They were indeed the familiar curves of a harp, the musical instrument for which these seals are named.

7

103

LANGUAGE SUPPORT

ESL Help students understand the words *scruffy* and *gooey*. Tell them *scruffy* means untidy, messy. A scruffy coat is one that goes every which way. It's not smooth. *Gooey* means sticky. A gooey coat is one that feels wet and slimy.

Write the words *scruffy* and *gooey* on the board. Ask students to suggest other items that have each of these qualities and write their responses under the correct heading on the board. For example, for *scruffy* they might suggest *a child's hair when it's washed but not combed* or *a lawn that needs mowing*. For *gooey* they might suggest *raw eggs* or *liquid glue*.

Minilesson

REVIEW/MAINTAIN

Summarize

Remind students that summarizing means paraphrasing the main points briefly.

- Ask students to imagine that they are Jonah Sobol.
- Have them think of what Jonah has done up to the moment he sees the newborn pup.

Activity Ask students to orally summarize Jonah's story so far. Urge them to be brief and to omit unimportant details.

Comprehension

(8) **PROBLEM AND SOLUTION** Nature sometimes finds solutions for problems. One problem for a baby seal is survival in such a cold climate. The first sentence on this page gives us one of nature's solutions. What is it? Can you find another solution that allows pups to survive in this cold place?

MODEL I can see that the newborn pups have a problem. They need to be warm. To solve this problem, nature has given them a small amount of baby fat to burn up. It also makes sure that newborn pups get a lot of milk from their mothers so that they can grow the thick layer of fat they will need.

To survive in this new world, harp seal pups are born with a small amount of baby fat which they immediately start to burn in order to give their bodies heat. But, they need their mothers' milk to grow the thick layer of blubber that will continue to protect them from the deep freeze that they are born into. We watched with wonder as the mother rolled onto her side, and the pup slid up toward her searching for the milk. The pup lay perfectly still, nursing without a break for ten minutes, as he would need to do five or six times each day.

The mother seals' milk is ten times richer than either cows' or humans' milk, and a well-fed pup will grow from twenty pounds at birth to almost eighty pounds by the time he is weaned at twelve days old.

104

Activity

Cross Curricular: Math

SEAL MATH Have students do "Seal Math."

- A pup grows from 20 pounds to 80 pounds in 12 days. How many pounds does a pup grow in 8 days?
(45 pounds)

- If Jonah weighs 50 pounds, how much heavier is he than a newborn pup?
(30 pounds)

- How much will four newborn pups weigh all together? (80 pounds) How about after 12 days? (320 pounds)

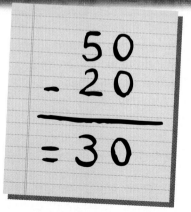

Before the pup finished nursing, the mother rubbed noses with him. This "kiss of recognition" was her way of familiarizing herself with the smell of her pup. A mother seal is often surrounded by dozens of pups and she must be able to identify her own by its unique scent or it will not survive. She has only enough milk for one pup and she will only nurse her very own.

105

Comprehension

9 **MAIN IDEA** Why does mother seal rub noses with her pup? (So she will be able to identify its scent.) **Why is this important?** (She only has enough milk for her own pup.) **Let's add to our charts.**

MAIN IDEAS	SUPPORTING DETAILS
Seals are great swimmers, but need to breathe air.	They are mammals.
	They hold their breath for long periods.
	They pop up every few minutes to breathe.
Mother seals care for their pups.	Mother identifies pup by its smell.
	Mother will only nurse its own pup.

P/i **CONTEXT CLUES** Read the third sentence on page 105. What kind of scent does a mother seal look for? (unique) Can you find any clues to the word's meaning? *Semantic Cues*

P/i PREVENTION/INTERVENTION

CONTEXT CLUES Help students determine the meaning of the word *unique.* You might focus their attention by asking:

- How many pups are usually surrounding a mother seal? (dozens)

- Why are the pups all around the mother seal? (They want to nurse.)

- How much milk does a mother seal have? (only enough for one pup)

- How does a mother seal know which pup is hers? (She knows the smell of her pup.)

- If a mother can tell which pup is hers by the smell, what does that tell you about the smell of each pup? (It is different.)

Using the answers to the questions, encourage students to determine the meaning of the word *unique.* (being the only one of its kind) *Semantic Cues*

Comprehension

10 This paragraph tells how a mother seal teaches her pup to swim. Who wants to volunteer to pantomime the roles of the mother seal and her baby? Act out the process for us. *Steps in a Process/Role-Play*

SELF-MONITORING STRATEGY

ASK FOR HELP If there's something you don't understand, stop and ask for help.

MODEL I've read this paragraph two times already, and I can't figure out which details are the important supporting ones. The paragraph is so long. I know it's about a mother seal and a baby seal swimming, but there are many other details. I'll ask my teacher to show me how to figure out what's important.

---

10 A few feet away we saw what appeared to be a mother seal giving her pup a swimming lesson. The mother nudged him toward the water, while the pup squealed and squealed. And then the pup

was in the water, floating and bobbing like a little cork. The pup had so much fat that he couldn't sink. "It's like he is wearing a life jacket," Jonah said, as the mother jumped in the water too. It was almost as if they were playing a game of tag. First the mother disappeared under the water. A few seconds later, she popped up in a different place. The pup squirmed and paddled to catch up to her. Then they rubbed noses.

Pups have to learn to swim well. Their home for most of the remainder of their lives is in the water, since harp seals spend only

106

Comprehension

 SUPPORTING DETAILS What details support this idea: *Pups have to learn to swim well?* (Most of pups' lives are spent in the water. Pups must survive on their own after two weeks. Pups must find food in the water.)

four to six weeks a year on the ice. By the time the pup is two weeks old, it is weaned from its mother's milk and has to find its own food in the chilly waters of the Atlantic. The weaning is sudden—without any warning, the mother slides into the water between nursings as she normally does, only this time she leaves forever, never to return to her pup. The two of them will always be part of the same seal herd, but the pup must quickly adjust to life on its own.

While the pups are being born and nursed, the males keep their distance, gathering in groups around breaks of open water. Once the pups are weaned, the female harp seals join the males for mating. The complete cycle of birth, nursing, and mating takes place in about two weeks, incredibly fast for such a large animal.

In April when the ice melts and breaks up, the entire seal colony will join together again to journey back north to their summer feeding grounds in the Arctic seas. The young pups, having lost their fine white coats by now, will straggle behind the main herd, feeding as they go on small shrimp. As they grow stronger and their swimming skills improve, they will be able to dive and catch small fish to add to their diet. When fully grown, these harp seals will weigh up to three hundred pounds.

11

107

LANGUAGE SUPPORT

ESL Call students' attention to the words *weaned* and *weaning,* which appear on this page. Explain that to *wean* means to take a person or an animal away from something it likes or thinks it needs. What was the baby seal weaned from? (its mother's milk) Who weaned it? (the mother)

Comprehension

(12) This selection is illustrated mostly with photographs of seals. The author could have chosen to include more photos of Jonah and himself. Why do you think he didn't do that? *Critical Thinking*

CULTURAL PERSPECTIVES

THE INUIT AND SEALS Explain: Not all people who have hunted seals wanted their skins to make slippers, gloves, or dolls. Before modern technology, the Inuit hunted seals and used nearly every part of a seal they caught. They ate seal meat. They sewed together seals' intestines to make warm, waterproof coats. They used seal skins and oil in building kayaks. Bones were made into tools.

Activity Have students act out a dialogue between Jonah Sobol and an Inuit hunter. ▶**Interpersonal**

Home for the pups for the next few years will be in the North Atlantic feeding grounds, just below the Arctic Circle. The pups will feed, grow, and develop their swimming skills until they are old enough to mate. In their fifth or sixth year of life, when autumn comes, they will know that it is their time to join the mature seals on the long swim south. Together, they will return to the ice where they were born. By the time that their lives come to an end, some twenty-five years later, most harp seals will have travelled over 75,000 miles, round and round through the ocean.

Jonah and I saw hundreds of seals. We spent hours and hours exploring on the ice. The sky grew dark in the late afternoon, and the pilots started warming the helicopter engines. Our day would soon be over. But there was still one thing Jonah wanted to do. "Dad," he said in a quiet voice, "could I please hold one seal before we go?"

We should have headed toward our helicopter, but instead, we walked in the other direction, over the long sloping ice ridge, in search of a friendly pup. There we found her—a beautiful whitecoat, round and contented with her first week of life. Slowly, Jonah approached her. When he was close he lay down to pet her. I went over and picked the seal up and placed her on Jonah's lap. "I can feel her breathing," Jonah said through the wide smile that now covered his face. "Her whiskers tickle and the soft white fur is like a warm blanket covering me."

It is sad to think that this same fur was what the hunters were seeking when they stalked the ice to slaughter these seals. The fur that they stripped from the whitecoats was turned into slippers, gloves, and even dolls. For twenty years people who cared about saving seals came out onto the ice to challenge

109

Comprehension

13 How does Jonah feel about seals? (Jonah wants to pet the seal.) How do hunters feel about seals? (The hunters wanted to kill them.) *Compare and Contrast*

Minilesson

REVIEW/MAINTAIN

Make Inferences

Remind students that sometimes readers can read between the lines and make inferences based upon what they already know.

- Ask students to think about the first sentence in the third paragraph.
- Why should Richard and Jonah have headed to their helicopter? What time of day was it? How cold was it?

Activity Ask students to orally finish the sentence "We should have headed toward our helicopter because. . . ."

Comprehension

 MAIN IDEA Sometimes it is important to read a paragraph all the way through before you can decide what its main idea is. Look back at the long paragraph that starts at the bottom of page 109 and continues on page 110. What do you think the main idea is?

MODEL The paragraph begins by telling about the hunters, and if I didn't read the whole thing, I might think the main idea is: *Hunters used to kill seals for their fur.* But if I read the whole paragraph, I could figure out a more accurate main idea: *People throughout the world tried to stop the hunting, and now some seals are protected.*

PHONICS AND DECODING Read the last word in the second line on page 110. (throughout) Slowly sound out the word. Do you hear sounds for all the letters? *Graphophonic Cues*

Writer's Craft

TEXT FEATURES

Explain: Sometimes a writer presents information in special ways to vary the text and keep the reader interested.

Example: Discuss the special text features used on page 111. Ask: How is this page different from other pages? (The page is titled. The photos have captions. There is only one column of text.)

Discuss how type styles set off the text. For example, bold type sets off the names of specific families of seals; italic type sets off the scientific name of harp seals.

 Have each partner find an example of special text features in *Seal Journey*. They can then explain the features to each other.

---

the hunters and to make them stop. They let people throughout the world know about this cruelty and asked them not to buy anything made from seal fur. As more people knew what was happening to the seal pups they joined together and stopped buying seal products. The hunters had no place to sell the fur. Only then did the killing stop here. In other places though, some seal hunting does continue, as hunters still stain the ice with the blood of these lovely animals. These harp seal pups, born in the Gulf of St. Lawrence, are the lucky ones. Now protected by laws, for the first time in hundreds of years this seal nursery is filled only with the cries of the hungry pups and not the thuds of the hunters' clubs.

It was now time to go. Jonah gently put the seal back down and gave her a soft pat. As he walked away he turned back toward her for one final look.

"Good-bye, seal," he said. "Now I know that dreams can come true."

As we flew back toward Prince Edward Island and looked down at the ice, its sharp edges began to soften and the harsh white glare turned into water-color splashes of pink and gray in the fading light. Soon the ice will melt and the seals will return north. During the hot summer months people will be sailing and swimming in this same wide channel. Next winter the ice will form again, calling the harp seals back. The magic of nature will bring more people here, too. Each year more and more adventurous tourists are journeying out onto the ice to experience the beauty of the seals. During these few short weeks people and seals can bring their worlds together. Somehow these seals seem to know that the people they encounter now are their protectors and there is no need to be afraid. This is how it should be.

110

PREVENTION/INTERVENTION

PHONICS AND DECODING
Remind students that sometimes more than one letter stands for a single sound.

• Write the letter *t* and the following groups of letters on separate index cards: *thr, ou, gh, ou.*

• Remind students that the letters *ou* can stand for different sounds: /u/, /ou/, /ù/, /ō/, and /ü/.

• Say the word slowly emphasizing the sounds represented by the letters *ou.*

• Point out that the letters *gh* are silent in the word *throughout.*

• Use the cards to create the word *throughout* and visually show the letters that work together. Then have students read the word together. *Graphophonic Cues*

More Seal Facts

Harp seals belong to the mammal group called pinnipeds. Pinnipeds are divided into three families:

Family Otariidae, which includes fur seals and sea lions, also known as "eared seals."

Family Odobenidae, which includes the walrus.

Family Phocidae, which includes all true seals.

True seals are monk seals, elephant seals, Antarctic seals, and northern true seals. They have rear flippers that extend behind their bodies. They are also known as "earless seals." The openings to their ears are small holes on the sides of their heads.

Harp seals are classified as northern true seals and their scientific name is *Phoca groenlandicus.*
Average adult weight—300 pounds
Average adult length—5 1/2 feet
Average lifespan—30 years

Harp seals live in three areas in the North Atlantic—the east coast of Canada near Newfoundland, in the White Sea off the coast of Russia, and between Yan Mayan and Svalbard, east of Greenland. Estimates of world population today vary from 2.25 million to 3.5 million.

Sea Lion

Walrus

Elephant Seal

Comprehension

15 What do you think the author's point of view is about hunting harp seals? (He is against it.) **How do you know?** (In the last paragraph of the story he says that people should protect harp seals.) **What do you think the author's purpose might have been in writing the story?** (To persuade people that hunting of seals should be stopped everywhere.) ***Author's Purpose, Point of View***

Comprehension

(16) **MAIN IDEA** Let's look back at the Main Ideas and Supporting Details chart.

MAIN IDEAS	SUPPORTING DETAILS
The life cycle of the harp seal is one of the great wonders of nature.	Each year seals make a journey of 3,000 miles.
	They swim through iceberg-filled water.
	Thousands of pups are born in the spring.
Seals are great swimmers, but need to breathe air.	They are mammals.
	They hold their breath for long periods.
	They pop up every few minutes to breathe.
Mother seals care for their pups.	Mother identifies pup by its smell.
	Mother will only nurse its own pup.

RETELL THE STORY Ask volunteers to tell the main ideas in the selection. Students may refer to their charts. *Summarize*

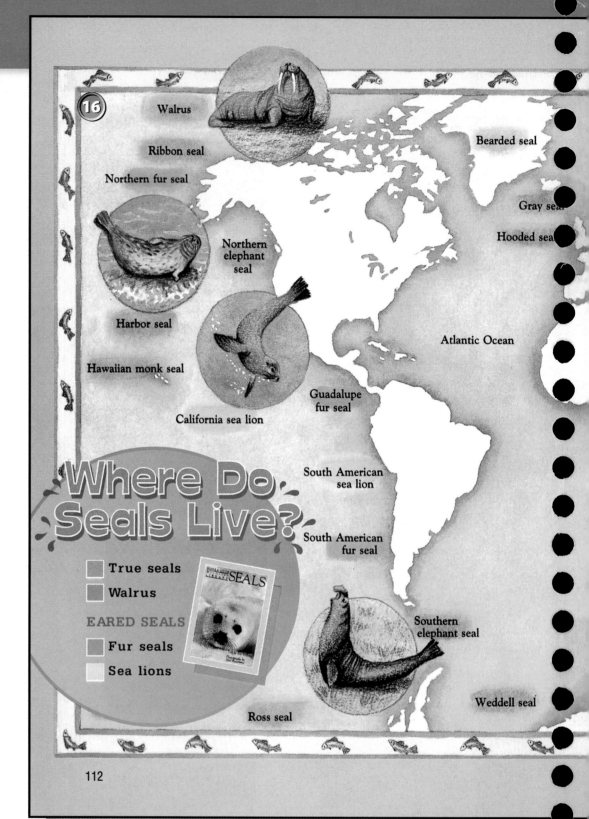

Where Do Seals Live?

☐ True seals
☐ Walrus
EARED SEALS
☐ Fur seals
☐ Sea lions

SEALS

112

STUDENT SELF-ASSESSMENT

- How did using the strategy of finding main ideas and supporting details help?

TRANSFERRING THE STRATEGY

- When might I use this strategy again? When could the chart help me again?

REREADING FOR *Fluency*

(PARTNERS) Have students choose a favorite paragraph to read to a partner. Encourage students to read with expression.

READING RATE When you evaluate rate, have the student read aloud from the story for one minute. Place a stick-on note after the last word read. Count the words read. To

evaluate students' performance, see the Running Record in the **Fluency Assessment** book.

(i) **Intervention** For leveled fluency lessons, passages, and norms charts, see **Skills Intervention Guide**, Part 4, Fluency.

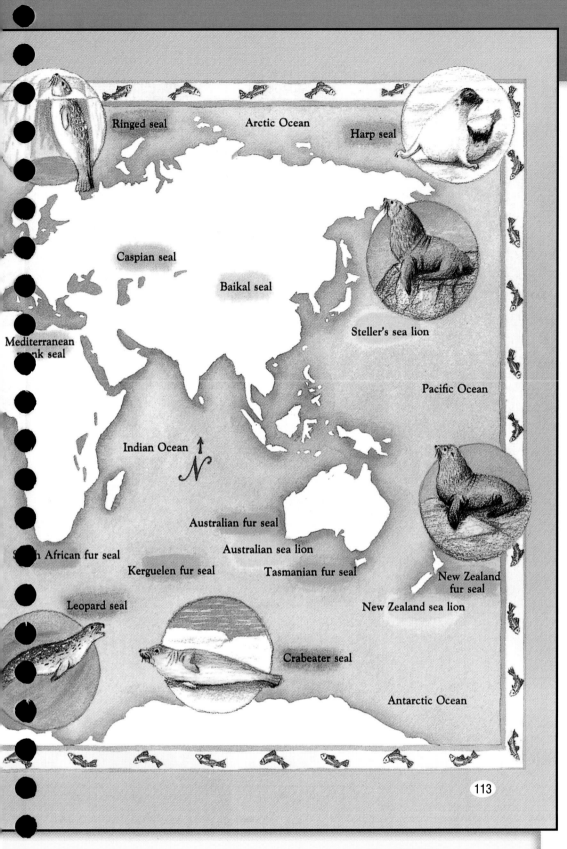

Pacific Ocean

Ringed seal — Arctic Ocean — Harp seal

Caspian seal

Baikal seal

Steller's sea lion

Mediterranean monk seal

Indian Ocean

Australian fur seal

Australian sea lion

South African fur seal

Kerguelen fur seal

Tasmanian fur seal

New Zealand fur seal

New Zealand sea lion

Leopard seal

Crabeater seal

Antarctic Ocean

113

Comprehension

Return to Predictions and Purposes

Review with students their story predictions and reasons for reading the story. Were their predictions correct? Did they find out what they wanted to know?

PREDICTIONS	WHAT HAPPENED
The story tells of a father and son visiting the home of seals.	Jonah and Richard Sobol spend a day at the harp seal nursery.
We will learn about mother seals and their babies.	Harp seals give birth to pups in the spring. The pups quickly grow, learn to swim, and set out on their own.

INFORMAL ASSESSMENT

Main Idea

HOW TO ASSESS

• Can students identify the main idea of a paragraph?

• Can students give details to support the main idea?

Students should be able to tell a main idea they learned about seals. They should also be able to give supporting details for the main idea.

FOLLOW UP If students have trouble thinking of a main idea about seals, help them brainstorm words and short phrases about what they learned. Then guide students to expand the words or phrases into complete thoughts.

If students have trouble remembering supporting details for main ideas, have them think about the main idea as you ask, "How do we know that?"

LITERARY RESPONSE

QUICK-WRITE Invite students to record their thoughts about the selection. The following questions may help them get started:

• How do you think it feels to be a seal?

• If you were Jonah, what would you have been most excited to see?

ORAL RESPONSE Have students share their thoughts and discuss what they found most interesting about the selection.

Story Questions

Have students discuss or write answers to the questions on page 114.

Answers:

1. Jonah and his father go to Canada to see harp seals. *Literal/Summarize*

2. The seals are thriving now that the hunting has stopped. *Inferential/Main Idea*

3. Sample answer: Photographs allow people to see how beautiful harp seals are. *Inferential/Draw Conclusions*

4. Sample answer: The harp seal is a very special animal. It should be protected. *Critical/Summarize*

5. Sample answer: They are both traveling with their fathers to wilderness areas. *Critical/Reading Across Texts*

Writing a Photo Essay For a full lesson related to this suggestion, see pages 117K–117L.

Story Questions & Activities

1 Why do Jonah and his father go to Canada?

2 How have the seals' lives improved since 1981?

3 How do the photographs give more information?

4 What is the main idea of this selection?

5 What do Jonah and Luke in "The Lost Lake" have in common? Explain your answer.

Write a Photo Essay

Jonah and his dad took a trip to see seals. Write about a trip you have taken. Describe where you went, what you did, and what you learned. Tell about events in order. Attach photos if you have them, or draw illustrations.

114

Meeting Individual Needs

EASY

Name_____ Date_____ **Reteach** 23

Vocabulary

Read each clue. Then find the vocabulary word in the row of letters and circle it.

| assured | horizon | jagged | mature | nursery | squealed |

1. grown up — b e t u m a t u r e p l s w
2. earth and sky boundary — l h o r i z o n j g f d a z c
3. told in a positive way — k a w j w a s s u r e d b c
4. an area for babies or young — h a y n u r s e r y l t e r
5. a high, shrill cry — r e w a r s q u e a l e d t
6. with sharp, uneven edges — m u w a j a g g e d l a c q

Story Comprehension **Reteach** 24

Circle the letter beside the answer to each question about "Seal Journey."

1. What is the topic of this selection?
   a. harp seals   b. polar bears
2. Which describes the setting?
   a. cold and icy   b. warm and rainy
3. What do mothers and their pups do to recognize each other?
   a. They lick each other.   b. They rub noses.
4. What special thing did Jonah get to do before going home?
   a. He held a pup.   b. He fed a pup.
5. Why were the pups killed in the past?
   a. Hunters wanted their white fur.
   b. The animals were disturbing people.

At Home: Have students draw a picture of a seal pup.
Book 4/Unit 1 Seal Journey 5

Reteach, 24

ON-LEVEL

Name_____ Date_____ **Practice** 24

Story Comprehension

Write an answer in the space provided for the questions about "Seal Journey."

1. Who is the photographer who is telling the story?
   Richard Sobol
2. Who is Jonah? He is Richard Sobol's son.
3. Where does the helicopter take Richard and Jonah?
   One hundred miles north of Prince Edward Island
4. Why are these seals called harp seals?
   They have markings on their backs that are curved like a harp.
5. How much does a baby seal weigh at the end of 12 days?
   The baby weighs about 80 pounds.
6. Why does the mother push the pup into the water?
   The pup must learn fast to swim and survive on its own in the water.
7. What happens to a seal pup after two weeks?
   Its mother goes off to join the males and the pups are on their own for good.
8. What happens in April when the ice melts?
   The whole seal colony, including the young pups, swims north to their Arctic feeding grounds.

24 At Home: Have students tell a family member about the lives of the harp seals.
Book 4/Unit 1 Seal Journey 8

Practice, 24

CHALLENGE

Name_____ Date_____ **Extend** 23

Vocabulary

| assured | jagged | nursery |
| horizon | mature | squealed |

Draw pictures to illustrate each of the words above. More than one word can be illustrated in each picture. Include a label or caption with each picture. Use a separate piece of paper if you need more space.
Captions or labels should show an understanding of vocabulary definitions.

Extend 24

Story Comprehension

Write a brief book review of "Seal Journey." What is the story about? Did you like it enough to tell your friends to read it? In the first paragraph, tell what "Seal Journey" is about. In the second paragraph, explain whether or not you liked the story and why. Use another piece of paper if you need more space.

Answers will vary, but should show student's comprehension of the story.

23–24 At Home: Have students tell a story for each of their vocabulary illustrations.
Book 4/Unit 1 Seal Journey

Extend, 24

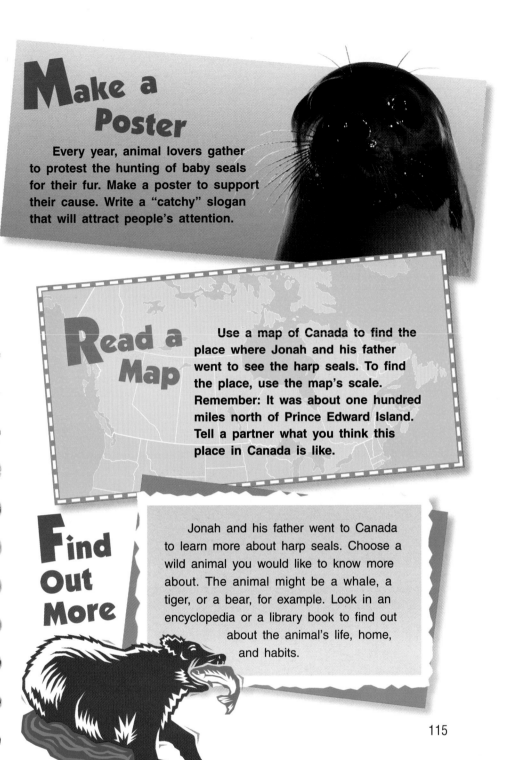

Make a Poster

Every year, animal lovers gather to protest the hunting of baby seals for their fur. Make a poster to support their cause. Write a "catchy" slogan that will attract people's attention.

Read a Map

Use a map of Canada to find the place where Jonah and his father went to see the harp seals. To find the place, use the map's scale. Remember: It was about one hundred miles north of Prince Edward Island. Tell a partner what you think this place in Canada is like.

Find Out More

Jonah and his father went to Canada to learn more about harp seals. Choose a wild animal you would like to know more about. The animal might be a whale, a tiger, or a bear, for example. Look in an encyclopedia or a library book to find out about the animal's life, home, and habits.

115

Story Activities

Make a Poster

Materials: large sheets of paper or poster-board, crayons, pencils, markers

GROUP Have groups brainstorm ideas for a catchy slogan. Encourage students to think about "catchy" slogans they have heard on television or read in newspapers and magazines. Ask them to consider what made those slogans effective.

Read a Map

Materials: map of Canada, ruler

PARTNERS Have students look at the scale on the map and estimate the distance between points. Then have them use the ruler to evaluate their estimates.

Find Out More

ONE **Research and Inquiry** Have students use resources in the media center to research a favorite animal. Ask students to make a list of details and facts that they discover.

inter**NET** **CONNECTION** Students can learn about animals by visiting **www.mhschool.com/reading**

FORMAL ASSESSMENT

After page 115, see Selection Assessment.

MATH: ESTIMATING DISTANCES The average harp seal swims over 75,000 miles during its life. Have students figure out how many times each rounded distance goes into 75,000 miles.

• the 4x400 meter Olympic Relay Race *1 mile* (75,000)

• distance across the United States *3,000 miles* (25)

• distance around the Earth *25,000 miles* (3)

To solve: Divide the distance a harp seal travels (75,000 miles) by the 1, 3,000, and 25,000 miles.

CHALLENGE

Study Skills

PARTS OF A BOOK

OBJECTIVES Students will use an index effectively.

PREPARE Read the passage with students. Display **Teaching Chart 21.**

TEACH Review how to use an index. Have a student circle the line of the index that shows the page number where a reader could find information about Russia.

PRACTICE Have students answer questions 1–5. **1.** pages 121, 127, 128, 133, 134; **2.** pages 127 and 133; **3.** page 122; **4.** pages 122–125 and 133; **5.** Sample answer: It tells you which pages to turn to.

ASSESS/CLOSE Have students use the index to answer these questions: Where is the first reference to harp seals? (page 121) Where is the first reference to Prince Edward Island? (page 122)

Study Skills

Use an Index

Suppose that you are reading a library book for a report about seals. You don't have much time, and you really want to know about one kind of seal—the harp seal. Where would you look in the book to find information quickly? You would look in the index.

The **index** is at the back of a book. It lists all the book's topics in alphabetical order. Next to each topic are the page numbers on which you will find information about your topic.

Greenland, 122
Harp seal, 121, 127, 128, 133, 134
Helicopter, 122–125, 133
Milk, seal, 128, 129, 131
Prince Edward Island, 122, 123, 134–135
Russia, 122
Whitecoats, 127, 133

Use the sample index to answer these questions.

1 On which pages would you find information about harp seals?

2 Where would you look to find out what a *whitecoat* is?

3 On which page would you find information about Greenland?

4 On which pages might you find information on how to travel to see the harp seals?

5 How can an index help you find information quickly?

Meeting Individual Needs

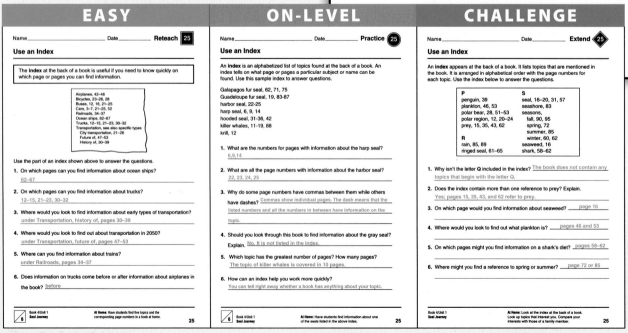

EASY	ON-LEVEL	CHALLENGE
Reteach, 25	Practice, 25	Extend, 25

Test Tip

Always read the directions carefully.

DIRECTIONS

Read the sample story. Then read each question about the story.

SAMPLE

Jim's Big Decision

Jim knew very little about raising tropical fish. But his friend Manny said he had been studying about them.

"Tropical fish live in a warmer climate than most other fish," Manny noted. "That's why you have to keep the water in their tank at a higher temperature."

"That makes sense," Jim said. He was afraid that caring for fish was going to be more complicated than he thought. He wasn't really sure if fish were the right pets for him to have.

"I can lend you the book I have," Manny said. He could see that Jim was unsure about getting a fish.

1 What is the main idea of the second paragraph?

  A The water is warm.

  B Manny has a book about fish.

  C Jim wants a fish.

  (D) Tropical fish need to live in a warm climate.

2 According to the story, why was Jim unsure about getting a fish?

  F He really wanted a dog.

  (G) He knew very little about them.

  H He didn't like fish.

  J He didn't know how to read.

117

Test Power

THE PRINCETON REVIEW

Read the Page

Direct students to read the story. Instruct students to pay attention to how the character feels.

Explain the Question

Question 1: This question asks students to find the main idea of the second paragraph. Have students refer back to the passage and summarize the paragraph in their own words before looking at the answer choices. As you read each answer choice as a group, discuss why an incorrect answer is incorrect even when it contains facts from the passage. The main idea of the second paragraph paraphrases the entire paragraph in a few words.

Question 2: This question requires students to draw a logical conclusion. Instruct students to refer back to the point in the passage when Jim was unsure.

Leveled Books

EASY

Run Fast, Fly Far

/û/ and /ü/

☑ **Main Idea**

☑ **Instructional Vocabulary:** *assured, horizon, jagged, mature, nursery, squealed*

Intervention ▶ **Skills**
Intervention Guide, for direct instruction and extra practice in vocabulary and comprehension

Answers to Story Questions

1. It is a distance of almost 20,000 miles.

2. Possible answer: The bird would be well cared for and have a better chance of being released in the wild.

3. Answers will vary but may include: the boys played and raced together, and Miko especially supported Kenu's desire to care for the bird; Miko knew Kenu would do the right thing for the bird by taking it to Elaine's Farm.

4. The story is about two boys' eagerness to nurture a wild bird until it could fend for itself; the boys knew they were not able to help the bird as much as a knowledgeable person, such as Elaine.

5. Answers will vary.

The *Story Questions and Activity* below appear in the *Easy Book.*

Story Questions and Activity

1. Approximately how far is an Arctic tern's round trip from the North to the South Pole and back again?

2. Why was it a good idea for Kenu to bring Jesse to Elaine's farm?

3. Think of the following sentence as a main idea and provide details to support it: Miko and Kenu were very good friends.

4. What is the story mostly about?

5. How were Kenu and Jonah from *Seal Journey* alike? How were they different?

Migrating Birds

Do some research about another migrating bird. Write a mini-report on it. Include a drawing of the bird and a map that shows a possible migration route.

from *Run Fast, Fly Far*

Guided Reading

PREVIEW AND PREDICT Have students preview the illustrations up to page 7, then predict what the story is about. Chart their ideas.

SET PURPOSES Have students write what they think they'll learn by reading this story. For example: *I'll learn about taking care of a baby tern.* Ask students to record their responses in their journals.

READ THE BOOK After students have read the story, use questions like the following to ensure understanding.

Page 2: How does Kenu protect the baby bird from the gulls? (Kenu puts the baby bird in his hat.) *Problem and Solution*

Page 5: What vowel sound do you hear in the words *loose* and *soon*? (/ü/) What letters represent this sound? (oo) *Phonics and Decoding*

Page 7: The main idea of this page seems to be that Jesse is improving. What details support this? (Sample answers: Jesse was in a bigger cage; she was covered in fluffy, white feathers; she was starting to walk.) *Main Idea*

Page 8: Kenu and Miko need to set Jesse free as soon as she is *mature* enough. How will they be able to tell when she's ready? (She'll be bigger, will have more feathers, and will be able to fly.) *Vocabulary*

Page 14: Why do you think Elaine wants to set Jesse free tomorrow? (It is time for the terns to fly south.) *Make Inferences*

RETURN TO PREDICTIONS AND PURPOSES Have students review their predictions. Which were accurate? Which were not? Did they find out what they wanted to learn as they read the story?

LITERARY RESPONSE Discuss these questions with students:

- What would you have done if you had found Jesse?

- Would you like to visit Elaine's nursery? Why or why not?

- Does it matter that Kenu and Miko didn't win their race? Explain your answer.

Also see the story questions and activity in *Run Fast, Fly Far*.

Leveled Books

INDEPENDENT

A Siren's Journey

☑ **Main Idea**

☑ **Instructional Vocabulary:** *assured, horizon, jagged, mature, nursery, squealed*

Guided Reading

PREVIEW AND PREDICT Have students preview the story up to page 7. Have them think about the illustrations and predict in their journals what they will learn.

SET PURPOSES Have students write some questions about humpback whales that they hope the story answers.

READ THE BOOK Have students read the story independently. Then use questions like the following to help them think about what they've read.

Page 4: The main idea on this page seems to be that humpback whales breathe through their blowholes. What details does the author include to support this main idea? (Sample answers: Blowholes are similar to our nostrils; when whales come up to breathe, they release air and water droplets from their blowholes.) *Main Idea*

Page 9: The humpback whales may use the sun and stars to find their way. How might they do that? (They might look at the sky and use what they see to point them in the right direction.) *Make Inferences*

Page 13: What's the main idea of this page? (Sample answer: Mother whales help calves survive.) *Main Idea*

Page 14: What clue words does the author include to help you understand the meaning of *nursery*? (young calves; young humpback whales) *Vocabulary*

RETURN TO PREDICTIONS AND PURPOSES Have students review their predictions and purposes for reading. Did they learn what they expected to? What did they learn that they didn't expect?

LITERARY RESPONSE Discuss these questions with students:

• If you were a humpback whale, what would you enjoy most about your life?

• Did you like learning about humpback whales? Why or why not?

• How are humpback whale mothers like human mothers, and how are they different?

Also see the story questions and activity in *A Siren's Journey.*

Answers to Story Questions

1. Humpback whales migrate to warm water to mate.
2. They use baleen. Baleen, a material similar to our nails, is used as a strainer to trap fish.
3. Male humpback whales may sing to attract females, to locate other whales in the distance, or to signal when it's time to return to the cooler waters.
4. Accept all reasonable responses, such as that humpback whales are unique and precious animals.
5. Answers will vary.

The *Story Questions and Activity* below appear in the *Independent Book.*

Story Questions and Activity

1. Why do humpback whales migrate to warm water?
2. How do humpback whales eat? Provide the main idea and the supporting details.
3. Why might humpback whales sing?
4. What is the main idea of the book?
5. If a humpback whale met one of the harp seals from *Seal Journey*, what do you think they might talk about?

Length and Weight

Humpback whales can weigh as much as 90,000 pounds and they can be up to 60 feet long. Based on this information, determine the weight and length of this humpback whale using YOU and YOUR CLASSMATES as the "unit of measurement."

• How many classmates would it take to equal the weight of this humpback whale?

• If you were to lie head to toe with classmates, how many of you would it take to equal 60 feet?

from *A Siren's Journey*

Leveled Books

CHALLENGE

Journey Against All Odds

☑ **Main Idea**

☑ **Instructional Vocabulary:**
assured, horizon, jagged, mature, nursery, squealed

written by Beth Terrill
illustrated by Lina Chesak

Answers to Story Questions

1. Salmon migrate back to the streams where they were born to spawn.
2. Salmon find their rivers and streams by using their sense of smell.
3. Salmon may be caught by predators or by people fishing; they may die because of pollution or water that is too warm for them.
4. This book is about the life of the salmon from stream to river to ocean and back again.
5. Answers should include migration but may vary.

The *Story Questions and Activity* below appear in the *Challenge Book.*

Story Questions and Activity

1. Why do salmon migrate back to the streams where they were born?
2. How do salmon find their rivers and streams?
3. What are some of the main ideas that explain why most salmon don't make it home?
4. What is the main idea of the book?
5. What do the harp seals in *Seal Journey* and the Pacific salmon discussed in this book have in common?

Life Cycle

Draw a diagram that depicts the life cycle of one salmon. Include labels on your diagram.

from Journey Against All Odds

Guided Reading

PREVIEW AND PREDICT Invite students to preview the story up to page 8. Have students look closely at the illustrations and make a Predictions chart of what the story may be about.

SET PURPOSES Have students write questions that they hope to have answered by reading the story.

READ THE BOOK After students have read the story independently, return to the text and apply the strategies, using questions like the following.

Page 3: One main idea on this page is: All salmon migrate. What are some supporting details? (They're born in freshwater streams; they migrate to the ocean.) *Main Idea*

Page 4: The writer compares the thousands of baby salmon in the river to a tiny *nursery*. What is a nursery? (A nursery is a place where small children are kept.) *Vocabulary*

Page 12: If the salmon come to a part of the river that's too shallow, they'll some- times wait for heavy rains. Why? (The water will rise and get deeper.) *Make Inferences*

Page 14: What is the main idea of the first three paragraphs on this page? (Sample answer: Some salmon have to swim up waterfalls.) *Main Idea*

RETURN TO PREDICTIONS AND PURPOSES Have students review their predictions and questions they hoped to get answered. Did the story teach them what they thought it would?

LITERARY RESPONSE Discuss these questions with students:

- If you were a salmon, what would be the hardest part of your life?
- Why is it important to learn about endangered animals?
- How might you and your friends help to keep salmon alive?

Also see the story questions and activity in *Journey Against All Odds.*

Bringing Groups Together

Anthology and Leveled Books

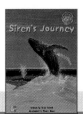

Connecting Texts

MIGRATION CHART Write the story titles on a chart. Discuss with students that although each book is about a different animal, they all focus on migration. Have students fill in some supporting details.

Seal Journey	Run Fast, Fly Far	A Siren's Journey	Journey Against All Odds
• Harp seals are born in Canada. • They travel to the northwest Atlantic. • Every autumn they return south.	• Arctic terns are born in the north. • In August, they fly to the South Pole. • In June, they return to Canada.	• Humpback whales are born in warm tropical waters. • In the summer, they migrate to cold polar waters. • Before the winter begins, they migrate to mate and give birth.	• Salmon are born in a freshwater stream. • After one to three years, they swim down the river to the ocean. • Mature salmon return home to spawn by swimming upstream.

Viewing/Representing

GROUP PRESENTATIONS Organize the class into groups, one for each of the four books. (For *Seal Journey*, combine students of different reading levels.) Have each group describe the main events and orally summarize their book.

AUDIENCE RESPONSE Ask students to listen to each group's presentation and to ask questions about anything they may not understand.

Research and Inquiry

MORE ABOUT LIFE CYCLES These four stories tell about the life cycles of harp seals, Arctic terns, humpback whales, and Pacific salmon. Have students select other animals and find out the following facts:

- What do they look like when they're born?

- What do they do when they're mature?

- What is their average size, weight, and lifespan?

- Have students make a Fact Wall of their life-cycle facts.

interNET CONNECTION To find out more about their sea animals, have students visit
www.mhschool.com/reading

117D

OBJECTIVES

Students will identify a main idea and supporting details.

Skills Finder

Main Idea

Introduce	95A-B
Review	117E-F, 127E-F
Test	Unit 1
Maintain	149, 291, 307, 623

TEACHING TIP

MANAGEMENT Many of the **Teaching Chart** passages can be reused to provide quick practice or review for other comprehension or vocabulary strategies. For example, some students may have had difficulty following the sequence of events in *Seal Journey*. Have partners reread "Jonah's Seal" and list three events in order.

SELF-SELECTED Reading

Students may choose from the following titles:

ANTHOLOGY

• Seal Journey

LEVELED BOOKS

• Run Fast, Fly Far

• A Siren's Journey

• Journey Against All Odds

Bibliography, pages T78–T79

Review Main Idea

PREPARE

Discuss Main Idea and Supporting Details

Review: To find the main idea of a paragraph, ask yourself: "What's the most important idea, the largest idea, in this paragraph?" Try the same strategy with a page, a chapter, or a whole book. Supporting details are facts or examples that help explain the main idea—or expand on it.

TEACH

Read "Jonah's Seal" and Model the Skill

Ask students to listen closely for main ideas and supporting details as you read the **Teaching Chart 22** passage with them.

Jonah's Seal

Jonah was careful not to upset the seal pup. He approached it slowly, so the pup wouldn't get frightened. He tried to avoid clunky motions a person might make walking on the ice. He didn't make a sound.

When he got to the pup, Jonah sat down on the ice. He felt an instant friendship with the beautiful seal baby. He imagined he saw the pup smile at him. He thought the pup seemed happy to get attention. "I think she likes me, Dad," he said.

Teaching Chart 22

Discuss the paragraphs in the teaching chart, looking for the main idea and the supporting details in each.

MODEL Each paragraph has a main idea with supporting details. In the first paragraph, I can tell how Jonah comes up to the seal. The details tell me Jonah was careful not to upset the pup.

PRACTICE

Find the Main Idea and Supporting Details

Have students circle the sentence that shows the main idea of the first paragraph. Ask them to underline details that support the main idea. Repeat with the second paragraph.

Then have groups decide what the main idea is for the entire story. (Jonah is careful as he forms a friendship with a seal.)

▶ **Logical/Interpersonal**

ASSESS/CLOSE

Write a New Story about a Child and a Seal

Tell children to imagine a child other than Jonah. Have them brainstorm ideas for a new two-paragraph story about a child and a seal. Remind them to decide beforehand what the main idea of the whole story will be—and what the main idea of each paragraph will be. Have groups share their stories with the class.

ALTERNATE TEACHING STRATEGY

MAIN IDEA

For a different approach to teaching this skill, see page T66.

Intervention ▶ **Skills Intervention Guide**, for direct instruction and extra practice in main ideas

Meeting Individual Needs for Comprehension

EASY	ON-LEVEL	CHALLENGE	LANGUAGE SUPPORT

EASY

Name_____ Date_____ Reteach **26**

Main Idea and Supporting Details

> Sometimes authors state the **main idea** and then give **details** to support it. Other times it is up to the reader to decide what the main idea is.

Read the paragraph. Then write the answers to the questions.

Americans have always loved sports. But the popularity of certain sports has changed over time. Baseball and football used to be the most popular sports in our country. Many people still play and enjoy these games. Today, however, millions of young people are playing soccer. Some schools have dropped football and replaced it with soccer. Gymnastics has also grown in popularity as have volleyball, ice and field hockey, and figure skating.

1. What is the main idea? The popularity of certain sports has changed over time.

2. What is one detail that supports the main idea? Possible answer: Today millions of young people are playing soccer.

3. What is another supporting detail? Possible answer: Some schools have dropped football and replaced it with soccer.

Read the statement that follows. Then answer the question.

Americans no longer care much about sports.

4. Is the statement true or false based on the paragraph above? false

At Home: Have students write a short paragraph about sports with a main idea and two supporting details.

26   Book 4/Unit 1   **Seal Journey** 4

ON-LEVEL

Name_____ Date_____ Practice **26**

Main Idea and Supporting Details

The **main idea** of a paragraph is its most important idea. **Details** in the paragraph help support the main idea. Read the paragraph below. Write the main idea, then the details that support the main idea.

Dogs are trained to do many different jobs. Some dogs are trained to help people who are blind or who can see only a little. They make it possible for people to do many things they couldn't do without them. Other dogs are trained to do police work. Dogs with a sharp sense of smell track people and search for dangerous items. Some dogs are used for hunting. Still other dogs help farmers herd sheep and cows. But many dogs are pets. They are playful. They may also help keep a home safe by barking when strangers come near.

1. Main idea: Dogs are trained to do many jobs.

2. Supporting detail: Some dogs are trained to help the blind or people with poor eyesight.

3. Supporting detail: Some dogs are trained to do police work.

4. Supporting detail: Dogs are also used for hunting.

5. Supporting detail: Some dogs are trained to help farmers herd their sheep and cows.

6. Supporting detail: Many dogs are pets. They are playful and often help keep a home safe by barking when strangers come near.

At Home: Have students write about the main idea of "Seal Journey."

26   Book 4/Unit 1   **Seal Journey** 6

CHALLENGE

Name_____ Date_____ Extend **26**

Main Idea and Supporting Details

Think about the details and facts that support the **main idea** of "Seal Journey." Write about three things that most impressed you in the story, and tell why they impressed you.

Answers will vary, but should cite main ideas and supporting details from the story.

Photographs have been important in making people aware of the cruelty toward baby harp seals. Think of an endangered animal that you would like to protect. State which animal you would protect. Tell why you would do this, using supporting details and facts.

Answers will vary, but should include supporting details and facts.

At Home: Discuss how photographs are important in making people aware of wildlife and their habitats.

26   Book 4/Unit 1   **Seal Journey** 5

LANGUAGE SUPPORT

Name_____ Date_____

My Seal Book

1. Number the pictures in the order each happened in *Seal Journey*. 2. Cut out the pictures. Color them if you want to. 3. Paste the pictures together to make your very own Seal Book.

30 Seal Journey • Language Support/Blackline Master 14   Grade 4

Reteach, 26   Practice, 26   Extend, 26   Language Support, 30

117F

OBJECTIVES

Students will make and explain inferences.

Skills Finder

Make Inferences

Introduce	41G-H
Review	65G-H, 117G-H, 515G-H, 535G-H, 567G-H
Test	Unit 1, Unit 5
Maintain	147, 197, 225, 495

TEACHING TIP

MANAGEMENT The Teaching Charts are designed to be used interactively with students. Be sure to have students underline or circle clues on the acetate overlay. The charts are also available on transparencies.

Review Make Inferences

PREPARE

Discuss Making Inferences

Explain: Readers use their own experiences plus "clues" from the text to make inferences about what is happening in a selection where the author has not been explicit.

TEACH

Read "On the Ice" and Model the Skill

Read the story "On the Ice." Ask students to consider how making inferences can help them understand the story better.

On the Ice

Dad and Juanita stepped out of the helicopter and onto the ice. Looking around at the bleak landscape, Juanita expected her teeth to start chattering, but they didn't. She was snug in her special outfit.

Juanita's clunky boots made walking easier than she had expected. When she'd first seen the surface, she'd thought she might have to make moves like a hockey player.

Dad pointed ahead, to thousands and thousands of seals. "This is really a different experience from a trip to the zoo, isn't it?" he said.

Teaching Chart 23

Ask a volunteer to look at the second sentence and read it aloud. Why did Juanita expect her teeth to start chattering? What inference does the author expect readers to make?

MODEL I know Juanita expected her teeth to chatter. From clues in the story, I know she's walking on ice. From my own experience, I know the temperature must have been very cold to freeze the water and turn it into ice.

ALTERNATE TEACHING
STRATEGY
....
MAKE INFERENCES
For a different approach to
teaching this skill, see page
T62.

PRACTICE

Make and Explain Inferences

GROUP

Invite volunteers to follow your model as they make and explain
other inferences about the story. Have them underline clues in the
story they used to make their inferences. Remind them to also
consider clues from their personal experience. ▶ **Logical**

ASSESS/CLOSE

Make an Inference

Tell students this story:

A boy sits outside on a summer day. He sees mosquitoes nearby.
Then his arm starts to itch.

Ask students to make an inference about why the boy's arm itched.

Intervention **Skills**
Intervention Guide, for direct
instruction and extra practice
in making inferences

Meeting Individual Needs for Comprehension

EASY	ON-LEVEL	CHALLENGE	LANGUAGE SUPPORT

EASY

Name_____ Date_____ Reteach **27**

Make Inferences

Good readers look for clues in the text that will help them understand what is
happening and how characters are feeling. This is called **making
inferences.**

Read the story. Then make inferences to answer the questions.

Brian turned around and around. Everywhere he looked there
was only sand. It seemed there were miles of nothing but sand.
Brian checked to see if his still had his hat on because he felt like he
was getting sunburned. His shirt felt glued to his body. He stretched
and could feel every bone in his body. It had been a long ride on the
camel. Even though he felt uncomfortable, he knew he would never
forget what he was seeing. After one last look, he waved goodbye to
the great pyramids.

Write the answer to each question.

1. Where is Brian? What clues let you know? the Egyptian desert; there was
sand everywhere; there were pyramids and camels

2. Is it hot or cold? How do you know? hot; He felt like he was getting
sunburned. His shirt stuck to his body.

3. How does Brian's body feel? How do you know? sore; achy; he could feel
every bone in his body.

4. Why does he feel this way? He had a long camel ride in the desert.

5. How does Brian feel as he looks around? Answers will vary. He probably
feels pleased to have the experience of seeing the great pyramids. At the
same time he feels uncomfortable physically.

Book 4/Unit 1
Seal Journey
At Home: Have students write about inferences they had
to make to figure out the plot of a favorite book or movie.
27

ON-LEVEL

Name_____ Date_____ Practice **27**

Make Inferences

An author doesn't always tell you why story characters do what they do.
Therefore, you must **make inferences** about characters' actions by
"reading between the lines." To make an inference, you can use clues
provided by the author and similar experiences that you have had or
heard about.

Read the story. Make an inference for each question.

Stacy, Gena, and their mom piled up the camping equipment near
the door.
"I'll help you put up the tent when we get there, Mom," said Stacy.
"I'm good at that."
Gena sighed as she dropped the knapsack. "I'll stay in the car until
you get that tent set up." Gena ran to give her best friend Hannah a
last-minute phone call. All her friends were going to Hannah's house
that afternoon. Everyone but Gena would be there. Gena sighed
again.
Stacy and her mom waited for Gena by the door. "I get excited
when I'm about to go camping," said Mom. "When I was little, I
couldn't wait to go. Luckily Gramma and Grandpa loved to camp too."

1. Who is going camping? Stacy, Gena, and their mom

2. How does Gena feel about going camping? How do you know?
She doesn't want to go. She's sighing and calling her friend to talk
about what they will be doing while she is out camping.

3. How does Stacy feel about the camping trip?
She seems enthusiastic. She looks forward to putting up the tent. She
waits with her mom by the door.

4. How might the girls' mom have gotten interested in camping?
She went camping a lot with her parents.

5. Who will enjoy the trip most? Stacy and her mom

Book 4/Unit 1
Seal Journey
At Home: Have students write a funny camping story.
27

CHALLENGE

Name_____ Date_____ Extend **27**

Make Inferences

Use clues in "Seal Journey" to **make inferences** about the story.
Answers will vary. Possible answers are given.

1. Why is a helicopter the only way for Jonah and his father to reach the seal
colony? It is probably the quickest way. So much ice might be
dangerous for boats.

2. What type of clothing do you think Jonah and his father wore?
Answers should include hats, boots, gloves or mittens, warm jackets,
waterproof or ski pants.

3. What type of supplies do you think that Jonah and his father took along for the
day? Possible answers may include film, camera supplies, food, water,
and extra clothes.

4. Why do you think that a mother seal's milk is so rich? The seal pups must
grow quickly, so they need extra nourishment. The mother seal's diet is
rich in nutrients, therefore, her milk will also be rich.

5. Do you think that Jonah's father ever held a baby seal, like his son did?
Explain. Yes, probably because he has visited and photographed the
seals before. Like his son, the father is very fond of the seals.

Book 4/Unit 1
Seal Journey
At Home: Have students guess memorable activities
the family has participated in together by giving a
series of clues.
27

LANGUAGE SUPPORT

Name_____ Date_____

If Pictures Could Talk

1. Each picture shows something that was described in Seal Journey.
2. Write a sentence under each picture that tells what each character in the story
might be thinking. 3. Color the pictures.

Jonah is in a helicopter seeing
Harp seals close up for the first time.

Jonah is gently holding
a seal pup.

A seal pup is nursing
with its mother.

Two seal pups are playing
in the water.

Grade 4
Language Support/Blackline Master 15 • Seal Journey **31**

Review Multiple-Meaning Words

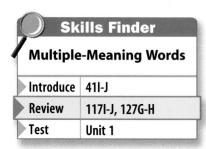

TESTED OBJECTIVES

Students will identify and understand multiple-meaning words and homographs.

Skills Finder

Multiple-Meaning Words

Introduce	41I–J
Review	117I–J, 127G–H
Test	Unit 1

TEACHING TIP

HOMOGRAPHS Tell students that to determine the meaning/pronunciation of a homograph, you must look carefully at its context within the sentence. It is also helpful to know whether the word functions as an action word, a naming word, or a describing word.
Semantic/Syntactic Cues

PREPARE

Discuss Multiple-Meaning Words and Homographs

Review: A multiple-meaning word has one spelling and one pronunciation, but more than one meaning. Homographs are spelled the same, but have different meanings, different pronunciations, and different functions in a sentence.

TEACH

Read the Passage and Model the Skill

Have students read the passage on **Teaching Chart 24.**

> **The Girl with the Bow in Her Hair**
>
> I have a friend who always wears a <u>bow</u> in her hair. Whenever I see her, I <u>bow</u>.
> One day, I tried to strike up a conversation with her, but she was busy reading. "I can't talk to you while I <u>read</u>," she said. I knew she was reading a book she had already <u>read</u>.
> "Why are you being <u>mean</u> to me?" I asked.
> "I'm sorry," she said. "I didn't <u>mean</u> to hurt your feelings."
>
> Teaching Chart 24

Help students identify multiple-meaning words and homographs.

MODEL I see the letters *b-o-w* twice in the first paragraph. I know this word can be pronounced /bou/ or /bō/. It is a homograph, because it has two different pronunciations and more than one meaning. One meaning refers to an action; the other names a thing. I can try both pronunciations and meanings in each sentence to see which one makes sense.

Identify Multiple-Meaning Words and Homographs

Have students underline the three pairs of common multiple-meaning words and homographs in the passage.

PRACTICE

Use Context Clues to Determine Meaning

GROUP

Ask volunteers to read the last two lines in the chart aloud. Have students tell the meaning of *mean* each time it is used. Encourage students to share the context clues they used to determine meaning. ▶ **Linguistic**

ASSESS/CLOSE

Identify Meanings

PARTNERS

Write these words on the chalkboard:

bat   lead   bass   wind

Have pairs write two meanings for each word and illustrate each. Invite them to share their illustrations with the class.

ALTERNATE TEACHING STRATEGY
....

MULTIPLE-MEANING WORDS

For a different approach to teaching this skill, see page T63.

Intervention ▶ **Skills**

Intervention Guide, for direct instruction and extra practice in multiple-meaning words

---

Meeting Individual Needs for Vocabulary

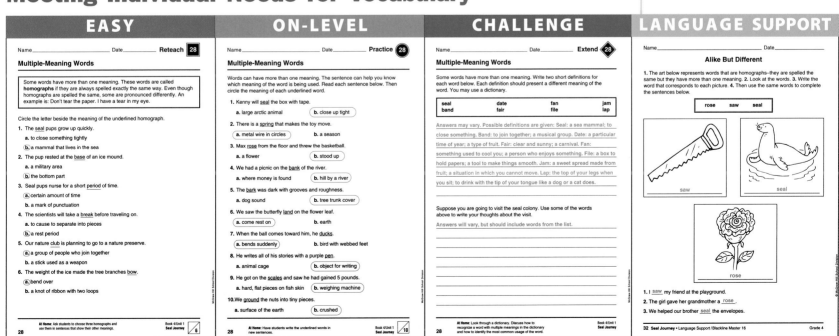

EASY	ON-LEVEL	CHALLENGE	LANGUAGE SUPPORT
Reteach, 28	Practice, 28	Extend, 28	Language Support, 32

Personal Narrative

GRAMMAR/SPELLING CONNECTIONS

See the 5-Day Grammar and Usage Plan on sentence combining, pages 117M–117N.

See the 5-Day Spelling Plan on words with /ū/ and /ü/, pages 117O–117P.

TEACHING TIP

Technology Word processing programs include a way to make "hard" page breaks. This function allows a writer working on a photo essay to type the text on a number of pages, thereby leaving room for illustrations.

Handwriting Remind students to use cursive writing for drafts and revisions. All letters should have the same slant. For clarity, the ascenders and descenders should not overlap. Explain the importance of legibility in writing.

Handwriting CD-ROM

Prewrite

WRITE A PHOTO ESSAY Present this writing assignment: Jonah and his dad took a trip to see seals. Write about a trip you have taken. Describe where you went, what you did, and what you learned. Tell about events in order. Attach photos, if you have them, or draw illustrations. Use facts or details to support your main idea.

BRAINSTORM IDEAS Have students brainstorm ideas for trips they might like to write about. This will be a photo essay, so urge them to think in pictures as well as words.

Strategy: Visualize and Draw Have students make rough sketches of scenes they would like to include. Suggest the following:

• Show planning and packing for the trip.

• Include the special or unusual highlights of the trip.

• Tell what you learned from the trip.

Draft

USE THE SKETCHES In their essays, students should include the strongest main ideas from their sketches and elaborate on them with details. They should take photos or make drawings that illustrate the specific text.

Revise

SELF-QUESTIONING Ask students to assess their drafts.

• Did I get across my main ideas?

• Did I tell and show details to support my main ideas?

• Have I presented events in the order they occurred?

Have partners exchange essays and recommend areas that need more detail.

Edit/Proofread

CHECK FOR ERRORS Students should reread their essays for spelling, grammar, and punctuation.

Publish

SHARE THE ESSAYS Students can exchange their completed essays with one another. Encourage them to discuss what they liked about each other's work.

Visiting Pandas

This summer Mom and I took a trip to the San Diego Zoo to see the Giant Pandas. We both think these big, black-and-white animals are really cool. We packed a lunch, brought sun hats and a camera, and took off in the car.

We headed for the zoo's panda exhibit where two Giant Pandas from China live. Bai Yun, the female, is nine years old. Her name means "white cloud." Shi Shi is sixteen. His name means "rock."

Bai Yun was eating bamboo. There was lots of it planted in her pen, along with other trees, logs, and a pool. Shi Shi was playing with the logs in his pen.

I had lots of questions. "Why are they kept apart?" I asked a zookeeper. "Pandas are used to living alone in the wild," she said. "But these two get together for a visit about once a week."

Presentation Ideas

TELL A STORY Have students tell a story about the place they went to. Encourage the audience to ask questions.

▶ **Speaking/Listening**

ACT OUT A SCENE Have students pantomime scenes from their essays. Encourage audience members to guess what they are seeing. ▶ **Viewing/Representing**

The Giant Panda lives on bamboo shoots.

Consider students' creative efforts, possibly adding a plus (+) for originality, wit, and imagination.

Viewing and Speaking

VIEWING STRATEGIES

Have students:
- tell the main ideas expressed in the photos or drawings.
- explain how details in the photos or drawings support those main ideas.

SPEAKING STRATEGIES

Encourage students to:
- tell why they included the photos or drawings they chose.
- ask questions suggested by the photos or drawings in student essays.

Scoring Rubric

Excellent	Good	Fair	Unsatisfactory
4: The writer • clearly gets across a main idea. • provides lots of interesting supporting facts and details. • combines text with pictures meaningfully. • presents events in a logical sequence.	**3:** The writer • tries to get across a main idea. • provides adequate supporting facts and details. • uses pictures and text well. • presents events in a mostly logical sequence.	**2:** The writer • does not succeed in getting a main idea across. • provides only some supporting facts and details. • does not always show relationship between pictures and text. • presents some events out of order.	**1:** The writer • has not formulated a main idea. • provides few supporting facts and details. • shows no relationship between pictures and text. • lacks a logical sequence of events.

Incomplete 0: The writer leaves the page blank or fails to respond to the writing task. The student does not address the topic or simply paraphrases the prompt. The response is illegible or incoherent.

For a 6-point or an 8-point scale, see pages T107–T108.

LANGUAGE SUPPORT

ESL Some English learners may have good visual ideas that they want to express in English. Have them organize their illustrations first. Then have them work with a native English speaking partner to brainstorm ways of putting their thoughts into complete sentences.

PORTFOLIO Invite students to include their photo essays or another writing project in their portfolios.

Meeting Individual Needs for Writing

EASY	ON-LEVEL	CHALLENGE
Snapshots Have students draw a series of "snapshots" that Jonah might have taken of the seals. Ask them to label each snapshot with a sentence or two.	**Letter** Have students imagine that they have gone on the trip with Richard and Jonah Sobol. Ask them to write a letter or E-mail to a friend or relative telling about what they saw and learned.	**Plan for a Trip** Have students select a wild animal that they would like to study. Ask them to write a plan for a study trip, outlining why they want to go, where they will look for the animal, and what they expect to see and how they will document their trip.

5 Day Grammar and Usage Plan

Have two students perform two different actions at the same time. Use one compound sentence to tell what they are doing.

DAILY LANGUAGE ACTIVITIES

Write the Daily Language Activities on the chalkboard each day or use **Transparency 4.** Have students orally combine the sentences, using conjunctions such as *while, if, where, because, unless, before, when, as if,* and *until.* For sample answers, see the transparency.

Day 1

1. Jonah looked. I took pictures.
2. You can hear seals. You listen.
3. The seals lay still. They were sleeping.

Day 2

1. We saw the place. The seals live.
2. They will die. Steps are taken.
3. He saw a seal. His dad saw it.

Day 3

1. He looks out the window. We fly.
2. We watched the seals. It got dark.
3. Jonah put down the seal. It was time to go.

Day 4

1. I was happy. The seals were safe.
2. I took pictures. I arrived.
3. The pup swims. It learns how.

Day 5

1. The seals head north. The ice melts.
2. Seals were hunted. People cared.
3. We walked softly. We were nervous.

DAY 1 — Introduce the Concept

Oral Warm-Up Ask students to list the conjunctions they have already learned. *(and, but, or)*

Introduce More Sentence Combining Remind them that a conjunction joins words or groups of words.

More Sentence Combining

- You can use conjunctions other than *and, but,* and *or* to combine sentences.
- Some conjunctions tell *where, when, why, how,* or *under what condition.*

Begin a chart of conjunctions that tell where *(where)*, when *(when, while, before, until)*, why *(because)*, how *(as if)*, and under what condition *(if, unless)*.

Present the Daily Language Activity. Have students choose four conjunctions and use them to write sentences.

 Assign the daily Writing Prompt on page 94C.

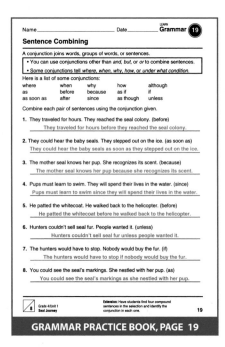

GRAMMAR PRACTICE BOOK, PAGE 19

DAY 2 — Teach the Concept

Review Sentence Combining Ask students to name words that can be used to combine sentences.

Introduce Complex Sentences The conjunctions *and, but,* and *or* form **compound sentences.** But what about sentences with other conjunctions?

Complex Sentences

- A sentence that contains two related ideas joined by a conjunction other than *and, but,* or *or* is called a **complex sentence.**

Display and discuss the following: **The pilot smiled as I boarded the plane.**

Present the Daily Language Activity. Have students write pairs of sentences using conjunctions other than *and, but,* or *or.* Invite them to exchange papers and write a complex sentence.

 Assign the daily Writing Prompt on page 94C.

GRAMMAR PRACTICE BOOK, PAGE 20

More Sentence Combining

DAY 3 — Review and Practice

Learn from the Literature Review sentence combining. Write the following complex sentence on the board, from the middle of page 98 of *Seal Journey:*

> **The first trip had been in 1981 when I set out to show the cruelty of the seal hunt that was then taking place.**

Ask students to identify the conjunction. Then have them remove the conjunction and turn the one sentence into two.

Find Complex Sentences Present the Daily Language Activity. Then have students look at page 109 of *Seal Journey.* Have them find complex sentences that use the conjunctions *until, where,* and *when.*

 Assign the daily Writing Prompt on page 94D.

DAY 4 — Review and Practice

Review Sentence Combining Write the conjunctions from the Daily Language Activity for Days 1–3 on the board. Ask students to choose one and use it to write a complex sentence. Then present the Daily Language Activity for Day 4.

Mechanics and Usage Display and discuss:

Quotations

- Use quotation marks at the beginning and end of a person's exact words.

- Do not use quotation marks when you do not use the speaker's exact words.

Use the following to help students understand when to use quotations:

He said, "I can't go."

He said he can't go.

 Assign the daily Writing Prompt on page 94D.

DAY 5 — Assess and Reteach

Assess Use the Daily Language Activity and page 23 of the **Grammar Practice Book** for assessment.

Reteach Invite students to play Sentence Tag. Have a volunteer begin a complex sentence by stating a main clause followed by a conjunction. For example, *I came home when. . . .* Then have the volunteer "tag" a student who will complete the sentence.

Have students add conjunctions, along with a sentence for each, to a Sentence Combining Bulletin Board.

Use page 24 of the **Grammar Practice Book** for additional reteaching.

 Assign the daily Writing Prompt on page 94D.

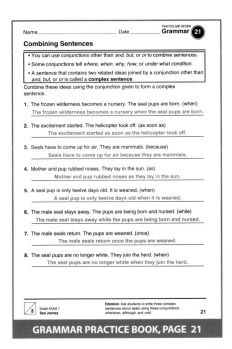

GRAMMAR PRACTICE BOOK, PAGE 21

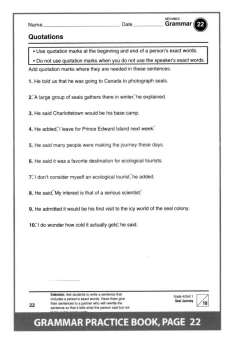

GRAMMAR PRACTICE BOOK, PAGE 22

GRAMMAR PRACTICE BOOK, PAGE 23

GRAMMAR PRACTICE BOOK, PAGE 24 **117N**

5 Day Spelling Plan

ESL Point out to students that the vowel sounds /ū/ and /ü/ are similar. Repeat the two sounds aloud, and then say words containing both sounds. (continue, gloomy, use, two) Have students identify which vowel sound is in each word.

DICTATION SENTENCES

Spelling Words

1. Did you bring your ruler to class?
2. We walked down the avenue.
3. A raccoon knocked over the can.
4. Some pigs got loose.
5. Mother has to commute a long way.
6. Please continue the story.
7. The boys looked gloomy.
8. The students started a unit about frogs.
9. Whose shoes are in the gym?
10. She has a good sense of humor.
11. Some paint will improve this room.
12. What a beautiful song!
13. The ice cube is cold.
14. She sits on a stool.
15. There was movement in the grass.
16. Rain will ruin that chair.
17. He plays the bugle.
18. Don't argue so much!
19. We live in a safe community.
20. A tuna is a fish.

Challenge Words

21. My friend assured me I looked pretty.
22. We saw a sail near the horizon.
23. The rocks are jagged.
24. That child is not mature.
25. She squealed when she saw the mouse.

DAY 1 — Pretest

Assess Prior Knowledge Use the Dictation Sentences at the left and **Spelling Practice Book** page 19 for the pretest. Allow students to correct their own papers. Students who require a modified list may be tested on the first ten words.

Spelling Words		Challenge Words
1. ruler	12. beautiful	21. **assured**
2. avenue	13. cube	22. **horizon**
3. raccoon	14. stool	23. **jagged**
4. loose	15. **move-**	24. **mature**
5. commute	**ment**	25. **squealed**
6. **continue**	16. ruin	
7. gloomy	17. bugle	
8. unit	18. argue	
9. whose	19. commu-	
10. humor	nity	
11. **improve**	20. tuna	

*Note: Words in **dark type** are from the story.*

Word Study On page 20 of the **Spelling Practice Book** are word study steps and an at-home activity.

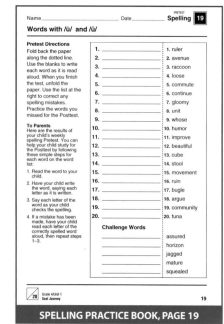

SPELLING PRACTICE BOOK, PAGE 19

WORD STUDY STEPS AND ACTIVITY, PAGE 20

DAY 2 — Explore the Pattern

Sort and Spell Words Say *cube* and *loose*. Ask students what vowel sound they hear in each word. (/ū/ and /ü/) Have students read the Spelling Words aloud and sort them as below.

Words with /ū/ Spelled

u	u-e	ue
unit	commute	avenue
humor	cube	continue
bugle		argue
community	**eau**	
	beautiful	

Words with /ü/ Spelled

u	oo	o-e
ruler	loose	whose
ruin	raccoon	improve
tuna	gloomy	movement
	stool	

Word Wall Have students create a word wall based on the word sort and add more words from their reading.

SPELLING PRACTICE BOOK, PAGE 21

Words with /ū/ and /ü/

DAY 3 — Practice and Extend

Word Meaning: Fill-Ins Organize students into pairs. Have the first student make up a sentence using one of the Spelling Words and then say the sentence aloud, leaving out the Spelling Word. See how long it takes the student's partner to fill in the blank with the correct spelling word. Then have the students switch roles. They can go back and forth, eventually making up sentences for all of the words.

If students need extra practice, have partners give each other a midweek test.

Glossary Use the Glossary to review illustrative sentences. Have partners:

- write each Challenge Word.

- copy the illustrative sentence that appears in the Glossary for each Challenge Word.

- write their own illustrative sentence for each Challenge Word.

DAY 4 — Proofread and Write

Proofread Sentences Write these sentences on the chalkboard, including the misspelled words. Ask students to proofread, circling incorrect spellings and writing the correct spellings. There are two spelling errors in each sentence.

> **Will the weather continu to impruve?**
> (continue, improve)
>
> **Whoose beutiful flowers are on the desk? (Whose, beautiful)**

Have students create additional sentences with errors for partners to correct.

 Have students use as many Spelling Words as possible in the daily Writing Prompt on page 94D. Remind students to proofread their writing for errors in spelling, grammar, and punctuation.

DAY 5 — Assess and Reteach

Assess Students' Knowledge Use page 24 of the **Spelling Practice Book** or the Dictation Sentences on page 117O for the posttest.

Personal Word List If students have trouble with any words in this lesson, have them add to their personal list in their journals. Suggest that students practice spelling and defining each of these words with a partner.

Students should refer to their word lists during later writing activities.

SPELLING PRACTICE BOOK, PAGE 22

Words with /ū/ and /ü/

PRACTICE AND EXTEND — Spelling 22

ruler	commute	whose	cube	bugle
avenue	continue	humor	stool	argue
raccoon	gloomy	improve	movement	community
loose	unit	beautiful	ruin	tuna

Complete each sentence below with a spelling word or words.

1. A king is the __ruler__ of a country.
2. I play the __bugle__ in the school marching band.
3. She knows __whose__ books these are.
4. The __raccoon__ sat on the tree branch and looked at me.
5. If I __continue__ to practice, I may make the baseball team.
6. The people who live in my __community__ are very friendly.
7. Put a leash on the dog, or he will get __loose__.
8. Many people __commute__ to work by train.
9. The nursery is just one __unit__ in the hospital.
10. He put an ice __cube__ in his drink.
11. A joke with good __humor__ can make you laugh.
12. The child stepped up on the __stool__ to reach the sink.

Synonym Alert!
Write the spelling word that has the same, or almost the same, meaning.

1. road — __avenue__
2. dark or sad — __gloomy__
3. disagree or fight — __argue__
4. motion — __movement__
5. pretty — __beautiful__
6. destroy — __ruin__
7. make better — __improve__
8. fish — __tuna__

22 — Challenge Extension: Have students write one sentence for each Challenge Word. — Grade 4/Unit 1 Seal Journey — 20

SPELLING PRACTICE BOOK, PAGE 23

Words with /ū/ and /ü/

PROOFREAD AND WRITE — Spelling 23

Proofreading Activity
There are six spelling mistakes in the paragraph below. Circle the misspelled words. Write the words correctly on the lines below.

The baby seal looked like a bootiful white ball of fur. It made a muvment toward its mother. Its mother will continu to feed it milk for twelve days. Seals eat small fish and shrimp, not big fish, like the toona. Soon the whole communeity of seals will swim north. It makes me sad and glumy to say goodbye to the baby seals.

1. __movement__ 3. __continue__ 5. __community__
2. __beautiful__ 4. __tuna__ 6. __gloomy__

Writing Activity
Think about an adventure you would like. Where would you go and what would you do? Write a paragraph using four spelling words in your writing.

10 — Grade 4/Unit 1 Seal Journey — 23

SPELLING PRACTICE BOOK, PAGE 24

Words with /ū/ and /ü/

POSTTEST — Spelling 24

Look at the words in each set below. One word in each set is spelled correctly. Use a pencil to fill in the circle next to the correct word. Before you begin, look at the sample sets of words. Sample A has been done for you. Do Sample B by yourself. When you are sure you know what to do, you may go on with the rest of the page.

Sample A — (A) ceaut (B) cuet (C) cutt (D) cute●
Sample B — (E) bute (F) boot (G) bote (H) byte

1. (A) unet (B) unitt (C) unit● (D) unyt
2. (E) commute● (F) comute (G) commut (H) commoot
3. (A) avenoo (B) avenue● (C) avenu (D) avenoe
4. (E) ruler● (F) rooler (G) rular (H) ruller
5. (A) byootiful (B) beatiful (C) beutiful (D) beautiful●
6. (E) loos (F) loose● (G) luose (H) looce
7. (A) woos (B) whos (C) whose● (D) whooz
8. (E) humor● (F) hoomor (G) humur (H) heumor
9. (A) kube (B) cyube (C) cube● (D) coobe
10. (E) continu (F) continyu (G) continooe (H) continue●
11. (A) rooin (B) ruine (C) ruin● (D) ruen
12. (E) raccune (F) raccoon● (G) raccun (H) raccoun
13. (A) improv (B) improov (C) improove (D) improve●
14. (E) glumy (F) gloomie (G) gloomy● (H) gloomey
15. (E) tuna● (F) tuona (G) toona (H) tunae
16. (E) byugle (F) boogle (G) bugel (H) bugle●
17. (A) stuol (B) stoole (C) stool● (D) stoul
18. (E) movement● (F) movment (G) moovement (H) muvement
19. (A) comyunity (B) community● (C) comoonity (D) comunity
20. (E) argoo (F) argyue (G) argue● (H) argu

24 — Grade 4/Unit 1 Seal Journey — 20

Cumulative Review with Expository Text

Time to Review

Anthology

Open Wide, Don't Bite!

Selection Summary Students will read about a dentist who works with some very special patients—animals. The unique problems of working on animals' teeth lead to some creative solutions.

Stories in Art focuses on the **comprehension** skill

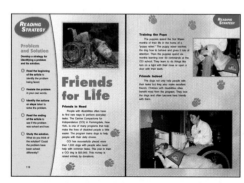

Reading Strategy applies the **comprehension** skill

Listening Library

INSTRUCTIONAL pages 120–127

Time to Reread

Reread Leveled Books

EASY
Lesson on pages 127A and 127D

INDEPENDENT
Lesson on pages 127B and 127D

🏠 *Take-Home version available*

CHALLENGE
Lesson on pages 127C and 127D

Leveled Practice

EASY

Reteach, 29–35 blackline masters with reteaching opportunities for each assessed skill

INDEPENDENT/ON-LEVEL

Practice, 29–35 workbook with Take-Home stories and practice opportunities for each assessed skill and story comprehension

CHALLENGE

Extend, 29–35 blackline masters that offer challenge activities for each assessed skill

Quizzes Prepared by Accelerated Reader®

WORKSTATION Activities

Language Arts .. Read Aloud, *118E*

Science . . . . Parts of a Tooth, *125*

Writing . . . . Personal Narrative, *124*

Art . . . . Create a Job Box, *125*
Draw a Poster, *125*

Research and Inquiry . . . . . . Find Out More, *125*

💻 **Internet Activities** . . . . www.mhschool.com/reading

Suggested
Lesson Planner

READING AND LANGUAGE ARTS

- **Comprehension**
- **Vocabulary**
- **Phonics/Decoding**
- **Study Skills**
- **Listening, Speaking, Viewing, Representing**

 DAY 1 *Focus on Reading and Skills*

 Read Aloud: Poetry, 118E
"The Dentist"

Develop Visual Literacy, 118

☑ Review Problem and Solution, 119A–119B
Teaching Chart 25
Reteach, Practice, Extend, 29

 Reading Strategy: Problem and Solution, 119
"Friends for Life"

ⓘ Intervention Program

DAY 2 *Read the Literature*

 Build Background, 120A
Develop Oral Language

Vocabulary, 120B–120C

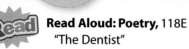

broad	healthy	reptiles
fangs	patients	skills

Teaching Chart 26
Word Building Manipulative Cards
Reteach, Practice, Extend, 30

 Read the Selection, 120–123
☑ Problem and Solution
☑ Make Inferences

Genre: Science Article, 121

ⓘ Intervention Program

- **Curriculum Connections**

 Link Works of Art, 118

Link Health/Science, 120A

- **Writing**

✏ **Writing Prompt:** Pretend you are the owner of an unusual pet. Describe in detail what a day would be like taking care of this animal.

✏ **Writing Prompt:** You are the dentist for the mountain lion on page 123. Describe the perfect dental office to accommodate this difficult patient.

📓 **Journal Writing,** 123
Quick-Write

- **Grammar**

Introduce the Concept: Run-on Sentences, 127M
Daily Language Activity
1. A dentist works hard he stays busy.
2. Some animals have flat teeth other animals have sharp teeth.
3. Sometimes cats break teeth this means trouble.

Grammar Practice Book, 25

Teach the Concept: Run-on Sentences, 127M
Daily Language Activity
1. The tiger is a big cat the housecat is small.
2. Beavers' teeth stay filed down they are always chewing.
3. Reptiles lose their teeth they are replaced.

Grammar Practice Book, 26

- **Spelling**

Pretest: Words from Health, 127O
Spelling Practice Book, 25, 26

Explore the Pattern: Words from Health, 127O
Spelling Practice Book, 27

Meeting Individual Needs

 = **Skill Assessed in Unit Test**

 Intervention Program Available

 **Read EVERY DAY**

DAY 3 — Read the Literature

 Rereading for Fluency, 122

Story Questions and Activities, 124–125
Reteach, Practice, Extend, 31

Study Skill, 126
 Parts of a Book
Teaching Chart 27
Reteach, Practice, Extend, 32

Test Power, 127

 **Read the Leveled Books,** 127A–127D
Guided Reading
Phonics Review
 **Comprehension Review**

 Intervention Program

 Activity Social Studies, 125

Writing Prompt: Compose a letter from Dr. Kertesz convincing a family why he would be the perfect dentist for their family pet.

Writing Process: Personal Narrative, 127K
Prewrite, Draft

Review and Practice: Run-on Sentences, 127N
Daily Language Activity
1. Monkeys pull back their lips they smile.
2. Wolves have pointed teeth they bite their food.

Grammar Practice Book, 27

Practice and Extend: Words from Health, 127P
Spelling Practice Book, 28

DAY 4 — Build and Review Skills

 Read **Read the Leveled Books and Self-Selected Books**

 Review Main Idea, 127E–127F
Teaching Chart 28
Reteach, Practice, Extend, 33
Language Support, 38

Review Multiple-Meaning Words, 127G–127H
Teaching Chart 29
Reteach, Practice, Extend, 34
Language Support, 39

 Intervention Program

 Activity Science, 125

Writing Prompt: You design habitats for animals in zoos or preserves. Write about the habitat you have created for a particular animal.

Writing Process: Personal Narrative, 127K
Revise
Meeting Individual Needs for Writing, 127L

Review and Practice: Run-on Sentences, 127N
Daily Language Activity
1. Lions can be mean medicine keeps them calm.
2. Teeth need to be cleaned diseases can start.

Grammar Practice Book, 28

Proofread and Write: Words from Health, 127P
Spelling Practice Book, 29

DAY 5 — Build and Review Skills

 Read **Read Self-Selected Books**

Review Antonyms and Synonyms, 127I–127J
Teaching Chart 30
Reteach, Practice, Extend, 35
Language Support, 40

Listening, Speaking, Viewing, Representing, 127L

Intervention Program

Writing Prompt: What's your favorite animal? Write a paragraph describing the animal and why you think it is more interesting than any other.

Writing Process: Personal Narrative, 127K
Edit/Proofread, Publish

Assess and Reteach: Run-on Sentences, 127N
Daily Language Activity
1. Big animals are easy patients their mouths are large.
2. Hand-holding calms a gorilla it visits the dentist.

Grammar Practice Book, 29, 30

Assess and Reteach: Words from Health, 127P
Spelling Practice Book, 30

118D

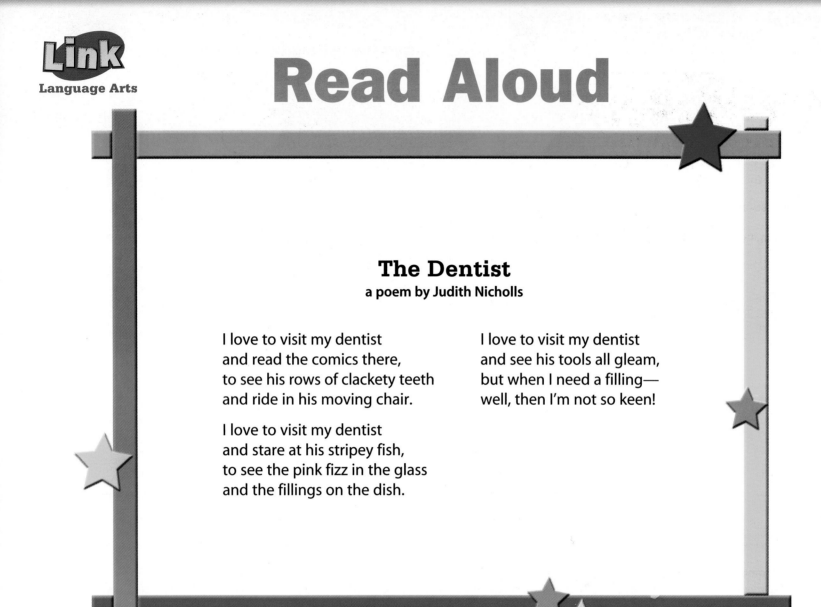

Read Aloud

Link Language Arts

The Dentist
a poem by Judith Nicholls

I love to visit my dentist
and read the comics there,
to see his rows of clackety teeth
and ride in his moving chair.

I love to visit my dentist
and stare at his stripey fish,
to see the pink fizz in the glass
and the fillings on the dish.

I love to visit my dentist
and see his tools all gleam,
but when I need a filling—
well, then I'm not so keen!

Oral Comprehension

LISTENING AND SPEAKING Read the poem aloud. Have students visualize the experience described. Ask:

• In the first two and a half stanzas, how does the poet feel about visiting the dentist's office?

• When does a shift in feeling occur? Why?

Then reread the poem. Discuss problem (fear) and solutions (overcoming fear) associated with a visit to the dentist.

GENRE STUDY: POETRY Discuss literary devices used in "The Dentist."

• The poem has three stanzas of four lines each. Note the ABCB rhyme scheme in each stanza.

• Discuss the lighthearted tone. Which words help set the tone?

Activity Read aloud the poem and have pairs of students pantomime the patient and dentist. Encourage students to express the tone of the poem through their actions. ▶ **Auditory/Kinesthetic**

Develop Visual Literacy

Stories in Art

When you first look at this Japanese painting you might see a fierce tiger. If you look again, you might see a landscape and crashing waves.

Look at this painting. What details do you notice about the tiger? Is the tiger ready to spring? If so, what problem could it bring to the land? To the people? How could the people solve the problem? Notice the waves. How could the rising water cause a problem?

Look at the painting again. How does it make you feel? Explain why.

Tiger
by Kishi Ganku, c. 1784
E. A. Barton Collection, England

118

Objective: Identify Problem and Solution

VIEWING In this painting, Kishi Ganku has evoked an apprehensive mood with his choice of subject and his use of bold brush strokes to create exciting patterns. Have students describe how they think the artist might have been feeling when he created this painting. Afterwards, ask how the brush strokes and patterns surrounding the tiger relate to the artist's feelings as well as their own.

Read the page with students, encouraging individual interpretations of the painting.

Ask students to identify problems and possible solutions they can observe in the painting. For example:

- The tiger springing could hurt people on the land.
- The rising water could cause floods.

REPRESENTING Have students create two paintings in a style similar to the original painting—one that shows a problem the tiger might have caused and one that shows how that problem was solved.

OBJECTIVES

TESTED

Students will read a passage to identify a problem and its solutions.

Skills Finder

Problem and Solution

Introduce	43A-B
Review	65E-F, 93G-H, 119A-B, 633A-B, 663E-F, 691G-H
Test	Unit 1, Unit 6
Maintain	411, 545

TEACHING TIP

PROBLEMS AND SOLUTIONS Point out to students that both fiction and nonfiction selections can include problems and solutions. In nonfiction selections, a problem may be described along with the ways people are working to solve it.

Review Problem and Solution

PREPARE

Discuss Problem and Solution

Ask volunteers to share a problem from the previous few days. How did they solve their problem? Explain that problems and solutions appear often in literature, both fiction and nonfiction, as well.

TEACH

Read the Passage and Model the Skill

Point out that when reading a story or article, it is useful to identify the problem or problems that the selection addresses. Readers should also look for any solution that is offered.

Stopping Cavities

What can you do to stop cavities—holes in the teeth—before they start?

One way to stop cavities is to brush your teeth in the morning, after every meal, and in the evening. You should floss once a day, too. Another way to stop cavities is to eat good foods without a lot of sugar.

Going to the dentist twice a year for a cleaning also helps to stop cavities.

If you do all these things, you are less likely to get cavities and more likely to have shiny, white teeth.

Teaching Chart 25

Display and read **Teaching Chart 25.** Ask: What problem does the selection describe? What are some solutions for the problem?

MODEL The first sentence tells me that the problem is stopping cavities. Because the problem is in question format, I know that I should look for solutions by answering the question.

Identify Problem and Solutions

Have a volunteer underline the problem in the passage. Then ask other volunteers to circle the solutions described by the author.

PRACTICE

Create a Problem and Solution Chart

Have students work in groups to survey each other about problems they have faced in the last few days and the solutions they found. Have students use a two-column Problem and Solution chart to record the problems and solutions.

▶ **Logical/Interpersonal**

GROUP

PROBLEM	SOLUTION
Jan lost her soccer shoes.	She searched the house to find them.
Billy's ride to school never came.	He rode his bike to school.
Ernesto didn't like his lunch.	He traded with Sam for another lunch.

ASSESS/CLOSE

Use a Problem and Solution Chart

Have students choose a favorite story and use a Problem and Solution chart to record the problems the main character faces and the attempts he or she makes to solve the problems. Encourage students to share their charts in small groups. ▶ **Logical/Interpersonal**

GROUP

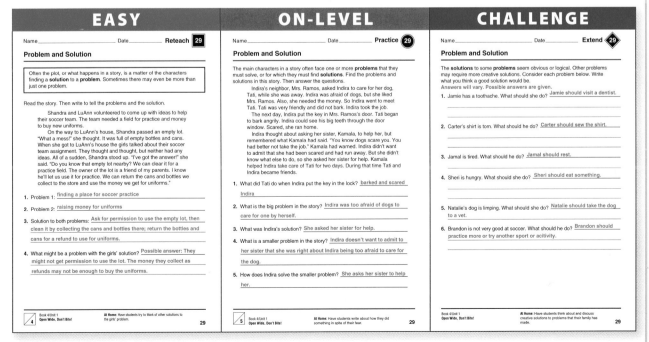

ALTERNATE TEACHING STRATEGY

PROBLEM AND SOLUTION

For a different approach to teaching this skill, see page T64.

Intervention ▶ **Skills Intervention Guide**, for direct instruction and extra practice in problem and solution

Meeting Individual Needs for Comprehension

EASY	ON-LEVEL	CHALLENGE

Reteach, 29   Practice, 29   Extend, 29

OBJECTIVES

Students will read a passage to identify a problem and its solutions.

Apply Problem and Solution

READING STRATEGY

Problem and Solution

Develop a strategy for identifying a problem and its solution.

1 Read the beginning of the article to identify the problem being faced.

2 Restate the problem in your own words.

3 Identify the actions or steps taken to solve the problem.

4 Read the ending of the article to see if the problem was solved and how.

5 Study the solution. What do you think of the solution? Could the problem have been solved differently?

119

Friends for Life

Friends in Need

People with disabilities often have to find new ways to perform everyday tasks. The Canine Companions for Independence (CCI) in Farmingdale, New York, is one of many programs that help make the lives of disabled people a little easier. The program trains dogs to help people with their daily chores.

CCI has successfully placed more than 1,600 dogs with people who need help with common tasks. The cost to train a CCI dog is $20,000. This money is raised entirely by donations.

READING STRATEGY

Training the Pups

The puppies spend the first fifteen months of their life in the home of a "puppy raiser." The puppy raiser teaches the dog how to behave and gives it lots of attention. Then the puppies spend six months learning over 50 commands at the CCI school. They learn to do things like turn on a light with their nose or open a door with their teeth.

Friends Indeed

The dogs not only help people with their tasks but they also make excellent friends. Children with disabilities often benefit most from the program. They love the dogs and often become best friends with them.

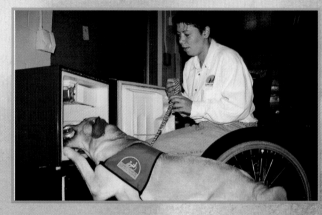

PREVIEW Have students preview "Friends for Life." Explain that problem-and-solution structures are used in nonfiction as well as fiction. A nonfiction article may tell about a real person or group with a problem and steps toward a solution.

SET PURPOSES Tell students to apply what they have learned about problem and solution as they read "Friends for Life."

APPLY THE STRATEGY Discuss this strategy for identifying problem and solution in a selection.

- Decide what the problem is.
- Explain the problem to yourself.
- Step-by-step, discover how the problem was solved.
- At the end of this article, was the problem solved? Were any new problems created?
- Decide if you think the solution was a good one. Were there better ways to solve the problem?

Activity Have each student create a Problem and Solution chart for the article.

Build Background

 Link
Science

Concept: Dental Hygiene

Open Wide, Don't Bite!

Evaluate Prior Knowledge

CONCEPT: DENTAL HYGIENE It is important for people to take good care of their teeth to avoid problems such as cavities, gum disease, tooth discoloration, and tooth loss.

EXPLORE AND CONSIDER DENTAL HYGIENE Have students compare healthy and unhealthy teeth by making a Venn diagram. ▶ **Logical/Visual**

HEALTHY TEETH		UNHEALTHY TEETH
Different	Alike	Different

white
no cavities
pink gums
no cracks or chips

need to be brushed
flossed
checked by the dentist

brown or yellow
cavities
bleeding gums
dying or dead teeth
cracks and/or chips

Graphic Organizer 14

DENTAL REPORT Have each student

WRITING ONE

look at his or her own teeth and mouth with a small mirror. Provide students with a "tooth map" from an encyclopedia that shows the location and name of each tooth. Ask students to use the map and their observations to write a dental report about their teeth.

Develop Oral Language

DISCUSS DENTAL HYGIENE Invite a

ESL local dentist to your classroom to discuss dental hygiene. Alternatively, you may want to bring in items associated with the maintenance of good dental hygiene: a toothbrush, dental floss, a fluoride mouthwash, a milk carton, and a green leafy vegetable such as kale. Hold up each object and ask a volunteer to name it. Write dental hygiene vocabulary on the chalkboard.

- **mouth**
- **teeth**
- **toothbrush**
- **dental floss**
- **mouthwash**
- **calcium**

Ask volunteers to pantomime the use of a toothbrush, dental floss, or mouthwash, to point to their mouth or teeth, and to explain the importance of calcium in maintaining healthy teeth and bones.

LANGUAGE SUPPORT

See the **Language Support Book**, pages 33–36, for teaching suggestions for Build Background.

BJECTIVES

Students will use context clues to determine the meanings of vocabulary words.

fangs
reptiles
patients
skills
healthy
broad

Vocabulary

Teach Vocabulary in Context

Identify Vocabulary Words Display **Teaching Chart 26** and read it with students. Have volunteers circle each vocabulary word and underline other words that are clues to its meaning.

Definitions

fangs (p. 123) sharp teeth

reptiles (p. 122) cold-blooded animals such as lizards

patients (p. 121) those who get care from a doctor or dentist

skills (p. 123) things you know how to do well

healthy (p. 123) well, not sick

broad (p. 122) wide

Animal Dentists

1. Have you ever had a <u>snake</u> show you its <u>sharp</u> (fangs?)
2. Well, if you're like most people, you try to stay away from close encounters with most (reptiles.) **3.** But for an animal dentist, <u>examining</u> slithery (patients) is just another day at the office. **4.** These special dentists use their <u>talents</u> and (skills) to keep our furry—and scaly—friends smiling. **5.** They know a (healthy) set of <u>teeth</u> and <u>gums</u> is essential for humans and animals alike. **6.** So next time you're in the zoo and a monkey or hippopotamus flashes you a (broad,) toothy grin, you can bet that there's an animal dentist nearby bursting with pride.

Teaching Chart 26

Story Words

These words from the selection may be unfamiliar. Before students read, have them check the meaning and pronunciation of each word in the Glossary, beginning on page 756, or in a dictionary.

• tusks, p. 121
• dentist, p. 121
• molars, p. 121

Discuss Meanings Ask questions like these to help students understand the meaning of each word:

• When do snakes use their fangs?
• Which animals are reptiles—alligators and crocodiles or hens and roosters?
• What kind of patients do vets have?
• What skills does it take to ride a bike?
• What foods make you feel most healthy?
• Why are bridges needed to cross broad rivers?

Practice

Synonyms

GROUP

Have a volunteer choose a vocabulary word and name synonyms for, or examples of, the word he or she chooses. Have the rest of the students name the word. ▶Auditory/Linguistic

patients   broad   reptiles

Word Building Manipulative Cards

Write Help-Wanted Ads

WRITING

Have students suppose they are zookeepers in need of an animal dentist. Have them write a "help wanted" advertisement that includes vocabulary words. ▶ Linguistic

Assess Vocabulary

Use Words in Context

PARTNERS

Have partners write each vocabulary word on a separate index card. Give partners three word cards apiece. Have them write a context sentence for each word, but direct them to leave a blank instead of writing the word itself. Next, have partners read each other's sentences and fill in the blanks. Finally, have them underline the context clues that helped them identify the missing word.

SPELLING/VOCABULARY CONNECTIONS
See Spelling Challenge Words, pages 1270–127P.

LANGUAGE SUPPORT

See the Language Support Book, pages 33–36, for teaching suggestions for Vocabulary.

Vocabulary PuzzleMaker

Provides vocabulary activities.

Meeting Individual Needs for Vocabulary

EASY

Name_____ Date_____ **Reteach** 30

Vocabulary

Write a word from the list to complete each sentence.

broad	fangs	patients	healthy	reptiles	skills

1. Doctors treat _____patients_____ with different problems.
2. Do you think a crocodile has a _____broad_____ smile?
3. The goal of a doctor is to keep people _____healthy_____.
4. Big cats have _____fangs_____ that help them grab and tear meat.
5. Medical schools teach doctors the _____skills_____ they need.
6. Crocodiles and lizards are _____reptiles_____.

Story Comprehension **Reteach** 31

Write complete sentences to answer the following questions about "Open Wide, Don't Bite!"

1. What kind of doctor is Dr. Kertesz?
   He is a dentist.
2. What does Dr. Kertesz do on Fridays?
   He sees his animal patients.
3. How does Dr. Kertesz keep animals from getting upset?
   He gives them medicine to keep them calm and pain-free.
4. What size animal is easiest for Dr. Kertesz to work on?
   large ones
5. How does Dr. Kertesz's work help animals?
   By keeping them healthier, he helps animals live longer.

30–31 At Home: Have students make a list of unusual occupations they know about. Book 4/Unit 1 Open Wide, Don't Bite! 5

ON-LEVEL

Name_____ Date_____ **Practice** 30

Vocabulary

Answer each question, and use the vocabulary word in your response.

1. **patients** What type of patients do veterinarians have?
   Patients include family pets and farm, zoo, or wild animals.
2. **healthy** Will exercise help to keep dogs healthy?
   Yes. To be healthy dogs need exercise.
3. **skills** What skills do you need to be a good basketball player?
   Possible answers include: ability to move quickly, to throw balls
   into baskets, to pass, and to dribble.
4. **broad** Does it make a difference if a path is narrow or broad?
   A broad path has room for many people to walk at once.
5. **reptiles** Name some animals that are reptiles.
   Crocodiles, alligators, lizards, and snakes are all reptiles.
6. **fangs** Which snake has poisonous fangs?
   A rattlesnake has poisonous fangs.

30 At Home: Have students write a paragraph using each vocabulary word in a sentence. Book 4/Unit 1 Open Wide, Don't Bite! 6

ON-LEVEL

Animal Doctor

Right now, my name is Lauren Ayana. When I grow up, my name is going to be Doctor Lauren Ayana, veterinarian to all animals.
I'm already working on my doctoring *skills*. I ask the veterinarian all kinds of questions when I take my pets to his office. I often check my cat and dog to make sure they seem *healthy*. I also care for two *reptiles*— a lizard and one snake with no *fangs*.
Some vets only treat pets or farm animals. That's too narrow for me. I plan to care for a very broad group of animals. My *patients* will include everything from pets to farm animals to wild animals.

1. Why is Lauren learning doctoring *skills*? She wants to be a veterinarian
   when she grows up.
2. Who does Lauren ask questions about keeping animals *healthy*?
   the veterinarian
3. What kind of animals does Lauren have in addition to her cat and dog?
   two reptiles—a lizard and a snake with no fangs
4. What kinds of *patients* are in the broad group Lauren plans to treat?
   She will be a doctor to all animals including pets,
   farm, and wild animals.
5. Why can you say Lauren will be a good veterinarian?
   She has a lot of pets and spends time taking care
   of them and learning about them.

5 Book 4/Unit 1 Open Wide, Don't Bite! At Home: Have students describe what a veterinarian does and tell what animals they would like to care for as a vet. 30a

CHALLENGE

Name_____ Date_____ **Extend** 30

Vocabulary

broad	patients	reptiles
fangs	healthy	skills

Write a short story using each of the vocabulary words.
Answers will vary, but should show correct use of vocabulary.

Story Comprehension **Extend** 31

Dr. Kertesz has both human patients and animal patients. How do you think the problems of his human patients and animal patients are alike? How do you think they are different?

Answers will vary. Possible answers may include some of the following.
Both probably have similar types of problems. The animals teeth may be in
worse condition since they do not visit a dentist regularly. Some animals
will have bigger or smaller mouths and teeth than humans do.

30–31 At Home: Have students discuss how they take care of their teeth and why it's important. Book 4/Unit 1 Open Wide, Don't Bite!

Reteach, 30   Practice, 30   Practice, 30a
                                          Take-Home Story

Extend, 30

Comprehension

Prereading Strategies

PREVIEW AND PREDICT Have students read the title and preview the article. Look at the section headings and captions for clues to the problems and solutions the article will address.

- What do all the animal photographs have in common?

- What problems might the person in the photographs be trying to solve?

- What do you think this article might be about? Why do you think so?

- How can you tell this is a nonfiction selection? (The people and animals shown in the pictures look real. The captions and titles contain explanations.) *Genre*

Have students record their predictions about what the article is about.

SET PURPOSES What do students think they will learn from this article? For example:

- What kinds of problems do animals have with their teeth?

- Who helps animals care for their teeth and what skills do they use?

TIME FOR KIDS
SPECIAL REPORT

Open Wide, Don't Bite!

120

Meeting Individual Needs · Grouping Suggestions for Strategic Reading

EASY	ON-LEVEL	CHALLENGE
Read Together Read the article with students or have them use the **Listening Library.** Have students use the Problem and Solution chart to record the problem described in the article and how the dentist might solve this problem. Comprehension prompts offer additional help with comprehension.	**Guided Instruction** Have students read the article together or independently. Use the Comprehension questions to aid in comprehension. Have students use the Problem and Solution chart to record notes about the article.	**Read Independently** Have students read the article independently. Remind them that a good reader tries to identify problems described in the text and their possible solutions. Have students create a Problem and Solution chart as on page 119B.

It Won't Hurt, Honest!

Meet a dentist who fixes sore fangs and tusks

Dr. Peter Kertesz examines a former dancing bear named Mitsos.

Dentist Peter Kertesz of London, England, has the wildest patients in the world. On Fridays, after a week of treating humans, Dr. Kertesz sees four-legged patients. And almost every one of them has *very* large teeth.

Kertesz belongs to a rare breed of dentists who treat animals, from aardvarks to zebras.

It all started when an animal doctor called the dentist to pull teeth from a housecat. Kertesz agreed to pull the cat's teeth. Soon he was taking on bigger cats—like lions, tigers, and jaguars.

The dentist didn't stop there, however. He went on to elephants (which have molars the size of bricks), camels, bears, monkeys, wolves, and even whales. He has treated about 50 kinds of animals in all. The dentist gives the animals medicine to keep them calm and pain-free.

When apes pull back their lips, they're smiling.

LANGUAGE SUPPORT

A blackline master of the Problem and Solution chart is available in the **Language Support Book.**

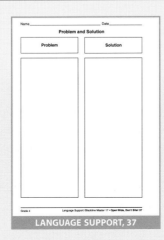

Comprehension

☑ **Apply Problem and Solution**

☑ **Apply Make Inferences**

STRATEGIC READING Before we begin reading, let's make Problem and Solution charts to help us record the problems described in the article, as well as the solutions an animal dentist might try. Some problems may only be identified in the article, without giving a solution.

1 **MAKE INFERENCES** Do you think a dentist for animals is paid well? Why do you think so? (Sample answer: Yes, because it takes a lot of talent and is sometimes a dangerous job.)

2 **PROBLEM AND SOLUTION** What does the dentist do to help animals stay calm and pain-free while he works? (He gives them medicine.)

Genre

Science Article

Explain that a science article appearing in a magazine such as *Time for Kids:*

• explains recent events, discoveries, or ideas.

• presents facts in a logical order.

• uses text features—for example, headings, sidebars, captions, charts, and diagrams—to offer additional information.

Activity After students read *Open Wide, Don't Bite!*, have them discuss the various ways information is presented, such as photos, captions, sidebars. Ask: Why is such variety of presentation important?

121

Comprehension

3 **MAKE INFERENCES** Based on what you read, would a hippo be an easy or a difficult patient? (Sample answer: It would be an easy patient because it has a large mouth.)

4 **PROBLEM AND SOLUTION** What kind of problems can tooth trouble cause for tigers? (Sample answer: Lack of food can weaken them and make them ready prey for other animals.) Use your Problem and Solution chart to organize the information in this article.

PROBLEM	SOLUTION
Keep animals calm and pain-free	Give medicine to calm and keep pain-free; hold some animals' hands to calm
Tooth trouble can affect hunting, eating, and mating	Dentist keeps animals' teeth healthy for longer life

ORGANIZE INFORMATION Ask volunteers to add one or two more problems to the chart. For problems that do not have solutions in the text, let students imagine their own solutions. Then have students use their charts to write the main idea and three supporting details for the article. *Summarize*

Hand-holding calms this gorilla when it visits the dentist.

Dr. Kertesz shows off his dental equipment.

DID YOU KNOW? SINK YOUR TEETH INTO THESE FACTS

◆ Reptiles lose and replace their teeth all the time.

◆ Vegetable-eating animals, such as elephants, giraffes, and sheep, have very broad, flat teeth. They use their teeth to mash up the plants they eat.

◆ Meat-eating animals (lions, tigers, and wolves) have long, pointed teeth. The sharp teeth make it easier for them to bite into their food.

◆ Cats and dogs have both kinds of teeth: sharp ones to bite into food and flat ones to crush or grind it.

◆ Rats' and beavers' teeth are always growing. Since they are always chewing on something, their teeth stay filed down to just the right size.

◆ Elephants grow six separate sets of teeth between birth and age 60.

REREADING FOR *Fluency*

PARTNERS Have students choose a favorite paragraph to read to a partner. Encourage students to read with expression.

READING RATE When you evaluate rate, have the student read aloud from the story for one minute. Place a stick-on note after the last word read. Count words read. To evaluate

students' performance, see the Running Record in the **Fluency Assessment** book.

i **Intervention** For leveled fluency lessons, passages, and norms charts, see **Skills Intervention Guide**, Part 4, Fluency.

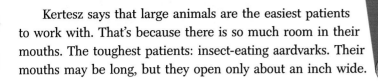
Kertesz says that large animals are the easiest patients to work with. That's because there is so much room in their mouths. The toughest patients: insect-eating aardvarks. Their mouths may be long, but they open only about an inch wide. ③

LIONS AND TIGERS AND BEARS . . . OH MY!

Kertesz has taken his dental skills to many countries. Most of his work is done for zoos. Circuses and animal hospitals also call on him. Kertesz has worked on Siberian tigers in Russia, an elephant in Spain, and a gorilla, a jaguar, badgers, deer, and foxes in England.

One bad tooth can keep a beast from hunting, eating, and even mating. Take a tiger, for example. It's one of the hungriest, meanest cats in the jungle—until it breaks a fang. This can mean big trouble. If a tiger can't eat, it will become weak and may become someone else's dinner. ④

Kertesz's dental work helps animals live longer and healthier lives. Even zoo animals, which are safer than animals in the wild, need healthy mouths. After all, diseases can start in the teeth or gums and spread throughout an animal's body. (And that's the whole "tooth"!)

The mountain lion's sharp teeth help it eat other animals.

FIND OUT MORE
Visit our website:
www.mhschool.com/reading

Based on an article in *TIME FOR KIDS*.   123

Comprehension

Return to Predictions and Purposes

Review with students the predictions they made about the article. Were their predictions correct? Did they find out what they wanted to know?

INFORMAL ASSESSMENT

PROBLEM AND SOLUTION

HOW TO ASSESS

- Ask students: What is the gorilla's problem on page 122? How is it solved?
- Ask students: How might a dentist solve the problem of a tiger with a broken fang?

Students should recognize that the gorilla is afraid. (problem) The problem is solved by hand-holding. They should recognize that animal dentists solve tooth problems much the same as human dentists do, but with some adjustment for the patients' features and needs.

FOLLOW UP If students have trouble identifying problems and solutions, name a problem described in the article and model possible solutions for the problem.

LITERARY RESPONSE

QUICK-WRITE Invite students to record questions they would like to ask an animal dentist.

RESEARCH AND INQUIRY Have groups do research to find out about a specific animal's teeth, such as a horse's or elephant's.

ORAL RESPONSE Have students share their journal responses with a group. Have groups discuss which parts of the article they found most interesting.

*inter*NET **CONNECTION** To learn more about animal teeth, have students go to *www.mhschool.com/reading*

Story Questions

Have students discuss or write answers to the questions on page 124.

Answers:

1. He treats animals' teeth. *Literal/Main Idea*

2. Sample answer: to keep their teeth and gums healthy *Inferential/Draw Conclusions*

3. Sample answer: emotional problems like fear, and physical problems like a small mouth *Inferential/Problem Solution*

4. Dentists who treat animals have to solve problems to do their jobs. *Critical/Summarize*

5. Sample answer: Dr. Dolittle would thank Dr. Kertesz on behalf of the animals. Dr. Kertesz would want to ask the animals where it hurts. *Critical/Reading Across Texts*

Write About an Experience For a full writing process lesson, see pages 127K–127L.

Story Questions & Activities

1. What unusual work does Dr. Peter Kertesz do?

2. Why would animals need a dentist?

3. What kinds of problems does Dr. Kertesz have to solve in order to do his work?

4. What is the main idea of this article?

5. Suppose that Dr. Kertesz met Dr. Dolittle. Dr. Dolittle is the doctor in books and movies who talks to the animals. What do you think the two men would say to each other? Why might Dr. Kertesz envy Dr. Dolittle's ability to understand animals?

Write About an Experience

Dr. Kertesz has had many interesting experiences with animals. Write about an experience you have had with an animal. Give details about what happened. Include how you felt about the experience.

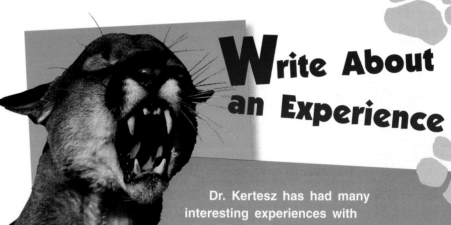

Meeting Individual Needs

EASY	ON-LEVEL	CHALLENGE
Name_____ Date_____ **Reteach** 30	Name_____ Date_____ **Practice** 31	Name_____ Date_____ **Extend** 30
Vocabulary	**Story Comprehension**	**Vocabulary**

EASY — Reteach 30

Vocabulary

Write a word from the list to complete each sentence.

| broad | fangs | patients | healthy | reptiles | skills |

1. Doctors treat ___patients___ with different problems.
2. Do you think a crocodile has a ___broad___ smile?
3. The goal of a doctor is to keep people ___healthy___
4. Big cats have ___fangs___ that help them grab and tear meat.
5. Medical schools teach doctors the ___skills___ they need.
6. Crocodiles and lizards are ___reptiles___

Story Comprehension — Reteach 31

Write complete sentences to answer the following questions about "Open Wide, Don't Bite!"

1. What kind of doctor is Dr. Kertesz?
   He is a dentist.
2. What does Dr. Kertesz do on Fridays?
   He sees his animal patients.
3. How does Dr. Kertesz keep animals from getting upset?
   He gives them medicine to keep them calm and pain-free.
4. What size animal is easiest for Dr. Kertesz to work on?
   large ones
5. How does Dr. Kertesz's work help animals?
   By keeping them healthier, he helps animals live longer.

At Home: Have students make a list of unusual occupations they know about.
30–31   Book 4/Unit 1 *Open Wide, Don't Bite!*

ON-LEVEL — Practice 31

Story Comprehension

Read statements 1 to 6 below. Write **T** for true if the statement describes "Open Wide, Don't Bite!" Write **F** for false if it does not.

1. ___T___ Peter Kertesz went to school to be a dentist for people.
2. ___F___ Kertesz treats only small cats, never tigers or lions.
3. ___T___ The dentist gives animals medicine so they won't feel pain.
4. ___T___ Large animals are easier for dentists to treat than small ones.
5. ___T___ A tiger can lose its life from one bad tooth.
6. ___T___ The teeth of beavers and rats never stop growing.

Write an answer for each question.

7. How was Dr. Kertesz the answer to another vet's problem?
   The vet didn't pull animal teeth and he needed someone to do that for a housecat he was treating.

8. Why do animals have different sizes and shapes of teeth?
   Special sizes and shapes of teeth are needed for the special food an animal eats. Vegetable-eating animals have short, broad teeth. Meat-eating animals have long, pointed teeth.

At Home: Have students write a short story about an animal dentist or a tiger.
31   Book 4/Unit 1 *Open Wide, Don't Bite!*

CHALLENGE — Extend 30

Vocabulary

| broad | patients | reptiles |
| fangs | healthy | skills |

Write a short story using each of the vocabulary words.
Answers will vary, but should show correct use of vocabulary.

Extend 31

Story Comprehension

Dr. Kertesz has both human patients and animal patients. How do you think the problems of his human patients and animal patients are alike? How do you think they are different?

Answers will vary. Possible answers may include some of the following. Both probably have similar types of problems. The animals teeth may be in worse condition since they do not visit a dentist regularly. Some animals will have bigger or smaller mouths and teeth than humans do.

At Home: Have students discuss how they take care of their teeth and why it's important.
30–31   Book 4/Unit 1 *Open Wide, Don't Bite!*

Reteach, 31   Practice, 31   Extend, 31

Create a Job Box

Dr. Kertesz is a trained dentist who works on people as well as on animals. How does someone become a dentist? What does a dentist do? Interview your dentist, or invite a dentist to speak to your class. Then create a job box with a group of other students. Use an index card to write a description of a dentist's job and training. Put the card in the box. Add other job descriptions as you read about them.

Draw a Poster

Everyone needs a good dentist. Draw a poster for an advertisement. Urge people and their pets to visit the dentist regularly. Look back at the article to get ideas for your ad.

Find Out More

Some of Dr. Kertesz's patients live in zoos. What are zoos like today? Start by visiting a local zoo to see how the animals live. If that isn't possible, use an encyclopedia, a video, or a book to learn more about modern zoos. Share what you learn with your classmates.

125

Story Activities

Create a Job Box

Materials: index cards, empty recipe card boxes, art supplies

GROUP Have groups decorate the outside of their boxes to reflect careers they are interested in. From time to time, have groups share information from their job box.

Draw a Poster

Materials: poster board; crayons, markers, or paint/paintbrushes

PARTNERS Have students display their posters during National Dental Hygiene Month (October) or during a similar educational day at your school.

Find Out More

RESEARCH AND INQUIRY Have groups brainstorm interesting ways to present their information, such as through a videotaped zoo trip, a written interview with a zoo-keeper, or an oral presentation that includes a handmade map of a modern zoo.

 *inter***NET CONNECTION** For more information on zoos, students can visit **www.mhschool.com/reading**

FORMAL ASSESSMENT

After page 127, see the Selection and Unit Assessments.

Activity

SCIENCE: PARTS OF A TOOTH Have students find information on and a diagram of a tooth. Then ask students to draw their own diagram of a tooth and label each part.

What to Look For Check responses to see that the student:

• draws an accurate diagram of a tooth.

• identifies and labels its major parts (root, crown, enamel, dentin, pulp).

CHALLENGE

125

Study Skills

PARTS OF A BOOK

OBJECTIVES Students will get information from headings, captions, and sidebars.

PREPARE Preview the book page's organization. Display **Teaching Chart 27.**

TEACH Point to the heading, caption, and sidebar. Say that these page organizers make information easier to find.

PRACTICE Have students answer questions 1–5. Review the answers with them. **1.** 2 **2.** 2, *Cleaning Your Teeth* and *How to Brush Your Teeth* **3.** to use an 18-inch piece of floss **4.** Sample answer: to keep these instructions separate from the rest of the article. **5.** by making it easier to find important information on a page

ASSESS/CLOSE Ask students to find the headings, captions, and sidebars in the article they just read.

Study Skills

Use Headings, Captions, and Sidebars

Hippos and dancing bears aren't the only ones who need to take care of their teeth. Look at this page from a book on dental health. Notice how the information is organized. **Headings** help you find information. **Captions** and **sidebars** contain additional facts.

Use an 18-inch piece of floss. Wrap the ends around one finger on each hand.

How to Brush Your Teeth
1. Use a soft toothbrush.
2. Angle the brush against your teeth.

Cleaning Your Teeth
If possible, brush teeth after every meal. Floss between and around your teeth once a day.

Use the sample page to answer these questions.

1. How many steps are listed for brushing your teeth?

2. How many headings are on this page? What are they?

3. Look at the drawing and read the caption. What additional information does the caption give you?

4. Why is information on brushing teeth in a sidebar?

5. How do headings, captions, and sidebars make reading easier?

Meeting Individual Needs

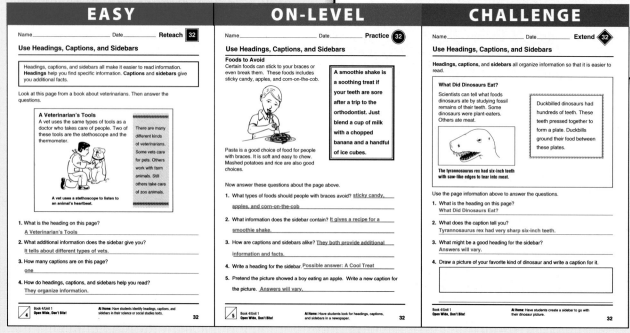

EASY	ON-LEVEL	CHALLENGE
Reteach, 32	Practice, 32	Extend, 32

TEST POWER

Test Tip

Put the passage in your own words.

DIRECTIONS

Read the sample story. Then read each question about the story.

SAMPLE

Attention: Neighborhood Kids

Mr. Kim needed assistance in fixing up his house. He offered neighborhood children a chance to complete chores and to earn points toward an outing. Mr. Kim said he would keep a record of the number of points <u>accumulated</u> by each child.

POSSIBLE OUTINGS:

The Beach:	90 points
The Fair:	60 points
The Theater:	40 points

POSSIBLE CHORES:

Wash Windows:	25 points
Paint Garage:	90 points
Paint Porch:	35 points

Kids can share chores and points. Three kids can go on each trip.

1 What is the story mostly about?

   A How kids can share points

   B How to go to the beach

   (C) How Mr. Kim finds helpers for his chores

   D How to wash the porch

2 In this story the word <u>accumulated</u> means—

   F wanted

   (G) earned

   H asked for

   J finished

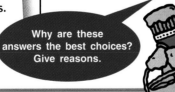

Why are these answers the best choices? Give reasons.

127

Test Power

Read the Page

Have students read *all* of the information on the poster and the story above the poster.

Discuss the Questions

Question 1: This question asks students what the story is *mostly* about. Wrong answer choices often include information that is stated in the passage, but the information is not what the passage is *mostly* about.

Question 2: This question requires students to define a word in context. Ask students to find the clues that will help them answer this question. The passage provides two clues: Mr. Kim offered children a chance to "earn points toward an outing" and said ". . . he would keep a record of the number of points . . ." Have students eliminate choices that are not supported by the text found near the underlined word.

Self-Selected Reading
Leveled Books

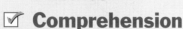

Intervention Guide, for direct instruction and extra practice in vocabulary and comprehension

Phonics

- short vowels
- long *a* and long *e*
- long *i* and long *o*
- /ū/ and /ü/

☑ Comprehension

- story elements
- problem and solution
- main idea and supporting details

Answers to Story Questions

Answers will vary and should include examples and details from the stories students have read.

EASY

Story Questions for Selected Reading

1. Who are the main characters in the story?
2. What problem did the main character face?
3. What was your favorite part of the story?
4. What was the story mainly about?
5. Did this story remind you of another story you have read? Explain how.

Draw a Comic Strip

Draw a comic strip of four events from the story.

EASY

UNIT SKILLS REVIEW

Phonics

☑ **Comprehension**

Help students self-select an Easy Book to read and apply phonics and comprehension skills.

Guided Reading

PREVIEW AND PREDICT Have students look at the first few illustrations in the book and predict what the story will be about. Chart their ideas. If the book has chapter headings, ask students to use the headings to help them make their predictions.

SET PURPOSES Have students write a few questions that they hope will be answered as they read the book. Have them share their purposes.

READ THE BOOK Use questions like the following to guide students' reading or to check comprehension after they have read the story independently.

- Where does the story take place? *Story Elements*
- How do the main characters solve their problem? *Problem and Solution*
- What clues does the author include to help you better understand the main character? *Make Inferences*

- What is the main idea of the story? What details does the author include to support this main idea? *Main Idea and Supporting Details*
- Look back through the story. Can you find examples of words with the long *a* or long *e* sound? *Phonics and Decoding*

RETURN TO PREDICTIONS AND PURPOSES Have students review their predictions and questions. Were their predictions accurate? Were their questions answered? For books with chapter headings, were the headings useful? How?

LITERARY RESPONSE Have students discuss questions like the following:

- How does the setting add to the story?
- What would be another good title for this book? Why?
- If you could write the next part of this story, what would happen next?

Self-Selected Reading
Leveled Books

INDEPENDENT

UNIT SKILLS REVIEW

☑ **Comprehension**

Help students self-select an Independent Book to read and apply comprehension skills.

Guided Reading

PREVIEW AND PREDICT Discuss the illustrations in the beginning of the book. As you scan the book, have students predict what the story will be about. If the book has chapter headings, ask students to use the headings to predict what will happen. Have students record their predictions in their journals.

SET PURPOSES Have students think about why they chose their selected books. Encourage them to record their reasons in their journals.

READ THE BOOK Use questions like the following to guide students' reading or to reinforce reading strategies after they have read the story independently.

- How is the setting important to the story? *Story Elements*

- What information does the author include to help you better understand the setting? *Story Elements*

- How is the problem in this book solved? *Problem and Solution*

- What is the main idea of the story? What details support this main idea? *Main Idea and Supporting Details*

RETURN TO PREDICTIONS AND PURPOSES Have students review their predictions and purposes for reading. Which predictions were close to what actually happened? Were their purposes met? For books with chapter headings, were the headings useful? How?

LITERARY RESPONSE The following questions will help focus students' responses:

- What new information did you learn from this story?

- What questions would you ask the author of this story?

- Would you tell a friend to read this story? Why or why not?

☑ **Comprehension**

- story elements
- problem and solution
- main idea and supporting details

Answers to Story Questions

Answers will vary and should include examples and details from the stories students have read.

INDEPENDENT

Story Questions for Selected Reading

1. Where does the story take place?
2. What are some of the problems presented in the story?
3. What part of the story is most exciting?
4. What are the main events of the story?
5. Have you read other stories about similar people or subjects? Does this story add anything new?

Write a Letter

Write a letter to a friend, describing the book you just read.

Self-Selected Reading
Leveled Books

☑ Comprehension

- story elements
- problem and solution
- main idea and supporting details

Answers to Story Questions

Answers will vary and should include examples and details from the stories students have read.

Story Questions for Selected Reading

1. What is the setting for the story?

2. What kinds of problems does the author present and how are they solved?

3. Do you think the events in this story really happened?

4. What are the major events in this story?

5. How did having read similar stories help you predict events in this story?

Write About an Experience

Write a paragraph about a problem you once had, and tell how you solved it.

CHALLENGE

UNIT SKILLS REVIEW

☑ Comprehension

Help students self-select a Challenge Book to read and apply comprehension skills.

Guided Reading

PREVIEW AND PREDICT Discuss the illustrations in the beginning of the book and have students scan the text. Ask them to predict what the story will be about. Have them record their predictions. If the book has chapter headings, ask students to use the headings to predict what will happen.

SET PURPOSES Have students write a few questions they hope will be answered in their selected book. Ask them to share their purposes.

READ THE BOOK Use questions like the following to reinforce reading strategies after students have read the story independently.

- What is the story mostly about? *Main Idea and Supporting Details*

- What details does the author include to support the main idea of the story? *Main Idea and Supporting Details*

- When is the main problem presented in the story? When is it solved? *Problem and Solution*

- How did your own experiences help you understand the story? *Make Inferences*

RETURN TO PREDICTIONS AND PURPOSES Discuss students' predictions and questions. Which predictions were close to the book's contents? For books with chapter headings, were the headings useful? How? Did students find out what they wanted to know?

LITERARY RESPONSE Have students discuss questions like the following:

- What was your favorite part of the book?

- If you were to give this book another title, what would it be? Why?

- What did you learn from reading this story?

Bringing Groups Together

Anthology and Leveled Books

Connecting Texts

PROBLEM SOLVING CHARTS
Have students discuss connections between the stories. For example, write these story titles horizontally across the tops of two separate charts: *The Stony Creek Bandit, Sukey Johnson Builds a House, Laura and the Great Quake,* and *Lost and Found.* Label one chart *Problems* and the other chart *Solutions.* Discuss with students the problems and solutions presented in each story and the solutions the characters found. Write student suggestions on the charts.

Problems

Stony Creek Bandit	Sukey Johnson Builds a House	Laura and the Great Quake	Lost and Found
• Someone is stealing items from camp.	• Sukey feels Latesha does not like her.	• Nonna is sad that she had to leave her home.	• Mark gets lost in the woods.

Solutions

Stony Creek Bandit	Sukey Johnson Builds a House	Laura and the Great Quake	Lost and Found
• The girls set a trap to catch the culprit.	• Sukey confronts Latesha.	• Laura and Daniele paint Nonna's ceiling.	• The park rangers find Mark.

Viewing/Representing

ILLUSTRATE A SCENE Have students break into groups in which they have all read some of the same titles. Students in each group can choose their favorite book and illustrate a scene showing a problem presented in their book. The caption to the illustration can explain the problem and its solution.

DISCUSS SOLUTIONS Give students time to study all the illustrations. Encourage them to ask questions to clarify problem and solution. Have students discuss why the solution was a good one and suggest any other possible solutions.

Research and Inquiry

CHOOSE A TOPIC Have students choose a topic related to several books to research, such as camping, migrant workers, weather forecasting, or cowboys. Then have them:

• list a few questions about their topics.

• think about ways to find information: encyclopedia, library books, magazines, organizations, or the Internet.

• make notes on index cards.

• create a poster to display their findings.

 To learn more about camping, migrant workers, weather forecasting, or cowboys, have students log on to ***www.mhschool.com/reading***

OBJECTIVES

Students will identify the main idea and supporting details in a passage.

Skills Finder

Main Idea

Introduce	95A-B
Review	117E-F, 127E-F
Test	Unit 1
Maintain	149, 291, 307, 623

LANGUAGE SUPPORT

ESL Use an illustration from a science or health book, or from an encyclopedia to show students which teeth are the *incisors*, the *cuspids*, and the *molars*.

SELF-SELECTED Reading

Students may choose from the following titles.

ANTHOLOGY

• Open Wide, Don't Bite!

LEVELED BOOKS

• All titles for the unit

Bibliography, pages T78–T79

Review Main Idea

PREPARE

Discuss Main Idea and Supporting Details

Review: The main idea is the most important idea in a selection. When the main idea is not stated directly, readers have to figure it out from information in the text. Supporting details are pieces of information that tell more about the main idea.

TEACH

Read the Passage and Model the Skill

Display **Teaching Chart 28**. Ask students to listen for the main idea of the passage as you read it aloud. Have students also listen for supporting details.

Tooth Types

Once you get all of your grown-up teeth, <u>you will have three kinds of teeth.</u> Teeth in the front of your mouth are called *incisors*. Incisors are thin with a flat edge for cutting food into chunks.

Behind the incisors are *cuspids*. Cuspids are more pointed for tearing food into smaller pieces.

Behind the cuspids are *molars*. Molars are wide and flat so you can chew and grind up the food to be swallowed.

As long as you take good care of your teeth, you'll be able to use *all* of them for a long time.

Teaching Chart 28

Model finding the main idea in the passage.

MODEL I know that main ideas are often stated at or near the beginning of a selection. The first sentence here tells me that the main idea of the article is that there are three basic kinds of permanent teeth.

Identify Main Idea and Supporting Details

ONE

Have a volunteer underline the phrase that tells the main idea. Have other volunteers circle phrases that offer supporting details. Have students use a Main Idea and Supporting Details chart to record information from the passage. Then ask students to think of other supporting details that might be included in an article about types of teeth, such as differences between human teeth and animal teeth.

▶ **Linguistic/Visual**

MAIN IDEA	SUPPORTING DETAILS
You will have three types of teeth.	Incisors cut food into chunks.
	Cuspids tear food into smaller pieces.
	Molars grind food for swallowing.

ASSESS/CLOSE

Form Main Idea and Supporting Details

PARTNERS

Ask students to develop an outline for a paragraph about caring for their teeth. Have them list a main idea and three supporting details. Then direct partners to exchange lists and identify each other's main idea and supporting details.

Meeting Individual Needs for Comprehension

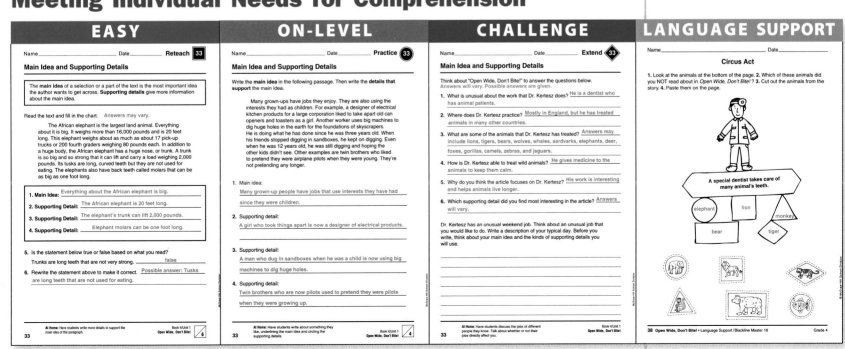

EASY	ON-LEVEL	CHALLENGE	LANGUAGE SUPPORT
Reteach, 33	Practice, 33	Extend, 33	Language Support, 38

PART 3

Build Skills

VOCABULARY

Students will:

- analyze multiple meanings of words to understand text.

- use words with multiple meanings.

Skills Finder

Multiple-Meaning Words

Introduce	41I-J
Review	117I-J, 127G-H
Test	Unit 1

TEACHING TIP

MULTIPLE-MEANING WORDS Give students examples of multiple-meaning words such as

- **wave:** to move your hand in a greeting; a high point on the surface of water; a vibrating motion; a sudden increase.

- **train:** a group of connected railroad cars; the back of a dress; a series of events; to coach; to make go in a certain direction.

Review Multiple-Meaning Words

PREPARE

Discuss Multiple-Meaning Words

Review: Words can have more than one meaning. If you see a familiar word that doesn't make sense in the sentence, think about other meanings the word might have. Also look for meaning clues in the words and sentences around the confusing word. Then read the sentence again with each "other" meaning until you find the meaning that makes sense.

TEACH

Read the Passage and Model the Skill

Display **Teaching Chart 29** and have students read it silently.

My Dentist

My dentist <u>treats</u> all kinds of people, from babies to grandparents. She is there whenever people <u>cry</u> for help.

My dentist wants me to have healthy teeth that won't <u>spread</u> germs to the <u>rest</u> of my body. When I get a cavity she <u>drills</u> my tooth and puts in a <u>filling</u>. She is very gentle, so the <u>shot</u> doesn't even hurt.

I like my dentist. She's really <u>cool</u>.

Teaching Chart 29

Model identifying and decoding a multiple-meaning word.

MODEL I'm not sure what the author means by *treats* in the first sentence. But by looking at the other words around *treats*, like *dentist* and *all kinds of people,* I can tell that the author uses *treats* to mean "to care for medically," not "to pay for someone else" or "give someone a treat."

PRACTICE

Identify Multiple-Meaning Words and Their Meanings

Have volunteers underline other words with multiple meanings. Have students write original sentences to show their understanding of the word's meaning in this context. ▶ **Linguistic/Visual**

ONE

ASSESS/CLOSE

Define Multiple-Meaning Words

Write the following sentence on the chalkboard. Ask groups to define the underlined words and identify context clues that helped suggest meanings.

The piano player played the wrong notes.

ALTERNATE TEACHING STRATEGY

MULTIPLE-MEANING WORDS

For a different approach to teaching this skill, see page T63.

i Intervention▶ Skills

Intervention Guide, for direct instruction and extra practice in multiple-meaning words

Meeting Individual Needs for Vocabulary

EASY

Name_____ Date_____ **Reteach 34**

Multiple-Meaning Words

Some words are spelled the same, but have **multiple meanings**. These words are called **homographs**. Use the clues before and after the underlined word in each sentence to figure out the correct meaning of the homograph.

Circle the letter beside the correct meaning for the underlined word.

1. The doctor keeps spare blankets in an oak <u>chest</u>.
 a. the front of the upper human body
 b. a box or piece of furniture

2. Can the doctor really operate on a <u>bug</u>?
 a. an insect
 b. a mistake in a computer program

3. Hold the kitten tightly so it doesn't <u>fall</u>.
 a. a season of the year
 b. to tumble to the ground

4. The <u>tip</u> of the needle was very sharp.
 a. money you leave for good service
 b. the point or end of an object

5. The dog must <u>fast</u> before the operation.
 a. to not eat
 b. quick

6. If your pets <u>tire</u> easily, they may be sick.
 a. get sleepy
 b. a rubber hoop around a wheel

Book 4/Unit 1
Open Wide, Don't Bite!
At Home: Ask students to think of three or four other words that have more than just one meaning. **34**

ON-LEVEL

Name_____ Date_____ **Practice 34**

Multiple-Meaning Words

Some words have **multiple-meanings**. The context of the sentence will tell you which meaning of the word is being used. Read each sentence below. Then circle the meaning of each underlined word.

1. She wears a blue <u>band</u> to hold her hair away from her face.
 a. group of musicians **b.** thin strip of cloth

2. Jeffrey <u>can</u> finish the race even though he is out of breath.
 a. is able to b. metal container

3. The <u>pitcher</u> on the table was filled with lemonade.
 a. container for pouring liquid b. baseball player

4. Hannah wrote the note on the yellow <u>slip</u>.
 a. slide suddenly **b.** small piece of paper

5. Tim sat at the <u>counter</u> eating a cheese sandwich.
 a. person listing numbers **b.** long table

6. The falling branch gave him a <u>blow</u> on the head.
 a. hard hit b. send air from the mouth

7. They had only one <u>match</u> left for two more nights in the woods.
 a. stick for starting fires b. things that go together

8. Maria and her sister liked to <u>lie</u> down and look at the stars.
 a. say something not true **b.** be in a flat position

9. They could see the <u>school</u> from the glass-bottom boat.
 a. place for learning **b.** group of fish

10. They stopped at the <u>toll</u> booth before they drove over the bridge.
 a. fee b. sound of a bell

Book 4/Unit 1
Open Wide, Don't Bite!
At Home: Have students write four sentences using two other words with multiple meanings. **34**

CHALLENGE

Name_____ Date_____ **Extend 34**

Multiple-Meaning Words

round	run	pack
sharp	store	rule

Each word above has **multiple meanings**. Write the word that fits the definitions below.

1. a group of something, such as animals; to put objects in a box
 pack

2. to move quickly; to be in charge of something _run_

3. a place where things are sold; to put things away until needed _store_

4. having a curved surface; a single outburst _round_

5. a statement or law; to govern, usually a country _rule_

6. sudden and dramatic; having a point or edge that cuts _sharp_

Write a paragraph about taking care of a pet—your own pet or someone else's. Include some of the words from the box above. Repeat the words in your writing by using their different meanings.

_____
_____
_____
_____
_____
_____
_____
_____

Book 4/Unit 1
Open Wide, Don't Bite!
At Home: Make up a short list of multiple-meaning words. Alternate using the words with each of their meanings to tell a story. **34**

LANGUAGE SUPPORT

Name_____ Date_____

A Silly Animal Story

1. Read the story below. 2. The words listed in the box below each have more than one meaning. 3. Use them to fill in the blanks and complete the story.

pull	room	room
mean	pull	pull
bear	bear	mean

The dentist opened her door and – surprise – into the _room_ came a little boy leading a big, hairy _bear_.

"Goodness!" cried the dentist, "What do you _mean_ by bringing that animal in here? Are you trying to _pull_ some kind of joke on me?"

"No," said the boy, "He has a toothache. I think you will have to _pull_ out his tooth."

"Well, all right," said the dentist. "Stand back and give me plenty of _room_." She held the creature down.

"Oh," cried the boy, I can not _bear_ to watch!"

"I am not trying to be _mean_," said the dentist, "but this will hurt." When he heard that, the creature roared, jumped up and ran out.

"Humph!" said the dentist, "That is not a _bear_ you have there. If you ask me, it is just a big chicken!"

Grade 4 Language Support / Blackline Master 19 • Open Wide, Don't Bite! **39**

Reteach, 34   Practice, 34   Extend, 34   Language Support, 39

OBJECTIVES

Students will:

- identify antonyms and synonyms.
- use antonyms and synonyms to define unfamiliar words.

Skills Finder

Antonyms and Synonyms

Introduce	65I-J
Review	93I-J, 127I-J, 663I-J, 691I-J, 723I-J
Test	Unit 1, Unit 6

TEACHING TIP

ANTONYMS AND SYNONYMS Share the following information with students.

- A synonym or antonym can appear either before or after its "match" in a sentence.

- The phrases *such as* and *for example* are common clues that synonyms will follow in a sentence.

Review Antonyms and Synonyms

PREPARE

Discuss Antonyms and Synonyms

Review: An *antonym* is a word or a group of words that means the opposite of another word. A *synonym* is a word or group of words that has the same or almost the same meaning as another word. Sometimes an antonym or a synonym can help you figure out the meaning of an unfamiliar word.

TEACH

Read the Passage and Model the Skill

Display and have students read **Teaching Chart 30** with you.

Fish and Reptile Teeth

Many fish and reptiles have (fascinating) teeth. One of the most <u>interesting</u> kinds is a set of teeth that grows on a fish or reptile's tongue. These creatures may also have teeth on the (roof) or <u>top,</u> of their mouths.

Some frogs grow an "egg tooth" to help them break out of their <u>weak,</u> (fragile) eggshell at birth. This tooth falls out just after birth and never returns.

Some reptiles, such as rattlesnakes, have (sharp) fangs to shoot poison into other animals. We could never do that with our <u>dull</u> teeth.

Teaching Chart 30

Demonstrate the use of a synonym as a context clue that helps to identify the meaning of an unfamiliar word.

MODEL I don't know what *fascinating* means. The words around it may offer a synonym or antonym as a clue to its meaning. When I read *interesting* in the next sentence, I see that *fascinating* is another word for *interesting*.

PRACTICE

Find Antonyms and Synonyms

GROUP

Circle the words *roof*, *fragile*, and *sharp*. Ask students to identify an antonym or synonym for each word. Have volunteers underline the antonym or synonym and explain their choices. ▶ **Linguistic**

ASSESS/CLOSE

Use Antonyms and Synonyms to Determine Meaning

PARTNERS

Write the following words on the chalkboard: *narrow*, *crush*, *pointy*. For each word have partners write two sentences—one in which an antonym for the word is used, the other in which a synonym is used. Have partners exchange papers when they are finished writing and underline and identify as either an antonym or a synonym the appropriate word in each sentence.

ALTERNATE TEACHING STRATEGY

ANTONYMS AND SYNONYMS

For a different approach to teaching this skill, see page T65.

i Intervention ▶ **Skills**

Intervention Guide, for direct instruction and extra practice in antonyms and synonyms

Meeting Individual Needs for Vocabulary

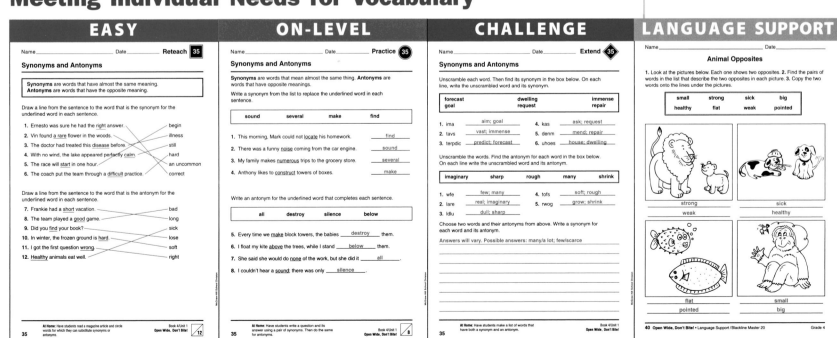

Reteach, 35   Practice, 35   Extend, 35   Language Support, 40

GRAMMAR/SPELLING
CONNECTIONS

See the 5-Day Grammar and Usage Plan on run-on sentences, pages 127M–127N.

See the 5-Day Spelling Plan on words from health, pages 127O–127P.

Personal Narrative

Prewrite

WRITE ABOUT AN EXPERIENCE
Present this writing assignment: Dr. Kertesz has had many interesting experiences with animals. Write about an experience you had with an animal. Give details about what happened. Include how you felt about the experience.

BRAINSTORM IDEAS Have students recall animals they have known or met. Suggest they think of places where they may have encountered animals, such as at home, on a farm, or in a zoo.

Strategy: Make a Chart Help students organize their ideas on a chart. Provide the following tips.

• Record vivid sensory details.

• List events in sequence; add feelings about each listed event.

• Highlight a problem that is central to the experience, and how it was solved.

PROBLEM	
EVENTS / FEELINGS →	DETAILS
SOLUTION	

Draft

USE THE CHART Encourage students to follow the sequence of events from their charts, first presenting the problem, then following a course of events to the solution. Remind students that they are writing about something that really happened.

Revise

SELF-QUESTIONING Ask students to assess their drafts for improvement.

• Did I include reactions to the experience?

• Have I presented the experience in a way that others will find interesting?

• Did I write from my own point of view?

Edit/Proofread

CHECK FOR ERRORS AND DETAILS
Students should reread their paragraphs for spelling, grammar, and punctuation.

Publish

SHARE THE EXPERIENCE Students can read their narratives aloud or exchange them with partners. Have class members tell the writer what was most engaging about his or her story.

> #### My Dog Bee Bee
>
> My dog Bee Bee is an amazing animal. She is smart and lively and has learned lots of tricks.
> The first time I saw Bee Bee she was dirty and so thin that her bones showed. She licked my hand and looked at me with sad eyes. Someone had abandoned her, the man at the pound said.
> We had the vet check Bee Bee out. Then we took her home and gave her lots of love and good food. Soon she was a happy healthy dog again. I'd have to say she is my best friend.

TEACHING TIP

Technology
Remind students to save a copy of their writing on a disk. This insures they will have a copy for future use.

Story Pattern Tell students their stories should follow a logical pattern with a beginning, a middle, and a conclusion. Using transition words will help move the story forward.

Handwriting CD-ROM

Presentation Ideas

CREATE A BOOK Have students draw pictures to go with their stories. Gather the visual images with their stories in a book called "Animals and Us."

▶ **Viewing/Representing**

DO A RADIO SHOW Let students take turns interviewing each other about their experiences. Encourage the audience to "call in" their questions and comments.

▶ **Speaking/Listening**

Consider students' creative efforts, possibly adding a plus (+) for originality, wit, and imagination.

Scoring Rubric

Excellent	Good	Fair	Unsatisfactory
4: The writer • clearly describes a problem and the events leading to its solution. • uses vivid and descriptive language to describe the experience. • writes from his or her point of view.	**3:** The writer • states a problem and solution. • adequately organizes supporting details. • usually writes from his or her point of view.	**2:** The writer • states the problem, but fails to state a solution. • presents few supporting details. • sometimes writes in the first person, from his or her point of view.	**1:** The writer • states the problem vaguely. • provides incomplete or unclear details. • writes in the third person.

Incomplete 0: The writer leaves the page blank or fails to respond to the writing task. The student does not address the topic or simply paraphrases the prompt. The response is illegible or incoherent.

For a 6-point or an 8-point scale, see pages T107–T108.

Meeting Individual Needs for Writing

EASY	ON-LEVEL	CHALLENGE
Comic Strip Have students divide a piece of paper into four sections. In each section, students should draw an illustration and write a sequence of descriptive sentences about their experience.	**Dialogue** Have students write a dialogue between themselves and an animal. Remind them to think about what the animal might actually want to say to them if it could speak. If students choose, they can present their dialogue in speech bubbles with appropriate illustrations.	**Brochure** Have students choose an animal that is not usually kept as a pet. Tell them to design a brochure to "sell" this pet to others. What traits are unique to this animal? How can students present these traits as positive features? Have them include an illustration and care instructions.

Listening and Speaking

LISTENING STRATEGIES

Ask students to read aloud their story. Have the others:

• jot down questions to ask the speaker.

• summarize the story.

SPEAKING STRATEGIES

As students read their paragraphs aloud, have them:

• vary volume and tone of voice to express how they feel.

• make eye contact with their listeners.

LANGUAGE SUPPORT

ESL Have students review the chart they made to organize their ideas. Ask them to use a dictionary or work with an English-fluent partner to create descriptive sentences for their stories.

PORTFOLIO Invite students to include their stories or another writing project in their portfolios.

5 Day Grammar and Usage Plan

DAILY LANGUAGE ACTIVITIES

Write the Daily Language Activities on the board each day or use **Transparency 5.** Have students respond orally. For answers, see the transparency.

Day 1

1. A dentist works hard he stays busy.
2. Some animals have flat teeth other animals have sharp teeth.
3. Sometimes cats break teeth this means trouble.

Day 2

1. The tiger is a big cat the housecat is small.
2. Beavers' teeth stay filed down they are always chewing.
3. Reptiles lose their teeth they are replaced.

Day 3

1. Monkeys pull back their lips they smile.
2. Wolves have pointed teeth they bite their food.

Day 4

1. Lions can be mean medicine keeps them calm.
2. Teeth need to be cleaned diseases can start.

Day 5

1. Big animals are easy patients their mouths are large.
2. Hand-holding calms a gorilla it visits the dentist.

Daily Language Transparency 5

DAY 1 — Introduce the Concept

Oral Warm-Up Read this aloud: *The dog growled he was angry.* Ask students to identify the two main ideas.

Introduce Run-on Sentences Run-on sentences contain too many ideas for one sentence. Present the following:

> ### Run-on Sentences
>
> - A **run-on sentence** joins together two or more sentences that should be written separately.
>
> - You can correct a run-on sentence by separating two complete ideas into two sentences.

Provide students with the following: *The tiger didn't eat it had a sore tooth. The tiger didn't eat. It had a sore tooth.*

Present the Daily Language Activity. Then have students write the sentences using correct punctuation.

 Assign the daily Writing Prompt on page 118C.

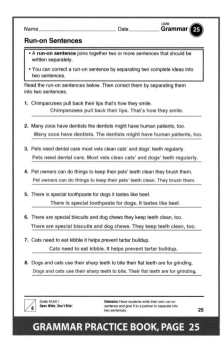

GRAMMAR PRACTICE BOOK, PAGE 25

DAY 2 — Teach the Concept

Review Run-on Sentences Ask students how to identify a run-on sentence and how it can be corrected.

More About Run-on Sentences Present the following:

> ### Run-on Sentences
>
> - You can correct a run-on sentence by rewriting it as a compound or complex sentence.

Provide students with these examples:

The map showed a road it was unpaved. The map showed a road, but it was unpaved.

We stayed inside the rain stopped. We stayed inside until the rain stopped.

Present the Daily Language Activity. Have students rewrite this: *The cat had a bad tooth the dentist fixed it.*

 Assign the daily Writing Prompt on page 118C.

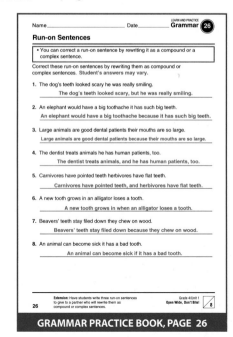

GRAMMAR PRACTICE BOOK, PAGE 26

127M *Open Wide, Don't Bite!*

Run-on Sentences

Learn from the Literature Review run-on sentences. Read this sentence from the top of page 123 of *Open Wide, Don't Bite!*

> **Their mouths may be long, but they open only about an inch wide.**

Ask students to identify the two ideas in this sentence and how they were joined.

Find Compound and Complex Sentences Present the Daily Language Activity and have students correct the sentences orally.

Have students look back though the selections in Unit 1 to find an example of a compound or a complex sentence. Ask students to copy the sentence. Then invite them to write the same sentence as a run-on sentence.

 Assign the daily Writing Prompt on page 118D.

Review Run-on Sentences Write three sentences from the Daily Language Activity for Days 1–3 on the chalkboard. Have students correct each sentence and explain how it was corrected. Then present the Daily Language Activity for Day 4.

Mechanics and Usage Before students begin the daily Writing Prompt on page 118D, review sentence punctuation. Display and discuss:

Sentence Punctuation

- Every sentence begins with a capital letter.
- Use the correct end mark for each sentence.

 Assign the daily Writing Prompt on page 118D.

Assess Use the Daily Language Activity and page 29 of the **Grammar Practice Book** for assessment.

Reteach Write the three rules for correcting a run-on sentence on the chalkboard. Have students work in pairs. Each student writes three run-on sentences that can be corrected following one of the rules. Students should trade papers and correct the sentences using proper punctuation.

Have students create a display with their repaired run-on sentences.

Use page 30 of the **Grammar Practice Book** for additional reteaching.

 Assign the daily Writing Prompt on page 118D.

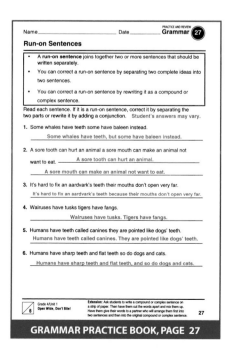

GRAMMAR PRACTICE BOOK, PAGE 27

GRAMMAR PRACTICE BOOK, PAGE 28

GRAMMAR PRACTICE BOOK, PAGE 29

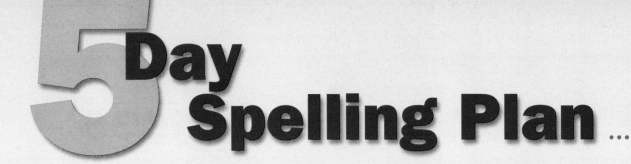

5 Day Spelling Plan

LANGUAGE SUPPORT

To help students understand the words in context, use visual cues to link spelling words together. For example, show students a picture or model of a tooth, and say: This tooth is a *molar*. The part you see is the *crown* and the *root* is below the *gums*. Discuss how each word is spelled.

DICTATION SENTENCES

Spelling Words

1. The dentist looked at my teeth.
2. Does a crown help your teeth?
3. The hospital is down the road.
4. My mother gave me medicine.
5. She eats a good diet.
6. She has clean gums.
7. The gland was sore.
8. I hurt the joint in my hand.
9. He has a fever.
10. He is chewing his dinner well.
11. I think with my brain.
12. My cavity hurts.
13. What is the name of the disease?
14. Plaque sticks to our teeth.
15. Lettuce has vitamins.
16. I have an ache in my arm.
17. He used a dental tool.
18. He works at the clinic.
19. The student passed the oral test.
20. Our molars are large teeth.

Challenge Words

21. The snake has sharp fangs.
22. A vet has many patients.
23. She has healthy teeth.
24. Turtles and snakes are reptiles.
25. He learned his skills in school.

DAY 1 Pretest

Assess Prior Knowledge Use the Dictation Sentences at the left and **Spelling Practice Book** page 25 for the pretest. Allow students to correct their own papers. Students who require a modified list may be tested on the first ten words.

Spelling Words		Challenge Words
1. **dentist**	11. brain	21. **fangs**
2. crown	12. cavity	22. **patients**
3. **hospital**	13. disease	23. **healthy**
4. **medicine**	14. plaque	24. **reptiles**
5. diet	15. vitamin	25. **skills**
6. **gums**	16. ache	
7. gland	17. **dental**	
8. joint	18. clinic	
9. fever	19. oral	
10. **chewing**	20. **molars**	

*Note: Words in **dark type** are from the story.*

Word Study On page 26 of the **Spelling Practice Book** are word study steps and an at-home activity.

DAY 2 Explore the Pattern

Sort and Spell Words Explain that all the spelling words relate to health in some way. Then say *crown, dentist,* and *hospital,* emphasizing the syllables in each word. Ask students if they can hear the number of syllables in each word. Have students read the Spelling Words aloud and sort them as below.

Words with		
One Syllable	Two Syllables	Three Syllables
crown	dentist	hospital
gums	diet	medicine
gland	fever	cavity
joint	chewing	vitamin
brain	disease	
plaque	dental	
ache	clinic	
	oral	
	molars	

Word Wall Have students create a word wall based on the word sort and add more words from their reading.

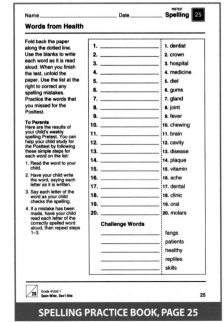

SPELLING PRACTICE BOOK, PAGE 25

WORD STUDY STEPS AND ACTIVITY, PAGE 26

SPELLING PRACTICE BOOK, PAGE 27

Words from Health

DAY 3 — Practice and Extend

Word Meaning: Definitions Remind students that a definition is the meaning of the word. Point out that some words have multiple meanings. Ask students to find as many Spelling Words with multiple meanings as they can. Write sentences for the words using the different meanings correctly.

If students need extra practice, have partners give each other a midweek test.

Glossary Review the basic parts of speech (noun, verb, adverb, adjective) and where these are found in a Glossary entry. Have partners:

- write each Challenge Word.

- look up the word and notice that some words can be used as more than one part of speech.

- write the parts of speech found for each word.

DAY 4 — Proofread and Write

Proofread Sentences Write these sentences on the chalkboard, including the misspelled words. Ask students to proofread, circling incorrect spellings and writing the correct spellings. There are two spelling errors in each sentence.

> **The dentist checked my molers for cavitys.** (molars, cavities)
>
> **Too much plack can cause desease.** (plaque, disease)

Have students create additional sentences with errors for partners to correct.

WRITING Have students use as many Spelling Words as possible in the daily Writing Prompt on page 118D. Remind students to proofread their writing for errors in spelling, grammar, and punctuation.

DAY 5 — Assess and Reteach

Assess Students' Knowledge Use page 30 of the **Spelling Practice Book** or the Dictation Sentences on page 127O for the posttest.

JOURNAL **Personal Word List** If students have trouble with any words in the lesson, have them add to their personal lists of troublesome words in their journals.

Have students write their own definitions for each word.

Students should refer to their word lists during later writing activities.

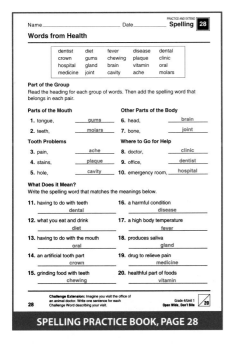

SPELLING PRACTICE BOOK, PAGE 28

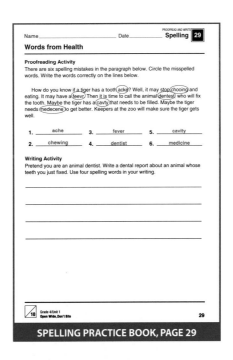

SPELLING PRACTICE BOOK, PAGE 29

SPELLING PRACTICE BOOK, PAGE 30

Wrap Up the Theme

Reflections
Stories let us share the experiences of others.

REVIEW THE THEME Remind students that all of the selections in this unit relate to the theme Reflections. Were students able to identify how story characters reflected upon or gave serious thought to their experiences? Ask students to name similar experiences or feelings they share with the characters in this unit.

READ THE POEM Read "I Ask My Mother to Sing" by Li-Young Lee aloud to students. As they listen, ask students to think about what the women are doing. After reading, discuss how the poem connects to the theme of Reflections. Ask students to explain how the author knows so much about the places in the poem.

LISTENING LIBRARY The poem is available on **audiocassette** and on **compact disc.**

MAKE CONNECTIONS Have students work in small groups to brainstorm a list of ways that the stories, poems, and the *Time for Kids* magazine article relate to the theme Reflections. Groups can then compare their lists as they share them with the class.

If students listened to any selection or poetry on audiocassette or compact disc, have them explain what they liked or disliked about experiencing the literature in that way.

128

LOOKING AT GENRE

Have students review *The Lost Lake* and *Open Wide, Don't Bite!* What makes *The Lost Lake* realistic fiction? What makes *Open Wide, Don't Bite!* nonfiction? Help students list the key characteristics of each literary form or genre. Can they name other realistic fiction or science articles that have these same characteristics?

REALISTIC FICTION *The Lost Lake*	SCIENCE ARTICLE *Open Wide, Don't Bite!*
• Story could really happen.	• Characters and setting are real.
• Characters and setting seem real.	• Reports on real people or events.
• Characters' actions seem believable.	

I Ask My Mother to Sing

She begins, and my grandmother joins her.
Mother and daughter sing like young girls.
If my father were alive, he would play
his accordion and sway like a boat.

I've never been in Peking, or the Summer Palace,
nor stood on the great Stone Boat to watch
the rain begin on Kuen Ming Lake, the picnickers
running away in the grass.

But I love to hear it sung;
how the waterlilies fill with rain until
they overturn, spilling water into water,
then rock back, and fill with more.

Both women have begun to cry.
But neither stops her song.

by Li-Young Lee

129

LEARNING ABOUT POETRY

Literary Devices: Figurative Language Read the poem aloud and ask students to close their eyes and picture the people and places in the poem. Point out how the author compares the women to young girls, helping the reader to visualize the characters. Have students read the poem aloud, looking for the simile the poet uses to describe her father.

Response Activity Have students draw a picture of one of the images they visualized while listening to the poem. As students share their drawings, discuss the words that sparked each image.

Research *and* Inquiry

Complete the Theme Project Have students work in teams to complete their group project. Remind them that the information they have collected about reflections from the recent past can be presented in many different ways. Encourage them to share the tasks of creating a class newspaper, making visual aids, or writing scripts so that each member of the team can contribute to the project.

Make a Classroom Presentation Have teams take turns presenting their projects. Be sure to include time for the audience to ask questions, make contributions, summarize, or reflect on ideas.

Draw Conclusions Have students draw conclusions about what they learned from researching and preparing their projects. Was the resource chart they made helpful? What other resources did they use? Did they find any information on the Internet? What conclusions have they made about their topic? Was their presentation effective? Finally, ask students if they learned anything about the past from listening to the stories of others. What conclusions can they make about what they have learned?

Ask More Questions/Revise Questions What additional questions do students now have about the past? What else would students like to find out? Do students have questions about other events that happened during the time periods they covered in their research? You might encourage the teams to continue their research and add information to their presentations.

129

Reading Social Studies

OBJECTIVES Students will:

- use the SQRRR strategy.
- use text features to make predictions and monitor comprehension.

FEATURES OF SOCIAL STUDIES TEXTS

- **headings**
- **special terms**
- **dates/numerical data**
- **diagrams and charts**
- **time lines**
- **photographs**
- **captions**
- **maps**

BUILD BACKGROUND

- Explain that the selections in this lesson come from a social studies textbook. The features in these selections often appear in social studies texts, other nonfiction books, and magazine articles.

- Review text features, such as headings in dark type, maps, photographs, and captions, and encourage students to look through their social studies textbooks and note some of these features.
- You may want to place other nonfiction books in a designated area for students to examine.
- Tell students that they will use a strategy called SQRRR (say *SQ3R*) to help them understand the variety of ways in which information is presented and to help them better understand and remember the information they read.

TEACHING TIP

Helping Students Read Social Studies

BUILD PRIOR KNOWLEDGE Social studies texts contain information from a variety of fields, including history, geography, politics, and anthropology. Information is also provided in pictures and on maps, charts, time lines, and diagrams. Absorbing all of this information may present quite a challenge. Encourage students to use prereading and study strategies. Help them use text format and features to understand information.

UNDERSTAND NEW VOCABULARY Social studies materials contain specialized vocabulary, such as *human resources*, abbreviations, and multiple-meaning words. Help students identify and learn terms by noticing special type, using context clues, looking for familiar word parts, and restating definitions in their own words.

UNDERSTAND CONCEPTS AND ORGANIZATION Figuring out the organization of a social studies text often helps students learn concepts. Looking at text headings will help students remember related parts of the topic. Summarizing the main ideas and important details will help students focus on important concepts.

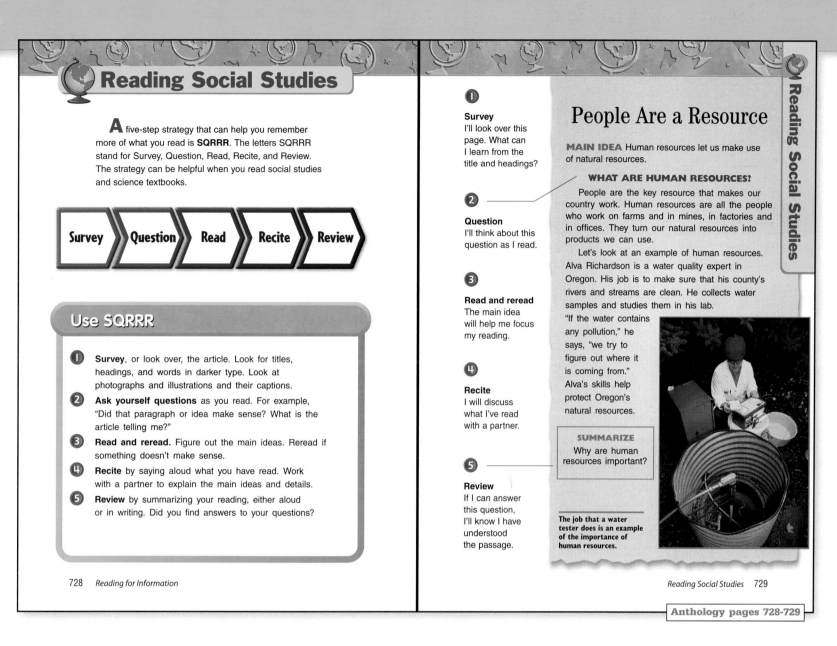

Reading Social Studies

A five-step strategy that can help you remember more of what you read is SQRRR. The letters SQRRR stand for Survey, Question, Read, Recite, and Review. The strategy can be helpful when you read social studies and science textbooks.

Survey > Question > Read > Recite > Review

Use SQRRR

① **Survey**, or look over, the article. Look for titles, headings, and words in darker type. Look at photographs and illustrations and their captions.

② **Ask yourself questions** as you read. For example, "Did that paragraph or idea make sense? What is the article telling me?"

③ **Read and reread.** Figure out the main ideas. Reread if something doesn't make sense.

④ **Recite** by saying aloud what you have read. Work with a partner to explain the main ideas and details.

⑤ **Review** by summarizing your reading, either aloud or in writing. Did you find answers to your questions?

728   *Reading for Information*

---

① **Survey**
I'll look over this page. What can I learn from the title and headings?

② **Question**
I'll think about this question as I read.

③ **Read and reread**
The main idea will help me focus my reading.

④ **Recite**
I will discuss what I've read with a partner.

⑤ **Review**
If I can answer this question, I'll know I have understood the passage.

People Are a Resource

MAIN IDEA Human resources let us make use of natural resources.

WHAT ARE HUMAN RESOURCES?

People are the key resource that makes our country work. Human resources are all the people who work on farms and in mines, in factories and in offices. They turn our natural resources into products we can use.

Let's look at an example of human resources. Alva Richardson is a water quality expert in Oregon. His job is to make sure that his county's rivers and streams are clean. He collects water samples and studies them in his lab.

"If the water contains any pollution," he says, "we try to figure out where it is coming from." Alva's skills help protect Oregon's natural resources.

SUMMARIZE
Why are human resources important?

The job that a water tester does is an example of the importance of human resources.

Reading Social Studies   729

Anthology pages 728-729

INTRODUCE Have students set purposes (to read for information). Say: The SQRRR plan is a good way to help you understand what you read in social studies. *SQRRR* stands for the first letter of the words on page 728: *Survey, Question, Read, Recite,* and *Review. (Set Purposes)*

Have volunteers read aloud the five steps of SQRRR. Explain that using SQRRR can become a regular part of reading social studies texts and other nonfiction materials. Stress that good readers develop the habit of reading strategically by:

• surveying the text.

• questioning and predicting.

• reading and then rereading if something doesn't make sense.

• telling someone what they read.

• summarizing.

PRACTICE Say: Here is a passage from a social studies textbook. The numbered items show how you might use SQRRR to understand the passage.

Have students read "People Are a Resource" and see how SQRRR is applied. Ask:

① **What does it mean to survey a page?** (to look quickly and not read every word)

② **How does the question in the heading help you to focus your reading?** (It identifies the topic, so I know to look for important details about the topic.)

③ **Why does it help to look for main ideas as you read?** (It helps to focus your reading.)

④ **Why is it important to explain the information in your own words?** (It will let me know if I really understood what I read.)

⑤ **Why would it be important to answer the question in the heading in your summary?** (It will help me remember the important information.)

129B

Reading for Information

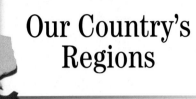

Our Country's Regions

Read Aloud

Four children wearing blindfolds were led to an elephant and asked to describe it. One said, "It is long and skinny like a snake." Another said, "It is thick like a tree trunk." The next said, "It is soft and floppy." The last said, "It is so big I can't get my arms around it." Who gave the best description?

Focus Activity

READ TO LEARN

How does studying regions help us learn about our country?

VOCABULARY

* region
* history

The Big Picture

The students all gave good descriptions of the elephant. But they were describing different parts. Trunk, legs, ears, and belly all look and feel different from each other. Yet without all of them the elephant would not be an elephant.

How would you describe the United States? Would you say it was warm or cold most of the year? Would you say it was a place of huge cities, small towns, or open spaces?

All of these things are true. It depends on what part you are describing. Let's look at the different parts of our country one at a time, like puzzle pieces. That way we can get to know each part better, and we'll have a better understanding of our country as a whole.

Five Regions

The puzzle pieces you just read about have a name. Geographers call each piece a **region** (REE jun). A region is an area with common features that set it apart from other areas. We will look at five regions of our country. Look at the map below. Which region do you live in?

Other people find it useful to divide the country into regions. For example, the U.S. Postal Service has its own set of regions. They use ten regions instead of five.

What other regions are you familiar with? Sports such as basketball have regional divisions. Teams in each region play each other. Then the winners from each region compete for a national championship.

Dividing the country into regions helps the Postal Service deliver mail quickly. Using regions helps geographers describe and understand our country.

REGIONS OF THE UNITED STATES

MAP WORK

We will learn about our country by studying the five **regions**.
1. Which region has the fewest states?
2. Which region looks smallest in area?
3. Find South Carolina. What region is it in?
4. Have you ever visited another state? What region was it in? Did you notice any differences from your state?

Anthology pages 730-731

APPLY Have students preview headings, subheadings, words in dark type, and other features of the text such as the map, photographs, and caption.

MODEL When I begin to survey this social studies selection, I see a number of special features in the text that help me understand it. The question in dark type at the far left of the first page helps me to understand the topic—regions of our country. Some key words are listed also. I expect that they will be explained in the text. I'll be sure to look for *region* and *history*.

Help students continue to survey the whole selection. Point out the Review Questions about "Our Country's Regions" at the end of page 733.

Ask: What part of SQRRR comes next? **(Question)** Stress the importance of using the headings in the text and one's own questions to monitor the reading and to make predictions about what will be explained next. Students may want to jot down some notes about key terms and questions.

Direct students to **Read, Recite,** and **Review.** Some students may want to work with a partner to discuss and summarize. Other students might spend more time studying the map and rereading.

What Makes a Region?

The five regions we will be studying are the Southeast, the Northeast, the Middle West, the Southwest, and the West. What kinds of common features define each region?

A Region's History

Each region is shaped by the people who have lived there. Each region has its own environment. Each region also has a **history**, a story of the past. Let's look at one example. The Southwest has long been the home of the Pueblo and Navajo Native Americans. For many years, it was part of the country of Mexico. The history of the Southwest makes it different from other regions.

A Region's Heritage

The settlers of the Southwest also helped form its culture. Many Southwesterners today have Mexican ancestors. Many places such as Mesa, Arizona, have names that come from Spanish, the language of Mexico. Even the foods of the Southwest show the region's Mexican heritage. In the United States, foods like tacos and chili were first eaten in the Southwest.

A clambake and a fiesta are both regional festivals. They celebrate what is special about each region.

Now you can eat these foods anywhere in our country. If you do, you are sharing the culture of the Southwest.

Regions Celebrate

People remember their heritage in celebrations and festivals. Fiestas help Southwesterners remember their Mexican heritage. Many Middle West towns hold Oktoberfests. These harvest festivals were brought by immigrants from Germany. A Northeastern clambake is a cookout that features seafood. It shows how important the sea is in the Northeast.

A Region's Environment

Each of the five regions also has its own special environment. The West is a region of high mountains. The Northeast has mountains that are lower and rounded. The Middle Western states have rich soil.

Of course, regions share parts of their environment. For example, the Southwest and the Southeast are both warm. Most of the Southwest, however, is very dry, while the Southeast gets plenty of rain. Differences in climate are another way that geographers define a region.

WHY IT MATTERS

You have learned how geographers divide the United States into five regions. Now you can read more to find out what makes each of these regions unique.

//// Reviewing Facts and Ideas

MAIN IDEAS

- A region is an area with common features that set it apart from other areas.
- The United States can be divided into five regions.
- Features of its environment, history, and culture make each region unique.

Review Questions

1. What is a region?
2. What are the five regions of the United States?
3. Did you follow each step in the SQRRR plan as you read? Did this help you to understand what kinds of features help define a region? Are there any steps you would repeat? Use the diagram on page 728 to be sure.

732 *Reading for Information*

Reading Social Studies 733

Anthology pages 732-733

ANSWERS TO REVIEW QUESTIONS

1. A region is an area with common features that set it apart from other areas.

2. The five regions of the United States are Southeast, Northeast, Middle West, Southwest, and West.

3. Answers will vary.

TRANSFER THE STRATEGY

Ask: How did using SQRRR help you to understand the social studies lesson? Can you name other subjects in which SQRRR would be useful?

Have volunteers use SQRRR to read news stories, magazine articles, and other nonfiction material.

Create a Brochure on Your Region

What to do:

- Plan with your classmates a brochure about your region. Remember that there are five features that define a region: history, cultural heritage, environment, climate, and geography.
- Decide on an Editor-in-Chief to help organize and make a written plan of the brochure.
- Work in 5 groups, with each group taking responsibility for researching one feature.
- Assign jobs within each group. Who will do the writing and who will do the graphics?
- Submit the work to the Editor-in-Chief when finished.
- Assemble the brochure.

129D

Personal Narrative

CONNECT TO LITERATURE In *The Lost Lake* Luke and his dad find a place that has a special meaning for them. In a class discussion, ask students to recall why the lake is special to the characters. How does this place make the characters feel? Ask students to think of ways that Luke and his dad could create a special place in their daily life at home.

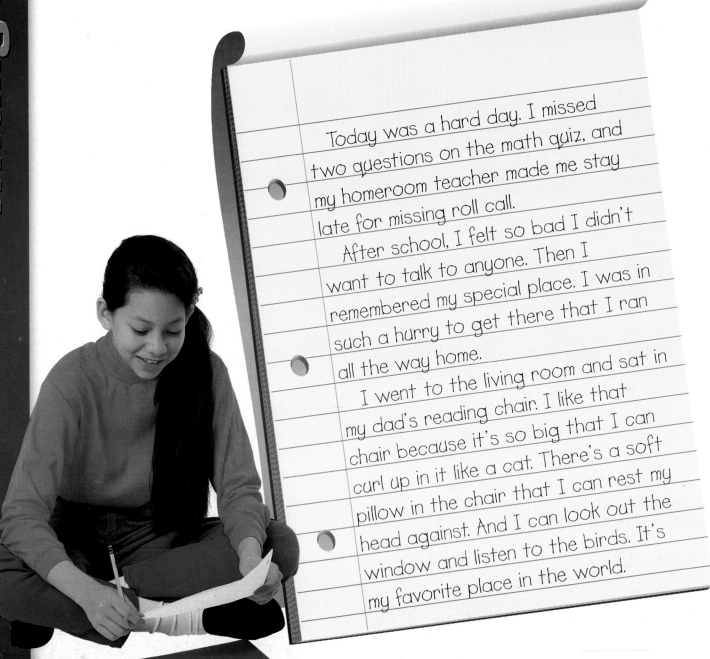

Today was a hard day. I missed two questions on the math quiz, and my homeroom teacher made me stay late for missing roll call.

After school, I felt so bad I didn't want to talk to anyone. Then I remembered my special place. I was in such a hurry to get there that I ran all the way home.

I went to the living room and sat in my dad's reading chair. I like that chair because it's so big that I can curl up in it like a cat. There's a soft pillow in the chair that I can rest my head against. And I can look out the window and listen to the birds. It's my favorite place in the world.

Prewrite

PURPOSE & AUDIENCE Have students write a personal narrative about a place that is special to them and their friends or family. Remind them to consider their purpose and audience when writing. What details about their special place will their readers find entertaining?

STRATEGY: BRAINSTORM Guide students to recall one experience that they had in their special place. Have them discuss aloud what they think makes people feel comfortable and happy in their own homes. Have one student make a board list of their comments.

Use **Writing Process Transparency 1A** to model a chart.

FEATURES OF PERSONAL NARRATIVE WRITING

- tells a story from personal experience
- has a beginning, middle, and end
- expresses the writer's feelings in a distinct personal voice

---

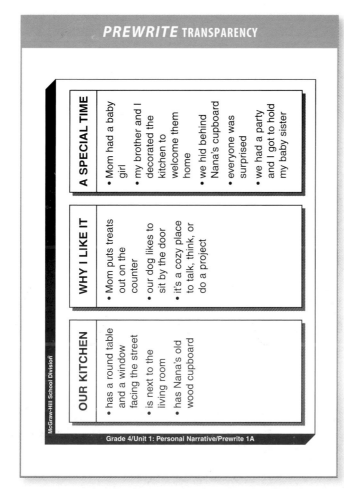

PREWRITE TRANSPARENCY

A SPECIAL TIME
- Mom had a baby girl
- my brother and I decorated the kitchen to welcome them home
- we hid behind Nana's cupboard
- everyone was surprised
- we had a party and I got to hold my baby sister

WHY I LIKE IT
- Mom puts treats out on the counter
- our dog likes to sit by the door
- it's a cozy place to talk, think, or do a project

OUR KITCHEN
- has a round table and a window facing the street
- is next to the living room
- has Nana's old wood cupboard

McGraw-Hill School Division

Grade 4/Unit 1: Personal Narrative/Prewrite 1A

Personal Narrative

Draft

STRATEGY: FREEWRITING Invite students to choose a strong memory as their story's starting point. Have them freely pour their thoughts onto the page, without editing for spelling or punctuation. Suggest that students write details for each of the five senses so that their writing will convey a strong feeling of place.

WORD CHOICE Have students circle several key words in their free writing such as names of characters, important objects, and actions. Then have them write one or more specific sensory words to describe the person, object, or action. Remind students that sensory words appeal to sight, sound, taste, touch, or smell. Words such as *tall and thin, buzzing, sweet, soft*, and *lemony* make images and feelings vivid and interesting.

Use **Writing Process Transparency 1B** as a model for discussion.

DRAFT TRANSPARENCY

everyone at our house seems to find reasons to be in the kitchen. Its got a round table and a window facing the yard. You can see the whole street from that window. Nana's old cubboard is there, too. My dad used to play hide and seek behind it. I like to do my homework there because our dog sits by the door and he's company. And mom always has a bowl of on the counter.

One of the best times we ever had was when mom brought home our baby sister? My brother and me decorated the whole kitchen with balloons and crepe paer streamers. We made punch and a cake and. Later on I got to hold my new sister Ellen. Every time I think about that day, I feel warm and happy inside,

McGraw-Hill School Division

Grade 4/Unit 1: Personal Narrative/Draft 1B

Revise

Have students review their writing for clarity and expressiveness. Ask them to be sure that the story's events are clear. You can have them team-read each other's work and share ideas to improve their stories.

Use **Writing Process Transparency 1C** for classroom discussion on the revision process.

STRATEGY: ELABORATION Have students compare first drafts with their prewriting charts to decide if they should add any additional information or sensory details to make the text clearer and richer. Encourage students to ask themselves the following questions:

- Do I like the way my narrative sounds when I read it out loud?

- Do my words express how I really feel?

- Have I described how the place looks, sounds, smells, and feels?

TEACHING **TIP**

TEACHER CONFERENCE
Work individually with students to elaborate upon the main idea in their writing. Use these questions as a base for a conferencing checklist:

- Do the place and people you've described seem real? Should you add more physical details to bring them to life?
- Have you described actions clearly? Can a reader follow your description of the events?
- Does your story have a beginning, middle and end?

***REVISE* TRANSPARENCY**

Our Kitchen
^

everyone at our house seems to find reasons to be in the kitchen. Its got a round table and a window facing the yard. You can see the whole street from that window. Nana's old cubboard is there, too. My dad used to play hide and seek
when he was little
behind it. I like to do my homework there because
^   *good*
our dog sits by the door and he's company. And
fruit and crackers
mom always has a bowl of on the counter.
^
One of the best times we ever had was when mom brought home our baby sister? My brother and me decorated the whole kitchen with balloons and crepe paer streamers. We made punch and a cake and. Later on I got to hold my new sister Ellen. Every time I think about that day, I feel warm and happy inside,

McGraw-Hill School Division

Grade 4/Unit 1: Personal Narrative/Revise 1C

129H

Personal Narrative

Edit/Proofread

After students finish making revisions, have them proofread for final corrections to the text.

GRAMMAR/SPELLING CONNECTIONS

See the 5-day Grammar and Usage Plans on compound and complex sentences, pp. 41M–41N, 65M–65N, 93M–93N, 117M–117N, and 127M–127N.

See the 5-day Spelling Plans, 41O–41P, 65O–65P, 93O–93P, 117O–117P, and 127O–127P.

GRAMMAR, MECHANICS, USAGE

- begin sentences with a capital letter
- correct use of periods, exclamation and question marks
- write in complete sentences
- correct use of subjects and predicates

Publish

CREATE AN ANTHOLOGY Combine students' work in a story anthology called "Our Special Places."

Use **Writing Process Transparency 1D** as a proofreading model, and **Writing Process Transparency 1E** to discuss presentation ideas for their writing.

PROOFREAD TRANSPARENCY

Our Kitchen

¶everyone at our house seems to find reasons to be in the kitchen. Its got a round table and a window facing the yard. You can see the whole street from that window. Nana's old cupboard is there, too. My dad used to play hide and seek behind it. when he was little I like to do my homework there because our dog sits by the door and he's company. good And mom always has a bowl of on the counter. fruit and crackers

One of the best times we ever had was when mom brought home our baby sister. My brother and me decorated the whole kitchen with balloons and crepe paper streamers. We made punch and a cake and. Later on I got to hold my new sister Ellen. Every time I think about that day, I feel warm and happy inside.

McGraw-Hill School Division

Grade 4/Unit 1: Personal Narrative/Proofread 1D

PUBLISH TRANSPARENCY

Our Kitchen

Everyone at our house seems to find reasons to be in the kitchen. It's got a round table and a window facing the yard. You can see the whole street from that window. Nana's old cupboard is there, too. My dad used to play hide and seek behind it when he was little. I like to do my homework there because our dog sits by the door, and he's good company. And Mom always has a bowl of fruit and crackers on the counter.

One of the best times we ever had was when Mom brought home our baby sister. My brother and I decorated the whole kitchen with balloons and crepe paper streamers. We made punch and a cake. Later on I got to hold my new sister, Ellen. Every time I think about that day, I feel warm and happy inside.

McGraw-Hill School Division

Grade 4/Unit 1: Personal Narrative/Publish 1E

Presentation Ideas

MAKE A DISPLAY Guide students to create a collage mural based on their stories. You can display the mural in the school library, with copies of the anthology for other students to read. ▶ **Viewing/Representing**

HAVE A CLASS DISCUSSION Have students read aloud from the anthology and then discuss each other's work. ▶ **Listening/Speaking**

Assessment

• Ask students to self-assess their writing. Present the personal narrative writing features on page 129F in question form on a chart.

• For a 6-point or an 8-point scale, see pages T107–T108.

Listening and Speaking

LISTENING STRATEGIES
• Face the speaker.
• Picture what the speaker is describing.
• Write questions to ask later.

SPEAKING STRATEGIES
• Speak in a clear, lively voice.
• Make eye contact with the audience.
• Vary volume and tone of voice to express feelings.
• Use gestures to engage the audience.

Scoring Rubric: 6-Trait Writing

4 Excellent

• **Ideas & Content** creates a focused, extensively-detailed picture of a place; expresses fresh insights about a sense of personal belonging.

• **Organization** unfolds a carefully-organized narrative, in a sequence that moves the reader smoothly through the text; ideas, sentences, and paragraphs are tied together.

• **Voice** conveys a reflective personal message that speaks directly to the reader; is deeply involved with the topic; shares a range of feelings.

• **Word Choice** uses both original and everyday language in a natural way; uses sophisticated vocabulary that creates a striking picture and brings the story to life.

• **Sentence Fluency** well-crafted simple and complex sentences flow in a smooth rhythm; dialogue, if used, sounds natural and strengthens the story; sentence lengths and patterns vary.

• **Conventions** is skilled in most writing conventions; correctly uses subjects, predicates, and sentence combining; proper use of the rules of English enhances clarity and narrative style.

3 Good

• **Ideas & Content** crafts a clear, substantial description of a place; details help convey key ideas and insights to the reader.

• **Organization** shows a well-planned narrative strategy; story is easy to follow; ideas are evenly tied together; events and details fit where they are placed.

• **Voice** makes a strong effort to share an original personal message; connects with the purpose and audience; attempts to explore a range of feelings.

• **Word Choice** uses words that fit the story and create an accurate picture of a place; experiments with some new words.

• **Sentence Fluency** crafts easy-to-follow sentences; may effectively use fragments and/or dialogue to enhance the story.

• **Conventions** spelling, capitalization, punctuation and usage are mostly correct; minor errors don't interfere with following the story; some editing may be needed.

2 Fair

• **Ideas & Content** attempts to describe a place, but may not elaborate clearly or may lose control of the narrative; details may be general or unrelated to the story.

• **Organization** may not craft a complete story structure, or may have trouble tying ideas together; reader may be confused by poorly-placed events or details.

• **Voice** tells a story, but in a predictable way; gets the basic message across, but does not seem very involved with the topic or the audience.

• **Word Choice** may not use words that convey strong feelings or images; some words are overused or may not fit the story purpose.

• **Sentence Fluency** simple sentences work, but may have trouble with more complicated structures; sentences are understandable, but may be choppy, rambling, or awkward.

• **Conventions** makes frequent, noticeable mistakes, which interfere with a smooth reading of the story; extensive editing is needed.

1 Unsatisfactory

• **Ideas & Content** does not tell a personal story; writer may go off in several directions without a sense of purpose.

• **Organization** writing is extremely hard to follow; story sequence, if any, is disorganized or incomplete; ideas and details are not tied together.

• **Voice** is not involved in sharing an experience with a reader; does not focus on anything of personal importance or interest; writing is flat and lifeless.

• **Word Choice** has a hard time finding the right words; may use words that do not fit the topic; some vocabulary detracts from the meaning of the text.

• **Sentence Fluency** sentences are incomplete, rambling, or confusing; may have trouble understanding how words and sentences fit together.

• **Conventions** makes repeated errors in spelling, word choice, punctuation and usage; sentence structures may be confused; few explicit connections made between ideas.

0 Incomplete: This piece is either blank, or fails to respond to the writing task. The topic is not addressed, or the student simply paraphrases the prompt. The response may be illegible or incoherent.

VOCABULARY

Have small groups choose three words and make a set of index cards for each. The first card shows the word, the second the definition, and the third an illustration. Have groups shuffle the cards and trade them with another group to put back in order.

Unit Review

The Lost Lake

brand-new	darted	muttered
compass	mug	talker

Amelia's Road

accidental	occasions	shortcut
labored	rhythms	shutters

Sarah, Plain and Tall

eerie	overalls	reins
huddled	pesky	squall

Seal Journey

assured	jagged	nursery
horizon	mature	squealed

Open Wide, Don't Bite!

broad	healthy	reptiles
fangs	patients	skills

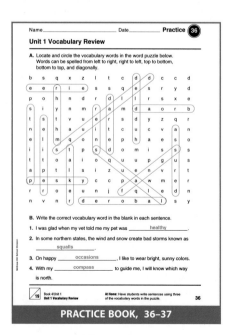

PRACTICE BOOK, 36–37

GRAMMAR

To review the unit's grammar skills, have students play Sentence Scramble. First write parts of sentences on separate sentence strips. Then give each student a sentence strip to hold and display. On command, students have two minutes to find one or more classmates to form a sentence. Read aloud the sentences formed and discuss the parts.

Unit Review

The Lost Lake
Sentences

Amelia's Road
Subjects and Predicates

Sarah, Plain and Tall
Sentence Combining

Seal Journey
More Sentence Combining

Open Wide, Don't Bite!
Run-on Sentences

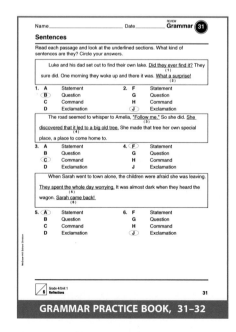

GRAMMAR PRACTICE BOOK, 31–32

SPELLING

![GROUP] Have students play Stick and Spell. Write the unit's spelling words on self-stick notes so that each syllable of a word is on a separate note. Use colored markers to show words that have the same vowel sound (e.g., red for long *a* words). Make a set for each group. Have students piece together the spelling words and organize them by common vowel sound.

Unit Review

Short Vowels
drank
wealth
fist
flock
couple

Long *a*, Long *e*
crayon
raisin
freight
zebra
rusty

Long *i*, Long *o*
title   below
supply   groan
tomato

/ū/ and /ü/
humor
commute
avenue
raccoon
movement

Health Words
plaque
diet
fever
medicine
vitamin

Spelling Practice Book

SPELLING PRACTICE BOOK, 31–32

☑ SKILLS & STRATEGIES

Comprehension
☑ Story Elements
☑ Make Inferences
☑ Problem and Solution
☑ Main Idea

Vocabulary Strategies
☑ Multiple-Meaning Words
☑ Antonyms and Synonyms

Study Skills
☑ Parts of a Book

Writing
☑ Personal Narrative

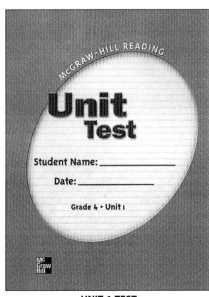

MCGRAW-HILL READING

Unit Test

Student Name: _____

Date: _____

Grade 4 • Unit 1

UNIT 1 TEST

Assessment
Follow-Up

Use the results of the informal and formal assessment opportunities in the unit to help you make decisions about future instruction.

SKILLS AND STRATEGIES	Reteaching Blackline Masters	Alternate Teaching Strategies	Skills Intervention Guide ⓘ
Comprehension			
Story Elements	1, 5, 15, 19	T60	✓
Make Inferences	6, 13, 27	T62	✓
Problem and Solution	8, 12, 20, 29	T64	✓
Main Idea	22, 26, 33	T66	✓
Vocabulary Strategy			
Multiple-Meaning Words	7, 28, 34	T63	✓
Antonyms and Synonyms	14, 21, 35	T65	✓
Study Skills			
Parts of a Book	4, 11, 18, 25, 32	T61	✓

	Alternate Writing Project–Easy	Unit Writing Process Lesson
Writing		
Personal Narrative	41L, 65L, 93L, 117L, 127L	129E

McGraw-Hill School
TECHNOLOGY

*inter***NET** **CONNECTION** Research and Inquiry Ideas.
Visit ***www.mhschool.com/reading***

Glossary

Introduce students to the Glossary by reading through the introduction and looking over the pages with them. Encourage the class to talk about what they see.

Words in a glossary, like words in a dictionary, are listed in **alphabetical order.** Point out the **guide words** at the top of each page that tell the first and last words appearing on that page.

Point out examples of **entries** and **main entries.** Read through a simple entry with the class, identifying each part. Have students note the order in which information is given: entry word(s), definition(s), example sentence, syllable division, pronunciation respelling, part of speech, plural/verb/adjective forms.

Note that if more than one definition is given for a word, the definitions are numbered. Note also the format used for a word that is more than one part of speech.

Review the parts of speech by identifying each in a sentence:

inter.	*adj.*	*n.*	*conj.*	*adj.*	*n.*
Wow!	A	dictionary	and	a	glossary

v.	*adv.*	*pron.*	*prep.*	*n.*
tell	almost	everything	about	words!

Explain the use of the **pronunciation key** (either the **short key,** at the bottom of every other page, or the **long key,** at the beginning of the glossary). Demonstrate the difference between **primary** stress and **secondary** stress by pronouncing a word with both.

Point out an example of the small triangle signaling a homophone. **Homophones** are words with different spellings and meanings but with the same pronunciation. Explain that a pair of words with the superscripts **1** and **2** are **homographs**—words that have the same spelling, but different origins and meanings, and in some cases, different pronunciations.

The **Word History** feature tells what language a word comes from and what changes have occurred in its spelling and/or meaning. Many everyday words have interesting and surprising stories behind them. Note that word histories can help us remember the meanings of difficult words.

Allow time for students to further explore the Glossary and make their own discoveries.

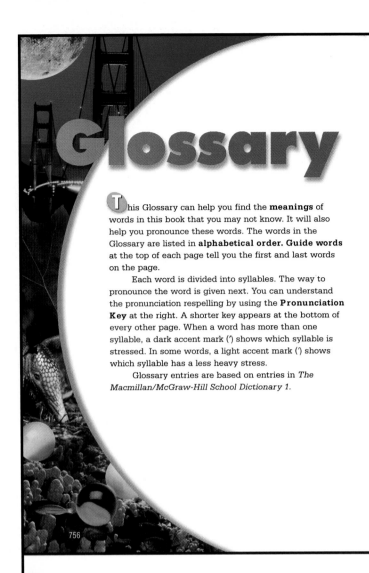

Glossary

This Glossary can help you find the **meanings** of words in this book that you may not know. It will also help you pronounce these words. The words in the Glossary are listed in **alphabetical order. Guide words** at the top of each page tell you the first and last words on the page.

Each word is divided into syllables. The way to pronounce the word is given next. You can understand the pronunciation respelling by using the **Pronunciation Key** at the right. A shorter key appears at the bottom of every other page. When a word has more than one syllable, a dark accent mark (′) shows which syllable is stressed. In some words, a light accent mark (′) shows which syllable has a less heavy stress.

Glossary entries are based on entries in *The Macmillan/McGraw-Hill School Dictionary 1*.

Sample Entry

Main entry — **adobe** A sandy kind of clay used to make bricks. Bits of straw are sometimes mixed with the clay, and the bricks are dried in the sun.

Example sentence — Many buildings in Mexico and the southwestern United States are made of *adobe*.

Definition

Syllable division — **a•do•be** (ə dō′ bē) *noun,* *plural* **adobes.**

Part of speech

Plural form   Pronunciation

a	at, bad	d	dear, soda, bad
ā	ape, pain, day, break	f	five, defend, leaf, off, cough, elephant.
ä	father, car, heart		
âr	care, pair, bear, their, where	g	game, ago, fog, egg
e	end, pet, said, heaven, friend	h	hat, ahead
ē	equal, me, feet, team, piece, key	hw	white, whether, which
i	it, big, English, hymn	j	joke, enjoy, gem, page, edge
ī	ice, fine, lie, my	k	kite, bakery, seek, tack, cat
îr	ear, deer, here, pierce	l	lid, sailor, feel, ball, allow
o	odd, hot, watch	m	man, family, dream
ō	old, oat, toe, low	n	not, final, pan, knife
ô	coffee, all, taught, law, fought	ng	long, singer, pink
ôr	order, fork, horse, story, pour	p	pail, repair, soap, happy
oi	oil, toy	r	ride, parent, wear, more, marry
ou	out, now	s	sit, aside, pets, cent, pass
u	up, mud, love, double	sh	shoe, washer, fish, mission, nation
ū	use, mule, cue, feud, few	t	tag, pretend, fat, button, dressed
ü	rule, true, food	th	thin, panther, both,
u̇	put, wood, should	th	this, mother, smooth
ûr	burn, hurry, term, bird, word, courage	v	very, favor, wave
		w	wet, weather, reward
ə	about, taken, pencil, lemon, circus	y	yes, onion
b	bat, above, job	z	zoo, lazy, jazz, rose, dogs, houses
ch	chin, such, match	zh	vision, treasure, seizure

756

757

Aa

abandon 1. To leave and not return; desert. The sailors *abandoned* the sinking ship. **2.** To give up completely. Because of heavy rain, we *abandoned* our picnic.
▲ Synonym: leave
a•ban•don (ə ban′ dən) *verb,* **abandoned, abandoning.**

> **Language Note**
> A **synonym** is a word with the same meaning as another word. A synonym for *abandon* is *desert.*

absorb 1. To soak up or take in. A towel *absorbed* the spilled water. **2.** To hold the interest of. The book about animals *absorbed* me.
ab•sorb (ab sôrb′ *or* ab zôrb′) *verb,* **absorbed, absorbing.**

accidental Not planned or expected; happening by chance. We did not know we would see each other; our meeting was *accidental.*
ac•ci•den•tal (ak′si den′təl) *adjective; adverb* **accidentally**.

admit 1. To make known that something is true; confess. They *admitted* that they had broken the lamp. **2.**To allow to enter; let in. We were *admitted* to the club last week.
ad•mit (ad mit′) *verb,* **admitted, admitting.**

affection A feeling of tenderness, fondness, or love. I have deep *affection* for my sister.
▲ Synonym: liking
af•fec•tion (ə fek′shən) *noun, plural* **affections.**

amazement Great surprise or wonder; astonishment. The people watching the whales swim by were filled with *amazement.*
a•maze•ment (ə māz′mənt) *noun.*

ancestor A person from whom one is descended. Your grandparents and great-grandparents are among your *ancestors.*
an•ces•tor (an′ses tər) *noun, plural* **ancestors.**

758

assure 1. To give confidence to. We *assured* the child that the dog was friendly. **2.** To state positively. I *assure* you that I won't be late.
as•sure (ə shu̇r′) *verb,* **assured, assuring.**

attendant A person who takes care of someone or provides service to other people. The *attendant* at the park showed us where we could rent a canoe.
at•ten•dant (ə ten′dənt) *noun, plural* **attendants.**

available 1. Possible to get. There are still a few seats available for the game. Strawberries become *available* in early summer. **2.** Ready for use or service. The telephone is now *available.*
a•vail•a•ble (ə vā′lə bəl) *adjective.*

awkward 1. Difficult or embarrassing. It was an *awkward* moment when the teacher found out that I hadn't done my homework. **2.** Lacking grace or poise in movement or behavior; clumsy or uncomfortable. The *awkward* colt had trouble standing up.
▲ Synonym: troublesome
awk•ward (ôk′wərd) *adjective; adverb,* **awkwardly.**

Bb

background 1. A person's experience or learning. Her *background* is in physics. **2.** The part of a picture that appears in the distance.
back•ground (bak′ground′) *noun, plural* **backgrounds**

ballerina A woman or girl who dances ballet.
bal•le•ri•na (bal′ə rē′ nə) *noun, plural* **ballerinas.**

barracks The building or buildings where soldiers live. The *barracks* are inspected every week. The word **barracks** may be used with a singular or a plural verb.
bar•racks (bar′eks) *plural noun.*

> at; āpe; fär; câre; end; mē; it; īce; pîerce; hot; ōld; sông; fôrk; oil; out; up; ūse; rüle; pu̇ll; tûrn; chin; sing; shop; thin; this; hw in white; zh in treasure. The symbol ə stands for the unstressed vowel sound in about, taken, pencil, lemon, and circus.

759

beloved Loved very much. The dog was *beloved* by the whole neighborhood.
be•lov•ed (bi luv′id *or* bi luvd′) *adjective.*

bid To offer to pay. We *bid* thirty-five dollars for the old desk at the auction. *Verb.*— An offer to pay money. The rug was sold to the person who made the highest *bid. Noun.*
bid (bid) *verb,* **bid,** *or* **bidden, bidding;** *noun, plural* **bids.**

biscuit 1. A small cake of baked dough. For breakfast, he had eggs, bacon, juice, and a *biscuit.* **2.** A cracker. Every afternoon, she has tea and *biscuits.*
bis•cuit (bis′kit) *noun, plural* **biscuits.**

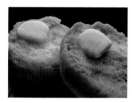

Word History
Cuit is the French word for "cooked." *Biscuit* comes from a 14th-century French word *bescuit,* meaning "twice-cooked bread."

brand-new Completely new. My aunt just bought a *brand-new* car.
brand-new (brand′nü *or* brand′nü) *adjective.*

brilliant 1. Very intelligent. That woman is a *brilliant* scientist. **2.** Very bright; sparkling. The North Star is a *brilliant* light in the sky.
bril•liant (bril′yənt) *adjective.*

brisk 1. Quick and lively. She walked at a *brisk* pace. **2.** Refreshing; keen; bracing. We walked in the *brisk* winter air.
brisk (brisk) *adjective,* **brisker, briskest.**

broad 1. Large from one side to the other side; wide. The side of the red barn is so *broad* that you can see it from a mile away. **2.** Wide in range; not limited. We have a *broad* knowledge of U.S. history.
broad (brôd) *adjective,* **broader, broadest.**

bulge To swell out. Because he put so many clothes in it, the suitcase *bulged. Verb.*— A rounded part that swells out. The rag made a *bulge* in the mechanic's back pocket. *Noun.*
bulge (bulj) *verb,* **bulged, bulging;** *noun, plural* **bulges;** *adjective,* **bulging.**

760

Cc

canoe To paddle or ride in a canoe. During the summer, they liked to go *canoeing* on the lake. *Verb.*— A light narrow boat, usually pointed at both ends and moved and steered with a paddle. The *canoe* tipped over when Eddie stood up. *Noun.*
ca•noe (kə nü′) *verb,* **canoed, canoeing;** *noun, plural* **canoes.**

captive A person or animal captured and held by force; prisoner. The police kept the *captive* in jail. *Noun.*—Held prisoner. The *captive* lion was kept in a cage. *Adjective.*
▲ Synonym: prisoner
cap•tive (kap′tiv) *noun, plural* **captives;** *adjective.*

captivity The state of being captive. Wolves live longer in *captivity* than in the wild.
cap•tiv•i•ty (kap ti′ və tē) *noun.*

celebration 1. The festivities carried on to observe or honor a special day or event. The wedding *celebration* is usually shared by friends and family. **2.** The act of celebrating. We went to the *celebration* of my cousin's graduation.
cel•e•bra•tion (sel′ ə brā′ shən) *noun, plural* **celebrations;** *adjective,* **celebratory.**

century A period of one hundred years. The time from 1651 to 1750 is one *century.*
century (sen′ chə rē) *noun, plural* **centuries**

challenge 1. Something calling for work, effort, and the use of one's talents. Chemistry is a real *challenge.* **2.** A call to take part in a contest or fight. In the days of duels, only a coward would refuse a *challenge. Noun.*—To question the truth or correctness of. They *challenged* my claim that bats are mammals. *Verb.*
chal•lenge (chal′ənj) *noun, plural* **challenges;** *verb,* **challenged, challenging.**

at; āpe; fär; câre; end; mē; it; īce; pîerce; hot; ōld; sông; fôrk; oil; out; up; ūse; rüle; pull; tûrn; chin; sing; shop; thin; this; hw in white; zh in treasure. The symbol ə stands for the unstressed vowel sound in about, taken, pencil, lemon, and circus.

761

---

chant A singing or shouting of words over and over. *Chants* usually have a strong rhythm. *Noun.* — To sing or shout in a chant. At the election rally, the group *chanted* the name of their favorite candidate. *Verb.*
chant (chant) *noun, plural* **chants;** *verb,* **chanted, chanting.**

Word History
Chant, as it is spelled today, is based on the Middle English word *chaunten.* The Latin word *cantare,* which means "to sing," is the original basis of the word.

circulate 1. To pass from person to person. Bills and coins have *circulated* in the United States since Colonial times. **2.** To move around widely among different places. The window fan *circulates* air around the room.
cir•cu•late (sûr′kyə lāt′) *verb,* **circulated, circulating.**

climate The average weather conditions of a place or region through the year. Climate includes average temperature, rainfall, humidity, and wind conditions. Southern California has a warm, mild *climate.*
cli•mate (klī′mit) *noun, plural* **climates.**

762

cling To stick closely. The wet pants were *clinging* to her legs.
cling (kling) *verb,* **clung, clinging.**

clipper 1. A tool used for cutting. Use *clippers* to cut your fingernails. **2.** A fast sailing ship. American *clippers* sailed all over the world.
clip•per (klip′ər) *noun, plural* **clippers.**

clover A small plant with leaves of three leaflets and rounded, fragrant flowers of white, red, or purple.
clo•ver (klō′vər) *noun, plural* **clovers.**

cluster To grow or group in a cluster. We all *clustered* around the campfire. *Verb.*— A number of things of the same kind that grow or are grouped together. Grapes grow in *clusters. Noun.*
clus•ter (klus′tər) *verb,* **clustered, clustering;** *noun, plural* **clusters.**

---

combine To join together; unite. We *combined* eggs, flour, and milk to make the batter. *Verb.* — A farm machine that harvests and threshes grain. *Noun.*
com•bine (kəm bīn′ *for verb;* kom′bin *for noun*) *verb,* **combined, combining;** *noun, plural* **combines.**

commercial An advertising message on radio or television. *Noun.*— Relating to business or trade. I plan to take *commercial* subjects in high school. *Adjective.*
com•mer•cial (kə mûr′shəl) *noun, plural* **commercials.**

communicate To exchange or pass along feelings, thoughts, or information. People *communicate* by speaking or writing.
com•mu•ni•cate (kə mū′ni kāt′) *verb,* **communicated, communicating.**

compare 1. To say or think that something is like something else. The writer *compared* the boom of big guns to the sound of thunder. **2.** To study in order to find out how persons or things are alike or different. We *compared* our watches and saw that your watch was five minutes ahead of mine.
com•pare (kəm pâr′) *verb,* **compared, comparing.**

compass 1. An instrument for showing directions; it has a magnetic needle that points to the north. Pilots, sailors, and many other people use compasses. The camper was able to get home because his *compass* showed him which way was west. **2.** An instrument for drawing circles or measuring distances, made up of two arms joined together at the top. One arm ends in a point and the other holds a pencil. Using a *compass,* the student was able to create a perfect circle on her drawing paper.
com•pass (kum′pəs) *noun, plural* **compasses.**

at; āpe; fär; câre; end; mē; it; īce; pîerce; hot; ōld; sông; fôrk; oil; out; up; ūse; rüle; pull; tûrn; chin; sing; shop; thin; this; hw in white; zh in treasure. The symbol ə stands for the unstressed vowel sound in about, taken, pencil, lemon, and circus.

763

complicated Hard to understand or do. The directions for putting together the bicycle were too *complicated* for me to follow.
▲ Synonym: difficult
com•pli•ca•ted (kom′pli kā′tid) *adjective.*

confusion 1. The condition of being confused; disorder. In my *confusion,* I gave the wrong answer. **2.** A mistaking of one person or thing for another. Mistaking John for his twin brother Tom is a common *confusion.*
con•fu•sion (kən fū′zhən) *noun, plural* **confusions.**

connect 1. To fasten or join together. *Connect* the trailer to the car. **2.** To consider as related; associate. We *connect* robins with spring.
con•nect (kə nekt′) *verb,* **connected, connecting.**

contain 1. To include as a part of. Candy *contains* sugar. **2.** To hold. The jar *contains* candy.
con•tain (kən tān′) *verb,* **contained, containing.**

coral A hard substance like stone, found in tropical seas. *Coral* is made up of the skeletons of tiny sea animals. *Coral* is beautiful when growing underwater, and it is very pretty as a decoration out of the water, too. *Noun.—* Having the color coral; pinkish red. She decided to use a *coral* nail polish. *Adjective.*
cor•al (kôr′əl) *noun, plural* **corals;** *adjective.*

county 1. One of the sections into which a state or country is divided. The longest bridge in the whole state is in that *county.* **2.** The people living in a county. Most of the *county* came to the fair.
coun•ty (koun′tē) *noun, plural* **counties.**

crate A box made of slats of wood. We broke up the old apple *crates* to use in our bonfire. *Noun.* —To pack in a crate or crates. The farmer *crated* the lettuce. *Verb.*
crate (krāt) *noun, plural* **crates;** *verb,* **crated, crating.**

764

crate

Dd

damage Harm that makes something less valuable or useful. The flood caused great *damage* to farms. *Noun.—* To harm or injure. Rain *damaged* the young plants. *Verb.*
dam•age (dam′ij) *noun, plural* **damages;** *verb,* **damaged, damaging.**

dart To move suddenly and quickly. The rabbit *darted* into the bushes. *Verb.—* A thin, pointed object that looks like a small arrow. He hit the target with each *dart* that he threw. *Noun.*
dart (därt) *verb,* **darted, darting;** *noun, plural* **darts.**

desire A longing; wish. I have always had a great *desire* to travel. *Noun.—*To wish for; long for. My sister *desires* a basketball more than anything. *Verb.*
de•sire (di zīr′) *noun, plural* **desires;** *verb,* **desired, desiring.**

crisscross To mark with crossing lines. The artist *crisscrossed* the paper with fine pencil marks.
criss•cross (kris′krôs) *verb,* **crisscrossed, crisscrossing.**

crumple 1. To press or crush into wrinkles or folds. He *crumpled* up the letter and threw it into the trash can. **2.** To fall down or collapse. The old shack *crumpled* when the bulldozer rammed it.
crum•ple (krum′pəl) *verb,* **crumpled, crumpling.**

cultured Having an appreciation of the arts, knowledge, and good taste and manners that are the result of education. The literature professor is a very *cultured* woman.
cul•tured (kul′chərd) *adjective.*

at; āpe; fär; câre; end; mē; it; īce; pîerce; hot; ōld; sông; fôrk; oil; out; up; ūse; rüle; púll; tûrn; chin; sing; shop; thin; <u>this</u>; hw in white; zh in treasure. The symbol ə stands for the unstressed vowel sound in about, taken, pencil, lemon, and circus.

765

destroy To ruin completely; wreck. The earthquake *destroyed* the city.
▲ Synonym: ruin
de•stroy (di stroi′) *verb,* **destroyed, destroying.**

disaster 1. An event that causes much suffering or loss. The flood was a *disaster.* **2.** Something that does not go right. My birthday party was a *disaster* because it rained.
▲ Synonym: catastrophe
dis•as•ter (di zas′tər) *noun, plural* **disasters.**

display To show or exhibit. The art museum is now *displaying* some of Monet's paintings. *Verb.* —A show or exhibit. A hug is a *display* of affection. *Noun.*
dis•play (dis plā′) *verb,* **displayed, displaying;** *noun, plural* **displays.**

ditch A long, narrow hole dug in the ground. Ditches are used to drain off water. After the rain shower, the *ditch* was full. *Noun.—* To make an emergency landing in water. No pilot wants to have to *ditch* an airplane. *Verb.*
ditch (dich) *noun, plural* **ditches;** *verb,* **ditched, ditching.**

downstage Toward the front of a theatrical stage. The prop was supposed to land *downstage* left. *Adverb or adjective.*
down•stage (doun′stāj′) *adverb; adjective.*

Ee

editor 1. A person who edits. The *editor* made changes in the book after talking with its author. **2.** A person who writes editorials. The newspaper *editor* wrote an article in favor of raising city taxes.
ed•i•tor (ed′i tər) *noun, plural* **editors.**

eerie Strange in a scary way; making people frightened or nervous. Walking through that abandoned house was an *eerie* experience.
▲ Synonym: creepy
ee•rie (îr′ē) *adjective,* **eerier, eeriest.**

766

eldest Born first; oldest. I am the *eldest* of three children.
el•dest (el′dist) *adjective.*

elegant Rich and fine in quality. The museum has a major display of *elegant* costumes.
▲ Synonym: tasteful
el•e•gant (el′i gənt) *adjective; noun,* **elegance;** *adverb,* **elegantly.**

> **Word History**
> The word *elegant* first appeared in the English language in the 15th century. The word comes from the Latin *eligere,* which means "to select."

endanger 1. To threaten with becoming extinct. Pollution is *endangering* many different species of animals. **2.** To put in a dangerous situation. The flood *endangered* the lives of hundreds of people.
▲ Synonym: risk
en•dan•ger (en dān′jər) *verb,* **endangered, endangering.**

endless 1. Having no limit or end; going on forever. The drive across the desert seemed *endless.* **2.** Without ends. A circle is *endless.*
end•less (end′lis) *adjective.*

enterprise Something that a person plans or tries to do. An *enterprise* is often something difficult or important. The search for the treasure was an exciting *enterprise.*
en•ter•prise (en′tər prīz′) *noun, plural* **enterprises.**

entertain 1. To keep interested and amused. The clown *entertained* the children. **2.** To have as a guest. They often *entertain* people in their house in the country.
en•ter•tain (en′tər tān′) *verb,* **entertained, entertaining.**

at; āpe; fär; câre; end; mē; it; īce; pîerce; hot; ōld; sông; fôrk; oil; out; up; ūse; rüle; púll; tûrn; chin; sing; shop; thin; <u>this</u>; hw in white; zh in treasure. The symbol ə stands for the unstressed vowel sound in about, taken, pencil, lemon, and circus.

767

errand 1. A short trip to do something. I have to run several *errands* this morning. **2.** Something a person is sent to do; the purpose of such a trip. Our *errand* was to buy the newspaper.
er•rand (er′ənd) *noun, plural* **errands.**

exist 1. To be found. Outside of zoos, polar bears *exist* only in arctic regions. **2.** To be real. I do not believe that ghosts *exist.*
ex•ist (eg zist′) *verb,* **existed, existing.**

expensive Having a high price; very costly. The town bought an *expensive* new fire engine.
▲ **Synonym:** costly
ex•pen•sive (ek spen′siv) *adjective.*

extinct 1. No longer existing. The dodo became *extinct* because people hunted it for food. **2.** No longer active. The village is built over an *extinct* volcano.
ex•tinct (ek stingkt′) *adjective; noun,* **extinction.**

extraordinary Very unusual; remarkable. The teacher said my friend had *extraordinary* talent.
ex•tra•or•di•nar•y (ek strôr′də ner′ē *or* ek′strə ôr′də ner′ē) *adjective.*

Ff

fang A long, pointed tooth. When trying to look threatening, a wolf shows its *fangs.*
fang (fang) *noun, plural* **fangs.**

feeble Not strong; weak. That is a *feeble* excuse.
fee•ble (fē′bəl) *adjective,* **feebler, feeblest;** *noun,* **feebleness;** *adverb,* **feebly.**

festival 1. A program of special activities or shows. We saw a foreign film at the film *festival.* **2.** A celebration or holiday. There were plenty of delicious foods to try at the street *festival.*
fes•ti•val (fes′tə vəl) *noun, plural* **festivals.**

768

foggy 1. Full of or hidden by fog; misty. Driving is dangerous on *foggy* days and nights. **2.** Confused or unclear. The ideas were *foggy* and the project needed more research to clear things up.
fog•gy (fôg′ē *or* fog′ē) *adjective,* **foggier, foggiest.**

footpath A trail or path for people to walk on. We walked on the *footpath* beside the road.
foot•path (fůt′path) *noun, plural* **footpaths.**

foul Very unpleasant or dirty. The water in the old well looked *foul. Adjective.* —A violation of the rules. The basketball player committed a *foul. Noun.*
▲ Another word that sounds like this is **fowl.**
foul (foul) *adjective,* **fouler, foulest;** *noun, plural* **fouls.**

fowl One of a number of birds used for food. Chicken, turkey, and duck are kinds of *fowl.* We always eat *fowl* for Thanksgiving dinner.
▲ Another word that sounds like this is **foul.**
fowl (foul) *noun, plural* **fowl** *or* **fowls.**

fowl

fragrance A sweet or pleasing smell. Roses have a beautiful *fragrance.*
▲ **Synonym:** smell
fra•grance (frā′grəns) *noun, plural* **fragrances.**

fray To separate into loose threads. Many years of wear had *frayed* the cuffs of the coat.
fray (frā) *verb,* **frayed, fraying.**

freeze 1. To harden because of the cold. When water *freezes,* it becomes ice. **2.** To cover or block with ice. The cold weather *froze* the pipes.
freeze (frēz) *verb,* **froze, frozen, freezing.**

at; āpe; fär; câre; end; mē; it; īce; pîerce;
hot; ōld; sông; fôrk; oil; out; up; ūse; rüle;
půll; tûrn; chin; sing; shop; thin; this; hw
in white; zh in treasure. The symbol ə
stands for the unstressed vowel sound in
about, taken, pencil, lemon, and circus.

769

fret To suffer emotional distress; irritation. My brother *frets* whenever he gets a low grade on a test. *Verb.* —One of the ridges fixed across the fingerboard of a stringed instrument such as a guitar. The notes get higher each time I move my finger up a *fret. Noun.*
fret (fret) *verb,* **fretted, fretting;** *noun, plural* **frets.**

Gg

gallon A unit of measure for liquids. A *gallon* equals four quarts, or about 3.8 liters.
gal•lon (gal′ən) *noun, plural* **gallons.**

garbage Things that are thrown out. All the spoiled food went into the *garbage.*
▲ **Synonym:** trash
gar•bage (gär′bij) *noun.*

generation 1. A group of persons born around the same time. My parents call us the younger *generation.* **2.** One step in the line of descent from a common ancestor. A grandparent, parent, and child make up three *generations.*
gen•er•a•tion (jen′ə rāsh′ən) *noun, plural* **generations.**

gild To cover with a thin layer of gold. The artist *gilded* the picture frame.
▲ Another word that sounds like this is **guild.**
gild (gild) *verb,* **gilded** *or* **gilt, gilding.**

girth The measurement around an object. The *girth* of the old redwood tree was tremendous.
girth (gûrth) *noun, plural* **girths.**

glint To sparkle or flash. Her eyes *glinted* with merriment.
glint (glint) *verb,* **glinted, glinting.**

glisten To shine with reflected light. The snow *glistened* in the sun.
glis•ten (glis′ən) *verb,* **glistened, glistening.**

glum Very unhappy or disappointed. Every member of the losing team looked *glum* after the game.
glum (glum) *adjective,* **glummer, glummest.**

770

gourd A rounded fruit related to the pumpkin or squash. Gourds grow on vines and have a hard outer rind. The hollow *gourd* hung above the tub of water.
gourd (gôrd) *noun, plural* **gourds.**

governess A woman who supervises and cares for a child, especially in a private household. The *governess* made sure the children were ready for bed.
gov•ern•ess (guv′ər nis) *noun, plural* **governesses.**

graze 1. To feed on growing grass. The sheep *grazed* on the hillside. **2.** To scrape or touch lightly in passing. The branch *grazed* the house when the wind blew.
graze (grāz) *verb,* **grazed, grazing.**

guilt 1. A feeling of having done something wrong; shame. I felt *guilt* because I got angry at a good friend. **2.** The condition or fact of having done something wrong or having broken the law. The evidence proved the robber's *guilt.*
▲ Another word that sounds like this is **gilt.**
guilt (gilt) *noun; adjective,* **guilty.**

Hh

harbor A sheltered place along a coast. Ships and boats often anchor in a *harbor. Noun.*—To give protection or shelter to. It is against the law to *harbor* a criminal. *Verb.*
har•bor (här′bər) *noun, plural* **harbors;** *verb,* **harbored, harboring.**

haul To pull or move with force; drag. We *hauled* the trunk up the stairs. *Verb.*— The act of hauling. It was an easy *haul* by truck. *Noun.*
▲ Another word that sounds like this is **hall.**
haul (hôl) *verb,* **hauled, hauling;** *noun, plural* **hauls.**

at; āpe; fär; câre; end; mē; it; īce; pîerce;
hot; ōld; sông; fôrk; oil; out; up; ūse; rüle;
půll; tûrn; chin; sing; shop; thin; this; hw
in white; zh in treasure. The symbol ə
stands for the unstressed vowel sound in
about, taken, pencil, lemon, and circus.

771

haze Mist, smoke, or dust in the air. The bridge was hidden in the *haze*.
haze (hāz) *noun, plural* **hazes.**

headlong 1. With the head first. The runner slid *headlong* into second base. **2.** In a reckless way; rashly. I rushed *headlong* into buying the bicycle.
head•long (hed′lông) *adverb.*

healthy Having or showing good health. She has a *healthy* outlook on life.
health•y (hel′thē) *adjective,* **healthier, healthiest.**

heave 1. To lift, raise, pull, or throw using force or effort. I *heaved* a rock across the stream. **2.** To utter in an effortful way. I *heaved* a sigh of relief.
heave (hēv) *verb,* **heaved, heaving.**

hilltop The top of a hill. From the *hilltop*, the hikers could see the smoke from the campfire.
hill•top (hil′top′) *noun, plural* **hilltops.**

horizon 1. The line where the sky and the ground or the sea seem to meet. The fishing boat headed out to sea just as the sun rose above the *horizon*. **2.** The limit of a person's knowledge, interests, or experience. You can widen your *horizons* by reading books.
hor•i•zon (hə rī′zən) *noun, plural* **horizons.**

huddle To gather close together in a bunch. The scouts *huddled* around the campfire to keep warm. *Verb.*—A group of people or animals gathered close together. The football players formed a *huddle* to plan their next play. *Noun.*
hud•dle (hud′əl) *verb,* **huddled, huddling;** *noun, plural* **huddles.**

772

Ii

iceberg A very large piece of floating ice that has broken off from a glacier. Only the tip of the *iceberg* is visible above the surface of the water.
ice•berg (is′bûrg′) *noun, plural* **icebergs.**

identify To find out or tell exactly who a person is or what a thing is; recognize. Can you *identify* this strange object?
▲ **Synonym:** recognize
i•den•ti•fy (i den′tə fī′) *verb,* **identified, identifying.**

ignorant 1. Not informed or aware. I wasn't wearing my watch, so I was *ignorant* of the time. **2.** Showing a lack of knowledge. The young cowhands were *ignorant* at first of how to brand cattle, but they learned quickly.
ig•no•rant (ig′nər ənt) *adjective.*

image 1. A person who looks very similar to someone else. That girl is the *image* of her mother. **2.** A picture or other likeness of a person or thing. A penny has an *image* of Abraham Lincoln on one side of it.
im•age (im′ij) *noun, plural* **images.**

importance The state of being important; having great value or meaning. Rain is of great *importance* to farmers, since crops can't grow without water.
im•por•tance (im pôr′təns) *noun.*

ingredient Any one of the parts that go into a mixture. Flour, eggs, sugar, and butter are the main *ingredients* of this cake.
in•gre•di•ent (in grē′dē ənt) *noun, plural* **ingredients.**

injury Harm or damage done to a person or thing. The accident caused an *injury* to my leg.
in•ju•ry (in′jə rē) *noun, plural* **injuries.**

inning One of the parts into which a baseball or softball game is divided. Both teams bat during an inning until three players on each team are put out. Our team won the game by scoring five runs in the last *inning*.
in•ning (in′ing) *noun, plural* **innings.**

at; āpe; fär; câre; end; mē; it; īce; pîerce; hot; ōld; sông; fôrk; oil; out; up; ūse; rūle; pull; tûrn; chin; sing; shop; thin; this; hw in white; zh in treasure. The symbol ə stands for the unstressed vowel sound in about, taken, pencil, lemon, and circus.

773

inspect To look at closely and carefully. The official *inspected* our car and declared it safe to drive.
▲ **Synonym:** examine
in•spect (in spekt′) *verb,* **inspected, inspecting.**

inspire 1. To stir the mind, feelings, or imagination of. The senator's speech *inspired* the audience. **2.** To fill with a strong, encouraging feeling. Success in school *inspired* me with hope for the future.
▲ **Synonym:** encourage
in•spire (in spir′) *verb,* **inspired, inspiring.**

instance An example; case. There are many *instances* of immigrants becoming famous Americans.
in•stance (in′stəns) *noun, plural* **instances.**

instinct A way of acting or behaving that a person or animal is born with and does not have to learn. Birds build nests by *instinct*.
in•stinct (in′stingkt′) *noun, plural* **instincts.**

Jj

jagged Having sharp points that stick out. Some eagles build nests on *jagged* cliffs.
jag•ged (jag′id) *adjective.*

Kk

keel To fall over suddenly; collapse. The heat in the crowded subway caused two people to *keel* over. *Verb.*— A wooden or metal piece that runs along the center of the bottom of many ships and boats. When we sailed through the shallow waters, the *keel* scraped along the bottom of the lake. *Noun.*
keel (kēl) *verb,* **keeled, keeling;** *noun, plural* **keels.**

774

knapsack A bag made of canvas, leather, nylon, or other material that is used for carrying clothes, books, equipment, or other supplies. A knapsack is strapped over the shoulders and carried on the back. Because she left her *knapsack* on the bus, she couldn't turn in her homework assignment.
▲ **Synonym:** backpack
knap•sack (nap′sak′) *noun, plural* **knapsacks.**

knowledge 1. An understanding that is gained through experience or study. I have enough *knowledge* of football to be able to follow a game. **2.** The fact of knowing. The *knowledge* that the car could slide on the icy road made the driver more careful.
knowl•edge (nol′ij) *noun.*

Ll

labor To do hard work. The two women *labored* over the quilt, hoping to finish it in time for the birthday party. *Verb.*—Hard work; toil. The farmers were tired after their *labor*. *Noun.*
la•bor (lā′bər) *verb,* **labored, laboring;** *noun, plural* **labors.**

launch To start something. The company *launched* its store with a big sale. *Verb.*—The act or process of launching. We watched the rocket *launch* on television. *Noun.*
launch (lônch) *verb,* **launched, launching;** *noun, plural* **launches.**

league 1. A number of people, groups, or countries joined together for a common purpose. Those two teams belong to the same *league*. **2.** A measure of distance used in the past, equal to about three miles. The army's camp was only two *leagues* from the city.
league (lēg) *noun, plural* **leagues.**

at; āpe; fär; câre; end; mē; it; īce; pîerce; hot; ōld; sông; fôrk; oil; out; up; ūse; rūle; pull; tûrn; chin; sing; shop; thin; this; hw in white; zh in treasure. The symbol ə stands for the unstressed vowel sound in about, taken, pencil, lemon, and circus.

775

linger To stay on as if not wanting to leave; move slowly. The fans *lingered* outside the stadium to see the team.
lin•ger (ling'gər) *verb*, **lingered, lingering.**

lodge A small house, cottage, or cabin. The hunters stayed at a *lodge* in the mountains. *Noun.*—To live in a place for a while. People *lodged* in the school during the flood. *Verb.*
lodge (loj) *noun, plural* **lodges;** *verb,* **lodged, lodging.**

loft 1. The upper floor, room, or space in a building. The artist cleaned his *loft.* **2.** An upper floor or balcony in a large hall or church. The choir sang in the choir *loft.*
loft (lôft) *noun, plural* **lofts.**

loosen 1. To make or become looser. *Loosen* your necktie. **2.** To set free or release. The dog had been *loosened* from its leash.
loosen (lü'sen) *verb,* **loosened, loosening.**

lurk 1. To lie hidden, especially in preparation for an attack. Snakes *lurk* under rocks. **2.** To move about quietly; sneak. Thieves *lurk* in the shadows.
lurk (lûrk) *verb,* **lurked, lurking.**

Mm

machine 1. A device that does a particular job, made up of a number of parts that work together. A lawn mower, a hair dryer, and a printing press are *machines.* **2.** A simple device that lessens the force needed to move an object. A lever and a pulley are simple *machines.*
ma•chine (mə shēn') *noun, plural* **machines.**

malachite A green mineral that is used for making ornaments.
mal•a•chite (mal'ə kīt') *noun.*

776

mammal A kind of animal that is warm-blooded and has a backbone. Human beings are *mammals.*
mam•mal (mam'əl) *noun, plural* **mammals.**

marine Having to do with or living in the sea. Whales are *marine* animals. *Adjective.*—A member of the Marine Corps. She joined the *Marines* after she graduated. *Noun.*
ma•rine (mə rēn') *adjective; noun, plural* **marines.**

marketplace A place where food and other products are bought and sold. In old towns the *marketplace* was often in a square.
mar•ket•place (mär'kit plās') *noun, plural* **marketplaces.**

marvel To feel wonder and astonishment. We *marveled* at the acrobat's skill. *Verb.*—A wonderful or astonishing thing. Space travel is one of the *marvels* of modern science. *Noun.*
mar•vel (mär'vəl) *verb,* **marveled, marveling;** *noun, plural* **marvels.**

mature Having reached full growth or development; ripe. When a puppy becomes *mature* it is called a dog. *Adjective.*—To become fully grown or developed. The tomatoes are *maturing* fast. *Verb.*
ma•ture (mə chur' *or* mə tur') *adjective; verb,* **matured, maturing.**

maze A confusing series of paths or passageways through which people may have a hard time finding their way. I got lost in the *maze* of hallways in my new school.
maze (māz) *noun, plural* **mazes.**

at; āpe; fär; câre; end; mē; it; īce; pîerce; hot; ōld; sông; fôrk; oil; out; up; ūse; rūle; pull; tûrn; chin; sing; shop; thin; this; hw in white; zh in treasure. The symbol ə stands for the unstressed vowel sound in about, taken, pencil, lemon, and circus.

777

memorize To learn by heart; fix in the memory. You can *memorize* the poem by reciting it over and over.
mem•o•rize (mem'ə rīz') *verb,* **memorized, memorizing.**

merely Nothing more than; only. Your explanations are *merely* excuses.
mere•ly (mîr'lē) *adverb.*

messenger A person who delivers messages or runs errands. The *messenger* was delayed by traffic.
mes•sen•ger (mes'ən jər) *noun, plural* **messengers.**

method 1. A way of doing something. Speaking on the telephone is a *method* of communicating. **2.** Order or system. I could not find what I wanted because the books had been shelved without *method.*
meth•od (meth'əd) *noun, plural* **methods.**

microscope A device for looking at things that are too small to be seen with the naked eye. It has one or more lenses that produce an enlarged image of anything viewed through it.
mi•cro•scope (mī'krə skōp') *noun, plural* **microscopes.**

microscope

mingle 1. To put or come together; mix; join. This stream *mingles* with others to form a river. **2.** To move about freely; join; associate. We *mingled* with the other guests.
min•gle (ming'gəl) *verb,* **mingled, mingling.**

molar Any one of the large teeth at the back of the mouth. *Molars* have broad surfaces for grinding food.
mo•lar (mō'lər) *noun, plural* **molars.**

moonscape View of the surface of the moon.
moon•scape (mün'skāp') *noun, plural* **moonscapes.**

mound A slightly raised area. The pitcher stands on the *mound* to pitch the ball. *Noun.*—To pile in a hill or heap. I like to *mound* ice cream on top of my pie. *Verb.*
mound (mound) *noun, plural* **mounds;** *verb,* **mounded, mounding.**

778

mug A large drinking cup with a handle, often made of pottery or metal. I drink tea out of my purple *mug. Noun.*—To attack and rob someone. A lady was *mugged* of all her belongings. *Verb.*
mug (mug) *noun, plural* **mugs;** *verb,* **mugged, mugging.**

mutter To speak in a low, unclear way with the mouth almost closed. I *muttered* to myself. *Verb.* —Oral sounds produced in a low, unclear way. There was a *mutter* of disapproval from the audience. *Noun.*
mut•ter (mut'ər) *verb,* **muttered, muttering;** *noun.*

Nn

native Originally living or growing in a region or country. Raccoons are *native* to America. *Adjective.* —A person who was born in a particular country or place. One of my classmates is a *native* of Germany. *Noun.*
na•tive (nā'tiv) *adjective; noun, plural* **natives.**

natural 1. Found in nature; not made by people; not artificial. *Natural* rock formations overlook the river. **2.** Existing from birth; not the result of teaching or training. Is your musical talent *natural,* or did you take lessons?
nat•u•ral (nach'ər əl) *adjective.*

neighbor A person, place, or thing that is next to or near another. Our *neighbor* took care of our dog while we were away.
neigh•bor (nā'bər) *noun, plural* **neighbors.**

newsletter A small publication containing news of interest to a special group of people. Our chess club publishes a monthly *newsletter.*
news•let•ter (nüz'let'ər) *noun, plural* **newsletters.**

at; āpe; fär; câre; end; mē; it; īce; pîerce; hot; ōld; sông; fôrk; oil; out; up; ūse; rūle; pull; tûrn; chin; sing; shop; thin; this; hw in white; zh in treasure. The symbol ə stands for the unstressed vowel sound in about, taken, pencil, lemon, and circus.

779

Glossary

G7

nip 1. To bite or pinch quickly and not hard. The parrot *nipped* my finger. **2.** To cut off by pinching. The gardener *nipped* the dead leaves off the plants.
nip (nip) *verb*, **nipped, nipping.**

nursery 1. A baby's bedroom. The baby's *nursery* was painted pink and blue. **2.** A place where young children are taken care of during the day.
nurs•er•y (nûr′sə rē) *noun*, *plural* **nurseries.**

occasion 1. An important or special event. The baby's first birthday was an *occasion*. **2.** A time when something happens. I have met that person on several *occasions*.
oc•ca•sion (ə kā′zhən) *noun*, *plural* **occasions.**

opponent A person or group that is against another in a fight, contest, or discussion. The soccer team beat its *opponent*.
▲ **Synonym:** enemy
op•po•nent (ə pō′nənt) *noun*, *plural* **opponents.**

orchard An area of land where fruit trees are grown. We picked apples in the apple *orchard*.
or•chard (ôr′chərd) *noun*, *plural* **orchards.**

organization 1. A group of people joined together for a particular purpose. The Red Cross is an international *organization*. **2.** The act of organizing. Who is responsible for the *organization* of the school dance?
or•gan•i•za•tion (ôr′gə nə zā′shən) *noun*, *plural* **organizations.**

original Relating to or belonging to the origin or beginning of something; first. The *original* owner of the house still lives there. *Adjective.* —Something that is original; not a copy, imitation, or translation. That painting is an *original* by Monet. *Noun.*
o•rig•i•nal (ə rij′ə nəl) *adjective*; *noun*, *plural* **originals.**

780

---

orphan A child whose parents are dead. The little *orphan* was raised by her grandparents. *Noun.* —To make an orphan of. The war *orphaned* many children. *Verb.*
or•phan (ôr′fən) *noun*, *plural* **orphans**; *verb*, **orphaned, orphaning.**

overalls Loose-fitting trousers with a piece that covers the chest and attached suspenders.
o•ver•alls (ō′vər ôlz′) *plural noun.*

overcome 1. To get the better of; beat or conquer. The tired runner couldn't *overcome* the others in the race. **2.** To get over or deal with. I *overcame* my fear of small spaces.
▲ **Synonym:** defeat
o•ver•come (ō′vər kum′) *verb*, **overcame, overcome, overcoming.**

overflow To be so full that the contents spill over. The bathtub *overflowed*. *Verb.*— Something that flows over. We mopped up the *overflow*. *Noun.*
o•ver•flow (ō′vər flō′ *for verb*; ō′vər flō′ *for noun*) *verb*, **overflowed, overflowing**; *noun.*

oxygen A colorless, odorless gas that makes up about one fifth of our air.
ox•y•gen (ok′si jən) *noun.*

Pp

pathway A course or route taken to reach a particular place. This *pathway* leads to the rose garden.
path•way (path′wā′) *noun*, *plural* **pathways.**

patient A person under the care or treatment of a doctor. The pediatrician had many *patients* to see. *Noun.*—Having or showing an ability to put up with hardship, pain, trouble, or delay without getting angry or upset. I tried to be *patient* while I waited in the line at the post office. *Adjective.*
pa•tient (pā′shənt) *noun*, *plural* **patients**; *adjective.*

at; āpe; fär; câre; end; mē; it; īce; pîerce; hot; ōld; sông; fôrk; oil; out; up; ūse; rūle; pull; tûrn; chin; sing; shop; thin; this; hw in white; zh in treasure. The symbol ə stands for the unstressed vowel sound in about, taken, pencil, lemon, and circus.

781

---

peddler One who carries goods from place to place and offers them for sale.
▲ **Synonym:** vendor
ped•dler (ped′lər) *noun*, *plural* **peddlers.**

percent The number of parts in every hundred. The symbol for *percent* when it is written with a number is %.
per•cent (pər sent′) *noun.*

permit To allow or let. My parents will not *permit* me to play outside after dark. *Verb.*—A written order giving permission to do something. You need a *permit* to fish here. *Noun.*
per•mit (pər mit′ *for verb*; pûr′mit *or* pər mit′ *for noun*) *verb*, **permitted, permitting**; *noun*, *plural* **permits.**

Word History
Permit comes from the Latin word *permittere*, "to let through."

pesky Troublesome or annoying. If that *pesky* fly does not stop buzzing in my ear, I'll swat it.
▲ **Synonym:** annoying
pes•ky (pes′kē) *adjective*, **peskier, peskiest.**

plantation A large estate or farm worked by laborers who live there. Cotton is grown on *plantations*.
plan•ta•tion (plan tā′shən) *noun*, *plural* **plantations.**

pod A part of a plant that holds a number of seeds as they grow. Beans and peas grow in *pods*.
pod (pod) *noun*, *plural* **pods.**

poisonous Containing a drug or other substance that harms or kills by chemical action. Many household chemicals are *poisonous*.
poi•son•ous (poi′zən əs) *adjective.*

poncho A cloak made of one piece of cloth or other material, with a hole in the middle for the head.
pon•cho (pon′chō) *noun*, *plural* **ponchos.**

782

---

portable Easy to carry from place to place. *Portable* computers are very popular.
port•a•ble (pôr′tə bəl) *adjective.*

portfolio 1. A case for carrying loose pictures, pamphlets, or papers. I placed all the pictures in my *portfolio*. **2.** A set of drawings or pictures bound in a book or a folder. I must get my *portfolio* ready for the meeting
port•fo•lio (pôrt fō′lē ō′) *noun*, *plural* **portfolios.**

pottery Pots, bowls, dishes, and other things made from clay. I made a bowl in *pottery* class.
pot•ter•y (pot′ə rē) *noun.*

pouch 1. A bag; sack. The mail carrier took the letters out of her *pouch*. **2.** A pocket of skin in some animals. Kangaroos and opossums carry their young in *pouches*.
pouch (pouch) *noun*, *plural* **pouches.**

prairie Flat or rolling land covered with grass, and with few or no trees.
prai•rie (prâr′ē) *noun*, *plural* **prairies.**

prairie

praise An expression of high regard and approval. The teacher had nothing but *praise* for the student's drawing. *Noun.*—To worship. The minister *praised* God in her sermon. *Verb.*
praise (prāz) *noun*, *plural* **praises**; *verb*, **praised, praising.**

prance 1. To spring forward on the hind legs. The colt *pranced* and leaped about the field. **2.** To move in a proud, happy way. The children *pranced* around the house in their fancy costumes.
prance (prans) *verb*, **pranced, prancing.**

at; āpe; fär; câre; end; mē; it; īce; pîerce; hot; ōld; sông; fôrk; oil; out; up; ūse; rūle; pull; tûrn; chin; sing; shop; thin; this; hw in white; zh in treasure. The symbol ə stands for the unstressed vowel sound in about, taken, pencil, lemon, and circus.

783

prejudice Hatred or unfair treatment of a particular group, such as members of a race or religion. *Noun.*—To cause to have prejudice. Being hurt once by a dentist *prejudiced* me against all dentists. *Verb.*
prej•u•dice (prej′ə dis) *noun, plural* **prejudices;** *verb,* **prejudiced, prejudicing.**

preserve To keep from being lost, damaged, or decayed; protect. It is important that we *preserve* our freedoms. *Verb.*—An area set aside for the protection of plants and animals. Rare birds and mammals breed in that nature *preserve. Noun.*
pre•serve (pri zûrv′) *verb,* **preserved, preserving;** *noun, plural* **preserves.**

pressure The force exerted by one thing pushing against another. The *pressure* of his foot on the gas pedal caused the car to go faster. *Noun.*—To urge strongly. The salesperson tried to *pressure* me into buying something I didn't need. *Verb.*
pres•sure (presh′ər) *noun, plural* **pressures;** *verb,* **pressured, pressuring.**

previously Before; at an earlier time. We had been introduced *previously.*
▲ **Synonym:** earlier
pre•vi•ous•ly (prē′vē əs lē) *adverb.*

quibble A minor dispute or disagreement. It's foolish to have a *quibble* over nothing. *Noun.* To engage in petty arguing. The two sisters *quibbled* for half an hour about who would take out the garbage. *Verb.*
quib•ble (kwi′bəl) *noun, plural* **quibbles;** *verb,* **quibbled, quibbling.**

racial Of or relating to a race of human beings. *Racial* prejudice is prejudice against people because of their race.
ra•cial (rā′shəl) *adjective; adverb,* **racially.**

ramp A sloping platform or passageway connecting two different levels.
ramp (ramp) *noun, plural* **ramps.**

784

reef A ridge of sand, rock, or coral at or near the surface of the ocean. We like to swim near the beautiful *reefs.*
reef (rēf) *noun, plural* **reefs.**

reference 1. A person or thing referred to; source of information. The encyclopedia was the *reference* for my report. **2.** A statement that calls or directs attention to something. The authors made a *reference* to their book.
ref•er•ence (ref′ər əns *or* ref′rəns) *noun, plural* **references.**

reflect 1. To give back an image of something. I saw myself *reflected* in the pond. **2.** To turn or throw back. Sand *reflects* light and heat from the sun.
re•flect (ri flekt′) *verb,* **reflected, reflecting.**

rein One of two or more narrow straps attached to a bridle or bit, used to guide and control a horse. The jockey held tightly to the horse's *reins. Noun.*—To guide, control, or hold back. The rider tried to *rein* in the galloping horse. *Verb.*
rein (rān) *noun, plural* **reins;** *verb,* **reined, reining.**

related 1. Belonging to the same family. You and your cousins are *related.* **2.** Having some connection. I have problems *related* to school.
re•la•ted (ri lā′tid) *adjective.*

at; āpe; fär; câre; end; mē; it; īce; pîerce; hot; ōld; sông; fôrk; oil; out; up; ūse; rūle; pull; tûrn; chin; sing; shop; thin; **th**is; hw in white; zh in treasure. The symbol ə stands for the unstressed vowel sound in about, taken, pencil, lemon, and circus.

785

release To set free; let go. The hostage was *released* after being held prisoner for ten days. *Verb.*—The act of releasing or the state of being released. The criminal's *release* from prison made headlines. *Noun.*
re•lease (ri lēs′) *verb,* **released, releasing;** *noun, plural* **releases.**

relieve 1. To free from discomfort or pain; comfort. The doctor gave me medicine to *relieve* my cough. **2.** To free from a job or duty. The lifeguards stayed on duty until they were *relieved.*
re•lieve (ri lēv′) *verb,* **relieved, relieving.**

reptile One of a class of cold-blooded animals with a backbone and dry, scaly skin, which move by crawling on their stomachs or creeping on short legs.
rep•tile (rep′təl *or* rep′tïl) *noun, plural* **reptiles.**

require 1. To have a need of. We all *require* food and sleep. **2.** To force, order, or demand. The law *requires* drivers to stop at a red light.
re•quire (ri kwïr′) *verb,* **required, requiring.**

research A careful study to find and learn facts. I did *research* in the library for my report. *Noun.*—To do research on or for. I *researched* my speech by reading many books on the subject. *Verb.*
re•search (ri sûrch′ *or* rē′sûrch′) *verb,* **researched, researching;** *noun, plural* **researches.**

resemble To be like or similar to. That hat *resembles* mine.
re•sem•ble (ri zem′bəl) *verb,* **resembled, resembling.**

resound 1. To be filled with sound. The stadium *resounded* with cheers. **2.** To make a loud, long, or echoing sound. Thunder *resounded* in the air.
re•sound (ri zound′) *verb,* **resounded, resounding.**

restless 1. Not able to rest. We got *restless* during the long speech. **2.** Not giving rest. The patient spent a *restless* night.
rest•less (rest′lis) *adjective; adverb,* **restlessly;** *noun,* **restlessness.**

786

rhythm A regular or orderly repeating of sounds or movements. We marched to the *rhythm* of drums.
rhythm (rith′əm) *noun, plural* **rhythms.**

roadblock A barrier or obstacle that prevents people or cars from passing through.
road•block (rōd′blok′) *noun, plural* **roadblocks.**

robot A machine that can do some of the same things that a human being can do.
ro•bot (rō′bət *or* rō′bot) *noun, plural* **robots.**

sacrifice The giving up of something for the sake of someone or something else. The parents made many *sacrifices* in order to send their children to college. *Noun.*—To offer as a sacrifice. Ancient peoples *sacrificed* animals to their gods. *Verb.*
sac•ri•fice (sak′rə fis′) *noun, plural* **sacrifices;** *verb,* **sacrificed, sacrificing;** *adjective,* **sacrificial.**

sage A very wise person, usually old and respected. *Noun.*— Having or showing great wisdom and sound judgment. My grandparents often give me *sage* advice. *Adjective.*
sage (sāj) *noun, plural* **sages;** *adjective,* **sager, sagest.**

sagebrush A plant that grows on the dry plains of western North America.
sage•brush (sāj′brush′) *noun.*

scamper To run or move quickly. The rabbit *scampered* into the woods.
scam•per (skam′pər) *verb,* **scampered, scampering.**

at; āpe; fär; câre; end; mē; it; īce; pîerce; hot; ōld; sông; fôrk; oil; out; up; ūse; rūle; pull; tûrn; chin; sing; shop; thin; **th**is; hw in white; zh in treasure. The symbol ə stands for the unstressed vowel sound in about, taken, pencil, lemon, and circus.

787

Glossary

G9

scribble To write or draw quickly or carelessly. I *scribbled* a note to my friend. *Verb.*—Writing or drawing that is made by scribbling. The paper was covered with messy *scribbles. Noun.*
 scrib•ble (skrib′əl) *verb,* **scribbled, scribbling;** *noun, plural* **scribbles;** *noun,* **scribbler.**

scuba (Self-Contained Underwater Breathing Apparatus) Equipment used for swimming underwater.
 scu•ba (skü′bə) *noun.*

sediment 1. Rocks, dirt, or other solid matter carried and left by water, glaciers, or wind. **2.** Small pieces of matter that settle at the bottom of a liquid. There was *sediment* at the bottom of the bottle.
 sed•i•ment (sed′ə mənt) *noun.*

segregation The practice of setting one group apart from another.
 seg•re•ga•tion (seg′ri gā′shən) *noun.*

settlement 1. A small village or group of houses. During the 1800s, pioneers built many *settlements* in the American West. **2.** The act of settling or the condition of being settled. The *settlement* of Jamestown took place in 1607.
 set•tle•ment (set′əl mənt) *noun, plural* **settlements.**

shanty A small, poorly built house; shack. During the Depression, many poor families lived in *shanties.*
 ▲ **Synonym:** shack
 shan•ty (shan′tē) *noun, plural* **shanties.**

shoreline The line where a body of water and the land meet. My friend has a house near the *shoreline.*
 shore•line (shôr′līn) *noun.*

shortcut 1. A quicker way of reaching a place. I took a *shortcut* to school. **2.** A way of doing something faster. Don't use any *shortcuts* in your science experiment.
 short•cut (shôrt′cut′) *noun, plural* **shortcuts.**

shriek A loud, sharp cry or sound. The child let out a *shriek* of laughter. *Noun.*—To utter a loud, sharp cry or sound. We all *shrieked* with laughter at her jokes. *Verb.*
 shriek (shrēk) *noun, plural* **shrieks;** *verb,* **shrieked, shrieking.**

788

shutter 1. A movable cover for a window, usually attached to the frame by hinges. *Shutters* are used to shut out light **2.** The part of a camera that snaps open and shuts quickly to let light onto the film when a picture is taken.
 shut•ter (shut′ər) *noun, plural* **shutters.**

siren A device that makes a loud, shrill sound, used as a signal or warning. Ambulances and police cars have *sirens.*
 si•ren (sī′rən) *noun, plural* **sirens.**

sketch A rough, quick drawing. The artist made several *sketches* of the model before starting the painting. *Noun.*—To make a sketch of. I *sketched* an old barn for my art class. *Verb.*
 sketch (skech) *verb,* **sketched, sketching;** *noun, plural* **sketches.**

> **Word History**
> *Sketch* comes from the Dutch word *schets* and the Italian word *schizzo,* meaning "splash." A sketch is often a rough drawing, a splash of an idea that will later become a detailed finished product.

skill The power or ability to do something. *Skill* comes with practice and experience.
 skill (skil) *noun, plural* **skills.**

skillet A shallow pan with a handle. A *skillet* is used for frying.
 skil•let (skil′it) *noun, plural* **skillets.**

skim 1. To remove from the surface of a liquid. The cook *skimmed* the fat from the soup. **2.** To read quickly. *Skim* the paper for the scores.
 skim (skim) *verb,* **skimmed, skimming.**

> at; āpe; fär; câre; end; mē; it; īce; pîerce; hot; ōld; sông; fôrk; oil; out; up; ūse; rüle; pùll; tûrn; chin; sing; shop; thin; this; hw in white; zh in treasure. The symbol ə stands for the unstressed vowel sound in about, taken, pencil, lemon, and circus.

789

smog A combination of smoke and fog in the air. *Smog* is found especially over cities where there are factories and many cars.
 smog (smog) *noun.*

> **Word History**
> The word *smog* was made using the first two letters of *smoke* and the last two letters of *fog.*

snout The front part of an animal's head, including nose, mouth, and jaws. My dog has a cute *snout.*
 snout (snout) *noun, plural* **snouts.**

soapsuds Water that is bubbly with soap. I like my bath to be filled with *soapsuds.*
 soap•suds (sōp′sudz′) *plural noun.*

soggy Very wet or damp; soaked. The soil was *soggy* after the rain.
 sog•gy (sog′ē) *adjective,* **soggier, soggiest.**

soot A black, greasy powder that forms when such fuels as wood, coal, and oil are burned. The old chimney was caked with *soot.*
 soot (sút *or* süt) *noun; adjective,* **sooty.**

spice The seeds or other parts of certain plants used to flavor food. Pepper, cloves, and cinnamon are spices. *Noun.*—To flavor with a spice or spices. I *spiced* the hamburgers. *Verb.*
 spice (spis) *noun, plural* **spices;** *verb,* **spiced, spicing;** *adjective,* **spicy.**

spike 1. Any sharp, pointed object or part that sticks out. Baseball shoes have *spikes* on the soles. **2.** A large, heavy nail used to hold rails to railroad ties. It was difficult to hammer in the railroad *spike.*
 spike (spik) *noun, plural* **spikes.**

sponge A simple water animal that has a body that is full of holes and absorbs water easily. The dried skeletons of some *sponge* colonies are used for cleaning and washing. *Noun.*—To clean with a sponge. We *sponged* and dried the dirty walls. *Verb.*
 sponge (spunj) *noun, plural* **sponges;** *verb,* **sponged, sponging.**

790

squall A strong gust of wind that arises very suddenly. Squalls often bring rain, snow, or sleet. We were forced indoors by a *squall* of snow.
 squall (skwôl) *noun, plural* **squalls.**

> **Word History**
> The word *squall* first appeared in the English language in 1699. It is probably based on the Swedish word *skval,* which means "rushing water."

squeal To make a loud, shrill cry or sound. The little pigs *squealed* with excitement. *Verb.* —A loud, shrill cry or sound. The *squeal* of the brakes hurt my ears. *Noun.*
 squeal (skwēl) *verb,* **squealed, squealing;** *noun, plural* **squeals.**

stake A stick or post pointed at one end so that it can be driven into the ground. The campers drove in *stakes* and tied the corners of the tent to them. *Noun.* — To fasten or hold up with a stake. The gardener *staked* the beans. *Verb.*
 ▲ Another word that sounds like this is **steak.**
 stake (stāk) *noun, plural* **stakes;** *verb,* **staked, staking.**

sterilize To make free of bacteria and microorganisms. The nurse *sterilized* the scalpels before the operation.
 ster•il•ize (ster′ə līz′) *verb,* **sterilized, sterilizing.**

stitch To make, fasten, or mend with stitches; sew. I *stitched* up the tear in my shirt. *Verb.*—One complete movement made with a needle and thread. *Noun.*
 stitch (stich) *verb,* **stitched, stitching;** *noun, plural* **stitches.**

strew To spread by scattering. I have to clean my room because my clothes are *strewn* all over the place.
 strew (strü) *verb,* **strewed, strewn, strewing.**

> at; āpe; fär; câre; end; mē; it; īce; pîerce; hot; ōld; sông; fôrk; oil; out; up; ūse; rüle; pùll; tûrn; chin; sing; shop; thin; this; hw in white; zh in treasure. The symbol ə stands for the unstressed vowel sound in about, taken, pencil, lemon, and circus.

791

stroll To walk in a slow, relaxed way. We *strolled* through the park. *Verb.* —A slow, relaxed walk. After dinner we took a *stroll. Noun.*
stroll (strōl) *verb,* **strolled, strolling;** *noun, plural* **strolls.**

sturdy Strong; hardy. Heavy trucks can drive on the *sturdy* bridge.
stur•dy (stûr′dē) *adjective,* **sturdier, sturdiest;** *adverb,* **sturdily;** *noun,* **sturdiness.**

success 1. A result hoped for; favorable end. The coach was pleased with the *success* of the game. **2.** A person or thing that does or goes well. The party was a big *success.*
suc•cess (sək ses′) *noun, plural* **successes;** *adjective,* **successful.**

sunrise The rising of the sun. We went to the beach to watch the *sunrise.*
sunrise (sun′rīz′) *noun, plural* **sunrises.**

swamp An area of wet land. The *swamp* looked scary and creepy. *Noun.* —To fill with water. High waves *swamped* the boat. *Verb.*
swamp (swomp) *noun, plural* **swamps;** *verb,* **swamped, swamping.**

swamp

talker One who exchanges spoken words in conversation. The two friends were great *talkers.*
talk•er (tôk′ ər) *noun, plural* **talkers**

teammate A person who is a member of the same team. We're basketball *teammates.*
team•mate (tēm′māt′) *noun, plural* **teammates.**

threat 1. A person or thing that might cause harm; danger. The outbreak of flu was a *threat* to the community. **2.** A statement of something that will be done to hurt or punish. The trespassers heeded our *threat.*
threat (thret) *noun, plural* **threats.**

ton A measure of weight equal to 2,000 pounds in the United States and Canada, and 2,240 pounds in Great Britain.
ton (tun) *noun, plural* **tons.**

tractor A vehicle with heavy tires or tracks. *Tractors* are used to pull heavy loads over rough ground.
trac•tor (trak′tər) *noun, plural* **tractors.**

tradition A custom or belief that is passed on from one generation to another.
tra•di•tion (trə dish′ən) *noun, plural* **traditions;** *adjective,* **traditional.**

travel To go from one place to another; to make a trip. We *traveled* through England. *Verb.* —The act of traveling. Camels are used for desert *travel. Noun.*
trav•el (trav′əl) *verb,* **traveled, traveling;** *noun, plural* **travels.**

tricorn A hat with the brim turned up on three sides.
tri•corn (trī′kôrn′) *noun, plural* **tricorns.**

tube A container of soft metal or plastic from which the contents are removed by squeezing. I need a new *tube* of toothpaste.
tube (tüb) *noun, plural* **tubes.**

tusk A long, pointed tooth that sticks out of each side of the mouth in certain animals. Elephants and walruses have *tusks.*
tusk (tusk) *noun, plural* **tusks.**

waddle To walk or move with short steps, swaying the body from side to side. The duck *waddled* across the yard. *Verb.*—A swaying or rocking walk. The audience laughed at the clown's *waddle. Noun.*
wad•dle (wod′əl) *verb,* **waddled, waddling;** *noun, plural* **waddles.**

at; āpe; fär; câre; end; mē; it; īce; pîerce; hot; ōld; sông; fôrk; oil; out; up; ūse; rüle; půll; tûrn; chin; sing; shop; thin; this; hw in white; zh in treasure. The symbol ə stands for the unstressed vowel sound in about, taken, pencil, lemon, and circus.

weary Very tired. The carpenter was *weary* after the day's hard work. *Adjective.*—To make or become weary; tire. The long walk *wearied* the children. *Verb.*
wea•ry (wîr′ē) *adjective,* **wearier, weariest;** *verb,* **wearied, wearying;** *adverb,* **wearily;** *noun,* **weariness.**

weird Strange or mysterious; odd. A *weird* sound came from the deserted old house.
▲ **Synonym:** peculiar
weird (wîrd) *adjective,* **weirder, weirdest;** *adverb,* **weirdly;** *noun,* **weirdness.**

wharf A structure built along a shore as a landing place for boats and ships; dock. We had to unload the boat once we reached the *wharf.*
wharf (hworf *or* wôrf) *noun, plural* **wharves** *or* **wharfs.**

whicker To neigh or whinny. The horse began *whickering* at the kids. *Verb.*—A neigh or whinny. The horse let out a *whicker. Noun.*
whick•er (hwi′kər) *verb,* **whickered, whickering;** *noun, plural* **whickers.**

whinny A soft neigh. We heard the *whinnies* of the horses. *Noun.* —To neigh in a low, gentle way. My horse *whinnied* when he saw me. *Verb.*
whin•ny (hwin′ē *or* win′ē) *verb,* **whinnied, whinnying;** *noun, plural* **whinnies.**

wildlife Wild animals that live naturally in an area. My favorite part of hiking is observing the *wildlife.*
wild•life (wīld′līf′) *noun.*

windowpane A framed sheet of glass in a window. I placed my candles by the *windowpane.*
win•dow•pane (win′dō pān′) *noun, plural* **windowpanes.**

wondrous Extraordinary; wonderful. The local theater put on a *wondrous* performance.
▲ **Synonym:** marvelous
won•drous (wun′drəs) *adjective;* *adverb,* **wondrously;** *noun,* **wondrousness.**

wrestle 1. To force by grasping. The champion *wrestled* his opponent to the mat. **2.** To struggle by grasping and trying to force and hold one's opponent to the ground, without punching. The children *wrestled* on the lawn.
wres•tle (res′əl) *verb,* **wrestled, wrestling.**

wriggle 1. To twist or turn from side to side with short, quick moves; squirm. The bored children *wriggled* in their seats. **2.** To get into or out of a position by tricky means. You always try to *wriggle* out of having to wash the dishes.
wrig•gle (rig′əl) *verb,* **wriggled, wriggling;** *adjective,* **wriggly.**

Word History
The word *wriggle* comes from the Old English word *wrigian,* which means "to turn."

at; āpe; fär; câre; end; mē; it; īce; pîerce; hot; ōld; sông; fôrk; oil; out; up; ūse; rüle; půll; tûrn; chin; sing; shop; thin; this; hw in white; zh in treasure. The symbol ə stands for the unstressed vowel sound in about, taken, pencil, lemon, and circus.

Glossary

G11

Cover Illustration: Terry Widener

The publisher gratefully acknowledges permission to reprint the following copyrighted material:

Autobiographical piece by Matt Christopher from PAUSES: AUTOBIOGRAPHICAL REFLECTIONS OF 101 CREATORS OF CHILDREN'S BOOKS by Lee Bennett Hopkins. Copyright © 1995 by Lee Bennett Hopkins. Used by permission of HarperCollins Children's Books, a division of HarperCollins Publishers.

Autobiographical piece by Robert Ballard from the book TALKING WITH ADVENTURERS by Pat and Linda Cummings. This excerpt copyright © 1998 by Robert Ballard. Used by permission of the National Geographic Society.

"The Bear and the Two Travelers" from MORE FABLES OF AESOP by Jack Kent. Copyright © 1974 by Jack Kent. Reprinted with the permission of Parents' Magazine Press.

"Beezus and Her Imagination" from BEEZUS AND RAMONA by Beverly Cleary (pp. 59–62). Copyright © 1955 by Beverly Cleary. Used by permission of Morrow Junior Books, a division of HarperCollins Publishers.

"The Biggest Problem (Is in Other People's Minds)" from FREE TO BE ... YOU AND ME AND FREE TO BE ... A FAMILY by Don Haynie. Copyright © 1987 by the Free to Be Foundation, Inc. Used by permission.

"Birdfoot's Grampa" from ENTERING ONANDAGA by Joseph Bruchac. Copyright © 1978 by Joseph Bruchac. Used by permission.

"Buffalo Dusk" by Carl Sandburg from THE COMPLETE POEMS OF CARL SANDBURG. Copyright © 1970, 1969 by Lilian Steichen Sandburg, Trustee. Reprinted by permission of Harcourt, Inc.

"Dakota Dugout" from DAKOTA DUGOUT by Ann Turner. Copyright © 1985 by Ann Turner. Reprinted with the permission of Simon & Schuster Books for Young Readers, an imprint of Simon & Schuster Children's Publishing Division.

"The Dentist" from ANOTHER FIRST POETRY BOOK by Judith Nicholls. Copyright © 1987 by Judith Nicholls. Reprinted by permission of the author.

"Don't Make a Bargain with a Fox" from THE KING OF THE MOUNTAINS: A TREASURY OF LATIN AMERICAN FOLK STORIES by M. A. Jagendorf and R. S. Boggs. Copyright © 1960 by M. A. Jagendorf and R. S. Boggs. Copyright renewed 1988 by Andre Jagendorf, Merna Alpert and R. S. Boggs. Used by permission of Random House Children's Books, a division of Random House, Inc.

"Earth Day Rap" by Doug Goodkin. Copyright © 1995. Used by permission of The McGraw-Hill Co., Inc.

"8,000 Stones" from 8,000 STONES: A CHINESE FOLKTALE by Diane Wolkstein. Text copyright © 1972 by Diane Wolkstein. Used by permission.

ACKNOWLEDGMENTS

The publisher gratefully acknowledges permission to reprint the following copyrighted material.

"Amelia's Road" by Linda Jacobs Altman, illustrated by Enrique O. Sanchez. Text copyright © 1993 by Linda Jacobs Altman. Illustrations copyright © 1993 by Enrique O. Sanchez. Permission granted by Lee & Low Books Inc., 95 Madison Avenue, New York, NY 10016.

"August 8" by Norman Jordan. From ABOVE MAYA, 1971, MAKE A JOYFUL SOUND, 1991, *Creative Classroom* magazine, 1995, *Connections* magazine, 1999.

"Baseball Saved Us" by Ken Mochizuki, illustrated by Dom Lee. Text copyright © 1993 by Ken Mochizuki. Illustrations copyright © 1993 by Dom Lee. Permission granted by Lee & Low Books Inc., 95 Madison Avenue, New York, NY 10016.

"Final Curve" from COLLECTED POEMS by Langston Hughes; Copyright © 1994 by the Estate of Langston Hughes. Reprinted by permission of Alfred A. Knopf, a Division of Random House, Inc.

"The Fox and the Guinea Pig"/"El zorro y el cuy" A Traditional Folk Tale translated by Mary Ann Newman, illustrated by Kevin Hawkes. Copyright © 1997 Macmillan/McGraw-Hill, a Division of the Educational and Professional Publishing Group of the McGraw-Hill Companies, Inc.

"The Garden We Planted Together" by Anuruddha Bose from A WORLD IN OUR HANDS. Reprinted with permission of A WORLD IN OUR HANDS by Peace Child Charitable Trust, illustrated by Sanjay Sinha ($15.95). Copyright © 1995 Tricycle Press (800-841-BOOK).

"Gluskabe and the Snow Bird" from FOUR ANCESTORS: STORIES, SONGS, AND POEMS FROM NATIVE NORTH AMERICA by Joseph Bruchac. Published by and reprinted with permission of Troll Communications, LLC.

"Grass Sandals/The Travels of Basho" by Dawnine Spivak, illustrated by Demi. Text copyright © 1997 by Dawnine Spivak, illustrations copyright © 1997 by Demi. Reprinted by permission of Atheneum Books for Young Readers, Simon and Schuster Children's Publishing Division. All rights reserved.

"The Hatmaker's Sign" by Candace Fleming, illustrated by Robert Andrew Parker. Text copyright © 1998 by Candace Fleming. Illustrations copyright © 1998 by Robert Andrew Parker. All rights reserved. Reprinted by permission of Orchard Books, New York.

"How to Tell the Top of a Hill" by John Ciardi from THE REASON FOR THE PELICAN. Copyright © 1959 by John Ciardi. Reprinted by permission of the Ciardi Family Trust, John L. Ciardi, Trustee.

"I Ask My Mother to Sing" by Li-Young Lee. Copyright © 1986 by Li-Young Lee. Reprinted from *Rose* with the permission of BOA Editions, Ltd., 260 East Ave., Rochester, NY 14604.

"Just a Dream" is from JUST A DREAM by Chris Van Allsburg. Copyright © 1990 by Chris Van Allsburg. Reprinted by permission of Houghton Mifflin Company.

"Justin and the Best Biscuits in the World" is from JUSTIN AND THE BEST BISCUITS IN THE WORLD by Mildred Pitts Walter. Copyright © 1986 by Mildred Pitts Walter. Used by permission of HarperCollins Publishers.

"Leah's Pony" by Elizabeth Friedrich, illustrated by Michael Garland. Text copyright © 1996 by Elizabeth Friedrich. Illustrations copyright © 1996 by Michael Garland. Used by permission of Boyds Mills Press.

"The Lost Lake" by Allen Say. Copyright © 1989 by Allen Say. Reprinted by permission of Houghton Mifflin Company. All rights reserved.

"The Malachite Palace" by Alma Flor Ada, translated by Rosa Zubizarreta, illustrated by Leonid Gore. Text copyright © 1998 by Alma Flor Ada, illustrations copyright © 1998 by Leonid Gore. Reprinted by permission of Atheneum Books for Young Readers, Simon and Schuster Children's Publishing Division. All rights reserved.

"Meet an Underwater Explorer" by Luise Woelflein. Reprinted from the June 1994 issue of RANGER RICK magazine, with the permission of the publisher, the National Wildlife Federation. Copyright © 1994 by the National Wildlife Federation.

"Mom's Best Friend" by Sally Hobart Alexander, photographs by George Ancona. Text copyright ©1992 by Sally Hobart Alexander. Photographs copyright © 1992 by George Ancona. Reprinted with permission of Simon & Schuster Books for Young Readers, Simon & Schuster Children's Publishing Division.

"My Poems" by Alan Barlow. From RISING VOICES: WRITINGS OF YOUNG NATIVE AMERICANS selected by Arlene B. Hirschfelder and Beverly R. Singer. Copyright © 1992. Published by Scribner's. Used by permission.

"On the Bus with Joanna Cole" excerpt from *On the Bus with Joanna Cole: A Creative Autobiography* by Joanna Cole with Wendy Saul. Copyright © 1996 by Joanna Cole. Published by Heinemann, a division of Reed Elsevier Inc. Reprinted by permission of the Publisher. Illustration on page 447 by Bruce Degen from THE MAGIC SCHOOL BUS INSIDE THE HUMAN BODY by Joanna Cole. Illustration copyright © 1989 by Bruce Degen. Reprinted with permission of Scholastic, Inc. THE MAGIC SCHOOL BUS is a registered trademark of Scholastic, Inc.

"Pat Cummings: My Story" reprinted with the permission of Simon & Schuster Books for Young Readers from TALKING WITH ARTISTS compiled and edited by Pat Cummings. Jacket illustration copyright © 1992 Pat Cummings. Copyright © 1992 Pat Cummings.

"A Place Called Freedom" by Scott Russell Sanders, illustrated by Thomas B. Allen. Text copyright © 1997 by Scott Russell Sanders, illustrations copyright © 1997 by Thomas B. Allen. Reprinted by permission of Atheneum Books for Young Readers, Simon and Schuster Children's Publishing Division. All rights reserved.

"The Poet Pencil" by Jesús Carlos Soto Morfin, translated by Judith Infante. From THE TREE IS OLDER THAN YOU ARE: A Bilingual Gathering of Poems and Stories from Mexico, selected by Naomi Shihab Nye. Copyright © 1995 Reprinted by permission of the author and María Guadalupe Morfin.

"The Rajah's Rice" from THE RAJAH'S RICE by David Barry, illustrated by Donna Perrone. Text Copyright © 1994 by David Barry. Art copyright © 1994 by Donna Perrone. Used with permission of W. H. Freeman and Company.

"Sarah, Plain and Tall" text excerpt from SARAH, PLAIN AND TALL by Patricia MacLachlan. Copyright © 1985 by Patricia MacLachlan. Reprinted by permission of HarperCollins Publishers. Cover permission for the Trophy Edition used by permission of HarperCollins Publishers.

"Scruffy: A Wolf Finds His Place in the Pack" by Jim Brandenburg. Copyright © 1996 by Jim Brandenburg. Published by arrangement with Walker Publishing Company, Inc.

"Seal Journey" From SEAL JOURNEY by Richard and Jonah Sobol. Copyright © 1993 Richard Sobol, text and photographs. Used by permission of Cobblehill Books, an affiliate of Dutton Children's Press, a division of Penguin USA, Inc.

"Teammates" from TEAMMATES by Peter Golenbock, text copyright © 1990 by Golenbock Communications, reprinted by permission of Harcourt, Inc.

"To" by Lee Bennett Hopkins from BEEN TO YESTERDAYS: Poems of a Life. Text copyright © 1995 by Lee Bennett Hopkins. Published by Wordsong/Boyds Mills Press. Reprinted by permission.

"The Toothpaste Millionaire" by Jean Merrill. Copyright © 1972 by Houghton Mifflin Company. Adapted and reprinted by permission of Houghton Mifflin Company. All rights reserved.

"Tortillas Like Africa" from CANTO FAMILIAR by Gary Soto. Copyright © 1995 Harcourt, Inc.

"Evergreen, Everblue" by Raffi. Copyright © 1990 Homeland Publishing, a division of Troubadour Records Ltd. Used by permission.

"Follow the Drinkin' Gourd," Words and Music by Ronnie Gilbert, Lee Hays, Fred Hellerman and Pete Seeger TRO- Copyright © 1951 (Renewed) Folkways Music Publishers, Inc., New York, New York. Used by permission.

"Fossils" from SOMETHING NEW BEGINS by Lilian Moore. Copyright © 1982 by Lilian Moore. Used by permission of Marian Reiner for the author.

Four haiku from CRICKET NEVER DOES: A COLLECTION OF HAIKU AND TANKA by Myra Cohn Livingston. Text copyright © 1977 by Myra Cohn Livingston. Used by permission of Margaret K. McElderry Books, an imprint of Simon & Schuster Children's Publishing Division.

"Whales" excerpt from WHALES by Seymour Simon. Copyright © 1989 by Seymour Simon. Reprinted by permission of HarperCollins Publishers.

"Yeh-Shen: A Cinderella Story from China" is from YEH-SHEN: A CINDERELLA STORY FROM CHINA by Ai-Ling Louie. Text copyright © 1982 by Ai-Ling Louie. Illustrations copyright © 1982 by Ed Young. Reprinted by permission of Philomel Books. Introductory comments by Ai-Ling Louie and used with her permission.

"Your World" by Georgia Douglas Johnson appeared originally in HOLD FAST TO DREAMS by Arna Bontemps. Originally published by Follett Publishing Company © 1969. Reprinted by permission of Pearson Learning.

Cover Illustration
Terry Widener

Illustration
Roberta Ludlow, 16-17; Jean and Mou-Sien Tseng, 128-129; David Ridley, 130-131; Elizabeth Rosen, 252-253; J. W. Stewart, 254-255; Bruno Paciulli, 372-373; Stefano Vitale, 408-419; Amy Vangsgard, 482-483; Susan Leopold, 484-485; Yoshi Miyake, 612-613; David Catrow, 666-687; B. J. Faulkner, 724-725; George Thompson, 758, 779; Rodica Prato, 762, 769; John Carrozza, 775, 789, 793.

Photography
5: m.r. Richard Sobol. 5: b.r. K. and K. Ammann/Bruce Coleman. 7: Lawrence Migdale/Photo Researchers, Inc. 9: Georg Gerster/Photo Researchers, Inc. 10: Jim Brandenburg/Minden Pictures. 11: t. Luise Woelflein. 12: George Ancona. 13: Marty Snyderman. 15: b. Galen Rowell/Corbis. 18—19: Owen Edgar Gallery, U.K./Fine Art Photographic Library, London/Art Resource, NY. 37: b.r. Courtesy, Allen Say. 42—43: © 2003 Artists Rights Society (ARS), New York/DACS, London/Bradford Art Galleries and Museums, West Yorkshire, U.K./The Bridgeman Art Library International. 44: t. Courtesy, Lee & Low Books. 44: b. Courtesy, Enrique O. Sanchez. 66: c. Superstock. 89: Courtesy, Patricia MacLachlan. 94: c. Shelburne Museum. 96: i. Courtesy, Richard Sobol. 111: t. Richard Sobol. 111: m. Richard Sobol. 111: b. Richard Sobol. 114: Richard Sobol. 115: Richard Sobol. 118: E.A. Barton Collection, The British Museum. 124: George Lepp/Corbis. 125: K. and K. Ammann/Bruce Coleman. 153: t. Courtesy, Mildred Pitts Walter. 153: b. Courtesy, Floyd Cooper. 158: © 1939 Turner Entertainment Company. All Rights Reserved./Photofest. 185: Courtesy/Minden Pictures, Chris Van Allsburg. 190: The Museum of Modern Art, New York/© Dorothea Lange Collection, Oakland Museum of California, City of Oakland. Gift of Paul S. Taylor. 192: t. Courtesy, Boyds Mills Press. 192: b. Courtesy, Boyds Mills Press. 216: Museo de Bellas Artes, Bilbao, Spain/Bridgeman Art Library International. 218: t. Courtesy, Lee & Low Books. 218: b. Courtesy, Lee & Low Books. 242: The British Museum, London/The Bridgeman Art Library International. 249: Lawrence Migdale/Photo Researchers. 250: Shelly Katz/TFK. 256: © Richard Estes/Licensed by VAGA, New York, NY/Marlborough Gallery, NY. 258: t. Courtesy, Orchard Books. 258: b. Courtesy, Orchard Books. 282: Hermitage Museum, St. Petersburg, Russia/Superstock. 294: Courtesy, Pat Cummings. 298: Canterbury Cathedral, Kent, UK/The Bridgeman Art Library International. 300: t. Courtesy, Dawnine Spivak. 300: b. Courtesy, Henry Holt and Company, Inc. 329: Susan Kuklin/Photo Researchers, Inc. 332: The Phillips Collection, Washington D.C. 334: t. Eva Sanders/Simon & Schuster Children's Division. 334: b. Alan Ferguson; courtesy, Ringling School of Art and Design, Sarasota, FL. 360: c. Cordon Art B. V. 367: Adrian Fisher. 370—71: Felicia Martinez/Photo Edit. 374: The Bridgeman Art Library International. 376: i. Anthony Bannister/Minden Pictures. 402: b.l. Jim Brandenburg/Minden Pictures. 403: E. Lemoine/Jacana Scientific Control/Photo Researchers, Inc. 406: The Heard Museum of Native Cultures and Art, Phoenix, AZ. 408: Courtesy, Fulcrum Publishing. 426—27: David Doubilet. 428: David Doubilet. 430—31: David Doubilet. 432: Doug Menuez. 433: b.r. Flip Schulke/Black Star. 434—45: b.l. Charles Nicklin/Al Giddings Images Inc. 435: i. Al Giddings Images Inc. 436: Al Giddings Images Inc. 438: b. Al Giddings Images Inc. 439: i. Courtesy, Luise Woelflein. 439: bkgd.

Stuart Westmoreland/Stone. 440: b.l. Charles Nicklin/Al Giddings Images Inc. 444: Courtesy, Estate of Alexander Calder/Artists Rights Society. 446: Courtesy, Joanna Cole. 455: Myron/Tony Stone Images. 456: Index Stock Photography. 462: Michael Orton/Tony Stone Images. 472—73: Natural History Museum, London/The Bridgeman Art Library International. 486: c. Christies Images. 488: i. Karen P. Hawkes; courtesy, Penguin Putnam Books for Young Readers. 516: Cary Herz Photography. 531: t. George Ancona. 531: b. Courtesy, George Ancona. 532: George Ancona. 536: Hermitage Museum, St. Petersburg, Russia/Art Resource, NY. 565: r. Chris Johns/National Geographic Society Image Collection. 565: l. E Hanumantha Rao/Photo Researchers, Inc. 568: Phoebe Beasley/Omni-Photo Communications. 595: r. Courtesy, Ai-Ling Louie. 595: l. Courtesy, Ed Young. 597: Georg Gerster/Photo Researchers, Inc. 600: Maas Gallery, London/The Bridgeman Art Library International. 606: Nick Caloyianis/National Geographic Society Image Collection. 610: t. Robb Kendrick/Aurora. 610: m.i. The Picture Cube/Index Stock Imagery. 610: b.i. Bob Daemmrich/The Image Works. 610—11: Visual Horizons/FPG International. 614—15: Jonathan Green Studios, Inc. 627: i. Courtesy, Peter Golebock. 632—33: Reproduced by kind permission of the Trustees of the Chester Beatty Library, Dublin. 634: b. Courtesy, HK Portfolio, Inc. 634: t. Courtesy, Alma Flor Ada. 661: l. Photo Researchers, Inc. 664: c. Motion Picture and Television Archives. 666: t. Courtesy, Jean Merrill. 666: b. Courtesy, David Catrow. 692: c. Superstock. 694—95: Al Giddings/Images Unlimited. 696—97: t. Minden Pictures. 696—97: b. Minden Pictures. 699: t. Minden Pictures. 708: Minden Pictures. 714: c. The Bridgeman Art Library Ltd. 721: i. Galen Rowell/Corbis.

READING STRATEGY
Illustration
Mike DiGiorgio, pp. 95, 601A; Diane Blasius, pp. 133A, 665—665A; Cedric Lucas, pp. 333—333A; Tom Leonard, pp. 425—425A; Debrah Wilson, p. 445A; Greg Harris, pp. 473—473A; John Wallner, pp. 487—487A; Fahimeh Amiri, pp. 537—537A; Oki Han, pp. 569—569A; Gail Piazza, pp. 633—633A;

Photography
Page 19 (inset), Bill Ivy/Stone; pages 19-19a, Dave G. Houser/Corbis; page 43, Hulton Getty; pages 43-43a, AP/Wide World Photos; pages 67-67a, Corbis/Bettmann; page 67a (top), George Eastman House/Lewis W. Hine/Archive Photos; pages 95-95a, Eric & David Hosking/Corbis; page 95a (inset), Hans Dieter Brandl/Frank Lane Picture Agency/Corbis; page 119, Mickey Pfleger/Photo 20-20/PictureQuest; page 119a, Courtesy Canine Companions for Independence; page 133-133a, John Loengard/Timepix; pages 159-159a (top), Erik Anderson/Stock Boston/PictureQuest; pages 159-159a (bottom), PhotoDisc; page 159a (inset), David Young-Wolf/PhotoEdit/PictureQuest; pages 191-191a, Charles Sleicher/Stone; page 217 (top), PhotoDisc; page 217 (bottom), Philip James Corwin/Corbis; pages 217-217a (top), Superstock; pages 217-217a (bottom), Duomo/Corbis; page 217a (top), Joe Patronite/The Image Bank; pages 243-243a, Peter Turnley/Corbis; pages 257-257a, Francis G. Mayer/Corbis; page 257a (bottom), Joe Viesti/Viesti Associates; page 283a, Courtesy Carmen Lomas Garza; pages 299-299a, John Warden/Stone; pages 361-361a, PhotoDisc; page 361a (top), Courtesy of the Staten Island Botanical Garden; page 375a (top), Ansel Adams Publishing Rights/Corbis; page 375a (bottom), Corbis; page 407, Araldo De Luca/Corbis; page 407a, Superstock; pages 517-517a, Hans Wolf/The Image Bank; page 517a (top), David Rubinger/Timepix; page 517a (bottom), S. Cordier/Photo Researchers; pages 601-601a, Jeff Hunter/The Image Bank; page 615 (inset), Corbis/Bettmann; pages 615-615a, Archive Photos/Timepix; page 615a (top), Flip Schulke/Corbis; pages 693-693a, Wolfgang Kaehler/Corbis; pages 715-715a (background), Larry Ulrich/Stone; pages 715-715a, James Carmichael/The Image Bank.

READING FOR INFORMATION, GLOSSARY
Table of Contents, pp. 726—727
Chess pieces   tl   Wides + Hall/FPG
Earth   mcl   M. Burns/Picture Perfect

"How It All Began" from THE STORY OF BASEBALL by Lawrence S. Ritter. Copyright © 1983, 1990 by Lawrence S. Ritter. Used by permission of Morrow Junior Books, a division of HarperCollins Publishers.

"Indians of the Plains" from WORLDS I KNOW AND OTHER POEMS by Myra Cohn Livingston. Text copyright © 1985 by Myra Cohn Livingston. Reprinted with the permission of Margaret K. McElderry Books, an imprint of Simon & Schuster Children's Publishing Division.

"Jackie Robinson" from FOLLOWERS OF THE NORTH STAR: RHYMES ABOUT AFRICAN AMERICAN HEROES, HEROINES, AND HISTORICAL TIMES by Susan Altman and Susan Lechner. Copyright © 1993 Childrens Press ®, Inc. Used by permission of Childrens Press.

"The Needle in the Haystack" from CRICKET MAGAZINE by John Hamma. Copyright © 1982 by John Hamma. Used by permission of Doris Hamma.

"Pack" text copyright © 1995 by Lee Bennett Hopkins from BEEN TO YESTERDAYS by Lee Bennett Hopkins. Reprinted by permission of Wordsong/Boyds Mills Press, Inc.

"The Paper Garden" from BREAKING THE SPELL: TALES OF ENCHANTMENT. Copyright © 1997, Kingfisher. Used by permission of the publisher, Larousse Kingfisher Chambers, Inc., New York.

"Rhodopis and Her Golden Sandals" from MULTICULTURAL FABLES AND FAIRY TALES by Tara McCarthy. Published by Scholastic Professional Books. Copyright © 1993 by Tara McCarthy. Reprinted by permission of Scholastic, Inc.

"Seal" from LAUGHING TIME by William Jay Smith. Copyright © 1990 by William Jay Smith. Used by permission of Farrar, Straus & Giroux, Inc.

"Spider in the Sky" by Anne Rose. Copyright © 1978 by Anne Rose. Used by permission of Harper Collins Publishers.

"Super-Goopy Glue" from THE NEW KID ON THE BLOCK by Jack Prelutsky. Text copyright © 1984 by Jack Prelutsky. Used by permission of Greenwillow Books, a division of HarperCollins Publishers.

"What's the Big Idea, Ben Franklin?" from WHAT'S THE BIG IDEA, BEN FRANKLIN? by Jean Fritz. Copyright © 1976 by Jean Fritz. Used by permission of Coward-McCann, a division of Penguin Putnam Inc.

"When Whales Exhale (Whale Watching)" from WHEN WHALES EXHALE AND OTHER POEMS by Constance Levy. Text copyright © 1996 by Constance King Levy. Used by permission of Margaret K. McElderry Books, an imprint of Simon & Schuster Children's Publishing Division.

"Windows of Gold" from WINDOWS OF GOLD AND OTHER GOLDEN TALES by Selma G. Lanes. Text copyright © 1989 by Selma G. Lanes. Reprinted with the permission of Simon and Schuster Books for Young Readers, an imprint of Simon and Schuster Children's Publishing Division.

"The Wolf" from THE RANDOM HOUSE BOOK OF POETRY FOR CHILDREN by Georgia Roberts Durston. Copyright © 1983. Used by permission of Random House.

ZB Font Method Copyright © 1996 Zaner-Bloser. Handwriting Models, Manuscript and Cursive. Used by permission.

Photography:
All photographs are by Macmillan/McGraw-Hill except as noted below.
page 129A left: Daniel Pangbourne Media/FPG.
page 129A right: M. Burns/Picture Perfect.
page 371A left: Jeff LePore/Natural Selection.
page 371A right: Stockbyte.

Pupil Edition (continued)

CD's	mcl	Michael Simpson/FPG
Newspapers	bl	Craig Orsini/Index Stock/PictureQuest
Clock	tc	Steve McAlister/The Image Bank
Kids circle	bc	Daniel Pangbourne Media/FPG
Pencils	tr	W. Cody/Corbis
Starfish	tc	Darryl Torckler/Stone
Keys	cr	Randy Faris/Corbis
Cells	br	Spike Walker/Stone
Stamps	tr	Michael W. Thomas/Focus Group/PictureQuest
Books	cr	Siede Preis/PhotoDisc
Sunflower	cr	Jeff LePore/Natural Selection
Mouse	br	Andrew Hall/Stone
Apples	tr	Siede Preis/PhotoDisc
Watermelons	br	Neil Beer/PhotoDisc
Butterfly	br	Stockbyte

All photographs are by Macmillan/McGraw-Hill (MMH); Stephen Ogilvy for MMH; and John Serafin for MMH, except as noted below:

p729 b.r.	United Sewerage Agency of Washington County
p732 t.r.	Anestis Diakopoulos/Stock Boston
p733 l.	Bob Daemmrich/Stock Boston
p737 m.i.r.	Cole Group/PhotoDisc
p737 m.i.l.	David Buffington/PhotoDisc
p737 bkgd.	PhotoLink/PhotoDisc (leaf bkgd.)
p739 t.c.	Biophoto Associates/Photo Researchers, Inc.
p739 t.l.	Biophoto Associates/Photo Researchers, Inc.
p739 b.l.	Photodisc
p739 m.l.	Ken Edwards/Photo Researchers, Inc
p739 m.r.	J.F. Gennaro/Photo Researchers, Inc.
p739 b.r.	PhotoDisc
p740	Jim Sugar Photography/Corbis
p743 t.l.	Biophoto Associates/Photo Researchers, Inc.
p743 m.l.	Biophoto Associates/Photo Researchers, Inc.
p743 t.r.	Barry Runk/Grant Heilman Photography, Inc.
p748 t.r.	PhotoDisc
p750 b.l.	CMCD/PhotoDisc
p756 l.	PhotoDisc
p759	Frank White/Liaison International
p760	Murray Photography/The Image Bank
p761	Guy Gillette/Photo Researchers
p763	Index Stock Photography, Inc.
p764	Jonathan Novrok/Photo Edit
p765	Farrell Grehan/Photo Researchers, Inc.
p767	Bokelberg/The Image Bank
p772 t.	Trehearne/Index Stock Photography, Inc.
p772 b.	Tony Freeman/Photo Edit
p776	Margo Taussig Pinkerton/Liaison International
p778	Charles D. Winters/Timeframe Photography, Inc./Photo Reseachers, Inc.
p780	Grant V. Faint/The Image Bank
p781	Harald Sund/The Image Bank
p782	Ron McMillan/Liaison International
p785 l.	Pete Seaward/Tony Stone Images
p785 r.	David R. Stoecklein/Tony Stone Images
p787	Michael Gallagher/Liaison International
p788	Charlie Ott/Photo Reseachers, Inc.
p790	Arvind Garg/Liaison International
p791	Cris Haigh/Tony Stone Images
p792	Peter Beney/The Image Bank
p794	Index Stock Photography, Inc.
p795	Ed Malitsky

Backmatter Contents

The Paper Garden
a folktale by Tony Ramsay

A long time ago, on a beautiful island that lay on the sea like a new moon, there was an emperor. He lived in a palace which looked out onto the loveliest garden in the East. It was a garden full of peacocks and cherry trees. It had a lake as smooth as glass. And most precious of all, lining its twisting paths, were rows of golden kushiri flowers, so rare they grew nowhere else in the world.

One day as the Emperor was sitting in his garden a breeze blew in over the kushiri beds and made their leaves rustle like paper kites. The Emperor sniffed the air. Then, bending low, he looked carefully at the lake which lay in the middle of his garden. What he saw made his nose wrinkle in anger.

"The wind!" he cried. "The wind is ruffling my lake!"

And sure enough the lake had changed. A moment before it had looked like a silver mirror. Now it was like a rumpled blanket where someone had been sleeping.

▶ "Stop!" cried the Emperor, waving his fist at the wind. "Stop, I command you!"

But the wind cared nothing for emperors and continued to blow across the beautiful lake.

At once the Emperor summoned the imperial masons. "You are to build a wall," he said. "A wall so high the wind cannot enter my garden. If any man leaves a hole where the least draft can creep in he'll be buried alive!"

So the masons set to work and built a wall a hundred feet high from stone blocks carved so carefully even the blade of a knife could not slip between them.

And once again the most beautiful lake in the East looked up at the sky like a mirror.

For a time the Emperor was content. Then one morning while he was looking for peacocks (even then they were becoming difficult to find) a cloud covered the sun and rain began to fall. As it fell

it pitter-pattered on the surface of the lake. And every drop made a circle that rippled outward until it reached the edge.

Once more the Emperor wrinkled his nose and grew angry.

"Stop!" cried the Emperor, waving his fist at the rain. "Stop, I command you!"

But the rain cared nothing for emperors and continued to fall on the beautiful lake.

This time he called his carpenters. "You must build a roof to keep out the rain," he cried. "And if any man leaves a hole where the least drop can creep in he'll be flung from the highest tower in the land!" So the carpenters set to work and built a roof of limewood over the garden.

But when the roof was finished no sunlight reached the lake and the flowers. The whole garden was dark as midnight. The carpenters were afraid the Emperor would be angry, so they chose the bravest among them to climb to the top and paint a yellow sun on the roofbeams. The paint was made of pure gold and shone down brightly on the lake below.

The Emperor was delighted. Now when he walked among the kushiri beds no breezes blew and ruffled the waters of the lake, and no rain pitter-pattered on the surface. He saw no peacocks now, but the lake was so beautiful he scarcely thought of them. But all was not well in the Emperor's garden.

Slowly the cherry trees began to lose their leaves. Leaf after leaf turned brown and fluttered to the ground.

Worse still, the kushiri flowers, which grew nowhere else in the world, had begun to shrivel. One by one they hung their heads and died.

The worried gardeners held a meeting in the summerhouse. All night long they argued until at last the chief gardener rose to his feet and said, "This is what we must do. We must cut flowers out of paper and paint them with the finest paints and stand them in the kushiri beds. We must make

Read Aloud   ▶ Continue reading here.

paper leaves and hang them in the cherry trees. If we don't do this, the Emperor will surely hang us from the cherry trees instead."

So the gardeners set to work, and in no time at all the whole garden was filled with paper flowers and paper trees. There was not a single cherry tree, a single kushiri plant left alive.

But even then the gardeners' troubles were not over. Without rain the lake began to shrink. Each day it became a little smaller, and they had to put glass around the edge so the Emperor would not notice. Quite soon where the lake had been there was nothing but a single sheet of glass looking up at a painted sun.

And still the Emperor walked in his garden.

One day at the height of summer he stopped by the lake. First he looked up, then he looked down. Then he bent close to the kushiri beds. For a long time he stood as if he was trying hard to remember something.

Then at last he called his gardeners and declared:

"There is a thief in the Imperial Gardens!"

"Why, master," said the chief gardener, "what has he stolen?"

The Emperor glared hard and his nose began to wrinkle.

"Someone has stolen the smell of the most beautiful garden under the sun."

"No," said the gardeners, "it's not possible!"

"There is no smell," said the Emperor, "in the whole garden."

One by one the gardeners sniffed.

"It's very faint," said one.

"Almost not there at all," said another. "But I think…yes, I'm almost sure I can smell something."

The Emperor wrinkled his nose and tried once more. Behind him the gardeners were muttering to themselves. "Yes, yes, I can definitely smell the cherry trees—or is it the kushiri flowers? Yes, perhaps it is the kushiri flowers after all."

At this the Emperor went to the nearest of the kushiri beds and sniffed hard. The leaves rustled as they always did, like paper kites. But there was no smell. He went closer and pushed his nose right into one of the flowers.

It was then something terrible happened.

The flowers had stood so long in the paper garden they were covered in a fine dust.

And when the Emperor sniffed, the dust went up his wrinkled nose.

"A-a-a-a…" went the Emperor.

The gardeners froze with fright.

"A-a-a-a-a-a…"

Some of them turned to hide. But it was no good. A sneeze was coming.

"A-a-a-a-a-a…"

And no ordinary sneeze. A huge sneeze such as only emperors are capable of.

"A-A-A-CHOO!"

When the Emperor sneezed his terrible sneeze the garden suddenly changed. All the paper flowers and the paper leaves on the trees, every last one of them, fluttered to the ground. In a moment the most beautiful garden in the East had disappeared. In its place was nothing but a sheet of glass and some scraps of paper settling on the dust.

Now, when the Emperor saw what had happened to his garden and the gardeners told him how the peacocks had left and the kushiri flowers had died, he was deeply moved.

He ordered his workmen to take away the roof with the painted sun. He told them to pull down the blocks of stone so carefully carved you could not slip the blade of a knife between them. Then he told them to throw everything into the sea.

When that was done he returned to the spot where his garden had once been, the loveliest garden in the East, where the peacocks had lived and the last kushiri plant had died.

"I have been a fool," he said. "And now I will be remembered as the emperor who killed the last kushiri plant in all the world."

For a long time he stood by the glass lake and wept. Imperial tears slipped down his wrinkled nose and fell to the ground.

When night came, the Emperor returned to his palace filled with a great sadness. And there the sadness grew in him until quite soon he died.

But that is not the end of our story.

For where the Emperor had stood his tears seeped into the earth and there they touched a seed. And the seed swelled and put out a tiny shoot. And the shoot pushed upward through the dark earth until it peeped out at the sun. The shoot began to grow. And if you had been there and had listened carefully, you would have heard a sound, a sound they thought had gone from the garden forever, a sound like the rustling of leaves. Or, like tiny paper kites flying in the wind….

Pack
a poem by Lee Bennett Hopkins

Pack
the boxes
into the car,
pile the dishes,
load in the clothes,
squeeze in the
pots and pans,
our two radios—
can't waste a space—
everything goes.

Crowd in the Mama,
the Daddy,
the sister,
jam in the brother,
make room for my toes—
can't waste a space—
everything goes.

Bundle the memories
we're moving today
from
Scranton, PA,
to
Newark, NJ.

Dakota Dugout
historical fiction by Ann Turner

Tell you about the prairie years? I'll tell you, child, how it was.

When Matt wrote, "Come!" I packed up all I had, cups and pots and dresses and rope, even Grandma's silver boot hook, and rode the clickety train to a cave in the earth, Matt's cave. Built from sod, you know, with a special iron plow that sliced the long earth strips. Matt cut them into bricks, laid them up, dug into a hill that was our first home.

I cried when I saw it. No sky came into that room, only a paper window that made the sun look greasy. Dirt fell on our bed, snakes sometimes, too, and the buffalo hide door could not keep out the wind or the empty cries in the long grass.

The birds visited me, there was no one else, with Matt all day in the fields. A hawk came, snake in its claws, a heron flapped by with wings like sails, and a sparrow jabbered the day long on a gray fence post. I jabbered back.

Winter came sudden. Slam-bang! the ground was iron, cattle breath turned to ice, froze their noses to the ground. We lost twelve in a storm and the wind scoured the dugout, *whish*-hush, *whish*-hush.

Spring, child, was teasing slow then quick, water booming in the lake, geese like yarn in the sky, green spreading faster than fire, and the wind blowing *shoosh*-hush, *shoosh*-hush.

First summer we watched the corn grow, strode around the field clapping hands. We saw dresses, buggies, gold in that grain until one day a hot wind baked it dry as an oven, *ssst-ssst*, *ssst-ssst*.

Matt sat and looked two whole days, silent and long.

Come fall we snuggled like beavers in our burrow, new grass on the floor, willows on our roof under the earth. I pasted newspaper on the walls, set the bread to bake on the coals, and the wind was quiet.

Corn grew finally, we got our dresses, buggies, some gold, built a clapboard house with windows like suns, floors I slipped on, and the empty sound of too many rooms. Didn't think I'd miss the taste of earth in the air. Now the broom went *whisp*-hush, and the clock tocked like a busy heart.

Talking brings it near again, the sweet taste of new bread in a Dakota dugout, how the grass whispered like an old friend, how the earth kept us warm.

Sometimes the things we start with are best.

Seal
by William Jay Smith

See how he dives
From the rocks with a zoom!
See how he darts
Through his watery room
Past crabs and eels
And green seaweed,
Past fluffs of sandy
Minnow feed!
See how he swims
With a swerve and a twist,
A flip of the flipper,
A flick of the wrist!
Quicksilver-quick,
Softer than spray,
Down he plunges
And sweeps away;
Before you can think,
Before you can utter
Words like "Dill pickle"
Or "Apple butter,"

Back up he swims
Past Sting Ray and Shark,
Out with a zoom,
A whoop, a bark;
Before you can say
Whatever you wish,
He plops at your side
With a mouthful of fish!

The Dentist
by Judith Nicholls

I love to visit my dentist
and read the comics there,
to see his rows of clackety teeth
and ride in his moving chair.

I love to visit my dentist
and stare at his stripey fish,
to see the pink fizz in the glass
and the fillings on the dish.

I love to visit my dentist
and see his tools all gleam,
but when I need a filling—
well, then I'm *not* so keen!

Annotated Workbooks (vertical text, left margin)

Name_____ Date_____ **Practice** ①

Story Elements

The **setting** is where and when a story takes place. The **characters** are the people in the story. Read this story. Then answer each question.

> The country store was a one-room shack half hidden by trees at the side of the road. Inside, Jen and her dad piled cans on a shelf. It was raining. The day was boring. "This morning is lasting forever," sighed Jen.
> Then the door flew open. "Hey, this is fun!" someone shouted. "Hi, my name is Maria. My mom's on the phone in the car. She sent me for camping food. You are so lucky to have your own store."
> Much later, Maria flew out the door, the same way she came in. "Next time, I'll stay longer," she shouted. "I'll help you work. It'll be fun!"
> Jen smiled at her dad. "That's a noisy girl," she said, "but I like her a lot." Then Jen looked at the shelves. "I'm going to arrange the cans," she said. "It'll be fun!"

1. What is the setting? <u>a country store on a rainy day</u>

2. Who are the three characters? <u>Jen, her dad, Maria</u>

3. At the start of the story, how is Jen feeling? <u>bored</u>

4. How does Maria feel about the store? <u>Answers will vary but may</u> <u>include: She feels excited, curious, enthusiastic.</u>

5. How is Jen feeling at the end of the story? <u>Answers will vary but may</u> <u>include: She is not bored. She sees the store through Maria's eyes.</u>

5 | Book 4/Unit 1 **The Lost Lake** | **At Home:** Have students fold a paper in half and draw a two-part story about someone who is bored and then finds something interesting to do. | 1

Name_____ Date_____ **Practice** ②

Vocabulary

Answer each question, using the vocabulary word before each question in your response. Answers will vary.

1. **compass** Why might a hiker find a compass helpful? <u>A compass helps a</u> <u>hiker locate directions.</u>

2. **darted** Why might a squirrel have darted across your path? <u>It might have</u> <u>darted because it was chased by a dog.</u>

3. **muttered** Why might you have trouble understanding what a person said if he or she muttered? <u>The muttered words would not be clear.</u>

4. **mug** How is a mug different from a plate? <u>A plate is flat and often</u> <u>holds food, a mug is a large cup that holds drinks.</u>

5. **talker** What does it mean when we say that someone is a talker? <u>We often mean that the person talks a lot without stopping.</u>

6. **brand-new** How many times has something been worn when it is brand-new? <u>When something is brand-new, it has never been worn.</u>

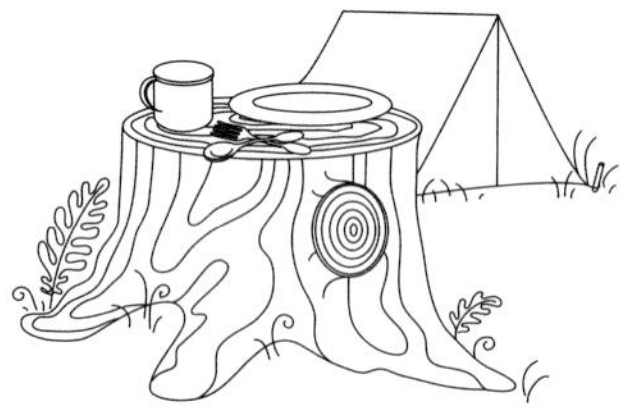

2 | **At Home:** Have students write sentences using each of the vocabulary words. | Book 4/Unit 1 **The Lost Lake** | 6

The Missing Compass

> My name is Irina. This morning I got a compass for my birthday. It was just what I wanted. I went outside to try it out. I never knew before that the back door of our house faced north.
> When Mom called me to come get a mug of lemonade, I left the compass in the grass. When I got back outside, it was gone. "Where is it?" I muttered. I began to get upset.
> Then I saw the neighbor's dog, Chichi. He always wanted to play. I watched as he darted around the yard making playful growls. He was quite a talker. And there, dangling from his mouth was my brand-new compass.
> The chase was on. I thought I'd never get the compass back, but Chichi saw my mug of lemonade on the steps. When he bent his head to drink it, I was able to grab the compass.

1. What gift did Irina get for her birthday? <u>a compass</u>

2. Where did she leave her brand-new gift? <u>in the grass</u>

3. How did Irina feel when she found her compass missing? <u>She was</u> <u>getting upset.</u>

4. How was Chichi moving? <u>He darted quickly around the yard.</u>

5. How did Irina's feelings change on her birthday? <u>First, she was happy to receive a compass.</u> <u>She grew upset when she lost it, but was</u> <u>happy again after she found it.</u>

5 | Book 4/Unit 1 **The Lost Lake** | **At Home:** Have students write how they feel when they lose something they like. | 2a

---

Name_____ Date_____ **Practice** ③

Story Comprehension

Read the statement below. Write **T** for true if the statement describes "The Lost Lake." Write **F** for false if the statement does not describe "The Lost Lake."

1. <u>F</u> Luke had lived with his Dad for many years.

2. <u>T</u> Luke had enjoyed cutting out pictures of mountains.

3. <u>F</u> Luke's Dad had never been camping before.

4. <u>T</u> Luke's Dad felt sad when they found Lost Lake.

5. <u>F</u> Luke's Dad didn't bring any food.

6. <u>T</u> Luke didn't know his dad could cook.

Write to tell why the following statements are not true. Answers may vary.

7. Luke was miserable sleeping in the tent. <u>Luke felt cozy and warm as the</u> <u>rain and wind beat against the side of the tent.</u>

8. Luke's dad still didn't talk much when they went back to the apartment in the city. <u>Luke tells his Dad he seems different now. He talks more.</u> <u>Dad says he will talk more from now on.</u>

3 | **At Home:** Have students fold a paper in quarters and draw four important parts of the story using speech balloons. Then have students show and tell the story to a family member. | Book 4/Unit 1 **The Lost Lake** | 8

The Lost Lake • PRACTICE

Name_____ Date_____ **Practice** 4

Use Parts of a Book

Books can have many different **parts.** Write the name of a book part to answer each question.

Front of the book	Back of the book
title page	glossary
table of contents	index

1. The author's name is found on the same page as the book title.

   On which page in the book can you find these names? _on the title page_

2. Which book part is like a small dictionary? _glossary_

3. How can you find the first page number of a chapter? _____
   Look in the table of contents.

4. Which part of a textbook gives a definition of a word? _glossary_

5. Which parts of a textbook are arranged in alphabetical order? _____
   the glossary and the index

6. Where would you look to find how many chapters a book has?
   in the table of contents

Book 4/Unit 1
The Lost Lake

At Home: Have students locate a book and discuss its parts with a family member.

4

Name_____ Date_____ **Practice** 5

Story Elements

Often a story's **setting** has a strong effect on how a **character** acts. In "The Lost Lake," Luke notices changes in his dad when they leave the city. In the chart below, make notes about what Luke's dad does and says in each setting. Then draw a conclusion about how he is different in the mountains.

Luke's Dad in the City

In his room
1. doesn't talk to Luke
2. busy with work

On the morning of the trip
3. wakes Luke early
4. quiet, grumpy

Luke's Dad in the Mountains

On the trail
5. makes jokes
6. whistles while he hikes

In the tent
7. shares his thoughts with Luke
8. decides to look for their own lake

In the forest
9. asks Luke what he is thinking
10. says he will talk more

Conclusions

11. In general, how does Luke's Dad act differently in the mountains?
    He talks to Luke more and shows more interest in him.

12. Does the change in Luke's Dad make sense to you? How?
    Yes. People often feel more relaxed when they get away.

5

At Home: Have students write a story where the main character's actions change.

Book 4/ Unit 1
The Lost Lake

12

Name_____ Date_____ **Practice** 6

Make Inferences

In "The Lost Lake," the author does not always explain what the characters are feeling or why they act as they do. Therefore, you must **make inferences** about their feelings and actions by "reading between the lines." To make an inference, you can use clues provided by the author and similar experiences that you have had or heard about.

Answer each question by making an inference. Use story clues or personal experience to make each inference. Answers will vary.

1. Why do you think Dad decided to take Luke camping? _He noticed nature_
   pictures Luke had put up and figured Luke might enjoy camping.

2. How do you think Dad felt when he and Luke arrived at the Lost Lake? How
   can you tell? _He felt disappointed. He didn't want to camp there with_
   all the people around.

3. Why do you think Luke suggested to Dad that they find their own lake?
   He wanted to make his Dad feel better. He liked the idea of finding a
   secret place as his father and grandfather had.

4. When Luke noted that Dad talked more in the mountains, why did Dad say,
   "I'll have to talk more often, then?" Why did Luke smile when his Dad said
   this? _He knew Luke liked it when he talked to him and wanted Luke_
   to feel happy. Luke smiled because he thought their life would be
   better in the future.

5. Why did Dad and Luke just gaze at "their" lake and not say anything?
   They felt content. They were happy to be alone together.

5
Book 4/Unit 1
The Lost Lake

At Home: Write about why Luke's Dad became glum when he saw other hikers ahead of him.

6

Name_____ Date_____ **Practice** 7

Multiple-Meaning Words

Many words are **multiple-meaning words,** or have more than one meaning. The context of the sentence will help you tell which meaning of the word is being used. Read each sentence below. Then circle the meaning of each underlined word.

1. Luke's Dad gave him a taste of the sweet coffee.
   a. good-tempered (b. sugary tasting)

2. I could see the mountain path snake through the trees.
   a. long, thin animals (b. wind around)

3. After he took out the camping stove, the knapsack was light.
   (a. not heavy) b. traffic signal

4. The boy crashed into a low-hanging branch.
   (a. limb of a tree) b. division of a library

5. It is important to train dogs not to chase animals in the woods.
   (a. teach) b. railroad cars

6. The man was patient as he waited for his son.
   (a. calm, not complaining) b. getting medical advice

7. A bat flew in the trees under the night sky.
   a. stick used in baseball (b. a flying animal)

8. They left the path and struck out for the wilderness.
   a. opposite of right (b. went away from)

9. In a second, the deer darted out of sight.
   a. after the first (b. one-sixtieth of a minute)

10. They would tire too quickly if their packs were too heavy.
    (a. need rest) b. part of a car wheel

7
At Home: Have students write sentences using words with different meanings.

Book 4/Unit 1
The Lost Lake

10

T7

The Lost Lake • RETEACH

Story Elements

Stories tell about **characters**. Characters can be people or animals. The **setting** is where and when a story takes place.

Read each story. Write the name of the main or most important character and tell what the setting is.

Tamika was upset. Her soccer team had just lost the big game. Now her victory camping trip to the lake would not happen. She stood on the soccer field shaking her head. Her coach smiled and said there would be other games to win.

1. Main Character _Tamika_

2. Setting _soccer field_

Our scout leader is great. At our scout meeting last night I think I may have made her unhappy. She asked us to name our favorite scout activities. I said I enjoyed the project we did cleaning up the empty lot. But I hated the fishing trip. Then she said she liked the fishing trip most.

3. Main Character _the speaker_

4. Setting _scout meeting last night_

You should see Willie's dog, Byron. This dog does all sorts of funny things. When Willie shines a flashlight, Byron chases the light all over the house. Byron likes to walk around with a towel in his mouth. Then he shakes his head throwing the towel over his face.

5. Main Character _Willie's dog, Byron_

6. Setting _Willie's house_

Book 4/Unit 1
The Lost Lake 6

At Home: Have students choose a setting in which to place themselves as the main character. Then have them tell a story with themselves in it.

1

Vocabulary

Read each clue. Then find the vocabulary word in the row of letters and circle it.

brand-new	compass	darted	mug	muttered	talker

1. never used   d e (b r a n d n e w) t s z

2. use it to find direction   b e (c o m p a s s) r n y

3. moved fast   r e t (d a r t e d) n g l y

4. big cup with handle   c a l (m u g) r e j d m l

5. spoke unclearly   w e (m u t t e r e d) l a r g a

6. one who talks   m a c (t a l k e r) a y d

6

Story Comprehension   **Reteach** 3

Write a ✔ next to every sentence that tells about "The Lost Lake."

_✔_ 1. Luke and Dad went on a camping trip.

____ 2. Dad often talked to Luke for hours at home.

____ 3. Dad liked to be with lots of other people at the lake.

_✔_ 4. Dad and Luke went looking for their own lake.

_✔_ 5. Dad was like a mountain goat on the trail.

_✔_ 6. Dad and Luke had to look out for bears.

____ 7. Luke never tired while hiking in the woods.

_✔_ 8. Dad and Luke got to know each other better on their trip.

2–3

At Home: Have students retell the story of "The Lost Lake" in their own words.

Book 4/Unit 1
The Lost Lake 8

Use Parts of a Book

Knowing the different **parts of a book** and how to use them can save time and provide important information.

On the lines below, write the letter that matches each book part with its description.

_c_ 1. Table of Contents   a. defines important words in a book

_b_ 2. Index   b. list of topics and important names in alphabetical order

_a_ 3. Glossary   c. list of chapters, unit titles, or selections

Circle the letter of the correct response.

4. In what part of a book would you look to find a word's pronunciation?

   a. index

   (b.) glossary

   c. table of contents

5. To find on which page a chapter begins, you would look at the

   a. index

   b. glossary

   (c.) table of contents

6. To find the page on which a topic is discussed, you would look at the

   (a.) index

   b. title page

   c. table of contents

Book 4/Unit 1
The Lost Lake 6

At Home: Have students write a table of contents for a book they would like to read, or perhaps write.

4

Story Elements

Knowing who the **characters** in a story are and what the **setting** is helps you better understand and enjoy the story.

Read each story. Circle the letter beside the correct response.

Jessica and her Mom were on their way to her Grandma's house at the lake. Jessica looked at Mom as she drove. Her Mom looked worried. Jessica looked at the road, then back at Mom. She realized that because grandma was ill, Mom now had to take care of Grandma as well as her own family.

1. Who are the main characters?

   (a.) Jessica and Mom   b. Grandma and Mom   c. Mom's family

Juan liked spending time with Freddie and his friends at the park. Freddie was fun to be with, but Juan didn't like it when the others started teasing the new boy, Hank. When Juan saw Hank about to run off, Juan walked over to him and asked him to come to his house.

2. What is the setting?

   a. Juan's house   (b.) neighborhood park   c. school yard

Dad and Dan usually went to the lake to fish, but not this time. Today they were at the ocean to catch some big, big fish. Neither said a word as each kept his eyes on the sparkling waves. The other fishers along the shore were silent and still, too, as they fished.

3. Who are the main characters?

   a. the other fishermen   (b.) Dad and Dan   c. the fish

4. What is the setting?

   (a.) the ocean   b. a lake   c. a boat

5

At Home: Have students choose a familiar story and change its setting to see how such a change affects the events of the story.

Book 4/Unit 1
The Lost Lake 4

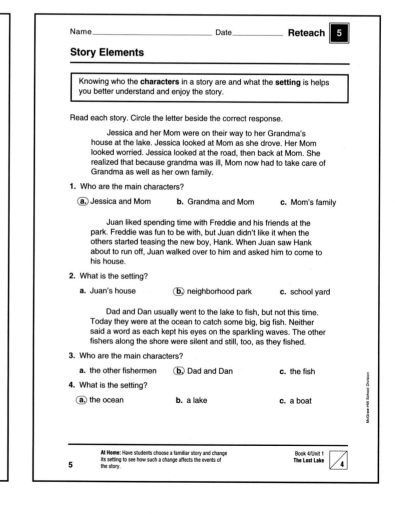

Name_____ Date_____ **Reteach** `6`

Make Inferences

> Authors do not always directly state what is happening or how characters are feeling in a story. Sometimes you have to use clues in the story and what you know from your own experiences to help you **make inferences**.

Read the story. Then write complete sentences to answer the questions.

> Lucas sat perfectly still as Ms. Sanchez returned the tests. Lucas had studied very hard. He had even missed a camping trip to spend more time studying. When Ms. Sanchez gave Alex his test, he looked at it, then crumpled it up. Jean took hers and kissed the paper. Lucas reached out and took his test from Ms. Sanchez. He took one quick look. Lucas just sat and grinned.

1. How did Alex do on the test? How do you know?

He probably did poorly because he crumpled up this test.

_____

2. How did Jean do? How do you know?

Jean probably did very well. She kissed the paper.

_____

3. Was Lucas happy with his test results? How do you know?

Yes. Lucas grinned.

_____

4. Why do you think the room was so quiet?

All the students probably were nervous about their grades.

_____

At Home: Have students explain how their own experiences in taking tests and finding out their grades helped them make inferences about the story.

Name_____ Date_____ **Reteach** `7`

Multiple-Meaning Words

> Some words have **multiple meanings**, or more than one meaning. Use the other words in the sentences below as clues to help you decide which meaning is correct.

Circle the letter beside the correct meaning for the underlined word.

1. The camper used a <u>saw</u> to cut the log.

  ⓐ a tool used to cut wood

  b. past tense of *see*

2. They got to the <u>park</u> early.

  ⓐ a recreation area

  b. to leave a car in a place for a time

3. He wondered if he had the <u>right</u> directions.

  ⓐ correct

  b. the opposite of left

4. His knapsack was <u>light</u>.

  ⓐ not heavy

  b. cause to catch fire

5. We could not <u>bear</u> the crowds at the lake.

  a. a large animal

  ⓑ put up with

6. It took just a <u>second</u> to the find the map.

  ⓐ a very short amount of time

  b. next after the first

At Home: Have students choose three of the underlined words to use in sentences that show their other meanings.

The Lost Lake • EXTEND

Name_____ Date_____ **Extend** ◆1

Story Elements

The **setting** is where and when the story takes place. Think about the setting of one of your favorite nature stories. Think about the details of the setting that you remember the most.

Write a paragraph describing the setting of the story. Where does the story take place? When does the story take place? How do the seasons of the year affect the setting? Explain what you like most about the setting. Include whether or not you would like to visit this place, and why.

Answers will vary, but should demonstrate an understanding of what the

setting of a story is.

_____
_____
_____
_____
_____
_____

Draw a picture showing you and a friend engaged in a fun activity in the setting. Show your picture to classmates and compare your favorite outdoor activities.

Book 4/Unit 1
The Lost Lake

At Home: Have students choose a favorite story and discuss the illustrations that show things that are unique to the settings.

1

Name_____ Date_____ **Extend** ◆2

Vocabulary

brand-new	compass	darted	mug	muttered	talker

Suppose that you are on a hiking trip with a group of friends. You are keeping a journal about your trip. Write three journal entries using some of the words in the box. Use a separate piece of paper if you need more space.

Answers will vary but should include at least four vocabulary words used

in the correct context and part of speech.

_____
_____
_____
_____
_____

Extend ◆3

Story Comprehension

Work with a partner. Choose one setting from "The Lost Lake." Write a short poem describing either Luke's or his father's feelings or reactions to the setting.

Answers will vary.

_____
_____
_____
_____
_____
_____
_____
_____

2–3

At Home: Read a poem about nature. Discuss how the poem reflects your feelings about nature.

Book 4/Unit 1
The Lost Lake

Name_____ Date_____ **Extend** ◆4

Use Parts of a Book

Suppose you wanted to write a book about favorite vacation spots in your state. There are several ways you could organize the information into chapters. One way would be to have a chapter for each region in the state. What are some other ways that the book could be organized?

Answers will vary. Some possibilities are by activity, by parks, by theme.

_____

Use one of the methods of organization to make a sample table of contents. Include two or three subheadings in each chapter to identify places, such as specific state parks. Will your book contain a glossary and an index? If so, be sure to include them in your table of contents.

Vacation Fun in My State
Table of Contents

Answers will vary.

_____
_____
_____
_____
_____
_____
_____
_____
_____
_____
_____

Now, on a separate piece of paper, design a title page for your book.

Book 4/Unit 1
The Lost Lake

At Home: Read through the table of contents of a book. List other ways that the book could be organized.

4

Name_____ Date_____ **Extend** ◆5

Story Elements

Characters are the people in a story. The characters in "The Lost Lake" are Luke and his father.

Select a situation in the story in which one of the characters might have acted differently. Write about how the story would be different because of the character's change. Would the outcome of the story change?

Answers will vary. Possible answers: Luke could have asked permission to

cut out the magazine pictures; if his father had said no, they may not have

gone on the camping trip. Luke could have refused the coffee; this would

probably not have affected the outcome. They could have stopped at the

Found Lake and never have discovered the Lost Lake.

_____
_____
_____
_____
_____
_____
_____
_____
_____
_____
_____
_____
_____

5

At Home: Have students choose a story and discuss how the story would be affected if one of the characters responded differently to a specific situation.

Book 4/Unit 1
The Lost Lake

The Lost Lake • EXTEND

Make Inferences

An **inference** is a conclusion that you are able to draw after considering the facts in a story and relating them to your personal experience.

Make inferences to answer the following questions.
Answers will vary. Possible answers are given.

1. In "The Lost Lake," Luke's father was not angry with him for cutting out the magazine pictures. Why do you think that Luke's father wasn't angry?
   His father liked the pictures. They made him think of when he used to camp or hike. He may have realized that Luke was bored.

2. Why do you think that Luke and his father did not talk much in the city?
   Luke did not want to bother his father. His father was used to living alone.

3. Why is it important that Luke's father had a compass when they went off the trail? so they would not get lost

4. Do you think that Luke's father was happy at the end of the story? Explain.
   Yes, they found a lake and they were alone. His father became more talkative.

5. Do you think that the camping trip brought Luke and his father closer together? Explain. Yes, they communicated more. Luke learned new things about his father.

6. Do you think that the camping trip was important to Luke? Why do you think so? Yes, he wrote the story to tell about it.

Book 4/Unit 1
The Lost Lake

At Home: Have students make and exchange a list of clues. Discuss what they are able to infer from the clues.

6

Multiple-Meaning Words

Multiple-meaning words are words that have more than one meaning even though they are spelled the same way. For example, consider the word *bear*. It can mean a large wild animal: The bear was eating berries in the woods. It can also mean that you cannot put up with something: He could not bear to hear the loud sirens.

Each of the words below are multiple-meaning words. Write two sentences for each word to show different meanings for the word.

1. bottle	3. glasses	5. lie	7. dip
2. cooler	4. tire	6. trail	8. stick

Answers will vary. Possible sentences are given. 1. She was tempted to bottle up her feelings to hide her disappointment. They took a water bottle on their hike. 2. The cooler is filled with soft drinks. It is cooler today than yesterday. 3. He put his glasses on to read. They took plastic glasses on the picnic. 4. Their car had a flat tire. The hike did not tire them out. 5. It's not good to tell a lie. The dog went to lie down in the shade. 6. The trail went along the lake shore. The leader told the others not to trail behind. 7. They took a dip in the pool. There was a dip in the road. 8. He like the unusual shape of the stick of wood. The stamp did not stick to the envelope.

At Home: Ask the student to think of other multiple-meaning words. Discuss whether the use of the word as a noun or as a verb changes the meaning of the word.

7

Book 4/Unit 1
The Lost Lake

The Lost Lake • GRAMMAR

Grammar 1 — LEARN

Name_____ Date_____

Sentences

- A **sentence** is a group of words that expresses a complete thought.
- A **sentence fragment** is a group of words that does not express a complete thought.
- Every sentence begins with a capital letter.
- A **statement** is a sentence that tells something. It ends with a period.
- A **question** is a sentence that asks something. It ends with a question mark.

Decide if each group of words makes a sentence. If it does, rewrite the sentence adding a capital letter and a period or a question mark.

1. it was too hot outside — It was too hot outside.

2. dad and Luke left in the morning
   Dad and Luke left in the morning.

3. when they hiked to Lost Lake
   _____

4. dad went up the trail — Dad went up the trail.

5. a mountain that no one else knew about
   _____

6. did they find a new "lost lake"
   Did they find a new "lost lake"?

Book 4 / Unit 1
The Lost Lake
6

Extension: Have students write two statements and two questions about an outdoor adventure.

1

Grammar 2 — LEARN & PRACTICE

Name_____ Date_____

Types of Sentences

- A **statement** is a sentence that tells something. It ends with a period.
- A **question** is a sentence that asks something. It ends with a question mark.
- A **command** tells or asks someone to do something. It ends with a period.
- An **exclamation** shows strong feeling. It ends with an exclamation mark.

Write **statement** if the sentence tells something. Write **question** if the sentence asks something. Write **command** if the sentence tells or asks someone to do something. Write **exclamation** if the sentence shows strong feeling. Then put the correct end mark at the end of each sentence.

1. Dad and Luke hiked to Lost Lake
   statement .

2. What did they find when they got there
   question ?

3. Put your pack on and let's go
   command .

4. Luke wanted to camp by the creek
   statement .

5. Look out for bears
   exclamation !

6. How did they find their special lake
   question ?

2

Extension: Have students think of a special place. Then have them write a statement, a question, a command, and an exclamation about it.

Book 4 / Unit 1
The Lost Lake
6

Grammar 3 — PRACTICE AND REVIEW

Name_____ Date_____

Write Sentences

Rewrite each sentence. Correct the sentence capitalization and punctuation.

1. have you ever hiked in the mountains.
   Have you ever hiked in the mountains?

2. try to imagine what it would be like?
   Try to imagine what it would be like.

3. wouldn't it be great to sleep outdoors.
   Wouldn't it be great to sleep outdoors?

4. put on your hiking boots?
   Put on your hiking boots.

5. let's hit the trail?
   Let's hit the trail!

6. we can reach the lake by nightfall
   We can reach the lake by nightfall.

7. shall we make camp on the shore.
   Shall we make camp on the shore?

8. i love the water.
   I love the water!

Book 4 / Unit 1
The Lost Lake
8

Extension: Have pairs of students choose a subject and take turns making up sentences about it. After each sentence, the student who is listening tells what kind of sentence it is.

3

Grammar 4 — MECHANICS

Name_____ Date_____

Using Capital Letters and End Marks

- Every sentence begins with a capital letter.
- A **statement** ends with a period.
- A **question** ends with a question mark.
- A **command** ends with a period.
- An **exclamation** ends with an exclamation mark.

Correct each sentence by changing any incorrect lower case letters to capital letters and by adding the correct end mark. Use the line provided for your answers.

1. the lake was high in the mountains — T .

2. how long did it take them to find it — H ?

3. it wasn't the lake Dad remembered — I .

4. it was too crowded — I !

5. dad would never stay there — D !

6. they kept hiking until they found a special place — T .

7. why was he different in the mountains — W ?

8. recall the things he did — R .

4

Extension: Have pairs of students look through books and magazines for examples of statements, questions, commands, and exclamations and copy an example of each.

Book 4 / Unit 1
The Lost Lake
8

The Lost Lake • GRAMMAR

Kinds of Sentences

A. Decide if the sentence is a statement, a question, a command, or an exclamation. Write what type of sentence it is, and add the correct end mark on the line.

1. Luke was staying with his Dad ____ statement;. ____

2. What did he do all day ____ question;? ____

3. Think about hiking ____ command;. ____

4. Where would you like to go ____ question;? ____

5. That sounds wonderful ____ exclamation;! ____

B. Add the correct punctuation to each of these sentences.

6. I'll take a hiking trip in the mountains ____ . ____

7. You wake up and discover a lake ____ . ____

8. Do you think that would be exciting ____ ? ____

9. I'd love to discover a lake ____ ! ____

10. Could I name it after myself ____ ? ____

McGraw-Hill School Division

Sentences and Punctuation Marks

- A **statement** is a sentence that tells something.

- A **question** is a sentence that asks something.

- A **command** tells or asks someone to do something.

- An **exclamation** shows strong feeling.

Mechanics

- Begin every sentence with a capital letter.

- A statement ends with a period.

- A question ends with a question mark.

- A command ends with a period.

- An exclamation ends with an exclamation mark.

Write each sentence correctly.

1. why did we wake up early

   Why did we wake up early?

2. we are going camping ____ We are going camping.

3. it was a long hike to the lake

   It was a long hike to the lake.

4. we found it ____ We found it!

5. were there many people

   Were there many people?

McGraw-Hill School Division

T13

The Lost Lake • SPELLING

Name_____ Date_____

Words with Short Vowels

Pretest Directions
Fold back the paper along the dotted line. Use the blanks to write each word as it is read aloud. When you finish the test, unfold the paper. Use the list at the right to correct any spelling mistakes. Practice the words you missed for the Posttest.

To Parents
Here are the results of your child's weekly spelling Pretest. You can help your child study for the Posttest by following these simple steps for each word on the word list:
1. Read the word to your child.
2. Have your child write the word, saying each letter as it is written.
3. Say each letter of the word as your child checks the spelling.
4. If a mistake has been made, have your child read each letter of the correctly spelled word aloud, and then repeat steps 1–3.

1. _____	1. drank
2. _____	2. rest
3. _____	3. ahead
4. _____	4. drink
5. _____	5. dock
6. _____	6. hung
7. _____	7. trouble
8. _____	8. magazines
9. _____	9. self
10. _____	10. deaf
11. _____	11. lift
12. _____	12. flock
13. _____	13. trust
14. _____	14. cousin
15. _____	15. cannon
16. _____	16. swept
17. _____	17. pleasant
18. _____	18. fist
19. _____	19. couple
20. _____	20. wealth

Challenge Words

_____ brand-new
_____ compass
_____ darted
_____ muttered
_____ talker

Name_____ Date_____

Words with Short Vowels

Using the Word Study Steps
1. LOOK at the word.
2. SAY the word aloud.
3. STUDY the letters in the word.
4. WRITE the word.
5. CHECK the word.

   Did you spell the word right?
   If not, go back to step 1.

Spelling Tip
Use words that you know how to spell to help you spell new words:

d<u>ri</u>p + th<u>ank</u> = drank

Word Scramble
Unscramble each set of letters to make a spelling word.

1. krind	drink	11. tilf	lift
2. nugh	hung	12. spewt	swept
3. kdoc	dock	13. stif	fist
4. fles	self	14. cloupe	couple
5. zagmainse	magazines	15. anconn	cannon
6. krand	drank	16. steapaln	pleasant
7. afde	deaf	17. sniocu	cousin
8. tres	rest	18. clofk	flock
9. broulet	trouble	19. sturt	trust
10. dahae	ahead	20. thalew	wealth

To Parents or Helpers
Using the Word Study Steps above as your child comes across any new words will help him or her learn to spell words effectively. Review the steps as you both go over this week's spelling words.
Go over the Spelling Tip with your child. Ask your child to think of words he or she knows that can help him or her spell other words on the list.
Help your child complete the spelling activity.

Name_____ Date_____

Words with Short Vowels

drank	dock	self	trust	pleasant
rest	hung	deaf	cousin	fist
ahead	trouble	lift	cannon	couple
drink	magazines	flock	swept	wealth

Sort each spelling word by finding the sound and spelling pattern to which it belongs. Write the word and circle the letter or letters that spell its vowel sound.

short a spelled
a
1. drank
2. cannon
3. magazines

short e spelled
e
4. rest
5. self
6. swept

short e spelled
ea
7. ahead
8. deaf
9. pleasant
10. wealth

short i spelled
i
11. drink
12. lift
13. fist

short o spelled
o
14. dock
15. flock

short u spelled
u
16. hung
17. trust

short u spelled
ou
18. trouble
19. cousin
20. couple

Sounds Alike
Write the spelling word that rhymes with each word below.

21. health ____wealth____   22. double ____trouble____

Name_____ Date_____

Words with Short Vowels

drank	dock	self	trust	pleasant
rest	hung	deaf	cousin	fist
ahead	trouble	lift	cannon	couple
drink	magazines	flock	swept	wealth

Complete each sentence with a spelling word.

1. These ____magazines____ always have funny stories I like to read.
2. Every morning, a large ____flock____ of birds visits my bird feeder.
3. I ____drank____ two glasses of milk this morning at breakfast.
4. A person's ____self____ is who they are and how they are special.
5. Last week, the students ____hung____ pictures on the classroom walls.
6. If you are in a hurry, you can go ____ahead____ of me in line.
7. I like to ____drink____ a glass of juice after school.
8. My ____cousin____ Bob is my Aunt Tilly's son.
9. The clown at the circus was shot from a ____cannon____.
10. He found the broom and ____swept____ the floor.

Define It!
Write the spelling words that have the same meanings as the words or phrases below.

11. take it easy or sleep ____rest____   14. a place to tie a boat ____dock____
12. two of something ____couple____   15. to raise up ____lift____
13. not able to hear ____deaf____   16. a tightly closed hand ____fist____

Challenge Extension: Ask students to write a "fill in the blank" sentence for each Challenge Word and then exchange papers with a partner to complete the sentences.

The Lost Lake • SPELLING

Name_____ Date_____

Words with Short Vowels

Proofreading Activity

There are six spelling mistakes in the letter below. Circle the misspelled words. Write the words correctly on the lines below.

Dear (Cusin) Bob,

 I had a wonderful time with my dad this summer. We hiked into the mountains. Dad hiked (ahede) of me because I had (truble) climbing. I had to stop and (reast) a lot. But soon we found a lake. We (draink) water right from the lake! Once I thought we were lost. Dad said we could (troust) his compass to help us find our way. And he was right. It was the best vacation I ever had.

See you soon,
Luke

1. ___cousin___   3. ___trouble___   5. ___drank___

2. ___ahead___   4. ___rest___   6. ___trust___

Writing Activity

Write a letter to a friend about a holiday or vacation you once had. Use four spelling words in your writing.

_____

_____

_____

_____

Name_____ Date_____

Words with Short Vowels

Look at the words in each set below. One word in each set is spelled correctly. Use a pencil to fill in the circle next to the correct word. Before you begin, look at the sample sets of words. Sample A has been done for you. Do Sample B by yourself. When you are sure you know what to do, you may go on with the rest of the page.

Sample A
- Ⓐ beest
- Ⓑ best
- Ⓒ beste
- Ⓓ biest

Sample B
- Ⓑ ring
- Ⓕ ringe
- Ⓖ raing
- Ⓗ reing

1.
- Ⓐ docke
- Ⓑ dock
- Ⓒ doick
- Ⓓ dok

2.
- Ⓔ cannin
- Ⓕ kannon
- Ⓖ cannon
- Ⓗ canin

3.
- Ⓐ drinke
- Ⓑ drienk
- Ⓒ drink
- Ⓓ drenk

4.
- Ⓔ trubble
- Ⓕ trouble
- Ⓖ troubel
- Ⓗ truble

5.
- Ⓐ ahead
- Ⓑ ahed
- Ⓒ ahaed
- Ⓓ ahede

6.
- Ⓔ lifft
- Ⓕ lift
- Ⓖ lifte
- Ⓗ liaft

7.
- Ⓐ silf
- Ⓑ sealf
- Ⓒ selfe
- Ⓓ self

8.
- Ⓔ huhng
- Ⓕ hung
- Ⓖ hunge
- Ⓗ hungh

9.
- Ⓐ riste
- Ⓑ rest
- Ⓒ reist
- Ⓓ reste

10.
- Ⓔ drenk
- Ⓕ draink
- Ⓖ draenk
- Ⓗ drank

11.
- Ⓐ megizines
- Ⓑ magazines
- Ⓒ magazanes
- Ⓓ magizins

12.
- Ⓔ deaf
- Ⓕ deef
- Ⓖ def
- Ⓗ daef

13.
- Ⓐ truste
- Ⓑ troust
- Ⓒ trost
- Ⓓ trust

14.
- Ⓔ flouck
- Ⓕ flock
- Ⓖ flok
- Ⓗ flocke

15.
- Ⓐ cousin
- Ⓑ cusin
- Ⓒ cousen
- Ⓓ cuzin

16.
- Ⓔ sweept
- Ⓕ swept
- Ⓖ swiept
- Ⓗ sweeped

17.
- Ⓐ welth
- Ⓑ weelth
- Ⓒ walth
- Ⓓ wealth

18.
- Ⓔ pleasant
- Ⓕ plesant
- Ⓖ pleasint
- Ⓗ plezant

19.
- Ⓐ feste
- Ⓑ fis
- Ⓒ fist
- Ⓓ fiste

20.
- Ⓔ cuple
- Ⓕ copple
- Ⓖ cuppel
- Ⓗ couple

Amelia's Road • PRACTICE

Problem and Solution

The **plot** is the events of a story. It often has a **problem** and a **solution**. The problem is the main idea of a story. A character must find a solution, or answer, to the problem. Read the story and answer the questions.

One by one, the kids in Ichiro's class stood up and told about a special talent. Everyone would take part. Soon it was Ichiro's turn. He gulped and then told his class that he was a good juggler and could juggle three balls at a time. Then the class asked Ichiro to juggle. "No problem," said Ichiro.

But there was a problem. Ichiro couldn't juggle. Last year, his big brother Yoshi tried to teach Ichiro to juggle, but Ichiro found it too hard to do.

Ichiro worried before remembering that he was a year older now. "Maybe I can do better," he thought. " I'll get Yoshi to help me try again." Sure enough, it worked. Juggling was easier now.

Three weeks later, Ichiro and Yoshi put on a show for the class. Yoshi did all the tricky stuff. No one noticed that Ichiro did only the simple tricks. The class thought Ichiro was great!

1. Who is the main character? Ichiro
2. What is the problem? Ichiro said he could juggle, but he can't.
3. What idea helped with the solution? Ichiro realized he's a year older. Maybe he would find juggling easier now
4. What was the solution? Ichiro got his brother to help him.
5. How did Ichiro's solution benefit the class? Answers will vary but should include giving a demonstration that the class enjoyed.

Vocabulary

Fill in each blank with the correct vocabulary word from the list at the top of the page.

accidental	labored	occasions	rhythm	shutters	shortcut

1. The little doors on the outside of windows are called __shutters__.
2. On some __occasions__ the doors are blown closed by the wind.
3. Doors are not supposed to close by themselves, so when they do, it is __accidental__.
4. The wind has a musical __rhythm__ when it blows things around outside.
5. We have all __labored__ to clean up after a windy day.
6. Cleaning up is hard work, and there is no __shortcut__.

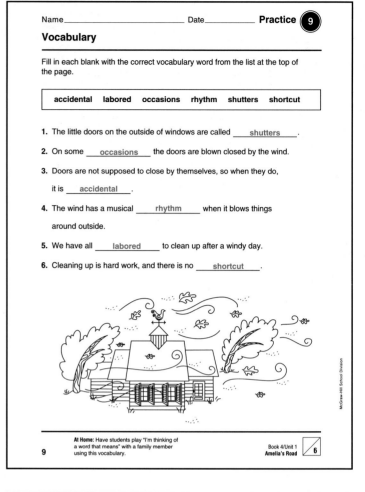

The Storm

The thunder made a loud crashing noise. Meg jumped and knocked over a plant. It was *accidental*, but as Meg *labored* to clean up the mess, she wished she didn't scare so easily.

Suddenly the rain began to come down heavily. Meg remembered that her window was open and raced to her room. She used her *shortcut*, the back stairs. Meg quickly closed *shutters* and window. Then she listened to the *rhythms* of the heavy rain. On *occasions* like this, Meg found comfort curling up on her bed with a favorite book—safe and dry.

1. What was *accidental*? Meg knocking over the plant.
2. What did Meg wish as she *labored* to clean up the mess? that she didn't scare so easily
3. Why did Meg take a *shortcut*? Meg wanted to close the window before the rain got in her room.
4. What did Meg do to comfort herself on stormy *occasions*? She curled up on her bed and read a book.
5. What did Meg not like about the storm? Possible answers include: she does not like the loud noise made by the thunder; she does not like the rain coming in the windows.

Story Comprehension

Answer the questions about "Amelia's Road."

1. What are los caminos? the roads
2. Why does Amelia hate los caminos? She hates the roads because she and her family are always on roads moving to a new place.
3. What does Amelia have to do before she goes to school? She has to pick apples from dawn to eight o'clock in the morning.
4. Why does Amelia like Mrs. Ramos more than the teacher at her last school? Mrs. Ramos remembered her name and gave her a red star. The other teacher never learned Amelia's name.
5. What did Amelia know she could always go back to? She could always return to the old tree near the accidental road.
6. For the first time, Amelia didn't cry when her family moved again. Why not? She had her special place that was permanent, the tree and the accidental road, which she knew would always be there.

Amelia's Road • PRACTICE

Name_____ Date_____ Practice 11

Use a Glossary

A **glossary** is like a small dictionary found at the back of the book.
It lists important or difficult words found in the book in alphabetical order.
The glossary gives the meanings and pronunciations of the words.

Here is part of a glossary. Use it to answer the questions.

mesquite A small, thorny flowering tree that
grows in desert regions. Mesquite trees can live with little water.
(mə sket´) noun

mural A picture painted directly on a wall or
ceiling. We painted a mural in the hallway of our school.
(mu´ rəl) noun,
plural **murals**

petroleum An oily flammable liquid made into
such products as gas to run cars and oil to heat buildings.
Petroleum is a valuable natural resource.
(pi tro´ lē əm) noun

1. Why does *mesquite* come before *mural*? They are alphabetized
according to the second letter in each word.

2. Which word names a natural resource? petroleum

3. How many syllables does *petroleum* have? four

4. What is a mural? A mural is a picture painted on a wall or ceiling.

5. Name two products made from petroleum. oil, gasoline

At Home: Have students write a glossary sentence
for each word. | 11

Name_____ Date_____ Practice 12

Problem and Solution

In most stories, the main character faces some kind of **problem** and must
find a **solution**, or a way to solve it. In "Amelia's Road," Amelia faces a big
problem and smaller ones. Answer each question about the story.
Answers may vary.

Problems

1. What was the problem with cabin number 12? It looked like every
other cabin.

2. What was the problem with Amelia going to so many different schools?
Amelia was in each school for such a short time that the teacher
didn't know her name and she didn't make friends.

3. What is the problem with Amelia's parents not knowing her birthday?
She feels lonely and different from the other children.

4. The big problem is how Amelia feels because her family moves so often.
How does she feel and why is it a problem? She feels sad and that
she never belongs. She wants something that is permanent and
something to call her own.

Solutions

5. What did Amelia find that she could call her own?
A permanent tree by the side of the accidental road.

6. What did Amelia do to make the road and tree her own home place?
She filled a box with "Amelia-things" and buried it under the tree.

12 | **At Home:** Have students write to describe a
problem and a solution.

Name_____ Date_____ Practice 13

Make Inferences

The author of a story doesn't always tell you what a character is feeling.
Sometimes you have to **make inferences**, or figure it out, based on what
the character says and does.

Answer each question. Tell what Amelia may be thinking. Answers may vary.

1. Why does Amelia cry every time her father takes out the map?
She cries because she doesn't want to move to a new place again
so soon.

2. What does Amelia think when she enters another grim, gray shanty
at the labor camp? She probably thinks about how ugly it is and
that she wishes she could live in a pretty place.

3. How does Amelia feel when she says she want to settle down and her
mother says, "Maybe someday." Amelia may think that is too good
to be true, and it will probably never happen.

4. How does Amelia feel when her parents can't remember when or where
she was born? She probably feels hurt and not very important.

5. Why is Amelia in such a good mood the day she finds the tree and
the accidental road? She had a good day at school.

6. How do you know Amelia can solve problems? She figured out by
herself how to feel better and how to make a place for herself.

At Home: Have students create a small box of things
that would make them feel special. | 13

Name_____ Date_____ Practice 14

Synonyms and Antonyms

Synonyms are words that mean almost the same thing. **Antonyms** are
words that have opposite meanings.

Write a synonym from the list to replace each underlined word.

labored	smiled	strange	cried

1. The baby <u>sobbed</u> when he was hungry. — cried

2. I have visited some <u>weird</u> places. — strange

3. The planters <u>worked</u> in the blazing sun. — labored

4. The friends <u>grinned</u> at each other when they won. — smiled

Write an antonym for the underlined word to complete each sentence.

relax	curved	temporary	beautiful

5. One road was <u>straight</u>, but the other was — curved .

6. The old cabin was <u>grim</u>, but the new house was — beautiful .

7. First Jeff would <u>worry</u>, then he would — relax .

8. A rock is a <u>permanent</u> thing, but a flower is — temporary .

14 | **At Home:** With a family member, have students list
other synonyms and antonyms for the underlined
words above.

Amelia's Road • RETEACH

Problem and Solution

Like someone in real life, a character in a story may have a **problem**. What the character does to find a **solution** to the problem makes up the **plot**, or main events, of the story.

Read the story. Then answer each question.

Sam felt left out. Willa and Lee were staying after school to build a rocket. Sam wanted to work on the rocket too.

Sam decided to ask Willa and Lee if he could help. They said sure, but that he would have to ask Mr. Ward, the science teacher. Mr. Ward said Sam could help if it was okay with his Mom that he stay after school. Sam called his Mom and she told Mr. Ward it was fine for Sam to stay.

Sam was a big help to Willa and Lee. He figured out how to get the rocket to blast-off. They launched the rocket the next day for the science class. All the kids cheered, and Sam was proud.

1. What was Sam's problem? <u>Sam wanted to work on the rocket, but no one had asked him.</u>

2. What did Sam do first to try to solve the problem? <u>He talked to Willa and Lee to find out if he could help with the work.</u>

3. What did Sam do next to help solve his problem? <u>He went to get Mr. Ward's permission to help with the rocket.</u>

4. What was the last thing Sam did to find a solution? <u>Sam asked his mother for permission to stay after school and she gave it.</u>

Book 4/Unit 1
Amelia's Road 4

At Home: Have students think of other ways Sam might have solved his problem.

8

Vocabulary

Use the words from the list to complete the sentence.

accidental	labored	occasions	rhythms	shortcut	shutters

1. She just happened to find the secret door; it was an <u>accidental</u> discovery.

2. The boys took a <u>shortcut</u> across the yard to catch the dog.

3. Birthdays are <u>occasions</u> I like to celebrate.

4. The farmers <u>labored</u> in the fields all day.

5. Our house has yellow <u>shutters</u> on all the windows.

6. We sat on shore and watched the <u>rhythms</u> of the waves.

6

Story Comprehension

Write the answers to these questions about "Amelia's Road."

1. Why did Amelia cry whenever her father took out the map? <u>She didn't want to move so much. She longed to be settled in a home.</u>

2. What work did Amelia do each morning before school? <u>She worked with her family to pick apples.</u>

3. How did Mrs. Ramos help Amelia at school? <u>She learned her name and asked her to share what was special to her.</u>

4. What happened by accident in the story? <u>Amelia found a footpath to a tree and an old metal box to put her treasures in.</u>

At Home: Have students write a paragraph about a place that is special to them.

9–10

Book 4/Unit 1
Amelia's Road 4

Use a Glossary

A **glossary**, which is like a small dictionary at the back of a book, can give you important information about a word you may not know. It tells:

the word's meaning as it is used in the book;

how to say the word correctly;

what part of speech the word is (noun, verb, and so on).

commotion A noisy confusion; disorder. When the campers disturbed the nesting birds, there was a *commotion*.
com•mo•tion (kə mō′ shən) *noun, plural* **commotions**

companion A person who often goes along with another; friend; comrade. We three campers were constant *companions* during the summer.
com•pan•ion (kəm pan′ yən) *noun, plural* **companions**

compass An instrument for showing directions. A *compass* has a magnetic needle that points to the north.
com•pass (kum′ pəs) *noun, plural* **compasses**

Use the part of a glossary shown above to answer the questions.

1. In what kind of order are the glossary words arranged?
alphabetical order

2. What does the word commotion mean?
noisy confusion; disorder

3. What is a compass helpful for?
finding direction

4. What part of speech are the three glossary words?
nouns

5. What is the plural form of *compass*?
compasses

Book 4/Unit 1
Amelia's Road 5

At Home: Have students make a four-word glossary for a favorite storybook to help younger readers enjoy the same book.

11

Problem and Solution

Knowing how to identify the **problem** a story character has and paying attention to how he or she goes about finding a **solution** will help you better understand the whole story.

Read the stories. Then write what the problems and the solutions are.

Sven is upset about his homework. He is trying to do a math problem but can't figure it out. He reads the directions over and over, but they don't make sense to him. Finally he gives up and goes to bed.

The next morning, Sven goes to school early so he can talk to his teacher. Mrs. Perry understands why Sven is confused and promises to teach the whole class how to solve the problem.

1. **Problem:** <u>Sven can't figure out how to do his math homework.</u>

2. **Solution:** <u>Sven asks his teacher for help, and she shows him and the class what to do.</u>

Tessa wants to add some new things to her special treasure box. She looks all over the house and can't find it in any of the usual places she keeps it.

Tessa sits down to think about where her box could be and remembers the last time she looked in it. She was at Lucia's house. She calls Lucia. The box is there!

3. **Problem:** <u>Tessa can't find her special treasure box.</u>

4. **Solution:** <u>Tessa thinks calmly about when she last had the box and calls Lucia who has the box.</u>

At Home: Have students make up a problem for a character. Then suggest they work with a friend to find some solutions.

12

Book 4/Unit 1
Amelia's Road 4

Amelia's Road • RETEACH

Make Inferences

> Sometimes you must read especially carefully to pick up clues about characters and events. When you use clues and what you know from your own life, you are **making inferences**.

The sunny room was filled with rows of plant experiments. There were books all along one wall. Margarita saw books about animals, the planets, electricity, and many other subjects. In the storage corner there were piles of safety goggles and plastic gloves. Margarita wasn't sure whether to go in or not. She just waited by the door.

The teacher waved for Margarita to come inside. He pointed to an empty seat and then introduced himself. Others in the room did the same. Before long, Margarita felt right at home.

Use clues in the story to answer the questions.

1. Where was Margarita? at school
_____

2. What kind of room was she looking into? science classroom
_____

3. How do you know what kind of room it was? There were rows of plant experiments, books on science topics, safety goggles

4. How do you think Margarita felt as she stood at the door? She may have felt shy, or nervous about entering the room.

5. How do you know Margarita was probably a new student? _____
The teacher and other students introduced themselves.

5 Book 4/Unit 1
Amelia's Road

At Home: Have students make up an oral story, giving clues about the setting but not identifying it directly. Ask them to have someone infer the setting.

13

Synonyms and Antonyms

> **Synonyms** are words that have almost the same meaning.
> **Antonyms** are words that have the opposite meaning.

Read each sentence. Write the word from the list that means almost the same as the underlined word.

stay	happiness	completed	rushed

1. She wants to remain in this town. ____stay____

2. I finished my drawing first. ____completed____

3. I hurried along the path to the lake. ____rushed____

4. The joy she showed made us smile. ____happiness____

Read each sentence. Write the word from the list that means the opposite of the underlined word.

curved	silent	cried	always

5. Follow the straight road north for two miles. ____curved____

6. The children were unusually noisy. ____silent____

7. She laughed just thinking of the movie. ____cried____

8. Marco is never late. ____always____

14 **At Home:** Have students list three pairs of synonyms and three pairs of antonyms.

Book 4/Unit 1
Amelia's Road 8

Amelia's Road • EXTEND

Name_____ Date_____ **Extend** 8

Problem and Solution

The main idea, or plan, of a story is called the plot. The plot may involve a **problem and solution**. Solutions to the problem can be simple and predictable or they can be more complicated and different from what you might expect.

Write a story about a problem that you were faced with and what the solution was.

Answers will vary but should include a problem and solution.

(blank lines)

Book 4/Unit 1
Amelia's Road

At Home: Have students retell the story they wrote with two different solutions to the problem.

8

Name_____ Date_____ **Extend** 9

Vocabulary

| accidental | occasions | shortcut | labored | rhythms | shutters |

Write three sentences using two of the vocabulary words in each sentence.

Answers will vary. Possible sentences are given. 1. The rhythms of the music made the time he labored in the fields go by quickly. 2. An accidental turn at the fork in the road led to a shortcut. 3. It was one of the many occasions that she walked by the house with the shutters.

Extend 10

Story Comprehension

Amelia found a special place beneath the tree at the end of the accidental road. She knew she would have to leave it soon. How did Amelia make herself feel better about having to leave?

Answers will vary. Possible answer: At her special place, Amelia buried a box filled with personal things. She told herself that she would be back.

Describe a place that is special to you.

Answers will vary.

9–10

At Home: Look at a map of your state. Select several destinations and determine how long it would take to drive to each place.

Book 4/Unit 1
Amelia's Road

Name_____ Date_____ **Extend** 11

Use a Glossary

A **glossary** is like a small dictionary in the back of a book. It explains the meaning of words or phrases used in the book. Glossary entries are alphabetized, and sometimes give the page number where the words or phrases can be found. A sentence from the book using the words or phrases also appears. Use the sample glossary below to answer each of the questions.

labor To work hard. Jasmine had to _labor_ for two hours on her science report. **la•bor** (lā′ bər) _verb._ (page 3)

labor union A group of workers organized to improve wages and working conditions. The _labor union_ demanded better housing conditions for the workers. **la•bor un•ion** (lā′ bər un′ yən) _noun, plural_ **labor unions.** (page 15)

landlord A person who owns and rents out property. The _landlord_ charges $500 per month for the house. **land•lord** (land′ lôrd) _noun, plural_ **landlords.** (page 8)

language The words and grammar that people often use to speak and write to each other. Some of the migrant workers speak the Spanish _language._ **lang•uage** (lang′ gwij) _noun, plural_ **languages.** (page 12)

leaflet A sheet of paper giving information. The volunteer handed a _leaflet_ to the worker. **leaf•let** (lēf′ lit) _noun, plural_ **leaflets.** (page 36)

long-term To do with a long period of time. The plan was for _long-term_ reform. **long-term** (long′ tûrm′) _adjective._ (page 48)

1. Where in the book would you find a reference to language?
page 12

2. If you wanted to add the word **landscape** to this glossary, between which two words would you place it? _between landlord and language_

3. Which words shown are **not** listed as nouns? _labor and long-term_

4. What is a leaflet? _a sheet of paper giving information_

5. Which word or phrase refers to an organized group? _labor union_

Book 4/Unit 1
Amelia's Road

At Home: Find a glossary in the back of one of your textbooks. Explain to someone at home how to use the glossary.

11

Name_____ Date_____ **Extend** 12

Problem and Solution

Most stories you read include a **problem and solution**. Some solutions present themselves through a sequence of events. Sometimes the main character solves the problem. Other times someone else solves the problem. Think about the sequence of events that led to the solution of Amelia's problem in "Amelia's Road."

1. Describe the sequence of events that led Amelia to discover her road.
Amelia went to school where her teacher gave everyone name tags. She drew a picture of her special house and got a star. She was so excited that she took a shortcut home and then found her road.

2. Amelia felt that she had found a home beneath the old tree. Was this a good solution to her problem? Explain.
Answers will vary. Possible answer: It was a temporary solution good for her at the time.

3. How did Amelia decide to make the place around the old tree her home?
She buried a treasure box near it and promised to come back.

4. Who solved Amelia's problem in the story? _Amelia_

5. Do you think the solution to Amelia's problem was a long-term solution for her? Explain. _Answers will vary. Possible answer: Yes, Amelia felt she had a special place now._

At Home: Discuss problems faced by real people and by fictional characters. Compare how different people or characters solve similar problems.

12

Book 4/Unit 1
Amelia's Road

T20 _Annotated Workbooks_

Amelia's Road • EXTEND

Name_____ Date_____ Extend **13**

Make Inferences

An **inference** is a conclusion that you draw after considering all the facts and relating them to your own experiences. Inferences can be important in a story because they help you understand a character's feelings, motivation, and actions. Consider Amelia in "Amelia's Road." Then make inferences to answer these questions.

1. Why do you think Amelia wanted to hurry home on the day she met her teacher, Mrs. Ramos? She wanted to tell her family about her wonderful day in school.

2. Do you think it bothered Amelia that her teacher did not bother to learn her name last year? Tell why. Yes, because it made Amelia feel unimportant and temporary.

3. Why did the teacher this year give name tags? She wanted everyone to get to know each other.

4. Why did Amelia save her name tag? It helped Amelia feel like she belonged someplace.

5. Why did Amelia bury her treasure box near the old tree? She felt like it was her home and her own special place.

6. Do you think that Amelia will return to her road? Explain. Amelia will probably return since this is such a special place to her.

At Home: Have students make inferences about what they will do at school the next day.

13

Name_____ Date_____ Extend **14**

Synonyms and Antonyms

Synonyms are words that have the same meaning. The words *rapid* and *quick* are synonyms. **Antonyms** are words that have opposite meanings. The words *weak* and *strong* are antonyms.

There are six pairs of synonyms in the box. Write the pairs of synonyms.

shack	faithful	conquer	talk	make	chat
teach	shanty	create	instruct	win	loyal

chat/talk; teach/instruct; conquer/win; shack/shanty; faithful/ loyal; create/make

Each word in the first box below has an antonym in the second box. Write each word and its antonym.

deep	cautious	noisy	bright	gradual

quiet	quick	shallow	reckless	dull

deep/shallow; cautious/reckless; noisy/quiet; bright/dull; gradual/quick

Write a short story using some of the pairs of synonyms and antonyms from your lists. Use a separate piece of paper to write your story.

14

At Home: Play a synonym/antonym game. Challenge each other to think up a synonym or an antonym for a given word.

Amelia's Road • GRAMMAR

Sentence Subjects

Remind students that the subject of a sentence tells whom or what the sentence is about.

- The **complete subject** includes all the words in the subject.
- The **simple subject** is the main word in the complete subject. It tells exactly whom or what the sentence is about.
- You can sometimes correct a sentence fragment by adding a subject.

Turn these sentence fragments into complete sentences by adding a subject. Answers will vary. A sample is provided.

1. Led to hard work
   Rebuilding the farm led to hard work.

2. Had to work too hard

3. Wanted a place to come home to

4. Found an accidental road

5. Led through a meadow

6. Stood at the end of the road

7. Gave name tags to everyone

8. Was full of "Amelia-things"

8 Book 4 / Unit 1
Amelia's Road

Extension: Ask students to write sentences. Then have them exchange sentences with a partner and underline all the words that make up the subject. 7

Sentence Predicates

Remind students that the predicate of a sentence tells what the subject does or is.

- The **complete predicate** includes all the words in the predicate.
- The **simple predicate** is the main word in the complete predicate. It tells exactly what the subject does or is.
- You can sometimes correct a sentence fragment by adding a predicate.

Turn these fragments into complete sentences by adding a predicate. Answers will vary. A sample is provided.

1. Everyone in Amelia's family
   Everyone in Amelia's family liked dogs.

2. All the apples

3. A white house with blue shutters

4. An old shade tree

5. Amelia's accidental road

6. All the new children in class

Write Complete Sentences

- The **subject** of a sentence tells whom or what the sentence is about.
- The **predicate** of a sentence tells what the subject does or is.

Complete each sentence fragment. Then tell if you added a subject or a predicate. Answers will vary.

1. Amelia and her family ———— predicate

2. Still felt sleepy ———— subject

3. Drew a picture of a pretty white house ———— subject

4. Everybody in the class ———— predicate

5. Danced for joy in the quiet meadow ———— subject

6. A narrow, rocky footpath ———— predicate

Sentence Punctuation

- A sentence begins with a capital letter.
- Sentences that make statements end with periods.

Read each group of words. If the words are a complete sentence, write a capital letter at the beginning and put a period at the end.

1. roads that led to strange places

2. they pick peaches in June
   They pick peaches in June.

3. a neat white house with blue shutters

4. the family followed the harvest
   The family followed the harvest.

5. now they picked apples
   Now they picked apples.

6. her teacher never learned her name
   Her teacher never learned her name.

7. a rocky path through the meadow

8. the old metal box was dented
   The old metal box was dented.

Amelia's Road • GRAMMAR

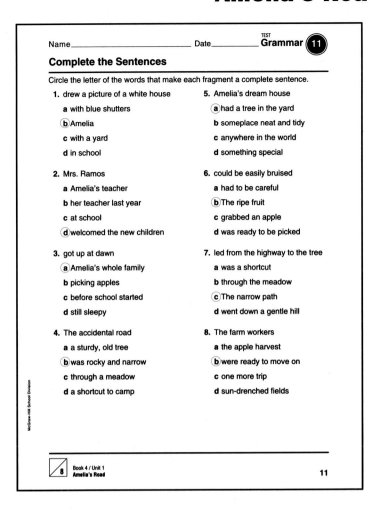

Complete the Sentences

Circle the letter of the words that make each fragment a complete sentence.

1. drew a picture of a white house
   a with blue shutters
   b Amelia
   c with a yard
   d in school

2. Mrs. Ramos
   a Amelia's teacher
   b her teacher last year
   c at school
   d welcomed the new children

3. got up at dawn
   a Amelia's whole family
   b picking apples
   c before school started
   d still sleepy

4. The accidental road
   a a sturdy, old tree
   b was rocky and narrow
   c through a meadow
   d a shortcut to camp

5. Amelia's dream house
   a had a tree in the yard
   b someplace neat and tidy
   c anywhere in the world
   d something special

6. could be easily bruised
   a had to be careful
   b The ripe fruit
   c grabbed an apple
   d was ready to be picked

7. led from the highway to the tree
   a was a shortcut
   b through the meadow
   c The narrow path
   d went down a gentle hill

8. The farm workers
   a the apple harvest
   b were ready to move on
   c one more trip
   d sun-drenched fields

McGraw-Hill School Division

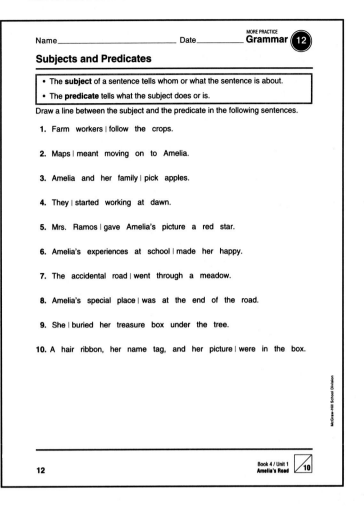

Subjects and Predicates

- The **subject** of a sentence tells whom or what the sentence is about.
- The **predicate** tells what the subject does or is.

Draw a line between the subject and the predicate in the following sentences.

1. Farm workers | follow the crops.

2. Maps | meant moving on to Amelia.

3. Amelia and her family | pick apples.

4. They | started working at dawn.

5. Mrs. Ramos | gave Amelia's picture a red star.

6. Amelia's experiences at school | made her happy.

7. The accidental road | went through a meadow.

8. Amelia's special place | was at the end of the road.

9. She | buried her treasure box under the tree.

10. A hair ribbon, her name tag, and her picture | were in the box.

McGraw-Hill School Division

Amelia's Road • SPELLING

Page 7

Words with Long *a* and Long *e*

Pretest Directions
Fold back the paper along the dotted line. Use the blanks to write each word as it is read aloud. When you finish the test, unfold the paper. Use the list at the right to correct any spelling mistakes. Practice the words you missed for the Posttest.

To Parents
Here are the results of your child's weekly spelling Pretest. You can help your child study for the Posttest by following these simple steps for each word on the word list:

1. Read the word to your child.
2. Have your child write the word, saying each letter as it is written.
3. Say each letter of the word as your child checks the spelling.
4. If a mistake has been made, have your child read each letter of the correctly spelled word aloud, then repeat steps 1–3.

1. _____	1. cape
2. _____	2. gray
3. _____	3. station
4. _____	4. rail
5. _____	5. freight
6. _____	6. agree
7. _____	7. teacher
8. _____	8. secret
9. _____	9. family
10. _____	10. cane
11. _____	11. crayon
12. _____	12. cable
13. _____	13. fail
14. _____	14. tea
15. _____	15. zebra
16. _____	16. rusty
17. _____	17. tray
18. _____	18. raisin
19. _____	19. bean
20. _____	20. tidy

Challenge Words

_____ accidental
_____ labored
_____ occasions
_____ rhythms
_____ shutters

Page 8

Words with Long *a* and Long *e*

Using the Word Study Steps

1. LOOK at the word.
2. SAY the word aloud.
3. STUDY the letters in the word.
4. WRITE the word.
5. CHECK the word.

Did you spell the word right? If not, go back to step 1.

Spelling Tip
Use words that you know how to spell to help you spell new words.

fr + eight = freight

Word Scramble
Unscramble each set of letters to make a spelling word.

1. greae	agree	11. tsury	rusty
2. lira	rail	12. eat	tea
3. giefrth	freight	13. neab	bean
4. epac	cape	14. diyt	tidy
5. rehatec	teacher	15. rabez	zebra
6. nace	cane	16. ialf	fail
7. maliyf	family	17. yarcno	crayon
8. yrag	gray	18. siainr	raisin
9. creets	secret	19. lebac	cable
10. sattnoi	station	20. yart	tray

To Parents or Helpers
Using the Word Study Steps above as your child comes across any new words will help him or her learn to spell words effectively. Review the steps as you both go over this week's spelling words.
Go over the Spelling Tip with your child. Ask your child to look at the spelling words and see if any of them contain smaller words that he or she knows how to spell.
Help your child complete the word scramble.

Page 9

Words with Long *a* and Long *e*

cape	freight	family	fail	tray
gray	agree	cane	tea	raisin
station	teacher	crayon	zebra	bean
rail	secret	cable	rusty	tidy

Pattern Power!
Sort each spelling word by finding the sound and spelling pattern to which it belongs. Write the word and circle the letter or letters that spell its vowel sound.

Long *a* spelled

a_e
1. cape
2. cane

ay
3. gray
4. crayon
5. tray

ai
6. rail
7. fail
8. raisin

a
9. station
10. cable

eigh
11. freight

Long *e* spelled

ee
12. agree

ea
13. teacher
14. tea
15. bean

e
16. secret
17. zebra

y
18. family
19. rusty
20. tidy

Page 10

Words with Long *a* and Long *e*

cape	freight	family	fail	tray
gray	agree	cane	tea	raisin
station	teacher	crayon	zebra	bean
rail	secret	cable	rusty	tidy

Complete each sentence below with a spelling word.

1. The bus __station__ is five miles from my house.
2. That __freight__ train carries food to the city.
3. If I mix white and black together, I will have the color __gray__.
4. It is not a __secret__ that she loves to dance.
5. Do you disagree, or __agree__ with me?
6. The new __teacher__ wrote her name on the chalkboard.
7. The dented metal looks red and __rusty__.
8. I will carry the cookies to the children on a __tray__.
9. Use a __crayon__ to color in your coloring book.
10. The newest, fastest trains run on only one __rail__.

What Does it Mean?
Write the spelling word that has the same, or almost the same meaning.

11. flunk	fail	15. seed of a plant	bean
12. neat	tidy	16. a dried fruit	raisin
13. relatives	family	17. hot drink	tea
14. striped animal	zebra	18. walking stick	cane

Challenge Extension: Have students create Challenge Word scrambles. Then have them swap them with a partner and solve each other's word scramble.

Amelia's Road • SPELLING

Page 11

Name_____ Date_____ **Spelling** 11
PROOFREAD AND WRITE

Words with Long *a* and Long *e*

Proofreading Activity

There are six spelling mistakes in the letter below. Circle the misspelled words. Write the words correctly on the lines below.

Dear Mrs. Ramos,

Thank you for being so nice to me. I want to tell you a (seecret). Even though my (femily) had to move to find work, I will come back to see you. I hope to build a small, (tiedy) house near the big tree. I will live there forever with my pretty, (grae) cat, Kitty. When I move into my wonderful house, I will not (fale) to come and see you. You are the best (teecher) I ever had.

Your student,
Amelia

1. _____secret_____   3. _____tidy_____   5. _____fail_____

2. _____family_____   4. _____gray_____   6. _____teacher_____

Writing Activity

Where would you like to live? Write a letter telling a friend what your place will look like. Use four spelling words in your writing.

_____

_____

_____

_____

Page 12

Name_____ Date_____ **Spelling** 12
POSTTEST

Words with Long *a* and Long *e*

Look at the words in each set below. One word in each set is spelled correctly. Use a pencil to fill in the circle next to the correct word. Before you begin, look at the sample sets of words. Sample A has been done for you. Do Sample B by yourself. When you are sure you know what to do, you may go on with the rest of the page.

Sample A
- (A) ranne
- (B) rane
- (C) rain ●
- (D) raine

Sample B
- (E) nete
- (F) neat
- (G) neit
- (H) neate

1.
- (A) teye
- (B) tea ●
- (C) tei
- (D) tae

2.
- (E) cane
- (F) cain ●
- (G) caine
- (H) ceane

3.
- (A) ugree
- (B) agrey
- (C) aggre
- (D) agree ●

4.
- (E) rason
- (F) raisin ●
- (G) raesin
- (H) raysin

5.
- (A) tidee
- (B) tyde
- (C) tidi
- (D) tidy ●

6.
- (E) crayon ●
- (F) craiyon
- (G) crayen
- (H) craon

7.
- (A) zibra
- (B) zebra ●
- (C) zeebra
- (D) zeabra

8.
- (E) capp
- (F) cape ●
- (G) caip
- (H) caipe

9.
- (A) station ●
- (B) staytion
- (C) stashun
- (D) steation

10.
- (E) trai
- (F) traye
- (G) tray ●
- (H) trei

11.
- (A) famile
- (B) family ●
- (C) familee
- (D) famely

12.
- (E) rale
- (F) rael
- (G) raile
- (H) rail ●

13.
- (A) teecher
- (B) teachur
- (C) teacher ●
- (D) taecher

14.
- (E) gray ●
- (F) grei
- (G) grai
- (H) graye

15.
- (A) frate
- (B) freight ●
- (C) freite
- (D) freaght

16.
- (E) cayble
- (F) caible
- (G) cable ●
- (H) cabl

17.
- (A) bean ●
- (B) beene
- (C) beane
- (D) bene

18.
- (E) seecret
- (F) secrete
- (G) seicret
- (H) secret ●

19.
- (A) rousty
- (B) rusty ●
- (C) ruste
- (D) rustey

20.
- (E) fale
- (F) faile
- (G) fayle
- (H) fail ●

McGraw-Hill School Division

Annotated Workbooks

Name_____ Date_____ **Practice** 15

Story Elements

The **plot** is what happens in the story. The **setting** is where and when the story takes place. The **characters** are the people in the story. Read this story and answer each question.

Tony was visiting his cousin, Manolo, who lived on a farm with horses. Tony, a city boy, loved the wide, open fields and the wooded trails. But horses made him nervous. All Manolo talked about was riding. But there was no way that Tony was going to get on a horse. They were so big!

Manolo kept asking Tony to ride. He promised Tony everything would be fine. By the third day, Tony gave in and agreed to go on a trail ride.

Manolo gave Tony a slow, gentle horse named Sam. Sam followed all of Tony's directions. He didn't gallop off or buck. Tony really liked his first ride. The next day Tony got up early so he could groom Sam and then ride him. Manolo had made a rider out of Tony, after all.

1. Who are the characters? Tony and Manolo

2. What is the setting? A farm in the country

3. In the first part of the story, Tony feels happy. Then things change and he is scared. Why? Manolo wants Tony to ride a horse.

4. In most plots, at least one of the characters changes. Who changed in this plot and how did it happen? Tony changed by not letting his fear keep him from riding.

5. What might happen the next time that Tony feels afraid to try something new? He might remember riding the horse and realize that if he forgets about his fear, trying new things can be fun.

5 Book 4/Unit 1
Sarah, Plain and Tall
At Home: Have students write a story in which someone tries something new and likes it.
15

Name_____ Date_____ **Practice** 16

Vocabulary

Write a vocabulary word to replace each underlined word.

reins	eerie	squall	huddled	pesky	overalls

1. At the bottom of the tree, baby squirrels <u>gathered closely</u> together to keep warm. huddled

2. Before the storm, a <u>strange, weird</u> stillness told us that the tornado was going to be even more frightening than we expected. eerie

3. The new rider sat on the horse and gave the <u>straps</u> a little wiggle to get the animal to move. reins

4. The <u>annoying</u> puppy kept whining for more food or a chance to go out and play. pesky

5. When a sudden <u>gigantic wind</u> brings rain along with it, everyone runs for the shelter of their homes. squall

6. The <u>pants with bib and straps</u> cover almost the whole body of the person wearing them. overalls

16 **At Home:** Have students write an eerie story using as many vocabulary words as possible.
Book 4/Unit 1
Sarah, Plain and Tall 6

PRAIRIE SQUALL

Sally heard the wind whistle across the prairie as she put on her *overalls* and ran out to her horse in the barnyard. She was frightened as *eerie* clouds darkened the sky. A brief *squall* blew rain into her eyes. Sally's horse was frightened, too, and gave her a hard time. Sally grabbed the horse's *reins* and led the animal into the barn. There the chickens were *pesky* and running around. But the cows *huddled* together, waiting for the storm to end.

1. What kind of clothing is Sally wearing? overalls

2. Define what the author means by "*eerie*". scary, frightening, dark

3. What word describes the behavior of the chickens in the barn? pesky

4. What did the other animals in the barn do during the storm? huddled

5. Why did Sally run so quickly out to the barnyard? Answers will vary but should mention that she knew the animals would be frightened and she wanted to get them into the barn where they would be dry.

5 Book 4/Unit 1
Sarah, Plain and Tall
At Home: Have students use the italicized words in new sentences.
16a

Name_____ Date_____ **Practice** 17

Story Comprehension

Write the names of the characters that fit each description.

1. All her life, she had lived near the sea. Sarah

2. They were neighbors who brought chickens. Matthew and Maggie

3. He doesn't remember his mother. Caleb

4. He brought roses for Sarah. Papa

5. She knew how to drive a wagon before Sarah did. Anna

6. They huddled in the barn during the squall. Sarah and the family

Answer each question.

7. Why is Caleb worried when Sarah drives away? He thinks she may be going to town to buy a train ticket. Then she will go back to her home, and Caleb will never see her again.

8. Why do you think it was so important to Sarah that she learn to ride a horse and drive a wagon? She would have more freedom to come and go and could go to town whenever she liked.

17 **At Home:** Have students write a new chapter in which Anna or Caleb teaches Sarah a new task.
Book 4/Unit 1
Sarah, Plain and Tall 8

Sarah, Plain and Tall • PRACTICE

Name_____ Date_____ **Practice 18**

Use a Table of Contents and Headings

Answer the questions about the table of contents and the following section.

Table of Contents

Weather on the Trails
The weather made life on the trail hard. If it was too hot, the animals could get sick. If it rained too much, the rivers would flood. Winter months were dangerous because of snow storms. But on cool, summer nights, families would gather around the campfire to cook, share food, and sing songs.

1. How many chapters are there in this book? _four_____

2. What are the two main parts of the book called? _units_____

3. How is the first unit different from the second unit? _____
   The first unit is about the trail west and covered wagon life; the
   second unit is about building a home on the prairie.

4. In which chapter might the heading "Weather on the Trails" be found?
   _____2_____

5. About how many pages are there in a chapter? _____20 pages_____

5 | Book 4/Unit 1
Sarah, Plain and Tall

At Home: Have students write unit and chapter heads for the topic of "Great Sports Stars."

18

Name_____ Date_____ **Practice 19**

Story Elements

Character and **setting** are closely linked to the **plot** of "Sarah, Plain and Tall." Sarah misses her home in Maine, but she also likes her new home on the prairie. Understanding what she likes about both places can help you understand Sarah's character.

In the chart below list what Sarah misses about her life in Maine and what she likes about her life on the prairie.

Misses About Maine	Likes About the Prairie
1. the sea	2. the family
3. her brother	4. neighbors
5. her aunts	6. chickens
7. her garden	8. Jack, the horse

9. Use the chart, the details from the selection, and your personal experience to describe the character of Sarah. _caring; sensitive; determined:_
   independent; shy; devoted; appreciates family, friends, and
   nature

10. Write a short description of the plot on the following lines. _____
    Answers will vary but should include: Anna and Caleb live on the
    prairie with their father. Sarah comes from her seaside home in
    Maine to visit and perhaps become their new mother. Everyone
    gets along well, but Sarah misses her home and the freedom she
    had there. Once she learns to ride a horse and drive a wagon, she
    feels free on the prairie, too. Everyone is happy because Sarah
    will stay with the family.

Name_____ Date_____ **Practice 20**

Problem and Solution

Read the story and answer each question. Answers may vary.

Molly found a ring on her way to play baseball. "What a pretty ring," thought Molly. "I should ask if anyone lost it." Then Molly heard the baseball coach call her name. She shoved the ring in her pocket and took off for baseball practice. Molly forgot all about the ring.

The next day, Molly heard Keisha say she'd lost her ring. Molly had left the ring at her house. She worried all that day because it was a day later and people might think she had wanted to keep the ring. Maybe she should just leave the ring at home and not mention it.

When Molly saw Keisha the next day, she knew she had to give the ring back. Keisha looked so sad. Molly knew it was better to give her the ring, no matter what the others said.

"My ring!" shouted Keisha as Molly handed her the ring. She hugged Molly. No one asked when Molly had found it. Everyone was just happy Keisha had her ring back. So was Molly!

1. What was Molly's problem?
   She found a ring and forgot to return it.

2. What solution did Molly think of at first?
   She could just leave the ring at home and forget about it.

3. How did Molly learn that leaving the ring at home was the wrong solution?
   Keisha looked so sad and really missed her ring.

4. What solution worked?
   Molly gave Keisha her ring.

5. What would your solution have been?
   Answers will vary but should mention returning the ring.

5 | Book 4/Unit 1
Sarah, Plain and Tall

At Home: Have students tell about a time they lost something that somebody needed and how that problem was solved.

20

Name_____ Date_____ **Practice 21**

Synonyms and Antonyms

Synonyms are words that mean almost the same thing. **Antonyms** are words that have opposite meanings.

Write a synonym from the list to replace each underlined word.

noisy	tender	teach	squall	thin

1. Hannah wore a skinny ribbon in her hair. _____thin_____

2. Tim's mom will show him how to do long division. _____teach_____

3. David was very gentle with his baby brother. _____tender_____

4. The loud music kept Jena from concentrating. _____noisy_____

5. A wind blew up just as the game started. _____squall_____

Write an antonym for the underlined word to complete each sentence.

cruel	silence	always	arrive	solution

6. First the room was filled with sound and then _____silence_____.

7. One twin was kind and the other one was _____cruel_____.

8. When Kevin has a problem, he finds a _____solution_____.

9. As we leave the cafeteria, another class will _____arrive_____.

10. I never eat peas, but I _____always_____ eat carrots.

21

At Home: Have students write a synonym for every underlined word in the pairs of antonyms.

Book 4/Unit 1
Sarah, Plain and Tall | 10

Sarah, Plain and Tall • RETEACH

Story Elements

> **Characters** = Who the story is about
> **Setting** = Where and when the story takes place
> **Plot** = What happens in the story

Read each story. Then write the answer to each question.

Alex lives on a dairy farm in Vermont. It is summer, and he is helping his Dad. They wake up early to milk the cows. Then they go out to the fields to cut hay. Alex is tired, but he knows they can't stop working. He has to help his Dad get the hay cut before a storm comes in. Finally, late in the afternoon, the hay is cut and they take a break in the cool house.

1. Who are the characters? Dad and Alex
   _____

2. What is the setting? Vermont dairy farm in summer
   _____

3. What are two things that happen in the story? Answers will vary, but may include: Alex and Dad milk the cows; they hurry to cut hay in the fields before a storm comes.

Louisa lives in an apartment in the city. It is school vacation, but Louisa can't sleep late because the street corner below is already busy and noisy. Louisa hears brakes screech and truck doors slam. She gets up and goes downstairs to have breakfast.

4. Who is the main character? Louisa
   _____

5. What is the setting? city apartment at school vacation time
   _____

6. What are two things that happen in the story? Answers will vary, but may include: noises prevent Louisa from sleeping late; Louisa gets up and goes to have breakfast.

Vocabulary

Read each clue. Then write the correct word from the list.

huddled	overalls	reins	squall	pesky	eerie

1. This word is an action word. huddled

2. This word names a piece of clothing. overalls

3. This word names a kind of storm. squall

4. This word describes annoying behavior. pesky

5. This word names something used with horses. reins

6. This word describes something strange and scary. eerie

6

Story Comprehension

Circle the letter beside the answer to each question about "Sarah, Plain and Tall."

1. Why did Sarah leave Maine and come to the prairie?
   a. to have a vacation   (b.) to answer Papa's ad

2. Who told Sarah there will always be things to miss?
   a. Papa   (b.) Maggie

3. How did Papa feel when Sarah helped with the roof?
   (a.) surprised   b. angry

4. What did Sarah want to learn to do?
   a. work in the field   (b.) drive a wagon

Use a Table of Contents and Headings

> The **table of contents** gives you an idea of what the chapters in a book are about. It also gives page numbers. **Headings** in a section of text also give you an idea of what you will read about.

Table of Contents
Chapter 1. History of Horses 6
Chapter 2. Work Horses 20
Chapter 3. Race Horses 32
Chapter 4. Wild Horses 40
Chapter 5. Ponies 52

Chapter 2   Work Horses

On the Farm
This breed of horses is the strongest and heaviest of all other horse breeds. Years ago these horses did the work that heavy farm machinery does today. They pulled wagons great distances and hauled plows through the fields.

Coach Horses
Another type of work horse is called the Heavy Harness Horse, or the Coach Horse. These horses are good for light farm work, pleasure riding, or pulling coaches or buggies.

Use the samples to answer these questions.

1. What is the whole book about? Possible answer: Horses, their history, types of horses, and ponies.

2. What is the title of Chapter 4? Wild Horses

3. To learn about ponies, which chapter would you read? Chapter 5

4. What is the first heading in Chapter 2? On the Farm

5. What page would you check to read about race horses? page 32

Story Elements

> As they read good readers keep track of the most important story elements: **characters**, **setting**, and the events that make up the **plot**.

Read the story. Then fill in the story map that follows.

Jackie spent most of the day at the department store. Her mom had suggested that she look for holiday gifts that didn't cost too much. Jackie wanted to find just the right gift for each of her three friends. And she did. She found a glass horse for Jennifer, a cloth purse for Ariel, and a book about lighthouses in Maine for René.

When Jackie returned home that evening, she and her mom went to work with lots of boxes and wrapping. They made each package as special as the gift inside. After dinner, Jackie was ready to deliver her gifts.

1. Characters	Jackie, mom
2. Setting # 1	department store during the day
3. Setting # 2	Jackie's home that evening
4. Event	Jackie goes to the department store.
5. Event	She finds three perfect gifts.
6. Event	She returns home.
7. Event	She wraps the gifts with her mother.
8. Ending	Jackie is ready to deliver the gifts.

Sarah, Plain and Tall • RETEACH

Problem and Solution

Sometimes one character's **problem** can affect other characters in the story. Often the other characters help find a **solution** to the problem.

Read the story. Then fill in the chart that follows.

Kelly wanted to get a pet. All her friends had pets.

Kelly had asked for a puppy for the past two birthdays, but she didn't get one. Her parents always seemed to avoid the issue. Kelly decided to explain to them how she felt.

Her mom and dad said there would be no one at home to walk the dog during the day. Dad asked, "What about a cat?"

But Kelly and her mom were worried that a cat would be too lonely by itself all day. "What about two kittens?" asked Dad. "They could keep each other company." Kelly liked the idea!

Kelly's Problem	Kelly's Solution
She wants a pet of her own.	1. She explains how she feels to her parents.
Mom and Dad's Problem	**Dad's Solution**
2. There would be no one to walk a dog.	3. Get a cat instead.
Mom and Kelly's Problem	**Dad's Solution**
4. The cat would be lonely.	5. Get two kittens.

At Home: Have students extend the story, adding new problems caused by the kittens and some possible solutions.

Synonyms and Antonyms

Synonyms are words that have almost the same meaning.
Antonyms are words that have the opposite meaning.

Read each sentence. Write the word from the list that means almost the same as the underlined word.

closed	glad	huge	smiled

1. After everyone was inside, we shut the door and _____closed_____ the windows.

2. Large clouds covered the sky and _____huge_____ drops of rain fell.

3. We were happy to be safe, and Papa was _____glad_____, too.

4. I grinned and Papa _____smiled_____ back.

Read each sentence. Write the word from the list that means the opposite of the underlined word.

softly	followed	dark	outside

5. The children talked loudly, but she spoke _____softly_____.

6. The light faded and we were left in the _____dark_____.

7. Inside it was calm, but _____outside_____ it was stormy.

8. Papa led the way to the house, and we _____followed_____.

At Home: Have students think of two pairs of synonyms and two pairs of antonyms to write in sentences.

Sarah, Plain and Tall • EXTEND

Extend 15

Name_____ Date_____ **Extend 15**

Story Elements

Suppose that you and your family are planning to move far away. Think about a short story you would write about the move. The **setting** of your story—where it takes place—should be your old home. Describe the setting of your story below.

Answers will vary but should demonstrate student's understanding of setting.

_____
_____
_____
_____
_____

If you moved, who would you miss the most? Think about how you would include that person as a **character** in your story. Describe the character and what, in particular, you would miss about him or her.

Answers will vary but should demonstrate student's understanding of character.

_____
_____
_____
_____
_____
_____
_____

Book 4/Unit 1
Sarah, Plain and Tall

At Home: Have students write a paragraph about where they would like to live and why.

15

Extend 16

Name_____ Date_____ **Extend 16**

Vocabulary

eerie	overalls	reins
huddled	pesky	squall

Suppose you were playing in a park far from your home when a storm comes. Think about how you might feel. Use some of the words above to write about what happened.

Answers will vary but should use vocabulary words correctly.

_____
_____
_____

Extend 17

Extend 17

Story Comprehension

Review "Sarah Plain and Tall." On the day Sarah drives to town, the other characters go about their usual daily activities. What do the other characters do while Sarah is gone?

Answers will vary. Possible answers: Jacob goes to work in the fields. Anna waters Sarah's plants and sweeps the porch. Caleb cleans the wood stove. Anna and Caleb take lunch to their father in the field. They feed the sheep. Anna sets the table. Jacob comes in from the field and lights the stove.

_____
_____

At Home: Discuss how the daily activities of a character from "Sarah, Plain and Tall" may be similar to or different from your daily activities.

16–17

Book 4/Unit 1
Sarah, Plain and Tall

Extend 18

Name_____ Date_____ **Extend 18**

Use a Table of Contents and Headings

Here is the **table of contents** from a book that recounts the story of a family's move west and their adventures. The table of contents contains chapter numbers, page numbers, and **headings** for chapter titles and titles of sections within each chapter. Use the table of contents to answer the questions below.

Table of Contents

1. What is the title of Chapter 2? What do you think the chapter is about? Tell why. *The Journey. It probably tells about the family's journey west and some of the difficulties they encountered. Some of the headings are clues that there were difficulties.*

2. On what page does Chapter 1 begin? How do you know? *page 3; the first page number for the chapter is page 3.*

3. How many section headings are there in Chapter 1? *3*

4. Write sample table of content entries for chapter 3. Include in your entries the chapter title and 3 subheads with page numbers. _____
_____
_____
_____

Book 4/Unit 1
Sarah, Plain and Tall

At Home: Look through several books at home. Discuss why some of the books have table of contents and some do not.

18

Extend 19

Name_____ Date_____ **Extend 19**

Story Elements

Think about Anna and Caleb in "Sarah, Plain and Tall." Both **characters** are afraid that Sarah is not going to come back when she goes to town alone. Why do you think they feel this way? How do Anna and Caleb feel about Sarah and why? Write a paragraph describing your thoughts. Include details to support your thoughts.

Answers will vary but should demonstrate student's understanding of character.

_____
_____
_____
_____
_____

Why do you think Sarah wanted to go to town alone? Did you think that she might not come back? Explain.

Answers will vary.

_____
_____
_____
_____
_____

On a piece of paper, illustrate a scene from "Sarah, Plain and Tall."

At Home: Have students look through a book with illustrations. Are the illustrations in color? Discuss how the illustrations enhance the story.

19

Book 4/Unit 1
Sarah, Plain and Tall

Sarah, Plain and Tall • EXTEND

Name_____ Date_____ **Extend** ◆20◆

Problem and Solution

Most **problems** have **solutions**. Often a problem can be solved more easily by working with someone than by working alone. Write about a problem in "Sarah, Plain and Tall" where the characters worked together to solve it.

Answers will vary. Possible answer: The roof needed repair. Sarah and

Jacob worked together to finish the work. The roof held through the

squalls.

_____

_____

_____

_____

_____

_____

Suppose your school needs some new art or sports supplies. Think of ways to help your school. Would you try to solve the problem by yourself or together with other people? Explain your decision.

Answers will vary but should demonstrate an understanding of problem

and solution.

_____

_____

_____

_____

_____

_____

_____

_____

Book 4/Unit 1
Sarah, Plain and Tall

At Home: Have students talk about daily problems students typically encounter. Discuss which problems are best solved alone and which problems are better solved with others.

20

Name_____ Date_____ **Extend** ◆21◆

Synonyms and Antonyms

Write your own synonyms for the words below.

| happen | party | confident | hard | pursue |

Possible answers: happen/occur; party/celebration; confident/certain;

pursue/chase; rigid/hard

_____

Write your own antonyms for the words below.

| hard | clean | happy | gather | success |

hard/soft; clean/dirty; happy/sad; gather/scatter; success/failure

_____

Begin a short story using at least three words from the first box of synonyms. Write three sentences. Then rewrite the sentences using the antonym of each word. How does your story change?

_____

_____

_____

_____

_____

_____

_____

_____

_____

_____

At Home: Make a list of common synonyms and antonyms.

21

Book 4/Unit 1
Sarah, Plain and Tall

T31

Sarah, Plain and Tall • GRAMMAR

Compound Sentences

- A **conjunction** joins words or groups of words. *And*, *but*, and *or* are conjunctions. Two related sentences can be joined with a comma and *and*, *but*, or *or*.
- A sentence that contains two sentences joined by *and*, *but*, or *or* is called a **compound sentence**.

Add a comma and *and*, *but*, or *or*, and combine each pair of sentences into one compound sentence. **Answers may vary**

1. The children laughed. The dogs barked.
   The children laughed, and the dogs barked.

2. The chickens were not hungry. They still continued to eat.
   The chickens were not hungry, but they still continued to eat.

3. Get the animals in the barn. They'll be lost in the storm.
   Get the animals in the barn, or they'll be lost in the storm.

4. Sarah had never driven a wagon. She was determined to learn.
   Sarah had never driven a wagon, but she was determined to learn.

5. Caleb looked frightened. Anna covered her ears.
   Caleb looked frightened, and Anna covered her ears.

6. They were afraid Sarah would leave. She came back.
   They were afraid Sarah would leave, but she came back.

7. Sarah missed the sea. She would miss the family more.
   Sarah missed the sea, but she would miss the family more.

8. Caleb couldn't be pesky. Sarah would leave.
   Caleb couldn't be pesky, or Sarah would leave.

8 Grade 4/Unit 1
Sarah, Plain and Tall
Extension: Have students write their own example of a compound sentence.
13

Compound Subjects and Predicates

- You can combine two sentences by joining two subjects or two predicates with *and* or *or*.
- A **compound subject** contains two or more simple subjects that have the same predicate.
- A **compound predicate** contains two or more simple predicates that have the same subject.

Combine each pair of sentences to form one sentence using a compound subject or a compound predicate.

1. Papa could teach Sarah to drive the wagon. Caleb could, too.
   Papa or Caleb could teach Sarah to drive the wagon.

2. The dogs barked. They ran out to meet the wagon.
   The dogs barked and ran out to meet the wagon.

3. The storm scattered the roses. It knocked over a tree.
   The storm scattered the roses and knocked over a tree.

4. Papa plowed the field. Sarah plowed the field.
   Papa and Sarah plowed the field.

5. Sarah had lived in Maine. She loved the sea.
   Sarah had lived in Maine and loved the sea.

6. Seal ignored the storm. Sarah's chickens ignored the storm.
   Seal and Sarah's chickens ignored the storm.

7. Rose had a flower name. Violet had a flower name.
   Rose and Violet had flower names.

8. Sarah drove to town. Sarah brought back presents.
   Sarah drove to town and brought back presents.

Extension: Have students write two sentences for a partner to combine into a sentence with a compound subject or predicate.
14
Grade 4/Unit 1
Sarah, Plain and Tall 8

Write Sentences

Add *and*, *but*, or *or* to combine each pair of sentences into one sentence that is a compound sentence or has a compound subject or predicate. **Answers may vary**

1. Anna wanted Sarah to stay. Caleb wanted Sarah to stay.
   Anna and Caleb wanted Sarah to stay.

2. Sarah kissed everyone good-bye. Sarah drove away.
   Sarah kissed everyone good-bye and drove away.

3. Sarah ran out into the storm. Papa followed her.
   Sarah ran out into the storm, and Papa followed her.

4. Thunder pounded. Lightning crackled.
   Thunder pounded, and lightning crackled.

5. Seal curled up in my lap. Seal went to sleep.
   Seal curled up in my lap and went to sleep.

6. Sarah was just going shopping. The children did not know that.
   Sarah was just going shopping, but the children did not know that.

7. Nick jumped into the wagon. Nick sat beside Sarah.
   Nick jumped into the wagon and sat beside Sarah.

8. Papa will drive the wagon. Sarah will drive the wagon.
   Papa and Sarah will drive the wagon.

8 Grade 4/Unit 1
Sarah, Plain and Tall
Extension: Have students write two sentences for a partner to combine into a sentence with a compound subject or predicate.
15

Punctuating Compound Sentences

- Use a comma before *and*, *but*, or *or* when you join two sentences to form a compound sentence.
- Begin every sentence with a capital letter.
- The second part of a compound sentence should not begin with a capital letter.

Correct each sentence. Write commas and capital letters where they are needed.

1. Papa gave Sarah daisies and she put them in her hair.
   Papa gave Sarah daisies, and she put them in her hair.

2. the neighbors came to help and Maggie brought plants.
   The neighbors came to help, and Maggie brought plants.

3. the women planted flowers and the men plowed the fields.
   The women planted flowers, and the men plowed the fields.

4. Sarah came by train and we went to meet her.
   Sarah came by train, and we went to meet her.

5. the sky was dark green and the air was still.
   The sky was dark green, and the air was still.

6. the work was done and the men came in from the field.
   The work was done, and the men came in from the field.

7. Sarah will stay and there will be a wedding.
   Sarah will stay, and there will be a wedding.

8. Sarah brought candles and they ate by candlelight.
   Sarah brought candles, and they ate by candlelight.

16
Extension: Have pairs of students look through books and magazines to find examples of compound sentences. Have students copy one example and then rewrite it as two sentences.
Grade 4/Unit 1
Sarah, Plain and Tall 8

Sarah, Plain and Tall • GRAMMAR

Sentence Combining

A. Add a comma and *and* to turn each pair of sentences into a compound sentence.

1. The wind howled. The dogs started to bark.

   The wind howled, and the dogs started to bark.

2. The rain stopped. The sun came out.

   The rain stopped, and the sun came out.

3. The whistle sounded. The train pulled into the station.

   The whistle sounded, and the train pulled into the station.

4. Nick sat beside Anna. Seal crawled into her lap.

   Nick sat beside Anna, and Seal crawled into her lap.

B. Combine each pair of sentences by joining their subjects or predicates with *and*.

5. Anna wanted Sarah to stay. Caleb wanted Sarah stay.

   Anna and Caleb wanted Sarah to stay.

6. Sarah took the wagon. Sarah went to town.

   Sarah took the wagon and went to town.

7. Old Bess pulled the wagon. Jack pulled the wagon.

   Old Bess and Jack pulled the wagon.

8. Caleb sat on the porch. Caleb played with his moon snail shell.

   Caleb sat on the porch and played with his moon snail shell

---

Combining Sentences

- A **compound sentence** contains two sentences joined by *and, but,* or *or.*
- A **compound subject** contains two or more simple subjects that have the same predicate.
- A **compound predicate** contains two or more simple predicates that have the same subject.

Mechanics

- In a compound sentence, use a comma before *and, but,* or *or* when you join two sentences.
- Begin every sentence with a capital letter.

Combine each pair of sentences to write one sentence that tells about the picture.

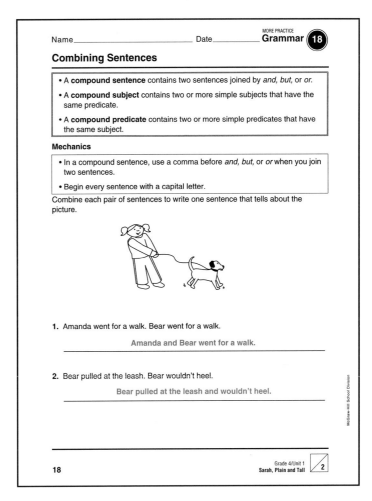

1. Amanda went for a walk. Bear went for a walk.

   Amanda and Bear went for a walk.

2. Bear pulled at the leash. Bear wouldn't heel.

   Bear pulled at the leash and wouldn't heel.

T33

Sarah, Plain and Tall • SPELLING

Name_____ Date_____

Words with Long *i* and Long *o*

Pretest Directions
Fold back the paper along the dotted line. Use the blanks to write each word as it is read aloud. When you finish the test, unfold the paper. Use the list at the right to correct any spelling mistakes. Practice the words you missed for the Posttest.

To Parents
Here are the results of your child's weekly spelling Pretest. You can help your child study for the Posttest by following these simple steps for each word on the word list:

1. Read the word to your child.

2. Have your child write the word, saying each letter as it is written.

3. Say each letter of the word as your child checks the spelling.

4. If a mistake has been made, have your child read each letter of the correctly spelled word aloud, then repeat steps 1–3.

1. _____	1. tiger
2. _____	2. drive
3. _____	3. reply
4. _____	4. roll
5. _____	5. note
6. _____	6. crow
7. _____	7. oak
8. _____	8. iron
9. _____	9. alike
10. _____	10. supply
11. _____	11. tomato
12. _____	12. stove
13. _____	13. below
14. _____	14. groan
15. _____	15. title
16. _____	16. pine
17. _____	17. overhead
18. _____	18. chose
19. _____	19. hollow
20. _____	20. file

Challenge Words

_____ eerie
_____ huddled
_____ pesky
_____ reins
_____ squall

Name_____ Date_____

Words with Long *i* and Long *o*

Using the Word Study Steps

1. LOOK at the word.

2. SAY the word aloud.

3. STUDY the letters in the word.

4. WRITE the word.

5. CHECK the word.

   Did you spell the word right?
   If not, go back to step 1.

> **Spelling Tip**
> Think of a word you know that has the same spelling pattern as the word you want to spell, such as a rhyming word.
>
> sn<u>ow</u>   r<u>ow</u>   cr<u>ow</u>

Find Rhyming Words
Circle the word in each row that rhymes with the spelling word in dark type.

1. **drive**	(alive)	brave		8. **supply**	supper	(fly)
2. **crow**	claw	(grow)		9. **groan**	spoon	(loan)
3. **pine**	(shine)	pain		10. **note**	not	(wrote)
4. **alike**	stick	(strike)		11. **tomato**	too	(potato)
5. **oak**	(soak)	bark		12. **stove**	(drove)	move
6. **below**	now	(throw)		13. **overhead**	bead	(dead)
7. **file**	fail	(mile)		14. **chose**	(those)	choose

Word Unscramble
Unscramble each set of letters to make a spelling word.

15. loowlh _____hollow_____   18. lolr _____roll_____

16. griet _____tiger_____   19. litte _____title_____

17. rino _____iron_____   20. pyrle _____reply_____

To Parents or Helpers
Using the Word Study Steps above as your child comes across any new words will help him or her learn to spell words effectively. Review the steps as you both go over this week's spelling words.
Go over the Spelling Tip with your child. Ask your child if he or she can think of any words that rhyme with one of the spelling words. Help your child complete the spelling activity.

Name_____ Date_____

Words with Long i and Long o

tiger	note	alike	below	overhead
drive	crow	supply	groan	chose
reply	oak	tomato	title	hollow
roll	iron	stove	pine	file

Write the spelling words with these spelling patterns.

Long *i* spelled   **Long *o* spelled**

i-e   *o*

1. _____drive_____   10. _____roll_____
2. _____alike_____   11. _____tomato_____
3. _____pine_____   12. _____overhead_____
4. _____file_____

i   *o-e*

5. _____tiger_____   13. _____note_____
6. _____iron_____   14. _____stove_____
7. _____title_____   15. _____chose_____

y   *ow*

8. _____reply_____   16. _____crow_____
9. _____supply_____   17. _____below_____
                             18. _____hollow_____

                                   oa

                             19. _____oak_____
                             20. _____groan_____

Name_____ Date_____

Words with Long *i* and Long *o*

tiger	note	alike	below	overhead
drive	crow	supply	groan	chose
reply	oak	tomato	title	hollow
roll	iron	stove	pine	file

Complete each sentence below with a spelling word.

1. If your shirt gets wrinkled, you can use my _____iron_____.

2. When I grow up, my mom will teach me to _____drive_____ a car.

3. A large black _____crow_____ flew into the clouds.

4. The _____title_____ of this story is Sarah, Plain and Tall.

5. The _____tiger_____ took a nap in its cage at the zoo.

6. Mom used the top of our _____stove_____ to fry onions.

7. Acorns are seeds from big _____oak_____ trees.

8. At the office, all papers are kept in a _____file_____.

9. A _____pine_____ tree has long, thin needles for leaves.

10. I keep a large _____supply_____ of dog food in the house.

What Does it Mean?
Write the spelling word that has the same, or almost the same, meaning.

11. empty _____hollow_____   15. under _____below_____

12. answer _____reply_____   16. above _____overhead_____

13. picked out _____chose_____ 17. moan _____groan_____

14. the same or similar _____alike_____ 18. letter _____note_____

Challenge Extension: Have students write fill-in sentences for each Challenge Word. Have each student exchange sentences with a partner and fill each other's sentences.

Sarah, Plain and Tall • SPELLING

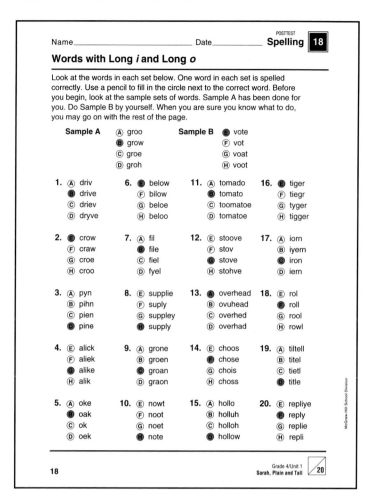

Words with Long *i* and Long *o*

Proofreading Activity

There are six spelling mistakes in the paragraph below. Circle the misspelled words. Write the words correctly on the lines below.

Sarah just got back from town. She brought us a ⟨suply⟩ of food for dinner. She cooked rich, delicious ⟨tomado⟩ soup on the ⟨stoov.⟩ Then she made us warm, brown dinner ⟨rowls.⟩ We ate outside, in the shade of the huge, old ⟨oke⟩ tree. ⟨Overhed⟩ the birds sang to each other in the branches. It was a wonderful day, and I was very happy.

1. _____supply_____ 3. _____stove_____ 5. _____oak_____

2. _____tomato_____ 4. _____rolls_____ 6. _____overhead_____

Writing Activity

Sarah liked to drive to town. Write a short story about a drive you would like to take. Use four spelling words in your writing.

_____

_____

_____

_____

Words with Long *i* and Long *o*

Look at the words in each set below. One word in each set is spelled correctly. Use a pencil to fill in the circle next to the correct word. Before you begin, look at the sample sets of words. Sample A has been done for you. Do Sample B by yourself. When you are sure you know what to do, you may go on with the rest of the page.

Sample A
- Ⓐ groo
- Ⓑ grow ●
- Ⓒ groe
- Ⓓ groh

Sample B
- Ⓔ vote ●
- Ⓕ vot
- Ⓖ voat
- Ⓗ voot

1.
- Ⓐ driv
- Ⓑ drive ●
- Ⓒ driev
- Ⓓ dryve

2.
- Ⓔ crow ●
- Ⓕ craw
- Ⓖ croe
- Ⓗ croo

3.
- Ⓐ pyn
- Ⓑ pihn
- Ⓒ pien
- Ⓓ pine ●

4.
- Ⓔ alick
- Ⓕ aliek
- Ⓖ alike ●
- Ⓗ alik

5.
- Ⓐ oke
- Ⓑ oak ●
- Ⓒ ok
- Ⓓ oek

6.
- Ⓔ below ●
- Ⓕ bilow
- Ⓖ beloe
- Ⓗ beloo

7.
- Ⓐ fil
- Ⓑ file ●
- Ⓒ fiel
- Ⓓ fyel

8.
- Ⓔ supplie
- Ⓕ suply
- Ⓖ suppley
- Ⓗ supply ●

9.
- Ⓐ grone
- Ⓑ groen
- Ⓒ groan ●
- Ⓓ graon

10.
- Ⓔ nowt
- Ⓕ noot
- Ⓖ noet
- Ⓗ note ●

11.
- Ⓐ tomado
- Ⓑ tomato ●
- Ⓒ toomatoe
- Ⓓ tomatoe

12.
- Ⓔ stoove
- Ⓕ stov
- Ⓖ stove ●
- Ⓗ stohve

13.
- Ⓐ overhead ●
- Ⓑ ovuhead
- Ⓒ overhed
- Ⓓ overhad

14.
- Ⓔ choos
- Ⓕ chose ●
- Ⓖ chois
- Ⓗ choss

15.
- Ⓐ hollo
- Ⓑ holluh
- Ⓒ holloh
- Ⓓ hollow ●

16.
- Ⓔ tiger ●
- Ⓕ tiegr
- Ⓖ tyger
- Ⓗ tigger

17.
- Ⓐ iorn
- Ⓑ iyern
- Ⓒ iron ●
- Ⓓ iern

18.
- Ⓔ rol
- Ⓕ roll ●
- Ⓖ rool
- Ⓗ rowl

19.
- Ⓐ tiltell
- Ⓑ titel
- Ⓒ tietl
- Ⓓ title ●

20.
- Ⓔ repliye
- Ⓕ reply ●
- Ⓖ replie
- Ⓗ repli

Practice 22

Name_____ Date_____ **Practice** 22

Main Idea and Supporting Details

The **main idea** tells you what a selection is all about. The **supporting details** in the selection help you to understand the main idea. Read this selection and answer each question.

Beavers are the engineers of the animal world. Engineers are people who use math and science to build bridges, tunnels, and building foundations and frames. Beavers build things, but they don't use math and science. They just know how to build dams and homes.

Beavers build dams to block river or pond water and make it deeper for their homes. Their homes, or lodges, stand partly below the water and partly above. These lodges have a front and back entrance. The lodge is made of logs and sticks plastered together with mud, grass, and moss. Beavers gather the building materials and float them to the lodge site along water channels they also build. Beavers work all the time, cutting down trees and branches to repair their lodges and dams.

1. What is the main idea? Beavers are like engineers because they build lodges and dams.

2. What supporting detail tells you why beavers are unlike engineers?
   Beavers build things but don't use math and science.

3. What supporting detail tells you about the materials beavers use?
   The lodge is made of logs, sticks, mud, grass, and moss.

4. Human engineers are supplied with building materials. Which supporting detail tells how beavers get their building materials? Beavers gather the materials and float them to the site along water channels.

5. Why do you think we use the expression "busy as a beaver"?
   Because beavers work constantly, we use the expression to describe people who are always busy.

5 Book 4/Unit 1 **Seal Journey**
At Home: Have students draw and label a home they would build.
22

Practice 23

Name_____ Date_____ **Practice** 23

Vocabulary

Substitute the correct word from the list for each underlined word or words.

nursery	squealed	assured	horizon	jagged	mature

1. The baby made a loud, shrill sound as it looked for its mother. squealed
   _____

2. In a snowstorm, we sometimes cannot see the line where the sky and land meet. horizon

3. The adult animals are almost always much bigger than the babies.
   mature

4. At night, sounds come from the place where babies are cared for.
   nursery

5. Some icebergs have sharply pointed edges. jagged
   _____

6. Many people are convinced that seals are harmless. assured
   _____

23
At Home: Have students write a paragraph using as many vocabulary words as possible.
Book 4/Unit 1 **Seal Journey** 6

A Place for a Boy and His Dog

On warm spring evenings, Matt likes to sit on the dock that stretches out into the lake. He looks at the line where the lake and the sky meet. Then the bright, orange sun sinks below the *horizon*. Sometimes the sunset forms a pattern of brilliant, *jagged* colors. Matt listens to the sounds in the woods behind him. With all the baby birds in the trees, it sounds like a *nursery*. Matt's puppy always *squealed* when he heard the baby birds. Now he's a *mature* dog and is used to those baby birds. Sitting in this beautiful place year after year makes Matt feel *assured* that he will always like it here.

1. What does Matt look at when he sits on the dock? the sun sinking below the horizon

2. What kind of pattern does the sunset form? a pattern of brilliant, jagged colors

3. Matt's dog *squealed* as a puppy but has stopped doing it now. Why?
   The puppy squealed when it heard the noise made by the baby birds. Now he's a mature dog used to hearing the baby birds.

4. What do the baby birds sound like? a nursery
   _____

5. What does Matt feel *assured* about? that he will always like sitting on the dock on a spring evening

5 Book 4/Unit 1 **Seal Journey**
At Home: Have students write a story with illustrations using some of the vocabulary words to describe a special and beautiful place.
23a

Practice 24

Name_____ Date_____ **Practice** 24

Story Comprehension

Write an answer in the space provided for the questions about "Seal Journey."

1. Who is the photographer who is telling the story?
   Richard Sobol

2. Who is Jonah? He is Richard Sobol's son.

3. Where does the helicopter take Richard and Jonah?
   One hundred miles north of Prince Edward Island

4. Why are these seals called harp seals?
   They have markings on their backs that are curved like a harp.

5. How much does a baby seal weigh at the end of 12 days?
   The baby weighs about 80 pounds.

6. Why does the mother push the pup into the water?
   The pup must learn fast to swim and survive on its own in the water.

7. What happens to a seal pup after two weeks?
   Its mother goes off to join the males and the pups are on their own for good.

8. What happens in April when the ice melts?
   The whole seal colony, including the young pups, swims north to their Arctic feeding grounds.

24
At Home: Have students tell a family member about the lives of the harp seals.
Book 4/Unit 1 **Seal Journey** 8

Seal Journey • PRACTICE

Use an Index

An **index** is an alphabetized list of topics found at the back of a book. An index tells on what page or pages a particular subject or name can be found. Use this sample index to answer questions.

Galapagos fur seal, 62, 71, 75
Guadeloupe fur seal, 19, 83-87
harbor seal, 22-25
harp seal, 6, 9, 14
hooded seal, 31-36, 42
killer whales, 11-19, 88
krill, 12

1. What are the numbers for pages with information about the harp seal?
6,9,14

2. What are all the page numbers with information about the harbor seal?
22, 23, 24, 25

3. Why do some page numbers have commas between them while others have dashes? Commas show individual pages. The dash means that the listed numbers and all the numbers in between have information on the topic.

4. Should you look through this book to find information about the gray seal? Explain. No. It is not listed in the index.

5. Which topic has the greatest number of pages? How many pages? The topic of killer whales is covered in 10 pages.

6. How can an index help you work more quickly?
You can tell right away whether a book has anything about your topic.

Main Idea and Supporting Details

The **main idea** of a paragraph is its most important idea. **Details** in the paragraph help support the main idea. Read the paragraph below. Write the main idea, then the details that support the main idea.

Dogs are trained to do many different jobs. Some dogs are trained to help people who are blind or who can see only a little. They make it possible for people to do many things they couldn't do without them. Other dogs are trained to do police work. Dogs with a sharp sense of smell track people and search for dangerous items. Some dogs are used for hunting. Still other dogs help farmers herd sheep and cows. But many dogs are pets. They are playful. They may also help keep a home safe by barking when strangers come near.

1. Main idea: Dogs are trained to do many jobs.

2. Supporting detail: Some dogs are trained to help the blind or people with poor eyesight.

3. Supporting detail: Some dogs are trained to do police work.

4. Supporting detail: Dogs are also used for hunting.

5. Supporting detail: Some dogs are trained to help farmers herd their sheep and cows.

6. Supporting detail: Many dogs are pets. They are playful and often help keep a home safe by barking when strangers come near.

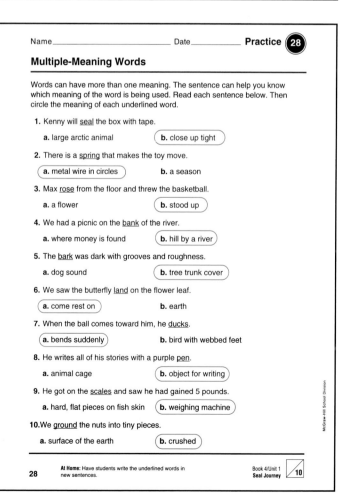

Make Inferences

An author doesn't always tell you why story characters do what they do. Therefore, you must **make inferences** about characters' actions by "reading between the lines." To make an inference, you can use clues provided by the author and similar experiences that you have had or heard about.

Read the story. Make an inference for each question.

Stacy, Gena, and their mom piled up the camping equipment near the door.
"I'll help you put up the tent when we get there, Mom," said Stacy. "I'm good at that."
Gena sighed as she dropped the knapsack. "I'll stay in the car until you get that tent set up." Gena ran to give her best friend Hannah a last-minute phone call. All her friends were going to Hannah's house that afternoon. Everyone but Gena would be there. Gena sighed again.
Stacy and her mom waited for Gena by the door. "I get excited when I'm about to go camping," said Mom. "When I was little, I couldn't wait to go. Luckily Gramma and Grandpa loved to camp too."

1. Who is going camping? Stacy, Gena, and their mom

2. How does Gena feel about going camping? How do you know?
She doesn't want to go. She's sighing and calling her friend to talk about what they will be doing while she is out camping.

3. How does Stacy feel about the camping trip?
She seems enthusiastic. She looks forward to putting up the tent. She waits with her mom by the door.

4. How might the girls' mom have gotten interested in camping?
She went camping a lot with her parents.

5. Who will enjoy the trip the most? Stacy and her mom

Multiple-Meaning Words

Words can have more than one meaning. The sentence can help you know which meaning of the word is being used. Read each sentence below. Then circle the meaning of each underlined word.

1. Kenny will seal the box with tape.
 a. large arctic animal   (**b.** close up tight)

2. There is a spring that makes the toy move.
 (**a.** metal wire in circles)   **b.** a season

3. Max rose from the floor and threw the basketball.
 a. a flower   (**b.** stood up)

4. We had a picnic on the bank of the river.
 a. where money is found   (**b.** hill by a river)

5. The bark was dark with grooves and roughness.
 a. dog sound   (**b.** tree trunk cover)

6. We saw the butterfly land on the flower leaf.
 (**a.** come rest on)   **b.** earth

7. When the ball comes toward him, he ducks.
 (**a.** bends suddenly)   **b.** bird with webbed feet

8. He writes all of his stories with a purple pen.
 a. animal cage   (**b.** object for writing)

9. He got on the scales and saw he had gained 5 pounds.
 a. hard, flat pieces on fish skin   (**b.** weighing machine)

10. We ground the nuts into tiny pieces.
 a. surface of the earth   (**b.** crushed)

Seal Journey • RETEACH

Main Idea and Supporting Details

> To find the **main idea**, ask yourself what the text you are reading is mostly about. Look for **supporting details** that tell more about the main idea.

Read the following and circle the letter beside the correct responses.

Recycling products is good for the environment. When we reuse paper, plastic and metal, fewer natural resources have to be used. Recycling also reduces garbage. It shows that people care about using our resources wisely. Almost everywhere in our country, communities are passing laws to make people recycle.

1. Which is the main idea?
   a. People should not waste plastic.
   b. Recycling is good for the environment.

2. Which is a supporting detail?
   a. Recycling reduces garbage.
   b. There are not enough natural resources.

3. Which is <u>not</u> a detail that tells more about the main idea?
   a. Almost everywhere communities are passing laws to make people recycle.
   b. Recycling helps people use resources wisely.

4. Which is <u>not</u> a fact according to the text?
   a. Recycling means fewer natural resources have to be used up.
   b. All people care about using our resources wisely.

Vocabulary

Read each clue. Then find the vocabulary word in the row of letters and circle it.

assured	horizon	jagged	mature	nursery	squealed

1. grown up — b e t u (m a t u r e) p l s w
2. earth and sky boundary — l (h o r i z o n) j g f d a z c
3. told in a positive way — k a w j w (a s s u r e d) b c
4. an area for babies or young — h a y (n u r s e r y) l t e r
5. a high, shrill cry — r e w a r (s q u e a l e d) t
6. with sharp, uneven edges — m u w a (j a g g e d) l a c q

6

Story Comprehension

Circle the letter beside the answer to each question about "Seal Journey."

1. What is the topic of this selection?
   a. harp seals   b. polar bears

2. Which describes the setting?
   a. cold and icy   b. warm and rainy

3. What do mothers and their pups do to recognize each other?
   a. They lick each other.   **b.** They rub noses.

4. What special thing did Jonah get to do before going home?
   a. He held a pup.   b. He fed a pup.

5. Why were the pups killed in the past?
   a. Hunters wanted their white fur.
   b. The animals were disturbing people.

Use an Index

> The **index** at the back of a book is useful if you need to know quickly on which page or pages you can find information.

Airplanes, 42–46
Bicycles, 23–26, 28
Buses, 12, 16, 21–25
Cars, 3–7, 21–25, 52
Railroads, 34–37
Ocean ships, 62–67
Trucks, 12–15, 21–23, 30–32
Transportation, see also specific types
   City transportation, 21–26
   Future of, 47–53
   History of, 30–39

Use the part of an index shown above to answer the questions.

1. On which pages can you find information about ocean ships?
   62–67

2. On which pages can you find information about trucks?
   12–15, 21–23, 30–32

3. Where would you look to find information about early types of transportation?
   under Transportation, history of, pages 30–39

4. Where would you look to find out about transportation in 2050?
   under Transportation, future of, pages 47–53

5. Where can you find information about trains?
   under Railroads, pages 34–37

6. Does information on trucks come before or after information about airplanes in the book? before

Main Idea and Supporting Details

> Sometimes authors state the **main idea** and then give **details** to support it. Other times it is up to the reader to decide what the main idea is.

Read the paragraph. Then write the answers to the questions.

Americans have always loved sports. But the popularity of certain sports has changed over time. Baseball and football used to be the most popular sports in our country. Many people still play and enjoy these games. Today, however, millions of young people are playing soccer. Some schools have dropped football and replaced it with soccer. Gymnastics has also grown in popularity as have volleyball, ice and field hockey, and figure skating.

1. What is the main idea? The popularity of certain sports has changed over time.

2. What is one detail that supports the main idea? Possible answer: Today millions of young people are playing soccer.

3. What is another supporting detail? Possible answer: Some schools have dropped football and replaced it with soccer.

Read the statement that follows. Then answer the question.

Americans no longer care much about sports.

4. Is the statement true or false based on the paragraph above?
   false

Seal Journey • RETEACH

Make Inferences

> Good readers look for clues in the text that will help them understand what is happening and how characters are feeling. This is called **making inferences**.

Read the story. Then make inferences to answer the questions.

Brian turned around and around. Everywhere he looked there was only sand. It seemed there were miles of nothing but sand. Brian checked to see if he still had his hat on because he felt like he was getting sunburned. His shirt felt glued to his body. He stretched and could feel every bone in his body. It had been a long ride on the camel. Even though he felt uncomfortable, he knew he would never forget what he was seeing. After one last look, he waved goodbye to the great pyramids.

Write the answer to each question.

1. Where is Brian? What clues let you know? <u>the Egyptian desert; there was</u> <u>sand everywhere; there were pyramids and camels</u>

2. Is it hot or cold? How do you know? <u>hot; He felt like he was getting</u> <u>sunburned. His shirt stuck to his body.</u>

3. How does Brian's body feel? How do you know? <u>sore; achy; he could feel</u> <u>every bone in his body.</u>

4. Why does he feel this way? <u>He had had a long camel ride in the desert.</u>

5. How does Brian feel as he looks around? <u>Answers will vary. He probably</u> <u>feels pleased to have the experience of seeing the great pyramids. At the</u> <u>same time he feels uncomfortable physically.</u>

Book 4/Unit 1
5 | **Seal Journey**

At Home: Have students write about inferences they had to make to figure out the plot of a favorite book or movie.

27

Multiple-Meaning Words

> Some words have more than one meaning. These words are called **homographs** if they are always spelled exactly the same way. Even though homographs are spelled the same, some are pronounced differently. An example is: Don't tear the paper. I have a tear in my eye.

Circle the letter beside the meaning of the underlined homograph.

1. The <u>seal</u> pups grow up quickly.
   a. to close something tightly
   (b.) a mammal that lives in the sea

2. The pup rested at the <u>base</u> of an ice mound.
   a. a military area
   (b.) the bottom part

3. Seal pups nurse for a short <u>period</u> of time.
   (a.) certain amount of time
   b. a mark of punctuation

4. The scientists will take a <u>break</u> before traveling on.
   a. to cause to separate into pieces
   (b.) a rest period

5. Our nature <u>club</u> is planning to go to a nature preserve.
   (a.) a group of people who join together
   b. a stick used as a weapon

6. The weight of the ice made the tree branches <u>bow</u>.
   (a.) bend over
   b. a knot of ribbon with two loops

28

At Home: Ask students to choose three homographs and use them in sentences that show their other meanings.

Book 4/Unit 1
Seal Journey | **6**

Seal Journey • EXTEND

Name_____ Date_____ **Extend** 22

Main Idea and Supporting Details

Are you good at a sport or other activity? Or have you ever had a fun summer vacation? Choose one of these two topics. Write about the best part of the activity or the vacation. Include at least three details to support your description.

Answers will vary but should include a main idea and supporting details.

_____
_____
_____
_____
_____
_____
_____
_____
_____

Suppose you wanted to illustrate the event you wrote about above with one photograph or a drawing. What details would be important to include? Describe the photo or drawing you would use.

Answers will vary but should include student's understanding of

photographs or drawings used as supporting details.

_____
_____
_____
_____
_____
_____
_____

Book 4/Unit 1
Seal Journey

At Home: Have students look through a photo album or scrapbook. Discuss how the photos help to recall special occasions.

22

Name_____ Date_____ **Extend** 23

Vocabulary

assured	jagged	nursery
horizon	mature	squealed

Draw pictures to illustrate each of the words above. More than one word can be illustrated in each picture. Include a label or caption with each picture. Use a separate piece of paper if you need more space.

Captions or labels should show an understanding of vocabulary definitions.

Extend 24

Story Comprehension

Write a brief book review of "Seal Journey." What is the story about? Did you like it enough to tell your friends to read it? In the first paragraph, tell what "Seal Journey" is about. In the second paragraph, explain whether or not you liked the story and why. Use another piece of paper if you need more space.

Answers will vary, but should show student's comprehension of the story.

_____
_____
_____
_____

23–24

At Home: Have students tell a story for each of their vocabulary illustrations.

Book 4/Unit 1
Seal Journey

Name_____ Date_____ **Extend** 25

Use an Index

An **index** appears at the back of a book. It lists topics that are mentioned in the book. It is arranged in alphabetical order with the page numbers for each topic. Use the index below to answer the questions.

P	S
penguin, 39	seal, 16–20, 31, 57
plankton, 46, 53	seashore, 83
polar bear, 28, 51–53	seasons,
polar region, 12, 20–24	fall, 90, 95
prey, 15, 35, 43, 62	spring, 72
	summer, 85
R	winter, 60, 62
rain, 85, 89	seaweed, 16
ringed seal, 61–65	shark, 58–62

1. Why isn't the letter **Q** included in the index? The book does not contain any topics that begin with the letter Q.

2. Does the index contain more than one reference to prey? Explain.
   Yes; pages 15, 35, 43, and 62 refer to prey.

3. On which page would you find information about seaweed? page 16

4. Where would you look to find out what plankton is? pages 46 and 53

5. On which pages might you find information on a shark's diet? pages 58–62

6. Where might you find a reference to spring or summer? page 72 or 85

Book 4/Unit 1
Seal Journey

At Home: Look at the index at the back of a book. Look up topics that interest you. Compare your interests with those of a family member.

25

Name_____ Date_____ **Extend** 26

Main Idea and Supporting Details

Think about the details and facts that support the **main idea** of "Seal Journey." Write about three things that most impressed you in the story, and tell why they impressed you.

Answers will vary, but should cite main ideas and supporting details from

the story.

_____
_____
_____
_____
_____
_____
_____
_____

Photographs have been important in making people aware of the cruelty toward baby harp seals. Think of an endangered animal that you would like to protect. State which animal you would protect. Tell why you would do this, using supporting details and facts.

Answers will vary, but should include supporting details and facts.

_____
_____
_____
_____
_____
_____
_____

26

At Home: Discuss how photographs are important in making people aware of wildlife and their habitats.

Book 4/Unit 1
Seal Journey

Seal Journey • EXTEND

Name_____ Date_____ Extend ◆27◆

Make Inferences

Use clues in "Seal Journey" to **make inferences** about the story.
Answers will vary. Possible answers are given.

1. Why is a helicopter the only way for Jonah and his father to reach the seal
colony? It is probably the quickest way. So much ice might be
dangerous for boats.

2. What type of clothing do you think Jonah and his father wore? _____
Answers should include hats, boots, gloves or mittens, warm jackets,
waterproof or ski pants.

3. What type of supplies do you think that Jonah and his father took along for the
day? Possible answers may include film, camera supplies, food, water,
and extra clothes.

4. Why do you think that a mother seal's milk is so rich? The seal pups must
grow quickly, so they need extra nourishment. The mother seal's diet is
rich in nutrients, therefore, her milk will also be rich.

5. Do you think that Jonah's father ever held a baby seal, like his son did?
Explain. Yes, probably because he has visited and photographed the
seals before. Like his son, the father is very fond of the seals.

McGraw-Hill School Division

Book 4/Unit 1
Seal Journey

At Home: Have students guess memorable activities
the family has participated in together by giving a
series of clues.

27

Name_____ Date_____ Extend ◆28◆

Multiple-Meaning Words

Some words have more than one meaning. Write two short definitions for
each word below. Each definition should present a different meaning of the
word. You may use a dictionary.

| seal | date | fan | jam |
| band | fair | file | lap |

Answers may vary. Possible definitions are given: Seal: a sea mammal; to
close something. Band: to join together; a musical group. Date: a particular
time of year; a type of fruit. Fair: clear and sunny; a carnival. Fan:
something used to cool you; a person who enjoys something. File: a box to
hold papers; a tool to make things smooth. Jam: a sweet spread made from
fruit; a situation in which you cannot move. Lap: the top of your legs when
you sit; to drink with the tip of your tongue like a dog or a cat does.

Suppose you are going to visit the seal colony. Use some of the words
above to write your thoughts about the visit.

Answers will vary, but should include words from the list.

_____
_____
_____
_____
_____
_____
_____
_____
_____
_____

McGraw-Hill School Division

28

At Home: Look through a dictionary. Discuss how to
recognize a word with multiple meanings in the dictionary
and how to identify the most common usage of the word.

Book 4/Unit 1
Seal Journey

Seal Journey • GRAMMAR

Page 19 (top left)

Name_____ Date_____ LEARN Grammar 19

Sentence Combining

A conjunction joins words, groups of words, or sentences.

- You can use conjunctions other than *and, but,* or *or* to combine sentences.
- Some conjunctions tell *where, when, why, how,* or *under what condition.*

Here is a list of some conjunctions:

where	when	why	how	although
as	before	because	as if	if
as soon as	after	since	as though	unless

Combine each pair of sentences using the conjunction given.

1. They traveled for hours. They reached the seal colony. (before)

   They traveled for hours before they reached the seal colony.

2. They could hear the baby seals. They stepped out on the ice. (as soon as)

   They could hear the baby seals as soon as they stepped out on the ice.

3. The mother seal knows her pup. She recognizes its scent. (because)

   The mother seal knows her pup because she recognizes its scent.

4. Pups must learn to swim. They will spend their lives in the water. (since)

   Pups must learn to swim since they will spend their lives in the water.

5. He patted the whitecoat. He walked back to the helicopter. (before)

   He patted the whitecoat before he walked back to the helicopter.

6. Hunters couldn't sell seal fur. People wanted it. (unless)

   Hunters couldn't sell seal fur unless people wanted it.

7. The hunters would have to stop. Nobody would buy the fur. (if)

   The hunters would have to stop if nobody would buy the fur.

8. You could see the seal's markings. She nestled with her pup. (as)

   You could see the seal's markings as she nestled with her pup.

8 Grade 4/Unit 1 Seal Journey

Extension: Have students find four compound sentences in the selection and identify the conjunction in each one.

19

Page 20 (top right)

Name_____ Date_____ LEARN AND PRACTICE Grammar 20

Complex Sentences

- A sentence that contains two related ideas joined by a conjunction other than *and, but,* or *or* is called a **complex sentence**.

Combine these ideas using the conjunction given to form a complex sentence.

1. The seals' swimming skills improve. They grow. (as)

   The seals' swimming skills improve as they grow.

2. The mother and pup rub noses. The pup nurses. (while)

   The mother and pup rub noses while the pup nurses.

3. Males keep their distance. Pups are being nursed. (while)

   Males keep their distance while pups are being nursed.

4. The seals journey back north. They spend the summer. (where)

   The seals journey back north where they spend the summer.

5. They will return to the ice. Autumn comes. (when)

   They will return to the ice when autumn comes.

6. Tourists want to see the whitecoats. That is what they came for. (since)

   Tourists want to see the whitecoats since that is what they came for.

7. The young pups feed on small shrimp. They swim along behind the herd. (as)

   The young pups feed on small shrimp as they swim along behind the herd.

8. Only twelve days pass. A seal pup is weaned. (before)

   Only twelve days pass before a seal pup is weaned.

9. The pup was still wet and yellow from its birth. They saw it. (when)

   The pup was still wet and yellow from its birth when they saw it.

10. We watched. The mother nudged the pup toward the water. (as)

    We watched as the mother nudged the pup toward the water.

20

Extension: Have students write their own complex sentences using each of these conjunctions: *where, before,* and *because.*

Grade 4/Unit 1 Seal Journey 10

Page 21 (bottom left)

Name_____ Date_____ PRACTICE AND REVIEW Grammar 21

Combining Sentences

- You can use conjunctions other than *and, but,* or *or* to combine sentences.
- Some conjunctions tell *where, when, why, how,* or *under what condition.*
- A sentence that contains two related ideas joined by a conjunction other than *and, but,* or *or* is called a **complex sentence**.

Combine these ideas using the conjunction given to form a complex sentence.

1. The frozen wilderness becomes a nursery. The seal pups are born. (when)

   The frozen wilderness becomes a nursery when the seal pups are born.

2. The excitement started. The helicopter took off. (as soon as)

   The excitement started as soon as the helicopter took off.

3. Seals have to come up for air. They are mammals. (because)

   Seals have to come up for air because they are mammals.

4. Mother and pup rubbed noses. They lay in the sun. (as)

   Mother and pup rubbed noses as they lay in the sun.

5. A seal pup is only twelve days old. It is weaned. (when)

   A seal pup is only twelve days old when it is weaned.

6. The male seal stays away. The pups are being born and nursed. (while)

   The male seal stays away while the pups are being born and nursed.

7. The male seals return. The pups are weaned. (once)

   The male seals return once the pups are weaned.

8. The seal pups are no longer white. They join the herd. (when)

   The seal pups are no longer white when they join the herd.

8 Grade 4/Unit 1 Seal Journey

Extension: Ask students to write three complex sentences about seals using these conjunctions: *whenever, although,* and *until.*

21

Page 22 (bottom right)

Name_____ Date_____ MECHANICS Grammar 22

Quotations

- Use quotation marks at the beginning and end of a person's exact words.
- Do not use quotation marks when you do not use the speaker's exact words.

Add quotation marks where they are needed in these sentences.

1. He told us that he was going to Canada to photograph seals.

2. "A large group of seals gathers there in winter," he explained.

3. He said Charlottetown would be his base camp.

4. He added, "I leave for Prince Edward Island next week."

5. He said many people were making the journey these days.

6. He said it was a favorite destination for ecological tourists.

7. "I don't consider myself an ecological tourist," he added.

8. He said, "My interest is that of a serious scientist."

9. He admitted it would be his first visit to the icy world of the seal colony.

10. "I do wonder how cold it actually gets," he said.

22

Extension: Ask students to write a sentence that includes a person's exact words. Have them give their sentences to a partner who will rewrite the sentence so that it tells what the person said but not in his or her exact words.

Grade 4/Unit 1 Seal Journey 10

Seal Journey • GRAMMAR

Complex Sentences

Choose the best conjunction to combine each pair of sentences.

1. There were holes in the ice ——— the seals would dive into the water.
   - a until
   - ⓑ where
   - c unless
   - d before

2. They could hear the baby seals ——— they stepped out onto the ice.
   - a unless
   - b as though
   - c until
   - ⓓ as soon as

3. Seals must come up for air ——— they are mammals.
   - a if
   - b unless
   - ⓒ because
   - d although

4. The pup couldn't sink ——— he had so much fat.
   - a before
   - b although
   - ⓒ because
   - d as if

5. A mother must find her own pup ——— she only has enough milk for one.
   - a if
   - ⓑ since
   - c when
   - d unless

Sentence Combining and Quotations

- You can use conjunctions other than *and, but,* or *or* to combine sentences.
- A sentence that contains two related ideas joined by a conjunction other than *and, but,* or *or* is called a **complex sentence**.

Mechanics

- Use quotation marks at the beginning and end of a person's exact words.
- Do not use quotation marks when you do not use the speaker's exact words.

A. Combine each pair of ideas to form a complex sentence. Answers may vary.

1. Jordan was sad. She read about hunters killing whitecoats.

   Jordan was sad when she read about hunters killing whitecoats.

2. That horror is over now. People fought to end seal hunting.

   That horror is over now because people fought to end seal hunting.

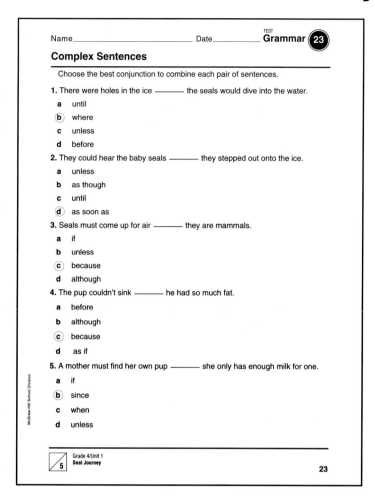

B. Look at the drawing above. Write what you think might be the boy's exact words. Write another sentence to tell what he says without using his exact words.

3. _____
   _____

4. _____
   _____

Seal Journey • SPELLING

Page 19 — PRETEST — Spelling 19

Name_____ Date_____ **Spelling 19**

Words with /ū/ and /ü/

Pretest Directions
Fold back the paper along the dotted line. Use the blanks to write each word as it is read aloud. When you finish the test, unfold the paper. Use the list at the right to correct any spelling mistakes. Practice the words you missed for the Posttest.

To Parents
Here are the results of your child's weekly spelling Pretest. You can help your child study for the Posttest by following these simple steps for each word on the word list:

1. Read the word to your child.
2. Have your child write the word, saying each letter as it is written.
3. Say each letter of the word as your child checks the spelling.
4. If a mistake has been made, have your child read each letter of the correctly spelled word aloud, then repeat steps 1–3.

#		#	Word
1.	_____	1.	ruler
2.	_____	2.	avenue
3.	_____	3.	raccoon
4.	_____	4.	loose
5.	_____	5.	commute
6.	_____	6.	continue
7.	_____	7.	gloomy
8.	_____	8.	unit
9.	_____	9.	whose
10.	_____	10.	humor
11.	_____	11.	improve
12.	_____	12.	beautiful
13.	_____	13.	cube
14.	_____	14.	stool
15.	_____	15.	movement
16.	_____	16.	ruin
17.	_____	17.	bugle
18.	_____	18.	argue
19.	_____	19.	community
20.	_____	20.	tuna

Challenge Words

_____ assured
_____ horizon
_____ jagged
_____ mature
_____ squealed

Grade 4/Unit 1
Seal Journey
19

Page 20 — AT HOME WORD STUDY — Spelling 20

Name_____ Date_____ **Spelling 20**

Words with /ū/ and /ü/

Using the Word Study Steps

1. LOOK at the word.
2. SAY the word aloud.
3. STUDY the letters in the word.
4. WRITE the word.
5. CHECK the word.

Did you spell the word right? If not, go back to step 1.

Spelling Tip
Keep an Alphabetical Personal Word List Notebook. Write words you often have trouble spelling.

Find and Circle
Where are the spelling words?

```
a a x x c o m m u t e x x g l o o m y a a b u n i t x v a v e n u e
a b r u l e r x x l o o s e y y z c o n t i n u e z z r a c c o o n a b z
s t o o l a b x x c u b e z z m o v e m e n t z z r u i n a b z z x x
a a w h o s e x x h u m o r z z b e a u t i f u l c c o m m u n i t y
x x b u g l e v v i m p r o v e y y a r g u e a b b c t u n a x y z z
```

To Parents or Helpers
Using the Word Study Steps above as your child comes across any new words will help him or her learn to spell words effectively. Review the steps as you both go over this week's spelling words.
Go over the Spelling Tip with your child. Ask him or her if he or she can think of words that are difficult to spell. Invite him or her to write it in a notebook.
Help your child find and circle the spelling words in the puzzle.

20
Grade 4/Unit 1
Seal Journey

Page 21 — EXPLORE THE PATTERN — Spelling 21

Name_____ Date_____ **Spelling 21**

Words with /ū/ and /ü/

ruler	commute	whose	cube	bugle
avenue	continue	humor	stool	argue
raccoon	gloomy	improve	movement	community
loose	unit	beautiful	ruin	tuna

Write each spelling words under the spelling pattern to which it belongs and circle the spelling pattern letter or letters.

/ū/ spelled u
1. unit
2. humor
3. bugle
4. community

/ū/ spelled u-e
5. commute
6. cube

/ū/ spelled ue
7. avenue
8. continue
9. argue

/ū/ spelled eau
10. beautiful

/ü/ spelled u
11. ruler
12. ruin
13. tuna

/ü/ spelled oo
14. loose
15. raccoon
16. gloomy
17. stool

/ü/ spelled o-e
18. whose
19. improve
20. movement

Grade 4/Unit 1
Seal Journey
21

Page 22 — PRACTICE AND EXTEND — Spelling 22

Name_____ Date_____ **Spelling 22**

Words with /ū/ and /ü/

ruler	commute	whose	cube	bugle
avenue	continue	humor	stool	argue
raccoon	gloomy	improve	movement	community
loose	unit	beautiful	ruin	tuna

Complete each sentence below with a spelling word or words.

1. A king is the _ruler_ of a country.
2. I play the _bugle_ in the school marching band.
3. She knows _whose_ books these are.
4. The _raccoon_ sat on the tree branch and looked at me.
5. If I _continue_ to practice, I may make the baseball team.
6. The people who live in my _community_ are very friendly.
7. Put a leash on the dog, or he will get _loose_.
8. Many people _commute_ to work by train.
9. The nursery is just one _unit_ in the hospital.
10. He put an ice _cube_ in his drink.
11. A joke with good _humor_ can make you laugh.
12. The child stepped up on the _stool_ to reach the sink.

Synonym Alert!
Write the spelling word that has the same, or almost the same, meaning.

1. road _avenue_
2. dark or sad _gloomy_
3. disagree or fight _argue_
4. motion _movement_
5. pretty _beautiful_
6. destroy _ruin_
7. make better _improve_
8. fish _tuna_

22
Challenge Extension: Have students write one sentence for each Challenge Word.
Grade 4/Unit 1
Seal Journey

T44 Annotated Workbooks

Seal Journey • SPELLING

Words with /ū/ and /ü/

Proofreading Activity

There are six spelling mistakes in the paragraph below. Circle the misspelled words. Write the words correctly on the lines below.

The baby seal looked like a (bootiful) white ball of fur. It made a (muvment) toward its mother. Its mother will (continu) to feed it milk for twelve days. Seals eat small fish and shrimp, not big fish, like the (toona). Soon the whole (communeity) of seals will swim north. It makes me sad and (glumy) to say goodbye to the baby seals.

1. _____movement_____   3. _____continue_____   5. _____community_____

2. _____beautiful_____   4. _____tuna_____   6. _____gloomy_____

Writing Activity

Think about an adventure you would like. Where would you go and what would you do? Write a paragraph using four spelling words in your writing.

_____

_____

_____

_____

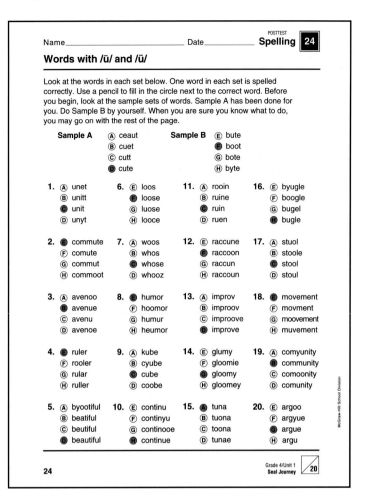

Words with /ū/ and /ü/

Look at the words in each set below. One word in each set is spelled correctly. Use a pencil to fill in the circle next to the correct word. Before you begin, look at the sample sets of words. Sample A has been done for you. Do Sample B by yourself. When you are sure you know what to do, you may go on with the rest of the page.

Sample A
- (A) ceaut
- (B) cuet
- (C) cutt
- (●) cute

Sample B
- (E) bute
- (●) boot
- (G) bote
- (H) byte

1.
- (A) unet
- (B) unitt
- (●) unit
- (D) unyt

2.
- (●) commute
- (F) comute
- (G) commut
- (H) commoot

3.
- (A) avenoo
- (B) avenue
- (C) avenu
- (D) avenoe

4.
- (●) ruler
- (F) rooler
- (G) rular
- (H) ruller

5.
- (A) byootiful
- (B) beatiful
- (C) beutiful
- (D) beautiful

6.
- (E) loos
- (●) loose
- (G) luose
- (H) looce

7.
- (A) woos
- (B) whos
- (●) whose
- (D) whooz

8.
- (●) humor
- (F) hoomor
- (G) humur
- (H) heumor

9.
- (A) kube
- (B) cyube
- (●) cube
- (D) coobe

10.
- (E) continu
- (F) continyu
- (G) continooe
- (●) continue

11.
- (A) rooin
- (B) ruine
- (●) ruin
- (D) ruen

12.
- (E) raccune
- (●) raccoon
- (G) raccun
- (H) raccoun

13.
- (A) improv
- (B) improov
- (C) improove
- (●) improve

14.
- (E) glumy
- (F) gloomie
- (●) gloomy
- (H) gloomey

15.
- (●) tuna
- (B) tuona
- (C) toona
- (D) tunae

16.
- (E) byugle
- (F) boogle
- (G) bugel
- (●) bugle

17.
- (A) stuol
- (B) stoole
- (●) stool
- (D) stoul

18.
- (●) movement
- (F) movment
- (G) moovement
- (H) muvement

19.
- (A) comyunity
- (●) community
- (C) comoonity
- (D) comunity

20.
- (E) argoo
- (F) argyue
- (●) argue
- (H) argu

Practice 29

Name_____ **Date**_____

Problem and Solution

The main characters in a story often face one or more **problems** that they must solve, or for which they must find **solutions**. Find the problems and solutions in this story. Then answer the questions.

　　Indira's neighbor, Mrs. Ramos, asked Indira to care for her dog, Tati, while she was away. Indira was afraid of dogs, but she liked Mrs. Ramos. Also, she needed the money. So Indira went to meet Tati. Tati was very friendly and did not bark. Indira took the job.

　　The next day, Indira put the key in Mrs. Ramos's door. Tati began to bark angrily. Indira could see his big teeth through the door window. Scared, she ran home.

　　Indira thought about asking her sister, Kamala, to help her, but remembered what Kamala had said. "You know dogs scare you. You had better not take the job." Kamala had warned. Indira didn't want to admit that she had been scared and had run away. But she didn't know what else to do, so she asked her sister for help. Kamala helped Indira take care of Tati for two days. During that time Tati and Indira became friends.

1. What did Tati do when Indira put the key in the lock? <u>barked and scared Indira</u>

2. What is the big problem in the story? <u>Indira was too afraid of dogs to care for one by herself.</u>

3. What was Indira's solution? <u>She asked her sister for help.</u>

4. What is a smaller problem in the story? <u>Indira doesn't want to admit to her sister that she was right about Indira being too afraid to care for the dog.</u>

5. How does Indira solve the smaller problem? <u>She asks her sister to help her.</u>

Book 4/Unit 1
Open Wide, Don't Bite! 5

At Home: Have students write about how they did something in spite of their fear.

29

Practice 30

Name_____ **Date**_____

Vocabulary

Answer each question, and use the vocabulary word in your response.

1. **patients** What type of patients do veterinarians have?
<u>Patients include family pets and farm, zoo, or wild animals.</u>

2. **healthy** Will exercise help to keep dogs healthy?
<u>Yes. To be healthy dogs need exercise.</u>

3. **skills** What skills do you need to be a good basketball player?
<u>Possible answers include: ability to move quickly, to throw balls into baskets, to pass, and to dribble.</u>

4. **broad** Does it make a difference if a path is narrow or broad?
<u>A broad path has room for many people to walk at once.</u>

5. **reptiles** Name some animals that are reptiles.
<u>Crocodiles, alligators, lizards, and snakes are all reptiles.</u>

6. **fangs** Which snake has poisonous fangs?
<u>A rattlesnake has poisonous fangs.</u>

30

At Home: Have students write a paragraph using each vocabulary word in a sentence.

Book 4/Unit 1
Open Wide, Don't Bite! 6

Animal Doctor

　　Right now, my name is Lauren Ayana. When I grow up, my name is going to be Doctor Lauren Ayana, veterinarian to all animals.

　　I'm already working on my doctoring *skills*. I ask the veterinarian all kinds of questions when I take my pets to his office. I often check my cat and dog to make sure they seem *healthy*. I also care for two *reptiles* — a lizard and one snake with no *fangs*.

　　Some vets only treat pets or farm animals. That's too narrow for me. I plan to care for a very broad group of animals. My *patients* will include everything from pets to farm animals to wild animals.

1. Why is Lauren learning doctoring *skills*? <u>She wants to be a veterinarian when she grows up.</u>

2. Who does Lauren ask questions about keeping animals *healthy*?
<u>the veterinarian</u>

3. What kind of animals does Lauren have in addition to her cat and dog?
<u>two reptiles—a lizard and a snake with no fangs</u>

4. What kinds of *patients* are in the broad group Lauren plans to treat?
<u>She will be a doctor to all animals including pets, farm, and wild animals.</u>

5. Why can you say Lauren will be a good veterinarian?
<u>She has a lot of pets and spends time taking care of them and learning about them.</u>

Book 4/Unit 1
Open Wide, Don't Bite! 5

At Home: Have students describe what a veterinarian does and tell what animals they would like to care for as a vet.

30a

Practice 31

Name_____ **Date**_____

Story Comprehension

Read statements 1 to 6 below. Write **T** for true if the statement describes "Open Wide, Don't Bite!" Write **F** for false if it does not.

1. ___T___ Peter Kertesz went to school to be a dentist for people.

2. ___F___ Kertesz treats only small cats, never tigers or lions.

3. ___T___ The dentist gives animals medicine so they won't feel pain.

4. ___T___ Large animals are easier for dentists to treat than small ones.

5. ___T___ A tiger can lose its life from one bad tooth.

6. ___T___ The teeth of beavers and rats never stop growing.

Write an answer for each question.

7. How was Dr. Kertesz the answer to another vet's problem?
<u>The vet didn't pull animal teeth and he needed someone to do that for a housecat he was treating.</u>

8. Why do animals have different sizes and shapes of teeth?
<u>Special sizes and shapes of teeth are needed for the special food an animal eats. Vegetable-eating animals have short, broad teeth. Meat-eating animals have long, pointed teeth.</u>

31

At Home: Have students write a short story about an animal dentist and a tiger.

Book 4/Unit 1
Open Wide, Don't Bite! 8

Annotated Workbooks

Open Wide, Don't Bite! • PRACTICE

Use Headings, Captions, and Sidebars

Foods to Avoid

Certain foods can stick to your braces or even break them. These foods includes sticky candy, apples, and corn-on-the-cob.

> A smoothie shake is a soothing treat if your teeth are sore after a trip to the orthodontist. Just blend a cup of milk with a chopped banana and a handful of ice cubes.

Pasta is a good choice of food for people with braces. It is soft and easy to chew. Mashed potatoes and rice are also good choices.

Now answer these questions about the page above.

1. What types of foods should people with braces avoid? sticky candy, apples, and corn-on-the-cob

2. What information does the sidebar contain? It gives a recipe for a smoothie shake.

3. How are captions and sidebars alike? They both provide additional information and facts.

4. Write a heading for the sidebar. Possible answer: A Cool Treat

5. Pretend the picture showed a boy eating an apple. Write a new caption for the picture. Answers will vary.

5 Book 4/Unit 1
Open Wide, Don't Bite!

At Home: Have students look for headings, captions, and sidebars in a newspaper.

32

Main Idea and Supporting Details

Write the **main idea** in the following passage. Then write the **details that support** the main idea.

Many grown-ups have jobs they enjoy. They are also using the interests they had as children. For example, a designer of electrical kitchen products for a large corporation liked to take apart old can openers and toasters as a girl. Another worker uses big machines to dig huge holes in the earth for the foundations of skyscrapers. He is doing what he has done since he was three years old. When his friends stopped digging in sandboxes, he kept on digging. Even when he was 12 years old, he was still digging and hoping the other kids didn't see. Other examples are twin brothers who liked to pretend they were airplane pilots when they were young. They're not pretending any longer.

1. Main idea:
   Many grown-up people have jobs that use interests they have had since they were children.

2. Supporting detail:
   A girl who took things apart is now a designer of electrical products.

3. Supporting detail:
   A man who dug in sandboxes when he was a child is now using big machines to dig huge holes.

4. Supporting detail:
   Twin brothers who are now pilots used to pretend they were pilots when they were growing up.

33 **At Home:** Have students write about something they like, underlining the main idea and circling the supporting details.

Book 4/Unit 1
Open Wide, Don't Bite! 4

Multiple-Meaning Words

Some words have **multiple-meanings**. The context of the sentence will tell you which meaning of the word is being used. Read each sentence below. Then circle the meaning of each underlined word.

1. She wears a blue band to hold her hair away from her face.
   a. group of musicians   **b. thin strip of cloth**

2. Jeffrey can finish the race even though he is out of breath.
   a. is able to   b. metal container

3. The pitcher on the table was filled with lemonade.
   a. container for pouring liquid   b. baseball player

4. Hannah wrote the note on the yellow slip.
   a. slide suddenly   **b. small piece of paper**

5. Tim sat at the counter eating a cheese sandwich.
   a. person listing numbers   **b. long table**

6. The falling branch gave him a blow on the head.
   a. hard hit   b. send air from the mouth

7. They had only one match left for two more nights in the woods.
   a. stick for starting fires   b. things that go together

8. Maria and her sister liked to lie down and look at the stars.
   a. say something not true   **b. be in a flat position**

9. They could see the school from the glass-bottom boat.
   a. place for learning   **b. group of fish**

10. They stopped at the toll booth before they drove over the bridge.
    a. fee   b. sound of a bell

10 Book 4/Unit 1
Open Wide, Don't Bite!

At Home: Have students write four sentences using two other words with multiple meanings.

34

Synonyms and Antonyms

Synonyms are words that mean almost the same thing. **Antonyms** are words that have opposite meanings.

Write a synonym from the list to replace the underlined word in each sentence.

sound	several	make	find

1. This morning, Mark could not locate his homework.   find

2. There was a funny noise coming from the car engine.   sound

3. My family makes numerous trips to the grocery store.   several

4. Anthony likes to construct towers of boxes.   make

Write an antonym for the underlined word that completes each sentence.

all	destroy	silence	below

5. Every time we make block towers, the babies destroy them.

6. I float my kite above the trees, while I stand below them.

7. She said she would do none of the work, but she did it all.

8. I couldn't hear a sound; there was only silence.

35 **At Home:** Have students write a question and its answer using a pair of synonyms. Then do the same for antonyms.

Book 4/Unit 1
Open Wide, Don't Bite! 8

Open Wide, Don't Bite! • RETEACH

Name_____ Date_____ **Reteach** `29`

Problem and Solution

> Often the plot, or what happens in a story, is a matter of the characters finding a **solution** to a **problem**. Sometimes there may even be more than just one problem.

Read the story. Then write to tell the problems and the solution.

Shandra and LuAnn volunteered to come up with ideas to help their soccer team. The team needed a field for practice and money to buy new uniforms.

On the way to LuAnn's house, Shandra passed an empty lot. "What a mess!" she thought. It was full of empty bottles and cans. When she got to LuAnn's house the girls talked about their soccer team assignment. They thought and thought, but neither had any ideas. All of a sudden, Shandra stood up. "I've got the answer!" she said. "Do you know that empty lot nearby? We can clear it for a practice field. The owner of the lot is a friend of my parents. I know he'll let us use it for practice. We can return the cans and bottles we collect to the store and use the money we get for uniforms."

1. Problem 1: _finding a place for soccer practice_

2. Problem 2: _raising money for uniforms_

3. Solution to both problems: _Ask for permission to use the empty lot, then_ _clean it by collecting the cans and bottles there; return the bottles and_ _cans for a refund to use for uniforms._

4. What might be a problem with the girls' solution? _Possible answer: They_ _might not get permission to use the lot. The money they collect as_ _refunds may not be enough to buy the uniforms._

`4` Book 4/Unit 1
Open Wide, Don't Bite!
At Home: Have students try to think of other solutions to the girls' problem.
29

Name_____ Date_____ **Reteach** `30`

Vocabulary

Write a word from the list to complete each sentence.

broad	fangs	patients	healthy	reptiles	skills

1. Doctors treat _____patients_____ with different problems.

2. Do you think a crocodile has a _____broad_____ smile?

3. The goal of a doctor is to keep people _____healthy_____.

4. Big cats have _____fangs_____ that help them grab and tear meat.

5. Medical schools teach doctors the _____skills_____ they need.

6. Crocodiles and lizards are _____reptiles_____.

`6`

Story Comprehension
Reteach `31`

Write complete sentences to answer the following questions about "Open Wide, Don't Bite!"

1. What kind of doctor is Dr. Kertesz?
   He is a dentist.

2. What does Dr. Kertesz do on Fridays?
   He sees his animal patients.

3. How does Dr. Kertesz keep animals from getting upset?
   He gives them medicine to keep them calm and pain-free.

4. What size animal is easiest for Dr. Kertesz to work on?
   large ones

5. How does Dr. Kertesz's work help animals?
   By keeping them healthier, he helps animals live longer.

At Home: Have students make a list of unusual occupations they know about.
30–31
Book 4/Unit 1
Open Wide, Don't Bite!
`5`

Name_____ Date_____ **Reteach** `32`

Use Headings, Captions, and Sidebars

> Headings, captions, and sidebars all make it easier to read information. **Headings** help you find specific information. **Captions** and **sidebars** give you additional facts.

Look at this page from a book about veterinarians. Then answer the questions.

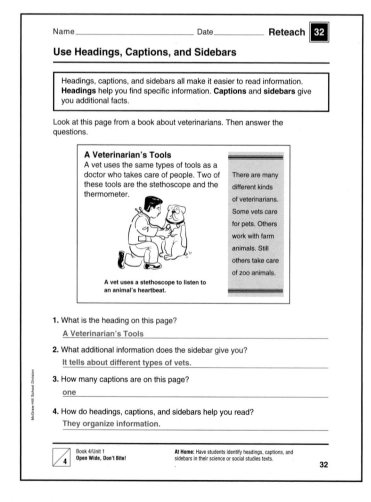

A Veterinarian's Tools
A vet uses the same types of tools as a doctor who takes care of people. Two of these tools are the stethoscope and the thermometer.

There are many different kinds of veterinarians. Some vets care for pets. Others work with farm animals. Still others take care of zoo animals.

A vet uses a stethoscope to listen to an animal's heartbeat.

1. What is the heading on this page?
   A Veterinarian's Tools

2. What additional information does the sidebar give you?
   It tells about different types of vets.

3. How many captions are on this page?
   one

4. How do headings, captions, and sidebars help you read?
   They organize information.

`4` Book 4/Unit 1
Open Wide, Don't Bite!
At Home: Have students identify headings, captions, and sidebars in their science or social studies texts.
32

Name_____ Date_____ **Reteach** `33`

Main Idea and Supporting Details

> The **main idea** of a selection or a part of the text is the most important idea the author wants to get across. **Supporting details** give more information about the main idea.

Read the text and fill in the chart. _Answers may vary._

The African elephant is the largest land animal. Everything about it is big. It weighs more than 16,000 pounds and is 20 feet long. This elephant weighs about as much as about 17 pick-up trucks or 200 fourth graders weighing 80 pounds each. In addition to a huge body, the African elephant has a huge nose, or trunk. A trunk is so big and so strong that it can lift and carry a load weighing 2,000 pounds. Its tusks are long, curved teeth but they are not used for eating. The elephants also have back teeth called molars that can be as big as one foot long.

1. Main Idea: _Everything about the African elephant is big._

2. Supporting Detail: _The African elephant is 20 feet long._

3. Supporting Detail: _The elephant's trunk can lift 2,000 pounds._

4. Supporting Detail: _Elephant molars can be one foot long._

5. Is the statement below true or false based on what you read?
   Trunks are long teeth that are not very strong. _____false_____

6. Rewrite the statement above to make it correct. _Possible answer: Tusks_ _are long teeth that are not used for eating._

At Home: Have students write more details to support the main idea of the paragraph.
33
Book 4/Unit 1
Open Wide, Don't Bite!
`6`

Open Wide, Don't Bite! • RETEACH

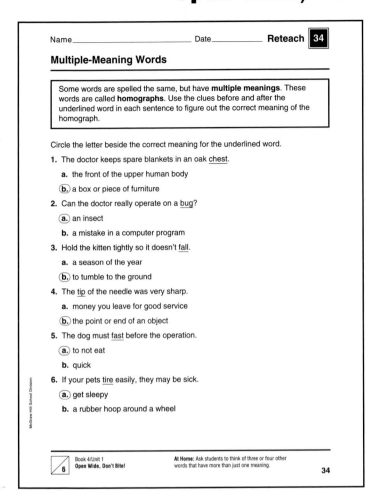

Multiple-Meaning Words

Some words are spelled the same, but have **multiple meanings**. These words are called **homographs**. Use the clues before and after the underlined word in each sentence to figure out the correct meaning of the homograph.

Circle the letter beside the correct meaning for the underlined word.

1. The doctor keeps spare blankets in an oak <u>chest</u>.
   - a. the front of the upper human body
   - (b.) a box or piece of furniture

2. Can the doctor really operate on a <u>bug</u>?
   - (a.) an insect
   - b. a mistake in a computer program

3. Hold the kitten tightly so it doesn't <u>fall</u>.
   - a. a season of the year
   - (b.) to tumble to the ground

4. The <u>tip</u> of the needle was very sharp.
   - a. money you leave for good service
   - (b.) the point or end of an object

5. The dog must <u>fast</u> before the operation.
   - (a.) to not eat
   - b. quick

6. If your pets <u>tire</u> easily, they may be sick.
   - (a.) get sleepy
   - b. a rubber hoop around a wheel

At Home: Ask students to think of three or four other words that have more than just one meaning.

34

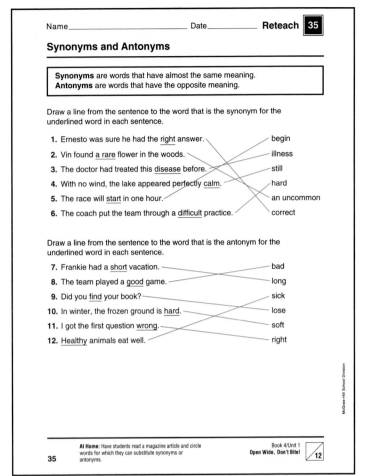

Synonyms and Antonyms

Synonyms are words that have almost the same meaning.
Antonyms are words that have the opposite meaning.

Draw a line from the sentence to the word that is the synonym for the underlined word in each sentence.

1. Ernesto was sure he had the <u>right</u> answer.
2. Vin found <u>a rare</u> flower in the woods.
3. The doctor had treated this <u>disease</u> before.
4. With no wind, the lake appeared perfectly <u>calm</u>.
5. The race will <u>start</u> in one hour.
6. The coach put the team through a <u>difficult</u> practice.

- begin
- illness
- still
- hard
- an uncommon
- correct

Draw a line from the sentence to the word that is the antonym for the underlined word in each sentence.

7. Frankie had a <u>short</u> vacation.
8. The team played a <u>good</u> game.
9. Did you <u>find</u> your book?
10. In winter, the frozen ground is <u>hard</u>.
11. I got the first question <u>wrong</u>.
12. <u>Healthy</u> animals eat well.

- bad
- long
- sick
- lose
- soft
- right

35 At Home: Have students read a magazine article and circle words for which they can substitute synonyms or antonyms.

Book 4/Unit 1
Open Wide, Don't Bite! 12

Open Wide, Don't Bite! • EXTEND

Problem and Solution

The **solutions** to some **problems** seem obvious or logical. Other problems may require more creative solutions. Consider each problem below. Write what you think a good solution would be.
Answers will vary. Possible answers are given.

1. Jamie has a toothache. What should she do? Jamie should visit a dentist.
_____
_____

2. Carter's shirt is torn. What should he do? Carter should sew the shirt.
_____
_____

3. Jamal is tired. What should he do? Jamal should rest.
_____

4. Sheri is hungry. What should she do? Sheri should eat something.
_____

5. Natalie's dog is limping. What should she do? Natalie should take the dog to a vet.

6. Brandon is not very good at soccer. What should he do? Brandon should practice more or try another sport or acitivity.
_____

Vocabulary

broad	patients	reptiles
fangs	healthy	skills

Write a short story using each of the vocabulary words.

Answers will vary, but should show correct use of vocabulary.
_____
_____
_____
_____
_____

Story Comprehension

Dr. Kertesz has both human patients and animal patients. How do you think the problems of his human patients and animal patients are alike? How do you think they are different?

Answers will vary. Possible answers may include some of the following.
Both probably have similar types of problems. The animals teeth may be in worse condition since they do not visit a dentist regularly. Some animals will have bigger or smaller mouths and teeth than humans do.
_____
_____

Use Headings, Captions, and Sidebars

Headings, captions, and **sidebars** all organize information so that it is easier to read.

What Did Dinosaurs Eat?

Scientists can tell what foods dinosaurs ate by studying fossil remains of their teeth. Some dinosaurs were plant-eaters. Others ate meat.

Duckbilled dinosaurs had hundreds of teeth. These teeth pressed together to form a plate. Duckbills ground their food between these plates.

The tyrannosaurus rex had six-inch teeth with saw-like edges to tear into meat.

Use the page information above to answer the questions.

1. What is the heading on this page?
What Did Dinosaurs Eat?
_____

2. What does the caption tell you?
Tyrannosaurus rex had very sharp six-inch teeth.
_____

3. What might be a good heading for the sidebar?
Answers will vary.
_____

4. Draw a picture of your favorite kind of dinosaur and write a caption for it.

Main Idea and Supporting Details

Think about "Open Wide, Don't Bite!" to answer the questions below.
Answers will vary. Possible answers are given.

1. What is unusual about the work that Dr. Kertesz does? He is a dentist who has animal patients.

2. Where does Dr. Kertesz practice? Mostly in England, but he has treated animals in many other countries.

3. What are some of the animals that Dr. Kertesz has treated? Answers may include lions, tigers, bears, wolves, whales, aardvarks, elephants, deer, foxes, gorillas, camels, zebras, and jaguars.

4. How is Dr. Kertesz able to treat wild animals? He gives medicine to the animals to keep them calm.

5. Why do you think the article focuses on Dr. Kertesz? His work is interesting and helps animals live longer.

6. Which supporting detail did you find most interesting in the article? Answers will vary.

Dr. Kertesz has an unusual weekend job. Think about an unusual job that you would like to do. Write a description of your typical day. Before you write, think about your main idea and the kinds of supporting details you will use.
_____
_____
_____
_____
_____

Open Wide, Don't Bite! • EXTEND

Multiple-Meaning Words

round	run	pack
sharp	store	rule

Each word above has **multiple meanings**. Write the word that fits the definitions below.

1. a group of something, such as animals; to put objects in a box
   <u>pack</u>

2. to move quickly; to be in charge of something <u>run</u>

3. a place where things are sold; to put things away until needed
   <u>store</u>

4. having a curved surface; a single outburst <u>round</u>

5. a statement or law; to govern, usually a country <u>rule</u>

6. sudden and dramatic; having a point or edge that cuts <u>sharp</u>

Write a paragraph about taking care of a pet—your own pet or someone else's. Include some of the words from the box above. Repeat the words in your writing by using their different meanings.

_____
_____
_____
_____
_____
_____
_____
_____
_____

Book 4/Unit 1
Open Wide, Don't Bite!

At Home: Make up a short list of multiple-meaning words. Alternate using the words with each of their meanings to tell a story.

34

Synonyms and Antonyms

Unscramble each word. Then find its synonym in the box below. On each line, write the unscrambled word and its synonym.

forecast	dwelling	immense
goal	request	repair

1. ima <u>aim; goal</u>   4. kas <u>ask; request</u>
2. tavs <u>vast; immense</u>   5. denm <u>mend; repair</u>
3. terpdic <u>predict; forecast</u>   6. uhoes <u>house; dwelling</u>

Unscramble the words. Find the antonym for each word in the box below. On each line write the unscrambled word and its antonym.

imaginary	sharp	rough	many	shrink

1. wfe <u>few; many</u>   4. tofs <u>soft; rough</u>
2. lare <u>real; imaginary</u>   5. rwog <u>grow; shrink</u>
3. ldlu <u>dull; sharp</u>

Choose two words and their antonyms from above. Write a synonym for each word and its antonym.

<u>Answers will vary. Possible answers: many/a lot; few/scarce</u>

_____
_____
_____
_____
_____
_____
_____
_____

35

At Home: Have students make a list of words that have both a synonym and an antonym.

Book 4/Unit 1
Open Wide, Don't Bite!

Open Wide, Don't Bite! • GRAMMAR

Grammar 25 — LEARN

Name_____ Date_____

Run-on Sentences

- A **run-on sentence** joins together two or more sentences that should be written separately.
- You can correct a run-on sentence by separating two complete ideas into two sentences.

Read the run-on sentences below. Then correct them by separating them into two sentences.

1. Chimpanzees pull back their lips that's how they smile.
   Chimpanzees pull back their lips. That's how they smile.

2. Many zoos have dentists the dentists might have human patients, too.
   Many zoos have dentists. The dentists might have human patients, too.

3. Pets need dental care most vets clean cats' and dogs' teeth regularly.
   Pets need dental care. Most vets clean cats' and dogs' teeth regularly.

4. Pet owners can do things to keep their pets' teeth clean they brush them.
   Pet owners can do things to keep their pets' teeth clean. They brush them.

5. There is special toothpaste for dogs it tastes like beef.
   There is special toothpaste for dogs. It tastes like beef.

6. There are special biscuits and dog chews they keep teeth clean, too.
   There are special biscuits and dog chews. They keep teeth clean, too.

7. Cats need to eat kibble it helps prevent tartar buildup.
   Cats need to eat kibble. It helps prevent tartar buildup.

8. Dogs and cats use their sharp teeth to bite their flat teeth are for grinding.
   Dogs and cats use their sharp teeth to bite. Their flat teeth are for grinding.

Grade 4/Unit 1
Open Wide, Don't Bite! — 8
Extension: Have students write their own run-on sentence and give it to a partner to separate into two sentences.
25

Grammar 26 — LEARN AND PRACTICE

Name_____ Date_____

Run-on Sentences

- You can correct a run-on sentence by rewriting it as a compound or a complex sentence.

Correct these run-on sentences by rewriting them as compound or complex sentences. Student's answers may vary.

1. The dog's teeth looked scary he was really smiling.
   The dog's teeth looked scary, but he was really smiling.

2. An elephant would have a big toothache it has such big teeth.
   An elephant would have a big toothache because it has such big teeth.

3. Large animals are good dental patients their mouths are so large.
   Large animals are good dental patients because their mouths are so large.

4. The dentist treats animals he has human patients, too.
   The dentist treats animals, and he has human patients, too.

5. Carnivores have pointed teeth herbivores have flat teeth.
   Carnivores have pointed teeth, and herbivores have flat teeth.

6. A new tooth grows in an alligator loses a tooth.
   A new tooth grows in when an alligator loses a tooth.

7. Beavers' teeth stay filed down they chew on wood.
   Beavers' teeth stay filed down because they chew on wood.

8. An animal can become sick it has a bad tooth.
   An animal can become sick if it has a bad tooth.

26
Extension: Have students write three run-on sentences to give to a partner who will rewrite them as compound or complex sentences.
Grade 4/Unit 1
Open Wide, Don't Bite! — 8

Grammar 27 — PRACTICE AND REVIEW

Name_____ Date_____

Run-on Sentences

- A **run-on sentence** joins together two or more sentences that should be written separately.
- You can correct a run-on sentence by separating two complete ideas into two sentences.
- You can correct a run-on sentence by rewriting it as a compound or complex sentence.

Read each sentence. If it is a run-on sentence, correct it by separating the two parts or rewrite it by adding a conjunction. Student's answers may vary.

1. Some whales have teeth some have baleen instead.
   Some whales have teeth, but some have baleen instead.

2. A sore tooth can hurt an animal a sore mouth can make an animal not want to eat. A sore tooth can hurt an animal.
   A sore mouth can make an animal not want to eat.

3. It's hard to fix an aardvark's teeth their mouths don't open very far.
   It's hard to fix an aardvark's teeth because their mouths don't open very far.

4. Walruses have tusks tigers have fangs.
   Walruses have tusks. Tigers have fangs.

5. Humans have teeth called canines they are pointed like dogs' teeth.
   Humans have teeth called canines. They are pointed like dogs' teeth.

6. Humans have sharp teeth and flat teeth so do dogs and cats.
   Humans have sharp teeth and flat teeth, and so do dogs and cats.

Grade 4/Unit 1
Open Wide, Don't Bite! — 6
Extension: Ask students to write a compound or complex sentence on a strip of paper. Then have them cut the words apart and mix them up. Have them give their words to a partner who will arrange them first into two sentences and then into the original compound or complex sentence.
27

Grammar 28 — MECHANICS

Name_____ Date_____

Sentence Punctuation

- Every sentence begins with a capital letter.
- Use the correct end mark for each sentence.

Add capital letters and punctuation to turn each set of words into a sentence. Answers may vary.

1. a tiger's teeth are long and sharp
   A tiger's teeth are long and sharp.

2. the tiger relies on them for hunting
   The tiger relies on them for hunting.

3. elephants have big, flat teeth
   Elephants have big, flat teeth.

4. they are good for eating grasses and hay
   They are good for eating grasses and hay.

5. plant-eaters have flat teeth for chewing and grinding
   Plant-eaters have flat teeth for chewing and grinding.

6. meat-eaters have long, pointed teeth for biting and tearing
   Meat-eaters have long, pointed teeth for biting and tearing.

7. animals' teeth match their diet
   Animals' teeth match their diet.

8. what do your teeth tell about your diet
   What do your teeth tell about your diet?

9. open wide
   Open wide!

10. what big teeth you have
    What big teeth you have!

28
Extension: Have pairs of students tape-record a brief conversation and then write down what they said, using capital letters and punctuation wherever needed.
Grade 4/Unit 1
Open Wide, Don't Bite! — 10

T52 *Annotated Workbooks*

Open Wide, Don't Bite! • GRAMMAR

Run-on Sentences

A. Correct these run-on sentences by separating them into two sentences.

1. A dentist was called to the zoo a tiger had a toothache.

   A dentist was called to the zoo. A tiger had a toothache.

2. The tiger's face was swollen it would not eat.

   The tiger's face was swollen. It would not eat.

3. The dentist fixed the tooth he did not pull it.

   The dentist fixed the tooth. He did not pull it.

4. The tiger felt better he was hungry again.

   The tiger felt better. He was hungry again.

5. The dentist went back to his office human patients were waiting.

   The dentist went back to his office. Human patients were waiting.

B. Rewrite the following run-on sentences as compound or complex sentences.

6. The bear growled it had a toothache.

   The bear growled because it had a toothache.

7. It would grow weak the tooth could be fixed.

   It would grow weak unless the tooth could be fixed.

8. The dentist went to the zoo he heard about it.

   The dentist went to the zoo as soon as he heard about it.

9. The tooth had to come out it was infected.

   The tooth had to come out because it was infected.

10. The bear lost a tooth it felt much better.

    The bear lost a tooth, but it felt much better.

Correcting Sentences

- A **run-on sentence** joins together two or more sentences that should be written separately.
- You can correct a run-on sentence by separating two complete ideas into two sentences.
- You can correct a run-on sentence by rewriting it as a compound or complex sentence.

Mechanics

- Begin every sentence with a capital letter.
- Use the correct end mark for each sentence.

Add capital letters and punctuation marks to turn each group of words into one or two sentences that tell about the picture above them.

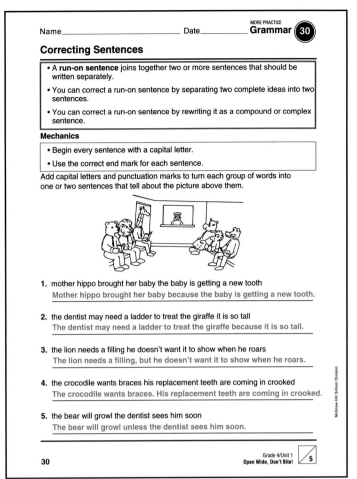

1. mother hippo brought her baby the baby is getting a new tooth

   Mother hippo brought her baby because the baby is getting a new tooth.

2. the dentist may need a ladder to treat the giraffe it is so tall

   The dentist may need a ladder to treat the giraffe because it is so tall.

3. the lion needs a filling he doesn't want it to show when he roars

   The lion needs a filling, but he doesn't want it to show when he roars.

4. the crocodile wants braces his replacement teeth are coming in crooked

   The crocodile wants braces. His replacement teeth are coming in crooked.

5. the bear will growl the dentist sees him soon

   The bear will growl unless the dentist sees him soon.

Open Wide, Don't Bite! • SPELLING

Words from Health

Fold back the paper along the dotted line. Use the blanks to write each word as it is read aloud. When you finish the test, unfold the paper. Use the list at the right to correct any spelling mistakes. Practice the words that you missed for the Posttest.

To Parents
Here are the results of your child's weekly spelling Pretest. You can help your child study for the Posttest by following these simple steps for each word on the list:

1. Read the word to your child.
2. Have your child write the word, saying each letter as it is written.
3. Say each letter of the word as your child checks the spelling.
4. If a mistake has been made, have your child read each letter of the correctly spelled word aloud, then repeat steps 1–3.

1. _____	1. dentist
2. _____	2. crown
3. _____	3. hospital
4. _____	4. medicine
5. _____	5. diet
6. _____	6. gums
7. _____	7. gland
8. _____	8. joint
9. _____	9. fever
10. _____	10. chewing
11. _____	11. brain
12. _____	12. cavity
13. _____	13. disease
14. _____	14. plaque
15. _____	15. vitamin
16. _____	16. ache
17. _____	17. dental
18. _____	18. clinic
19. _____	19. oral
20. _____	20. molars

Challenge Words

_____ fangs
_____ patients
_____ healthy
_____ reptiles
_____ skills

Words from Health

Using the Word Study Steps

1. LOOK at the word.
2. SAY the word aloud.
3. STUDY the letters in the word.
4. WRITE the word.
5. CHECK the word.

Did you spell the word right? If not, go back to step 1.

Spelling Tip
Keep an Alphabetical Personal Word List Notebook. Write words you often have trouble spelling.

Word Scramble
Unscramble each set of letters to make a spelling word.

1. wronc	crown	11. stentid	dentist
2. tojin	joint	12. vityca	cavity
3. whignec	chewing	13. mugs	gums
4. inbar	brain	14. slarom	molars
5. splohati	hospital	15. heac	ache
6. iedt	diet	16. refev	fever
7. edesias	disease	17. nideicem	medicine
8. niccil	clinic	18. loar	oral
9. nimtaiv	vitamin	19. ledant	dental
10. ndagl	gland	20. qlaupe	plaque

To Parents or Helpers
Using the Word Study Steps above as your child comes across any new words will help him or her learn to spell words effectively. Review the steps as you both go over this week's spelling words.
Go over the Spelling Tip with your child. Help him or her spell new words by practicing words written in a Personal Word List.
Help your child complete the spelling activity.

Words from Health

dentist	diet	fever	disease	dental
crown	gums	chewing	plaque	clinic
hospital	gland	brain	vitamin	oral
medicine	joint	cavity	ache	molars

Word Sort
Write the spelling words with these spelling patterns.

one syllable

1. crown
2. gums
3. gland
4. joint
5. brain
6. plaque
7. ache

two syllables

8. dentist
9. diet
10. fever
11. chewing
12. disease
13. dental
14. clinic
15. oral
16. molars

three syllables

17. hospital
18. medicine
19. cavity
20. vitamin

Rhyme Time
Write the spelling word that rhymes with each word below.

1. plane — brain
2. mental — dental
3. track — plaque
4. take — ache
5. sand — gland
6. gravity — cavity

Words from Health

dentist	diet	fever	disease	dental
crown	gums	chewing	plaque	clinic
hospital	gland	brain	vitamin	oral
medicine	joint	cavity	ache	molars

Part of the Group
Read the heading for each group of words. Then add the spelling word that belongs in each pair.

Parts of the Mouth

1. tongue, — gums
2. teeth, — molars

Other Parts of the Body

6. head, — brain
7. bone, — joint

Tooth Problems

3. pain, — ache
4. stains, — plaque
5. hole, — cavity

Where to Go for Help

8. doctor, — clinic
9. office, — dentist
10. emergency room, — hospital

What Does it Mean?
Write the spelling word that matches the meanings below.

11. having to do with teeth — dental
12. what you eat and drink — diet
13. having to do with the mouth — oral
14. an artificial tooth part — crown
15. grinding food with teeth — chewing
16. a harmful condition — disease
17. a high body temperature — fever
18. produces saliva — gland
19. drug to relieve pain — medicine
20. healthful part of foods — vitamin

Challenge Extension: Imagine you visit the office of an animal doctor. Write one sentence for each Challenge Word describing your visit.

Open Wide, Don't Bite! • SPELLING

Words from Health

Proofreading Activity

There are six spelling mistakes in the paragraph below. Circle the misspelled words. Write the words correctly on the lines below.

How do you know if a tiger has a tooth acke? Well, it may stop chooing and eating. It may have a feevr. Then it is time to call the animal dentest who will fix the tooth. Maybe the tiger has a cavty that needs to be filled. Maybe the tiger needs medecene to get better. Keepers at the zoo will make sure the tiger gets well.

1. _____ache_____   3. _____fever_____   5. _____cavity_____

2. _____chewing_____   4. _____dentist_____   6. _____medicine_____

Writing Activity

Pretend you are an animal dentist. Write a dental report about an animal whose teeth you just fixed. Use four spelling words in your writing.

_____

_____

_____

_____

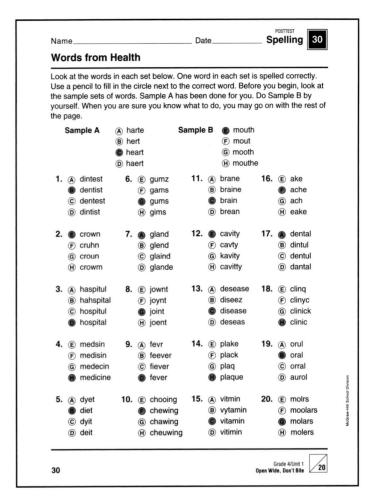

Words from Health

Look at the words in each set below. One word in each set is spelled correctly. Use a pencil to fill in the circle next to the correct word. Before you begin, look at the sample sets of words. Sample A has been done for you. Do Sample B by yourself. When you are sure you know what to do, you may go on with the rest of the page.

Sample A
- Ⓐ harte
- Ⓑ hert
- ● heart
- Ⓓ haert

Sample B
- ● mouth
- Ⓕ mout
- Ⓖ mooth
- Ⓗ mouthe

1.
- Ⓐ dintest
- ● dentist
- Ⓒ dentest
- Ⓓ dintist

2.
- ● crown
- Ⓕ cruhn
- Ⓖ croun
- Ⓗ crowm

3.
- Ⓐ haspitul
- Ⓑ hahspital
- Ⓒ hospitul
- Ⓓ hospital

4.
- Ⓔ medsin
- Ⓕ medisin
- Ⓖ medecin
- Ⓗ medicine

5.
- Ⓐ dyet
- ● diet
- Ⓒ dyit
- Ⓓ deit

6.
- Ⓔ gumz
- Ⓕ gams
- Ⓖ gums
- Ⓗ gims

7.
- Ⓐ gland
- Ⓑ glend
- Ⓒ glaind
- Ⓓ glande

8.
- Ⓔ jownt
- Ⓕ joynt
- ● joint
- Ⓗ joent

9.
- Ⓐ fevr
- Ⓑ feever
- Ⓒ fiever
- Ⓓ fever

10.
- Ⓔ chooing
- Ⓕ chewing
- Ⓖ chawing
- Ⓗ cheuwing

11.
- Ⓐ brane
- Ⓑ braine
- Ⓒ brain
- Ⓓ brean

12.
- Ⓔ cavity
- Ⓕ cavvy
- Ⓖ kavity
- Ⓗ cavitty

13.
- Ⓐ desease
- Ⓑ diseez
- Ⓒ disease
- Ⓓ deseas

14.
- Ⓔ plake
- Ⓕ plack
- Ⓖ plaq
- Ⓗ plaque

15.
- Ⓐ vitmin
- Ⓑ vytamin
- Ⓒ vitamin
- Ⓓ vitimin

16.
- Ⓔ ake
- ● ache
- Ⓖ ach
- Ⓗ eake

17.
- Ⓐ dental
- Ⓑ dintul
- Ⓒ dentul
- Ⓓ dantal

18.
- Ⓔ clinq
- Ⓕ clinyc
- Ⓖ clinick
- ● clinic

19.
- Ⓐ orul
- Ⓑ oral
- Ⓒ orral
- Ⓓ aurol

20.
- Ⓔ molrs
- Ⓕ moolars
- Ⓖ molars
- Ⓗ molers

Unit 1 Review • PRACTICE and RETEACH

Name_____ Date_____ **Practice** 36

Unit 1 Vocabulary Review

A. Locate and circle the vocabulary words in the word puzzle below. Words can be spelled from left to right, right to left, top to bottom, bottom to top, and diagonally.

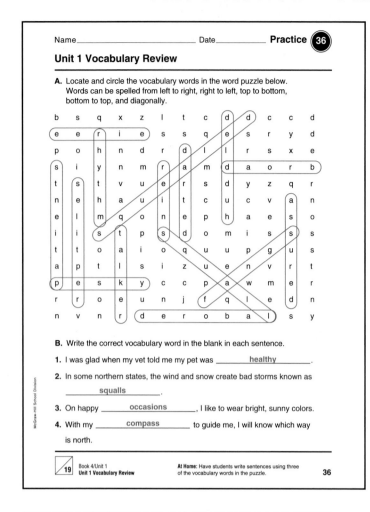

B. Write the correct vocabulary word in the blank in each sentence.

1. I was glad when my vet told me my pet was _____healthy_____.

2. In some northern states, the wind and snow create bad storms known as _____squalls_____.

3. On happy _____occasions_____, I like to wear bright, sunny colors.

4. With my _____compass_____ to guide me, I will know which way is north.

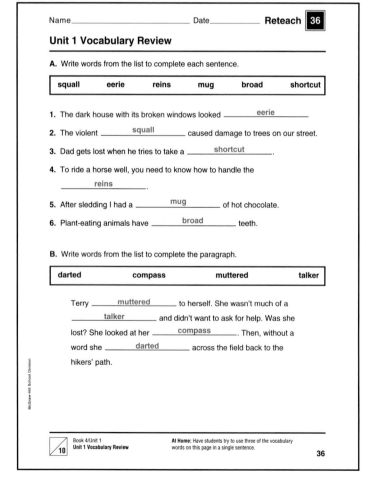

19 Book 4/Unit 1
Unit 1 Vocabulary Review

At Home: Have students write sentences using three of the vocabulary words in the puzzle.

36

Name_____ Date_____ **Practice** 37

Unit 1 Vocabulary Review

Answer each question using the underlined vocabulary word.

1. How can you feel <u>assured</u> that you will pass the test?
   I can feel assured that I will pass by studying hard.

2. Which path is the <u>shortcut</u> to your house?
   The path that goes through the park is the shortcut.

3. What does the weather person mean by a <u>squall</u>?
   The weather person is talking about a big wind.

4. How many <u>patients</u> will your doctor help today?
   My doctor may help as many as 20 patients.

5. Is it true that they <u>labored</u> hard to clean up the yard?
   Yes. They labored all morning and afternoon.

6. Has he learned the <u>skills</u> to be a great basketball player?
   He has great basketball skills, and he keeps working on them.

7. Where is that <u>eerie</u> and mournful sound coming from?
   That eerie sound is coming from the foghorn at the lighthouse.

8. Is the ice on the rink too rough and <u>jagged</u> for skating?
   No. It is only jagged around the edges of the rink.

9. What are the most important <u>occasions</u> in your life?
   My most important occasions are my birthday and Father's Day.

10. Did you mean to say that or was it <u>accidental</u>?
    It wasn't accidental. I meant what I said.

At Home: Have students write about something they did, using as many of the vocabulary words as possible.

37

Book 4/Unit 1
Unit 1 Vocabulary Review 10

Name_____ Date_____ **Reteach** 36

Unit 1 Vocabulary Review

A. Write words from the list to complete each sentence.

squall	eerie	reins	mug	broad	shortcut

1. The dark house with its broken windows looked _____eerie_____

2. The violent _____squall_____ caused damage to trees on our street.

3. Dad gets lost when he tries to take a _____shortcut_____.

4. To ride a horse well, you need to know how to handle the _____reins_____.

5. After sledding I had a _____mug_____ of hot chocolate.

6. Plant-eating animals have _____broad_____ teeth.

B. Write words from the list to complete the paragraph.

darted	compass	muttered	talker

Terry _____muttered_____ to herself. She wasn't much of a _____talker_____ and didn't want to ask for help. Was she lost? She looked at her _____compass_____. Then, without a word she _____darted_____ across the field back to the hikers' path.

10 Book 4/Unit 1
Unit 1 Vocabulary Review

At Home: Have students try to use three of the vocabulary words on this page in a single sentence.

36

Name_____ Date_____ **Reteach** 37

Unit 1 Vocabulary Review

A. Read each question. Choose a word from the list to answer the question. Write your answer on the line.

assured	fangs	nursery	patients	horizon

1. If you are on a boat and you see where the sky and sea meet, what are you seeing? _____horizon_____

2. If you see a tiger without its long front teeth, what is it missing? _____fangs_____

3. Where do newborn babies sleep in the hospital? _____nursery_____

4. If someone told you positively that you were right, what would you feel? _____assured_____

5. When people visit a doctor for treatment, what are they called? _____patients_____

B. Read each clue. Then find the vocabulary word in the row of letters and circle it.

shutters	overalls	labored	huddled	pesky

1. worked very hard   m a q (l a b o r e d) s e c v

2. crowded together   j (h u d d l e d) n e r s c

3. work clothes   t h u e s r (o v e r a l l s)

4. window covers   b a w c (s h u t t e r s) p a z

5. synonym for *annoying*   n o t m d (p e s k y) l a r j

37 **At Home:** Have students look for vocabulary in newspapers and magazines they read and keep a list of the sentences the words are used in.

Book 4/Unit 1
Unit 1 Vocabulary Review 10

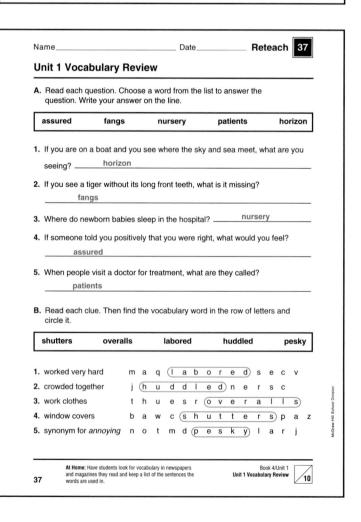

Unit 1 Review • EXTEND and GRAMMAR

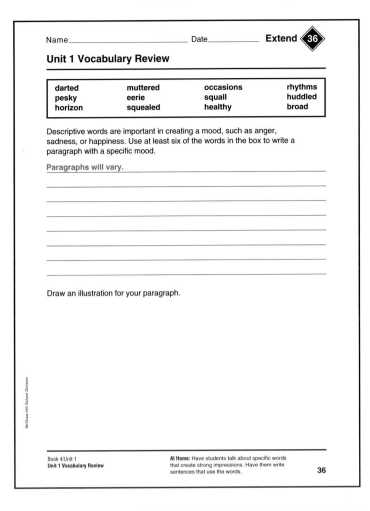

Name_____ Date_____ **Extend** 36

Unit 1 Vocabulary Review

darted	muttered	occasions	rhythms
pesky	eerie	squall	huddled
horizon	squealed	healthy	broad

Descriptive words are important in creating a mood, such as anger, sadness, or happiness. Use at least six of the words in the box to write a paragraph with a specific mood.

Paragraphs will vary.

_____

_____

_____

_____

_____

_____

_____

Draw an illustration for your paragraph.

Book 4/Unit 1
Unit 1 Vocabulary Review

At Home: Have students talk about specific words that create strong impressions. Have them write sentences that use the words.

36

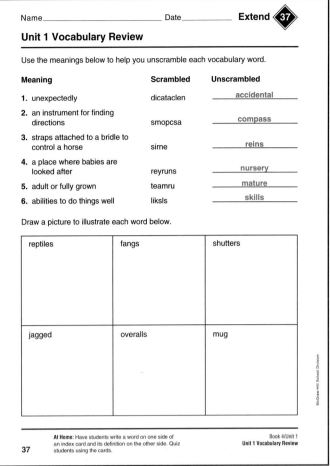

Name_____ Date_____ **Extend** 37

Unit 1 Vocabulary Review

Use the meanings below to help you unscramble each vocabulary word.

Meaning	Scrambled	Unscrambled
1. unexpectedly	dicataclen	accidental
2. an instrument for finding directions	smopcsa	compass
3. straps attached to a bridle to control a horse	sirne	reins
4. a place where babies are looked after	reyruns	nursery
5. adult or fully grown	teamru	mature
6. abilities to do things well	liksls	skills

Draw a picture to illustrate each word below.

reptiles	fangs	shutters
jagged	overalls	mug

37

At Home: Have students write a word on one side of an index card and its definition on the other side. Quiz students using the cards.

Book 4/Unit 1
Unit 1 Vocabulary Review

Name_____ Date_____ REVIEW **Grammar** 31

Sentences

Read each passage and look at the underlined sections. What kind of sentences are they? Circle your answers.

> Luke and his dad set out to find their own lake. <u>Did they ever find it?</u> They
> (1)
> sure did. One morning they woke up and there it was. <u>What a surprise!</u>
> (2)

1. A Statement
   (B) Question
   C Command
   D Exclamation

2. F Statement
   G Question
   H Command
   (J) Exclamation

> The road seemed to whisper to Amelia, "<u>Follow me.</u>" So she did. <u>She
> (3)
> discovered that it led to a big old tree.</u> She made that tree her own special
> (4)
> place, a place to come home to.

3. A Statement
   B Question
   (C) Command
   D Exclamation

4. (F) Statement
   G Question
   H Command
   J Exclamation

> When Sarah went to town alone, the children were afraid she was leaving.
> <u>They spent the whole day worrying.</u> It was almost dark when they heard the
> (5)
> wagon. <u>Sarah came back!</u>
> (6)

5. (A) Statement
   B Question
   C Command
   D Exclamation

6. F Statement
   G Question
   H Command
   (J) Exclamation

6
Grade 4/Unit 1
Reflections

31

Name_____ Date_____ REVIEW **Grammar** 32

Sentences

Read the passage and look at the underlined sentences. Is there a mistake? If there is, how do you correct it? Circle your answer.

> Baby seals used to be hunted for their beautiful white fur. <u>Those sweet baby
> (7)
> seals with big dark eyes.</u> People thought hunting them was terrible and cruel.
> <u>They worked to stop the hunting. They succeeded.</u>
> (8)

7. A Add a subject.
   (B) Add a predicate.
   C Join two sentences with *and.*
   D No mistake.

8. F Add a subject.
   G Add a predicate.
   (H) Join two sentences with *and.*
   J No mistake.

> Humans share lots of things with animals. <u>Might share a dentist.</u> <u>There are
> (9)
> dentists who have human patients. They have animal patients, too.</u>
> (10)

9. (A) Add a subject.
   B Add a predicate.
   C Join two sentences with *and.*
   D No mistake.

10. F Add a subject.
    G Add a predicate.
    (H) Join two sentences with *and.*
    J No mistake.

32

Grade 4/Unit 1
Reflections
10

Unit 1 Review • SPELLING

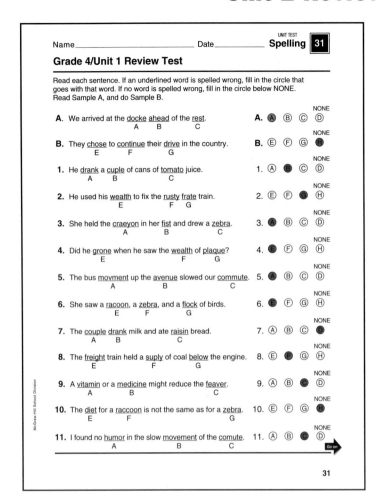

Name_____ Date_____

Grade 4/Unit 1 Review Test

Read each sentence. If an underlined word is spelled wrong, fill in the circle that goes with that word. If no word is spelled wrong, fill in the circle below NONE. Read Sample A, and do Sample B.

A. We arrived at the <u>docke</u> <u>ahead</u> of the <u>rest</u>.　　A. ⒶⒷ Ⓒ Ⓓ NONE
　　　　　　　A　　　　B　　　　C

B. They <u>chose</u> to <u>continue</u> their <u>drive</u> in the country.　B. Ⓔ Ⓕ Ⓖ ● NONE
　　E　　　　F　　　　G

1. He <u>drank</u> a <u>cuple</u> of cans of <u>tomato</u> juice.　1. Ⓐ ● Ⓒ Ⓓ NONE
　　A　　　B　　　　　　C

2. He used his <u>wealth</u> to fix the <u>rusty</u> <u>frate</u> train.　2. Ⓔ Ⓕ ● Ⓗ NONE
　　　　　　E　　　　　　　F　　G

3. She held the <u>craeyon</u> in her <u>fist</u> and drew a <u>zebra</u>.　3. ● Ⓑ Ⓒ Ⓓ NONE
　　　　　　　A　　　　　B　　　　　　C

4. Did he <u>grone</u> when he saw the <u>wealth</u> of <u>plaque</u>?　4. ● Ⓕ Ⓖ Ⓗ NONE
　　　　E　　　　　　　　　F　　　　G

5. The bus <u>movment</u> up the <u>avenue</u> slowed our <u>commute</u>.　5. ● Ⓑ Ⓒ Ⓓ NONE
　　　　　　A　　　　　B　　　　　　　　　C

6. She saw a <u>racoon</u>, a <u>zebra</u>, and a <u>flock</u> of birds.　6. ● Ⓕ Ⓖ Ⓗ NONE
　　　　　　E　　　　F　　　　　G

7. The <u>couple</u> <u>drank</u> milk and ate <u>raisin</u> bread.　7. Ⓐ Ⓑ Ⓒ ● NONE
　　　A　　B　　　　　　　C

8. The <u>freight</u> train held a <u>suply</u> of coal <u>below</u> the engine.　8. Ⓔ ● Ⓖ Ⓗ NONE
　　　E　　　　　　F　　　　G

9. A <u>vitamin</u> or a <u>medicine</u> might reduce the <u>feaver</u>.　9. Ⓐ Ⓑ ● Ⓓ NONE
　　A　　　　B　　　　　　　C

10. The <u>diet</u> for a <u>raccoon</u> is not the same as for a <u>zebra</u>.　10. Ⓔ Ⓕ Ⓖ ● NONE
　　　E　　　F　　　　　　　　　　G

11. I found no <u>humor</u> in the slow <u>movement</u> of the <u>comute</u>.　11. Ⓐ Ⓑ ● Ⓓ NONE
　　　　　A　　　　　B　　　　　C

Go on →

Name_____ Date_____

Grade 4 Unit 1 Review Test

12. He gave the <u>raccoon</u> some <u>medisin</u> to reduce its <u>fever</u>. 12. Ⓔ ● Ⓖ Ⓗ NONE
　　　　　　E　　　　　F　　　　　　　　G

13. A man with <u>humor</u> shared my <u>commute</u> up the <u>avenue</u>. 13. Ⓐ Ⓑ Ⓒ ● NONE
　　　　　A　　　　　　　B　　　　　　C

14. The <u>couple</u> had a <u>tytle</u> added to the <u>plaque</u>. 14. Ⓔ ● Ⓖ Ⓗ NONE
　　　E　　　　F　　　　　　G

15. I am on a <u>raizin</u> and <u>tomato</u> <u>diet</u>. 15. ● Ⓑ Ⓒ Ⓓ NONE
　　　　A　　　　B　　C

16. The <u>fever</u> caused the lady to <u>groan</u> and make a <u>fiste</u>. 16. Ⓔ Ⓕ ● Ⓗ NONE
　　　E　　　　　　　　F　　　　　　　G

17. She held a <u>rusty</u> nail and a <u>crayon</u> in her <u>fist</u>. 17. Ⓐ Ⓑ Ⓒ ● NONE
　　　　A　　　　　B　　　　　C

18. This <u>raisin</u> will <u>supply</u> you with a <u>vitamen</u>. 18. Ⓔ Ⓕ Ⓖ ● NONE
　　E　　　　F　　　　　　G

19. I saw the <u>movement</u> of the <u>flock</u> down the <u>avenu</u>. 19. Ⓐ Ⓑ ● Ⓓ NONE
　　　A　　　　B　　　　　C

20. This book's <u>title</u> is "<u>Wealth</u> and <u>Humer</u>." 20. Ⓔ Ⓕ ● Ⓗ NONE
　　　E　　　　F　　　G

21. He <u>drank</u> juice and took a <u>vitamin</u> during his <u>dyet</u>. 21. Ⓐ Ⓑ ● Ⓓ NONE
　　　A　　　　B　　　　　C

22. We heard a <u>rustie</u> wheel <u>groan</u> in the street <u>below</u>. 22. ● Ⓕ Ⓖ Ⓗ NONE
　　　E　　　　F　　　　　G

23. The <u>freight</u> train carried a <u>supply</u> of <u>medicine</u>. 23. Ⓐ Ⓑ Ⓒ NONE
　　A　　　　　B　　　　C

24. The <u>plaque</u> had a <u>title</u> that said "Best <u>Tomatoe</u>." 24. Ⓔ Ⓕ ● Ⓗ NONE
　　　E　　　　F　　　　　G

25. The <u>freight</u> train ran <u>beloew</u> the <u>flock</u> of birds. 25. Ⓐ ● Ⓒ Ⓓ NONE
　　A　　　　B　　　　C

Story Elements

OBJECTIVES Students will analyze character and setting by comparing and contrasting. They will explore various settings and characters through illustrations and descriptions.

Alternate Activities

Visual

CHARACTER COMPARISON IN THE ROUND

Materials: heavy construction paper, scissors, glue, crayons or markers

Have students create dioramas in the round to compare story characters.

- Have students brainstorm characteristics of two characters. Encourage them to think about ways the characters are alike and ways they are different.

- Ask students to cut out two equal circles from construction paper, about the size of a dinner plate. On one circle, have them draw and write about one character. On the other, have them draw and write about the other character.

- Show students how to fold a flap forward at the bottom of each circle. Have them glue the circles back to back to make the stand-up diorama.

- Encourage students to share their dioramas with classmates.
  ▶ **Spatial**

Kinesthetic

SETTING PROJECTION

Materials: overhead transparency film, overhead transparency markers

Have students draw a setting on an overhead transparency film. They will project the setting and use it as a background for a mini-dramatization.

- Organize students into small groups. Give each group an overhead transparency film.

- Encourage students to visualize a story scene whose setting was important to the story. Have them discuss why the setting played a key role in the scene.

- Ask students to work together to draw the setting on the overhead transparency film.

- Invite groups of students to project their drawing on the screen. Have them perform a mini-dramatization of the scene while they stand in front of the screen.
  ▶ **Bodily/Kinesthetic**

Auditory

MYSTERY SETTINGS

Have students describe to one another a setting of a memorable scene.

- Organize students into partners. Without revealing their choice to their partner, have each student think about a scene in which the setting was important to that part of the story.

- Have students take turns describing the setting for their partner. Encourage them to use descriptive language and details, explaining not only how the place looks, but also how it feels, sounds, and smells.

- Have partners guess the place being described and talk about how the scene might have been different had it occurred in a different place.
  ▶ **Linguistic**

See Reteach 1, 5, 15, 19

Parts of a Book

OBJECTIVES Students will explore parts of a book by writing captions, generating and sorting questions, and creating a music video about parts of a book.

Alternate Activities

Kinesthetic

TABLEAUS WITH CAPTIONS

 GROUP **Materials:** sentence strips, markers

Have students work together to create captions for tableaus.

- Organize students into small groups. Assign pairs of groups to work together.
- Have each pair of groups brainstorm a scene from the story that they would like to act out.
- Ask one group in each pair to arrange themselves in the tableau. Have the other group imagine that the tableau is a photo in a book and generate a caption for it.
- Invite one group member to record the caption on a sentence strip.
- Then have groups in each pair switch roles.
- Encourage all groups to perform their tableaus and display their assigned captions.
  ▶ Bodily/Kinesthetic

Visual

PARTS-OF-A-BOOK SORT

GROUP **Materials:** construction paper, markers, scissors

Have students create a pocket chart and questions to review parts of a book.

- Review the parts of a book, including table of contents, glossary, and index.
- Organize students into small groups.

- Have them create a mini-pocket chart from a piece of construction paper. Show them how to fold the piece of paper lengthwise and staple it in three sections to make pockets. Have students label each pocket: *table of contents, glossary, index.*

 WRITING Have students work together to write question cards that can be answered by telling which part of a book to use to find the information. For example, students might write, *Where would you find the meaning of* inferno?

- After groups generate six question cards, have them mix up the cards and exchange with another group. Have groups work together to read and sort the cards.
  ▶ Interpersonal

Auditory

PARTS-OF-A-BOOK MUSIC VIDEO

GROUP Have students work in groups to create a music video about a specific book part.

- Organize students into small groups and assign each group a part of a book: *glossary, table of contents, index,* or *captions.*
- Have students work together to create a "music video" dramatization using singing and movement to explain the function of their part of the book.
- Invite students to perform their music videos.
  ▶ Musical

See Reteach 4, 11, 18, 25, 32

Make Inferences

OBJECTIVES Students will make inferences by identifying common sounds on a tape, by viewing pictures that reveal a character's identity, and by noticing details in classmates' poses.

Alternate Activities

Auditory

SOUND ID

Materials: cassette recorder, cassette tapes

GROUP

Have students work together to identify recorded sounds.

- Prepare a cassette tape of common household or classroom sounds, such as water running, a pencil being sharpened, and so on.

- Ask students to listen to the tape and to make inferences to identify the sounds. Encourage students to discuss how they were able to identify each sound.

▶ **Interpersonal**

Kinesthetic

PANTOMIME SNAPSHOTS

GROUP

Have students make inferences about an activity as they see classmates posed, as if in a snapshot.

- Ask a volunteer to stand at the front of the room with eyes closed.

- Without naming the activity, pantomime an action such as eating, painting, or driving. Have students join you in the pantomime.

- Call "Snapshot!" and have students freeze in position. Have the volunteer look and make an inference to name the activity being performed.

▶ **Bodily/Kinesthetic**

Visual

CHARACTER COLLAGE

Materials: magazines, scissors

ONE

Have students cut pictures from magazines to create a character's collection of objects. Other students will make inferences about the character based on the photos.

- Have each student select a character from a story they have recently read. Encourage them to think about things associated with the person, such as things he or she wore, used as tools, and so on.

- Have students create a poster of pictures either drawn or cut from magazines to represent the person.

- Invite students to share their collages. Encourage other students to make inferences about the character represented based on the collection of pictures. Have students try to guess the identity of the character.

▶ **Spatial**

See Reteach 6, 13, 27

Multiple-Meaning Words

OBJECTIVES Students will provide definitions for multiple-meaning words by participating in a "game show," playing a variation of hopscotch, and creating a pull-through manipulative.

Alternate Activities

Visual

MULTIPLE-MEANING PULL-THROUGHS

Materials: oak tag, markers, paper, scissors

ONE Have students make a pull-through game to use multiple-meaning words in context.

- Cut a square of oak tag for each student. Show them how to cut two parallel slits in the cutout. Give each student a strip of paper the same width as the slits.

- Have students choose a multiple-meaning word with at least three meanings.

- Show students how to feed the paper strip through the slits in the square to reveal one area at a time. Have them write one definition in each area.

- Have students use their strips to practice using the word in sentences according to its meaning.
  ▶ **Spatial**

Auditory

MULTIPLE-MEANING WORD GAME SHOW

Materials: index cards, marker, timer

PARTNERS Students will provide definitions for multiple-meaning words in a timed segment.

- On separate index cards, write multiple-meaning words.

- Organize students into pairs, and have one pair play the game at a time.

- Set the timer for one minute. Show a word card. When partners list at least two meanings for the word, they earn a point. Have partners play to see how many points they can earn in one minute.
  ▶ **Linguistic**

Kinesthetic

MULTIPLE-MEANING HOPSCOTCH

Materials: chalk; stone or other marker

GROUP Students will play a variation of hopscotch and use multiple-meaning words in sentences.

- In an outdoor area, show students how to draw a hopscotch grid with four squares. In each square, write a multiple-meaning word.

- Have groups of students take turns playing the game. Students must use the word their marker lands on in a sentence. As other students land on the same word, encourage them to use another meaning of the word.
  ▶ **Bodily/Kinesthetic**

See Reteach 7, 28, 34

Problem and Solution

OBJECTIVES Students will list examples of problems and solutions from literature. They will attempt to solve a problem both independently and in a group, and compare the two approaches.

Alternate Activities

Auditory

EXAMPLES-FROM-LITERATURE GAME

GROUP **Materials:** index cards, markers

Assign groups to provide examples of either problems or solutions from literature they have read. Other groups will respond by naming the corresponding solutions or problems.

- Organize students into two groups and assign them to brainstorm either problems or solutions. Encourage students to think about examples in literature they have read. Have one group member record on index cards the examples the group generates.

- Create a *Problem-Solution* grid on chart paper. Have groups take turns sharing an example and placing it in the correct place on the chart. Have members of the other group write the corresponding problem or solution to complete the chart.
  ▶ **Linguistic**

Kinesthetic

PUZZLING PROBLEMS AND SOLUTIONS

GROUP **Materials:** pattern blocks

Have students work independently, then in a group, to solve a problem with pattern blocks. They will compare the two approaches to problem solving.

- Set up a center with pattern blocks and a complex pattern for students to replicate. Have students rotate through the center independently and attempt to solve the problem by creating the pattern shown.

- Then organize students into small groups. Provide each group with pattern blocks and a new, equally challenging pattern to replicate. Have students work together to solve the problem.
  ▶ **Logical/Mathematical**

Visual

"TO DO" LISTS

ONE **Materials:** paper, pencils

Have students create a "to do" list for themselves, a story character, or a person from history. The list should show problems the person wants to solve and possible solutions.

- Ask students to think about a problem they, a story character, or a person from history has had.

WRITING Have students write a "to do" list for the person of their choice that details problems and suggests possible solutions. Encourage students to prioritize the items on their lists.

- Invite students to display their lists.
  ▶ **Logical/Mathematical**

See Reteach 8, 12, 20, 29

Antonyms and Synonyms

OBJECTIVES **Students will pantomime antonym and synonym word pairs, create a synonym chain, and use antonyms to retell an oral story.**

Alternate Activities

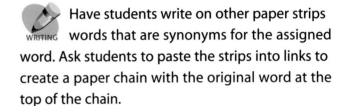

Kinesthetic

ANTONYM AND SYNONYM ALIEN ADVENTURES

 PARTNERS Have students pantomime pairs of words to emphasize how they are similar or opposite.

- Organize students into pairs. Have them imagine they are in charge of teaching an outer-space alien as much of the English language as they can in ten minutes.

- Explain to students that this particular type of alien learns best by learning words in pairs that are antonyms or synonyms.

- Have students pretend to teach the alien words by pantomiming the meanings of word pairs, such as *high–low, fast–slow, cry–weep, smile–grin.*
  ▶ **Bodily/Kinesthetic**

Visual

SYNONYM CHAINS

 GROUP **Materials:** construction paper, markers
Have students work together to make a paper chain to link words that are synonyms.

- Organize students into groups. Give each group a strip of paper that has a word written on it. Choose words for which there are many synonyms, such as *nice, good, walk.*

 WRITING Have students write on other paper strips words that are synonyms for the assigned word. Ask students to paste the strips into links to create a paper chain with the original word at the top of the chain.

- Display the chains in the classroom. Encourage students to refer to them during independent writing assignments.
  ▶ **Spatial**

Auditory

HEARING THE OPPOSITE

 PARTNERS Have students rephrase sentences to state the opposite.

- Organize students into pairs. Give students a story starter and encourage them to collaborate to tell two oral stories.

- The first partner begins the story. At a stopping point, the other partner takes a turn, retelling the story from the beginning, and including as many antonyms as possible.

- The first partner continues with the original story. Then the other partner retells it with antonyms, until the two stories are complete.
  ▶ **Linguistic**

See Reteach 14, 21, 35

Main Idea

OBJECTIVES Students will use main idea and supporting details to tell oral stories. They will identify main idea and supporting details through mimed presentations and through writing.

Auditory

COLLABORATIVE STORIES

Materials: index cards, markers

GROUP Have students collaborate to tell oral stories about a provided main idea. They will weave together the main idea and supporting details.

• Prepare index cards with main ideas for stories, such as *A girl and her mother learn about one another while stargazing*; or, *A family survives a house fire because of planning and practicing.*

• Organize students into small groups. Have each group select a card and read it aloud. Have group members take turns contributing a sentence to the story to build on the main idea with supporting details.

▶ **Interpersonal**

Visual

TRI-FOLDS

Materials: cardboard or oak tag, markers

ONE Have students create tri-fold displays to show the main idea and supporting details of a story.

• Have each student select a story they have recently read and think about the main idea and supporting details.

• Give each student a piece of oak tag or cardboard. Have them fold it to divide it into thirds.

WRITING In the center section, have students write to summarize the main idea of the story. Suggest that students create illustrations to enhance their writing. On the outer folds, have students write about and draw supporting details of the story.

• Invite students to share and display their boards.

▶ **Linguistic**

Kinesthetic

MAIN-IDEA MIME

Materials: stories or articles

GROUP Students will read a brief passage and work together to present a pantomime of the main idea. Other students will try to guess the content of the dramatization.

• Organize students into small groups. Distribute to each group a brief story or nonfiction article. Have students read the passage and discuss the main idea.

• Ask students to work together to present a pantomime of the main idea for classmates. Encourage classmates to guess what each group is dramatizing.

• Have each group read its passage aloud and verbalize the main idea.

▶ **Bodily/Kinesthetic**

See Reteach 22, 26, 33

A Communication Tool

Although typewriters and computers are readily available, many situations continue to require handwriting. Tasks such as keeping journals, completing forms, taking notes, making shopping or organizational lists, and the ability to read hand-written manuscript or cursive writing are a few examples of practical application of this skill.

BEFORE YOU BEGIN

Before children begin to write, certain fine motor skills need to be developed. Examples of activities that can be used as warm-up activities are:

- **Simon Says** Play a game of Simon Says using just finger positions.
- **Finger Plays and Songs** Sing songs that use Signed English, American Sign Language or finger spelling.
- **Mazes** Mazes are available in a wide range of difficulty. You can also create mazes that allow children to move their writing instruments from left to right.

Determining Handedness

Keys to determining handedness in a child:

- Which hand does the child eat with? This is the hand that is likely to become the dominant hand.
- Does the child start coloring with one hand and then switch to the other? This may be due to fatigue rather than lack of hand preference.
- Does the child cross midline to pick things up or use the closest hand? Place items directly in front of the child to see if one hand is preferred.
- Does the child do better with one hand or the other?

The Mechanics of Writing

DESK AND CHAIR

- Chair height should allow for the feet to rest flat on the floor.
- Desk height should be two inches above the level of the elbows when the child is sitting.
- The chair should be pulled in allowing for an inch of space between the child's abdomen and the desk.
- Children sit erect with the elbows resting on the desk.
- Children should have models of letters on the desk or at eye level, not above their heads.

PAPER POSITION

- **Right-handed children** should turn the paper so that 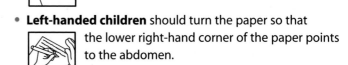 the lower left-hand corner of the paper points to the abdomen.

- **Left-handed children** should turn the paper so that the lower right-hand corner of the paper points to the abdomen.

- The nondominant hand should anchor the paper near the top so that the paper doesn't slide.

- The paper should be moved up as the child nears the bottom of the paper. Many children won't think of this and may let their arms hang off the desk when they reach the bottom of a page.

The Writing Instrument Grasp

For handwriting to be functional, the writing instrument must be held in a way that allows for fluid dynamic movement.

FUNCTIONAL GRASP PATTERNS

- **Tripod Grasp** With open web space, the writing instrument is held with the tip of the thumb and the index finger and rests against the side of the third finger. The thumb and index finger form a circle.

- **Quadrupod Grasp** With open web space, the writing instrument is held with the tip of the thumb and index finger and rests against the fourth finger. The thumb and index finger form a circle.

INCORRECT GRASP PATTERNS

- **Fisted Grasp** The writing instrument is held in a fisted hand.

- **Pronated Grasp** The writing instrument is held diagonally within the hand with the tips of the thumb and index finger on the writing instrument but with no support from other fingers.

- **Five-Finger Grasp** The writing instrument is held with the tips of all five fingers.

TO CORRECT WRITING INSTRUMENT GRASPS

- Have children play counting games with an eye dropper and water.
- Have children pick up small objects with a tweezer.
- Do counting games with children picking up small coins using just the thumb and index finger.

FLEXED OR HOOKED WRIST

- The writing instrument can be held in a variety of grasps with the wrist flexed or bent. This is typically seen with left-handed writers but is also present in some right-handed writers. To correct wrist position, have children check their writing posture and paper placement.

Evaluation Checklist

Functional writing is made up of two elements, legibility and functional speed.

LEGIBILITY

MANUSCRIPT

Formation and Strokes

- ☑ Does the child begin letters at the top?
- ☑ Do circles close?
- ☑ Are the horizontal lines straight?
- ☑ Do circular shapes and extender and descender lines touch?
- ☑ Are the heights of all upper-case letters equal?
- ☑ Are the heights of all lower-case letters equal?
- ☑ Are the lengths of the extenders and descenders the same for all letters?

Directionality

- ☑ Are letters and words formed from left to right?
- ☑ Are letters and words formed from top to bottom?

Spacing

- ☑ Are the spaces between letters equidistant?
- ☑ Are the spaces between words equidistant?
- ☑ Do the letters rest on the line?
- ☑ Are the top, bottom and side margins even?

CURSIVE

Formation and Strokes

- ☑ Do circular shapes close?
- ☑ Are the downstrokes parallel?
- ☑ Do circular shapes and downstroke lines touch?
- ☑ Are the heights of all upper-case letters equal?
- ☑ Are the heights of all lower-case letters equal?
- ☑ Are the lengths of the extenders and descenders the same for all letters?
- ☑ Do the letters which finish at the top join the next letter? (*l, o, v, w*)
- ☑ Do the letters which finish at the bottom join the next letter? (*a, c, d, h, i, k, l, m, n, r, s, t, u, x*)
- ☑ Do letters with descenders join the next letter? (*f, g, j, p, q, y, z*)
- ☑ Do all letters touch the line?
- ☑ Is the vertical slant of all letters consistent?

Directionality

- ☑ Are letters and words formed from left to right?
- ☑ Are letters and words formed from top to bottom?

Spacing

- ☑ Are the spaces between letters equidistant?
- ☑ Are the spaces between words equidistant?
- ☑ Do the letters rest on the line?
- ☑ Are the top, bottom and side margins even?

SPEED

The prettiest handwriting is not functional for classroom work if it takes the child three times longer than the rest of the class to complete work assignments. After the children have been introduced to writing individual letters, begin to add time limitations to the completion of copying or writing assignments. Then check the child's work for legibility.

Handwriting Models—Manuscript

A B C D E F G H

I J K L M N O P

Q R S T U V W

X Y Z

a b c d e f g h

i j k l m n o p

q r s t u v w

x y z

Handwriting Models—Cursive

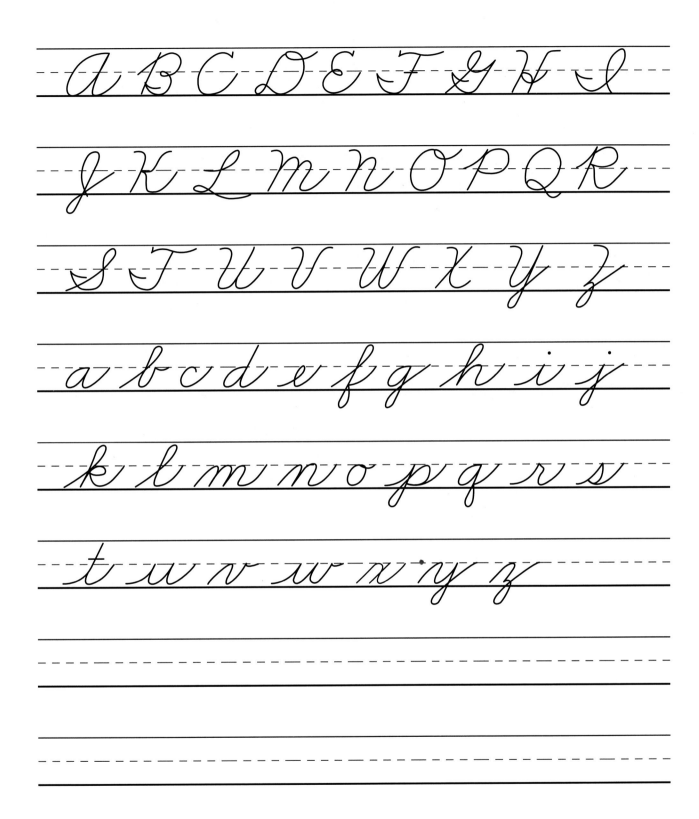

Handwriting Models—Slant

A B C D E F G H

I J K L M N O P

Q R S T U V W

X Y Z

a b c d e f g h

i j k l m n o p

q r s t u v w

x y z

Handwriting Practice

Selection Titles | Honors, Prizes, and Awards

TO
Unit 1, p. 16
by *Lee Bennett Hopkins*

Poet: Lee Bennett Hopkins, winner of Golden Kite Honor Book Award (1995), Christopher Award (1996) for *Been to Yesterday: Poems of a Life*

THE LOST LAKE
Unit 1, p. 20
by *Allen Say*

Author/Illustrator: Allen Say, winner of Christopher Award (1985) for *How My Parents Learned to Eat*; Boston Globe-Horn Book Award (1988), Caldecott Honor, ALA Notable (1989) for *The Boy of the Three-Year Nap*; Caldecott Medal, Boston Globe-Horn Book Award, ALA Notable, New York Times Best Illustrated (1994) for *Grandfather's Journey*

AMELIA'S ROAD
Unit 1, p. 44
by *Linda Jacobs Altman*
Illustrated by *Enrique O. Sanchez*

Illustrator: Enrique O. Sanchez, winner of Parent's Choice Award (1993) for *Abuela's Weave*

SARAH, PLAIN AND TALL
Unit 1, p. 68
by *Patricia MacLachlan*
Illustrated by *Burton Silverman*

Golden Kite Award for Fiction, IRA-CBC Children's Choice, School Library Best of the Best (1985), Newbery Medal, Christopher Award, Scott O'Dell Historical Fiction Award (1986)

SEAL JOURNEY
Unit 1, p. 96
by *Richard and Jonah Sobol*
Photographs by *Richard Sobol*

Outstanding Science Trade Book for Children (1994)

JUSTIN AND THE BEST BISCUITS IN THE WORLD
Unit 2, p. 134
by *Mildred Pitts Walter*
Illustrated by *Floyd Cooper*

Coretta Scott King Award (1987)
Illustrator: Floyd Cooper, winner of Coretta Scott King Honor (1995) for *Meet Danitra Brown*

JUST A DREAM
Unit 2, p. 160
by *Chris Van Allsburg*

Author/Illustrator: Chris Van Allsburg, winner of ALA Notable, Caldecott Medal (1982) for *Jumanji*; ALA Notable (1984) for *The Wreck of the Zephyr*; ALA Notable, Boston Globe-Horn Book Honor, Caldecott Medal (1986) for *The Polar Express*; NSTA Outstanding Science Trade Book for Children (1988), IRA-CBC Children's Choice (1989) for *Two Bad Ants*; ALA Notable (1994) for *The Sweetest Fig*

Selection Titles	Honors, Prizes, and Awards
LEAH'S PONY Unit 2, p. 192 by *Elizabeth Friedrich* Illustrated by *Michael Garland*	**National Council of Trade Books Award, Golden Kite Award, Parent's Magazine Best Book of the Year, IRA Teacher's Choice Award (1997), Texas Bluebonnet Award (1997-98)**
BASEBALL SAVED US Unit 2, p. 218 by *Ken Mochizuki* Illustrated by *Dom Lee*	**Parent's Choice Award (1993)**
THE HATMAKER'S SIGN Unit 3, p. 258 by *Candace Fleming* Illustrated by *Robert Andrew Parker*	**Illustrator: Robert Andrew Parker,** winner of Caldecott Honor (1970) for *Pop Corn and Ma Goodness*
PAT CUMMINGS: MY STORY Unit 3, p. 284 by *Pat Cummings*	**Boston Globe-Horn Book Award (1992), ALA Notable (1993)**
GRASS SANDALS: THE TRAVELS OF BASHO Unit 3, p. 300 by *Dawnine Spivak* Illustrated by *Demi*	**National Council of Trade Books Award (1998)** **Illustrator: Demi,** winner of the New York Times Best Illustrated Children's Books of the Year (1985) for *The Nightingale*
A PLACE CALLED FREEDOM Unit 3, p. 334 by *Scott Russell Sanders* Illustrated by *Thomas B. Allen*	**Notable Children's Book in the Field of Social Studies (1998)**
FINAL CURVE Unit 4, p. 372 by *Langston Hughes*	**Poet: Langston Hughes,** winner of Witter Bynner Prize (1926); Harmon Foundation Literature Award (1931); Guggenheim Fellowship (1935); American Academy of Arts and Letters Grant (1946); Spingarn Medal (1960)

Selection Titles	Honors, Prizes, and Awards
 **SCRUFFY** Unit 4, p. 376 by *Jim Brandenburg*	**Author/Photographer: Jim Brandenburg,** winner ALA Best Book for Young Adults Award, Orbis Picture Award for Outstanding Non-fiction Honor Book, Minnesota Book Award (1994) for *To the Top of the World: Adventures with Arctic Wolves*; Parent's Choice Award, Outstanding Science Trade Book for Children, John Burroughs List of Outstanding Nature Books for Children (1995) for *Sand and Fog: Adventures in South Africa*; ALA Best Book for Young Adults (1996) for *An American Safari: Adventures on the North American Prairie*
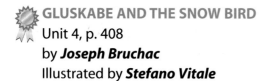 **GLUSKABE AND THE SNOW BIRD** Unit 4, p. 408 by *Joseph Bruchac* Illustrated by *Stefano Vitale*	**Author: Joseph Bruchac,** winner of the Skipping Stones Honor Award for Multicultural Children's Literature (1997) for *Four Ancestors*
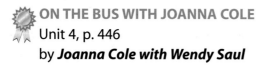 **ON THE BUS WITH JOANNA COLE** Unit 4, p. 446 by *Joanna Cole with Wendy Saul*	**Author: Joanna Cole,** winner of Washington Children's Choice Picture Book Award, Colorado Children's Book Award (1989) for *The Magic School Bus at the Waterworks*; Parenting's Reading Magic Awards (1989) for *The Magic School Bus Inside the Human Body*
 **TORTILLAS LIKE AFRICA** Unit 4, p. 482 by *Gary Soto*	**Poet: Gary Soto,** winner of Academy of American Poets Award (1975); American Book Award (1984) for *Living Up the Street*; California Library Association's John And Patricia Beatty Award, Best Books for Young Adults Awards (1991) for *Baseball in April and Other Stories*; Américas Book Award, Honorable Mention (1995) for *Chato's Kitchen*; Américas Book Award, Commended List (1995) for *Canto Familiar*; (1996) for *The Old Man and His Door*; (1997) for *Buried Onions*
 **HOW TO TELL THE TOP OF A HILL** Unit 5, p. 484 by *John Ciardi*	**Poet: John Ciardi,** winner of New York Times Best Illustrated Children's Books of the Year (1959) for *The Reason for the Pelican*; (1960) for *Scruffy The Pup*; (1966) for *The Monster Den: Or, Look What Happened at My House—and to It*; ALA Best Book Award (1961) for *I Met a Man*; (1963) for *John Plenty and Fiddler Dan: A New Fable of the Grasshopper and the Ant*; National Council of Teachers of English Award for Excellence in Poetry for Children (1982)

Selection Titles	Honors, Prizes, and Awards
MOM'S BEST FRIEND Unit 5, p. 518 by *Sally Hobart Alexander* Photographs by *George Ancona*	**Author: Sally Hobart Alexander**, winner of Christopher Award (1995) for *Taking Hold: My Journey Into Blindness*
YEH-SHEN Unit 5, p. 570 retold by **Ai-Ling Louie** Illustrated by **Ed Young**	**ALA Notable, School Library Journal Best Books of the Year (1982), Boston Globe-Horn Book Honor (1983)** **Illustrator: Ed Young,** winner of Caldecott Honor (1968) for *The Emperor and the Kite*; Boston Globe-Horn Book Honor (1984) for *The Double Life of Pocahontas*; NCSS Notable Children's Book Award (1989), Caldecott Medal, Boston Globe-Horn Book Award, ALA Notable (1990) for *Lon Po Po*; ALA Notable (1991) for *Mice Are Nice*; ALA Notable (1992) for *All Of You Was Singing*; ALA Notable, Boston Globe-Horn Book Award, Caldecott Honor (1993) for *Seven Blind Mice;* ALA Notable (1994) for *Sadako*; National Council for Social Studies Notable Children's Book Awards (1998) for *Genesis* and *Voices of the Heart*
TEAMMATES Unit 6, p. 616 by *Peter Golenbock* Illustrated by **Paul Bacon**	**Author: Peter Golenbock,** winner of National Council of Trade Books in Social Studies Award; Redbook Children's Picture Book Award (1990)
THE MALACHITE PALACE Unit 6, p. 634 by *Alma Flor Ada* Illustrated by *Leonid Gore*	**Author: Alma Flor Ada,** winner of Christopher Award (1992) for *The Gold Coin*
WHALES Unit 6, p. 694 by *Seymour Simon*	**Author: Seymour Simon,** winner of ALA Notable (1985) for *Moon*; (1986) for *Saturn*; (1987) for *Mars*; (1993) for *Our Solar System* and *Snakes*; Texas Blue Bonnet Master List (1996–97) for *Sharks*; NSTA Outstanding Science Tradebook for Children (1997) for *The Heart*
DECISIONS Unit 6, p. 724 by *Angela Shelf Medearis*	**Poet: Angela Shelf Medearis,** winner IRA-Teacher's Choice Award, Primary Grades (1995) for *Our People*

THE LOST LAKE

AMELIA'S ROAD

Trade Books

Additional fiction and nonfiction trade books related to each selection can be shared with students throughout the unit.

Remember to allow time each day for students in small and large groups to share and discuss favorite books and authors. Also have students choose their own reading based on their preference of genre and knowledge of author's style and themes.

Marven of the Great North Woods
Kathryn Lasky, illustrated by Kevin Hawkes (Harcourt Brace, 1997)

Marven experiences life in a logging camp when his parents send him away to escape the influenza epidemic of 1918. *Historical Fiction*

Like Jake and Me
Mavis Jukes, illustrated by Lloyd Bloom (Alfred A. Knopf, 1987)

Filled with admiration but somewhat intimidated by his stepfather, Alex learns that everyone is afraid of something and is given the opportunity to show his own courage. *Realistic Fiction*

Joey Pigza Loses Control
Jack Gantos (Farrar, Straus and Giroux, 2000)

In this Newbery Honor Book, Joey Pigza becomes reacquainted with his father during a six-week summertime visit. *Realistic Fiction*

The Lotus Seed
Sherry Garland, illustrated by Tatsuro Kiuchi (Voyager Picture Book, 1997)

Forced to leave Vietnam, a young girl takes a lotus seed with her to America. When finally planted by her grandson, it blossoms with beauty and hope. *Realistic Fiction*

Going Home
Eve Bunting, illustrated by David Diaz (HarperCollins, 1996)

When migrant parents take the family back to their Mexican village for Christmas, the children experience the richness of their heritage. *Realistic Fiction*

Under the Royal Palms
Alma Flor Ada (Atheneum Books, 1998)

Reading this book—a collection of stories and reminiscences from the author's childhood on the island of Cuba—may help children discover the stories of their own lives. *Autobiography*

Technology

Multimedia resources can be used to enhance students' understanding of the selections.

Remind students to compare the film version of a favorite book with the book itself.

 Runaway Ralph *((SVE/Churchill) Video, 40 min.* Ralph runs away and is caught up in many adventures.

 Three Days on a River in a Red Canoe *(GPN/Reading Rainbow) Video, 30 min.* Camping out proves to be both fun and exciting.

 Meanwhile Back at the Ranch *(GPN/Reading Rainbow) Video, 30 min.* When Rancher Hicks goes to town in search of excitement, he misses all the excitement that is going on back home.

 Hispanic Americans Tell Their Story *(SVE/Churchill) Video, 13 min.* Famous Hispanic Americans share their life stories and experiences.

 Living on a String *(Phoenix/BFA) Video, 25 min.* Two boys from the south island of New Zealand share stories about their lives.

 Victor *(SVE/Churchill) Video, 27 min.* A young Mexican boy faces the everyday difficulties of life when his family emigrates to the United States.

SARAH, PLAIN AND TALL

Keepers
Jeri Hanel Watts, illustrated by Felicia Marshall (Lee & Low, 1997)

Kenyon's love of baseball, his grandmother, and the wonderful stories she tells combine to weave a tale of how he becomes the next "keeper" in his family. *Realistic Fiction*

Skylark
Patricia MacLachlan (HarperTrophy, 1997)

When the popular characters from *Sarah, Plain and Tall* are plagued by drought, Sarah takes the children to her home in Maine, where they experience the sea. *Historical Fiction*

On the Banks of Plum Creek
Laura Ingalls Wilder, illustrated by Garth Williams (HarperCollins, 1976)

Leaving the little house on the prairie, Laura and her family experience a new, though not uneventful, way of life in Minnesota. *Autobiographical Story*

 Sarah, Plain and Tall (SRA/McGraw-Hill) Video, 29 min. A dramatization of the story.

 Sarah, Plain and Tall (Hallmark Home Entertainment) Video, 98 min. An award-winning adaptation of the novel by Patricia MacLachlan.

 Sarah, Plain and Tall, Write On! Series (Educational Software) Computer software Apple, Macintosh, IBM PC. A writing program based on *Sarah, Plain and Tall.*

SEAL JOURNEY

Seal Surfer
Michael Foreman (Harcourt Brace, 1996)

After witnessing the birth of a seal, Ben develops a special relationship with a seal and discovers they have a lot in common. *Realistic Fiction*

Antarctic Journal
Jennifer Owings Dewey (HarperCollins, 2001)

The author recounts her experiences in the great Antarctic wilderness, where she spent four months at a research station writing and drawing. *Nonfiction*

Our Wet World
Sneed B. Collard III, illustrated by James M. Needham (Charlesbridge, 1998)

An overview of Earth's diverse and beautiful underwater ecosystems. *Nonfiction*

 Seals (SVE/Churchill) Video, 22 min. Shows seals' migration and social patterns.

 Jack, the Seal, and the Sea (GPN/Reading Rainbow) Video, 30 min. A man finds an ailing seal and learns the necessity of preserving the oceans and marine life.

 The Arctic (SVE/Churchill) Video, 13 min. A visit to the Arctic during spring when many of the animals there are raising their offspring.

OPEN WIDE, DON'T BITE!

I Want to Be a Veterinarian
Stephanie Maze and Catherine O'Neill Grace (Harcourt, 1999)

Filled with photographs and information about veterinary medicine, this book talks about different kinds of careers in animal healthcare. *Nonfiction*

Animal Rescue:
The Best Job There Is
Susan E. Goodman (Simon & Schuster, 2000)

John Walsh travels the world rescuing animals from floods, earthquakes, and fires. This book recounts some of his adventures. *Biography*

Tooth Decay and Cavities
Dr. Alvin Silverstein, et al. (Franklin Watts, 2000)

An easy-to-read, well-presented book on dental care, with just the right number of facts, illustrations, and diagrams. *Nonfiction*

 Dive to the Coral Reefs (GPN/Reading Rainbow) Video, 30 min. A "reef doctor" recounts his experiences repairing damaged coral reefs.

 The Little Animal Doctor (Phoenix/BFA) Video, 25 min. Brett talks about his experiences living and working in an animal sanctuary.

 I Can Be an Animal Doctor (Cloud 9, distributed by LibraryVideo) CD-ROM, Windows, Macintosh. Students interact with on-screen animals to see what it takes to become a veterinarian.

Publishers Directory

Aladdin Paperbacks
(Imprint of Simon & Schuster Children's Publishing)

Annick Press
(Imprint of Firefly, Ltd.)

Atheneum
(Imprint of Simon & Schuster Children's Publishing)

Avon Books
(Division of Hearst Corp.)
1350 Ave. of the Americas
New York, NY 10019
(212) 261-6800 • (800) 238-0658
Fax (800) 223-0239
www.avonbooks.com

Bantam Doubleday Dell Books for Young Readers
(Imprint of Random House)

Beech Tree Books
(Imprint of William Morrow & Co.)

Blackbirch Press
260 Amity Road
Woodbridge, CT 06525
(203) 387-7525 • (800) 831-9183
www.blackbirch.com

Blue Sky Press
(Imprint of Scholastic)

Bradbury Press
(Imprint of Simon & Schuster Children's Publishing)

BridgeWater Books
(Distributed by Penguin Putnam Inc.)

Candlewick Press
2067 Massachusetts Avenue
Cambridge, MA 02140
(617) 661-3330 • Fax (617) 661-0565
www.candlewick.com

Carolrhoda Books
(Division of Lerner Publications Co.)

Cartwheel Books
(Imprint of Scholastic)

Charlesbridge Publishing Inc.
85 Main Street
Watertown, MA 02472
(617) 926-0329 • (800) 225-3214
Fax (617) 926-5720
www.charlesbridge.com

Children's Book Press
246 First St., Suite 101
San Francisco, CA 94105
(415) 995-2200 • Fax (415) 995-2222

Children's Press (Division of Grolier, Inc.)
P.O. Box 1795
Danbury, CT 06816-1333
(800) 621-1115 • www.grolier.com

Chronicle Books
85 Second Street, Sixth Floor
San Francisco, CA 94105
(415) 537-3730 • Fax (415) 537-4460
(800) 722-6657
www.chroniclebooks.com

Clarion Books
(Imprint of Houghton Mifflin, Inc.)
215 Park Avenue South
New York, NY 10003
(212) 420-5800 • (800) 225-3362
www.houghtonmifflinbooks.com/clarion

Crabtree Publishing Co.
350 Fifth Ave., Suite 3308
New York, NY 10118
(212) 496-5040 • (800) 387-7650
Fax (800) 355-7166
www.crabtree-pub.com

Crowell (Imprint of HarperCollins)

Crown Publishing Group
(Imprint of Random House)

Delacorte
(Imprint of Random House)

Dial Books
(Imprint of Penguin Putnam Inc.)

Discovery Enterprises, Ltd.
31 Laurelwood Dr.
Carlisle, MA 01741
(978) 287-5401 • (800) 729-1720
Fax (978) 287-5402

Disney Press
(Division of Disney Book Publishing, Inc.,
A Walt Disney Co.)
114 Fifth Ave.
New York, NY 10011
(212) 633-4400 • Fax (212) 633-4833
www.disneybooks.com

Dorling Kindersley (DK Publishing)
95 Madison Avenue
New York, NY 10016
(212) 213-4800 • Fax (212) 213-5290
(888) 342-5357 • www.dk.com

Doubleday (Imprint of Random House)

E. P. Dutton Children's Books
(Imprint of Penguin Putnam Inc.)

Farrar, Straus and Giroux
19 Union Square West
New York, NY 10003
(212) 741-6900 • Fax (212) 741-6973
(888) 330-8477

Firefly Books, Ltd.
PO Box 1338
Endicott Station
Buffalo, NY 14205
(416) 499-8412 • Fax (800) 565-6034
(800) 387-5085
www.firefly.com

First Avenue Editions
(Imprint of Lerner Publishing Group)

Four Winds Press
(Imprint of Macmillan, see Simon &
Schuster Children's Publishing)

Franklin Watts, Inc.
Affiliate of Grolier Company
90 Sherman Turnpike
Danbury, CT 06816
(203) 797-3500 • Fax (203) 797-6986
www.publishing.grolier.com

Greenwillow Books
(Imprint of William Morrow & Co, Inc.)

Gulliver Green Books
(Imprint of Harcourt Brace & Co.)

Harcourt Brace & Co.
6277 Sea Harbor Drive
Orlando, FL 32887
(407) 345-2000 • (800) 225-5425

Harper & Row (Imprint of HarperCollins)

HarperCollins Children's Books
1350 Avenue of the Americas
New York, NY 10019
(212) 261-6500 • Fax (212) 261-6689
(800) 242-7737
www.harperchildrens.com

Harper Trophy
(Imprint of HarperCollins)

Holiday House
425 Madison Avenue
New York, NY 10017
(212) 688-0085 • Fax (212) 421-6134

Henry Holt and Company
115 West 18th Street
New York, NY 10011
(212) 886-9200 • (212) 633-0748
(888) 330-8477 • www.henryholt.com/byr/

Houghton Mifflin
222 Berkeley Street
Boston, MA 02116
(617) 351-5000 • Fax (617) 351-1125
(800) 225-3362
www.houghtonmifflinbooks.com

Hyperion Books
(Division of ABC, Inc.)
77 W. 66th Street, Eleventh Floor
New York, NY 10023
(212) 456-0100 • (800) 343-9204
www.disney.com

Just Us Books
356 Glenwood Avenue
E. Orange, NJ 07017
(973) 672-7701 • Fax (973) 677-7570
www.justusbooks.com

Kane/Miller Book Publishers
P.O. Box 310529
Brooklyn, NY 11231-0529
(718) 624-5120 • Fax (718) 858-5452
www.kanemiller.com

Alfred A. Knopf
(Imprint of Random House)

Lee & Low Books
95 Madison Avenue, Room 606
New York, NY 10016
(212) 779-4400 • Fax (212) 683-1894

Lerner Publications Co.
241 First Avenue North
Minneapolis, MN 55401
(612) 332-3344 • Fax (612) 332-7615
(800) 328-4929 • www.lernerbooks.com

Little, Brown & Co.
3 Center Plaza
Boston, MA 02108
(617) 227-0730 • Fax (617) 263-2864
(800) 759-0190 • www.littlebrown.com

Lothrop Lee & Shepard
(Imprint of William Morrow & Co.)

Macmillan
(Imprint of Simon & Schuster
Children's Publishing)

McGraw-Hill Publishing Group
1221 Avenue of the Americas
New York, NY 10020
(212) 512-2000

Meredith Books
1615 Locust Street
Des Moines, IA 50309-3023
(505) 284-3000

Millbrook Press, Inc.
2 Old New Milford Road
Brookfield, CT 06804
(203) 740-2220 • (800) 462-4703
Fax (203) 740-2526
www.millbrookpress.com

Mindfull Publishing
177 W. Norfolk Road
Norfolk, CT 06850
(203) 831-0855 • Fax (203) 853-2943

William Morrow & Co.
(Imprint of HarperCollins)

Morrow Junior Books
(Imprint of HarperCollins)

National Geographic Society
1145 17th Street, NW
Washington, DC 20036
(800) 638-4077
www.nationalgeographic.com

Orchard Books (A Grolier Company)
95 Madison Avenue
New York, NY 10016
(212) 951-2600 • Fax (212) 213-6435
www.grolier.com

Penguin Putnam, Inc.
375 Hudson Street
New York, NY 10014
(212) 366-2000 • Fax (212) 366-2666
(800) 631-8571
www.penguinputnam.com

Philomel Books
(Imprint of Penguin Putnam, Inc.)

Pippin Press
Gracie Station, Box 1347
229 E. 85th Street
New York, NY 10028
(212) 288-4920 • Fax (732) 225-1562

Price Stern Sloan
(Imprint of Penguin Putnam, Inc.)

Puffin Books
(Imprint of Penguin Putnam, Inc.)

G.P. Putnam's Sons Publishing
(Imprint of Penguin Putnam, Inc.)

Random House
1540 Broadway
New York, NY 10036
(212) 782-9000 • Fax (212) 782-9452
(800) 200-3552
www.randomhouse.com/kids

Rising Moon
(Imprint of Northland Publishing)

Scholastic
555 Broadway
New York, NY 10012
(212) 343-7500 • Fax (212) 965-7442
(800) SCHOLASTIC • www.scholastic.com

Sierra Club Books for Children
85 Second Street, Second Floor
San Francisco, CA 94105-3441
(415) 977-5500 • Fax (415) 977-5793
(800) 935-1056
www.sierraclub.org/books

Silver Burdett Press
(Division of Pearson Education)
299 Jefferson Rd.
Parsippany, NJ 07054-0480
(973) 739-8000 • (800) 848-9500
www.sbgschool.com

Simon & Schuster Children's Books
1230 Avenue of the Americas
New York, NY 10020
(212) 698-7200 • (800) 223-2336
www.simonsays.com/kidzone

Sunburst
(Imprint of Farrar, Straus & Giroux)

Tricycle Press
(Division of Ten Speed Press)
P.O. Box 7123
Berkeley, CA 94707
(510) 559-1600 • (800) 841-2665
Fax (510) 559-1637
www.tenspeed.com

Viking Children's Books
(Imprint of Penguin Putnam Inc.)

Voyager
(Imprint of Harcourt Brace & Co.)

Walker & Co.
435 Hudson Street
New York, NY 10014
(212) 727-8300 • (212) 727-0984
(800) AT-WALKER

Watts Publishing
(Imprint of Grolier Publishing;
see Children's Press)

Westcliffe Publishers, Inc.
2650 S. Zuni Street
Englewood, CO 80110-1145
(303) 935-0900 • (800) 523-3692

Yearling Books
(Imprint of Random House)

Directory of Resources

Multimedia Resources

AIMS Multimedia
9710 DeSoto Avenue
Chatsworth, CA 91311-4409
(800) 367-2467
www.AIMS-multimedia.com

Ambrose Video and Publishing
28 West 44th Street, Suite 2100
New York, NY 10036
(800) 526-4663 • Fax (212) 768-9282
www.AmbroseVideo.com

BFA Educational Media
(see Phoenix Learning Group)

Brittannica
310 South Michigan Avenue
Brittanica Center
Chicago, IL 60604-4293
(800) 621-3900 • Fax (800) 344-9624

Broderbund
(Parsons Technology;
also see The Learning Company)
500 Redwood Blvd.
Novato, CA 94997
(800) 474-8840 • www.broderbund.com

Carousel Film and Video
250 Fifth Avenue, Suite 204
New York, NY 10001
(212) 683-1660 • Fax (212) 683-1662
e-mail: carousel@pipeline.com

CBS/Fox Video
1330 Avenue of the Americas
New York, NY 10019
(800) 457-0686

Coronet/MTI
(see Phoenix Learning Group)

Direct Cinema, Ltd.
P.O. Box 10003
Santa Monica, CA 90410-1003
(800) 525-0000 • Fax (310) 396-3233

Encyclopaedia Britannica Educational Corp.
310 South Michigan Avenue
Chicago, IL 60604
(800) 554-9862 • www.eb.com

ESI/Educational Software Institute
4213 S. 94th Street
Omaha, NE 68127
(800) 955-5570 • Fax (402) 592-2071
www.edsoft.com

GPN/Reading Rainbow
University of Nebraska-Lincoln
P.O. Box 80669
Lincoln, NE 68501-0669
(800) 228-4630 • Fax (800) 306-2330
www.gpn.unl.edu

Hallmark Home Entertainment
6100 Wilshire Blvd.
Suite 1400
Los Angeles, CA 90048
(213) 634-3000 • Fax (213) 549-3760

LibraryVideo Company
P.O. Box 580
Wynnewood, PA 19096
(800) 843-3620 • Fax (610) 645-4040

Listening Library
A subsidiary of Random House
One Park Avenue
Greenwich, CT 06870-1727
(800) 243-4504 • www.listeninglib.com

Macmillan/McGraw-Hill
(see SRA/McGraw-Hill)

Marshmedia
P.O. Box 8082
Shawnee Mission, KS 66208
(800) 821-3303 • Fax (816) 333-7421
www.marshmedia.com

MECC
(see The Learning Company)

National Geographic Society Educational Services
P.O. Box 10597
Des Moines, IA 50340-0597
(800) 368-2728 • Fax (515) 362-3366
www.nationalgeographic.com/education

PBS Video
1320 Braddock Place
Alexandria, VA 22314
(800) 344-3337 • www.pbs.org

Phoenix/BFA Films and Videos
(see Phoenix Learning Group)

The Phoenix Learning Group
Phoenix/BFA Films & Video
2348 Chaffee Drive
St. Louis, MO 63146
(800) 221-1274 • Fax (314) 569-2834

Pied Piper (see AIMS Multimedia)

Rainbow Educational Video
4540 Preslyn Drive
Raleigh, NC 27615
(800) 331-4047 • Fax (314) 569-2834
www.rainbowedumedia.com

Social Studies School Service
10200 Jefferson Boulevard
P.O. Box 802
Culver City, CA 90232-0802
(800) 421-4246 • Fax (310) 839-2249
www.socialstudies.com

SRA/McGraw-Hill
220 Danieldale Road
De Soto, TX 75115
(800) 843-8855 • Fax (972) 228-1982
www.sra4kids.com

SVE/Churchill Media
6677 North Northwest Highway
Chicago, IL 60631
(800) 829-1900 • Fax (800) 624-1678
www.svemedia.com

Tom Snyder Productions (also see ESI)
80 Coolidge Hill Rd.
Watertown, MA 02472
(800) 342-0236 • Fax (800) 304-1254
www.teachtsp.com

Troll Associates
100 Corporate Drive
Mahwah, NJ 07430
(800) 929-8765 • Fax (800) 979-8765
www.troll.com

United Learning
1560 Sherman Avenue
Suite 100
Evanston, IL 60201
(800) 323-9084 • Fax (847) 328-6706

Zenger Media
(see Social Studies School Service)

UNIT 1

Vocabulary | Spelling

THE LOST LAKE

Vocabulary
- brand-new
- compass
- darted
- mug
- muttered
- talker

Words with Short Vowels

drank	hung	lift	swept
rest	trouble	flock	pleasant
ahead	**magazines**	trust	fist
drink	self	cousin	couple
dock	deaf	cannon	wealth

AMELIA'S ROAD

Vocabulary
- accidental
- labored
- occasions
- rhythms
- shortcut
- shutters

Words with long *a* and long *e*

cape	agree	crayon	**rusty**
gray	**teacher**	cable	tray
station	secret	fail	raisin
rail	**family**	tea	bean
freight	cane	zebra	**tidy**

SARAH, PLAIN AND TALL

Vocabulary
- eerie
- huddled
- overalls
- pesky
- reins
- squall

Words with long *i* and long *o*

tiger	**crow**	tomato	pine
drive	oak	**stove**	**overhead**
reply	iron	below	chose
roll	alike	groan	hollow
note	supply	title	file

SEAL JOURNEY

Vocabulary
- assured
- horizon
- jagged
- mature
- nursery
- squealed

Words with /ū/ and /ü/

ruler	**continue**	**improve**	ruin
avenue	gloomy	beautiful	bugle
raccoon	unit	cube	argue
loose	whose	stool	community
commute	humor	**movement**	tuna

TIME FOR KIDS: OPEN WIDE, DON'T BITE!

Vocabulary
- broad
- fangs
- patients
- healthy
- reptiles
- skills

Words from Health

dentist	**gums**	brain	ache
crown	gland	cavity	**dental**
hospital	joint	disease	clinic
medicine	fever	plaque	oral
diet	**chewing**	vitamin	**molars**

Boldfaced words appear in the selection.

UNIT 2

Vocabulary

Spelling

JUSTIN AND THE BEST BISCUITS IN THE WORLD

Vocabulary
- festival
- guilt
- inspecting
- lingered
- pranced
- resounded

Spelling — Syllable Patterns

biscuit	cabin	local	**razor**
clover	plastic	mustard	fancy
public	radar	pupil	limit
oven	mitten	sofa	**famous**
bandage	**knapsack**	**welcome**	item

JUST A DREAM

Vocabulary
- bulging
- crumpled
- foul
- haze
- shrieking
- waddled

Spelling — Words with Consonant Clusters

blank	bridge	brand	credit
daring	**float**	among	darling
claim	plank	flatter	flutter
flour	classified	**clothesline**	clatter
crack	cradle	bridle	cruise

LEAH'S PONY

Vocabulary
- bidding
- clustered
- county
- glistened
- overflowing
- sturdy

Spelling — Words with Consonant Clusters

thrill	sprint	stern	stung
spruce	spare	spectacle	sparkle
stand	threw	strap	stress
speed	**stranger**	thrifty	special
stretch	springtime	street	steak

BASEBALL SAVED US

Vocabulary
- crate
- ditches
- endless
- glinting
- inning
- mound

Spelling — Plurals

cities	engines	eyelashes	**sunglasses**
mistakes	**soldiers**	**uniforms**	groceries
foxes	ranches	batteries	loaves
babies	hobbies	calves	**mattresses**
knives	yourselves	**shovels**	ferries

TIME FOR KIDS: WILL HER NATIVE LANGUAGE DISAPPEAR?

Vocabulary
- backgrounds
- century
- communicate
- extinct
- generations
- native

Spelling — Words from Social Studies

language	accent	folktale	symbol
history	tribe	practice	guide
pottery	human	**relatives**	totem
study	custom	interview	colony
spoken	village	region	**prints**

Boldfaced words appear in the selection.

UNIT 3

Vocabulary

Spelling

THE HATMAKER'S SIGN

admitted
brisk
displaying
elegantly
strolling
wharf

Words with /ou/ and /oi/

oily	royalty	**aloud**	**however**
annoy .	bounce	tower	appointment
around	**bowing**	avoid	scout
growl	moist	employ	powder
disappoint	enjoyment	**lookout**	noun

PAT CUMMINGS: MY STORY

exist
image
inspire
loft
reference
sketch

Words with / u̇ / and /yu̇ /

curious	**should**	**would**	woolen
pure	furious	bulldozer	pudding
fully	cure	soot	goodness
sure	handful	tour	pulley
wooden	crooked	butcher	overlook

GRASS SANDALS: THE TRAVELS OF BASHO

chanted
nipped
pouch
restless
scribbled
stitching

Work with Digraphs

changed	south	**cloth**	whittle
watch	chimney	**themselves**	thoughtful '
fresh	scratch	crunch	birch
shoulder	shove	batch	switch
whatever	wheat	harsh	theater

A PLACE CALLED FREEDOM

fretted
gourd
plantation
settlement
sunrise
weary

Adding -ed and -ing

freed	**carried**	shedding	varied
hugged	**believed**	sledding	**arrived**
emptied	dimmed	magnified	plugging
figured	studied	wedged	rising
budding	providing	rotting	**celebrated**

TIME FOR KIDS: TWISTED TRAILS

challenge
combine
contained
entertaining
mazes
requires

Words from the Arts

designs	art	assemble	mold
artist	create	craft	easel
building	**master**	express	plaster
activity	poster	arrange	masterpiece
museum	statue	**professional**	exhibit

Boldfaced words appear in the selection.

UNIT 4

	Vocabulary	**Spelling**

SCRUFFY: A WOLF FINDS HIS PLACE IN THE PACK

Vocabulary: affection, climate, clinging, injury, methods, threat

Words with /ô/ and /ôr/

awful	**toward**	false	dawn
daughter	already	jaw	hoarse
roar	brought	offer	war
order	**form**	sauce	board
office	author	**chorus**	cough

GLUSKABE AND THE SNOW BIRD

Vocabulary: confusion, freeze, hilltop, lodge, messenger, praised

Words with /är/ and /âr/

apart	repair	starve	therefore
hardly	**careful**	barber	dairy
yarn	scare	carnival	hare
army	somewhere	carpet	**prepare**
marbles	wear	unfair	pear

MEET AN UNDERWATER EXPLORER

Vocabulary: connected, endangered, haul, overcome, poisonous, sponge

Words with /îr/ and /ûr/

fern	mere	**worse**	period
curve	cheer	swirl	insert
worst	serious	**gear**	purpose
shirt	germ	sincerely	twirling
clear	burst	volunteer	spear

ON THE BUS WITH JOANNA COLE

Vocabulary: abandon, absorb, available, original, research, traditional

Compound Words

bedroom	backyard	**outline**	**whirlwinds**
anymore	railroad	windowpane	loudspeaker
everybody	forever	**evergreens**	northwest
classroom	bathtub	grandparents	thunderstorm
anyway	homemade	**photocopy**	bedspread

TIME FOR KIDS: EARTH'S FIRST CREATURES

Vocabulary: ancestors, disaster, microscope, snout, spikes, weird

Words from Science

shells	**discovered**	mineral	kelp
crabs	cast	dolphin	caterpillar
liquid	lobster	**systems**	depth
fact	**hatch**	clam	skeleton
butterfly	expert	imprint	fungus

Boldfaced words appear in the selection.

UNIT 5

	Vocabulary	Spelling

THE FOX AND THE GUINEA PIG

Vocabulary
- **amazement**
- **destroyed**
- **eldest**
- **fowl**
- **stake**
- **strewn**

Words with /s/ and /f/

mess	rough	**laughter**	alphabet
sorry	certain	citizen	triumph
balance	telephone	advice	careless
police	**surprise**	photograph	tough
classic	elephant	cider	**enormous**

MOM'S BEST FRIEND

Vocabulary
- **clippers**
- **errands**
- **instinct**
- **memorizing**
- **relieved**
- **sirens**

Words with /ər/ and /chər/

brother	**pictures**	member	anchor
honor	odor	nature	pasture
either	enter	tender	chapter
popular	vinegar	visitor	suffer
number	capture	polar	**furniture**

THE RAJAH'S RICE

Vocabulary
- **attendants**
- **awkwardly**
- **celebration**
- **knowledge**
- **released**
- **spice**

Words with /əl/ and /ən/

final	pencil	reason	**medical**
uncle	lion	gentle	evil
several	**taken**	total	listen
model	simple	settle	common
terrible	women	level	cotton

YEH-SHEN: A CINDERELLA STORY FROM CHINA

Vocabulary
- **beloved**
- **bid**
- **desire**
- **heaved**
- **marveled**
- **permit**

Contractions

that's	there's	they'll	it'll
he'll	couldn't	weren't	hadn't
wasn't	he'd	here's	they'd
what's	could've	she'd	where's
I'd	let's	who's	wouldn't

TIME FOR KIDS: CAN WE RESCUE THE REEFS?

Vocabulary
- **coral**
- **damage**
- **loosened**
- **percent**
- **reefs**
- **ton**

Words from Science

rescue	**dying**	**seaweed**	adapt
survive	shelter	**creatures**	locate
channel	extreme	dissolve	assist
vessel	**danger**	motion	future
expose	protect	feature	**divers**

Boldfaced words appear in the selection.

UNIT 6

	Vocabulary	Spelling

TEAMMATES

Vocabulary: circulated, extraordinary, launched, opponents, organizations, teammate

Words with Silent Letters

knew	writer	knead	stalk
climb	knob	plumber	kneel
calm	numb	chalk	**sought**
although	delight	midnight	thorough
knight	wren	wreck	wrestle

THE MALACHITE PALACE

Vocabulary: cultured, feeble, fragrance, mingled, resembled, scampered

Homophones and Homographs

seen	scene	peak	pale
great	beet	post	grave
light	bowl	pail	berry
beat	grate	bury	**peek**
lean	fan	punch	**dates**

THE TOOTHPASTE MILLIONAIRE

Vocabulary: brilliant, commercials, expensive, gallon, ingredient, successful

Words with Suffixes

useless	motionless	fairness	hopeless
entertainment	description	government	**production**
construction	measurement	protection	enjoyable
adjustable	adorable	dependable	greatness
darkness	breathless	sickness	

WHALES

Vocabulary: identify, mammals, marine, pods, preserve, related

Words with Prefixes

redo	inactive	nonstop	rewind
unkind	**international**	refill	unsure
disappear	unlucky	uncertain	disagree
reread	dislike	interstate	reheat
nonfat	unpack	incomplete	nonsense

TIME FOR KIDS: SAVING THE EVERGLADES

Vocabulary: compares, importance, instance, lurk, soggy, wildlife

Words from Math

area	minute	**amount**	quart
hundreds	noon	cylinder	decade
size	cone	zero	rectangle
billions	yard	figure	era
weight	edge	calendar	length

Boldfaced words appear in the selection.

Listening, Speaking, Viewing, Representing

☑ Tested Skill

Tinted panels show skills, strategies, and other teaching opportunities

LISTENING	K	1	2	3	4	5	6
Learn the vocabulary of school (numbers, shapes, colors, directions, and categories)							
Identify the musical elements of literary language, such as rhymes, repetition, onomatopoeia, alliteration, assonance							
Determine purposes for listening (get information, solve problems, enjoy and appreciate)							
Understand and follow directions							
Listen critically and responsively; recognize barriers to effective listening							
Ask and answer relevant questions (for clarification; to follow up on ideas)							
Listen critically to interpret and evaluate							
Listen responsively to stories and other texts read aloud, including selections from classic and contemporary works							
Connect and compare own experiences, feelings, ideas, and traditions with those of others							
Apply comprehension strategies in listening activities							
Understand the major ideas and supporting evidence in spoken messages							
Participate in listening activities related to reading and writing (such as discussions, group activities, conferences)							
Listen to learn by taking notes, organizing, and summarizing spoken ideas							
Know personal listening preferences							

SPEAKING	K	1	2	3	4	5	6
Uses repetition, rhyme, and rhythm in oral texts (such as in reciting songs, poems, and stories with repeating patterns)							
Learn the vocabulary of school (numbers, shapes, colors, directions, and categories)							
Use appropriate language, grammar, and vocabulary learned to describe ideas, feelings, and experiences							
Ask and answer relevant questions (for clarification; to follow up on ideas)							
Communicate effectively in everyday situations (such as discussions, group activities, conferences, conversations)							
Demonstrate speaking skills (audience, purpose, occasion, clarity, volume, pitch, intonation, phrasing, rate, fluency)							
Clarify and support spoken messages and ideas with objects, charts, evidence, elaboration, examples							
Use verbal communication in effective ways when, for example, making announcements, giving directions, or making introductions							
Use nonverbal communication in effective ways such as eye contact, facial expressions, gestures							
Retell a story or a spoken message by summarizing or clarifying							
Connect and compare own experiences, ideas, and traditions with those of others							
Determine purposes for speaking (inform, entertain, compare, describe, give directions, persuade, express personal feelings and opinions)							
Recognize differences between formal and informal language							
Demonstrate skills of reporting and providing information							
Demonstrate skills of interviewing, requesting and providing information							
Apply composition strategies in speaking activities							
Monitor own understanding of spoken message and seek clarification as needed							

VIEWING	K	1	2	3	4	5	6
Demonstrate viewing skills (focus attention, organize information)							
Understand and use nonverbal cues							
Respond to audiovisual media in a variety of ways							
Participate in viewing activities related to reading and writing							
Apply comprehension strategies in viewing activities, including main idea and details							
Recognize artists' craft and techniques for conveying meaning							
Interpret information from various formats such as maps, charts, graphics, video segments, technology							
Knows various types of mass media (such as film, video, television, billboards, and newspapers)							
Evaluate purposes of various media, including mass media (information, appreciation, entertainment, directions, persuasion)							
Use media, including mass media, to compare ideas, information, and points of view							

REPRESENTING	K	1	2	3	4	5	6
Select, organize, or produce visuals to complement or extend meanings							
Produce communication using appropriate media to develop a class paper, multimedia or video reports							
Show how language, medium, and presentation contribute to the message							

Reading: Alphabetic Principle, Sounds/Symbols

☑ Tested Skill

☐ Tinted panels show skills, strategies, and other teaching opportunities

PRINT AWARENESS	K	1	2	3	4	5	6
Know the order of the alphabet							
Recognize that print represents spoken language and conveys meaning							
Understand directionality (tracking print from left to right; return sweep)							
Understand that written words and sentences are separated by spaces							
Know the difference between individual letters and printed words							
Understand that spoken words are represented in written language by specific sequence of letters							
Recognize that there are correct spellings for words							
Know the difference between capital and lowercase letters							
Recognize how readers use capitalization and punctuation to comprehend							
Recognize the distinguishing features of a letter, word, sentence, paragraph							
Understand appropriate book handling							
Recognize that parts of a book (such as cover/title page and table of contents) offer information							

PHONOLOGICAL AWARENESS	K	1	2	3	4	5	6
Listen for environmental sounds							
Identify spoken words and sentences							
Divide spoken sentence into individual words							
Produce rhyming words and distinguish rhyming words from nonrhyming words							
Identify, segment, and combine syllables within spoken words							
Blend and segment onsets and rimes							
Identify and isolate the initial, medial, and final sound of a spoken word							
Add, delete, or substitute sounds to change words (such as *cow* to *how*, *pan* to *fan*)							
Blend sounds to make spoken words							
Segment one-syllable spoken words into individual phonemes							

PHONICS AND DECODING	K	1	2	3	4	5	6
Alphabetic principle: Letter/sound correspondence	☑	☑	☑				
Blending CVC words	☑	☑					
Segmenting CVC words	☑						
Blending CVC, CVCe, CCVC, CVCC, CVVC words	☑	☑	☑				
Segmenting CVC, CVCe, CCVC, CVCC, CVVC words and sounds	☑	☑	☑				
Initial and final consonants: /n/n, /d/d, /s/s, /m/m, /t/t, /k/c, /f/f, /r/r, /p/p, /l/l, /k/k, /g/g, /b/b, /h/h, /w/w, /v/v, /ks/x, /kw/qu, /j/j, /y/y, /z/z	☑	☑					
Initial and medial short vowels: *a, i, u, o, e*	☑	☑	☑				
Long vowels: *a-e, i-e, o-e, u-e* (vowel-consonant-e)		☑	☑				
Long vowels, including *ay, ai; e, ee, ie, ea; o, oa, oe, ow; i, y, igh*		☑	☑				
Consonant Digraphs: *sh, th, ch, wh*		☑					
Consonant Blends: continuant/continuant, including *sl, sm, sn, fl, fr, ll, ss, ff*		☑					
Consonant Blends: continuant/stop, including *st, sk, sp, ng, nt, nd, mp, ft*		☑					
Consonant Blends: stop/continuant, including *tr, pr, pl, cr, tw*		☑					
Variant vowels: including /ù/oo; /ô/a, *aw, au*; /ü/ue, *ew*		☑	☑				
Diphthongs, including /ou/ou, *ow*; /oi/oi, *oy*		☑	☑				
r-controlled vowels, including /âr/are; /ôr/or, ore; /îr/ear			☑				
Soft *c* and soft *g*			☑				
nk		☑	☑				
Consonant Digraphs: *ck*	☑	☑					
Consonant Digraphs: *ph, tch, ch*			☑				
Short *e: ea*			☑				
Long *e: y, ey*			☑				
/ü/oo		☑	☑				
/är/ar; /ûr/ir, ur, er		☑	☑				
Silent letters: including *l, b, k, w, g, h, gh*			☑				
Schwa: /ər/er; /ən/en; /əl/le;			☑				
Reading/identifying multisyllabic words		☑	☑				
Using graphophonic cues							

Reading: Vocabulary/Word Identification

Tinted panels show skills, strategies, and other teaching opportunities

WORD STRUCTURE	K	1	2	3	4	5	6
Common spelling patterns							
Syllable patterns							
Plurals		🗹					
Possessives		🗹					
Contractions		🗹					
Root, or base, words and inflectional endings (-s, -es, -ed, -ing)		🗹	🗹	🗹		🗹	
Compound Words		🗹	🗹	🗹	🗹	🗹	🗹
Prefixes and suffixes (such as un-, re-, dis-, non-; -ly, -y, -ful, -able, -tion)			🗹	🗹	🗹	🗹	🗹
Root words and derivational endings				🗹	🗹	🗹	🗹

WORD MEANING	K	1	2	3	4	5	6
Develop vocabulary through concrete experiences, word walls, other people							
Develop vocabulary through selections read aloud							
Develop vocabulary through reading							
Cueing systems: syntactic, semantic, graphophonic							
Context clues, including semantic clues (word meaning), syntactical clues (word order), and graphophonic clues	🗹	🗹	🗹	🗹	🗹	🗹	🗹
High-frequency words (such as the, a, and, said, was, where, is)	🗹	🗹					
Identify words that name persons, places, things, and actions							
Automatic reading of regular and irregular words							
Use resources and references (dictionary, glossary, thesaurus, synonym finder, technology and software, and context)							
Classify and categorize words							
Synonyms and antonyms				🗹	🗹	🗹	🗹
Multiple-meaning words				🗹		🗹	🗹
Figurative language				🗹	🗹	🗹	🗹
Decode derivatives (root words, such as like, pay, happy with affixes, such as dis-, pre-, un-)							
Systematic study of words across content areas and in current events							
Locate meanings, pronunciations, and derivations (including dictionaries, glossaries, and other sources)							
Denotation and connotation							🗹
Word origins as aid to understanding historical influences on English word meanings							
Homophones, homographs							
Analogies							🗹
Idioms							

Reading: Comprehension

PREREADING STRATEGIES	K	1	2	3	4	5	6
Preview and predict							
Use prior knowledge							
Set and adjust purposes for reading							
Build background							

MONITORING STRATEGIES	K	1	2	3	4	5	6
Adjust reading rate							
Reread, search for clues, ask questions, ask for help							
Visualize							
Read a portion aloud, use reference aids							
Use decoding and vocabulary strategies							
Paraphrase							
Create story maps, diagrams, charts, story props to help comprehend, analyze, synthesize and evaluate texts							

(continued on next page)

(Reading: Comprehension continued)

SKILLS AND STRATEGIES	K	1	2	3	4	5	6
Recall story details, including character and setting	☑	☑					
Use illustrations	☑	☑					
Distinguish reality and fantasy	☑	☑	☑				
Classify and categorize	☑						
Make predictions	☑	☑	☑	☑	☑	☑	☑
Recognize sequence of events (tell or act out)	☑	☑	☑	☑	☑	☑	☑
Recognize cause and effect	☑	☑	☑	☑	☑	☑	☑
Compare and contrast	☑	☑	☑	☑	☑	☑	☑
Summarize	☑	☑	☑	☑	☑	☑	☑
Make and explain inferences		☑	☑	☑	☑	☑	☑
Draw conclusions		☑	☑	☑	☑	☑	☑
Distinguish important and unimportant information				☑	☑	☑	☑
Recognize main idea and supporting details	☑	☑	☑	☑	☑	☑	☑
Form conclusions or generalizations and support with evidence from text			☑	☑	☑	☑	☑
Distinguish fact and opinion (including news stories and advertisements)				☑	☑	☑	☑
Recognize problem and solution				☑	☑	☑	☑
Recognize steps in a process		☑	☑	☑	☑	☑	☑
Make judgments and decisions				☑	☑	☑	☑
Distinguish fact and nonfact				☑	☑	☑	☑
Recognize techniques of persuasion and propaganda							☑
Evaluate evidence and sources of information, including checking other sources and asking experts							☑
Identify similarities and differences across texts (including topics, characters, problems, themes, cultural influences, treatment, scope, or organization)							
Practice various questions and tasks (test-like comprehension questions)							
Paraphrase and summarize to recall, inform, and organize							
Answer various types of questions (open-ended, literal, interpretative, test-like such as true-false, multiple choice, short-answer)							
Use study strategies to learn and recall (preview, question, reread, and record)							

LITERARY RESPONSE	K	1	2	3	4	5	6
Listen to stories being read aloud							
React, speculate, join in, read along when predictable and patterned selections are read aloud							
Respond to a variety of stories and poems through talk, movement, music, art, drama, and writing							
Show understanding through writing, illustrating, developing demonstrations, and using technology							
Connect ideas and themes across texts							
Support responses by referring to relevant aspects of text and own experiences							
Offer observations, make connections, speculate, interpret, and raise questions in response to texts							
Interpret text ideas through journal writing, discussion, enactment, and media							

TEXT STRUCTURE/LITERARY CONCEPTS	K	1	2	3	4	5	6
Distinguish forms and functions of texts (lists, newsletters, signs)							
Use text features to aid comprehension							
Understand story structure							
Identify narrative (for entertainment) and expository (for information)							
Distinguish fiction from nonfiction, including fact and fantasy							
Understand literary forms (stories, poems, plays, and informational books)							
Understand literary terms by distinguishing between roles of author and illustrator							
Understand title, author, and illustrator across a variety of texts							
Analyze character, character's motive, character's point of view, plot, setting, style, tone, mood		☑	☑	☑	☑	☑	☑
Compare communication in different forms							
Understand terms such as *title, author, illustrator, playwright, theater, stage, act, dialogue,* and *scene*							
Recognize stories, poems, songs, myths, legends, folktales, fables, tall tales, limericks, plays, biographies, autobiographies							
Judge internal logic of story text							
Recognize that authors organize information in specific ways							
Recognize author's purpose: to inform, influence, express, or entertain							
Describe how author's point of view affects text				☑	☑	☑	☑
Recognize biography, historical fiction, realistic fiction, modern fantasy, informational texts, and poetry							
Analyze ways authors present ideas (cause/effect, compare/contrast, inductively, deductively, chronologically)							
Recognize literary techniques such as imagery, repetition, flashback, foreshadowing, symbolism							

(continued on next page)

(Reading: Comprehension continued)

VARIETY OF TEXT	K	1	2	3	4	5	6
Read a variety of genres and understand their distinguishing features							
Use expository and other informational texts to acquire information							
Read for a variety of purposes							
Select varied sources when reading for information or pleasure							
Know preferences for reading literary and nonfiction texts							
FLUENCY							
Read regularly in independent-level and instructional-level materials							
Read orally with fluency from familiar texts							
Self-select independent-level reading							
Read silently for increasing periods of time							
Demonstrate characteristics of fluent and effective reading							
Adjust reading rate to purpose							
Read aloud in selected texts, showing understanding of text and engaging the listener							
CULTURES							
Connect own experience with culture of others							
Compare experiences of characters across cultures							
Articulate and discuss themes and connections that cross cultures							
CRITICAL THINKING							
Experiences (comprehend, apply, analyze, synthesize, evaluate)							
Make connections (comprehend, apply, analyze, synthesize, evaluate)							
Expression (comprehend, apply, analyze, synthesize, evaluate)							
Inquiry (comprehend, apply, analyze, synthesize, evaluate)							
Problem solving (comprehend, apply, analyze, synthesize, evaluate)							
Making decisions (comprehend, apply, analyze, synthesize, evaluate)							

Study Skills

INQUIRY/RESEARCH AND STUDY STRATEGIES	K	1	2	3	4	5	6
Follow and give directions							
Use alphabetical order							
Use text features and formats to help understand text (such as boldface, italic, or highlighted text; captions; headings and subheadings; numbers or symbols)							
Use study strategies to help read text and to learn and recall information from text (such as preview text, set purposes, and ask questions; use SQRRR; adjust reading rate; skim and scan; use KWL)							
Identify/frame and revise questions for research							
Obtain, organize, and summarize information: classify, take notes, outline, web, diagram							
Evaluate research and raise new questions							
Use technology for research and/or to present information in various formats							
Follow accepted formats for writing research, including documenting sources							
Use test-taking strategies							
Use text organizers (book cover; title page—title, author, illustrator; contents; headings; glossary; index)		☑	☑	☑	☑	☑	☑
Use graphic aids, such as maps, diagrams, charts, graphs, schedules, calendars		☑	☑	☑	☑	☑	☑
Read and interpret varied texts, such as environmental print, signs, lists, encyclopedia, dictionary, glossary, newspaper, advertisement, magazine, calendar, directions, floor plans, online resources		☑	☑	☑	☑	☑	☑
Use print and online reference sources, such as glossary, dictionary, encyclopedia, telephone directory, technology resources, nonfiction books		☑	☑	☑	☑	☑	☑
Recognize Library/Media center resources, such as computerized references; catalog search—subject, author, title; encyclopedia index		☑	☑	☑	☑	☑	☑

Writing

MODES AND FORMS	K	1	2	3	4	5	6
Interactive writing							
Descriptive writing			☑				
Personal narrative			☑	☑	☑	☑	☑
Writing that compares		☑	☑	☑	☑	☑	☑
Explanatory writing			☑	☑	☑	☑	☑
Persuasive writing				☑	☑	☑	☑
Writing a story		☑	☑	☑	☑	☑	☑
Expository writing; research report		☑	☑	☑	☑	☑	☑
Write using a variety of formats, such as advertisement, autobiography, biography, book report/report, comparison-contrast, critique/review/editorial, description, essay, how-to, interview, invitation, journal/log/notes, message/list, paragraph/multi-paragraph composition, picture book, play (scene), poem/rhyme, story, summary, note, letter							

PURPOSES/AUDIENCES							
Dictate sentences and messages such as news and stories for others to write							
Write labels, notes, and captions for illustrations, possessions, charts, and centers							
Write to record, to discover and develop ideas, to inform, to influence, to entertain							
Exhibit an identifiable voice							
Use literary devices (suspense, dialogue, and figurative language)							
Produce written texts by organizing ideas, using effective transitions, and choosing precise wording							

PROCESSES							
Generate ideas for self-selected and assigned topics using prewriting strategies							
Develop drafts							
Revise drafts for varied purposes, elaborate ideas							
Edit for appropriate grammar, spelling, punctuation, and features of published writings							
Proofread own writing and that of others							
Bring pieces to final form and "publish" them for audiences							
Use technology to compose, revise, and present text							
Select and use reference materials and resources for writing, revising, and editing final drafts							

SPELLING							
Spell own name and write high-frequency words							
Words with short vowels (including CVC and one-syllable words with blends CCVC, CVCC, CCVCC)							
Words with long vowels (including CVCe)							
Words with digraphs, blends, consonant clusters, double consonants							
Words with diphthongs							
Words with variant vowels							
Words with r-controlled vowels							
Words with /ər/, /əl/, and /ən/							
Words with silent letters							
Words with soft c and soft g							
Inflectional endings (including plurals and past tense and words that drop the final e and double a consonant when adding -ing, -ed)							
Compound words							
Contractions							
Homonyms							
Suffixes such as -able, -ly, -ful, or -less, and prefixes such as dis-, re-, pre-, or un-							
Spell words ending in -tion and -sion, such as station and procession							
Accurate spelling of root or base words							
Orthographic patterns and rules such as keep/can; sack/book; out/now; oil/toy; match/speech; ledge/cage; consonant doubling, dropping e, changing y to i							
Multisyllabic words using regularly spelled phonogram patterns							
Syllable patterns (including closed, open, syllable boundary patterns)							
Synonyms and antonyms							
Words from Social Studies, Science, Math, and Physical Education							
Words derived from other languages and cultures							
Use resources to find correct spellings, synonyms, and replacement words							
Use conventional spelling of familiar words in writing assignments							
Spell accurately in final drafts							

(continued on next page)

(Writing continued)

☑ Tested Skill

☐ Tinted panels show skills, strategies, and other teaching opportunities

GRAMMAR AND USAGE

	K	1	2	3	4	5	6
Understand sentence concepts (word order, statements, questions, exclamations, commands)							
Recognize complete and incomplete sentences							
Nouns (common, proper, singular, plural, irregular plural, possessives)							
Verbs (action, helping, linking, irregular)							
Verb tense (present, past, future, perfect, and progressive)							
Pronouns (possessive, subject and object, pronoun-verb agreement)							
Use objective case pronouns accurately							
Adjectives							
Adverbs that tell how, when, where							
Subjects, predicates							
Subject-verb agreement							
Sentence combining							
Recognize sentence structure (simple, compound, complex)							
Synonyms and antonyms							
Contractions							
Conjunctions							
Prepositions and prepositional phrases							

PENMANSHIP

	K	1	2	3	4	5	6
Write each letter of alphabet (capital and lowercase) using correct formation, appropriate size and spacing							
Write own name and other important words							
Use phonological knowledge to map sounds to letters to write messages							
Write messages that move left to right, top to bottom							
Gain increasing control of penmanship, pencil grip, paper position, beginning stroke							
Use word and letter spacing and margins to make messages readable							
Write legibly by selecting cursive or manuscript as appropriate							

MECHANICS

	K	1	2	3	4	5	6
Use capitalization in sentences, proper nouns, titles, abbreviations and the pronoun I							
Use end marks correctly (period, question mark, exclamation point)							
Use commas (in dates, in addresses, in a series, in letters, in direct address)							
Use apostrophes in contractions and possessives							
Use quotation marks							
Use hyphens, semicolons, colons							

EVALUATION

	K	1	2	3	4	5	6
Identify the most effective features of a piece of writing using class/teacher-generated criteria							
Respond constructively to others' writing							
Determine how his/her own writing achieves its purpose							
Use published pieces as models for writing							
Review own written work to monitor growth as writer							

Scoring Chart

The Scoring Chart is provided for your convenience in grading your students' work.

- Find the column that shows the total number of items.
- Find the row that matches the number of items answered correctly.
- The intersection of the two rows provides the percentage score.

TOTAL NUMBER OF ITEMS

NUMBER CORRECT	1	2	3	4	5	6	7	8	9	10	11	12	13	14	15	16	17	18	19	20	21	22	23	24	25	26	27	28	29	30
1	100	50	33	25	20	17	14	13	11	10	9	8	8	7	7	6	6	6	5	5	5	5	4	4	4	4	4	4	3	3
2		100	67	50	40	33	29	25	22	20	18	17	15	14	13	13	12	11	11	10	10	9	9	8	8	8	7	7	7	7
3			100	75	60	50	43	38	33	30	27	25	23	21	20	19	18	17	16	15	14	14	13	13	12	12	11	11	10	10
4				100	80	67	57	50	44	40	36	33	31	29	27	25	24	22	21	20	19	18	17	17	16	15	15	14	14	13
5					100	83	71	63	56	50	45	42	38	36	33	31	29	28	26	25	24	23	22	21	20	19	19	18	17	17
6						100	86	75	67	60	55	50	46	43	40	38	35	33	32	30	29	27	26	25	24	23	22	21	21	20
7							100	88	78	70	64	58	54	50	47	44	41	39	37	35	33	32	30	29	28	27	26	25	24	23
8								100	89	80	73	67	62	57	53	50	47	44	42	40	38	36	35	33	32	31	30	29	28	27
9									100	90	82	75	69	64	60	56	53	50	47	45	43	41	39	38	36	35	33	32	31	30
10										100	91	83	77	71	67	63	59	56	53	50	48	45	43	42	40	38	37	36	34	33
11											100	92	85	79	73	69	65	61	58	55	52	50	48	46	44	42	41	39	38	37
12												100	92	86	80	75	71	67	63	60	57	55	52	50	48	46	44	43	41	40
13													100	93	87	81	76	72	68	65	62	59	57	54	52	50	48	46	45	43
14														100	93	88	82	78	74	70	67	64	61	58	56	54	52	50	48	47
15															100	94	88	83	79	75	71	68	65	63	60	58	56	54	52	50
16																100	94	89	84	80	76	73	70	67	64	62	59	57	55	53
17																	100	94	89	85	81	77	74	71	68	65	63	61	59	57
18																		100	95	90	86	82	78	75	72	69	67	64	62	60
19																			100	95	90	86	83	79	76	73	70	68	66	63
20																				100	95	91	87	83	80	77	74	71	69	67
21																					100	95	91	88	84	81	78	75	72	70
22																						100	96	92	88	85	81	79	76	73
23																							100	96	92	88	85	82	79	77
24																								100	96	92	89	86	83	80
25																									100	96	93	89	86	83
26																										100	96	93	90	87
27																											100	96	93	90
28																												100	97	93
29																													100	97
30																														100

Personal Narrative

6-Point Writing Rubric

6. Exceptional

- **Ideas & Content** crafts an appealing, elaborately detailed story about a special place at home.
- **Organization** unfolds a thoughtfully planned story line; sequence moves a reader smoothly through events from beginning to end; ideas are connected.
- **Voice** shows unusual originality; uses a range of emotions to express why the place is special; communicates effectively for the purpose and audience.
- **Word Choice** creatively uses accurate, specific words to paint a clear picture of characters and events.
- **Sentence Fluency** crafts creative, effective sentences that flow in a smooth rhythm; may experiment effectively with fragments, dialogue, or other devices.
- **Conventions** is skilled in most writing conventions; proper use of the rules of English enhances clarity, meaning, and narrative style; editing is largely unnecessary.

5. Excellent

- **Ideas & Content** creates a cohesive, focused picture of a special place at home, with carefully chosen details.
- **Organization** unfolds a consistent, careful structure, in a sequence that helps a reader follow the events; ideas are connected.
- **Voice** shows originality and a strong personal message that speaks directly to the reader and matches purpose and audience.
- **Word Choice** makes thoughtful use of challenging and everyday words that paint a picture in the reader's mind.
- **Sentence Fluency** crafts varied, capable sentences that flow naturally; dialogue, if used, sounds natural and strengthens the story.
- **Conventions** is skilled in most writing conventions; text is easy to follow and understand; little editing is needed.

4. Good

- **Ideas & Content** crafts a solid, clear personal story; details help convey the main idea of a special place.
- **Organization** has a well-planned story line; ideas are connected; has a clear beginning and ending.
- **Voice** makes a strong effort to share an authentic personal message with the reader; writing style matches the purpose and audience.
- **Word Choice** shows an overall clarity of expression; has effective control of both new and everyday words.
- **Sentence Fluency** crafts careful, easy-to-follow sentences; may successfully use dialogue to strengthen the story; has better control of simple sentences.
- **Conventions** may make some errors in spelling, capitalization, punctuation or usage, which do not interfere with following the text; some editing is needed.

3. Fair

- **Ideas & Content** attempts to write a personal story; details may be general or unrelated to topic; some ideas are unclear or do not fit.
- **Organization** may not have a clear structure, or may have trouble tying ideas together; reader may be confused by poorly-placed ideas or details.
- **Voice** attempts to match writing style to the purpose; may convey the basic message, without a sense of personal involvement with topic or audience.
- **Word Choice** may not experiment with any new words; may not attempt to use words that create a colorful picture for the reader.
- **Sentence Fluency** may have trouble with complex sentences; most sentences are understandable, but some rereading may be needed to follow the story.
- **Conventions** has some minor problems with conventions; makes enough noticeable mistakes to prevent a smooth reading of the story.

2. Poor

- **Ideas & Content** writing is somewhat vague; may present events or details without a clear narrative purpose.
- **Organization** extreme lack of structure interferes with following the story; beginning or ending may be missing, fragmented, or undeveloped.
- **Voice** is not involved in sharing anything of personal importance; does not reach out to a reader; writing is flat or lifeless.
- **Word Choice** does not use words that express clear feelings or pictures; some words may detract from the meaning of the story.
- **Sentence Fluency** incomplete, rambling, or confusing sentences may interfere with following the text.
- **Conventions** repeated errors in spelling, word choice, punctuation, and usage make the paper hard to read; extensive editing is needed.

1. Unsatisfactory

- **Ideas & Content** does not tell a personal story; writing may go off in several directions, without a sense of purpose; few connections are made between ideas.
- **Organization** extreme disorganization interferes with understanding the text; there may be no evident structure at all.
- **Voice** does not address an audience, or does not attempt to share understandable feelings and ideas.
- **Word Choice** uses words that do not convey clear pictures, or are confusing to the reader; no new words are attempted.
- **Sentence Fluency** constructs incomplete or confusing sentences; text is hard to read and understand; words, ideas, and sentences do not fit together.
- **Conventions** severe errors in most or all conventions interfere with readability; some parts of the text may be impossible to follow or understand.

0 Incomplete: This piece is either blank, or fails to respond to the writing task. The topic is not addressed, or the student simply paraphrases the prompt. The response may be illegible or incoherent.

Personal Narrative

8-Point Writing Rubric

8	7	6	5	4	3	2	1
The writer	The writer	The writer	The writer	The writer	The writer	The writer	The writer
• has crafted an outstandingly well-developed and highly organized personal narrative that communicates a definite sense of purpose and audience. • conveys a full-bodied picture of an event through the use of transitions and detailed descriptions. • adeptly uses innovative figurative language, vivid imagery, and authentic expression of feelings to recreate the event. • frequently uses sophisticated vocabulary and complex sentence structure to enhance meaning.	• presents a well-developed and consistently organized personal narrative with a strong overall sense of purpose and audience. • conveys an authentic, clear picture of an event through the use of transitions and descriptions. • often uses figurative language, thoughtful imagery, and expression of feelings. • often uses advanced vocabulary and a variety of sentence structures to maintain high interest.	• presents an organized, cohesive personal narrative with a consistent sense of purpose and audience. • details a good overall picture of the event through the use of some transitions and the development of satisfactory descriptions. • uses some thoughtful figurative language, imagery, and expression of feelings, though elaboration is not always consistent. • chooses meaningful vocabulary and varies sentence structure to add interest to the narrative.	• has crafted a personal narrative of satisfactory organization with a general sense of audience and purpose. • sometimes uses transitions to connect events. • sometimes uses elaboration to enhance descriptions. • occasionally uses figurative language and imagery, but may not fully explain thoughts and feelings related to the event. • uses familiar grade-appropriate vocabulary, but does not consistently vary sentence structure.	• has made an adequate attempt at organizing a personal narrative, though sense of audience and purpose are not always consistent. • demonstrates limited use of transitions, and misses opportunities to elaborate on important descriptions. • articulates a good opening statement or paragraph, but may lose focus soon thereafter. • uses some solid imagery, but omits descriptions of important thoughts and feelings. • may make mistakes in grammar, usage, and mechanics that somewhat detract from readability.	• chooses a good topic to share in a personal narrative, but does not adequately organize events or fully develop ideas. • does not adequately use transitions, and provides limited descriptions of important observations and experiences. • may not develop an opening sentence or paragraph. • frequently misses the opportunity to provide images, thoughts, and feelings. • displays problems with organization. • makes mistakes in grammar, usage, and mechanics that distract the reader from fully understanding the narrative.	• makes a largely unsuccessful attempt to construct a personal narrative out of personal experience. • has not explained events in logical sequence; writing is often unfocused. • does not use transitions or descriptions to communicate important events. • fails to use figurative language; vocabulary is simplistic. • exhibits serious lack of language control.	• has not successfully developed a personal narrative. • has not articulated a main idea, or overall focus, for the piece. • does not use transitions, imagery, or descriptions in the writing. • uses limited, below-grade-level vocabulary to explain events. • demonstrates lack of language control severe enough to impair reader understanding of the main idea.

0 Incomplete: This piece is either blank, or fails to respond to the writing task. The topic is not addressed, or the student simply paraphrases the prompt. The response may be illegible or incoherent.

Notes

Notes

Notes

Notes

Notes

Notes

Notes

Notes

Notes

Notes